PEARSON CUSTOM BUSINESS RESOURCES

ACCT 2200
Principles of Accounting I
Kean University

PEARSON

ISBN 10: 1-269-66181-7
ISBN 13: 978-1-269-66181-2

PEARSON

Table of Contents

Accounting and the Business Environment

Accounting and the Business Environment

Coffee, Anyone?

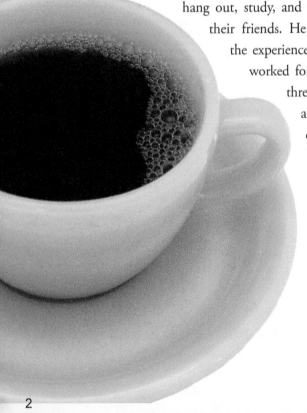

Aiden Jackson stared at the list the banker had given him during their meeting. *Business plan, cash flow projections, financial statements, tax returns.* Aiden had visited with the banker because he had a dream of opening a coffee shop across the street from campus. He knew there was a need; students were always looking for a place to hang out, study, and visit with their friends. He also had the experience. He had worked for the past three years as a manager of a coffee shop in a neighboring town. Aiden needed one thing, though—money. He had saved a small amount of money from his job and received several contributions from family and friends, but he still didn't have enough to open the business. He had decided the best option was to get a loan from his bank. After the meeting, Aiden felt overwhelmed and unsure of the future of his business.

You might think that Aiden was facing an impossible situation, but you'd be wrong. Almost every new business faces a similar situation. The owner starts with an inspiration, and then he or she needs to provide enough continuous cash flow to build the business. In addition, the owner has to make decisions such as: *Should we expand to another location? Do we have enough money to purchase a new coffee roaster? How do I know if the business made a profit?*

So how does Aiden get started? Keep reading. That's what accounting teaches you.

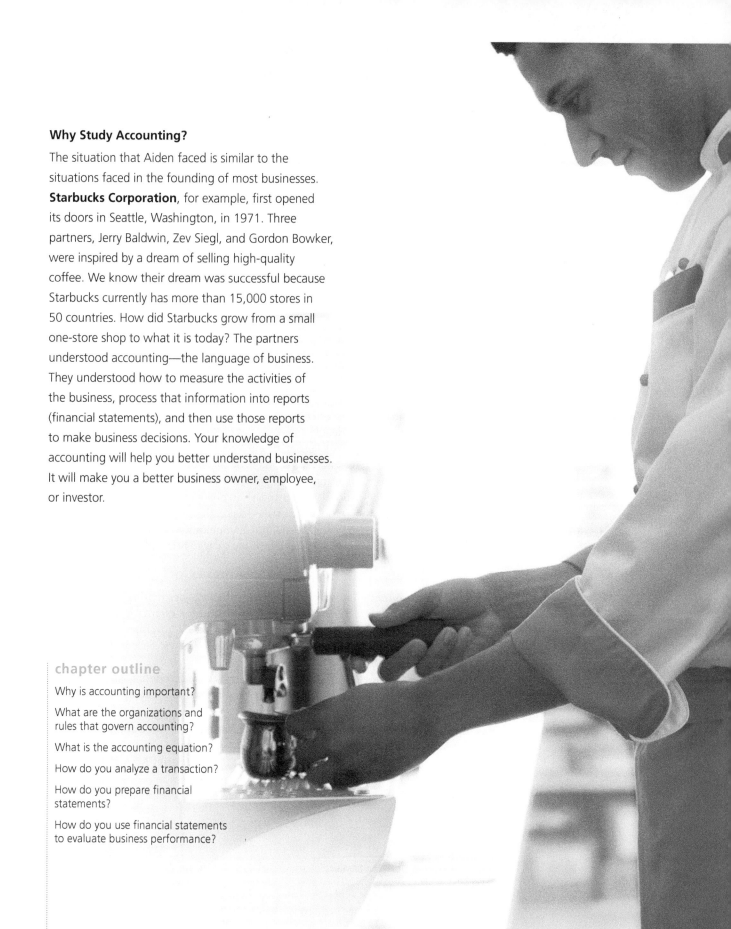

Why Study Accounting?

The situation that Aiden faced is similar to the situations faced in the founding of most businesses. **Starbucks Corporation**, for example, first opened its doors in Seattle, Washington, in 1971. Three partners, Jerry Baldwin, Zev Siegl, and Gordon Bowker, were inspired by a dream of selling high-quality coffee. We know their dream was successful because Starbucks currently has more than 15,000 stores in 50 countries. How did Starbucks grow from a small one-store shop to what it is today? The partners understood accounting—the language of business. They understood how to measure the activities of the business, process that information into reports (financial statements), and then use those reports to make business decisions. Your knowledge of accounting will help you better understand businesses. It will make you a better business owner, employee, or investor.

chapter outline

Why is accounting important?

What are the organizations and rules that govern accounting?

What is the accounting equation?

How do you analyze a transaction?

How do you prepare financial statements?

How do you use financial statements to evaluate business performance?

Learning Objectives

1. Explain why accounting is important and list the users of accounting information

2. Describe the organizations and rules that govern accounting

3. Describe the accounting equation, and define assets, liabilities, and equity

4. Use the accounting equation to analyze transactions

5. Prepare financial statements

6. Use financial statements and return on assets (ROA) to evaluate business performance

WHY IS ACCOUNTING IMPORTANT?

Learning Objective 1

Explain why accounting is important and list the users of accounting information

Accounting

The information system that measures business activities, processes the information into reports, and communicates the results to decision makers.

You've heard the term *accounting*, but what exactly is it? Accounting is the information system that measures business activities, processes the information into reports, and communicates the results to decision makers. Accounting is the language of business. The better you understand the language of business, the better you can manage your own business, be a valuable employee, or make wise investments.

We tend to think of accountants as boring and dry. However, accounting is much more than simple recordkeeping or bookkeeping. Today's accountants participate in a broad range of activities such as the investigation of financial evidence, the development of computer programs to process accounting information, and the communication of financial results to interested parties. The knowledge of accounting is used every day to help make business decisions.

Decision Makers: The Users of Accounting Information

Financial Accounting

The field of accounting that focuses on providing information for external decision makers.

Managerial Accounting

The field of accounting that focuses on providing information for internal decision makers.

We can divide accounting into two major fields—financial accounting and managerial accounting. Financial accounting provides information for external decision makers, such as outside investors, lenders, customers, and the federal government. Managerial accounting focuses on information for internal decision makers, such as the company's managers and employees.

Exhibit 1 illustrates the difference between financial accounting and managerial accounting. Regardless of whether they are external or internal to the company, all decision

Exhibit 1 | Decision Making: Financial versus Managerial Accounting

Financial Accounting	Managerial Accounting
External Decision Makers:	**Internal Decision Makers:**
Should I invest in the business? Is the business profitable? Should we lend money to the business? Can the business pay us back?	How much money should the business budget for production? Should the business expand to a new location? How do actual costs compare to budgeted costs?

makers need information to make the best choices. The bigger the decision, the more information decision makers need. Let's look at some ways in which various people use accounting information to make important decisions.

Individuals

How much cash do you have? How much do you need to save each month to retire at a certain age or pay for your children's college education? Accounting can help you answer questions like these. By using accounting information, you can manage your money, evaluate a new job, and better decide whether you can afford to buy a new computer. Businesses need accounting information to make similar decisions.

Businesses

Business owners use accounting information to set goals, measure progress toward those goals, and make adjustments when needed. The financial statements give owners the information they need to help make those decisions. Financial statements are helpful when, for example, a business owner wants to know whether his or her business has enough cash to purchase another computer.

Investors

Outside investors who have some ownership interest often provide the money to get a business going. Suppose you're considering investing in a business. How would you decide whether it is a good investment? In making this decision, you might try to predict the amount of income you would earn on the investment. Also, after making an investment, investors can use a company's financial statements to analyze how their investment is performing.

You might have the opportunity to invest in the stock market through your company's retirement plan. Which investments should you pick? Understanding a company's financial statements will help you decide. You can view the financial statements of large companies that report to the SEC by logging on to **http://finance.yahoo.com**, **www.google.com/finance**, or the Security and Exchange Commission's EDGAR database (**www.sec.gov/edgar.shtml**).

Creditors

Any person or business to whom a business owes money is a creditor. Before extending credit to a business, a creditor evaluates the company's ability to make the payments by reviewing its financial statements. Creditors follow the same process when you need to borrow money for a new car or a house. The creditor reviews accounting data to determine your ability to make the loan payments. What does your financial position tell the creditor about your ability to pay the loan? Are you a good risk for the bank?

Taxing Authorities

Local, state, and federal governments levy taxes. Income tax is calculated using accounting information. Good accounting records can help individuals and businesses take advantage of lawful deductions. Without good records, the IRS can disallow tax deductions, resulting in a higher tax bill plus interest and penalties.

The Accounting Profession

What do businesses such as Amazon.com, Walmart, or even your local sandwich shop across from campus have in common? They all need accountants! That is why a degree in accounting opens so many doors upon graduation.

You've probably heard of a CPA before. Certified public accountants, or CPAs, are licensed professional accountants who serve the general public. CPAs work for public

IFRS

Accounting is alive! As businesses evolve and the type of business transactions change, so must the language of business. The most significant changes in the business world in the last decade have been the huge increases in international commerce. Because more business is conducted internationally, decision-makers are looking for an international accounting language.

Look for more information about International Financial Reporting Standards (IFRS) in these elements.

Creditor
Any person or business to whom a business owes money.

Certified Public Accountants (CPAs)
Licensed professional accountants who serve the general public.

What if I < want more information about becoming a CPA or CMA?

Certified Management Accountants (CMAs)
Certified professionals who specialize in accounting and financial management knowledge. They typically work for a single company.

Recently, the AICPA added a certification program in international accounting for those CPAs who want to specialize in global commerce.

accounting firms, businesses, government entities, or educational institutions. What does it take to be a CPA? Although requirements vary between states, to be certified in a profession, one must meet the educational and/or experience requirements *and* pass a qualifying exam. The American Institute of Certified Public Accountants (AICPA) website (**www.thiswaytocpa.com**) contains a wealth of information about becoming a CPA, career opportunities, and exam requirements.

Certified management accountants, or **CMAs**, are certified professionals who specialize in accounting and financial management knowledge. Generally, CMAs work for a single company. You can find information about becoming a CMA, how a CMA differs from a CPA, and why employers are recognizing the CMA certification on the Institute of Management Accountants (IMA) website (**www.imanet.org**). It's worth spending the time and energy for accountants to get certified—certified accountants generally make 10–15% more than their non-certified colleagues when they enter the work force.

Studying accounting and becoming certified professionally can lead to a financially secure job. According to Robert Half's *2012 Salary Guide*, the top positions in demand that rely on accounting skills are controllers, financial analysts, tax accountants, auditors, cost accountants, and business systems analysts. How much do these types of accountants make? Exhibit 2 provides a snapshot of the earning potential for key positions.

Accountants generally work either in public, private, or governmental accounting. Public accounting involves services such as auditing and tax preparation. Well-known public accounting firms include Ernst & Young, Deloitte, PwC, and KPMG. Private accounting involves working for a single company such as Amazon.com, Walmart, or Dell. Other accountants work for the federal or state governments. Wherever accountants work, demand for their services is high. According to the U.S. Department of Labor's *Occupational Outlook Handbook 2010–2011*, the federal government expects faster than average employment growth for accountants and auditors from 2008–2018.

Exhibit 2 | **Comparison of Accounting Positions**

Position	Job Description	Salary Range
Controllers	Compile financial statements, interact with auditors, and oversee regulatory reporting.	$82,750–$199,000
Financial analysts	Review financial data and help to explain the story behind the numbers.	$38,000–$114,500
Business systems analysts	Use accounting knowledge to create computer systems.	$44,250–$107,250
Tax accountants	Help companies navigate tax laws.	$41,500–$114,750
Auditors	Perform reviews of companies to ensure compliance to rules and regulations.	$42,500–$171,750
Cost accountants	Typically work in a manufacturing business. Help analyze accounting data.	$40,000–$103,750

> Try It!

Match the accounting terminology to the definitions.

1.	Certified management accountants	**a.**	the information system that measures business activities, processes that information into reports, and communicates the results to decision makers
2.	Accounting	**b.**	licensed professional accountants who serve the general public
3.	Managerial accounting	**c.**	any person or business to whom a business owes money
4.	Certified public accountants	**d.**	the field of accounting that focuses on providing information for internal decision makers
5.	Financial accounting	**e.**	certified professionals who work for a single company
6.	Creditor	**f.**	the field of accounting that focuses on providing information for external decision makers

Check your answers at the end of the chapter.

For more practice, see Short Exercise S-1. MyAccountingLab

WHAT ARE THE ORGANIZATIONS AND RULES THAT GOVERN ACCOUNTING?

All professions have regulations. Let's look at the organizations and rules that govern the accounting profession.

Governing Organizations

In the United States, the **Financial Accounting Standards Board (FASB)**, a privately funded organization, oversees the creation and governance of accounting standards. The FASB works with governmental regulatory agencies like the **Securities and Exchange Commission (SEC)**. The SEC is the U.S. governmental agency that oversees the U.S. financial markets. It also oversees those organizations that set standards (like the FASB). The FASB also works with congressionally created groups like the Public Company Accounting Oversight Board (PCAOB) and private groups like the AICPA, IMA, and International Accounting Standards Board (IASB).

Generally Accepted Accounting Principles

The guidelines for accounting information are called **Generally Accepted Accounting Principles (GAAP)**. GAAP is the main U.S. accounting rule book and is currently created and governed by the FASB. In order to use and prepare financial statements, it's important that we understand GAAP. GAAP rests on a conceptual framework that identifies the objectives, characteristics, elements, and implementation of financial statements and creates the acceptable accounting practices. The primary objective of financial reporting is to provide information useful for making investment and lending decisions. To be useful, information must be relevant and have faithful representation.[1] Relevant information allows

Learning Objective 2
Describe the organizations and rules that govern accounting.

Financial Accounting Standards Board (FASB)
The private organization that oversees the creation and governance of accounting standards in the United States.

Securities and Exchange Commission (SEC)
U.S. governmental agency that oversees the U.S. financial markets.

Generally Accepted Accounting Principles (GAAP)
Accounting guidelines, currently formulated by the *Financial Accounting Standards Board (FASB)*; the main U.S. accounting rule book.

---

[1] This wording was changed from relevant and reliable by the *Statement of Financial Accounting Concepts No. 8.*

users of the information to make a decision. Information that is faithfully representative is complete, neutral, and free from error. These basic accounting assumptions and principles are part of the foundation for the financial reports that companies present.

The Economic Entity Assumption

Economic Entity Assumption
An organization that stands apart as a separate economic unit.

The most basic concept in accounting is that of the economic entity assumption. An economic (business) entity is an organization that stands apart as a separate economic unit. We draw boundaries around each entity to keep its affairs distinct from those of other entities. An entity refers to one business, separate from its owners.

In order to demonstrate the economic entity assumption and several other concepts in this chapter, we will use a fictitious business—Smart Touch Learning—an e-learning business that specializes in providing online courses in accounting, economics, marketing, and management.

Assume Sheena Bright started the business by contributing capital of $30,000. Following the economic entity assumption, Smart Touch Learning recorded the $30,000 separately from Sheena's personal assets, such as her clothing and car. To mix the $30,000 of business cash with her personal assets would make it difficult to measure the success or failure of Smart Touch Learning. The economic entity assumption requires that each organization be separate from other businesses and from the owner.

A business can be organized as a sole proprietorship, partnership, corporation, or limited-liability company (LLC). Exhibit 3 summarizes the similarities and differences among the four types of business organizations.

Cost Principle
A principle that states that acquired assets and services should be recorded at their actual cost.

Sole Proprietorship
A business with a single owner.

Partnership
A business with two or more owners and not organized as a corporation.

Corporation
A business organized under state law that is a separate legal entity.

Limited-Liability Company (LLC)
A company in which each member is only liable for his or her own actions.

The Cost Principle

The cost principle states that acquired assets and services should be recorded at their actual cost (also called *historical cost*). The cost principle means we record a transaction at

Exhibit 3 | **Business Organizations**

	Sole Proprietorship	Partnership	Corporation	Limited-Liability Company (LLC)
Definition	A business with a single owner	A business with two or more owners and not organized as a corporation	A business organized under state law that is a separate legal entity	A company in which each member is only liable for his or her own actions
Number of owners	One (called the proprietor)	Two or more (called partners)	One or more (called stockholders)	One or more (called members or partners)
Life of the organization	Terminates at owner's choice or death	Terminates at a partner's choice or death	Indefinite	Indefinite
Personal liability of the owner(s) for the business's debts	Owner is personally liable	Partners are personally liable	Stockholders are not personally liable	Members are not personally liable
Taxation	Not separate taxable entities. The owner pays tax on the proprietorship's earnings.	Partnership is not taxed. Instead partners pay tax on their share of the earnings.	Separate taxable entity. Corporation pays tax.	LLC is not taxed. Instead members pay tax on their share of earnings.
Type of business	Small businesses	Professional organizations of physicians, attorneys, and accountants	Large multinational businesses	An alternative to the partnership

the amount shown on the receipt—the actual amount paid. Even though the purchaser may believe the price is a bargain, the item is recorded at the price actually paid and not at the "expected" cost. For example, assume our fictitious company Smart Touch Learning purchased land for $20,000. The owner, Sheena Bright, might believe the land is instead worth $25,000. The cost principle requires that Smart Touch Learning record the land at $20,000, not $25,000.

The cost principle also holds that the accounting records should continue reporting the historical cost of an asset over its useful life. Why? Because cost is a reliable measure. Suppose Smart Touch Learning holds the land for six months. During that time land prices rise, and the land could be sold for $30,000. Should its accounting value—the figure on the books—be the actual cost of $20,000 or the current market value of $30,000? By the cost principle, the accounting value of the land would remain at the actual cost of $20,000.

The Going Concern Assumption

Another reason for measuring assets at historical cost is the going concern assumption. This assumes that the entity will remain in operation for the foreseeable future. Under the going concern assumption, accountants assume that the business will remain in operation long enough to use existing resources for their intended purpose.

The Monetary Unit Assumption

In the United States, we record transactions in dollars because the dollar is the medium of exchange. The value of a dollar changes over time, and a rise in the price level is called *inflation*. During periods of inflation, a dollar will purchase less. But accountants assume that the dollar's purchasing power is stable. This is the basis of the monetary unit assumption, which requires that the items on the financial statements be measured in terms of a monetary unit.

International Financial Reporting Standards

The concepts and principles that we have discussed so far apply to businesses that follow U.S. GAAP and are traded on a U.S. stock exchange, such as the New York Stock Exchange. The SEC requires that U.S. businesses follow U.S. GAAP. Currently, though, the SEC is investigating endorsing International Financial Reporting Standards (IFRS), which are published by the International Accounting Standards Board (IASB). IFRS is a set of global accounting standards that are used or required by more than 120 nations. They are generally less specific and based more on principle than U.S. GAAP. IFRS leaves more room for professional judgment. For example, unlike U.S. GAAP, IFRS allows periodic revaluation of certain assets and liabilities to restate them to market value, rather than keeping them at historical cost.

What would it mean if the SEC endorsed IFRS? Endorsement involves a process of slowly incorporating IFRS into the U.S. financial system with the ultimate goal of U.S. GAAP being in line with IFRS. The current timeline shows reporting under IFRS could start as early as 2015 or 2016.

Ethics in Accounting and Business

Ethical considerations affect accounting. Investors and creditors need relevant and faithfully representative information about a company that they are investing in or lending money to. Companies want to be profitable and financially strong to attract investors and attempt to present their financial statements in a manner that portrays the business in the best possible way. Sometimes these two opposing viewpoints can cause conflicts of interest. For example, imagine a company that is facing a potential million-dollar lawsuit due to a defective product. The company might not want to share this information

IFRS

Under international reporting standards, the company would be allowed to restate and report the land at $30,000. The ability to report assets and liabilities at their current fair value each year under international standards is a significant difference from U.S. rules.

Going Concern Assumption
Assumes that the entity will remain in operation for the foreseeable future.

Monetary Unit Assumption
The assumption that requires the items on the financial statements to be measured in terms of a monetary unit.

International Financial Reporting Standards (IFRS)
A set of global accounting guidelines, formulated by the *International Accounting Standards Board (IASB)*.

International Accounting Standards Board (IASB)
The private organization that oversees the creation and governance of *International Financial Reporting Standards (IFRS)*.

Audit
An examination of a company's financial statements and records.

Sarbanes-Oxley Act (SOX)
Requires companies to review internal control and take responsibility for the accuracy and completeness of their financial reports.

with investors because it would potentially hurt the business's profitability. On the other hand, investors would want to know about the pending lawsuit so that they could make an informed decision about investing in the business. To handle these conflicts of interest and to provide reliable information, the SEC requires publicly held companies to have their financial statements audited by independent accountants. An **audit** is an examination of a company's financial statements and records. The independent accountants then issue an opinion that states whether or not the financial statements give a fair picture of the company's financial situation.

The vast majority of accountants do their jobs professionally and ethically, but we often don't hear about them. Unfortunately, only those who cheat make the headlines. In recent years we have seen many accounting scandals.

In response to the Enron and WorldCom reporting scandals, the U.S. government took swift action. It passed the **Sarbanes-Oxley Act (SOX)**, intended to curb financial scandals. SOX requires companies to review internal control and take responsibility for the accuracy and completeness of their financial reports. In addition, SOX made it a criminal offense to falsify financial statements. The Sarbanes-Oxley Act also created a new watchdog agency, the Public Company Accounting Oversight Board (PCAOB), to monitor the work of independent accountants who audit public companies. More recent scandals, such as the Bernie Madoff scandal in which Mr. Madoff pleaded guilty to defrauding thousands of investors by filing falsified trading reports, have further undermined the public's faith in financial reporting. This may result in more legislation for future reporting.

 Try It!

Match the accounting terminology to the definitions.

7. Cost principle	**a.** oversees the creation and governance of accounting standards in the United States
8. GAAP	**b.** requires an organization to be a separate economic unit
9. Faithful representation	**c.** oversees U.S. financial markets
10. SEC	**d.** states that acquired assets and services should be recorded at their actual cost
11. FASB	**e.** creates International Financial Reporting Standards
12. Monetary unit assumption	**f.** the main U.S. accounting rule book
13. Economic entity assumption	**g.** assumes that an entity will remain in operation for the foreseeable future
14. Going concern assumption	**h.** assumes that items on the financial statements are recorded in a monetary unit
15. IASB	**i.** requires information to be complete, neutral, and free from material error

Check your answers at the end of the chapter.

For more practice, see Short Exercises S-2 through S-5. MyAccountingLab

WHAT IS THE ACCOUNTING EQUATION?

The basic tool of accounting is the accounting equation. It measures the resources of a business (what the business owns or has control of) and the claims to those resources (what the business owes to creditors and to the owner). The accounting equation is made up of three parts—assets, liabilities, and equity—and shows how these three parts are related. Assets appear on the left side of the equation, and the liabilities and equity appear on the right side.

Assets = Liabilities + Equity

Remember, the accounting equation is an equation—so the left side of the equation always equals the right side of the equation.

Example: If a business has assets of $230,000 and liabilities of $120,000, its equity must be $110,000 ($230,000 − $120,000).

Assets	=	Liabilities	+	Equity
$230,000	=	$120,000	+	?
$230,000	=	$120,000	+	$110,000

Assets

An asset is an economic resource that is expected to benefit the business in the future. Assets are something the business owns or has control of that has value. Cash, merchandise inventory, furniture, and land are examples of assets.

Liabilities

Claims to those assets come from two sources: liabilities and equity. Liabilities are debts that are owed to creditors. Liabilities are something the business owes and represent the creditors' claims on the business's assets. For example, a creditor who has loaned money to a business has a claim to some of the business's assets until the business pays the debt. Many liabilities have the word *payable* in their titles. Examples include accounts payable, notes payable, and salaries payable.

Equity

The owner's claim to the assets of the business are called equity (also called owner's equity). Equity represents the amount of assets that are left over after the company has paid its liabilities. It is the company's net worth.

Equity increases with owner contributions and revenues. Owner contributions are referred to as owner's capital. An owner can contribute cash or other assets (such as equipment) to the business and receive capital. Equity is also increased by revenues. Revenues are earnings that result from delivering goods or services to customers. Examples of revenues are sales revenue, service revenue, and rent revenue.

Equity decreases with expenses and owner withdrawals. Expenses are the cost of selling goods or services. Expenses are the opposite of revenues and, therefore, decrease

Learning Objective 3
Describe the accounting equation, and define assets, liabilities, and equity

Accounting Equation
The basic tool of accounting, measuring the resources of the business (what the business owns or has control of) and the claims to those resources (what the business owes to creditors and to the owner). Assets = Liabilities + Equity

Assets
Economic resources that are expected to benefit the business in the future. Something the business owns or has control of.

Liabilities
Debts that are owed to *creditors*.

Equity
The owner's claim to the assets of the business.

Owner's Capital
Owner contributions to a business.

Revenues
Amounts earned from delivering goods or services to customers.

Expenses
The cost of selling goods or services.

equity. Examples of expenses are rent expense, salaries expense, advertising expense, and utilities expense.

Owner's withdrawals or drawings are payments of equity (usually of cash) to the owner. Withdrawals are not expenses because they are personal and are not related to the business. An owner may or may not make withdrawals from the business. Owner withdrawals are the opposite of owner contributions and, therefore, decrease equity.

Owner's Withdrawals
Payments of equity to the owner.

Equity can be broken out into the four components shown in the expanded accounting equation:

$$\text{Assets} = \left\{ \text{Liabilities} + \underline{\hspace{1cm}\text{Equity}\hspace{1cm}} \right.$$

Owner's Capital − Owner's Withdrawals + Revenues − Expenses

Businesses strive for net income. When revenues are greater than expenses, the result of operations is a profit or net income. When expenses are greater than revenues, the result is a net loss.

Net Income
The result of operations that occurs when total revenues are greater than total expenses.

Net Loss
The result of operations that occurs when total expenses are greater than total revenues.

> Try It!

16. Using the expanded accounting equation, solve for the missing amount.

Assets	$71,288
Liabilities	2,260
Owner's Capital	?
Owner's Withdrawal	14,420
Revenues	53,085
Expenses	28,675

Check your answer at the end of the chapter.

For more practice, see Short Exercises S-6 through S-8. MyAccountingLab

HOW DO YOU ANALYZE A TRANSACTION?

Learning Objective 4
Use the accounting equation to analyze transactions

Accounting is based on actual transactions. A transaction is any event that affects the financial position of the business *and* can be measured reliably. Transactions affect what the company has or owes or its net worth. Many events affect a company, including economic booms and recessions. Accountants, however, do not record the effects of those events. An accountant records only those events that have dollar amounts that can be measured reliably, such as the purchase of a building, a sale of merchandise, and the payment of rent.

Transaction
An event that affects the financial position of the business and can be measured reliably in dollar amounts.

What are some of your personal transactions? You may have bought a car. Your purchase was a transaction. If you are making payments on an auto loan, your payments are also transactions.

Transaction Analysis for Smart Touch Learning

To illustrate accounting for a business, we'll use Smart Touch Learning, the business introduced earlier. We'll account for the transactions of Smart Touch Learning, during November 2014, and show how each transaction affects the accounting equation.

Transaction 1—Owner Contribution

Sheena Bright starts the new business as a sole proprietorship named Smart Touch Learning. The e-learning business receives $30,000 cash from the owner, Sheena Bright, and the business gave capital to her. The effect of this transaction on the accounting equation of the business is as follows:

Assets		Liabilities	+	Equity
Cash				Bright, Capital
(1) +30,000	=			+30,000

Let's take a close look at the transaction above following these steps:

Step 1: Identify the accounts and the account type. Each transaction must have at least two accounts but could have more. *The two accounts involved are Cash (Asset) and Bright, Capital (Equity).*

Step 2: Decide if each account increases or decreases. Remember to always view this from the *business's* perspective, and not from the owner's or customer's perspective. *Cash increases.* The business has more cash than it had before. *Bright, Capital increases.* The business received a $30,000 contribution.

Step 3: Determine if the accounting equation is in balance. For each transaction, the amount on the left side of the equation must equal the amount on the right side. *$30,000 = $30,000*

Transaction 2—Purchase of Land for Cash

The business purchases land for an office location, paying cash of $20,000. This transaction affects the accounting equation of Smart Touch Learning as follows:

	Assets			Liabilities	+	Equity
	Cash	+	Land		+	Bright, Capital
Bal.	$30,000			=		$30,000
(2)	−20,000		+20,000			
Bal.	$10,000	+	$20,000			$30,000

Let's review the transaction using the steps we learned:

Step 1: Identify the accounts and the account type. *The two accounts involved are Cash (Asset) and Land (Asset).*

Step 2: Decide if each account increases or decreases. *Cash decreases.* The business paid cash. *Land increases.* The business now has land.

Step 3: Determine if the accounting equation is in balance. *$10,000 + $20,000 = $30,000*

Transaction 3—Purchase of Office Supplies on Credit

Smart Touch Learning buys office supplies on account (credit), agreeing to pay $500 within 30 days. This transaction increases both the assets and the liabilities of the business, as follows:

	Assets					Liabilities	+	Equity
	Cash	+	Office Supplies	+	Land	Accounts Payable	+	Bright, Capital
Bal.	$10,000			+	$20,000			$30,000
(3)			+500			+500		
Bal.	$10,000	+	$500	+	$20,000	$500	+	$30,000

(with = between Assets and Liabilities + Equity)

Accounts Payable
A short-term liability that will be paid in the future.

Step 1: Identify the accounts and the account type. *The two accounts involved are Office Supplies (Asset) and Accounts Payable (Liability).* Office Supplies is an asset, not an expense, because the supplies aren't used up now, but will be in the future. The liability created by purchasing "on account" is an accounts payable, which is a short-term liability that will be paid in the future. A payable is always a liability.

Step 2: Decide if each account increases or decreases. *Office Supplies increases.* The business now has more office supplies than it had before. *Accounts Payable increases.* The business now owes more than it did before.

Step 3: Determine if the accounting equation is in balance. *$10,000 + $500 + $20,000 = $500 + $30,000*

> *Notice how the steps help when analyzing transactions. It's important that, as you are learning, you use the steps to complete the transactions. Moving forward, try writing the steps out yourself before looking at the transaction analysis.*

Transaction 4—Earning of Service Revenue for Cash

Smart Touch Learning earns service revenue by providing training services for clients. The business earns $5,500 of revenue and collects this amount in cash. The effect on the accounting equation is an increase in Cash and an increase in Service Revenue as follows:

	Assets					Liabilities	+	Equity		
	Cash	+	Office Supplies	+	Land	Accounts Payable	+	Bright, Capital	+	Service Revenue
Bal.	$10,000	+	$500	+	$20,000	$500	+	$30,000		
(4)	+5,500									+5,500
Bal.	$15,500	+	$500	+	$20,000	$500	+	$30,000	+	$5,500

(with = between Assets and Liabilities + Equity)

A revenue transaction grows the business, as shown by the increases in assets and equity.

Transaction 5—Earning of Service Revenue on Account

Smart Touch Learning performs a service for clients who do not pay immediately. The business receives the clients' promise to pay $3,000 within one month. This promise is an asset, an accounts receivable, because the business expects to collect the cash in the future. In accounting, we say that Smart Touch Learning performed this service *on account*. It is in performing the service (doing the work), not collecting the cash, that the company *earns* the revenue. As in transaction 4, increasing revenue increases equity. Smart Touch Learning records the earning of $3,000 of revenue on account, as follows:

Accounts Receivable
The right to receive cash in the future from customers for goods sold or for services performed.

		Assets				=	Liabilities	+		Equity	
	Cash	+ Accounts Receivable	+ Office Supplies	+	Land		Accounts Payable	+	Bright, Capital	+	Service Revenue
Bal.	$15,500		+ $500	+	$20,000		$500	+	$30,000	+	$5,500
(5)		+3,000									+3,000
Bal.	$15,500 +	$3,000	+ $500	+	$20,000		$500	+	$30,000	+	$8,500

Transaction 6—Payment of Expenses with Cash

The business pays $3,200 in cash expenses: $2,000 for office rent and $1,200 for employee salaries. The effects on the accounting equation are as follows:

		Assets				=	Liabilities	+			Equity		
	Cash	+ Accounts Receivable	+ Office Supplies	+	Land		Accounts Payable	+	Bright, Capital	+ Service Revenue	− Rent Expense	− Salaries Expense	
Bal.	$15,500 +	$3,000	+ $500	+	$20,000		$500	+	$30,000	+ $8,500			
(6)	−3,200										−2,000	−1,200	
Bal.	$12,300 +	$3,000	+ $500	+	$20,000		$500	+	$30,000	+ $8,500	− $2,000	− $1,200	

Expenses have the opposite effect of revenues. Expenses shrink the business, as shown by the decreased balances of assets and equity. Each expense is recorded separately. We record the cash payment in a single amount for the sum of the expenses: $3,200 ($2,000 + $1,200). Notice that the accounting equation remains in balance ($12,300 + $3,000 + $500 + $20,000 = $500 + $30,000 + $8,500 − $2,000 − $1,200).

Transaction 7—Payment on Account (Accounts Payable)

The business pays $300 to the store from which it purchased office supplies in transaction 3. In accounting, we say that the business pays $300 *on account*. The effect on the accounting equation is a decrease in Cash and a decrease in Accounts Payable, as shown here:

		Assets				=	Liabilities	+			Equity		
	Cash	+ Accounts Receivable	+ Office Supplies	+	Land		Accounts Payable	+	Bright, Capital	+ Service Revenue	− Rent Expense	− Salaries Expense	
Bal.	$12,300 +	$3,000	+ $500	+	$20,000		$500	+	$30,000	+ $8,500	− $2,000	− $1,200	
(7)	−300						−300						
Bal.	$12,000 +	$3,000	+ $500	+	$20,000		$200	+	$30,000	+ $8,500	− $2,000	− $1,200	

The payment of cash on account has no effect on the amount of Office Supplies (Asset). Smart Touch Learning has not increased the amount of its office supplies; instead, it is paying off a liability (Accounts Payable decreased $300) with cash (Cash decreased $300). To record an increase to Office Supplies, in this transaction, would be accounting for the purchase of office supplies twice. We have already recorded the purchase of office supplies in transaction 3; in this transaction, we are now ready to record only the payment on account.

Transaction 8—Collection on Account (Accounts Receivable)

In transaction 5, the business performed services for clients on account. Smart Touch Learning now collects $2,000 from a client. We say that Smart Touch Learning collects the cash *on account*. The business will record an increase in the asset Cash. Should it also record an increase in Service Revenue? No, because the business already recorded the revenue when it earned the revenue in transaction 5. The phrase "collect cash on account" means to record an increase in Cash and a decrease in Accounts Receivable. Accounts Receivable is decreased because the $2,000 that the business was to collect at some point in the future is being collected today. The effect on the accounting equation is as follows:

		Assets						Liabilities	+			Equity		
	Cash	+ Accounts Receivable	+ Office Supplies	+ Land				Accounts Payable	+ Bright, Capital	+ Service Revenue	− Rent Expense	− Salaries Expense
Bal.	$12,000 +	$3,000	+ $500	+ $20,000		=		$200	+ $30,000	+ $8,500	− $2,000	− $1,200
(8)	+2,000	−2,000										
Bal.	$14,000 +	$1,000	+ $500	+ $20,000				$200	+ $30,000	+ $8,500	− $2,000	− $1,200

This transaction is recorded as an increase in one asset (Cash) and a decrease in another asset (Accounts Receivable). Is the accounting equation still in balance? Yes. As long as you record an increase and decrease of the same amount on one side of the accounting equation, the accounting equation remains in balance. In other words, total assets, liabilities, and equity are all unchanged from the preceding total. Why? Because Smart Touch Learning exchanged one asset (Cash) for another (Accounts Receivable), causing a zero effect on the total amount of assets in the accounting equation ($+\$2,000 - \$2,000 = \$0$).

Transaction 9—Owner Withdrawal of Cash

Sheena Bright withdraws $5,000 cash from the business. The effect on the accounting equation is:

		Assets						Liabilities	+				Equity		
	Cash	+ Accounts Receivable	+ Office Supplies	+ Land				Accounts Payable	+ Bright, Capital	− Bright, Withdrawals	+ Service Revenue	− Rent Expense	− Salaries Expense
Bal.	$14,000 +	$1,000	+ $500	+ $20,000		=		$200	+ $30,000		+ $8,500	− $2,000	− $1,200
(9)	−5,000									−5,000			
Bal.	$9,000 +	$1,000	+ $500	+ $20,000				$200	+ $30,000	− $5,000	+ $8,500	− $2,000	− $1,200

The owner withdrawal decreases the business's cash and equity. *Withdrawals do not represent an expense because they are not related to the earning of revenue. Therefore, owner's withdrawals do not affect the business's net income or net loss.*

A summary of all nine transactions for Smart Touch Learning is presented in Exhibit 4.

Exhibit 4 | Analysis of Transactions, Smart Touch Learning

1. Smart Touch Learning received $30,000 cash and gave capital to Sheena Bright, owner.
2. Paid $20,000 cash for land.
3. Bought $500 of office supplies on account.
4. Received $5,500 cash from clients for service revenue earned.
5. Performed services for clients on account, $3,000.
6. Paid cash expenses: office rent, $2,000; employee salaries, $1,200.
7. Paid $300 on the accounts payable created in transaction 3.
8. Collected $2,000 on the accounts receivable created in transaction 5.
9. Owner withdrew cash of $5,000.

	Assets						Liabilities	+			Equity					
	Cash	+	Accounts Receivable	+	Office Supplies	+	Land		Accounts Payable	+	Bright, Capital	−	Bright, Withdrawals	+	Service Revenue	−	Rent Expense	−	Salaries Expense
(1)	+30,000										+30,000						
(2)	−20,000						+20,000										
Bal.	$10,000					+	$20,000				$30,000						
(3)					+500				+500								
Bal.	$10,000			+	$500	+	$20,000		$500	+	$30,000						
(4)	+5,500														+5,500		
Bal.	$15,500			+	$500	+	$20,000		$500	+	$30,000			+	$5,500		
(5)			+3,000												+3,000		
Bal.	$15,500	+	$3,000	+	$500	+	$20,000		$500	+	$30,000			+	$8,500		
(6)	−3,200															−2,000	−1,200
Bal.	$12,300	+	$3,000	+	$500	+	$20,000		$500	+	$30,000			+	$8,500	−	$2,000	−	$1,200
(7)	−300								−300								
Bal.	$12,000	+	$3,000	+	$500	+	$20,000		$200	+	$30,000			+	$8,500	−	$2,000	−	$1,200
(8)	+2,000		−2,000														
Bal.	$14,000	+	$1,000	+	$500	+	$20,000		$200	+	$30,000			+	$8,500	−	$2,000	−	$1,200
(9)	−5,000												−5,000				
Bal.	$ 9,000	+	$1,000	+	$500	+	$20,000		$200	+	$30,000	−	$5,000	+	$8,500	−	$2,000	−	$1,200

$30,500

$30,500

Try It!

17. Using the information provided, analyze the affects of Lawlor Lawn Service's transactions on the accounting equation.

May 1	Received $1,700 and gave capital to Eric Lawlor.
May 3	Purchased a mower on account, $1,440.
May 5	Performed lawn services for client on account, $200.
May 17	Paid $60 cash for gas used in mower.
May 28	Eric Lawlor withdrew cash of $300.

Check your answers at the end of the chapter.

For more practice, see Short Exercises S-9 and S-10. MyAccountingLab

HOW DO YOU PREPARE FINANCIAL STATEMENTS?

Learning Objective 5
Prepare financial statements

We have now recorded Smart Touch Learning's transactions, and they are summarized in Exhibit 4. Notice how total assets equal total liabilities plus equity ($30,500 = $30,500).

But a basic question remains: How will people actually use this information? The information in Exhibit 4 does not tell a lender whether Smart Touch Learning can pay off a loan. The data in the exhibit do not tell whether the business is profitable.

To address these important questions, we need financial statements. **Financial statements** are business documents that are used to communicate information needed to make business decisions. There are four financial statements prepared. These statements are prepared in the order listed:

Financial Statements
Business documents that are used to communicate information needed to make business decisions.

Income Statement
Reports the *net income* or *net loss* of the business for a specific period.

Statement of Owner's Equity
Shows the changes in the owner's capital account for a specific period.

Balance Sheet
Reports on the assets, liabilities, and owner's equity of the business as of a specific date.

Statement of Cash Flows
Reports on a business's cash receipts and cash payments for a specific period.

1. **Income statement**—Answers the question of whether the business is profitable. The income statement summarizes an entity's revenues and expenses and reports the net income or net loss for a specific period.
2. **Statement of owner's equity**—Answers the question of how the business uses its earnings. Did the owner withdraw the earnings or did he or she keep the earnings to further invest in the business? The statement of owner's equity shows the changes in the owner's capital account for a specific period. The owner's capital account increases by owner's contributions and net income and decreases by owner's withdrawals and net losses.
3. **Balance sheet**—Answers the questions of the amount of assets a business has and who can claim those assets—creditors or owners. The balance sheet is the accounting equation reporting the assets, liabilities, and owner's equity of the business as of a specific date.
4. **Statement of cash flows**—Answers the question of whether the business generates enough cash to pay its bills. The statement of cash flows reports on a business's cash receipts and cash payments for a specific period.

Income Statement

Let's start by reviewing the income statement. The income statement (also called the *statement of earnings*) presents a summary of a business entity's revenues and expenses for a period of time, such as a month, quarter, or year. The income statement tells us whether the business enjoyed net income or suffered a net loss. Remember:

- Net income means total revenues are greater than total expenses.
- Net loss means total expenses are greater than total revenues.

It's important to remember that the only two types of accounts that are reported on the income statement are revenues and expenses. Exhibit 5 shows the income statement for Smart Touch Learning. Every income statement contains similar information.

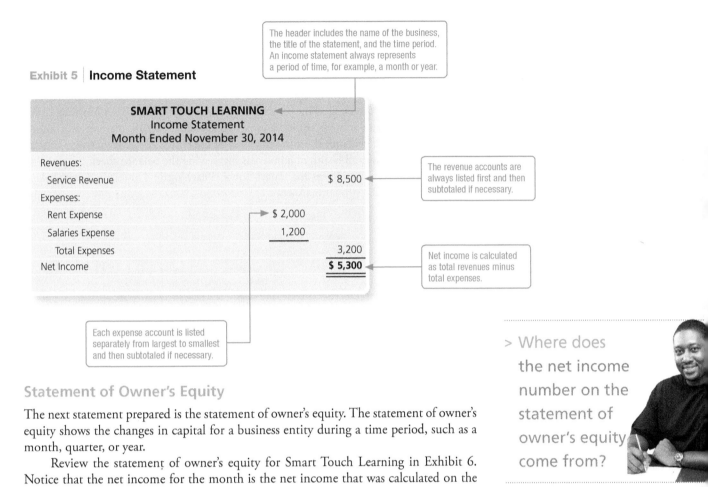

Exhibit 5 | **Income Statement**

The header includes the name of the business, the title of the statement, and the time period. An income statement always represents a period of time, for example, a month or year.

SMART TOUCH LEARNING
Income Statement
Month Ended November 30, 2014

Revenues:		
Service Revenue		$ 8,500
Expenses:		
Rent Expense	$ 2,000	
Salaries Expense	1,200	
Total Expenses		3,200
Net Income		**$ 5,300**

The revenue accounts are always listed first and then subtotaled if necessary.

Net income is calculated as total revenues minus total expenses.

Each expense account is listed separately from largest to smallest and then subtotaled if necessary.

Statement of Owner's Equity

The next statement prepared is the statement of owner's equity. The statement of owner's equity shows the changes in capital for a business entity during a time period, such as a month, quarter, or year.

Review the statement of owner's equity for Smart Touch Learning in Exhibit 6. Notice that the net income for the month is the net income that was calculated on the

> Where does the net income number on the statement of owner's equity come from?

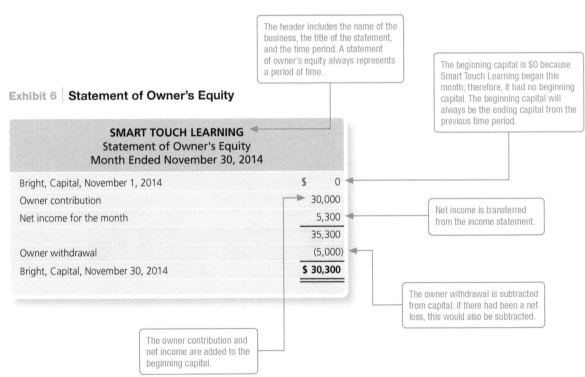

Exhibit 6 | **Statement of Owner's Equity**

The header includes the name of the business, the title of the statement, and the time period. A statement of owner's equity always represents a period of time.

SMART TOUCH LEARNING
Statement of Owner's Equity
Month Ended November 30, 2014

Bright, Capital, November 1, 2014	$ 0
Owner contribution	30,000
Net income for the month	5,300
	35,300
Owner withdrawal	(5,000)
Bright, Capital, November 30, 2014	**$ 30,300**

The beginning capital is $0 because Smart Touch Learning began this month; therefore, it had no beginning capital. The beginning capital will always be the ending capital from the previous time period.

Net income is transferred from the income statement.

The owner withdrawal is subtracted from capital. If there had been a net loss, this would also be subtracted.

The owner contribution and net income are added to the beginning capital.

income statement. This is the main reason why the income statement is prepared before the statement of owner's equity. The net income must first be calculated on the income statement and then carried to the statement of owner's equity.

Balance Sheet

What does < the balance sheet tell an investor or creditor?

The balance sheet (also called the *statement of financial position*) lists a business entity's assets, liabilities, and owner's equity as of a specific date, usually the end of a month, quarter, or year. The balance sheet is a snapshot of the entity. An investor or creditor can quickly assess the overall health of a business by viewing the balance sheet.

Review the balance sheet for Smart Touch Learning in Exhibit 7. Every balance sheet is prepared in a similar manner.

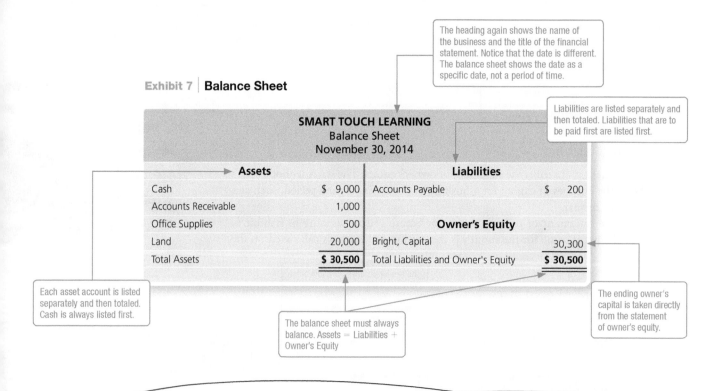

Exhibit 7 | **Balance Sheet**

The heading again shows the name of the business and the title of the financial statement. Notice that the date is different. The balance sheet shows the date as a specific date, not a period of time.

Liabilities are listed separately and then totaled. Liabilities that are to be paid first are listed first.

SMART TOUCH LEARNING
Balance Sheet
November 30, 2014

Assets		Liabilities	
Cash	$ 9,000	Accounts Payable	$ 200
Accounts Receivable	1,000		
Office Supplies	500	**Owner's Equity**	
Land	20,000	Bright, Capital	30,300
Total Assets	**$ 30,500**	Total Liabilities and Owner's Equity	**$ 30,500**

Each asset account is listed separately and then totaled. Cash is always listed first.

The balance sheet must always balance. Assets = Liabilities + Owner's Equity

The ending owner's capital is taken directly from the statement of owner's equity.

When you are preparing the financial statements, start by identifying which account goes on which statement. Each account will only go on one statement, except for Capital and Cash. For example, Service Revenue is only reported on the income statement. Liabilities, such as Accounts Payable, are only reported on the balance sheet. Cash and Capital appear on two statements. Cash is reported on the balance sheet and statement of cash flows, and Capital is reported on the statement of owner's equity and balance sheet.

>Ethics What constitutes manipulating financial statements?

The board of directors of Xiaping Trading Company is meeting to discuss the past year's results before releasing financial statements to the bank. Wai Lee, the company owner, comments, "This has not been a good year! Revenue is down and expenses are way up. If we are not careful, we will report a loss for the third year in a row. I can temporarily transfer some land that I own into the company's name, and that will beef up our balance sheet. Brent, as accountant, can you shave $500,000 from expenses? Then we can probably get the bank loan that we need." What should Brent do? What would you do if you were Brent?

Solution

Brent should remind Wai Lee that the intent of the financial statements is to tell the truth about the company's performance and financial position. If Wai Lee does not intend to leave the land in the business, then she should not transfer it to the business for the sole intent of increasing the assets and equity of the business.

It is possible that Brent could "shave expenses" legally, if it meant reducing the amount of expenses that the business had. But if Wai Lee meant that Brent should reclassify expenses or delay the recognition of expenses in an effort to boost net income, then this would be false and dishonest.

Statement of Cash Flows

The statement of cash flows reports the cash coming in (positive amounts) and the cash going out (negative amounts) during a period. It only reports transactions that involve cash because it reports the net increase or decrease in *cash* during the period and the ending *cash* balance. If a transaction does not involve cash, such as the purchase of land with a mortgage, it will not be reported on the statement of cash flows.

The statement of cash flows is divided into three distinct sections: operating, investing, and financing. *Operating activities* involve cash receipts for services provided and cash payments for expenses paid. *Investing activities* include the purchase and sale of land and equipment for cash. The third section, *financing activities*, includes cash contributions by the owner and withdrawals of cash by the owner.

Take a look at the statement of cash flows for Smart Touch Learning (Exhibit 8). Notice the important items that every statement of cash flows contains.

> Would the purchase of land with a mortgage be reported on the statement of cash flows?

Accounting and the Business Environment

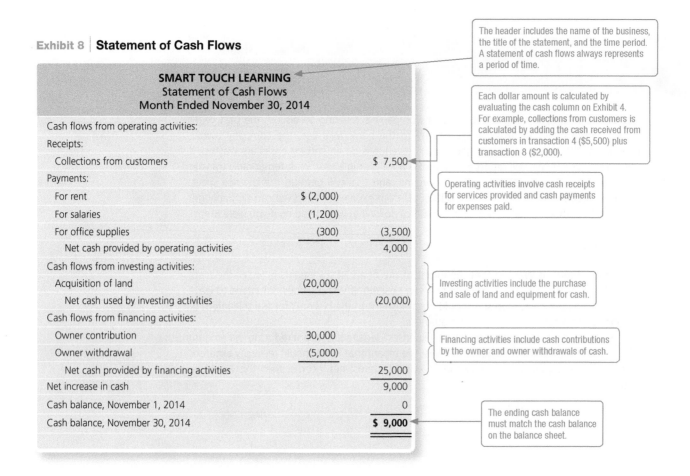

Exhibit 8 | Statement of Cash Flows

SMART TOUCH LEARNING
Statement of Cash Flows
Month Ended November 30, 2014

Cash flows from operating activities:		
Receipts:		
Collections from customers		$ 7,500
Payments:		
For rent	$ (2,000)	
For salaries	(1,200)	
For office supplies	(300)	(3,500)
Net cash provided by operating activities		4,000
Cash flows from investing activities:		
Acquisition of land	(20,000)	
Net cash used by investing activities		(20,000)
Cash flows from financing activities:		
Owner contribution	30,000	
Owner withdrawal	(5,000)	
Net cash provided by financing activities		25,000
Net increase in cash		9,000
Cash balance, November 1, 2014		0
Cash balance, November 30, 2014		$ 9,000

The header includes the name of the business, the title of the statement, and the time period. A statement of cash flows always represents a period of time.

Each dollar amount is calculated by evaluating the cash column on Exhibit 4. For example, collections from customers is calculated by adding the cash received from customers in transaction 4 ($5,500) plus transaction 8 ($2,000).

Operating activities involve cash receipts for services provided and cash payments for expenses paid.

Investing activities include the purchase and sale of land and equipment for cash.

Financing activities include cash contributions by the owner and owner withdrawals of cash.

The ending cash balance must match the cash balance on the balance sheet.

> Try It!

18. Using the following information, complete the income statement, statement of owner's equity, and balance sheet for DR Painting for the month of March 2015. The business began operations on March 1, 2015.

Accounts Receivable	$ 1,400	Salaries Expense	800
Accounts Payable	1,000	Service Revenue	7,000
Cash	22,300	Office Supplies	1,800
Owner contribution during March	40,000	Truck	20,000
Owner withdrawal during March	1,500	Utilities Expense	200
Richardson, Capital, March 1, 2015	0		

Check your answers at the end of the chapter.

For more practice, see Short Exercises S-11 through S-15. MyAccountingLab

HOW DO YOU USE FINANCIAL STATEMENTS TO EVALUATE BUSINESS PERFORMANCE?

Each of the financial statements provides different information about the company to the users of the financial statements. Exhibit 9 summarizes the information provided and the purpose of each financial statement.

Learning Objective 6

Use financial statements and return on assets (ROA) to evaluate business performance

Exhibit 9 | **Information Provided by Financial Statements**

Financial Statement	Information Provided and Purpose
Income statement	Provides information about profitability for a particular period for the company.
Statement of owner's equity	Informs users about how much of the earnings were kept and reinvested in the company.
Balance sheet	Provides valuable information to financial statement users about economic resources the company has (assets) as well as debts the company owes (liabilities). Allows decision makers to determine their opinion about the financial position of the company.
Statement of cash flows	Reports on a business's cash receipts and cash payments for a period of time.

Green Mountain Coffee Roasters, Inc.

In this chapter, we have reviewed the transactions and financial statements of Smart Touch Learning, a fictitious company. Now it's time to apply what we have learned to a real-world company. We will review the financial statements of **Green Mountain Coffee Roasters, Inc.** You will learn how to analyze its financial statements and apply the concepts presented in this chapter.

Take a moment to review the 2011 financial statements for Green Mountain in Appendix A, located online at **http://investor.gmcr.com/annuals.cfm**. Let's start by identifying the financial statements that we've discussed in this chapter. The income statement is presented on page F-4 of the Annual Report and is called the Consolidated Statements of Operations. Notice that the income statement calculates net income (revenue minus expenses). Green Mountain's net income for the year ending September 24, 2011, was $199,501,000.

Next the balance sheet is presented on page F-3 of the Annual Report. Can you find assets, liabilities, and equity? As we have learned in this chapter, Green Mountain's assets of $3,197,887,000 are equal to its liabilities and equity, $3,197,887,000.

Return on Assets (ROA)

One of the many tools that users of financial statements can use to determine how well a company is performing is the company's return on assets (ROA). Return on assets measures how profitably a company uses its assets. Return on assets is calculated by dividing net income by average total assets. Average total assets is calculated by adding the beginning and ending total assets for the time period and then dividing by two.

Return on Assets (ROA)

Measures how profitably a company uses its assets. Net income / Average total assets.

> Return on assets = Net income / Average total assets
> Average total assets = (Beginning total assets + Ending total assets) / 2

> Decisions — How can individuals make decisions about investing in the stock market?

Lori Cummings just inherited $10,000 from her grandmother. She has decided that she will invest the money in the stock market. She is thinking about investing in one of her favorite clothing stores. The problem is she can't decide between Urban Outfitters or The Gap.

How should Lori decide between the companies? What resources should she use?

Solution

Lori should begin by reviewing the financial statements of each business. She can locate them on the companies' websites or on the Securities and Exchange Commission's website (**www.sec.gov/edgar.shtml**). She should review the income statement and compare net income. Which business was more profitable? She should look at the balance sheet, carefully reviewing each part of the accounting equation. What was the dollar amount of assets? How much debt does the business have? In addition, she could go online and research the individual companies using a website such as Yahoo! Finance. These websites provide news and information about the company, such as current headlines, key statistics, and industry comparisons.

Lori should also consider diversifying her investment. Diversifying involves investing in more than one company and in a variety of industries and companies of different sizes. Diversification reduces the risk of an investment. Lori should consider investing half of the $10,000 in a company in a different industry, such as her favorite restaurant or food manufacturer.

Let's take a moment to calculate Green Mountain's ROA and measure how profitably it uses its assets. On its 2011 income statement, Green Mountain reported net income of $199,501 (in thousands). The corporation reported beginning total assets (found on the balance sheet) of $1,370,574 (in thousands) and ending total assets of $3,197,887 (in thousands). Green Mountain's return on assets for 2011 is:

$$\text{Return on assets} = \$199{,}501 / ((\$1{,}370{,}574 + \$3{,}197{,}887) / 2)$$
$$= \$199{,}501 / \$2{,}284{,}231^*$$
$$= 8.7\%^*$$

*rounded

How do we as an investor know if 8.7% is good or bad? We have to compare the return on assets of competing companies such as Caribou Coffee Company, Inc., **Starbucks Corporation**, and Dunkin' Brands Group, Inc. What if we told you that Dunkin' Brands Group, Inc.'s return on assets was 1.1%? Due to Green Mountain's higher ROA, we now know that Green Mountain has a stronger return on its assets than does Dunkin'. What does this mean? It means that Green Mountain produces more profit per every dollar of assets than Dunkin' does. As you learn more about accounting, you will explore more financial tools that are available to help investors evaluate a company's performance. Only after an investor looks at the big picture of a company will he or she have a good sense of the company's investment potential.

> Try It!

19. Using the following information, calculate the return on assets (ROA).

Net income	$ 5,000
Total assets, November 1, 2015	76,000
Total assets, November 30, 2015	80,250

Check your answer at the end of the chapter.

For more practice, see Short Exercise S-16. MyAccountingLab

REVIEW

> Things You Should Know

1. Why is accounting important?

- It's the language of business.
- Accounting is used by decision makers including individuals, businesses, investors, creditors, and taxing authorities.
- Accounting can be divided into two major fields: financial accounting and managerial accounting.
- Financial accounting is used by external decision makers and managerial accounting is used by internal decision makers.
- All businesses need accountants. Accountants work in private, public, and governmental jobs.
- Accountants can be licensed as either a certified public accountant (CPA) or certified management accountant (CMA).

2. What are the organizations and rules that govern accounting?

- Generally Accepted Accounting Principles (GAAP) are the rules that govern accounting in the United States.
- The Financial Accounting Standards Board (FASB) is responsible for the creation and governance of accounting standards (GAAP).
  - Economic entity assumption: Requires an organization to be a separate economic unit such as a sole proprietorship, partnership, corporation, or limited-liability company.
  - Cost principle: Acquired assets and services should be recorded at their actual cost.
  - Going concern assumption: Assumes that an entity will remain in operation for the foreseeable future.
  - Monetary unit assumption: Assumes financial transactions are recorded in a monetary unit.

3. What is the accounting equation?

- Assets = Liabilities + Equity
  - Assets: Items the business owns or controls (examples: cash, furniture, land)
  - Liabilities: Items the business owes (examples: accounts payable, notes payable, salaries payable)
  - Equity: Owner's claim to the assets (examples: owner's capital, owner's withdrawal, revenues, expenses)

4. **How do you analyze a transaction?**

- A transaction affects the financial position of a business and can be reliably measured.

- Transactions are analyzed using three steps:

  Step 1: Identify the accounts and account type (Asset, Liability, or Equity).

  Step 2: Decide whether each account increases or decreases.

  Step 3: Determine whether the accounting equation is in balance.

5. **How do you prepare financial statements?**

- Financial statements are prepared in the following order:

  1. Income Statement:
     - Reports the net income or net loss of a business for a specific period.
     - Revenues − Expenses = Net Income or Net Loss

  2. Statement of Owner's Equity:
     - Reports on the changes in owner's capital for a specific period.
     - Capital, Beginning + Owner Contributions + Net Income − Owner Withdrawals − Net Loss = Capital, Ending

  3. Balance Sheet:
     - Reports on an entity's assets, liabilities, and owner's equity as of a specific date.
     - Assets = Liabilities + Equity

  4. Statement of Cash Flows:
     - Reports on a business's cash receipts and cash payments during a period.
     - Includes three sections: Cash flows from operating activities, cash flows from investing activities, and cash flows from financing activities.

6. **How do you use financial statements to evaluate business performance?**

- Income statement evaluates profitability.

- Statement of owner's equity studies the amount of earnings that were kept and reinvested in the company.

- Balance sheet details the economic resources the company owns as well as debts the company owes.

- Statement of cash flows shows the change in cash.

- Return on assets (ROA) = Net income / Average total assets

> Summary Problem

Ron Smith opens an apartment-locator business near a college campus. The company will be named Campus Apartment Locators. During the first month of operations, July 2015, the business completes the following transactions:

a. Smith contributes $35,000 to the business. The business gives capital to Smith.

b. Purchases $350 of office supplies on account.

c. Pays cash of $30,000 to acquire a lot next to campus.

d. Locates apartments for clients and receives cash of $1,900.

e. Pays $100 on the accounts payable the business created in transaction b.

f. Pays cash expenses for office rent, $400, and utilities, $100.

g. Smith withdrew cash of $1,200.

Requirements

1. Analyze the preceding transactions in terms of their effects on the accounting equation of Campus Apartment Locators. Use Exhibit 4 as a guide.

2. Prepare the income statement, statement of owner's equity, and balance sheet of the business after recording the transactions.

3. Calculate the return on assets (ROA).

> Solution

Requirement 1

	Assets				=	Liabilities	+	Equity									
	Cash	+	Office Supplies	+	Land		Accounts Payable	+	Smith, Capital	−	Smith, Withdrawals	+	Service Revenue	−	Rent Expense	−	Utilities Expense
(a)	+35,000								+35,000								
(b)			+350				+350										
Bal.	$35,000	+	$350				$350	+	$35,000								
(c)	−30,000				+30,000												
Bal.	$5,000	+	$350	+	$30,000		$350	+	$35,000								
(d)	+1,900												+1,900				
Bal.	$6,900	+	$350	+	$30,000		$350	+	$35,000			+	$1,900				
(e)	−100						−100										
Bal.	$6,800	+	$350	+	$30,000		$250	+	$35,000			+	$1,900				
(f)	−500														−400		−100
Bal.	$6,300	+	$350	+	$30,000		$250	+	$35,000			+	$1,900	−	$400	−	$100
(g)	−1,200										−1,200						
Bal.	$5,100	+	$350	+	$30,000		$250	+	$35,000	−	$1,200	+	$1,900	−	$400	−	$100

$35,450

$35,450

Requirement 2

CAMPUS APARTMENT LOCATORS
Income Statement
Month Ended July 31, 2015

Revenues:		
Service Revenue		$ 1,900
Expenses:		
Rent Expense	$ 400	
Utilities Expense	100	
Total Expenses		500
Net Income		$ 1,400

CAMPUS APARTMENT LOCATORS
Statement of Owner's Equity
Month Ended July 31, 2015

Smith, Capital, July 1, 2015	$ 0
Owner contribution	35,000
Net income for the month	1,400
	36,400
Owner withdrawal	(1,200)
Smith, Capital, July 31, 2015	$ 35,200

CAMPUS APARTMENT LOCATORS
Balance Sheet
July 31, 2015

Assets		Liabilities	
Cash	$ 5,100	Accounts Payable	$ 250
Office Supplies	350		
Land	30,000	**Owner's Equity**	
		Smith, Capital	35,200
Total Assets	$ 35,450	Total Liabilities and Owner's Equity	$ 35,450

Requirement 3

ROA = Net income / Average total assets
Average total assets = (Beginning total assets + Ending total assets) / 2
Average total assets = ($0 + $35,450) / 2 = $17,725
ROA = $1,400 / $17,725 = 0.079 = 7.9%*

*rounded

Key Terms

Accounting

The information system that measures business activities, processes the information into reports, and communicates the results to decision makers.

Accounting Equation

The basic tool of accounting, measuring the resources of the business (what the business owns or has control of) and the claims to those resources (what the business owes to creditors and to the owner). Assets = Liabilities + Equity.

Accounts Payable

A short-term liability that will be paid in the future.

Accounts Receivable

The right to receive cash in the future from customers for goods sold or for services performed.

Assets

Economic resources that are expected to benefit the business in the future. Something the business owns or has control of.

Audit

An examination of a company's financial statements and records.

Balance Sheet

Reports on the assets, liabilities, and owner's equity of the business as of a specific date.

Certified Management Accountants (CMAs)

Certified professionals who specialize in accounting and financial management knowledge. They typically work for a single company.

Certified Public Accountants (CPAs)

Licensed professional accountants who serve the general public.

Corporation

A business organized under state law that is a separate legal entity.

Cost Principle

A principle that states that acquired assets and services should be recorded at their actual cost.

Creditor

Any person or business to whom a business owes money.

Economic Entity Assumption

An organization that stands apart as a separate economic unit.

Equity

The owner's claim to the assets of the business.

Expenses

The cost of selling goods or services.

Financial Accounting

The field of accounting that focuses on providing information for external decision makers.

Financial Accounting Standards Board (FASB)

The private organization that oversees the creation and governance of accounting standards in the United States.

Financial Statements

Business documents that are used to communicate information needed to make business decisions.

Generally Accepted Accounting Principles (GAAP)

Accounting guidelines, currently formulated by the *Financial Accounting Standards Board (FASB)*; the main U.S. accounting rule book.

Going Concern Assumption

Assumes that the entity will remain in operation for the foreseeable future.

Income Statement

Reports the *net income* or *net loss* of the business for a specific period.

International Accounting Standards Board (IASB)

The private organization that oversees the creation and governance of *International Financial Reporting Standards (IFRS)*.

International Financial Reporting Standards (IFRS)

A set of global accounting guidelines, formulated by the *International Accounting Standards Board (IASB)*.

Liabilities

Debts that are owed to *creditors*.

Limited-Liability Company (LLC)

A company in which each member is only liable for his or her own actions.

Managerial Accounting

The field of accounting that focuses on providing information for internal decision makers.

Monetary Unit Assumption

The assumption that requires the items on the financial statements to be measured in terms of a monetary unit.

Net Income

The result of operations that occurs when total revenues are greater than total expenses.

Net Loss

The result of operations that occurs when total expenses are greater than total revenues.

Owner's Capital

Owner contributions to a business.

Owner's Withdrawals

Payments of equity to the owner.

Partnership
A business with two or more owners and not organized as a corporation.

Return on Assets (ROA)
Measures how profitably a company uses its assets. Net income / Average total assets.

Revenues
Amounts earned from delivering goods or services to customers.

Sarbanes-Oxley Act (SOX)
Requires companies to review internal control and take responsibility for the accuracy and completeness of their financial reports.

Securities and Exchange Commission (SEC)
U. S. governmental agency that oversees the U.S. financial markets.

Sole Proprietorship
A business with a single owner.

Statement of Cash Flow
Reports on a business's cash receipts and cash payments for a specific period.

Statement of Owner's Equity
Shows the changes in the owner's capital account for a specific period.

Transaction
An event that affects the financial position of the business and can be measured reliably in dollar amounts.

> Quick Check

1. Accounting is the information system that

   a. measures business activities.

   b. communicates the results to decision makers.

   c. processes information into reports.

   d. All of the above.

   Learning Objective 1

2. Which of the following is not an external user of a business's financial information?

   a. Taxing authorities

   b. Customers

   c. Employee

   d. Investors

   Learning Objective 1

3. Generally Accepted Accounting Principles (GAAP) are currently formulated by the

   a. Financial Accounting Standards Board (FASB).

   b. Securities and Exchange Commission (SEC).

   c. Institute of Management Accountants (IMA).

   d. American Institute of Certified Public Accountants (AICPA).

   Learning Objective 2

4. Which type of business organization is owned by only one owner?

   a. Corporation

   b. Partnership

   c. Sole proprietorship

   d. Items a, b, and c are all correct.

   Learning Objective 2

5. Which of the following characteristics best describes a corporation?

   a. A business with a single owner

   b. Is not taxed

   c. Stockholders not personally liable for entity's debts

   d. Not a separate taxable entity

   Learning Objective 2

6. Which of the following requires accounting information to be complete, neutral, and free from material error?

   a. Faithful representation concept
   b. Cost principle
   c. Economic entity assumption
   d. Going concern assumption

7. At the end of a recent year, Global Cleaning Service, a full-service house and office cleaning service, had total assets of $3,630 and equity of $2,280. How much were Global Cleaning Service's liabilities?

   a. $5,910
   b. $3,630
   c. $1,350
   d. $2,280

8. Consider the overall effects on Global Cleaning Service from selling and performing services on account for $6,400 and paying expenses totaling $2,500. What is Global Cleaning Service's net income or net loss?

   a. Net income of $3,900
   b. Net loss of $3,900
   c. Net income of $6,400
   d. Net income of $8,900

9. Assume that Global Cleaning Service performed cleaning services for a department store on account for $180. How would this transaction affect Global Cleaning Service's accounting equation?

   a. Increase both assets and liabilities by $180
   b. Increase both assets and equity by $180
   c. Increase both liabilities and equity by $180
   d. Decrease liabilities by $180 and increase equity by $180

10. The balance sheet reports the

    a. financial position on a specific date.
    b. results of operations on a specific date.
    c. financial position for a specific period.
    d. results of operations for a specific period.

11. Assume Global Cleaning Service had net income of $570 for the year. Global Cleaning Service's beginning and ending total assets were $4,520 and $4,180, respectively. Calculate Global Cleaning Service's return on assets (ROA).

    a. 12.6%
    b. 13.6%
    c. 13.1%
    d. 7.63%

Check your answers at the end of the chapter.

ASSESS YOUR PROGRESS

> Review Questions

1. What is accounting?

2. Briefly describe the two major fields of accounting.

3. Describe the various types of individuals who use accounting information and how they use that information to make important decisions.

4. What are two certifications available for accountants? Briefly explain each certification.

5. What is the role of the Financial Accounting Standards Board (FASB)?

6. Explain the purpose of Generally Accepted Accounting Principles (GAAP), including the organization currently responsible for the creation and governance of these standards.

7. Describe the similarities and differences among the four different types of business entities discussed in the chapter.

8. A business purchases an acre of land for $5,000. The current market value is $5,550 and the land was assessed for property tax purposes at $5,250. What value should the land be recorded at, and which accounting principle supports your answer?

9. What does the going concern assumption mean for a business?

10. Which concept states that accounting information should be complete, neutral, and free from material error?

11. Financial statements in the United States are reported in U.S. dollars. What assumption supports this statement?

12. Explain the role of the International Accounting Standards Board (IASB) in relation to International Financial Reporting Standards (IFRS).

13. What is the accounting equation? Briefly explain each of the three parts.

14. What are the two ways that equity increases? What are the two ways that equity decreases?

15. How is net income calculated? Define revenues and expenses.

16. What are the steps used when analyzing a business transaction?

17. List the four financial statements. Briefly describe each statement.

18. What is the calculation for return on assets (ROA)? Explain what ROA measures.

Accounting and the Business Environment

> Short Exercises

Learning Objective 1

S-1 Identifying users of accounting information

For each user of accounting information, identify if the user would use financial accounting (FA) or managerial accounting (MA).

a. investor

b. banker

c. Internal Revenue Service

d. manager of the business

e. owner

f. stockholder

g. human resources director

h. creditor

Learning Objective 2

S-2 Determining organizations that govern accounting

Suppose you are starting a business, Wholly Shirts, to imprint logos on T-shirts. In organizing the business and setting up its accounting records, you take your information to a CPA to prepare financial statements for the bank. Name the organization that governs the majority of the guidelines that the CPA will use to prepare financial statements for Wholly Shirts. What are those guidelines called?

Learning Objective 2

S-3 Identifying types of business organizations

Chloe Michaels plans on opening Chloe Michaels Floral Designs. She is considering the various types of business organizations and wishes to organize her business with unlimited life and wants owners of the business to not be held personally liable for the business's debts. Additionally, Chloe wants the business to be a separate taxable entity. Which type of business organization will meet Chloe's needs best?

Learning Objective 2

S-4 Identifying types of business organizations

You would like to start a cellular telephone equipment service business. You are considering organizing the business as a sole proprietorship. Identify the advantages and disadvantages of owning a sole proprietorship.

Learning Objective 2

S-5 Applying accounting assumptions and principles

Michael McNamee is the proprietor of a property management company, Apartment Exchange, near the campus of Pensacola State College. The business has cash of $8,000 and furniture that cost $9,000 and has a market value of $13,000. The business debts include accounts payable of $6,000. Michael's personal home is valued at $400,000 and his personal bank account has a balance of $1,200. Consider the accounting principles and assumptions discussed in the chapter and identify the principle or assumption that best matches the situation:

a. Michael's personal assets are not recorded on the Apartment Exchange's balance sheet.

b. The Apartment Exchange records furniture at its cost of $9,000, not its market value of $13,000.

c. The Apartment Exchange reports its financial statements in U.S. dollars.

d. Michael expects the Apartment Exchange to remain in operations for the foreseeable future.

S-6 Using the accounting equation

Learning Objective 3

Hill Country Handyman Services has total assets for the year of $12,500 and total liabilities of $8,240.

Requirements

1. Use the accounting equation to solve for equity.
2. If next year assets increased by $3,200 and equity decreased by $1,890, what would be the amount of total liabilities for Hill Country Handyman Services?

S-7 Using the accounting equation

Learning Objective 3

Jacob's Overhead Doors reports the following financial information:

Assets	$45,800
Liabilities	15,230
Owner's Capital	28,700
Owner's Withdrawal	7,000
Revenues	10,890
Expenses	?

Requirements

1. Use the accounting equation to solve for the missing information.
2. Did Jacob's Overhead Doors report net income or net loss?

S-8 Identifying accounts

Learning Objective 3

Consider the following accounts:

a. Accounts Payable
b. Cash
c. Owner's Capital
d. Accounts Receivable
e. Rent Expense
f. Service Revenue
g. Office Supplies
h. Owner's Withdrawal
i. Land
j. Salaries Expense

Identify each account as Asset (A), Liability (L), or Equity (E).

Learning Objective 4

S-9 Using the accounting equation to analyze transactions

Turtle Creek Kennel earns service revenue by caring for the pets of customers. Turtle Creek Kennel is owned and operated by Ethan Martin. During the past month, Turtle Creek Kennel has the following transactions:

a. Received $320 cash for service revenue earned.

b. Paid $125 cash for salaries expense.

c. Ethan contributed $1,000 to the business in exchange for capital.

d. Earned $440 for service revenue, but the customer has not paid Turtle Creek Kennel yet.

e. Received utility bill of $65, which will be paid next month.

f. Ethan withdrew $80 cash.

Indicate the effects of the business transactions on the accounting equation for Turtle Creek Kennel. Transaction (a) is answered as a guide.

a. Increase asset (Cash); Increase equity (Service Revenue)

Learning Objective 4

S-10 Using the accounting equation to analyze transactions

Extreme Inflatables earns service revenue by providing party planning services and inflatable playscapes. Extreme Inflatables is owned and operated by Emma Gonzalez. During the past month, Extreme Inflatables has the following transactions:

a. Emma contributed $8,000 to the business in exchange for capital.

b. Purchased equipment for $2,000 on account.

c. Paid $300 for office supplies.

d. Earned and received $1,500 cash for service revenue.

e. Paid $200 for wages to employees.

f. Emma withdrew $500 cash.

g. Earned $2,000 for services provided. Customer has not yet paid.

h. Paid $800 for rent.

i. Received a bill for $150 for the monthly utilities. The bill has not yet been paid.

Indicate the effects of the business transactions on the accounting equation for Extreme Inflatables. Transaction (a) is answered as a guide.

a. Increase asset (Cash); Increase equity (Gonzalez, Capital)

Learning Objective 5

S-11 Identifying accounts on the financial statements

Consider the following accounts:

a. Accounts Payable

b. Cash

c. Owner's Capital

d. Accounts Receivable

e. Rent Expense

f. Service Revenue

g. Office Supplies

h. Owner's Withdrawal

i. Land

j. Salaries Expense

Identify the financial statement (or statements) that each account would appear on. Use I for Income Statement, OE for Statement of Owner's Equity, and B for Balance Sheet.

Use the following information to answer S-12 through S-14.

Elegant Arrangements has just completed operations for the year ended December 31, 2014. This is the third year of operations for the company. The following data have been assembled for the business:

Insurance Expense	$ 4,000	Salaries Expense	$42,000
Service Revenue	74,000	Accounts Payable	6,800
Utilities Expense	1,100	Office Supplies	2,100
Rent Expense	13,000	Rose, Withdrawals	3,900
Rose, Capital, Jan. 1, 2014	10,500	Accounts Receivable	5,500
Cash	4,700	Equipment	15,000

S-12 Preparing the income statement

Prepare the income statement of Elegant Arrangements for the year ended December 31, 2014.

Learning Objective 5

S-13 Preparing the statement of owner's equity

Prepare the statement of owner's equity of Elegant Arrangements for the year ended December 31, 2014.

Learning Objective 5

S-14 Preparing the balance sheet

Prepare the balance sheet of Elegant Arrangements as of December 31, 2014.

Learning Objective 5

S-15 Preparing the statement of cash flows

Main Street Homes had the following cash transactions for the month ended July 31, 2014.

Learning Objective 5

Cash receipts:	
Collections from customers	$20,000
Owner contribution	8,000
Cash payments:	
Rent	3,000
Utilities	1,500
Salaries	2,100
Purchase of equipment	10,750
Owner withdrawals	5,250
Cash balance, July 1, 2014	12,500
Cash balance, July 31, 2014	17,900

Prepare the statement of cash flows for Main Street Homes for the month ended July 31, 2014.

S-16 Calculating Return on Assets (ROA)

Advanced Water Services had net income for the month of October of $30,000. Assets as of the beginning and end of the month totaled, $355,000, and $345,000, respectively. Calculate Advanced Water Services' return on assets (ROA) for the month of October.

Learning Objective 6

> Exercises

Learning Objective 1

E-17 Identifying users of accounting information

For each of the users of accounting information, identify whether the user is an external decision maker (E) or an internal decision maker (I):

a. customer

b. company manager

c. Internal Revenue Service

d. lender

e. investor

f. controller

g. cost accountant

h. SEC

Learning Objective 2

E-18 Using accounting vocabulary

Consider the following accounting terms and definitions and match each term to the definition:

1. Sole proprietorship	a. Set of global accounting guidelines, formulated by the IASB
2. Faithful representation	b. Holds that fair market value should not be used over actual costs
3. Partnership	
4. IFRS	c. Stands for Financial Accounting Standards Board
5. Corporation	d. Owner is referred to as a proprietor
6. Audit	e. Asserts that accounting information should be complete, neutral, and free from material error
7. Cost principle	
8. FASB	f. An examination of a company's financial statements and records
9. Creditors	
10. SEC	g. Has two or more owners (called partners)
	h. U.S. governmental agency that oversees the U.S. financial markets
	i. Type of entity that is designed to limit personal liability exposure of owners to the entity's debts
	j. Person or business lending money

E-19 Using accounting vocabulary

Learning Objectives 3, 5

Consider the following accounting terms and definitions and match each term to the definition:

1. Accounting equation
2. Asset
3. Balance sheet
4. Expense
5. Income statement
6. Liability
7. Net income
8. Net loss
9. Revenue
10. Statement of cash flows
11. Statement of owner's equity

a. An economic resource that is expected to be of benefit in the future

b. Debts that are owed to creditors

c. Excess of total expenses over total revenues

d. Excess of total revenues over total expenses

e. The basic tool of accounting, stated as Assets = Liabilities + Equity

f. Decreases in equity that occur in the course of selling goods or services

g. Increases in equity that occur in the course of selling goods or services

h. Reports on a business's cash receipts and cash payments during a period

i. Reports on an entity's assets, liabilities, and equity as of a specific date

j. Reports on an entity's revenues, expenses, and net income or loss for the period

k. Report that shows the changes in capital for a period of time.

E-20 Using the accounting equation

Learning Objective 3

Compute the missing amount in the accounting equation for each entity from the financial information presented:

	Assets	Liabilities	Equity
New Rock Gas	$?	$24,000	$50,000
DJ Video Rentals	75,000	?	32,000
Corner Grocery	100,000	53,000	?

E-21 Using the accounting equation

Learning Objective 3

Great City Builders' balance sheet data at May 31, 2014, and June 30, 2014, follow:

	May 31, 2014	June 30, 2014
Total assets	$177,000	$213,000
Total liabilities	122,000	144,000

For each of the following situations with regard to owner's contributions and withdrawals of the business, compute the amount of net income or net loss during June 2014.

a. The owner contributed $6,000 in the business and made no withdrawals.

b. The owner made no contributions. The owner withdrew cash of $10,000.

c. The company owner made contributions of $18,000 and withdrew cash of $20,000.

39

Accounting and the Business Environment

Learning Objective 3

E-22 Using the accounting equation

Bob Auto Repairs started 2014 with total assets of $19,000 and total liabilities of $9,000. At the end of 2014, Bob's total assets stood at $27,000, and total liabilities were $13,000.

Requirements

1. Did the owner's equity of Bob Auto Repairs increase or decrease during 2014? By how much?
2. Identify the four possible reasons that owner's equity can change.

Learning Objective 3

E-23 Using the accounting equation

During 2014, Serenity Creek Spa reported revenue of $21,000. Total expenses for the year were $14,000. Serenity Creek Spa ended the year with total assets of $30,000, and it owed debts totaling $14,000. At year-end 2013, the business reported total assets of $23,000 and total liabilities of $14,000.

Requirements

1. Compute Serenity Creek Spa's net income for 2014.
2. Did Serenity Creek Spa's equity increase or decrease during 2014? By how much?

Learning Objective 3

E-24 Using the accounting equation

The records of Felix Company show the following at December 31, 2014:

Beginning:		Equity:	
Assets	$ 45,000	Owner contributions	$ 0
Liabilities	29,000	Owner withdrawals	19,000
Ending:		Revenues	242,000
Assets	$ 55,000	Expenses	?
Liabilities	38,000		

Requirements

1. Compute the missing amount for Felix Company. You will need to work through total owner's equity.
2. Did Felix earn a net income or suffer a net loss for the year? Compute the amount.

Learning Objective 4

E-25 Using the accounting equation to analyze transactions

As the manager of a Papa Sam's restaurant, you must deal with a variety of business transactions. Give an example of a transaction that has each of the following effects on the accounting equation:

a. Increase one asset and decrease another asset.

b. Decrease an asset and decrease equity.

c. Decrease an asset and decrease a liability.

d. Increase an asset and increase equity.

e. Increase an asset and increase a liability.

E-26 Using the accounting equation to analyze business transactions

Learning Objective 4

Indicate the effects of the following business transactions on the accounting equation of Viviani Video store. Transaction (a) is answered as a guide.

a. Received cash of $8,000 from owner and gave capital.

   Answer: Increase asset (Cash); Increase equity (Viviani, Capital)

b. Earned video rental revenue on account, $1,800.

c. Purchased office furniture on account, $400.

d. Received cash on account, $600.

e. Paid cash on account, $100.

f. Rented videos and received cash of $300.

g. Paid monthly office rent of $900.

h. Paid $200 cash to purchase office supplies.

E-27 Using the accounting equation to analyze business transactions

Learning Objective 4

Indicate the effects of the following business transactions on the accounting equation for Shane's Roasted Peanuts, a supplier of snack foods. Transaction (a) is answered as a guide.

a. Shane's Roasted Peanuts received cash from the owner and gave capital to Shane.

   Answer: Increase asset (Cash); Increase equity (Shane, Capital)

b. Cash purchase of land for a building site.

c. Paid cash on accounts payable.

d. Purchased equipment; signed a note payable.

e. Performed service for a customer on account.

f. Employees worked for the week but will be paid next Tuesday.

g. Received cash from a customer on accounts receivable.

h. Borrowed money from the bank.

i. Owner withdrew cash.

j. Incurred utilities expense on account.

Learning Objective 4

E-28 Using the accounting equation to analyze business transactions

The analysis of the first eight transactions of All-in-One Accounting Service follows. Describe each transaction.

			Assets					Liabilities	+				Equity			
	Cash	+	Accounts Receivable	+ Equipment				Accounts Payable	+	Larrison, Capital	−	Larrison, Withdrawals	+	Service Revenue	−	Salaries Expense
1	+31,000									+31,000						
2			+3,800											+3,800		
Bal.	$31,000	+	$3,800							$31,000			+	$3,800		
3				+13,400				+13,400								
Bal.	$31,000	+	$3,800	+ $13,400				$13,400	+	$31,000			+	$3,800		
4	+190		−190		=											
Bal.	$31,190	+	$3,610	+ $13,400				$13,400	+	$31,000			+	$3,800		
5	−410			+410												
Bal.	$30,780	+	$3,610	+ $13,810				$13,400	+	$31,000			+	$3,800		
6	−8,000							−8,000								
Bal.	$22,780	+	$3,610	+ $13,810				$5,400	+	$31,000			+	$3,800		
7	+790													+790		
Bal.	$23,570	+	$3,610	+ $13,810				$5,400	+	$31,000			+	$4,590		
8	−1,500															−1,500
Bal.	$22,070	+	$3,610	+ $13,810				$5,400	+	$31,000			+	$4,590	−	$1,500

Learning Objective 4

E-29 Using the accounting equation to analyze business transactions

Caren Smith opened a medical practice. During July, the first month of operation, the business, titled Caren Smith, M.D., experienced the following events:

July 6	Smith contributed $55,000 in the business by opening a bank account in the name of C. Smith, M.D. The business gave capital to Smith.
9	Paid $46,000 cash for land.
12	Purchased medical supplies for $1,800 on account.
15	Officially opened for business.
20	Paid cash expenses: employees' salaries, $1,600; office rent, $900; utilities, $100.
31	Earned service revenue for the month, $8,000, receiving cash.
31	Paid $1,100 on account.

Analyze the effects of these events on the accounting equation of the medical practice of Caren Smith, M.D., using the following format:

		Assets					Liabilities	+				Equity					
Cash	+	Medical Supplies	+	Land	=		Accounts Payable	+	Smith, Capital	−	Smith, Withdrawals	+ Service Revenue	− Salaries Expense	−	Rent Expense	−	Utilities Expense

E-30 Preparing the financial statements

Learning Objective 5

Evan O'Brien publishes a travel magazine. In need of cash, the business applies for a loan with National Bank. The bank requires borrowers to submit financial statements. With little knowledge of accounting, Evan O'Brien, the proprietor, does not know how to proceed.

Requirements

1. What are the four financial statements that Evan will need to prepare?

2. Is there a specific order in which the financial statements must be prepared?

3. Explain how to prepare each statement.

Use the following information to answer E-31 through E-33.

The account balances of Wilson Towing Service at June 30, 2014, follow:

Equipment	$13,600	Service Revenue	$11,200
Office Supplies	900	Accounts Receivable	6,200
Notes Payable	6,900	Accounts Payable	3,000
Rent Expense	550	Wilson, Capital, June 1, 2014	2,950
Cash	1,900	Salaries Expense	1,900
Wilson, Withdrawals	1,000		

E-31 Preparing the income statement

Learning Objective 5

Net Income $8,750

Requirements

1. Prepare the income statement for Wilson Towing Service for the month ending June 30, 2014.

2. What does the income statement report?

E-32 Preparing the statement of owner's equity

Learning Objective 5

Ending Capital $12,700

Requirements

1. Prepare the statement of owner's equity for Wilson Towing Service for the month ending June 30, 2014. Assume the owner made a contribution of $2,000 on June 15, 2014.

2. What does the statement of owner's equity report?

E-33 Preparing the balance sheet

Learning Objective 5

Total Assets $22,600

Requirements

1. Prepare the balance sheet for Wilson Towing Service as of June 30, 2014.

2. What does the balance sheet report?

Use the following information to answer E-34 through E-36.

The asset, liabilities, and equities of Davis Design Studio have the following balances at December 31, 2014. The owner began the year with a $33,300 capital balance and contributed $15,000 and withdrew $54,400 during the year.

Notes Payable	$10,900	Office Furniture	$ 49,000
Rent Expense	23,000	Utilities Expense	6,900
Cash	3,600	Accounts Payable	3,200
Office Supplies	4,500	Service Revenue	158,300
Salaries Expense	65,000	Accounts Receivable	8,600
Property Tax Expense	1,500	Miscellaneous Expense	4,200

Learning Objective 5

Net Income $57,700

E-34 Preparing the income statement

Prepare the income statement for Davis Design Studio for the year ending December 31, 2014.

Learning Objective 5

Ending Capital $51,600

E-35 Preparing the statement of owner's equity

Prepare the statement of owner's equity for Davis Design Studio for the year ending December 31, 2014.

Learning Objective 5

Total Assets $65,700

E-36 Preparing the balance sheet

Prepare the balance sheet for Davis Design Studio as of December 31, 2014.

Learning Objective 5

E-37 Preparing the statement of cash flows

For each transaction, identify the appropriate section on the statement of cash flows to report the transaction. Choose from: Cash flows from operating activities (O), Cash flows from investing activities (I), Cash flows from financing activities (F), or Is not reported on the statement of cash flows (X). If reported on the statement, decide whether the transaction should be shown as a positive cash flow (+) or a negative cash flow (–):

a. The business received cash from the owner in exchange for capital.

b. Paid cash on accounts payable for office supplies purchased.

c. Performed services for a customer on account.

d. The owner withdrew cash.

e. Received cash from a customer for services performed.

f. Purchased equipment with cash.

g. Paid rent for the month.

h. Purchased land; signed a note payable.

i. Paid employees wages for the week.

j. Incurred utility expense on account

E-38 Preparing the statement of cash flows

Learning Objective 5

Decrease in cash $5,050

Java Food Equipment Company had the following transactions for the month ending February 28, 2014. Java's cash balance on February 1, 2014 was $13,750.

Feb. 1	The owner contributed an additional $10,000 cash to the business in exchange for capital.
7	Purchased equipment for $2,600 on account.
14	Paid $15,000 cash for land.
17	Paid cash expenses: employees' salaries, $800; office rent, $1,000; utilities, $250.
23	The owner withdrew $2,000.
26	Earned service revenue for the month, $4,000, receiving cash.

Prepare the statement of cash flows of Java Food Equipment Company for the month ended February 28, 2014.

E-39 Calculating Return on Assets (ROA)

Learning Objective 6

Alpha Appliance Service had net income for the year of $35,000. In addition, the balance sheet reports the following balances:

	Jan. 1, 2014	Dec. 31, 2014
Notes Payable	$ 50,000	$ 71,500
Cash	35,000	55,000
Office Furniture	28,000	50,000
Building	150,000	150,000
Accounts Payable	10,000	8,500
Wright, Capital	180,000	240,000
Accounts Receivable	2,600	18,800
Equipment	20,000	45,000
Office Supplies	4,400	1,200

Calculate the return on assets (ROA) for Alpha Appliance Service for the year ending December 31, 2014.

> Problems **Group A**

Learning Objective 4

Total Assets $27,900

P-40A Using the accounting equation for transaction analysis

Matilda Crone owns and operates a public relations firm called Dance Fever. The following amounts summarize her business on August 31, 2014:

	Assets					Liabilities	+				Equity			
	Cash + Accounts + Office + Land				=	Accounts	+	Crone,	−	Crone,	+ Service	− Rent	− Advertising	
	Receivable Supplies					Payable		Capital		Withdrawals	Revenue	Expense	Expense	
Bal.	$2,300 + $3,000 + $0		+$14,000			$8,000	+	$11,300						

During September 2014, the business completed the following transactions:

a. Matilda Crone contributed $13,000 cash in exchange for capital.

b. Performed service for a client and received cash of $900.

c. Paid off the beginning balance of accounts payable.

d. Purchased office supplies from OfficeMax on account, $600.

e. Collected cash from a customer on account, $2,300.

f. Matilda withdrew $1,600.

g. Consulted for a new band and billed the client for services rendered, $5,500.

h. Recorded the following business expenses for the month:

Paid office rent: $1,200.

Paid advertising: $600.

Analyze the effects of the transactions on the accounting equation of Dance Fever using the format presented above.

Learning Objective 4

Total Assets $19,425

P-41A Using the accounting equation for transaction analysis

Christopher Turner started a new business, Turner Gymnastics, and completed the following transactions during December:

Dec. 1	Christopher contributed $21,000 cash in exchange for capital.
2	Received $3,500 cash from customers for services performed.
5	Paid $200 cash for office supplies.
9	Performed services for a customer and billed the customer for services rendered, $2,000.
10	Received $300 bill for utilities due in two weeks.
15	Paid for advertising in the local paper, $325.
20	Paid utility bill received on Dec. 10.
25	Collected cash from customer billed on Dec. 9.
28	Paid rent for the month, $2,000.
28	Paid $1,250 to assistant for wages.
30	Received $1,800 cash from customers for services performed.
31	Christopher withdrew $5,000 cash from the business.

Analyze the effects of the transactions on the accounting equation of Turner Gymnastics using a format similar to Exhibit 4.

P-42A Preparing financial statements

Learning Objective 5

1. Net Income $86,900

Presented here are the accounts of Gate City Answering Service for the year ended December 31, 2014.

Land	$ 8,000	Owner contribution, 2014	$ 28,000
Notes Payable	32,000	Accounts Payable	11,000
Property Tax Expense	2,600	Accounts Receivable	1,000
Wayne, Withdrawals	30,000	Advertising Expense	15,000
Rent Expense	13,000	Building	145,200
Salaries Expense	65,000	Cash	3,000
Salaries Payable	1,300	Equipment	16,000
Service Revenue	192,000	Insurance Expense	2,500
Office Supplies	10,000	Interest Expense	7,000
Wayne, Capital, 12/31/13	54,000		

Requirements

1. Prepare Gate City Answering Service's income statement.
2. Prepare the statement of owner's equity.
3. Prepare the balance sheet.

P-43A Preparing financial statements

Learning Objective 5

b. Ending Capital $76,000

Studio Photography works weddings and prom-type parties. The balance of Ansel, Capital was $16,000 at December 31, 2013. At December 31, 2014, the business's accounting records show these balances:

Insurance Expense	$ 8,000	Accounts Receivable	$ 8,000
Cash	37,000	Notes Payable	12,000
Accounts Payable	7,000	Ansel, Capital, Dec. 31, 2014	?
Advertising Expense	3,000	Salaries Expense	25,000
Service Revenue	80,000	Equipment	50,000
Ansel, Withdrawals	13,000	Owner contribution, 2014	29,000

Prepare the following financial statements for Studio Photography for the year ended December 31, 2014:

a. Income statement
b. Statement of owner's equity
c. Balance sheet

Accounting and the Business Environment

P-44A Preparing financial statements

The bookkeeper of Greener Landscaping prepared the company's balance sheet while the accountant was ill. The balance sheet contains numerous errors. In particular, the bookkeeper knew that the balance sheet should balance, so he plugged in the owner's equity amount needed to achieve this balance. The owner's equity is incorrect. All other amounts are right, but some are out of place. Prepare a corrected balance sheet.

GREENER LANDSCAPING
Balance Sheet
Month Ended November 30, 2014

Assets		Liabilities	
Cash	$ 4,900	Accounts Receivables	$ 2,200
Office Supplies	600	Tum, Withdrawals	10,000
Land	34,200	Service Revenue	39,000
Salaries Expense	2,800	Property Tax Expense	2,600
Office Furniture	6,100	Accounts Payable	2,700
Notes Payable	24,200		
Rent Expense	300	**Owner's Equity**	
		Tum, Capital	16,600
Total Assets	**$ 73,100**	Total Liabilities	**$ 73,100**

P-45A Using the accounting equation for transaction analysis and preparing financial statements

Alex Shore recently opened his own accounting firm, which he operates as a sole proprietorship. The name of the new entity is Alex Shore, CPA. Shore experienced the following events during the organizing phase of the new business and its first month of operations in 2014:

Feb. 5	Shore deposited $50,000 in a new business bank account titled Alex Shore, CPA. The business gave capital to Shore.
6	Paid $100 cash for letterhead stationery for new office.
7	Purchased office furniture for the office on account, $9,700.
10	Consulted with tax client and received $2,000 for services rendered.
11	Paid utilities, $200.
12	Finished tax hearings on behalf of a client and submitted a bill for accounting services, $17,000.
18	Paid office rent, $1,500.
25	Received amount due from client that was billed on February 12.
27	Paid full amount of accounts payable created on February 7.
28	Shore withdrew cash of $1,000.

Requirements

1. Analyze the effects of the events on the accounting equation of the sole proprietorship of Alex Shore, CPA. Use a format similar to Exhibit 4.

2. Prepare the following financial statements:

    a. Income statement

    b. Statement of owner's equity

    c. Balance sheet

P-46A Using the accounting equation for transaction analysis and preparing financial statements

Learning Objectives 4, 5

2c. Total Assets $110,480

Angela Peters recently opened her own law office, which she operates as a sole proprietorship. The name of the new entity is Angela Peters, Attorney. Peters experienced the following events during the organizing phase of the new business and its first month of operation, March 2014. Some of the events were personal and did not affect the law practice. Others were business transactions and should be accounted for by the business.

Mar. 1	Sold personal investment in eBay stock, which she had owned for several years, receiving $31,000 cash.
2	Deposited the $31,000 cash from the sale of the eBay stock in her personal bank account.
3	Deposited $89,000 cash in a new business bank account titled Angela Peters, Attorney. The business gave capital to Peters.
5	Paid $400 cash for ink cartridges for the printer.
7	Purchased computer for the law office, agreeing to pay the account, $9,300, within three months.
9	Received $2,000 cash from customers for services rendered.
15	Received bill from *The Lawyer* for magazine subscription, $120.
23	Finished court hearings on behalf of a client and submitted a bill for legal services, $13,500, on account.
28	Paid bill from *The Lawyer*.
30	Paid utilities, $1,200.
31	Received $3,000 cash from clients billed on Mar 23.
31	Peters withdrew cash of $2,000.

Requirements

1. Analyze the effects of the preceding events on the accounting equation of the sole proprietorship of Angela Peters, Attorney. Use a format similar to Exhibit 4.

2. Prepare the following financial statements:

    a. Income statement

    b. Statement of owner's equity

    c. Balance sheet

Accounting and the Business Environment

> Problems **Group B**

Learning Objective 4

Total Assets $22,400

P-47B Using the accounting equation for transaction analysis

Missy Collins owns and operates a public relations firm called Top 40. The following amounts summarize her business on August 31, 2014:

		Assets				Liabilities	+				Equity			
Cash	+ Accounts +	Office +	Land		=	Accounts	+	Collins, −	Collins,	+ Service	− Rent	− Advertising		
	Receivable	Supplies				Payable		Capital	Withdrawals	Revenue	Expense	Expense		
Bal.	$2,100 +	$2,000 +	$0	+ $10,000		$6,000	+	$8,100						

During September 2014, the business completed the following transactions:

a. Missy Collins contributed $10,000 cash in exchange for capital.

b. Performed service for a client and received cash of $1,000.

c. Paid off the beginning balance of accounts payable.

d. Purchased office supplies from OfficeMax on account, $700.

e. Collected cash from a customer on account, $500.

f. Missy withdrew $1,900.

g. Consulted for a new band and billed the client for services rendered, $5,800.

h. Recorded the following business expenses for the month:

Paid office rent: $900.

Paid advertising: $400.

Analyze the effects of the transactions on the accounting equation of Top 40 using the format presented above.

Learning Objective 4

Total Assets $34,925

P-48B Using the accounting equation for transaction analysis

Anna Taylor started a new business, Taylor Gymnastics, and completed the following transactions during December:

Dec. 1	Anna contributed $30,000 cash in exchange for capital.
2	Received $4,000 cash from customers for services performed.
5	Paid $100 cash for office supplies.
9	Performed services for a customer and billed the customer for services rendered, $3,000.
10	Received $200 bill for utilities due in two weeks.
15	Paid for advertising in the local paper, $125.
20	Paid utility bill received on Dec. 10.
25	Collected cash from customer billed on Dec. 9.
28	Paid rent for the month, $1,500.
28	Paid $1,050 to assistant for wages.
30	Received $2,800 cash from customers for services performed.
31	Anna withdrew $2,000 cash from the business.

Analyze the effects of the transactions on the accounting equation of Taylor Gymnastics using a format similar to Exhibit 4.

P-49B Preparing financial statements

Learning Objective 5

Presented here are the accounts of Quick and EZ Delivery for the year ended December 31, 2014:

1. Net Income $82,100

Land	$ 7,000	Owner contribution, 2014	$ 32,000
Notes Payable	30,000	Accounts Payable	14,000
Property Tax Expense	2,900	Accounts Receivable	1,700
Trott, Withdrawals	32,000	Advertising Expense	17,000
Rent Expense	13,000	Building	137,900
Salaries Expense	69,000	Cash	6,000
Salaries Payable	500	Equipment	17,000
Service Revenue	192,000	Insurance Expense	2,000
Office Supplies	8,000	Interest Expense	6,000
Trott, Capital, 12/31/13	51,000		

Requirements

1. Prepare Quick and EZ Delivery's income statement.
2. Prepare the statement of owner's equity.
3. Prepare the balance sheet.

P-50B Preparing financial statements

Learning Objective 5

Photo Gallery works weddings and prom-type parties. The balance of Leibovitz, Capital was $17,000 at December 31, 2013. At December 31, 2014, the business's accounting records show these balances:

b. Ending Capital $84,000

Insurance Expense	$ 9,000	Accounts Receivable	$ 6,000
Cash	26,000	Notes Payable	14,000
Accounts Payable	4,000	Leibovitz, Capital, Dec. 31, 2014	?
Advertising Expense	2,000	Salaries Expense	21,000
Service Revenue	78,000	Equipment	70,000
Leibovitz, Withdrawals	14,000	Owner contribution, 2014	35,000

Prepare the following financial statements for Photo Gallery for the year ended December 31, 2014:

a. Income statement

b. Statement of owner's equity

c. Balance sheet

Accounting and the Business Environment

Learning Objective 5

Total Assets $41,700

P-51B Preparing financial statements

The bookkeeper of Outdoor Life Landscaping prepared the company's balance sheet while the accountant was ill. The balance sheet contains numerous errors. In particular, the bookkeeper knew that the balance sheet should balance, so he plugged in the owner's equity amount needed to achieve this balance. The owner's equity is incorrect. All other amounts are right, but some are out of place. Prepare a corrected balance sheet.

OUTDOOR LIFE LANDSCAPING
Balance Sheet
Month Ended July 31, 2014

Assets		Liabilities	
Cash	$ 5,000	Accounts Receivables	$ 2,300
Office Supplies	800	Kamp, Withdrawals	8,000
Land	28,400	Service Revenue	39,200
Salaries Expense	3,500	Property Tax Expense	2,000
Office Furniture	5,200	Accounts Payable	2,800
Notes Payable	26,400		
Rent Expense	700	**Owner's Equity**	
		Kamp, Capital	15,700
Total Assets	**$ 70,000**	Total Liabilities	**$ 70,000**

Learning Objectives 4, 5

2c. Total Assets $37,950

P-52B Using the accounting equation for transaction analysis and preparing financial statements

Aaron Woody recently opened his own accounting firm, which he operates as a sole proprietorship. The name of the new entity is Aaron Woody, CPA. Woody experienced the following events during the organizing phase of the new business and its first month of operations in 2014.

Feb. 5	Woody deposited $31,000 in a new business bank account titled Aaron Woody, CPA. The business gave capital to Woody.
6	Paid $200 cash for letterhead stationery for new office.
7	Purchased office furniture for the office on account, $9,500.
10	Consulted with tax client and received $3,000 for services rendered.
11	Paid utilities, $150.
12	Finished tax hearings on behalf of a client and submitted a bill for accounting services, $14,000.
18	Paid office rent, $1,900.
25	Received amount due from client that was billed on February 12.
27	Paid full amount of accounts payable created on February 7.
28	Woody withdrew cash of $8,000.

Requirements

1. Analyze the effects of the events on the accounting equation of the sole proprietorship of Aaron Woody, CPA. Use a format similar to Exhibit 4.

2. Prepare the following financial statements:

   a. Income statement

   b. Statement of owner's equity

   c. Balance sheet

P-53B Using the accounting equation for transaction analysis and preparing financial statements

Learning Objectives 4, 5

2b. Ending Capital $122,020

Aimee Griffin recently opened her own law office, which she operates as a sole proprietorship. The name of the new entity is Aimee Griffin, Attorney. Griffin experienced the following events during the organizing phase of the new business and its first month of operation, December 2014. Some of the events were personal and did not affect the law practice. Others were business transactions and should be accounted for by the business.

Dec. 1	Sold personal investment in eBay stock, which she had owned for several years, receiving $33,000 cash.
2	Deposited the $33,000 cash from the sale of the eBay stock in her personal bank account.
3	Deposited $109,000 cash in a new business bank account titled Aimee Griffin, Attorney. The business gave capital to Griffin.
5	Paid $900 cash for ink cartridges for the printer.
7	Purchased computer for the law office, agreeing to pay the account, $9,200, within three months.
9	Received $3,000 cash from customers for services rendered.
15	Received bill from *The Lawyer* for magazine subscription, $80.
23	Finished court hearings on behalf of a client and submitted a bill for legal services, $17,000, on account.
28	Paid bill from *The Lawyer*.
30	Paid utilities, $1,900.
31	Received $4,000 cash from clients billed on Dec. 23.
31	Griffin withdrew cash of $5,000.

Requirements

1. Analyze the effects of the preceding events on the accounting equation of the sole proprietorship of Aimee Griffin, Attorney. Use a format similar to Exhibit 4.

2. Prepare the following financial statements:

   a. Income statement

   b. Statement of owner's equity

   c. Balance sheet

> Continuing Problem

3. Ending Capital $18,400

P-54 Using the accounting equation for transaction analysis, preparing financial statements, and calculating return on assets (ROA)

Davis Consulting began operations and completed the following transactions during December, 2014:

Dec. 2	Owner contributed $18,000 cash in exchange for capital.
2	Paid monthly office rent, $550.
3	Paid cash for a computer, $1,800. This equipment is expected to remain in service for five years.
4	Purchased office furniture on account, $4,200. The furniture should last for five years.
5	Purchased office supplies on account, $900.
9	Performed consulting service for a client on account, $1,500.
12	Paid utilities expenses, $250.
18	Performed service for a client and received cash of $1,100.
21	Received $1,400 in advance for client service to be performed over the next 30 days. (This increases the Unearned Revenue account which is a liability.)
21	Hired an administrative assistant to be paid $2,055 on the 20th day of each month. The secretary begins work immediately.
26	Paid $400 on account.
28	Collected $300 on account.
30	Davis withdrew $1,400.

Requirements

1. Analyze the effects of Davis Consulting's transactions on the accounting equation. Use the format of Exhibit 4, and include these headings: Cash; Accounts Receivable; Office Supplies; Equipment; Furniture; Accounts Payable; Unearned Revenue; Davis, Capital; Davis, Withdrawals; Service Revenue; Rent Expense; and Utilities Expense.

2. Prepare the income statement of Davis Consulting for the month ended December 31, 2014.

3. Prepare the statement of owner's equity for the month ended December 31, 2014.

4. Prepare the balance sheet as of December 31, 2014.

5. Calculate the return on assets for Davis Consulting.

CRITICAL THINKING

> Decision Cases

Decision Case 1

Let's examine a case using Greg's Tunes and Sal's Silly Songs. It is now the end of the first year of operations, and both owners—Sally Siegman and Greg Moore—want to know how well they came out at the end of the year. Neither business kept complete accounting records and neither owner made any withdrawals. Moore and Siegman throw together the following data at year end:

Sal's Silly Songs:	
Total assets	$23,000
Owner contribution	8,000
Total revenues	35,000
Total expenses	22,000
Greg's Tunes:	
Total liabilities	$10,000
Owner contribution	6,000
Total expenses	44,000
Net income	9,000

Working in the music business, Moore has forgotten all the accounting he learned in college. Siegman majored in English literature, so she never learned any accounting. To gain information for evaluating their businesses, they ask you several questions. For each answer, you must show your work to convince Moore and Siegman that you know what you are talking about.

Requirements

1. Which business has more assets?
2. Which business owes more to creditors?
3. Which business has more owner's equity at the end of the year?
4. Which business brought in more revenue?
5. Which business is more profitable?
6. Which of the foregoing questions do you think is most important for evaluating these two businesses? Why?
7. Which business looks better from a financial standpoint?

Decision Case 2

Dave and Reba Guerrera saved all their married life to open a bed and breakfast (B&B) named Tres Amigos. They invested $100,000 of their own money and the company gave capital to them. The business then got a $100,000 bank loan for the $200,000 needed to get started. The company bought a run-down old Spanish colonial home in Tucson for $80,000. It cost another $50,000 to renovate. They found most of the furniture at antique shops and flea markets—total cost was $20,000. Kitchen equipment cost $10,000, and a computer system cost $2,000.

Prior to the grand opening, the banker requests a report on their activities thus far. Tres Amigos' bank statement shows a cash balance of $38,000. Dave and Reba believe that the $38,000 represents net income for the period, and they feel pretty good about the results of their business. To better understand how well they are doing, they prepare the following income statement for presentation to the bank:

TRES AMIGOS BED AND BREAKFAST
Income Statement
Six Months Ended June 30, 2015

Revenues:		
Contributions by owner	$ 100,000	
Bank loan	100,000	
Total revenues		$ 200,000
Expenses:		
Cost of the house	80,000	
Renovation to the house	50,000	
Furniture expense	20,000	
Kitchen equipment expense	10,000	
Computer expense	2,000	
Total expenses		162,000
Net income		$ 38,000

Requirements

1. Suppose you are the Guerreras' banker, and they have given you this income statement. Would you congratulate them on their net income? If so, explain why. If not, how would you advise them to measure the net income of the business? Does the amount of cash in the bank measure net income? Explain.

2. Prepare Tres Amigos' balance sheet from their data. There is no net income or loss yet.

> Ethical Issue 1

The tobacco companies have paid billions because of smoking-related illnesses. In particular, Philip Morris, a leading cigarette manufacturer, paid more than $3,000,000,000 in settlement payments in one year.

Requirements

1. Suppose you are the chief financial officer (CFO) responsible for the financial statements of Philip Morris. What ethical issue would you face as you consider what to report in your company's annual report about the cash payments? What is the ethical course of action for you to take in this situation?

2. What are some of the negative consequences to Philip Morris for not telling the truth? What are some of the negative consequences to Philip Morris for telling the truth?

> Fraud Case 1

Exeter is a building contractor on the Gulf Coast. After losing a number of big lawsuits, it was facing its first annual net loss as the end of the year approached. The owner, Hank Snow, was under intense pressure from the company's creditors to report positive net income for the year. However, he knew that the controller, Alice Li, had arranged a short-term bank loan of $10,000 to cover a temporary shortfall of cash. He told Alice to record the incoming cash as "construction revenue" instead of a loan. That would nudge the company's income into positive territory for the year, and then, he said, the entry could be corrected in January when the loan was repaid.

Requirements

1. How would this action affect the year-end income statement? How would it affect the year-end balance sheet?

2. If you were one of the company's creditors, how would this fraudulent action affect you?

> Financial Statement Case 1

This case focuses on the financial statements of a real company—**Starbucks Corporation**, a premier roaster and retailer of specialty coffee. As you work the case, you will gain confidence in your ability to use the financial statements of real companies.

Visit **www.pearsonhighered.com/Horngren** to view a link to the Starbucks Corporation Fiscal 2011 Annual Report.

Requirements

1. How much in cash (including cash equivalents) did Starbucks Corporation have on October 2, 2011?

2. What were the company's total assets at October 2, 2011? At October 3, 2010?

3. Write the company's accounting equation at October 2, 2011, by filling in the dollar amounts:

$$\text{Assets} = \text{Liabilities} + \text{Equity}$$

4. Identify total net sales (revenues) for the year ended October 2, 2011. How much did total revenue increase or decrease from 2010 to 2011?

5. How much net income (net earnings) or net loss did Starbucks earn for 2011 and for 2010? Based on net income, was 2011 better or worse than 2010?

6. Calculate Starbucks Corporation's return on assets as of October 2, 2011.

7. How did Starbucks Corporation's return on assets compare to **Green Mountain Coffee Roasters, Inc.'s** return on assets?

> Team Projects

Team Project 1

You are opening Quail Creek Pet Kennel. Your purpose is to earn a profit, and you organize as a sole proprietorship.

Requirements

1. Make a detailed list of 10 factors you must consider to establish the business.

2. Identify 10 or more transactions that your business will undertake to open and operate the kennel.

3. Prepare the Quail Creek Pet Kennel income statement, statement of owner's equity, and balance sheet at the end of the first month of operations. Use made-up figures and include a complete heading for each financial statement. Date the balance sheet as of January 31, 20XX.

4. Discuss how you will evaluate the success of your business and how you will decide whether to continue its operation.

Team Project 2

You are promoting a rock concert in your area. Your purpose is to earn a profit, and you organize Concert Enterprises as a sole proprietorship.

Requirements

1. Make a detailed list of 10 factors you must consider to establish the business.

2. Describe 10 of the items your business must arrange in order to promote and stage the rock concert.

3. Prepare your business's income statement, statement of owner's equity, and balance sheet on June 30, 20XX, immediately after the rock concert. Use made-up amounts, and include a complete heading for each financial statement. For the income statement and the statement of owner's equity, assume the period is the three months ended June 30, 20XX.

4. Assume that you will continue to promote rock concerts if the venture is successful. If it is unsuccessful, you will terminate the business within three months after the concert. Discuss how you will evaluate the success of your venture and how you will decide whether to continue in business.

> Communication Activity 1

Using 25 words or fewer, illustrate the accounting equation and explain each part of the accounting equation.

MyAccountingLab	**For a wealth of online resources, including exercises, problems, media, and immediate tutorial help, please visit** www.myaccountinglab.com.

Try It! Solutions

1.	e	9.	i
2.	a	10.	c
3.	d	11.	a
4.	b	12.	h
5.	f	13.	b
6.	c	14.	g
7.	d	15.	e
8.	f		

16.

Assets			Liabilities	+				Equity				
					Owner's Capital	−	Owner's Withdrawals	+	Revenues	−	Expenses	
$71,288	=		$2,260	+	?	−	$14,420	+	$53,085	−	$28,675	
$71,288			$2,260	+	**$59,038**	−	$14,420	+	$53,085	−	$28,675	

17.

	Assets					Liabilities	+			Equity			
	Cash	+	Accounts Receivable	+	Equipment	Accounts Payable	+	Lawlor, Capital	−	Lawlor, Withdrawals	+	Service Revenue	−	Gas Expense
May 1	+ 1,700							+1,700					
Bal.	$1,700							$1,700					
3					+1,440	+1,440							
Bal.	$1,700			+	$1,440	$1,440	+	$1,700					
5			+200									+200	
Bal.	$1,700	+	$200	+	$1,440	$1,440	+	$1,700			+	$200	
17	−60												−60
Bal.	$1,640	+	$200	+	$1,440	$1,440	+	$1,700			+	$200	−	$60
28	−300									−300			
Bal.	$1,340	+	$200	+	$1,440	$1,440	+	$1,700	−	$300	+	$200	−	$60

$2,980 = $2,980

18.

DR PAINTING Income Statement Month Ended March 31, 2015		
Revenues:		
Service Revenue		$ 7,000
Expenses:		
Salaries Expense	$ 800	
Utilities Expense	200	
Total Expenses		1,000
Net Income		$ 6,000

DR PAINTING
Statement of Owner's Equity
Month Ended March 31, 2015

Richardson, Capital, March 1, 2015	$	0
Owner contribution		40,000
Net income for the month		6,000
		46,000
Owner withdrawals		(1,500)
Richardson, Capital, March 31, 2015		**$ 44,500**

DR PAINTING
Balance Sheet
March 31, 2015

Assets		Liabilities	
Cash	$ 22,300	Accounts Payable	$ 1,000
Accounts Receivable	1,400		
Office Supplies	1,800	**Owner's Equity**	
Truck	20,000	Richardson, Capital	44,500
Total Assets	**$ 45,500**	Total Liabilities and Owner's Equity	**$ 45,500**

19.   Return on assets = Net income / Average total assets
      = $5,000 / [($76,000 + $80,250) / 2]
      = 6.4%

> Quick Check Answers

1. d   **2.** c   **3.** a   **4.** c   **5.** c   **6.** a   **7.** c   **8.** a   **9.** b   **10.** a   **11.** c

Glossary

Accounting. The information system that measures business activities, processes the information into reports, and communicates the results to decision makers.

Accounting Equation. The basic tool of accounting, measuring the resources of the business (what the business owns or has control of) and the claims to those resources (what the business owes to creditors and to the owner). Assets = Liabilities + Equity.

Accounts Payable. A short-term liability that will be paid in the future.

Accounts Receivable. The right to receive cash in the future from customers for goods sold or for services performed.

Assets. Economic resources that are expected to benefit the business in the future. Something the business owns or has control of.

Audit. An examination of a company's financial statements and records.

Balance Sheet. Reports on the assets, liabilities, and owner's equity of the business as of a specific date.

Certified Management Accountants (CMAs). Certified professionals who specialize in accounting and financial management knowledge. They typically work for a single company.

Certified Public Accountants (CPAs). Licensed professional accountants who serve the general public.

Corporation. A business organized under state law that is a separate legal entity.

Cost Principle. A principle that states that acquired assets and services should be recorded at their actual cost.

Creditor. Any person or business to whom a business owes money.

Economic Entity Assumption. An organization that stands apart as a separate economic unit.

Equity. The owner's claim to the assets of the business.

Expenses. The cost of selling goods or services.

Financial Accounting. The field of accounting that focuses on providing information for external decision makers.

Financial Accounting Standards Board (FASB). The private organization that oversees the creation and governance of accounting standards in the United States.

Financial Statements. Business documents that are used to communicate information needed to make business decisions.

Generally Accepted Accounting Principles (GAAP). Accounting guidelines, currently formulated by the *Financial Accounting Standards Board (FASB)*; the main U.S. accounting rule book.

Going Concern Assumption. Assumes that the entity will remain in operation for the foreseeable future.

Income Statement. Reports the *net income* or *net loss* of the business for a specific period.

International Accounting Standards Board (IASB). The private organization that oversees the creation and governance of *International Financial Reporting Standards (IFRS)*.

International Financial Reporting Standards (IFRS). A set of global accounting guidelines, formulated by the *International Accounting Standards Board (IASB)*.

Liabilities. Debts that are owed to creditors.

Limited-Liability Company (LLC). A company in which each member is only liable for his or her own actions.

Managerial Accounting. The field of accounting that focuses on providing information for internal decision makers.

Monetary Unit Assumption. The assumption that requires the items on the financial statements to be measured in terms of a monetary unit.

Net Income. The result of operations that occurs when total revenues are greater than total expenses.

Net Loss. The result of operations that occurs when total expenses are greater than total revenues.

Owner's Capital. Owner contributions to a business.

Owner's Withdrawals. Payments of equity to the owner.

Partnership. A business with two or more owners and not organized as a corporation.

Return on Assets (ROA). Measures how profitably a company uses its assets. Net income / Average total assets.

Revenues. Amounts earned from delivering goods or services to customers.

Sarbanes-Oxley Act (SOX). Requires companies to review internal control and take responsibility for the accuracy and completeness of their financial reports.

Securities and Exchange Commission (SEC). U. S. governmental agency that oversees the U.S. financial markets.

Sole Proprietorship. A business with a single owner.

Statement of Cash Flow. Reports on a business's cash receipts and cash payments for a specific period.

Statement of Owner's Equity. Shows the changes in the owner's capital account for a specific period.

Transaction. An event that affects the financial position of the business and can be measured reliably in dollar amounts.

Photo Credits

Credits are listed in order of appearance.

Photo 1 (top): Fotolia
Photo 2 (middle): Bragin Alexey/Shutterstock
Photo 3 (bottom): Barbara Tripp/Shutterstock
Photo 4: Corbis Super RF/Alamy
Photo 5: Monkey Business Images/Shutterstock
Photo 6 (top): Iodrakon/Shutterstock
Photo 7 (bottom): Shutterstock
Photo 8: Lisa F. Young/Shutterstock
Photo 9: Rido/Shutterstock
Photo 10: Mike Flippo/Shutterstock

Recording Business Transactions

From Chapter 2 of *Horngren's Accounting*, Tenth edition. Tracie Nobles, Brenda Mattison, Ella Mae Matsumura. Copyright © 2014 by Pearson Education, Inc. All rights reserved.

Recording Business Transactions

Where's the Money?

Rachel Long scoured through the stacks of printouts. She had been hired to work on an embezzlement (stealing cash or assets of an entity) case for an local school district. The chief financial officer had called her because he suspected one of his employees was stealing money from the PTA (Parent Teacher Association). Rachel loved working on embezzlement cases. She enjoyed searching through the financial statements, identifying a problem, and then finding the transactions that documented the embezzlement. Rachel knew that if she looked deep enough she would find the evidence that money was stolen. She always treated these cases as a puzzle that needed to be solved.

Sometimes businesses are unfortunate enough to have employees steal from them, and they need help in identifying the thief and providing enough evidence to turn the matter over to a law enforcement agency. Businesses often turn to an accountant, such as Rachel, who specializes in fraud, often called a certified fraud examiner. In addition, businesses hire accountants to help protect their assets by identifying potential problems in their recordkeeping and control of cash and assets.

Where will Rachel start looking when she begins searching for the stolen money? She'll start at the source, by reviewing documents such as invoices, sales receipts, and bank deposit slips. She will then review the transactions that were recorded (or not recorded) from those documents. These two pieces will help Rachel determine whether money was stolen from the school district and how the embezzlement occurred. It's important to Rachel that she not only catches the thief, but also helps the school district prevent losses in the future. She will use her knowledge and experience in accounting to help her.

Why Is Recording Business Transactions Important?

Accounting is based on transactions. The recording of those transactions is based on source documents that provide the proof of the financial position of the business. The lack of that proof can lead to discoveries of stolen money and fictitious financial statements. As an example, when an employee at WorldCom, Inc., a long distance telephone company, found a $500 million accounting entry without any evidence to support it, it led to the discovery of a $3.8 billion fraud. The recording of transactions from source documents is the first step in the accounting process—and one of the most important. In this chapter you learn about source documents and how to record transactions.

chapter outline

What is an account?

What is double-entry accounting?

How do you record transactions?

What is the trial balance?

How do you use the debt ratio to evaluate business performance?

Learning Objectives

1. Explain accounts as they relate to the accounting equation and describe common accounts

2. Define debits, credits, and normal account balances using double-entry accounting and T-accounts

3. Record transactions in a journal and post journal entries to the ledger

4. Prepare the trial balance and illustrate how to use the trial balance to prepare financial statements

5. Use the debt ratio to evaluate business performance

Sheena Bright of Smart Touch Learning started out by recording her company's business transactions in terms of the accounting equation. That procedure works well when learning how to analyze transactions, but it's not a method in which a real-world business actually records transactions. In this chapter, you learn a more efficient way to capture business transactions. First, we need to start with a review of the accounting equation.

WHAT IS AN ACCOUNT?

Learning Objective 1

Explain accounts as they relate to the accounting equation and describe common accounts

The basic tool of accounting is the accounting equation:

$$\text{Assets = Liabilities + Equity}$$

The accounting equation is made up of three parts or categories: assets, liabilities, and equity. Each category contains accounts. An **account** is the detailed record of all increases and decreases that have occurred in an individual asset, liability, or equity during a specified period.

Account

A detailed record of all increases and decreases that have occurred in an individual asset, liability, or equity during a specific period.

Assets

Assets are economic resources that are expected to benefit the business in the future—something the business owns or has control of that has value. Exhibit 1 contains a list of asset accounts that most businesses use.

Exhibit 1 | **Asset Accounts**

Account Name	Explanation
Cash	A business's money. Includes bank balances, bills, coins, and checks.
Accounts Receivable	A customer's promise to pay in the future for services or goods sold. Often described as "On Account."
Notes Receivable	A *written* promise that a customer will pay a fixed amount of money and *interest* by a certain date in the future. Usually more formal than an Accounts Receivable.
Prepaid Expense	A payment of an expense in advance. It is considered an asset because the prepayment provides a benefit in the future. Examples of prepaid expenses are *Prepaid Rent*, *Prepaid Insurance*, and *Office Supplies*.
Equipment, Furniture, and Fixtures	The cost of equipment, furniture, and fixtures (such as light fixtures and shelving). A business has a separate asset account for each type.
Building	The cost of an office building, a store, or a warehouse.
Land	The cost of land a business uses in operations.

Notes Receivable
A written promise that a customer will pay a fixed amount of money and interest by a certain date in the future.

Prepaid Expense
A payment of an expense in advance.

Liabilities

A *liability* is a debt—that is, something the business owes. A business generally has fewer liability accounts than asset accounts. Exhibit 2 contains examples of common liability accounts.

You might be confused by the difference between the asset account, Accounts Receivable, and the liability account, Accounts Payable. An easy way to remember the distinction between these two accounts involves the words *Receivable* and *Payable*. A *receivable* involves a future *receipt* of cash. A *payable* involves a future *payment* of cash.

> I get confused by the difference between Accounts Receivable and Accounts Payable. Is there an easy way to remember these two accounts?

Exhibit 2 | **Liability Accounts**

Account Name	Explanation
Accounts Payable	A promise made by the business to pay a debt in the future. Arises from a credit purchase.
Notes Payable	A *written* promise made by the business to pay a debt, usually involving *interest,* in the future.
Accrued Liability	An amount owed but not paid. A specific type of payable such as *Taxes Payable*, *Rent Payable*, and *Salaries Payable*.
Unearned Revenue	Occurs when a company receives cash from a customer but has not provided the product or service. The promise to provide services or deliver goods in the future.

Notes Payable
A written promise made by the business to pay a debt, usually involving interest, in the future.

Accrued Liability
A liability for which the business knows the amount owed but the bill has not been paid.

Unearned Revenue
A liability created when a business collects cash from customers in advance of providing services or delivering goods.

Equity

The owner's claim to the assets of the business is called equity or owner's equity. As shown in Exhibit 3, a company has separate accounts for each element of equity.

Exhibit 3 | **Equity Accounts**

Account Name	Explanation
Capital	Represents the net contributions of the owner in the business. Increases equity.
Owner Withdrawals	Distributions of cash or other assets to the owner. Decreases equity.
Revenues	Earnings that result from delivering goods or services to customers. Increases equity. Examples include *Service Revenue* and *Rent Revenue*.
Expenses	The cost of selling goods or services. Decreases equity. Examples include *Rent Expense*, *Wages Expense*, and *Utilities Expense*.

Chart of Accounts

Chart of Accounts
A list of all of a company's accounts with their account numbers.

Companies need a way to organize their accounts. They use a **chart of accounts** to do this. A chart of accounts lists all company accounts along with the account numbers. The chart of accounts for Smart Touch Learning appears in Exhibit 4. Account numbers are just shorthand versions of the account names. One account number equals one account name—just like your Social Security number is unique to you.

> It can be confusing to choose the correct account to use when there are multiple accounts that sound similar. As an example, let's think about rent. There are four types of rent accounts: Prepaid Rent (asset), Rent Payable (liability), Rent Revenue (equity), or Rent Expense (equity). It is important that we understand the definition of each type of account so that we can use the account correctly. Prepaid Rent represents a _prepayment_ of cash for renting a building _in the future_. Rent Payable represents a _debt owed_ for renting a building _currently_ and Rent Expense represents the _cost_ of renting a building _currently_. Rent Revenue, on the other hand, relates to the _earning_ of revenue related to renting the building to a tenant _currently_.

Account numbers usually have two or more digits. Assets are often numbered beginning with 1, liabilities with 2, owner's equity with 3, revenues with 4, and expenses with 5. The second and third digits in an account number indicate where the account fits within the category. For example, if Smart Touch Learning is using three-digit account numbers, Cash may be account number 101, the first asset account. Accounts Receivable may be account number 111, the second asset. Accounts Payable may be number 201, the first liability. When numbers are used, all accounts are numbered by this system. However, each company chooses its own account numbering system.

Notice in Exhibit 4 the gap in account numbers between 121 and 141. Smart Touch Learning may need to add another asset account in the future. For example, the business may start selling some type of inventory and want to use account number 131 for Merchandise Inventory. So, the chart of accounts will change as the business evolves.

Exhibit 4 | Chart of Accounts—Smart Touch Learning

Balance Sheet Accounts		
Assets	**Liabilities**	**Equity**
101 Cash	201 Accounts Payable	301 Bright, Capital
111 Accounts Receivable	211 Salaries Payable	311 Bright, Withdrawals
121 Notes Receivable	221 Interest Payable	
141 Office Supplies	231 Unearned Revenue	
151 Furniture	241 Notes Payable	
171 Building		
191 Land		

Income Statement Accounts (Part of Equity)	
Revenues	**Expenses**
401 Service Revenue	501 Rent Expense
411 Interest Revenue	511 Salaries Expense
	521 Utilities Expense
	531 Advertising Expense

Worldwide, accounting systems are based on the same equation: Assets = Liabilities + Equity. Or, in Spanish: Activos = Pasivos + Patrimonio Neto. And, accounts are the building blocks for all accounting systems.

The chart of accounts varies from business to business, though many account names are common to all companies. For example, you will find Cash on every company's chart of accounts. The chart of accounts contains the list of account names you will use to record a transaction.

Ledger

In addition to a chart of accounts, companies need a way to show all of the increases and decreases in each account along with their balances. Companies use a ledger to fulfill this task. A ledger is a collection of all the accounts, the changes in those accounts, and their balances.

A chart of accounts and a ledger are similar in that they both list the account names and account numbers of the business. A ledger, though, provides more detail. It includes the increases and decreases of each account for a specific period and the balance of each account at a specific point in time.

Ledger
The record holding all the accounts of a business, the changes in those accounts, and their balances.

Consider the following accounts and identify each as an asset (A), liability (L), or equity (E).

1. Rent Expense
2. Brock, Capital
3. Furniture
4. Service Revenue
5. Prepaid Insurance
6. Accounts Payable
7. Unearned Revenue
8. Notes Receivable
9. Brock, Withdrawals
10. Insurance Expense

Check your answers at the end of the chapter.

> What is the difference between a chart of accounts and a ledger?

For more practice, see Short Exercise S-1. MyAccountingLab

WHAT IS DOUBLE-ENTRY ACCOUNTING?

Learning Objective 2
Define debits, credits, and normal account balances using double-entry accounting and T-accounts

Double-Entry System
A system of accounting in which every transaction affects at least two accounts.

Previously you learned that every transaction must be recorded into at least two accounts. For example, when an owner contributes money in exchange for capital, the two accounts involved are Cash and Owner's Capital. Accounting uses this **double-entry system** to record the dual effects of each transaction. A transaction would be incomplete if only one side were recorded.

Consider a cash purchase of office supplies. What are the dual effects? A cash purchase of office supplies:

1. Increases the account Office Supplies (you received office supplies)
2. Decreases Cash (you gave cash).

The T-Account

T-Account
A summary device that is shaped like a capital *T* with debits posted on the left side of the vertical line and credits on the right side of the vertical line.

A shortened form of the ledger is called the **T-account** because it takes the form of the capital letter *T*. The vertical line divides the account into its left and right sides, with the account name at the top. For example, the Cash T-account appears as follows:

Account name

Cash

Debit (DR) | Credit (CR)

Debit
The left side of a T-account.

Credit
The right side of a T-account.

The left side of the T-account is called the **debit** side, and the right side is called the **credit** side. To become comfortable using these terms, remember the following: Debits go on the left; credits go on the right. Debit is abbreviated as DR and Credit is abbreviated as CR.

Increases and Decreases in the Accounts

How we record increases and decreases to an account is determined by the account type (asset, liability, or equity). For any given account, increases are recorded on one side and decreases are recorded on the opposite side. The following T-accounts provide a summary:

Assets			Liabilities		+	Equity	
↑	↓		↓	↑		↓	↑
Debit	Credit		Debit	Credit		Debit	Credit

In other words, assets are always increased with a *debit* and decreased with a *credit*. Liabilities and equity are always increased with a *credit* and decreased with a *debit*. Whether an account is increased or decreased by a debit or a credit depends on the type of account. Debits are not "good" or "bad." Neither are credits. Debits are not always increases or always decreases—neither are credits. The only thing a designation as a debit or credit means is where the item is placed—on the left or right side of the T-account.

In a computerized accounting information system, the computer interprets debits and credits as increases or decreases, based on the account type. For example, a computer reads a debit to Cash as an increase, because it is an asset account. The computer reads a debit to Accounts Payable as a decrease, because it is a liability account.

Example: Assume a business wants to record an increase of $30,000 to the Cash account. The business would record a debit to Cash as follows:

Cash

Debit ——→ 30,000

Cash is an asset account and, remember, asset accounts are increased with debits.

Example: What if the business, instead, wanted to record a decrease of $20,000 to the Cash account? The business would record a credit to Cash because Cash is an asset account and asset accounts are decreased with credits:

Cash

20,000 ◄—— Credit

Expanding the Rules of Debit and Credit

As we have noted, equity contains four account types: Owner's Capital, Owner's Withdrawals, Revenues, and Expenses. Owner's Capital and Revenues increase equity, whereas Owner's Withdrawals and Expenses decrease equity. We must now expand the accounting equation and the rules of debits and credits to include all elements of equity:

					Equity					
Assets	=	**Liabilities**	+	**Owner's Capital**	–	**Owner's Withdrawals**	+	**Revenues**	–	**Expenses**
↑ Debit | ↓ Credit		↓ Debit | ↑ Credit		↓ Debit | ↑ Credit		↑ Debit | ↓ Credit		↓ Debit | ↑ Credit		↑ Debit | ↓ Credit

Notice in the expanded accounting equation that Owner's Withdrawals and Expenses record increases and decreases opposite of Owner's Capital and Revenues. This is because increases in Owner's Withdrawals and Expenses decrease equity.

The Normal Balance of an Account

All accounts have a normal balance. An account's *normal balance* appears on the side—either debit or credit—where we record an *increase* (↑) in the account's balance. For example, assets are increased with a debit, so the normal balance is a debit. Liabilities and equity are increased with a credit so the normal balance is a credit. Expenses and Owner's Withdrawal are equity accounts that have normal debit balances—unlike the other equity accounts. They have debit balances because they decrease equity. Owner's Capital and Revenues have a normal balance of credit. Let's look again at the accounting equation, this time with the normal balances marked:

Normal Balance
The balance that appears on the increase side of an account.

					Equity					
Assets	=	**Liabilities**	+	**Owner's Capital**	–	**Owner's Withdrawals**	+	**Revenues**	–	**Expenses**
↑ Debit | ↓ Credit		↓ Debit | ↑ Credit		↓ Debit | ↑ Credit		↑ Debit | ↓ Credit		↓ Debit | ↑ Credit		↑ Debit | ↓ Credit
Normal Balance			**Normal Balance**			**Normal Balance**	**Normal Balance**			**Normal Balance**	**Normal Balance**

An account with a normal debit balance may occasionally have a credit balance. That indicates a negative amount in the account. For example, Cash will have a credit balance if the business overdraws its bank account. Also, the liability, Accounts Payable—a normal credit balance account—could have a debit balance if the company overpays its accounts payable. In other cases, a non-normal account balance indicates an error. For example, a credit balance in Office Supplies, Furniture, or Buildings is an error because negative amounts of these assets make no sense.

Exhibit 5 summarizes the rules of debit and credit, and the normal balances for each account type.

Exhibit 5 | **Rules of Debit and Credit and Normal Balances for Each Account Type**

Account Type	Increases	Decreases	Normal Balance
Assets	Debit	Credit	Debit
Expenses	Debit	Credit	Debit
Owner's Withdrawals	Debit	Credit	Debit
Liabilities	Credit	Debit	Credit
Revenues	Credit	Debit	Credit
Owner's Capital	Credit	Debit	Credit

> Any easy way to remember the rules of debits and credits is to memorize this helpful sentence. _All elephants will love rowdy children._ The first three words in the sentence will help you remember that _a_ssets, _e_xpenses, and _w_ithdrawals all have normal debit balances. The last three words in the sentence will remind you that _l_iabilities, _r_evenues, and _c_apital all have normal credit balances.

Determining the Balance of a T-Account

T-accounts can be used to determine the amount remaining in an account or the *balance* of the account. To illustrate, let's look at the following Cash T-Account:

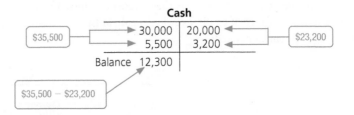

The balance of this Cash account is $12,300. This is calculated by adding each side of the account separately ($35,500 and $23,200) and then subtracting the smaller number from the larger number ($35,500 − $23,200). The balance ($12,300) is always reported on the side with the larger number.

> Try It!

For each account, identify if the change would be recorded as a debit (DR) or credit (CR).

11. Increase to Cash	16. Increase to Interest Revenue
12. Decrease to Accounts Payable	17. Increase to Rent Expense
13. Increase to Brock, Capital	18. Decrease to Office Supplies
14. Increase to Unearned Revenue	19. Increase to Prepaid Rent
15. Decrease to Accounts Receivable	20. Increase to Notes Payable

Check your answers at the end of the chapter.

For more practice, see Short Exercises S-2 and S-3.   MyAccountingLab

HOW DO YOU RECORD TRANSACTIONS?

In this text, we provide you with the transactions. In a real-world business, because of the faithful representation concept, accountants would need to provide evidence for those transactions.

Learning Objective 3

Record transactions in a journal and post journal entries to the ledger

Source Documents—The Origin of the Transactions

Accountant use **source documents** to provide the evidence and data for recording transactions. For example, consider Sheena Bright's contribution of $30,000 to the business. Exhibit 6 illustrates the transaction. In that exhibit, Smart Touch Learning received $30,000 and deposited it in the bank. The business then gave capital to Sheena Bright. The check received and the bank deposit slip are the source documents that show the amount of cash received by the business and the capital contribution of the owner, Sheena Bright. Based on these documents, the business can determine how to record this transaction.

Source Document

Provides the evidence and data for accounting transactions.

Exhibit 6 | Flow of Accounting Data

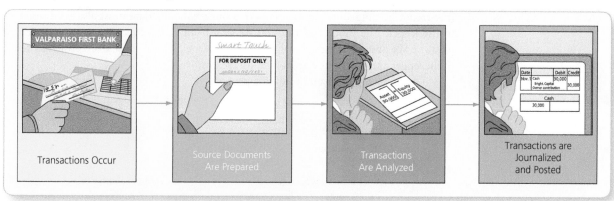

>Ethics   Are receipts really important?

Elijah Morris, assistant manager for Red's American Burger Restaurant, is responsible for purchasing equipment and supplies for the restaurant. Elijah recently purchased a $4,000 commercial-grade refrigerator for the restaurant, but he can't find the receipt. Elijah purchased the refrigerator with personal funds and is asking to be reimbursed by the restaurant. Hannah, the restaurant's accountant, has said that she is unsure if the business can reimburse Elijah without a receipt. Elijah suggests: "Hannah, it won't really matter if I have a receipt or not. You've seen the refrigerator in the restaurant, so you know I purchased it. What difference is a little receipt going to make?"

What should Hannah do? What would you do?

Solution

Hannah should not reimburse Elijah until she receives the receipt—the source document. Elijah could have purchased the refrigerator for less than the amount he is asking in reimbursement. Source documents provide the evidence of the amount of the transaction. If either an auditor or the owner of the restaurant investigated the $4,000 purchase, he or she would need to see the source document to verify the transaction. If Elijah truly cannot find the receipt, Hannah should ask for an alternative source document such as a credit card or bank statement that shows evidence of the purchase. In addition, Elijah should be warned about using personal funds to purchase equipment for the business.

Other source documents that businesses use include the following:

- **Purchase invoices**—Documents that tell the business how much and when to pay a vendor for purchases on account, such as office supplies.
- **Bank checks**—Documents that illustrate the amount and date of cash payments.
- **Sales invoice**—A document provided to a client when a business sells services or goods; tells the business how much revenue to record.

Journalizing and Posting Transactions

After accountants review the source documents, they are then ready to record the transactions. Transactions are first recorded in a journal, which is the record of transactions in date order.

Journalizing a transaction records the data only in the journal—but not in the ledger (the record holding all of the accounts of a business). The data must also be transferred to the ledger. The process of transferring data from the journal to the ledger is called posting. We post from the journal to the ledger. Debits in the journal are posted as debits in the ledger and credits as credits—no exceptions.

The following diagram shows this process:

Journal
A record of transactions in date order.

Posting
Transferring data from the journal to the ledger.

Date		Debit	Credit
Nov.1	Cash	30,000	
	Bright, Capital		30,000
	Owner contribution		

Transactions are recorded in a journal.

Cash	
30,000	

Data is posted (transferred) to the ledger.

You have learned steps to use when analyzing accounting transactions. Use a modified version of those steps to help when recording transactions in the journal and then posting the journal entries to the ledger. The journalizing and posting process has five steps:

Step 1: Identify the accounts and the account type (asset, liability, or equity).

Step 2: Decide whether each account increases or decreases using the rules of debits and credits.

Step 3: Record the transaction in the journal.

Step 4: Post the journal entry to the ledger.

Step 5: Determine whether the accounting equation is in balance.

Let's begin by journalizing the first transaction of Smart Touch Learning.

Transaction 1—Owner Contribution

On November 1, the e-learning agency receives $30,000 cash from the owner, Sheena Bright, and the business gave capital to her.

Step 1: Identify the accounts and the account type. The two accounts involved are Cash (Asset) and Bright, Capital (Equity).

Step 2: Decide whether each account increases or decreases using the rules of debits and credits. Both accounts increase by $30,000. Reviewing the rules of debits and credits, we use the accounting equation to help determine debits and credits for each account. Cash is an asset account and it is increasing, we will record a debit to Cash. Bright, Capital is an equity account and it is increasing, we will record a credit to Bright, Capital.

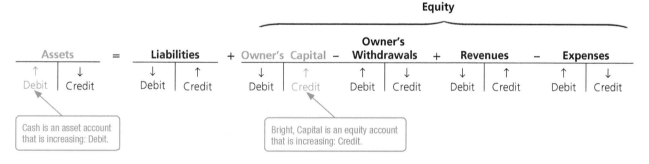

Step 3: Record the transaction in the journal. The recording of a transaction in the journal creates a journal entry. The journal entry for Transaction 1 is illustrated below. Notice that each journal entry contains four parts.

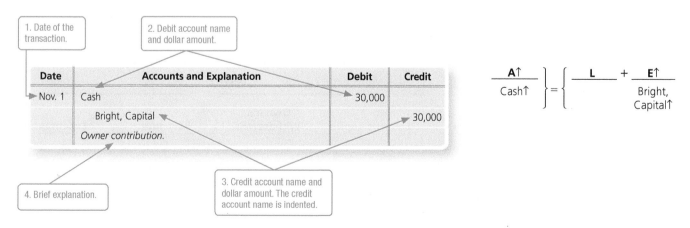

Step 4: Post the journal entry to the ledger. When transactions are posted from the journal to the ledger, the dollar amount is transferred from the debit and credit columns to the specific account. The date of the journal entry is also transferred to the T-accounts in the ledger. In a computerized system, this step is completed automatically when the transaction is recorded in the journal.

Date	Accounts and Explanation	Debit	Credit
Nov. 1	Cash	30,000	
	Bright, Capital		30,000
	Owner contribution.		

Cash		Bright, Capital	
Nov. 1 30,000			30,000 Nov. 1

Step 5: Determine if the accounting equation is in balance.

Assets		Liabilities	+	Equity
Cash	=			Bright, Capital
(1) + 30,000				+ 30,000

To help reinforce your learning of the account types, we will illustrate the transaction in the margin. We will indicate the accounts and account type (Step 1) and whether each account is increasing or decreasing (Step 2). These notations would not normally show up in a journal, but we have included them here to reinforce the rules of debit and credit.

Let's look at Transaction 2 for Smart Touch Learning and apply the steps we just learned.

Transaction 2—Purchase of Land for Cash

On November 2, Smart Touch Learning paid $20,000 cash for land.

Step 1: Identify the accounts and the account type. The two accounts involved are Cash (Asset) and Land (Asset).

Step 2: Decide whether each account increases or decreases using the rules of debits and credits. Cash decreases. The business paid cash. Therefore, we credit Cash. The land increased, so we debit the Land account.

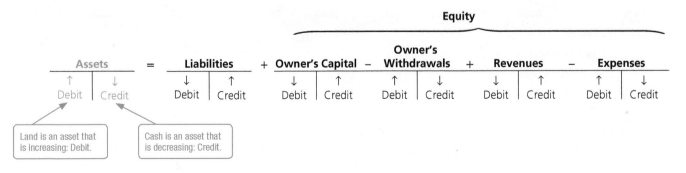

Step 3: Record the transaction in the journal.

Date	Accounts and Explanation	Debit	Credit
Nov. 2	Land	20,000	
	Cash		20,000
	Paid cash for land.		

$$\left.\frac{A\uparrow\downarrow}{\substack{\text{Land}\uparrow \\ \text{Cash}\downarrow}}\right\} = \left\{ \frac{L}{} + \frac{E}{} \right.$$

Step 4: Post the journal entry to the ledger.

Cash				Land	
Nov. 1	30,000	20,000	Nov. 2	Nov. 2	20,000

Step 5: Determine whether the accounting equation is in balance.

	Assets				Liabilities	+	Equity
	Cash	+	Land			+	Bright, Capital
Bal.	$30,000						$30,000
(2)	−20,000		+20,000				
Bal.	$10,000	+	$20,000				$30,000

We will now record journal entries for several more transactions for Smart Touch Learning. Now that you understand the steps, try to write the steps yourself before looking at the journal entry. Remember, if you need help, we'll provide the effect on the accounting equation in the margin.

Transaction 3—Purchase of Office Supplies on Credit

Smart Touch Learning buys $500 of office supplies on account on November 3.

The supplies will benefit Smart Touch Learning in future periods, so they are an asset to the company until they are used. The asset Office Supplies increased, so we debit Office Supplies. The liability Accounts Payable increased, so we credit Accounts Payable.

Date	Accounts and Explanation	Debit	Credit
Nov. 3	Office Supplies	500	
	Accounts Payable		500
	Purchased office supplies on account.		

$$\left.\frac{A\uparrow}{\substack{\text{Office} \\ \text{Supplies}\uparrow}}\right\} = \left\{ \frac{L\uparrow}{\substack{\text{Accounts} \\ \text{Payable}\uparrow}} + \frac{E}{} \right.$$

Office Supplies			Accounts Payable	
Nov. 3	500		500	Nov. 3

Transaction 4—Earning of Service Revenue for Cash

On November 8, Smart Touch Learning collected cash of $5,500 for service revenue that the business earned by providing e-learning services for clients.

    The asset Cash increased, so we debit Cash. Revenue increased, so we credit Service Revenue.

$$\underbrace{\frac{A\uparrow}{\text{Cash}\uparrow}}{} = \left\{ \underbrace{\quad L \quad}{} + \underbrace{\frac{E\uparrow}{\substack{\text{Service} \\ \text{Revenue}\uparrow}}}{} \right.$$

Date	Accounts and Explanation	Debit	Credit
Nov. 8	Cash	5,500	
	Service Revenue		5,500
	Performed services and received cash.		

	Cash		
Nov. 1	30,000	20,000	Nov. 2
Nov. 8	5,500		

Service Revenue	
5,500	Nov. 8

Transaction 5—Earning of Service Revenue on Account

On November 10, Smart Touch Learning performed services for clients, for which the clients will pay the company later. The business earned $3,000 of service revenue on account.

    This transaction increased Accounts Receivable, so we debit this asset. Service Revenue is increased with a credit.

$$\underbrace{\frac{A\uparrow}{\substack{\text{Accounts} \\ \text{Receivable}\uparrow}}}{} = \left\{ \underbrace{\quad L \quad}{} + \underbrace{\frac{E\uparrow}{\substack{\text{Service} \\ \text{Revenue}\uparrow}}}{} \right.$$

Date	Accounts and Explanation	Debit	Credit
Nov. 10	Accounts Receivable	3,000	
	Service Revenue		3,000
	Performed services on account.		

Accounts Receivable	
Nov. 10 3,000	

Service Revenue	
5,500	Nov. 8
3,000	Nov. 10

    Notice the differences and the similarities between Transactions 4 and 5. In both transactions, Service Revenue was increased (credited) because in both cases the company had earned revenue. However, in Transaction 4, the company was paid at the time of service. In Transaction 5, on the other hand, the company will receive cash later (Accounts Receivable). This difference is key, because the amount of revenue is not determined by when the company *receives* cash. Revenues are recorded when the company *does* the work or provides the service.

Transaction 6—Payment of Expenses with Cash

Smart Touch Learning paid the following cash expenses on November 15: Office rent, $2,000 and employee salaries, $1,200. We need to debit each expense account to record its increase and credit Cash for the total decrease.

Date	Accounts and Explanation	Debit	Credit
Nov. 15	Rent Expense	2,000	
	Salaries Expense	1,200	
	Cash		3,200
	Paid cash expenses.		

$$A\downarrow \left.\begin{array}{c} \\ \text{Cash}\downarrow \\ \\ \end{array}\right\} = \left\{\begin{array}{c} L + E\downarrow \\ \text{Rent Expense}\uparrow \\ \text{Salaries Expense}\uparrow \end{array}\right.$$

Cash

Nov. 1	30,000	20,000	Nov. 2
Nov. 8	5,500	3,200	Nov. 15

Rent Expense

Nov. 15	2,000	

Salaries Expense

Nov. 15	1,200	

Notice that the journal entry has three accounts involved—two debits and one credit. This is a compound journal entry. A compound journal entry has more than two accounts, but total debits still must equal total credits.

Before we move to the next transaction, let's take a moment and carefully look at expenses. In Transaction 6, we recorded a debit to the expense accounts. The accounting equation and the rules of debits and credits state that a debit to an expense account increases the account.

We are recording an increase to the expense account because the business has more expenses now then it had before. But remember, the overall effect on the accounting equation is that increases in expenses decrease equity. An easy way to think about it is that we are increasing a negative account.

Compound Journal Entry

A journal entry that is characterized by having multiple debits and/or multiple credits.

> I thought expenses decreased equity, but we are debiting the expense that records an increase to the account.

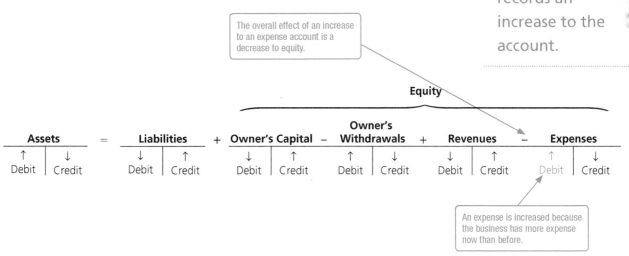

The overall effect of an increase to an expense account is a decrease to equity.

An expense is increased because the business has more expense now than before.

Transaction 7—Payment on Account (Accounts Payable)

On November 21, Smart Touch Learning paid $300 on the accounts payable created in Transaction 3. The payment decreased cash, so we credit Cash. The payment decreased Accounts Payable, so we debit that liability.

$$\underline{\quad A\downarrow \quad} \left.\vphantom{\begin{matrix}a\\b\end{matrix}}\right\} = \left\{\vphantom{\begin{matrix}a\\b\end{matrix}}\right. \underline{\quad L\downarrow \quad} + \underline{\quad E \quad}$$

Cash↓ = Accounts Payable↓

Date	Accounts and Explanation	Debit	Credit
Nov. 21	Accounts Payable	300	
	Cash		300
	Paid cash on account.		

	Cash				Accounts Payable		
Nov. 1	30,000	20,000	Nov. 2	Nov. 21	300	500	Nov. 3
Nov. 8	5,500	3,200	Nov. 15				
		300	Nov. 21				

Notice that after recording this transaction and posting to the Accounts Payable account, the balance of Accounts Payable is $200 ($500 − $300). This is the new balance that the business owes to its creditor.

Transaction 8—Collection on Account (Accounts Receivable)

On November 22, Smart Touch Learning collected $2,000 cash from a client in Transaction 5. Cash is increased, so we debit Cash. Accounts Receivable is decreased, so we credit Accounts Receivable. *Note:* This transaction has no effect on revenue; the related revenue was recorded in Transaction 5.

$$\underline{\quad A\downarrow\uparrow \quad} \left.\vphantom{\begin{matrix}a\\b\\c\end{matrix}}\right\} = \left\{\vphantom{\begin{matrix}a\\b\\c\end{matrix}}\right. \underline{\quad L \quad} + \underline{\quad E \quad}$$

Cash↑
Accounts Receivable↓

Date	Accounts and Explanation	Debit	Credit
Nov. 22	Cash	2,000	
	Accounts Receivable		2,000
	Received cash on account.		

	Cash				Accounts Receivable		
Nov. 1	30,000	20,000	Nov. 2	Nov. 10	3,000	2,000	Nov. 22
Nov. 8	5,500	3,200	Nov. 15				
Nov. 22	2,000	300	Nov. 21				

Transaction 9—Owner Withdrawal of Cash

On November 25, Sheena Bright withdrew cash of $5,000. The withdrawal decreased the entity's cash, so we credit Cash. The withdrawal also decreased equity. Decreases in equity that result from owner withdrawals are debited to the owner's withdrawal account, so we debit Bright, Withdrawals.

Date	Accounts and Explanation	Debit	Credit
Nov. 25	Bright, Withdrawals	5,000	
	Cash		5,000
	Owner withdrawal.		

$$\underline{\text{A}\downarrow} \quad \} = \{ \quad \underline{\text{L}} \quad + \quad \underline{\text{E}\downarrow}$$

Cash↓ ‖ Bright, Withdrawals↑

	Cash				Bright, Withdrawals	
Nov. 1	30,000	20,000	Nov. 2	Nov. 25	5,000	
Nov. 8	5,500	3,200	Nov. 15			
Nov. 22	2,000	300	Nov. 21			
		5,000	Nov. 25			

Transaction 10—Prepaid Expenses

On December 1, Smart Touch Learning prepays three months' office rent of $3,000 ($1,000 per month $\times$ 3 months). The prepayment of the rent is recorded to the Prepaid Rent account (Asset). It is recorded as an asset because Smart Touch Learning will receive a benefit in the future. The asset, Prepaid Rent, is increasing, so we will need to debit it. Cash is decreasing and will be recorded as a credit.

Date	Accounts and Explanation	Debit	Credit
Dec. 1	Prepaid Rent	3,000	
	Cash		3,000
	Paid rent in advance.		

$$\underline{\text{A}\downarrow\uparrow} \quad \} = \{ \quad \underline{\text{L}} \quad + \quad \underline{\text{E}}$$

Prepaid Rent↑ Cash↓

	Cash				Prepaid Rent	
Nov. 1	30,000	20,000	Nov. 2	Dec. 1	3,000	
Nov. 8	5,500	3,200	Nov. 15			
Nov. 22	2,000	300	Nov. 21			
		5,000	Nov. 25			
		3,000	Dec. 1			

Transaction 11—Payment of Expense with Cash

On December 1, Smart Touch Learning paid employee salaries of $1,200. Salaries Expense will be debited to record its increase and Cash will be credited for the decrease.

$$\left.\frac{A\downarrow}{\text{Cash}\downarrow}\right\} = \left\{\frac{L}{} + \frac{E\downarrow}{\substack{\text{Salaries}\\ \text{Expense}\uparrow}}\right.$$

Date	Accounts and Explanation	Debit	Credit
Dec. 1	Salaries Expense	1,200	
	Cash		1,200
	Paid salaries.		

Cash

Nov. 1	30,000	20,000	Nov. 2
Nov. 8	5,500	3,200	Nov. 15
Nov. 22	2,000	300	Nov. 21
		5,000	Nov. 25
		3,000	Dec. 1
		1,200	Dec. 1

Salaries Expense

Nov. 15	1,200
Dec. 1	1,200

Transaction 12—Purchase of Building with Notes Payable

On December 1, Smart Touch Learning purchased a $60,000 building in exchange for a notes payable. The building will benefit the business in the future, so it is recorded as an asset to the company. The asset Building is increased, so we debit Building. The liability Notes Payable increased, so we credit Notes Payable.

$$\left.\frac{A\uparrow}{\text{Building}\uparrow}\right\} = \left\{\frac{L\uparrow}{\substack{\text{Notes}\\ \text{Payable}\uparrow}} + \frac{E}{}\right.$$

Date	Accounts and Explanation	Debit	Credit
Dec. 1	Building	60,000	
	Notes Payable		60,000
	Purchase of building with note.		

Building

Dec. 1	60,000

Notes Payable

60,000	Dec. 1

Transaction 13—Owner Contribution

On December 2, Smart Touch Learning received a contribution of furniture with a fair market value of $18,000 from Sheena Bright. In exchange, Smart Touch Learning gave Bright capital. The furniture will benefit the company in the future, so it is recorded as an asset. The asset Furniture is increasing, so we debit it. Bright, Capital is also increasing and is recorded as a credit.

Date	Accounts and Explanation	Debit	Credit
Dec. 2	Furniture	18,000	
	Bright, Capital		18,000
	Owner contribution of furniture.		

$$\underset{\text{Furniture}\uparrow}{\underline{\text{A}\uparrow}} \left.\right\} = \left\{ \underline{\quad\text{L}\quad} + \underset{\substack{\text{Bright,}\\\text{Capital}\uparrow}}{\underline{\text{E}\uparrow}} \right.$$

Furniture				Bright, Capital	
Dec. 2	18,000			30,000	Nov. 1
				18,000	Dec. 2

Transaction 14—Accrued Liability

On December 15, Smart Touch Learning received a telephone bill for $100 and will pay this expense next month. There is no cash payment now. This is an accrued liability. Remember, an accrued liability is a liability for which the business knows the amount owed but the bill has not been paid. The Utilities Expense increased, so we debit this expense. The liability (Utilities Payable) increased, so we credit Utilities Payable. Alternatively, we could credit Accounts Payable instead of Utilities Payable.

Date	Accounts and Explanation	Debit	Credit
Dec. 15	Utilities Expense	100	
	Utilities Payable		100
	Accrued utility liability.		

$$\underline{\quad\text{A}\quad} \left.\right\} = \left\{ \underset{\substack{\text{Utilities}\\\text{Payable}\uparrow}}{\underline{\text{L}\uparrow}} + \underset{\substack{\text{Utilities}\\\text{Expense}\uparrow}}{\underline{\text{E}\downarrow}} \right.$$

Utilities Payable			Utilities Expense	
	100	Dec. 15	Dec. 15	100

Transaction 15—Payment of Expense With Cash

On December 15, Smart Touch Learning paid employee salaries of $1,200. Salaries Expense will be debited to record its increase and Cash will be credited for the decrease.

$$\left.\frac{A\downarrow}{Cash\downarrow}\right\} = \left\{\quad \frac{L}{} + \frac{E\downarrow}{\substack{Salaries \\ Expense\uparrow}}\right.$$

Date	Accounts and Explanation	Debit	Credit
Dec. 15	Salaries Expense	1,200	
	Cash		1,200
	Paid salaries.		

		Cash				Salaries Expense	
Nov. 1	30,000	20,000	Nov. 2	Nov. 15	1,200	
Nov. 8	5,500	3,200	Nov. 15	Dec. 1	1,200	
Nov. 22	2,000	300	Nov. 21	Dec. 15	1,200	
		5,000	Nov. 25			
		3,000	Dec. 1			
		1,200	Dec. 1			
		1,200	Dec. 15			

Transaction 16—Unearned Revenue

On December 21, a law firm engages Smart Touch Learning to provide e-learning services and agrees to pay $600 in advance. Smart Touch Learning will receive cash but has not yet performed the services. Cash increased, so we debit Cash. The promise to perform services in the future will be recorded as Unearned Revenue, a liability account. Unearned Revenue is increasing, so we credit it. Notice that we did not record revenue. Revenue is not recorded until Smart Touch Learning provides the services.

$$\left.\frac{A\uparrow}{Cash\uparrow}\right\} = \left\{\quad \frac{L\uparrow}{\substack{Unearned \\ Revenue\uparrow}} + \frac{E}{}\right.$$

Date	Accounts and Explanation	Debit	Credit
Dec. 21	Cash	600	
	Unearned Revenue		600
	Collected cash for future services.		

		Cash			Unearned Revenue	
Nov. 1	30,000	20,000	Nov. 2		600	Dec. 21
Nov. 8	5,500	3,200	Nov. 15			
Nov. 22	2,000	300	Nov. 21			
Dec. 21	600	5,000	Nov. 25			
		3,000	Dec. 1			
		1,200	Dec. 1			
		1,200	Dec. 15			

Transaction 17—Earning of Service Revenue for Cash

On December 28, Smart Touch Learning collected cash of $8,000 for Service Revenue that the business earned by providing e-learning services for clients.

Date	Accounts and Explanation	Debit	Credit
Dec. 28	Cash	8,000	
	Service Revenue		8,000
	Performed services and received cash.		

$$\left.\frac{A\uparrow}{Cash\uparrow}\right\} = \left\{\frac{L}{} + \frac{E\uparrow}{\substack{Service \\ Revenue\uparrow}}\right.$$

	Cash		
Nov. 1	30,000	20,000	Nov. 2
Nov. 8	5,500	3,200	Nov. 15
Nov. 22	2,000	300	Nov. 21
Dec. 21	600	5,000	Nov. 25
Dec. 28	8,000	3,000	Dec. 1
		1,200	Dec. 1
		1,200	Dec. 15

	Service Revenue	
	5,500	Nov. 8
	3,000	Nov. 10
	8,000	Dec. 28

The Ledger Accounts After Posting

Exhibit 7 shows the T-accounts of Smart Touch Learning after posting the journal entries from the journal to the ledger. The accounts are grouped under their headings. Notice that at December 31, Smart Touch Learning has assets of $114,700 ($12,200 + $1,000 + $500 + $3,000 + $18,000 + $60,000 + $20,000), liabilities of $60,900 ($200 + $100 + $600 + $60,000), and equity of $53,800 ($48,000 − $5,000 + $16,500 − $2,000 − $3,600 − $100). The accounting equation is in balance ($114,700 = $60,900 + $53,800).

Exhibit 7 | Smart Touch Learning's Accounts After Posting Journal Entries in November and December

Assets = Liabilities + Equity

Assets

Cash

Nov. 1	30,000	20,000	Nov. 2
Nov. 8	5,500	3,200	Nov. 15
Nov. 22	2,000	300	Nov. 21
Dec. 21	600	5,000	Nov. 25
Dec. 28	8,000	3,000	Dec. 1
		1,200	Dec. 1
		1,200	Dec. 15
Bal.	12,200		

Accounts Receivable

Nov. 10	3,000	2,000	Nov. 22
Bal.	1,000		

Office Supplies

Nov. 3	500	
Bal.	500	

Prepaid Rent

Dec. 1	3,000	
Bal.	3,000	

Furniture

Dec. 2	18,000	
Bal.	18,000	

Building

Dec. 1	60,000	
Bal.	60,000	

Land

Nov. 2	20,000	
Bal.	20,000	

$114,700

Liabilities

Accounts Payable

Nov. 21	300	500	Nov. 3
		200	Bal.

Utilities Payable

	100	Dec. 15
	100	Bal.

Unearned Revenue

	600	Dec. 21
	600	Bal.

Notes Payable

	60,000	Dec. 1
	60,000	Bal.

$60,900

Equity

Bright, Capital

	30,000	Nov. 1
	18,000	Dec. 2
	48,000	Bal.

Bright, Withdrawals

Nov. 25	5,000	
Bal.	5,000	

Service Revenue

	5,500	Nov. 8
	3,000	Nov. 10
	8,000	Dec. 28
	16,500	Bal.

Rent Expense

Nov. 15	2,000	
Bal.	2,000	

Salaries Expense

Nov. 15	1,200	
Dec. 1	1,200	
Dec. 15	1,200	
Bal.	3,600	

Utilities Expense

Dec. 15	100	
Bal.	100	

$53,800

The Four-Column Account: An Alternative to the T-Account

The ledger accounts illustrated thus far appear as T-accounts, with the debits on the left and the credits on the right. The T-account clearly separates debits from credits and is used for teaching. An alternative to using the T-account is the four-column account. The four-column account still has debit and credit columns, but it also adds two additional columns that are used to determine a running balance. Exhibit 8 shows the Cash T-account and the Cash four-column account for Smart Touch Learning.

The first pair of Debit/Credit columns is for transaction amounts posted to the account from the journal, such as the $30,000 debit. The second pair of Debit/Credit columns shows the balance of the account as of each date. Because the four-column format provides more information, it is used more often in practice than the T-account. Notice that the balance after the last transaction on December 28 is $12,200, which is the same balance calculated in the T-account.

Do you notice the column labeled *Post Ref.* in the four-column account in Exhibit 8? This column is used in the posting process. When the information is transferred from the journal to the ledger, a posting reference (Post Ref.) is added. This allows a user of the financial data to trace the amount in the ledger back to

Exhibit 8 | **T-Account Versus Four-Column Account**

Cash

Nov. 1	30,000	20,000	Nov. 2
Nov. 8	5,500	3,200	Nov. 15
Nov. 22	2,000	300	Nov. 21
Dec. 21	600	5,000	Nov. 25
Dec. 28	8,000	3,000	Dec. 1
		1,200	Dec. 1
		1,200	Dec. 15
Bal.	12,200		

The Debit or Credit for each transaction.

The balance of the account after each transaction.

CASH					Account No. 101	
Date	Item	Post Ref.	Debit	Credit	Balance	
					Debit	Credit
2014						
Nov. 1		J1	30,000		30,000	
Nov. 2		J1		20,000	10,000	
Nov. 8		J1	5,500		15,500	
Nov. 15		J1		3,200	12,300	
Nov. 21		J1		300	12,000	
Nov. 22		J1	2,000		14,000	
Nov. 25		J1		5,000	9,000	
Dec. 1		J2		3,000	6,000	
Dec. 1		J2		1,200	4,800	
Dec. 15		J2		1,200	3,600	
Dec. 21		J2	600		4,200	
Dec. 28		J2	8,000		12,200	

the journal. In a computerized system, the user would be able to click on the posting reference to view the related journal entry. Exhibit 9 shows the posting and associated posting references for Transaction 1 of Smart Touch Learning. Remember, in a computerized environment, this process is completed automatically when the user enters the journal entry.

Exhibit 9 | Posting References

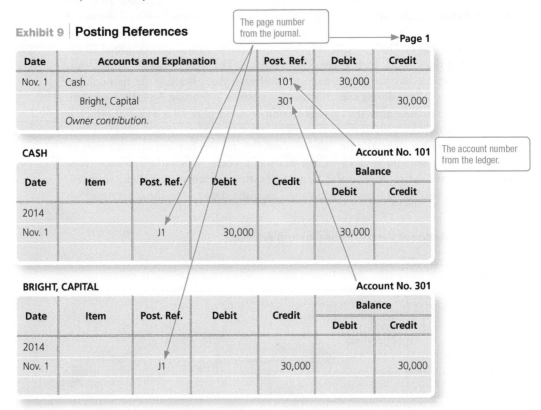

The page number from the journal. ➜ Page 1

Date	Accounts and Explanation	Post. Ref.	Debit	Credit
Nov. 1	Cash	101	30,000	
	Bright, Capital	301		30,000
	Owner contribution.			

CASH   **Account No. 101**

The account number from the ledger.

Date	Item	Post. Ref.	Debit	Credit	Balance Debit	Balance Credit
2014						
Nov. 1		J1	30,000		30,000	

BRIGHT, CAPITAL   **Account No. 301**

Date	Item	Post. Ref.	Debit	Credit	Balance Debit	Balance Credit
2014						
Nov. 1		J1		30,000		30,000

> Try It!

21. EMB Consulting Services had the following transactions for the month of November. Journalize the transactions and include an explanation with each entry.

Nov. 1	The business received $10,000 cash and gave capital to Eloise Martinez, the owner.
15	Purchased office supplies on account, $400.
18	Paid advertising bill, $150.
20	Received $1,000 from customers for services rendered.
28	Martinez withdrew $500 from the business.

Check your answers at the end of the chapter.

For more practice, see Short Exercises S-4 through S-7. MyAccountingLab

WHAT IS THE TRIAL BALANCE?

After the transactions are recorded in the journal and then posted to the ledger, a trial balance can be prepared. The trial balance summarizes the ledger by listing all the accounts with their balances—assets first, followed by liabilities, and then equity. In a manual accounting system, the trial balance provides an accuracy check by showing whether total debits equal total credits. In all types of systems, the trial balance is a useful summary of the accounts and their balances because it shows the balances on a specific date for all accounts in a company's accounting system. Exhibit 10 is the trial balance of Smart Touch Learning at December 31, 2014.

Learning Objective 4
Prepare the trial balance and illustrate how to use the trial balance to prepare financial statements

Trial Balance
A list of all ledger accounts with their balances at a point in time.

Exhibit 10 | **Trial Balance**

SMART TOUCH LEARNING
Trial Balance
December 31, 2014

Account Title	Balance Debit	Credit
Cash	$ 12,200	
Accounts Receivable	1,000	
Office Supplies	500	
Prepaid Rent	3,000	
Furniture	18,000	
Building	60,000	
Land	20,000	
Accounts Payable		$ 200
Utilities Payable		100
Unearned Revenue		600
Notes Payable		60,000
Bright, Capital		48,000
Bright, Withdrawals	5,000	
Service Revenue		16,500
Rent Expense	2,000	
Salaries Expense	3,600	
Utilities Expense	100	
Total	$ 125,400	$ 125,400

The trial balance and the balance sheet are not the same. Make sure you understand the differences between these two documents. A trial balance verifies the equality of debits and credits and is an internal document used only by employees of the company. The balance sheet, on the other hand, presents the business's accounting equation and is a financial statement that can be used by both internal and external users.

Preparing Financial Statements From the Trial Balance

In addition to proving the equality of debits and credits, the trial balance is also used to prepare the financial statements. The account balances are taken directly from the trial balance and are used to prepare the income statement, statement of owner's equity, and balance sheet. In Exhibit 11 we present the financial statements for the two months ended December 31, 2014, for Smart Touch Learning.

Exhibit 11 | Smart Touch Learning's Financial Statements

SMART TOUCH LEARNING
Income Statement
Two Months Ended December 31, 2014

Revenues:		
Service Revenue		$ 16,500
Expenses:		
Salaries Expense	$ 3,600	
Rent Expense	2,000	
Utilities Expense	100	
Total Expenses		5,700
Net Income		$ 10,800

SMART TOUCH LEARNING
Statement of Owner's Equity
Two Months Ended December 31, 2014

Bright, Capital, November 1, 2014	$ 0
Owner contribution	48,000
Net income for the two months	10,800
	58,800
Owner withdrawal	(5,000)
Bright, Capital, December 31, 2014	$ 53,800

SMART TOUCH LEARNING
Balance Sheet
December 31, 2014

Assets		Liabilities	
Cash	$ 12,200	Accounts Payable	$ 200
Accounts Receivable	1,000	Utilities Payable	100
Office Supplies	500	Unearned Revenue	600
Prepaid Rent	3,000	Notes Payable	60,000
Furniture	18,000	Total Liabilities	60,900
Building	60,000		
Land	20,000	**Owner's Equity**	
		Bright, Capital	53,800
Total Assets	$ 114,700	Total Liabilities and Owner's Equity	$ 114,700

Correcting Trial Balance Errors

Throughout the accounting process, total debits should always equal total credits. If they do not, there is an error. Computerized accounting systems eliminate many errors because most software will not let you make a journal entry that does not balance. But computers cannot *eliminate* all errors because humans can input the wrong data.

Balancing errors can be detected by computing the difference between total debits and total credits on the trial balance. Then perform one or more of the following actions:

1. **Search the trial balance for a missing account.** For example, suppose the accountant omitted the Bright, Withdrawals account from the trial balance in Exhibit 10. Total debits would then be $120,400 ($125,400 − $5,000). Trace each account from the ledger to the trial balance, and you will locate the missing account.
2. **Divide the difference between total debits and total credits by 2.** A debit treated as a credit, or vice versa, doubles the amount of the error. Suppose the accountant

posted a $500 credit as a debit. Total debits contain the $500, and total credits omit the $500. The out-of-balance amount is $1,000. Dividing the difference by 2 identifies the $500 amount of the transaction. Then search the journal or ledger for a $500 transaction and trace it to the account affected.

3. **Divide the out-of-balance amount by 9.** If the result is evenly divisible by 9, the error may be a *slide* (example: writing $1,000 as $100 or writing $100 as $1,000) or a *transposition* (example: listing $1,200 as $2,100). Suppose, for example, that the accountant entered the $5,000 Bright, Withdrawals as $50,000 on the trial balance. This is a slide-type error. Total debits would differ from total credits by $45,000 ($50,000 − $5,000 = $45,000). Dividing $45,000 by 9 yields $5,000, the correct amount of the withdrawals. Look for an account in the ledger with a $5,000 balance until you reach the Bright, Withdrawals account. You have then found the error.

Total debits can equal total credits on the trial balance; however, there still could be errors in individual account balances because an incorrect account might have been selected in an individual journal entry.

22. Using the following accounts and their balances, prepare the trial balance for Cooper Furniture Repair as of December 31, 2015.

Cash	$ 7,000	Advertising Expense	$ 1,200
Unearned Revenue	4,500	Utilities Expense	800
Equipment	10,000	Rent Expense	5,000
Service Revenue	8,000	Accounts Payable	2,300
Miller, Capital	12,200	Miller, Withdrawals	3,000

Check your answers at the end of the chapter.

For more practice, see Short Exercise S-8. MyAccountingLab

HOW DO YOU USE THE DEBT RATIO TO EVALUATE BUSINESS PERFORMANCE?

Evaluating a company's return on assets (Net income / Average total assets) can help in determining how well a company is performing. In this chapter, you learn about another tool that can be used when reviewing financial statements. The **debt ratio** shows the proportion of assets financed with debt and is calculated by dividing total liabilities by total assets. It can be used to evaluate a business's ability to pay its debts.

> Debt ratio = Total liabilities / Total assets

Learning Objective 5
Use the debt ratio to evaluate business performance

Debt Ratio
Shows the proportion of assets financed with debt. Total liabilities / Total assets.

Think about the accounting equation (Assets = Liabilities + Equity). The equation shows who can claim the assets. The liabilities represent the claims of the creditors and the equity represents the claim of the owner. Companies that have a high percentage of liabilities are at greater risk of default. If they are unable to pay their creditors as the amounts become due, the creditors have the right to claim the assets. The debt ratio calculates the percentage of assets that are financed with liabilities.

Let's look at **Green Mountain Coffee Roasters, Inc.** and evaluate its ability to pay its debts. On its 2011 balance sheet (located in), Green Mountain reported (in thousands) total liabilities of $1,285,672 ($471,374 + $575,969 + $189,637 + $27,184 + $474 + $21,034) and total assets of $3,197,887. The debt ratio for Green Mountain as of September 24, 2011 follows:

$$\text{Debt ratio} = \text{Total liabilities} / \text{Total assets}$$
$$= \$1,285,672 / \$3,197,887 = 0.40 = 40.0\%$$

A debt ratio of 40.0% means that a little less than half the assets of Green Mountain are financed with debt. The other 60.0% (100% − 40.0%) are financed by investors of the corporation. What is an acceptable debt ratio depends on the industry average. The coffee and tea manufacturing industry typically has an average debt ratio of around 41.2%. Green Mountain's debt ratio is slightly lower than the industry average. The debt ratio indicates the risk of a company. The higher the debt ratio, the higher the risk. All liabilities must eventually be paid, and the debt ratio is one indication of the ability of the company to fulfill these obligations.

> Decisions — Would you purchase equipment with debt?

Jackson Russell works as a district sales manager for a large pharmaceutical sales company. Jackson would like to purchase a new high-tech marketing display that he will be able to use at upcoming medical conferences. The marketing display will allow his customers to access up-to-date information and research statistics on the pharmaceuticals that his company sells by using multiple touch screen computers. He believes that the marketing display will significantly increase the sales revenue of the products he sells. The only problem is that the marketing display will cost $50,000, and he does not have the cash in his budget to purchase the display. Jackson will need to purchase the display using debt, which will increase the district's debt ratio from 20% to 58%. Jackson is aware that his company closely monitors the district's debt ratio and has a policy that the district must maintain a ratio below 55%. Should Jackson purchase the equipment?

Solution

If the company has a policy that the district's debt ratio must remain below 55%, then Jackson should not purchase the equipment. However, there might be a way to structure the purchase so that the district's debt ratio would stay below 55%. Jackson either needs to incur less debt or increase his total assets. He could do this in several possible ways. One alternative might be for Jackson to pay for part of the display equipment with cash and only finance part of it with debt. Even putting as little as $10,000 cash down on the equipment would keep the debt ratio below 55%. Another alternative might be for his district to recognize revenue. If there are open sales opportunities that his employees could close, they might be able to increase total assets (and revenue), and, thereby, decrease the debt ratio.

> Try It!

23. Using the following accounts and their balances, calculate the debt ratio for Cooper Furniture Repair as of December 31, 2015.

Cash	$ 7,000	Advertising Expense	$ 1,200
Unearned Revenue	4,500	Utilities Expense	800
Equipment	10,000	Rent Expense	5,000
Service Revenue	8,000	Accounts Payable	2,300
Miller, Capital	12,200	Miller, Withdrawals	3,000

Check your answer at the end of the chapter.

For more practice, see Short Exercise S-9.   MyAccountingLab

REVIEW

> Things You Should Know

1. What is an account?

- An account is a detailed record of all increases and decreases that have occurred in an individual asset, liability, or equity during a specific period.

- Common asset accounts: Cash, Accounts Receivable, Notes Receivable, Prepaid Expenses, Land, Building, Furniture

- Common liability accounts: Accounts Payable, Notes Payable, Taxes Payable, Salaries Payable, Unearned Revenue

- Common equity accounts: Owner's Capital, Owner's Withdrawals, Revenues, Expenses

- A chart of accounts lists a company's accounts along with account numbers.

- A ledger shows the increases and decreases in each account along with their balances.

2. What is double-entry accounting?

- Double-entry accounting requires transactions to be recorded into at least two accounts.

- The T-account is shaped like a capital "T" with debits posted to the left side of vertical line and credits posted to the right side of the vertical line.

- Debit = Left

- Credit = Right

- Assets, Owner's Withdrawals, and Expenses are increased with a debit and decreased with a credit.

- Liabilities, Owner's Capital, and Revenues are increased with a credit and decreased with a debit.

- The normal balance of an account is the increase side of an account.

3. How do you record transactions?

- Source documents provide the evidence and data for transactions.

- Transactions are recorded in a journal and then the journal entries are posted (transferred) to the ledger.

- Transactions are journalized and posted using five steps:

  Step 1: Identify the accounts and the account type.

  Step 2: Decide whether each account increases or decreases using the rules of debits and credits.

  Step 3: Record the transaction in the journal.

  Step 4: Post the journal entry to the ledger.

  Step 5: Determine whether the accounting equation is in balance.

4. What is the trial balance?

- The trial balance summarizes the ledger by listing all the accounts with their balances.

- Assets are listed first, followed by liabilities, and then equity.

- The trial balance ensures that debits equal credits and is used to prepare the financial statements.

5. How do you use the debt ratio to evaluate business performance?

- The debt ratio can be used to evaluate a business's ability to pay its debts.

- Debt ratio = Total liabilities / Total assets

> Summary Problem

The trial balance of Harper Service Center as of February 28, 2015 follows:

HARPER SERVICE CENTER Trial Balance February 28, 2015		
	Balance	
Account Title	**Debit**	**Credit**
Cash	$ 26,000	
Accounts Receivable	4,500	
Office Supplies	0	
Land	0	
Accounts Payable		$ 2,000
Utilities Payable		0
Unearned Revenue		0
Notes Payable		0
Harper, Capital		28,500
Harper, Withdrawals	0	
Service Revenue		0
Salaries Expense	0	
Rent Expense	0	
Interest Expense	0	
Utilities Expense	0	
Total	$ 30,500	$ 30,500

Recording Business Transactions

During March, the business engaged in the following transactions:

Mar. 2	Borrowed $45,000 from the bank and signed a note payable in the name of the business.
4	Paid cash of $40,000 to acquire land.
9	Performed services for a customer and received cash of $5,000.
13	Purchased office supplies on account, $300.
15	Performed services for a customer on account, $2,600.
18	Paid $1,200 on account.
21	Paid the following cash expenses: salaries, $3,000; rent, $1,500; and interest, $400.
25	Received $3,100 from customer on account.
27	Received a $200 utility bill that will be paid next month.
29	Received $1,500 for services to be performed next month.
30	Harper withdrew cash of $1,800.

Requirements

1. Open the accounts listed in the trial balance using the balances indicated. Use the T-account format.

2. Journalize each transaction including explanations.

3. Post the journal entries to the ledger (use T-account format).

4. Prepare the trial balance of Harper Service Center as of March 31, 2015.

> Solution

Requirement 1

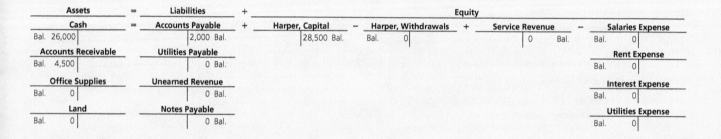

Requirement 2

Date	Accounts and Explanation	Debit	Credit
Mar. 2	Cash	45,000	
	Notes Payable		45,000
	Borrowed cash on notes payable.		
4	Land	40,000	
	Cash		40,000
	Purchased land with cash.		
9	Cash	5,000	
	Service Revenue		5,000
	Performed services and received cash.		
13	Office Supplies	300	
	Accounts Payable		300
	Purchased office supplies on account.		
15	Accounts Receivable	2,600	
	Service Revenue		2,600
	Performed services on account.		
18	Accounts Payable	1,200	
	Cash		1,200
	Paid cash on account.		
21	Salaries Expense	3,000	
	Rent Expense	1,500	
	Interest Expense	400	
	Cash		4,900
	Paid cash expenses.		
25	Cash	3,100	
	Accounts Receivable		3,100
	Received cash on account.		
27	Utilities Expense	200	
	Utilities Payable		200
	Received utility bill.		
29	Cash	1,500	
	Unearned Revenue		1,500
	Collected cash for future services.		
30	Harper, Withdrawals	1,800	
	Cash		1,800
	Owner withdrawal.		

Requirement 3

Assets	=	Liabilities	+				Equity			

Cash

Bal.	26,000	40,000	Mar. 4
Mar. 2	45,000	1,200	Mar.18
Mar. 9	5,000	4,900	Mar. 21
Mar. 25	3,100	1,800	Mar. 30
Mar. 29	1,500		
Bal.	32,700		

Accounts Receivable

Bal.	4,500	3,100	Mar. 25
Mar. 15	2,600		
Bal.	4,000		

Office Supplies

Bal.	0		
Mar. 13	300		
Bal.	300		

Land

Bal.	0		
Mar. 4	40,000		
Bal.	40,000		

Accounts Payable

Mar.18	1,200	2,000	Bal.
		300	Mar. 13
		1,100	Bal.

Utilities Payable

		0	Bal.
		200	Mar. 27
		200	Bal.

Unearned Revenue

		0	Bal.
		1,500	Mar. 29
		1,500	Bal.

Notes Payable

		0	Bal.
		45,000	Mar. 2
		45,000	Bal.

Harper, Capital

		28,500	Bal.
		28,500	Bal.

Harper, Withdrawals

Bal.	0		
Mar. 30	1,800		
Bal.	1,800		

Service Revenue

		0	Bal.
		5,000	Mar. 9
		2,600	Mar. 15
		7,600	Bal.

Salaries Expense

Bal.	0		
Mar. 21	3,000		
Bal.	3,000		

Rent Expense

Bal.	0		
Mar. 21	1,500		
Bal.	1,500		

Interest Expense

Bal.	0		
Mar. 21	400		
Bal.	400		

Utilities Expense

Bal.	0		
Mar. 27	200		
Bal.	200		

Requirement 4

HARPER SERVICE CENTER
Trial Balance
March 31, 2015

Account Title	Balance Debit	Balance Credit
Cash	$ 32,700	
Accounts Receivable	4,000	
Office Supplies	300	
Land	40,000	
Accounts Payable		$ 1,100
Utilities Payable		200
Unearned Revenue		1,500
Notes Payable		45,000
Harper, Capital		28,500
Harper, Withdrawals	1,800	
Service Revenue		7,600
Salaries Expense	3,000	
Rent Expense	1,500	
Interest Expense	400	
Utilities Expense	200	
Total	$ 83,900	$ 83,900

> Key Terms

Account
A detailed record of all increases and decreases that have occurred in an individual asset, liability, or equity during a specific period.

Accrued Liability
A liability for which the business knows the amount owed but the bill has not been paid.

Chart of Accounts
A list of all of a company's accounts with their account numbers.

Compound Journal Entry
A journal entry that is characterized by having multiple debits and/or multiple credits.

Credit
The right side of a T-account.

Debit
The left side of a T-account.

Debt Ratio
Shows the proportion of assets financed with debt. Total liabilities / Total assets.

Double-Entry System
A system of accounting in which every transaction affects at least two accounts.

Journal
A record of transactions in date order.

Ledger
The record holding all the accounts of a business, the changes in those accounts, and their balances.

Normal Balance
The balance that appears on the increase side of an account.

Notes Receivable
A written promise that a customer will pay a fixed amount of money and interest by a certain date in the future.

Notes Payable
A written promise made by the business to pay a debt, usually involving interest, in the future.

Posting
Transferring data from the journal to the ledger.

Prepaid Expense
A payment of an expense in advance.

Source Document
Provides the evidence and data for accounting transactions.

T-Account
A summary device that is shaped like a capital *T* with debits posted on the left side of the vertical line and credits on the right side of the vertical line.

Trial Balance
A list of all the ledger accounts with their balances at a point in time.

Unearned Revenue
A liability created when a business collects cash from customers in advance of providing services or delivering goods.

> Quick Check

1. The detailed record of the changes in a particular asset, liability, or owner's equity is called

   a. an account.
   b. a journal.
   c. a ledger.
   d. a trial balance.

   Learning Objective 1

2. Which of the following accounts is a liability?

   a. Accounts Receivable
   b. Service Revenue
   c. Unearned Revenue
   d. Prepaid Rent Expense

   Learning Objective 1

3. The left side of an account is used to record which of the following?

   a. Debit or credit, depending on the type of account
   b. Increases
   c. Credits
   d. Debits

   Learning Objective 2

Recording Business Transactions

4. Which of the following statements is correct?
   a. Prepaid Expenses are decreased with a debit.
   b. Unearned Revenue is increased with a debit.
   c. Rent Expense is increased with a credit.
   d. Accounts Payable is increased with a credit.

5. Your business purchased office supplies of $2,500 on account. The journal entry to record this transaction is as follows:

a.
| Office Supplies | 2,500 | |
| Accounts Receivable | | 2,500 |

b.
| Office Supplies | 2,500 | |
| Accounts Payable | | 2,500 |

c.
| Accounts Payable | 2,500 | |
| Office Supplies | | 2,500 |

d.
| Cash | 2,500 | |
| Accounts Payable | | 2,500 |

6. Sedlor Properties purchased office supplies on account for $800. Which journal entry records the payment of those office supplies?

a.
| Accounts Payable | 800 | |
| Accounts Receivable | | 800 |

b.
| Accounts Payable | 800 | |
| Cash | | 800 |

c.
| Cash | 800 | |
| Accounts Payable | | 800 |

d.
| Office Supplies | 800 | |
| Cash | | 800 |

7. Posting a $2,500 purchase of office supplies on account appears as follows:

Learning Objective 3

a.

Cash		Office Supplies	
	2,500	2,500	

b.

Office Supplies		Accounts Payable	
	2,500	2,500	

c.

Office Supplies		Accounts Receivable	
2,500			2,500

d.

Office Supplies		Accounts Payable	
2,500			2,500

8. Pixel Copies recorded a cash collection on account by debiting Cash and crediting Accounts Payable. What will the trial balance show for this error?

Learning Objective 4

   a. Cash is overstated
   b. Liabilities are overstated
   c. Expenses are overstated
   d. The trial balance will not balance

9. Which sequence correctly summarizes the accounting process?

Learning Objectives 3, 4

   a. Journalize transactions, post to the accounts, prepare a trial balance
   b. Journalize transactions, prepare a trial balance, post to the accounts
   c. Post to the accounts, journalize transactions, prepare a trial balance
   d. Prepare a trial balance, journalize transactions, post to the accounts

10. Nathville Laundry reported assets of $800 and equity of $480. What is Nathville's debt ratio?

Learning Objective 5

   a. 60%
   b. 40%
   c. 67%
   d. Not enough information is provided

Check your answers at the end of the chapter.

ASSESS YOUR PROGRESS

> Review Questions

1. Identify the three categories of the accounting equation and list at least four accounts associated with each category.

2. What is the purpose of the chart of accounts? Explain the numbering typically associated with the accounts.

3. What does a ledger show? What's the difference between a ledger and the chart of accounts?

4. Accounting uses a double-entry system. Explain what this sentence means.

5. What is a T-account? On which side is the debit? On which side is the credit? Where does the account name go on a T-account?

6. When are debits increases? When are debits decreases?

7. When are credits increases? When are credits decreases?

8. Identify which types of accounts have a normal debit balance and which types of accounts have a normal credit balance.

9. What are source documents? Provide examples of source documents that a business might use.

10. Where are transactions initially recorded?

11. Explain the five steps in journalizing and posting transactions.

12. What are the four parts of a journal entry?

13. What is involved in the posting process?

14. What is the purpose of the trial balance?

15. What is the difference between the trial balance and the balance sheet?

16. If total debits equal total credits on the trial balance, is the trial balance error-free? Explain your answer.

17. What is the calculation for the debt ratio? Explain what the debt ratio evaluates.

> Short Exercises

S-1 Identifying accounts
Learning Objective 1

Consider the following accounts:

a. Notes Receivable

b. Nations, Capital

c. Prepaid Insurance

d. Notes Payable

e. Rent Revenue

f. Taxes Payable

g. Rent Expense

h. Furniture

i. Nations, Withdrawals

j. Unearned Revenue

Identify each account as an asset (A), liability (L), or equity (E).

S-2 Identifying increases and decreases in accounts
Learning Objective 2

For each account, identify whether the changes would be recorded as a debit (DR) or credit (CR).

a. Increase to Accounts Receivable

b. Decrease to Unearned Revenue

c. Decrease to Cash

d. Increase to Interest Expense

e. Increase to Salaries Payable

f. Decrease to Prepaid Rent

g. Increase to Perez, Capital

h. Increase to Notes Receivable

i. Decrease to Accounts Payable

j. Increase to Interest Revenue

S-3 Identifying normal balances
Learning Objective 2

For each account, identify whether the normal balance is a debit (DR) or credit (CR).

a. Notes Payable

b. Harris, Withdrawals

c. Service Revenue

d. Land

e. Unearned Revenue

f. Harris, Capital

g. Utilities Expense

h. Office Supplies

i. Advertising Expense

j. Interest Payable

Learning Objective 3

S-4 Journalizing transactions

Ned Brown opened a medical practice in San Diego, California, and had the following transactions during the month of January.

Jan. 1	The business received $29,000 cash and gave capital to Brown.
2	Purchased medical supplies on account, $14,000.
4	Performed services for patients receiving $1,400.
12	Paid monthly office rent of $2,600.
15	Recorded $8,000 revenue for services rendered to patients on account.

Journalize the transactions of Ned Brown, M.D. Include an explanation with each entry.

Learning Objective 3

S-5 Journalizing transactions

Texas Sales Consultants completed the following transactions during the latter part of January:

Jan. 22	Performed services for customers on account, $8,000.
30	Received cash on account from customers, $7,000.
31	Received a utility bill, $180, which will be paid during February.
31	Paid monthly salary to salesman, $2,000.
31	Received $1,500 for 3 months of consulting service to be performed starting in February.
31	The owner, Dylan Hansen, withdrew $1,000 from the business.

Journalize the transactions of Texas Sales Consultants. Include an explanation with each journal entry.

Learning Objective 3

S-6 Calculating the balance of a T-account

Accounts Payable			
May 2	6,000	14,000	May 1
May 22	12,000	1,000	May 5
		7,000	May 15
		500	May 23

Calculate the Accounts Payable balance.

S-7 Journalizing transactions and posting to T-accounts

Learning Objective 3

Kenneth Dolkart Optical Dispensary completed the following transactions during the latter part of March:

Mar. 15	Purchased office supplies on account, $3,400
28	Paid $1,200 on account.

Requirements

1. Journalize the transactions of Kenneth Dolkart Optical Dispensary. Include an explanation with each journal entry.

2. Open the following accounts (use T-account format): Cash (Beginning Balance of $14,000), Office Supplies, and Accounts Payable. Post the journal entries from Requirement 1 to the accounts and compute the balance in each account.

S-8 Preparing a trial balance

Learning Objective 4

Oakland Floor Coverings reported the following summarized data at December 31, 2014. Accounts appear in no particular order, and all have normal balances.

Service Revenue	$34,000	Salaries Payable	$12,000
Equipment	45,000	Salaries Expense	2,000
Rent Expense	14,000	Cash	8,000
Oakland, Capital	22,000	Accounts Receivable	4,000
Accounts Payable	2,000	Interest Payable	6,000
Oakland, Withdrawals	1,800	Utilities Expense	1,200

Prepare the trial balance of Oakland Floor Coverings at December 31, 2014.

S-9 Calculating debt ratio

Learning Objective 5

Professional Carpet Care had the following total assets, liabilities, and equity as of October 31.

Assets	$230,000
Liabilities	69,000
Equity	161,000

What is Professional Carpet Care's debt ratio as of October 31?

> Exercises

E-10 Using accounting vocabulary

Match the accounting terms with the corresponding definitions.

1. Posting
2. Account
3. Debit
4. Journal
5. Chart of accounts
6. Trial balance
7. Normal balance
8. Ledger
9. Credit
10. Compound journal entry

a. A detailed record of all increases and decreases that have occurred in a particular asset, liability, or equity during a period

b. The record holding all the accounts of a business, the changes in those accounts, and their balances

c. A journal entry that is characterized by having multiple debits and/or multiple credits

d. A record of transactions in date order

e. Left side of a T-account

f. Side of an account where increases are recorded

g. Transferring amounts from the journal to the ledger

h. Right side of a T-account

i. A list of all accounts with their balances at a point in time

j. A list of all accounts with their account numbers

E-11 Creating a chart of accounts

Richard Autobody Shop has the following accounts:

Accounts Payable	Service Revenue
Cash	Equipment
Utilities Expense	Richard, Capital
Automotive Supplies	Advertising Expense
Richard, Withdrawals	Unearned Revenue

Create a chart of accounts for Richard Autobody Shop using the standard numbering system. Each account is separated by a factor of 10. For example, the first asset account will be 100 and the next asset account will 110.

E-12 Identifying accounts, increases in accounts, and normal balances

a. Interest Revenue
b. Accounts Payable
c. Chapman, Capital
d. Office Supplies
e. Advertising Expense
f. Unearned Revenue
g. Prepaid Rent
h. Utilities Expense
i. Chapman, Withdrawals
j. Service Revenue

Requirements

1. Identify each account as asset (A), liability (L), or equity (E).
2. Identify whether the account is increased with a debit (DR) or credit (CR).
3. Identify whether the normal balance is a debit (DR) or credit (CR).

E-13 Identifying increases and decreases in accounts and normal balances

Learning Objective 2

Insert the missing information into the accounting equation. Signify increases as Incr. and decreases as Decr.

(a)	=	Liabilities	+		(b)	

Assets	=	(c)	+	Owner's Capital	−	(d)	+	Revenues	−	Expenses
(e) Debit	Decr. (n)	Decr. (o)	(f) Credit	(g) (p)	(h) Credit	(i) (q)	(j) Credit	(k) Debit	(l) Credit	Incr. (r)	(m) Credit

E-14 Identifying source documents

Learning Objective 3

For each transaction, identify a possible source document.

a. The business received $20,000 cash and gave capital to the owner.
b. Purchased office supplies on account, $500.
c. Recorded $1,000 revenue for services rendered to customers.

E-15 Analyzing and journalizing transactions

Learning Objective 3

As the manager of Mighty Fine Mexican Restaurant, you must deal with a variety of business transactions. Provide an explanation for the following transactions:

a. Debit Equipment and credit Cash.
b. Debit Fernandez, Withdrawals and credit Cash.
c. Debit Wages Payable and credit Cash.
d. Debit Equipment and credit Fernandez, Capital.
e. Debit Cash and credit Unearned Revenue.
f. Debit Advertising Expense and credit Cash.
g. Debit Cash and credit Service Revenue.

Recording Business Transactions

Use the following information to answer Exercises E-16 and E-17.

The following transactions occurred for London Engineering:

Jul. 2	Received $10,000 contribution from Bill London, owner, in exchange for capital.
4	Paid utilities expense of $400.
5	Purchased equipment on account, $2,100.
10	Performed services for a client on account, $2,000.
12	Borrowed $7,000 cash, signing a notes payable.
19	The owner, Bill London, withdrew $500 cash from the business.
21	Purchased office supplies for $800 and paid cash.
27	Paid the liability from July 5.

Learning Objective 3

E-16 Analyzing and journalizing transactions

Journalize the transactions of London Engineering. Include an explanation with each journal entry. Use the following accounts: Cash; Accounts Receivable; Office Supplies; Equipment; Accounts Payable; Notes Payable; London, Capital; London, Withdrawals; Service Revenue; Utilities Expense.

Learning Objective 3

3. Cash Balance $13,200

E-17 Posting journal entries to T-accounts

Requirements

1. Open the following T-accounts for London Engineering: Cash; Accounts Receivable; Office Supplies; Equipment; Accounts Payable; Notes Payable; London, Capital; London, Withdrawals; Service Revenue; Utilities Expense.

2. Post the journal entries to the T-accounts. Also transfer the dates to the T-accounts.

3. Compute the July 31 balance for each account.

Use the following information to answer Exercises E-18 and E-19.

The following transactions occurred for Ward Technology Solutions:

May 1	The business received cash of $75,000 and gave capital to Zoe Ward, the owner.
2	Purchased office supplies on account, $500.
4	Paid $53,000 cash for building and land. The building had a fair market value of $45,000.
6	Performed services for customers and received cash, $2,600.
9	Paid $400 on accounts payable.
17	Performed services for customers on account, $2,500.
19	Paid rent expense for the month, $900.
20	Received $1,200 from customers for services to be performed next month.
21	Paid $500 for advertising in next month's *IT Technology* magazine.
23	Received $1,900 cash on account from a customer.
31	Incurred and paid salaries, $1,100.

E-18 Analyzing and journalizing transactions

Learning Objective 3

Journalize the transactions of Ward Technology Solutions. Include an explanation with each journal entry. Use the following accounts: Cash; Accounts Receivable; Office Supplies; Prepaid Advertising; Building; Land; Accounts Payable; Unearned Revenue; Ward, Capital; Service Revenue; Rent Expense; Salaries Expense.

E-19 Posting journal entries to four-column accounts

Learning Objective 3

Requirements

2. Cash Balance $24,800

1. Open four-column accounts using the following account numbers: Cash, 110; Accounts Receivable, 120; Office Supplies, 130; Prepaid Advertising, 140; Building, 150; Land, 160; Accounts Payable, 210; Unearned Revenue, 220; Ward, Capital, 310; Service Revenue, 410; Rent Expense, 510; Salaries Expense, 520.

2. Post the journal entries to the four-column accounts and determine the balance in the account after each transaction. Assume that the journal entries were recorded on page 10 of the journal. Make sure to complete the Post. Ref. columns in the journal and ledger.

E-20 Analyzing transactions from T-accounts

Learning Objective 3

The first nine transactions of North-West Airplane Repair have been posted to the T-accounts. Provide an explanation for each of the nine transactions.

E-21 Journalizing transactions from T-accounts

Learning Objective 3

In December 2015, the first five transactions of Adams' Lawn Care Company have been posted to the T-accounts. Prepare the journal entries that served as the sources for the five transactions. Include an explanation for each entry.

Learning Objective 4

Total Debits $210,000

E-22 Preparing a trial balance

The accounts of Atkins Moving Company follow with their normal balances as of August 31, 2015. The accounts are listed in no particular order.

Atkins, Capital	$ 72,000	Trucks	$ 132,000
Insurance Expense	600	Fuel Expense	3,000
Accounts Payable	4,000	Atkins, Withdrawals	5,400
Service Revenue	80,000	Utilities Expense	500
Building	48,000	Accounts Receivable	8,800
Advertising Expense	400	Notes Payable	54,000
Salaries Expense	7,000	Office Supplies	300
Cash	4,000		

Prepare Atkins' trial balance as of August 31, 2015.

Learning Objective 4

Total Debits $74,500

E-23 Preparing a trial balance from T-accounts

The T-accounts of McDonald Farm Equipment Repair follow as of May 31, 2015.

Prepare McDonald Farm Equipment Repair's trial balance as of May 31, 2015.

E-24 Journalizing transactions, posting journal entries to four-column accounts, and preparing a trial balance

Learning Objectives 3, 4

3. Total Debits $25,550

The following transactions occurred during the month for Teresa Parker, CPA:

Jun. 1	Parker opened an accounting firm by contributing $14,000 cash and office furniture with a fair market value of $5,200 in exchange for capital.
5	Paid monthly rent of $1,500.
9	Purchased office supplies on account, $900.
14	Paid employee's salary, $1,700.
18	Received a bill for utilities to be paid next month, $250.
21	Paid $700 of the accounts payable created on June 9.
25	Performed accounting services on account, $5,900.
28	Parker withdrew cash of $6,700.

Requirements

1. Open the following four-column accounts of Teresa Parker, CPA: Cash, 110; Accounts Receivable, 120; Office Supplies, 130; Office Furniture, 140; Accounts Payable, 210; Utilities Payable, 220; Parker, Capital, 310; Parker, Withdrawals, 320; Service Revenue, 410; Salaries Expense, 510; Rent Expense, 520; Utilities Expense, 530.

2. Journalize the transactions and then post the journal entries to the four-column accounts. Keep a running balance in each account. Assume the journal entries are recorded on page 10 of the journal.

3. Prepare the trial balance as of June 30, 2015.

E-25 Analyzing accounting errors

Learning Objective 4

Danielle Neylon has trouble keeping her debits and credits equal. During a recent month, Danielle made the following accounting errors:

a. In preparing the trial balance, Danielle omitted a $7,000 notes payable. The debit to Cash was correct.

b. Danielle posted a $90 Utilities Expense as $900. The credit to Cash was correct.

c. In recording an $800 payment on account, Danielle debited Furniture instead of Accounts Payable.

d. In journalizing a receipt of cash for service revenue, Danielle debited Cash for $1,200 instead of the correct amount of $120. The credit was correct.

e. Danielle recorded a $540 purchase of office supplies on account by debiting Office Supplies and crediting Accounts Payable for $450.

Requirements

1. For each of these errors, state whether total debits equal total credits on the trial balance.

2. Identify each account that has an incorrect balance, and the amount and direction of the error (such as "Accounts Receivable $500 too high").

Learning Objective 4

Total Debits $40,250

E-26 Correcting errors in a trial balance

The accountant for Metro Painting Specialists is having a hard time preparing the trial balance as of November 30, 2015:

METRO PAINTING SPECIALISTS Trial Balance November 30, 2015		
	Balance	
Account Title	Debit	Credit
Painting Equipment	$ 14,500	
Cash	12,600	
Accounts Receivable	1,200	
Advertising Expense	550	
White, Withdrawals		$ 7,000
Accounts Payable		3,500
Rent Expense	1,800	
White, Capital	15,000	
Service Revenue		19,750
Unearned Revenue	2,000	
Salaries Expense	2,100	
Office Supplies		200
Utilities Expense	300	
Total	$ 50,050	$ 30,450

Prepare the corrected trial balance as of November 30, 2015. Assume all amounts are correct and all accounts have normal balances.

Learning Objective 4

Total Debits $34,700

E-27 Correcting errors in a trial balance

The following trial balance of Joy McDowell Tutoring Service as of May 31, 2015, does not balance.

JOY MCDOWELL TUTORING SERVICE Trial Balance May 31, 2015		
	Balance	
Account Title	Debit	Credit
Cash	$ 3,000	
Accounts Receivable	2,000	
Office Supplies	600	
Computer Equipment	15,800	
Accounts Payable		$ 11,100
Utilities Payable		300
McDowell, Capital		11,600
McDowell, Withdrawals	10,000	
Service Revenue		9,800
Salaries Expense	1,700	
Rent Expenses	700	
Utilities Expense	500	
Total	$ 34,300	$ 32,800

Investigation of the accounting records reveals that the bookkeeper:

a. Recorded a $500 cash revenue transaction by debiting Accounts Receivable. The credit entry was correct.

b. Posted a $1,000 credit to Accounts Payable as $100.

c. Did not record Utilities Expense or the related Utilities Payable in the amount of $400.

d. Understated McDowell, Capital by $600.

Prepare the corrected trial balance as of May 31, 2015, complete with a heading; journal entries are not required.

E-28 Calculating the debt ratio

Learning Objective 5

Total Assets $170,250

John Hill, M.D. reported the following trial balance as of September 30, 2015.

JOHN HILL, M.D. Trial Balance September 30, 2015		
	Balance	
Account Title	**Debit**	**Credit**
Cash	$ 35,000	
Accounts Receivable	7,250	
Office Supplies	3,000	
Office Equipment	25,000	
Building	80,000	
Land	20,000	
Accounts Payable		$ 2,000
Utilities Payable		935
Unearned Revenue		14,000
Notes Payable		75,000
Hill, Capital		100,000
Hill, Withdrawals	50,000	
Service Revenue		52,915
Salaries Expense	23,500	
Utilities Expense	800	
Advertising Expense	300	
Total	$ 244,850	$ 244,850

Calculate the debt ratio for John Hill, M.D.

> Problems Group A

Learning Objectives 3, 4

2. Cash Balance $69,880

P-29A Journalizing transactions, posting journal entries to T-accounts, and preparing a trial balance

Vernon Yung practices medicine under the business title Vernon Yung, M.D. During July, the medical practice completed the following transactions:

Jul. 1	Yung contributed $68,000 cash to the business in exchange for capital.
5	Paid monthly rent on medical equipment, $560.
9	Paid $16,000 cash to purchase land to be used in operations.
10	Purchased office supplies on account, $1,600.
19	Borrowed $23,000 from the bank for business use. Yung signed a note payable to the bank in the name of the business.
22	Paid $1,300 on account.
28	The business received a bill for advertising in the daily newspaper to be paid in August, $240.
31	Revenues earned during the month included $6,500 cash and $5,800 on account.
31	Paid employees' salaries $2,500, office rent $1,000, and utilities, $400. Record as a compound entry.
31	The business received $1,140 for medical screening services to be performed next month.
31	Yung withdrew cash of $7,000.

The business uses the following accounts: Cash; Accounts Receivable; Office Supplies; Land; Accounts Payable; Advertising Payable; Unearned Revenue; Notes Payable; Yung, Capital; Yung, Withdrawals; Service Revenue; Salaries Expense; Rent Expense; Utilities Expense; and Advertising Expense.

Requirements

1. Journalize each transaction. Explanations are not required.

2. Post the journal entries to the T-accounts, using transaction dates as posting references in the ledger accounts. Label the balance of each account *Bal*.

3. Prepare the trial balance of Vernon Yung, M.D. as of July 31, 2015.

P-30A Journalizing transactions, posting journal entries to T-accounts, and preparing a trial balance

Learning Objectives 3, 4

4. Total Debits $50,050

Doris Stewart started her practice as a design consultant on September 1, 2015. During the first month of operations, the business completed the following transactions:

Sep. 1	Received $42,000 cash and gave capital to Stewart.
4	Purchased office supplies, $700, and furniture, $1,900, on account.
6	Performed services for a law firm and received $1,400 cash.
7	Paid $24,000 cash to acquire land to be used in operations.
10	Performed services for a hotel and received its promise to pay the $1,000 within one week.
14	Paid for the furniture purchased on September 4 on account.
15	Paid assistant's semimonthly salary, $1,490.
17	Received cash on account, $400.
20	Prepared a design for a school on account, $700.
25	Received $1,800 cash for design services to be performed in October.
28	Received $2,100 cash for consulting with Plummer & Gordon.
29	Paid $1,200 cash for a 12-month insurance policy starting on October 1.
30	Paid assistant's semimonthly salary, $1,490.
30	Paid monthly rent expense, $650.
30	Received a bill for utilities, $350. The bill will be paid next month.
30	Stewart withdrew cash of $3,000.

Requirements

1. Record each transaction in the journal using the following account titles: Cash; Accounts Receivable; Office Supplies; Prepaid Insurance; Furniture; Land; Accounts Payable; Utilities Payable; Unearned Revenue; Stewart, Capital; Stewart, Withdrawals; Service Revenue; Salaries Expense; Rent Expense; Utilities Expense. Explanations are not required.

2. Open a T-account for each of the accounts.

3. Post the journal entries to the T-accounts, using transaction dates as posting references in the ledger accounts. Label the balance of each account *Bal.*

4. Prepare the trial balance of Doris Stewart, Designer, as of September 30, 2015.

Learning Objectives 3, 4

3. Cash Balance $14,140

P-31A Journalizing transactions, posting journal entries to four-column accounts, and preparing a trial balance

Trevor Moore opened a law office on January 1, 2015. During the first month of operations, the business completed the following transactions:

Jan. 1	Moore contributed $59,000 cash to the business, Trevor Moore, Attorney. The business gave capital to Moore.
3	Purchased office supplies, $600, and furniture, $2,000, on account.
4	Performed legal services for a client and received $1,300 cash.
7	Purchased a building, $100,000, and land, $20,000. The business paid $40,000 cash and signed a note payable to the bank for the remaining amount.
11	Prepared legal documents for a client on account, $700.
15	Paid assistant's semimonthly salary, $1,180.
16	Paid for the office supplies purchased on January 3 on account.
18	Received $2,400 cash for helping a client sell real estate.
19	Defended a client in court and billed the client for $800.
25	Received a bill for utilities, $400. The bill will be paid next month.
29	Received cash on account, $700.
30	Paid $2,400 cash for a 12-month insurance policy starting on February 1.
30	Paid assistant's semimonthly salary, $1,180.
31	Paid monthly rent expense, $1,500.
31	Moore withdrew cash of $2,400.

Requirements

1. Record each transaction in the journal, using the following account titles: Cash; Accounts Receivable; Office Supplies; Prepaid Insurance; Furniture; Building; Land; Accounts Payable; Utilities Payable; Notes Payable; Moore, Capital; Moore, Withdrawals; Service Revenue; Salaries Expense; Rent Expense; and Utilities Expense. Explanations are not required.

2. Open the following four-column accounts including account numbers: Cash, 101; Accounts Receivable, 111; Office Supplies, 121; Prepaid Insurance, 131; Furniture, 141; Building, 151; Land, 161; Accounts Payable, 201; Utilities Payable, 211; Notes Payable, 221; Moore, Capital, 301; Moore, Withdrawals, 311; Service Revenue, 411; Salaries Expense, 511; Rent Expense, 521; and Utilities Expense, 531.

3. Post the journal entries to four-column accounts in the ledger, using dates, account numbers, journal references, and posting references. Assume the journal entries were recorded on page 1 of the journal.

4. Prepare the trial balance of Trevor Moore, Attorney, at January 31, 2015.

P-32A Journalizing transactions, posting journal entries to four-column accounts, and preparing a trial balance

The trial balance of Sam Mitchell, CPA, is dated January 31, 2015:

Learning Objectives 3, 4

3. Accounts Receivable Balance $8,800

SAM MITCHELL, CPA
Trial Balance
January 31, 2015

Account Title	Balance Debit	Balance Credit
Cash	$ 7,000	
Accounts Receivable	10,500	
Office Supplies	600	
Furniture	0	
Automobile	0	
Land	17,000	
Accounts Payable		$ 4,700
Unearned Revenue		0
Mitchell, Capital		30,400
Mitchell, Withdrawals	0	
Service Revenue		0
Salaries Expense	0	
Rent Expense	0	
Total	$ 35,100	$ 35,100

During February, the business completed the following transactions:

Feb. 4	Collected $4,000 cash from a client on account.
8	Performed tax services for a client on account, $4,600.
13	Paid $2,400 on account.
14	Purchased furniture on account, $3,000.
15	Mitchell contributed his personal automobile to the business in exchange for capital. The automobile had a market value of $8,500.
18	Purchased office supplies on account, $900.
19	Received $2,300 for tax services performed on February 8.
20	Mitchell withdrew cash of $2,200.
21	Received $2,300 cash for consulting work completed.
24	Received $1,000 cash for accounting services to be completed next month.
27	Paid office rent, $500.
28	Paid employee salary, $1,600.

Requirements

1. Record the February transactions in the journal. Use the following accounts: Cash; Accounts Receivable; Office Supplies; Furniture; Automobile; Land; Accounts Payable; Unearned Revenue; Mitchell, Capital; Mitchell, Withdrawals; Service Revenue; Salaries Expense; and Rent Expense. Include an explanation for each entry.

2. Open the four-column ledger accounts listed in the trial balance, together with their balances as of January 31. Use the following account numbers: Cash, 11; Accounts Receivable, 12; Office Supplies, 13; Furniture, 14; Automobile, 15; Land, 16; Accounts Payable, 21; Unearned Revenue, 22; Mitchell, Capital, 31; Mitchell, Withdrawals, 32; Service Revenue, 41; Salaries Expense, 51; and Rent Expense, 52.

3. Post the journal entries to four-column accounts in the ledger, using dates, account numbers, journal references, and posting references. Assume the journal entries were recorded on page 5 of the journal.

4. Prepare the trial balance of Sam Mitchell, CPA, at February 28, 2015.

Learning Objective 4

P-33A Correcting errors in a trial balance

Total Debits $115,400

The trial balance of Smart Tots Child Care does not balance.

<table>
<tr><td colspan="3" align="center">SMART TOTS CHILD CARE
Trial Balance
August 31, 2015</td></tr>
<tr><td></td><td colspan="2" align="center">Balance</td></tr>
<tr><td>Account Title</td><td align="center">Debit</td><td align="center">Credit</td></tr>
<tr><td>Cash</td><td>$ 7,700</td><td></td></tr>
<tr><td>Accounts Receivable</td><td>7,000</td><td></td></tr>
<tr><td>Office Supplies</td><td>700</td><td></td></tr>
<tr><td>Prepaid Insurance</td><td>800</td><td></td></tr>
<tr><td>Equipment</td><td>87,000</td><td></td></tr>
<tr><td>Accounts Payable</td><td></td><td>$ 3,000</td></tr>
<tr><td>Notes Payable</td><td></td><td>50,000</td></tr>
<tr><td>Tilley, Capital</td><td></td><td>51,700</td></tr>
<tr><td>Tilley, Withdrawals</td><td>4,400</td><td></td></tr>
<tr><td>Service Revenue</td><td></td><td>4,700</td></tr>
<tr><td>Salaries Expense</td><td>3,600</td><td></td></tr>
<tr><td>Rent Expense</td><td>500</td><td></td></tr>
<tr><td>Total</td><td>$ 111,700</td><td>$ 109,400</td></tr>
</table>

The following errors are detected:

a. Cash is understated by $1,000.

b. A $4,000 debit to Accounts Receivable was posted as a credit.

c. A $1,000 purchase of office supplies on account was neither journalized nor posted.

d. Equipment was incorrectly transferred from the ledger as $87,000. It should have been transferred as $78,500.

e. Salaries Expense is overstated by $200.

f. A $400 cash payment for advertising expense was neither journalized nor posted.

g. A $200 owner's withdrawal of cash was incorrectly journalized as $2,000.

h. Service Revenue was understated by $5,000.

i. A 12-month insurance policy was posted as a $1,200 credit to Prepaid Insurance. Cash was posted correctly.

Prepare the corrected trial balance as of August 31, 2015. Journal entries are not required.

P-34A Correcting errors in a trial balance

The trial balance for Treasure Hunt Exploration Company does not balance.

Learning Objective 4

Total Debits $83,100

TREASURE HUNT EXPLORATION COMPANY Trial Balance February 28, 2015		
	Balance	
Account Title	**Debit**	**Credit**
Cash	$ 6,300	
Accounts Receivable	6,000	
Office Supplies	400	
Computers	22,300	
Exploration Equipment	49,000	
Accounts Payable		$ 2,800
Notes Payable		18,500
Jones, Capital		50,000
Jones, Withdrawals	4,000	
Service Revenue		4,100
Salaries Expense	1,400	
Rent Expense	800	
Advertising Expense	900	
Utilities Expense	800	
Total	$ 91,900	$ 75,400

Recording Business Transactions

The following errors were detected:

a. The Cash balance is overstated by $5,000.

b. Rent Expense of $340 was erroneously posted as a credit rather than a debit.

c. A $6,800 credit to Service Revenue was not posted.

d. A $400 debit to Accounts Receivable was posted as $40.

e. The balance of Utilities Expense is understated by $70.

f. A $900 purchase of office supplies on account was neither journalized nor posted.

g. Computers should be $16,490.

Prepare the corrected trial balance at February 28, 2015. Journal entries are not required.

Learning Objectives 4, 5

P-35A Preparing financial statements from the trial balance and calculating the debt ratio

2. Ending Capital Balance $27,300

The trial balance as of July 31, 2015, for Sharon Silver, Registered Dietician, is presented below:

SHARON SILVER, REGISTERED DIETICIAN Trial Balance July 31, 2015		
	Balance	
Account Title	**Debit**	**Credit**
Cash	$ 36,200	
Accounts Receivable	9,100	
Office Supplies	1,800	
Prepaid Insurance	2,000	
Equipment	13,000	
Accounts Payable		$ 3,300
Unearned Revenue		1,500
Notes Payable		30,000
Silver, Capital		23,150
Silver, Withdrawals	2,300	
Service Revenue		8,800
Salaries Expense	1,700	
Rent Expense	500	
Utilities Expense	150	
Total	$ 66,750	$ 66,750

Requirements

1. Prepare the income statement for the month ended July 31, 2015.

2. Prepare the statement of owner's equity for the month ended July 31, 2015. The beginning balance of capital was $0 and the owner contributed $23,150 during the month.

3. Prepare the balance sheet as of July 31, 2015.

4. Calculate the debt ratio as of July 31, 2015.

> Problems **Group B**

P-36B Journalizing transactions, posting journal entries to T-accounts, and preparing a trial balance

Learning Objectives 3, 4

2. Cash Balance $64,120

Vince Rockford practices medicine under the business title Vince Rockford, M.D. During March, the medical practice completed the following transactions:

Mar. 1	Rockford contributed $74,000 cash to the business in exchange for capital.
5	Paid monthly rent on medical equipment, $560.
9	Paid $24,000 cash to purchase land to be used in operations.
10	Purchased office supplies on account, $1,300.
19	Borrowed $19,000 from the bank for business use. Rockford signed a note payable to the bank in the name of the business.
22	Paid $900 on account.
28	The business received a bill for advertising in the daily newspaper to be paid in April, $120.
31	Revenues earned during the month included $7,100 cash and $4,700 on account.
31	Paid employees' salaries $2,000, office rent $1,600, and utilities, $320. Record as a compound entry.
31	The business received $1,400 for medical screening services to be performed next month.
31	Rockford withdrew cash of $8,000.

The business uses the following accounts: Cash; Accounts Receivable; Office Supplies; Land; Accounts Payable; Advertising Payable; Unearned Revenue; Notes Payable; Rockford, Capital; Rockford, Withdrawals; Service Revenue; Salaries Expense; Rent Expense; Utilities Expense; and Advertising Expense.

Requirements

1. Journalize each journal entries. Explanations are not required.
2. Post the journal entries to the T-accounts, using transaction dates as posting references in the ledger accounts. Label the balance of each account *Bal.*
3. Prepare the trial balance of Vince Rockford, M.D. as of March 31, 2015.

Learning Objectives 3, 4

4. Total Debits $41,950

P-37B Journalizing transactions, posting journal entries to T-accounts, and preparing a trial balance

Beth Nelson started her practice as a design consultant on November 1, 2015. During the first month of operations, the business completed the following transactions:

Nov. 1	Received $34,000 cash and gave capital to Nelson.
4	Purchased office supplies, $500, and furniture, $1,900, on account.
6	Performed services for a law firm and received $1,200 cash.
7	Paid $25,000 cash to acquire land to be used in operations.
10	Performed services for a hotel and received its promise to pay the $1,200 within one week.
14	Paid for the furniture purchased on November 4 on account.
15	Paid assistant's semimonthly salary, $1,080.
17	Received cash on account, $500.
20	Prepared a design for a school on account, $800.
25	Received $1,800 cash for design services to be performed in December.
28	Received $2,200 cash for consulting with Plummer & Gordon.
29	Paid $2,400 cash for a 12-month insurance policy starting on December 1.
30	Paid assistant's semimonthly salary, $1,080.
30	Paid monthly rent expense, $830.
30	Received a bill for utilities, $250. The bill will be paid next month.
30	Nelson withdrew cash of $2,700.

Requirements

1. Record each transaction in the journal using the following account titles: Cash; Accounts Receivable; Office Supplies; Prepaid Insurance; Furniture; Land; Accounts Payable; Utilities Payable; Unearned Revenue; Nelson, Capital; Nelson, Withdrawals; Service Revenue; Salaries Expense; Rent Expense; Utilities Expense. Explanations are not required.

2. Open a T-account for each of the accounts.

3. Post the journal entries to the T-accounts, using transaction dates as posting references in the ledger accounts. Label the balance of each account *Bal.*

4. Prepare the trial balance of Beth Nelson, Designer, as of November 30, 2015.

P-38B Journalizing transactions, posting journal entries to four-column accounts, and preparing a trial balance

Learning Objectives 3, 4

3. Service Revenue Balance $5,400

Vince Perez opened a law office on April 1, 2015. During the first month of operations, the business completed the following transactions:

Apr. 1	Perez contributed $62,000 cash to the business, Vince Perez, Attorney. The business gave capital to Perez.
3	Purchased office supplies, $500, and furniture, $2,000, on account.
4	Performed legal services for a client and received $1,900 cash.
7	Purchased a building, $120,000, and land, $30,000. The business paid $50,000 cash and signed a note payable to the bank for the remaining amount.
11	Prepared legal documents for a client on account, $1,100.
15	Paid assistant's semimonthly salary, $920.
16	Paid for the office supplies purchased on April 3 on account.
18	Received $1,700 cash for helping a client sell real estate.
19	Defended a client in court and billed the client for $700.
25	Received a bill for utilities, $300. The bill will be paid next month.
28	Received cash on account, $800.
29	Paid $1,200 cash for a 12-month insurance policy starting on May 1.
29	Paid assistant's semimonthly salary, $920.
30	Paid monthly rent expense, $730.
30	Perez withdrew cash of $2,700.

Requirements

1. Record each transaction in the journal, using the following account titles: Cash; Accounts Receivable; Office Supplies; Prepaid Insurance; Furniture; Building; Land; Accounts Payable; Utilities Payable; Notes Payable; Perez, Capital; Perez, Withdrawals; Service Revenue; Salaries Expense; Rent Expense; and Utilities Expense. Explanations are not required.

2. Open the following four-column accounts including account numbers: Cash, 101; Accounts Receivable, 111; Office Supplies, 121; Prepaid Insurance, 131; Furniture, 141; Building, 151; Land, 161; Accounts Payable, 201; Utilities Payable, 211; Notes Payable, 221; Perez, Capital, 301; Perez, Withdrawals, 311; Service Revenue, 411; Salaries Expense, 511; Rent Expense, 521; and Utilities Expense, 531.

3. Post the journal entries to four-column accounts in the ledger, using dates, account numbers, journal references, and posting references. Assume the journal entries were recorded on page 1 of the journal.

4. Prepare the trial balance of Vince Perez, Attorney, at April 30, 2015.

Learning Objectives 3, 4

3. Cash Balance $12,800

P-39B Journalizing transactions, posting journal entries to four-column accounts, and preparing a trial balance

The trial balance of John Hilton, CPA, is dated March 31, 2015:

JOHN HILTON, CPA
Trial Balance
March 31, 2015

Account Title	Balance Debit	Balance Credit
Cash	$ 5,000	
Accounts Receivable	8,100	
Office Supplies	800	
Furniture	0	
Automobile	0	
Land	14,000	
Accounts Payable		$ 4,200
Unearned Revenue		0
Hilton, Capital		23,700
Hilton, Withdrawals	0	
Service Revenue		0
Salaries Expense	0	
Rent Expense	0	
Total	$ 27,900	$ 27,900

During April, the business completed the following transactions:

Apr. 4	Collected $7,000 cash from a client on account.
8	Performed tax services for a client on account, $5,000.
13	Paid $2,500 on account.
14	Purchased furniture on account, $4,000.
15	Hilton contributed his personal automobile to the business in exchange for capital. The automobile had a market value of $10,500.
18	Purchased office supplies on account, $600.
19	Received $2,100 for tax services performed on April 8.
20	Hilton withdrew cash of $2,300.
21	Received $2,100 cash for consulting work completed.
24	Received $3,000 cash for accounting services to be completed next month.
27	Paid office rent, $300.
28	Paid employee salary, $1,300.

Requirements

1. Record the April transactions in the journal using the following accounts: Cash; Accounts Receivable; Office Supplies; Furniture; Automobile; Land; Accounts Payable; Unearned Revenue; Hilton, Capital; Hilton, Withdrawals; Service Revenue; Salaries Expense; and Rent Expense. Include an explanation for each entry.

2. Open the four-column ledger accounts listed in the trial balance, together with their balances as of March 31. Use the following account numbers: Cash, 11; Accounts Receivable, 12; Office Supplies, 13; Furniture, 14; Automobile, 15; Land, 16; Accounts Payable, 21; Unearned Revenue, 22; Hilton, Capital, 31; Hilton, Withdrawals, 32; Service Revenue, 41; Salaries Expense, 51; and Rent Expense, 52.

3. Post the journal entries to four-column accounts in the ledger, using dates, account numbers, journal references, and posting references. Assume the journal entries were recorded on page 5 of the journal.

4. Prepare the trial balance of John Hilton, CPA, at April 30, 2015.

P-40B Correcting errors in a trial balance

The trial balance of Building Blocks Child Care does not balance.

Learning Objective 4

Total Debits $117,700

BUILDING BLOCKS CHILD CARE Trial Balance May 31, 2015		
	Balance	
Account Title	**Debit**	**Credit**
Cash	$ 6,300	
Accounts Receivable	3,000	
Office Supplies	700	
Prepaid Insurance	400	
Equipment	88,000	
Accounts Payable		$ 7,000
Notes Payable		50,000
Estella, Capital		50,800
Estella, Withdrawals	2,600	
Service Revenue		4,700
Salaries Expense	3,200	
Rent Expense	700	
Total	$ 104,900	$ 112,500

Recording Business Transactions

The following errors are detected:

a. Cash is understated by $4,000.

b. A $2,000 debit to Accounts Receivable was posted as a credit.

c. A $1,200 purchase of office supplies on account was neither journalized nor posted.

d. Equipment was incorrectly transferred from the ledger as $88,000. It should have been transferred as $87,700.

e. Salaries Expense is overstated by $100.

f. A $300 cash payment for advertising expense was neither journalized nor posted.

g. A $100 owner's withdrawal of cash was incorrectly journalized as $1,000.

h. Service Revenue was understated by $4,000.

i. A 12-month insurance policy was posted as a $2,000 credit to Prepaid Insurance. Cash was posted correctly.

Prepare the corrected trial balance as of May 31, 2015. Journal entries are not required.

Learning Objective 4

P-41B Correcting errors in a trial balance

The trial balance for Ocean Divers Exploration Company does not balance.

Total Debits $83,400

OCEAN DIVERS EXPLORATION COMPANY
Trial Balance
July 31, 2015

Account Title	Balance Debit	Balance Credit
Cash	$ 6,600	
Accounts Receivable	9,000	
Office Supplies	200	
Computers	22,600	
Exploration Equipment	46,000	
Accounts Payable		$ 2,900
Notes Payable		18,900
Indiana, Capital		50,100
Indiana, Withdrawals	1,000	
Service Revenue		4,900
Salaries Expense	1,800	
Rent Expense	100	
Advertising Expense	100	
Utilities Expense	700	
Total	$ 88,100	$ 76,800

The following errors were detected:

a. The Cash balance is overstated by $1,000.

b. Rent Expense of $300 was erroneously posted as a credit rather than a debit.

c. A $6,000 credit to Service Revenue was not posted.

d. A $500 debit to Accounts Receivable was posted as $50.

e. The balance of Utilities Expense is understated by $90.

f. A $600 purchase of office supplies on account was neither journalized nor posted.

g. Computers should be $17,160.

Prepare the corrected trial balance at July 31, 2015. Journal entries are not required.

P-42B Preparing financial statements from the trial balance and calculating the debt ratio

Learning Objectives 4, 5

1. Net Income $5,000

The trial balance as of July 31, 2015 for Shermana Peters, Registered Dietician, is presented below:

SHERMANA PETERS, REGISTERED DIETICIAN Trial Balance July 31, 2015		
	Balance	
Account Title	**Debit**	**Credit**
Cash	$ 36,800	
Accounts Receivable	5,500	
Office Supplies	1,400	
Prepaid Insurance	1,000	
Equipment	16,000	
Accounts Payable		$ 3,700
Unearned Revenue		2,500
Notes Payable		30,000
Peters, Capital		21,700
Peters, Withdrawals	2,200	
Service Revenue		7,000
Salaries Expense	1,500	
Rent Expense	300	
Utilities Expense	200	
Total	**$ 64,900**	**$ 64,900**

Requirements

1. Prepare the income statement for the month ended July 31, 2015.

2. Prepare the statement of owner's equity for the month ended July 31, 2015. The beginning balance of capital was $0 and the owner contributed $21,700 during the month.

3. Prepare the balance sheet as of July 31, 2015.

4. Calculate the debt ratio as of July 31, 2015.

> Continuing Problem

3. Cash Balance $16,400

P-43 Journalizing transactions, posting to T-accounts, and preparing a trial balance

Davis Consulting completed the following transactions during December 2014:

Dec. 2	Owner contributed $18,000 cash in exchange for capital.
2	Paid monthly office rent, $550.
3	Paid cash for a computer, $1,800. This equipment is expected to remain in service for five years.
4	Purchased office furniture on account, $4,200. The furniture should last for five years.
5	Purchased office supplies on account, $900.
9	Performed consulting service for a client on account, $1,500.
12	Paid utilities expenses, $250.
18	Performed service for a client and received cash of $1,100.
21	Received $1,400 in advance for client service to be performed in the future.
21	Hired an administrative assistant to be paid $2,055 on the 20th day of each month. The secretary begins work immediately.
26	Paid $400 on account.
28	Collected $300 on account.
30	Davis withdrew cash of $1,400.

Requirements

1. Journalize the transactions, using the following accounts: Cash; Accounts Receivable; Office Supplies; Equipment; Furniture; Accounts Payable; Unearned Revenue; Davis, Capital; Davis, Withdrawals; Service Revenue; Rent Expense; and Utilities Expense. Explanations are not required.

2. Open a T-account for each of the accounts.

3. Post the journal entries to the T-accounts and calculate account balances. Formal posting references are not required.

4. Prepare a trial balance as of December 31, 2014.

5. Prepare the income statement of Davis Consulting for the month ended December 31, 2014.

6. Prepare the statement of owner's equity for the month ended December 31, 2014.

7. Prepare the balance sheet as of December 31, 2014.

8. Calculate the debt ratio for Davis Consulting.

> Practice Set

P-44 Journalizing transactions, posting to T-accounts, and preparing a trial balance

3. Cash Balance $73,100

Consider the following transactional data for the first month of operations for Shine King Cleaning.

Nov. 1	Evan Hudson contributed $35,000 and his truck, with a market value of $8,000, to the business in exchange for capital.
2	The business paid $2,000 to Pleasant Properties for November through February rent. (Debit Prepaid Rent)
3	Paid $2,400 for a business insurance policy for the term November 1, 2015 through October 31, 2016. (Debit Prepaid Insurance)
4	Purchased cleaning supplies on account, $270.
5	Purchased on account an industrial vacuum cleaner costing $1,000. The invoice is payable November 25.
7	Paid $1,200 for a computer and printer.
9	Performed cleaning services on account in the amount of $3,000.
10	Received $100 for services rendered on November 9.
15	Paid employees, $500.
16	Received $3,600 for a 1-year contract beginning November 16 for cleaning services to be provided. Contract begins November 16, 2015, and ends November 15, 2016. (Credit Unearned Revenue)
17	Provided cleaning services and received $800 cash.
18	Received a utility bill for $175 with a due date of December 4, 2015. (Use Accounts Payable)
20	Borrowed $40,000 from bank with interest rate of 9% per year.
21	Received $900 on account for services performed on November 9.
25	Paid $500 on account for vacuum cleaner purchased on November 5.
29	Paid $100 for advertising.
30	Hudson withdrew cash of $600.

Requirements

1. Journalize the transactions, using the following accounts: Cash; Accounts Receivable; Cleaning Supplies; Prepaid Rent; Prepaid Insurance; Equipment; Truck; Accounts Payable; Unearned Revenue; Notes Payable; Hudson, Capital; Hudson, Withdrawals; Service Revenue; Salaries Expense; Advertising Expense; and Utilities Expense. Explanations are not required.

2. Open a T-account for each account.

3. Post the journal entries to the T-accounts and calculate account balances. Formal posting references are not required.

4. Prepare a trial balance as of November 30, 2015.

CRITICAL THINKING

> Decision Cases

Decision Case 1

Your friend, Dean McChesney, requested that you advise him on the effects that certain transactions will have on his business, A-Plus Travel Planners. Time is short, so you cannot journalize the transactions. Instead, you must analyze the transactions without a journal. McChesney will continue the business only if he can expect to earn a monthly net income of $6,000. The business completed the following transactions during June:

a. McChesney deposited $10,000 cash in a business bank account to start the company. The company gave capital to McChesney.

b. Paid $300 cash for office supplies.

c. Incurred advertising expense on account, $700

d. Paid the following cash expenses: secretary's salary, $1,400; office rent, $1,000.

e. Earned service revenue on account, $8,800.

f. Collected cash from customers on account, $1,200.

Requirements

1. Open the following T-accounts: Cash; Accounts Receivable; Office Supplies; Accounts Payable; McChesney, Capital; Service Revenue; Salaries Expense; Rent Expense; and Advertising Expense.

2. Post the transactions directly to the accounts without using a journal. Record each transaction by letter. Calculate account balances.

3. Prepare a trial balance at June 30, 2016.

4. Compute the amount of net income or net loss for this first month of operations. Would you recommend that McChesney continue in business?

Decision Case 2

Answer the following questions. Consider each question separately.

Requirements

1. Explain the advantages of double-entry bookkeeping instead of recording transactions in terms of the accounting equation to a friend who is opening a used book store.

2. When you deposit money in your bank account, the bank credits your account. Is the bank misusing the word *credit* in this context? Why does the bank use the term *credit* to refer to your deposit, instead of *debit*?

> Ethical Issue 1

Better Days Ahead, a charitable organization, has a standing agreement with First National Bank. The agreement allows Better Days Ahead to overdraw its cash balance at the bank when donations are running low. In the past, Better Days Ahead managed funds wisely and rarely used this privilege. Jacob Henson has recently become the president of Better Days. To expand operations, Henson acquired office equipment and spent large amounts on fundraising. During Henson's presidency, Better Days Ahead has maintained a negative bank balance of approximately $10,000.

What is the ethical issue in this situation, if any? State why you approve or disapprove of Henson's management of Better Days Ahead's funds.

> Fraud Case 1

Roy Akins was the accounting manager at Zelco, a tire manufacturer, and he played golf with Hugh Stallings, the CEO, who was something of a celebrity in the community. The CEO stood to earn a substantial bonus if Zelco increased net income by year-end. Roy was eager to get into Hugh's elite social circle; he boasted to Hugh that he knew some accounting tricks that could increase company income by simply revising a few journal entries for rental payments on storage units. At the end of the year, Roy changed the debits from "rent expense" to "prepaid rent" on several entries. Later, Hugh got his bonus, and the deviations were never discovered.

Requirements

1. How did the change in the journal entries affect the net income of the company at year-end?

2. Who gained and who lost as a result of these actions?

> Financial Statement Case 1

Visit **www.pearsonhighered.com/Horngren** to view a link to the **Starbucks Corporation** Fiscal 2011 Annual Report.

Requirement

1. Calculate the debt ratio for Starbucks Corporation as of October 2, 2011.

2. How did the debt ratio for Starbucks Corporation compare to the debt ratio for **Green Mountain Coffee Roasters, Inc.**? Discuss.

> Team Project 1

Contact a local business and arrange with the owner to learn what accounts the business uses.

Requirements

1. Obtain a copy of the business's chart of accounts.

2. Prepare the company's financial statements for the most recent month, quarter, or year. (You may omit the statement of cash flows.) You may use either made-up account balances or balances supplied by the owner.

If the business has a large number of accounts within a category, combine related accounts and report a single amount on the financial statements. For example, the company may have several Cash accounts. Combine all cash amounts and report a single Cash amount on the balance sheet.

You will probably encounter numerous accounts that you have not yet learned. Deal with these as best you can.

Keep in mind that the financial statements report the balances of the accounts listed in the company's chart of accounts, either by individual account or in summarized categories. Therefore, the financial statements must be consistent with the chart of accounts.

> Communication Activity 1

In 35 words or fewer, explain the difference between a debit and a credit, and explain what the normal balance of the six account types is.

MyAccountingLab | **For a wealth of online resources, including exercises, problems, media, and immediate tutorial help, please visit** www.myaccountinglab.com.

Try It! Solutions

1.	E	11.	DR
2.	E	12.	DR
3.	A	13.	CR
4.	E	14.	CR
5.	A	15.	CR
6.	L	16.	CR
7.	L	17.	DR
8.	A	18.	CR
9.	E	19.	DR
10.	E	20.	CR

21.

Date	Accounts and Explanation	Debit	Credit
Nov. 1	Cash	10,000	
	Martinez, Capital		10,000
	Owner contribution.		
15	Office Supplies	400	
	Accounts Payable		400
	Purchased office supplies on account.		
18	Advertising Expense	150	
	Cash		150
	Paid advertising expense.		
20	Cash	1,000	
	Service Revenue		1,000
	Performed services and received cash.		
28	Martinez, Withdrawals	500	
	Cash		500
	Owner withdrawal.		

22.

COOPER FURNITURE REPAIR Trial Balance December 31, 2015		
	Balance	
Account Title	**Debit**	**Credit**
Cash	$ 7,000	
Equipment	10,000	
Accounts Payable		$ 2,300
Unearned Revenue		4,500
Miller, Capital		12,200
Miller, Withdrawals	3,000	
Service Revenue		8,000
Rent Expense	5,000	
Advertising Expense	1,200	
Utilities Expense	800	
Total	**$ 27,000**	**$ 27,000**

23.

Total assets = $7,000 + $10,000 = $17,000

Total liabilities = $2,300 + $4,500 = $6,800

Debt ratio = Total liabilities / Total assets = $6,800 / $17,000 = 0.40 = 40%

> Quick Check Answers

1. a **2.** c **3.** d **4.** d **5.** b **6.** b **7.** d **8.** b **9.** a **10.** b

Glossary

Account. A detailed record of all increases and decreases that have occurred in an individual asset, liability, or equity during a specific period.

Accrued Liability. A liability for which the business knows the amount owed but the bill has not been paid.

Chart of Accounts. A list of all of a company's accounts with their account numbers.

Compound Journal Entry. A journal entry that is characterized by having multiple debits and/or multiple credits.

Credit. The right side of a T-account.

Debit. The left side of a T-account.

Debt Ratio. Shows the proportion of assets financed with debt. Total liabilities / Total assets.

Double-Entry System. A system of accounting in which every transaction affects at least two accounts.

Journal. A record of transactions in date order.

Ledger. The record holding all the accounts of a business, the changes in those accounts, and their balances.

Normal Balance. The balance that appears on the increase side of an account.

Notes Receivable. A written promise that a customer will pay a fixed amount of money and interest by a certain date in the future.

Notes Payable. A written promise made by the business to pay a debt, usually involving interest, in the future.

Posting. Transferring data from the journal to the ledger.

Prepaid Expense. A payment of an expense in advance.

Source Document. Provides the evidence and data for accounting transactions.

T-Account. A summary device that is shaped like a capital *T* with debits posted on the left side of the vertical line and credits on the right side of the vertical line.

Trial Balance. A list of all the ledger accounts with their balances at a point in time

Unearned Revenue. A liability created when a business collects cash from customers in advance of providing services or delivering goods.

Photo Credits

The Adjusting Process

From Chapter 3 of *Horngren's Accounting*, Tenth edition. Tracie Nobles, Brenda Mattison, Ella Mae Matsumura. Copyright © 2014 by Pearson Education, Inc. All rights reserved.

The Adjusting Process

Where's My Bonus?

Liam Mills was surprised when he opened his mail. He had just received his most recent quarterly bonus check from his employer, Custom Marketing, and the check was smaller than he expected. Liam worked as a sales manager and was responsible for product marketing and implementation in the southwest region of the United States. He was paid a monthly salary but also received a 3% bonus for all revenue generated from advertising services provided to customers in his geographical area. He was counting on his fourth quarter (October–December) bonus check to be large enough to pay off the credit card debt he had accumulated over the holiday break. It had been a great year-end for Liam. He had closed several open accounts, successfully signing sev-

eral annual advertising contracts. In addition, because of his negotiating skills, he was able to collect half of the payments for services up front instead of waiting for his customers to pay every month. Liam expected that his bonus check would be huge because of this new business, but it wasn't.

The next day, Liam stopped by the accounting office to discuss his bonus check. He was surprised to learn that his bonus was calculated by the revenue earned by his company through December 31. Although Liam had negotiated to receive half of the payments up front, the business had not yet earned the revenue from those payments. Custom Marketing will not record revenue earned until the advertising services have been performed. Eventually Liam will see the new business reflected in his bonus check, but he'll have to wait until the revenue has been earned.

How Was Revenue Earned Calculated?

At the end of a time period (often December 31), companies are required to accurately report revenues earned and expenses incurred during that time period. In order to do this, the company reviews the account balances as of the end of the time period and determines whether any adjustments are needed. For example, CC Media Holdings, Inc., the parent company of radio giant Clear Channel Communications and Clear Channel Outdoor Holdings, an outdoor advertising agency, must determine the amount of revenue earned from open advertising contracts. These contracts can cover only a few weeks or up to several years. Only the amount earned in the current time period is reported as revenue on the income statement. *Adjusting the books* is the process of reviewing and adjusting the account balances so that amounts on the financial statements are reported accurately. This is what we will learn in this chapter.

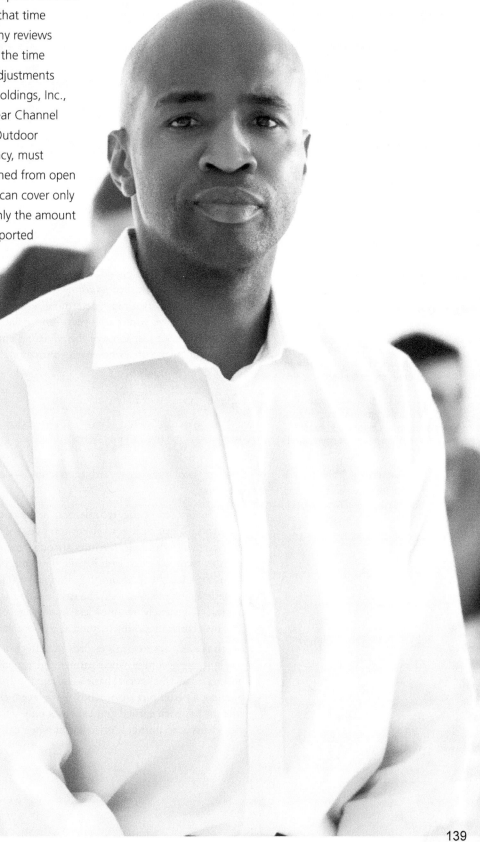

chapter outline

What is the difference between cash basis accounting and accrual basis accounting?

What concepts and principles apply to accrual basis accounting?

What are adjusting entries and how do we record them?

What is the purpose of the adjusted trial balance and how do we prepare it?

What is the impact of adjusting entries on the financial statements?

How could a worksheet help in preparing adjusting entries and the adjusted trial balance?

What is an alternative treatment of recording prepaid expenses and unearned revenues? (Appendix A)

Learning Objectives

1 Differentiate between cash basis accounting and accrual basis accounting

2 Define and apply the time period concept, revenue recognition, and matching principles

3 Explain the purpose of and journalize and post adjusting entries

4 Explain the purpose of and prepare an adjusted trial balance

5 Identify the impact of adjusting entries on the financial statements

6 Explain the purpose of a worksheet and use it to prepare adjusting entries and the adjusted trial balance

7 Understand the alternative treatments of recording prepaid expenses and unearned revenues (Appendix A)

In this chapter, we'll explore the accounting cycle by learning how to update the accounts at the end of the period. This process is called adjusting the books, and it requires special journal entries called *adjusting entries*. For example, you learn how, at the end of a particular period, you must determine how many office supplies you have used and how much you owe your employees—and make adjusting entries to account for these amounts. These are just some of the adjusting entries you need to make before you can see the complete picture of how well your company performed during a period of time.

WHAT IS THE DIFFERENCE BETWEEN CASH BASIS ACCOUNTING AND ACCRUAL BASIS ACCOUNTING?

There are two ways to record transactions—cash basis accounting or accrual basis accounting.

- **Cash basis accounting** records only transactions with cash: cash receipts and cash payments. When cash is received, revenues are recorded. When cash is paid, expenses are recorded. As a result, revenues are only recorded when cash is received and expenses are only recorded when cash is paid. The cash basis of accounting is not allowed under Generally Accepted Accounting Principles (GAAP); however, small businesses will sometimes use this method. The cash method is an easier accounting method to follow because it generally requires less knowledge of accounting concepts and principles. The cash basis accounting method also does a good job of tracking a business's cash flow.

- **Accrual basis accounting** records the effect of each transaction as it occurs—that is, revenues are recorded when earned and expenses are recorded when incurred. Most businesses use the accrual basis as covered in this text. The accrual basis of accounting provides a better picture of a business's revenues and expenses. It records revenue only when it has been earned and expenses only when they have been incurred. Under accrual basis accounting, it is irrelevant when cash is received or paid.

Cash Basis Accounting
Accounting method that records revenue only when cash is received and expenses only when cash is paid.

Accrual Basis Accounting
Accounting method that records revenue when earned and expenses when incurred.

Learning Objective 1
Differentiate between cash basis accounting and accrual basis accounting

If cash basis < accounting is not allowed by GAAP, why would a business choose to use this method?

Example Suppose on May 1, Smart Touch Learning paid $1,200 for insurance for the next 6 months ($200 per month). This prepayment represents insurance coverage for May through October. Under the cash basis method, Smart Touch Learning would record Insurance Expense of $1,200 on May 1. This is because the cash basis method records an expense when cash is paid. Alternatively, accrual basis accounting requires the company to prorate the expense. Smart Touch Learning would record a $200 expense every month from May through October. This is illustrated as follows:

	Cash basis		Accrual basis	
Cash Payment Made	May 1:	$1,200	May 1:	$1,200
Expense Recorded	May 1:	$1,200	May 31:	$ 200
			June 30:	200
			July 31:	200
			August 31:	200
			September 30:	200
			October 31:	200
Total Expense Recorded		$1,200		$1,200

Now let's see how the cash basis and the accrual basis methods account for revenues.

Example Suppose on April 30, Smart Touch Learning received $600 for services to be performed for the next 6 months (May through October). Under the cash basis method, Smart Touch Learning would record $600 of revenue when the cash is received on April 30. The accrual basis method, though, requires the revenue to be recorded only when it is earned. Smart Touch Learning would record $100 of revenue each month for the next six months beginning in May.

	Cash basis		Accrual basis	
Cash Received	April 30:	$600	April 30:	$600
Revenue Recorded	April 30:	$600	May 31:	$100
			June 30:	100
			July 31:	100
			August 31:	100
			September 30:	100
			October 31:	100
Total Revenue Recorded		$600		$600

Notice that under both methods, cash basis and accrual basis, the total amount of revenues and expenses recorded by October 31 was the same. The major difference between a cash basis accounting system and an accrual basis accounting system is the timing of recording the revenue or expense.

> Try It!

Total Pool Services earned $130,000 of service revenue during 2014. Of the $130,000 earned, the business received $105,000 in cash. The remaining amount, $25,000, was still owed by customers as of December 31. In addition, Total Pool Services incurred $85,000 of expenses during the year. As of December 31, $10,000 of the expenses still needed to be paid. In addition, Total Pool Services prepaid $5,000 cash in December 2014 for expenses incurred during the next year.

1. Determine the amount of service revenue and expenses for 2014 using a cash basis accounting system.
2. Determine the amount of service revenue and expenses for 2014 using an accrual basis accounting system.

Check your answers at the end of the chapter.

For more practice, see Short Exercises S-1 and S-2.   MyAccountingLab

WHAT CONCEPTS AND PRINCIPLES APPLY TO ACCRUAL BASIS ACCOUNTING?

Learning Objective 2
Define and apply the time period concept, revenue recognition, and matching principles

As we have seen, the timing and recognition of revenues and expenses is the key difference between the cash basis and accrual basis methods of accounting. This difference can be explained by understanding the time period concept and the revenue recognition and matching principles.

The Time Period Concept

Smart Touch Learning will know with 100% certainty how well it has operated only if the company sells its assets, pays its liabilities, and gives any leftover cash to its owner(s). For obvious reasons, it is not practical to measure income this way. Because businesses need periodic reports on their affairs, the time period concept assumes that a business's activities can be sliced into small time segments and that financial statements can be prepared for specific periods, such as a month, quarter, or year.

The basic accounting period is one year, and most businesses prepare annual financial statements. The twelve month accounting period used for the annual financial statements is called a fiscal year. For most companies, the annual accounting period is the calendar year, from January 1 through December 31. Other companies use a fiscal year that ends on a date other than December 31. The year-end date is usually the low point in business activity for the year. Retailers are a notable example. For instance, Wal-Mart Stores, Inc. and J. C. Penney Company, Inc. use a fiscal year that ends on January 31 because the low point of their business activity comes about a month after the holidays.

Time Period Concept
Assumes that a business's activities can be sliced into small time segments and that financial statements can be prepared for specific periods, such as a month, quarter, or year.

Fiscal Year
An accounting year of any twelve consecutive months that may or may not coincide with the calendar year.

The Revenue Recognition Principle

The revenue recognition principle tells accountants the following things:

- *When* to record revenue—that is, when to make a journal entry for revenue
- The *amount* of revenue to record

Revenue Recognition Principle
Requires companies to record revenue when it has been earned and determines the amount of revenue to record.

> **Decisions**   What would be the most appropriate fiscal year?

Molly Kielman is the owner of Summertime Day Camp. She has just started her business and is deciding between using a calendar year or a noncalendar year for her financial statements. Because the majority of her business will be during the months of June and July, she is thinking about using a fiscal year-end of August 31. What fiscal year-end should Molly use for her new business?

Solution

From an accounting perspective, Molly should align her year-end date with the lowest point of activity in her business, August 31. Typically, businesses that are highly seasonal, such as Molly's, will not use a calendar year-end. This allows the business to more accurately reflect the revenue and expenses of the business because there are fewer transactions and complications.

Alternative Solution

Molly's tax advisor might suggest an alternative answer of December 31. If Molly is operating her business as a sole proprietorship, the business and the owner must both file a tax return using the same year-end. Most individuals do not file a tax return using a year-end other than December 31. Choosing a fiscal year-end, such as August 31, might unnecessarily complicate her individual tax return.

When to Record Revenue

The revenue recognition principle requires companies to record revenue when it has been earned—but not before. Revenue has been earned when the business has delivered a good or service to the customer, not necessarily when the business receives the cash from the customer. The earnings process is complete when the company has done everything required by the sale agreement regardless of whether cash is received.

The Amount of Revenue to Record

Revenue is recorded for the actual selling price of the item or service transferred to the customer. Suppose that in order to obtain a new client, Smart Touch Learning performs e-learning services for the discounted price of $100. Ordinarily, the business would have charged $200 for this service. How much revenue should the business record? Smart Touch Learning charged only $100, so the business records $100 of revenue.

The Matching Principle

The **matching principle** (sometimes called the *expense recognition principle*) guides accounting for expenses and ensures the following:

- All expenses are recorded when they are incurred during the period.

- Expenses are matched against the revenues of the period.

> **Matching Principle**
> Guides accounting for expenses, ensures that all expenses are recorded when they are incurred during the period, and matches those expenses against the revenues of the period.

To match expenses against revenues means to subtract expenses incurred during one month from revenues earned during that same month. The goal is to compute an accurate net income or net loss for the time period.

There is a natural link between some expenses and revenues. For example, Smart Touch Learning pays a commission to the employee who sells the e-learning company's services. The commission expense is directly related to the e-learning company's revenue earned. Other expenses are not so easy to link to revenues. For example, Smart Touch Learning's monthly rent expense occurs regardless of the revenues earned that month. The matching principle tells us to identify those expenses with a particular period, such as a month or a year, when the related revenue occurred. The business will record rent expense each month based on the rental agreement.

> Try It!

Match the accounting terminology to the definitions.

3. Time period concept	**a.** requires companies to record revenue when it has been earned and determines the amount of revenue to record
4. Revenue recognition principle	**b.** assumes that a business's activities can be sliced into small time segments and that financial statements can be prepared for specific periods
5. Matching principle	**c.** guides accounting for expenses, ensures that all expenses are recorded when they are incurred during the period, and matches those expenses against the revenues of the period.

Check your answers at the end of the chapter.

For more practice, see Short Exercises S-3 and S-4.   MyAccountingLab

WHAT ARE ADJUSTING ENTRIES AND HOW DO WE RECORD THEM?

Learning Objective 3

Explain the purpose of and journalize and post adjusting entries

The end-of-period process begins with the trial balance. Exhibit 1 is the unadjusted trial balance of Smart Touch Learning at December 31, 2014.

Exhibit 1 | Unadjusted Trial Balance

SMART TOUCH LEARNING Unadjusted Trial Balance December 31, 2014		
	Balance	
Account Title	**Debit**	**Credit**
Cash	$ 12,200	
Accounts Receivable	1,000	
Office Supplies	500	
Prepaid Rent	3,000	
Furniture	18,000	
Building	60,000	
Land	20,000	
Accounts Payable		$ 200
Utilities Payable		100
Unearned Revenue		600
Notes Payable		60,000
Bright, Capital		48,000
Bright, Withdrawals	5,000	
Service Revenue		16,500
Rent Expense	2,000	
Salaries Expense	3,600	
Utilities Expense	100	
Total	$ 125,400	$ 125,400

This *unadjusted trial balance* lists the revenues and expenses of the e-learning company for November and December. But these amounts are incomplete because they omit various revenue and expense transactions. Accrual basis accounting requires the business to review the unadjusted trial balance and determine whether any additional revenues and expenses need to be recorded. Are there revenues that Smart Touch Learning has earned that haven't been recorded yet? Are there expenses that have occurred that haven't been journalized?

For example, consider the Office Supplies account in Exhibit 1. Smart Touch Learning uses office supplies during the two months. This reduces the office supplies on hand (an asset) and creates an expense (Supplies Expense). It is a waste of time to record Supplies Expense every time office supplies are used. But by December 31, enough of the $500 of Office Supplies on the unadjusted trial balance (Exhibit 1) have probably been used that we need to adjust the Office Supplies account. This is an example of why we need to adjust some accounts at the end of the accounting period.

An **adjusting entry** is completed at the end of the accounting period and records revenues to the period in which they are earned and expenses to the period in which they occur. Adjusting entries also update the asset and liability accounts. Adjustments are needed to properly measure two things:

Adjusting Entry
An entry made at the end of the accounting period that is used to record revenues to the period in which they are earned and expenses to the period in which they occur.

1. Net income (loss) on the income statement
2. Assets and liabilities on the balance sheet

There are two basic categories of adjusting entries: *prepaids* and *accruals*. In a prepaid adjustment, the cash payment occurs before an expense is incurred or the cash receipt occurs before the revenue is earned. Prepaids are also called *deferrals* because the recognition of revenue or expense is deferred to a date after the cash is received or paid. Accrual adjustments are the opposite. An accrual records an expense before the cash is paid or it records the revenue before the cash is received.

The two basic categories of adjusting entries can be further separated into four types:

1. Prepaid expenses (prepaid)
2. Unearned revenues (prepaid)
3. Accrued expenses (accrual)
4. Accrued revenues (accrual)

The focus of this chapter is on learning how to account for these four types of adjusting entries.

Prepaid Expenses

Prepaid expenses are advance payments of future expenses. Prepaid expenses are always paid for before they are used up. Such payments are considered assets rather than expenses until they are used up. When the prepayment is used up, the used portion of the asset becomes an expense via an adjusting entry.

Prepaid Rent

For example, Smart Touch Learning prepaid three months' office rent of $3,000 ($1,000 per month × 3 months) on December 1, 2014. The entry to record the payment was as follows:

Date	Accounts and Explanation	Debit	Credit
Dec. 1	Prepaid Rent	3,000	
	Cash		3,000
	Paid rent in advance.		

A↑↓		L	+	E
Prepaid Rent ↑				
Cash ↓				

After posting, Prepaid Rent has a $3,000 debit balance.

Prepaid Rent

Dec. 1	3,000

Throughout December, Prepaid Rent maintains this balance. But $3,000 is *not* the amount of Prepaid Rent for the balance sheet at December 31. Why?

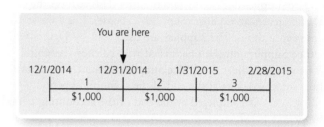

As of December 31, Prepaid Rent should be decreased for the amount that has been used up. The used-up portion is one month of the three months prepaid, or one-third of the prepayment. Recall that an asset that has expired is an *expense*. The adjusting entry transfers $1,000 ($3,000 × 1/3) from Prepaid Rent to Rent Expense. The adjusting entry is as follows:

$$\underset{\substack{\text{Prepaid}\\\text{Rent↓}}}{\underline{\textbf{A↓}}} \Big\} = \Big\{ \underline{\textbf{L}} + \underset{\substack{\text{Rent}\\\text{Expense↑}}}{\underline{\textbf{E↓}}}$$

Date	Accounts and Explanation	Debit	Credit
Dec. 31	Rent Expense	1,000	
	Prepaid Rent		1,000
	To record rent expense.		

After posting, Prepaid Rent and Rent Expense show correct ending balances:

	Prepaid Rent			**Rent Expense**	
Dec. 1	3,000	1,000 Dec. 31	Nov. 15	2,000	
			Dec. 31	1,000	
Bal.	2,000		Bal.	3,000	

The Prepaid Rent is an example of an asset that was overstated prior to journalizing and posting the adjusting entry. Notice that the ending balance in Prepaid Rent is now $2,000. Because Prepaid Rent is an asset account for Smart Touch Learning, it should contain only two more months of rent on December 31 (for January and February). So we have $1,000 rent per month times two months equals the $2,000 Prepaid Rent balance.

If Smart Touch Learning had prepaid insurance, the same type of analysis would apply to the prepayment of three months of insurance. The only difference is in the account titles. Prepaid Insurance would be used instead of Prepaid Rent, and Insurance Expense would be used instead of Rent Expense.

Office Supplies

Office supplies are also accounted for as prepaid expenses. Let's look at another example. On November 3, Smart Touch Learning purchased $500 of office supplies on account.

The December 31 trial balance, therefore, still lists Office Supplies with a $500 debit balance. But Smart Touch Learning's December 31 balance sheet should *not* report office supplies of $500. Why not?

During November and December, the e-learning company used office supplies to conduct business. The cost of the supplies used becomes *Supplies Expense*. To measure Supplies Expense, the business first counts the office supplies on hand at the end of December. This is the amount of the asset still owned by the business. Assume that office supplies costing $100 remain on December 31. Then, the business uses the Office Supplies T-account to determine the value of the supplies that were used:

So, we can solve for the office supplies used as follows:

Office Supplies Balance before Adjustment – Office Supplies Used = Office Supplies on Hand
$500 – Office Supplies Used = $100
Office Supplies Used = $400

The December 31 adjusting entry updates Office Supplies and records Supplies Expense for November and December as follows:

Date	Accounts and Explanation	Debit	Credit
Dec. 31	Supplies Expense	400	
	Office Supplies		400
	To record office supplies used.		

$$A\downarrow \left.\begin{array}{l}\text{Office}\\ \text{Supplies}\downarrow\end{array}\right\} = \left\{\begin{array}{l}L \quad + \quad E\downarrow\\ \qquad\quad \text{Supplies}\\ \qquad\quad \text{Expense}\uparrow\end{array}\right.$$

After posting the adjusting entry, the December 31 balance of Office Supplies is correctly reflected as $100 and the Supplies Expense is correctly reflected as $400.

Office Supplies
Nov. 3   500 | 400   Dec. 31
Bal.   100 |

Supplies Expense
Dec. 31   400 |
Bal.   400 |

The Office Supplies account then enters January with a $100 balance. If the adjusting entry for Office Supplies had not been recorded, the asset would have been overstated and Supplies Expense would have been understated. In making the adjusting entry, the correct balance of Office Supplies, $100, is now reported on the balance sheet as of December 31 and the income statement is correctly reporting an expense of $400.

Depreciation

Plant assets are long-lived, tangible assets used in the operation of a business. Examples include land, buildings, equipment, furniture, and automobiles. As a business uses these assets, their value and usefulness decline. The decline in usefulness of a plant asset is

Plant Assets
Long-lived, tangible assets, such as land, buildings, and equipment, used in the operation of a business.

an expense, and accountants systematically spread the asset's cost over its useful life. The allocation of a plant asset's cost over its useful life is called depreciation. For example, a business might pay cash for an automobile when purchased, but the automobile will last for years, so depreciation allocates the cost spent on the car over the time the business uses the car. All plant assets are depreciated. However, land is the exception. We record no depreciation for land, as its value typically does not decline with use.

Depreciation
The process by which businesses spread the allocation of a plant asset's cost over its useful life.

Similarity to Prepaid Expenses The concept of accounting for plant assets is similar to that of prepaid expenses. The major difference is the length of time it takes for the asset to be used up. Prepaid expenses usually expire within a year, but plant assets remain useful for several years. As a business uses its plant assets, an adjusting entry is required to allocate the assets' cost. The adjusting entry records the cost allocation to an expense account called *Depreciation Expense.*

Let's review an example for Smart Touch Learning. On December 2, the business received a contribution of furniture with a market value of $18,000 from Sheena Bright. In exchange, Smart Touch Learning gave Bright capital and made the following journal entry:

$$\left.\begin{array}{c} \underline{\text{A}\uparrow} \\ \text{Furniture}\uparrow \end{array}\right\} = \left\{\begin{array}{ccc} \underline{\text{L}} & + & \underline{\text{E}\uparrow} \\ & & \text{Bright,} \\ & & \text{Capital}\uparrow \end{array}\right.$$

Date	Accounts and Explanation	Debit	Credit
Dec. 2	Furniture	18,000	
	Bright, Capital		18,000
	Owner contribution of furniture.		

After posting, the Furniture account has an $18,000 balance:

Furniture

Dec. 2 18,000	

Residual Value
The value of a depreciable asset at the end of its useful life.

Straight-line Method
A depreciation method that allocates an equal amount of depreciation each year. (Cost − Residual value) / Useful life.

Smart Touch Learning believes the furniture will remain useful for five years, and at the end of five years, Smart Touch Learning believes the furniture will be worthless. The value of a depreciable asset at the end of its useful life is called the residual value. Smart Touch Learning will use the straight-line method to compute the amount of depreciation. The straight-line method allocates an equal amount of depreciation each year and is calculated as

Straight-line depreciation = (Cost − Residual value) / Useful life

Smart Touch Learning will calculate the depreciation of the furniture for the month of December as

Straight-line depreciation = (Cost − Residual value) / Useful life
= ($18,000 − $0) / 5 years
= $3,600 per year / 12 months = $300 per month

Depreciation expense for December is recorded by the following adjusting entry:

Date	Accounts and Explanation	Debit	Credit
Dec. 31	Depreciation Expense—Furniture	300	
	Accumulated Depreciation—Furniture		300
	To record depreciation on furniture.		

$$A\downarrow \left.\begin{array}{c} \text{Accumulated} \\ \text{Depreciation—} \\ \text{Furniture}\uparrow \end{array}\right\} = \left\{\begin{array}{c} L + E\downarrow \\ \text{Depreciation} \\ \text{Expense—} \\ \text{Furniture}\uparrow \end{array}\right.$$

The Accumulated Depreciation Account Notice that in the above adjusting entry for depreciation, we credited Accumulated Depreciation—Furniture and *not* the asset account Furniture. Why? We need to keep the original cost of the furniture separate from the accumulated depreciation because of the cost principle. Managers can then refer to the Furniture account to see how much the asset originally cost. This information may help decide how much to sell the asset for in the future or how much to pay for new furniture. The Accumulated Depreciation account is the sum of all depreciation expense recorded for the depreciable asset to date. Accumulated Depreciation will increase (accumulate) over time.

Accumulated Depreciation is a contra asset, which means that it is an asset account with a normal credit balance. Contra means opposite. A contra account has two main characteristics:

- A contra account is paired with and is listed immediately after its related account in the chart of accounts and associated financial statement.
- A contra account's normal balance (debit or credit) is the opposite of the normal balance of the related account.

For example, Accumulated Depreciation—Furniture is the contra account that follows the Furniture account on the balance sheet. The Furniture account has a normal debit balance, so Accumulated Depreciation—Furniture, a contra asset, has a normal credit balance.

> When recording depreciation, why don't we record a credit to the Furniture account?

Accumulated Depreciation
The sum of all the depreciation expense recorded to date for a depreciable asset.

Contra Account
An account that is paired with, and is listed immediately after, its related account in the chart of accounts and associated financial statement, and whose normal balance is the opposite of the normal balance of the related account.

A business may have a separate Accumulated Depreciation account for each depreciable asset. Because Smart Touch Learning has both a Building and a Furniture account, it also has these two accounts: Accumulated Depreciation—Building, and Accumulated Depreciation—Furniture. However, small companies often have only one Accumulated Depreciation account for all their depreciable assets.

After posting the depreciation, the accounts appear as follows:

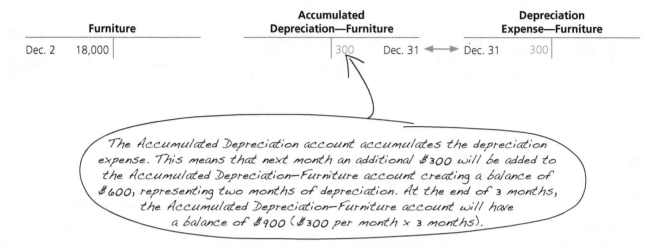

Furniture		Accumulated Depreciation—Furniture		Depreciation Expense—Furniture	
Dec. 2 18,000			300 Dec. 31	Dec. 31 300	

The Accumulated Depreciation account accumulates the depreciation expense. This means that next month an additional $300 will be added to the Accumulated Depreciation—Furniture account creating a balance of $600, representing two months of depreciation. At the end of 3 months, the Accumulated Depreciation—Furniture account will have a balance of $900 ($300 per month × 3 months).

Book Value

A depreciable asset's cost minus accumulated depreciation.

Book Value The balance sheet reports both Furniture and Accumulated Depreciation—Furniture. Because it is a contra account, Accumulated Depreciation—Furniture is subtracted from Furniture. The resulting net amount (cost minus accumulated depreciation) of a plant asset is called its book value. The book value represents the cost invested in the asset that the business has not yet expensed. For Smart Touch Learning's furniture, the book value is as follows:

Book value of furniture:	
Furniture	$18,000
Less: Accumulated Depreciation—Furniture	(300)
Book value of furniture	$17,700

Depreciation on the building purchased on December 1 would be recorded in a similar manner. Suppose that the monthly depreciation is $250. The following adjusting entry would record depreciation for December:

A↓   L + E↓
Accumulated   Depreciation
Depreciation—   Expense—
Building↑   Building↑

Date	Accounts and Explanation	Debit	Credit
Dec. 31	Depreciation Expense—Building	250	
	Accumulated Depreciation—Building		250
	To record depreciation on building.		

Remember, an increase in a contra asset, such as Accumulated Depreciation, decreases total assets. This is because a contra asset has a credit balance and credits decrease assets.

Had Smart Touch Learning not recorded the adjusting entries for depreciation on the furniture and building, plant assets would have been overstated and expenses would have been understated. After recording the adjusting entries, plant assets are reported at the correct net amount, as shown on the December 31 partial balance sheet in Exhibit 2.

Exhibit 2 | Plant Assets on the Balance Sheet of Smart Touch Learning

SMART TOUCH LEARNING Balance Sheet (Partial) December 31, 2014		
Plant Assets:		
Furniture	$ 18,000	
Less: Accumulated Depreciation—Furniture	(300)	$ 17,700
Building	60,000	
Less: Accumulated Depreciation—Building	(250)	59,750
Land		20,000
Plant Assets, Net		**$ 97,450**

Unearned Revenues

Remember, unearned revenues occur when the company is paid cash before it does the work or delivers a product to earn that cash. The company owes a product or a service to the customer, or it owes the customer his or her money back. Only after completing the job or delivering the product does the business *earn* the revenue. Because of this delay, unearned revenue is a liability and is also called deferred revenue.

Suppose, for example, a law firm engages Smart Touch Learning to provide e-learning services for the next thirty days, agreeing to pay $600 in advance. Smart Touch Learning collected the amount on December 21 and recorded the following entry:

Deferred Revenue
A liability created when a business collects cash from customers in advance of completing a service or delivering a product.

Date	Accounts and Explanation	Debit	Credit
Dec. 21	Cash	600	
	Unearned Revenue		600
	Collected cash for future services.		

$$\left.\frac{A\uparrow}{\text{Cash}\uparrow}\right\} = \left\{\frac{L\uparrow}{\substack{\text{Unearned}\\\text{Revenue}\uparrow}} + \frac{E}{}\right.$$

The liability account, Unearned Revenue, now shows that Smart Touch Learning owes $600 in services.

Unearned Revenue

	600 Dec. 21

During the last 10 days of the month—December 22 through December 31—Smart Touch Learning will *earn* approximately one-third (10 days divided by 30 days) of the $600, or $200. Therefore, Smart Touch Learning makes the following adjusting entry to record earning $200 of revenue:

Date	Accounts and Explanation	Debit	Credit
Dec. 31	Unearned Revenue	200	
	Service Revenue		200
	To record service revenue earned that was collected in advance.		

This adjusting entry shifts $200 from the liability account to the revenue account. Service Revenue increases by $200, and Unearned Revenue decreases by $200. Now both accounts are up-to-date at December 31:

Unearned Revenue					Service Revenue	
Dec. 31	200	600	Dec. 21		5,500	Nov. 8
		400	Bal.		3,000	Nov. 10
					8,000	Dec. 28
					200	Dec. 31
					16,700	Bal.

Had the adjusting entry not been made, the liability, Unearned Revenue, would be overstated and Service Revenue would be understated.

Accrued Expenses

Accrued Expense
An expense that the business has incurred but has not yet paid.

Businesses often incur expenses before paying for them. The term **accrued expense** refers to an expense of this type. An accrued expense hasn't been paid for yet. Consider an employee's salary. Salaries Expense grows as the employee works, so the expense is said to *accrue*. Another accrued expense is interest expense on a note payable. Interest accrues as time passes on the note. An accrued expense always creates an accrued liability.

Companies do not make daily or weekly journal entries to accrue expenses. Instead, they wait until the end of the accounting period. They make an adjusting entry to bring each expense (and the related liability) up to date for the financial statements.

Accrued Salaries Expense

Smart Touch Learning pays its employee a monthly salary of $2,400—half on the 15th and half on the first day of the next month. Here is a calendar for December and three days in January with the two paydays circled:

December 2014						
Sunday	Monday	Tuesday	Wednesday	Thursday	Friday	Saturday
	Dec 1	2	3	4	5	6
7	8	9	10	11	12	13
14	(15) Pay Day	16	17	18	19	20
21	22	23	24	25	26	27
28	29	30	31	Jan 1 Pay Day	2	3

During December, the company paid the first half-month salary on Monday, December 15, and made this entry:

Date	Accounts and Explanation	Debit	Credit
Dec. 15	Salaries Expense	1,200	
	Cash		1,200
	Paid salaries.		

$$\left.\frac{A\downarrow}{Cash\downarrow}\right\} = \left\{\frac{L}{} + \frac{E\downarrow}{\text{Salaries Expense}\uparrow}\right.$$

The December 15 entry records only the first half of December's salaries expense. The second payment of $1,200 will occur on January 1; however, the expense was incurred in December, so the expense must be recorded in December. On December 31, Smart Touch Learning makes the following adjusting entry:

Date	Accounts and Explanation	Debit	Credit
Dec. 31	Salaries Expense	1,200	
	Salaries Payable		1,200
	To accrue salaries expense.		

$$\left.\frac{A}{}\right\} = \left\{\frac{L\uparrow}{\substack{\text{Salaries}\\\text{Payable}\uparrow}} + \frac{E\downarrow}{\substack{\text{Salaries}\\\text{Expense}\uparrow}}\right.$$

After posting, both Salaries Expense and Salaries Payable are up to date:

Salaries Payable				Salaries Expense		
	1,200	Dec. 31		Nov. 15	1,200	
	1,200	Bal.		Dec. 1	1,200	
				Dec. 15	1,200	
				Dec. 31	1,200	
				Bal.	4,800	

Salaries Expense shows a full two months' salary, and Salaries Payable shows the liability owed at December 31. This is an example of a liability that was understated before the adjusting entry was made. It also is an example of the matching principle: We are recording December's Salaries Expense in December so it will be reported on the same income statement as December's revenues.

Future Payment of Accrued Salaries Expense The adjusting entry at December 31 creates a liability that will eventually be paid. In this case, Smart Touch Learning will pay its employee the second half of December's wages on January 1. Because the expense has already been recorded, Smart Touch Learning will not record the expense again. To do so would record the expense twice, thus overstating the expense account. Instead, the business will decrease the amount of the liability, Salaries Payable, with a debit and record the cash payment. On January 1, Smart Touch Learning would record the following journal entry:

$$\frac{A\downarrow}{Cash\downarrow} \Big\} = \Big\{ \frac{L\downarrow}{\substack{Salaries \\ Payable\downarrow}} + \underline{\quad E\quad}$$

Date	Accounts and Explanation	Debit	Credit
Jan. 1	Salaries Payable	1,200	
	Cash		1,200
	To record payment of accrued expense.		

Don't confuse this entry with an adjusting entry. Adjusting entries are recorded only at the end of the accounting period and are used either to record revenue earned or expenses incurred. This entry is a journal entry. It is simply recording an everyday business transaction—the payment of salaries previously accrued.

In this example, the amount paid for salaries was equal to the amount of the liability in the adjusting entry. Sometimes, however, the amount paid might be different than the liability in the adjusting entry. For example, assume that instead of making a payment for salaries on January 1, Smart Touch Learning doesn't make the payment until January 5. By delaying the payment, Smart Touch Learning incurs additional days of salaries expense. The journal entry to record the payment on January 5 will not only decrease the payable recorded in the adjusting entry but will also record any additional expense incurred.

Accrued Interest Expense

Borrowing money creates an additional liability for a Note Payable. Smart Touch Learning purchased a $60,000 building in exchange for a loan. Smart Touch Learning signed a one-year loan and recorded the following entry using the Notes Payable account:

$$\frac{A\uparrow}{Building\uparrow} \Big\} = \Big\{ \frac{L\uparrow}{\substack{Notes \\ Payable\uparrow}} + \underline{\quad E\quad}$$

Date	Accounts and Explanation	Debit	Credit
Dec. 1	Building	60,000	
	Notes Payable		60,000
	Purchase of building with note.		

>Ethics When should accrued expenses be recorded?

Evan is in the process of recording the adjusting entries for Green Landscaping Services. Bob Green, the owner, has asked Evan to record all of the adjusting entries except for accrued expenses. Bob has a meeting with the banker on Monday to apply for a business loan. Bob knows that the banker will review his balance sheet and income statement. Bob is concerned that by recording the accrued expenses, his liabilities will be significantly higher on the balance sheet and a net loss will be reported on the income statement (due to higher expenses). Bob has instructed Evan to delay recording the accrued expenses until after his meeting with the banker. What should Evan do?

Solution

Failing to record the adjusting entries for accrued expenses violates the matching principle. Recording the expenses now (before Monday) accurately matches the occurrence of the expenses with the revenues that were created during that period. If Evan does not record the adjusting entries, the financial statements will not accurately represent the financial position or operating performance of the business. The banker could be tricked into lending the company money. Then, if the business could not repay the loan, the bank would lose—all because the banker relied on incorrect accounting information supplied by the company.

Interest on this note is payable one year later, on December 1, 2015. Although the company won't make the interest payment for a year, the company must record the amount of interest expense that has been incurred by December 31, 2014. The company will make an adjusting entry to record interest expense for one month (December 1–December 31). Assume one month's interest expense on this note is $100. The December 31 adjusting entry to accrue interest expense is as follows:

Date	Accounts and Explanation	Debit	Credit
Dec. 31	Interest Expense	100	
	Interest Payable		100
	To accrue interest expense.		

$$A \Bigg\} = \begin{cases} L\uparrow & + & E\downarrow \\ \text{Interest} & & \text{Interest} \\ \text{Payable}\uparrow & & \text{Expense}\uparrow \end{cases}$$

Notice that the adjusting entry records a credit to the liability, Interest Payable. This is because the interest payment will not be made until next year; therefore, Smart Touch Learning owes interest to the bank. Had the adjusting entry not been recorded, liabilities and expenses would have been understated. After posting, Interest Expense and Interest Payable now have the following correct balances:

Interest Payable			Interest Expense	
	100	Dec. 31	Dec. 31	100
	100	Bal.	Bal.	100

Accrued Revenues

As we have just seen, expenses can occur before a company makes a cash payment for them, which creates an accrued expense. Similarly, businesses can earn revenue before they receive the cash. This creates an accrued revenue, which is a revenue that has been earned but for which the cash has not yet been collected.

Assume that Smart Touch Learning is hired on December 15 to perform e-learning services, beginning on December 16. Under this agreement, the business will earn $1,600 monthly and receive payment on January 15. At the date of hiring, Smart Touch Learning does not record a journal entry because revenue has not yet been earned. During December, it will earn half a month's fee, $800, for work December 16 through December 31. On December 31, Smart Touch Learning makes the following adjusting entry to record the revenue earned December 16 through December 31:

Date	Accounts and Explanation	Debit	Credit
Dec. 31	Accounts Receivable	800	
	Service Revenue		800
	To accrue service revenue.		

The adjusting entry records the earned revenue and brings the balance of the Service Revenue account to $17,500. In addition, the adjusting entry records an additional $800 receivable. Smart Touch Learning did not record cash because the business has not yet received payment on the services provided. The cash will not be received until January 15. Smart Touch Learning's account balances after posting the adjusting entry are:

Accounts Receivable				Service Revenue		
Nov. 10	3,000	2,000	Nov. 22		5,500	Nov. 8
Dec. 31	800				3,000	Nov. 10
					8,000	Dec. 28
Bal.	1,800				200	Dec. 31
					800	Dec. 31
					17,500	Bal.

Without the adjustment, Smart Touch Learning's financial statements would understate both an asset, Accounts Receivable, and a revenue, Service Revenue.

Future Receipt of Accrued Revenues The adjusting entry on December 31 records revenue earned for half a month and also creates an accounts receivable. When Smart Touch Learning receives the payment on January 15, the business will record the following entry:

Revenue for Jan. 1–Jan. 15

Date	Accounts and Explanation	Debit	Credit
Jan. 15	Cash	1,600	
	Service Revenue		800
	Accounts Receivable		800
	Performed services and received cash.		

Accounts Receivable created from the adjusting entry.

Notice that on January 15, Smart Touch Learning only records revenue for the remaining half of the month (January 1–January 15). Smart Touch Learning recognizes that $800 of revenue was already recorded in December. The entry on January 15 removes the accounts receivable and records the remaining revenue. If the business had incorrectly recorded $1,600 of Service Revenue on January 15, the revenue would have been overstated in January.

Exhibit 3 summarizes the adjusting entries for prepaids and accruals.

Exhibit 3 | Prepaid and Accrual Adjustments

The adjusting entries and account balances after posting for Smart Touch Learning at December 31 are shown in Exhibit 4.

- Panel A gives the data for each adjustment.
- Panel B shows the adjusting entries.
- Panel C shows the T-accounts and balances after posting.

Exhibit 4 | **Journalizing and Posting the Adjusting Entries of Smart Touch Learning**

Panel A: Information for Adjustments

a. Prepaid rent expired, $1,000.
b. Supplies used, $400.
c. Depreciation on furniture, $300.
d. Depreciation on building, $250.
e. Service revenue that was collected in advance and now has been earned, $200.

f. Accrued salaries expense, $1,200.
g. Accrued interest on note, $100.
h. Accrued service revenue, $800.

Panel B: Adjusting Entries

Date	Accounts and Explanation	Debit	Credit
(a) Dec. 31	Rent Expense	1,000	
	Prepaid Rent		1,000
	To record rent expense.		
(b) 31	Supplies Expense	400	
	Office Supplies		400
	To record office supplies used.		
(c) 31	Depreciation Expense—Furniture	300	
	Accumulated Depreciation—Furniture		300
	To record depreciation on furniture.		
(d) 31	Depreciation Expense—Building	250	
	Accumulated Depreciation—Building		250
	To record depreciation on building.		
(e) 31	Unearned Revenue	200	
	Service Revenue		200
	To record service revenue earned that was collected in advance.		
(f) 31	Salaries Expense	1,200	
	Salaries Payable		1,200
	To accrue salaries expense.		
(g) 31	Interest Expense	100	
	Interest Payable		100
	To accrue interest expense.		
(h) 31	Accounts Receivable	800	
	Service Revenue		800
	To accrue service revenue.		

Panel C: Account Balances After Posting

Assets = Liabilities + Equity

Assets

Cash

Nov. 1	30,000	20,000	Nov. 2
Nov. 8	5,500	3,200	Nov. 15
Nov. 22	2,000	300	Nov. 21
Dec. 21	600	5,000	Nov. 25
Dec. 28	8,000	3,000	Dec. 1
		1,200	Dec. 1
		1,200	Dec. 15
Bal.	12,200		

Accounts Receivable

Nov. 10	3,000	2,000	Nov. 22
Dec. 31	800		
Bal.	1,800		

Office Supplies

Nov. 3	500	400	Dec. 31
Bal.	100		

Prepaid Rent

Dec. 1	3,000	1,000	Dec. 31
Bal.	2,000		

Furniture

Dec. 2	18,000		
Bal.	18,000		

Accumulated Depreciation—Furniture

		300	Dec. 31
		300	Bal.

Building

Dec. 1	60,000		
Bal.	60,000		

Accumulated Depreciation—Building

		250	Dec. 31
		250	Bal.

Land

Nov. 2	20,000		
Bal.	20,000		

$113,550

Liabilities

Accounts Payable

Nov. 21	300	500	Nov. 3
		200	Bal.

Utilities Payable

		100	Dec. 15
		100	Bal.

Salaries Payable

		1,200	Dec. 31
		1,200	Bal.

Interest Payable

		100	Dec. 31
		100	Bal.

Unearned Revenue

Dec. 31	200	600	Dec. 21
		400	Bal.

Notes Payable

		60,000	Dec. 1
		60,000	Bal.

$62,000

Equity

Bright, Capital

		30,000	Nov. 1
		18,000	Dec. 2
		48,000	Bal.

Bright, Withdrawals

Nov. 25	5,000		
Bal.	5,000		

Service Revenue

		5,500	Nov. 8
		3,000	Nov. 10
		8,000	Dec. 28
		200	Dec. 31
		800	Dec. 31
		17,500	Bal.

Rent Expense

Nov. 15	2,000		
Dec. 31	1,000		
Bal.	3,000		

Salaries Expense

Nov. 15	1,200		
Dec. 1	1,200		
Dec. 15	1,200		
Dec. 31	1,200		
Bal.	4,800		

Supplies Expense

Dec. 31	400		
Bal.	400		

Utilities Expense

Dec. 15	100		
Bal.	100		

Depreciation Expense—Furniture

Dec. 31	300		
Bal.	300		

Depreciation Expense—Building

Dec. 31	250		
Bal.	250		

Interest Expense

Dec. 31	100		
Bal.	100		

$51,550

> Try It!

Startech Surveillance Services had the following adjustments as of the end of the year.

a. Equipment depreciation was $1,500.

b. $700 of advertising expense was incurred but not paid. (Use Advertising Payable.)

c. Office Supplies on hand at the end of the year totaled $250. The beginning balance of Office Supplies was $600.

d. $1,200 of rent revenue was earned but not recorded or received.

e. Unearned revenue of $3,000 has been earned.

6. For each situation, indicate which category (prepaid or accrual) of adjustment is described.

7. Journalize the adjusting entry needed.

Check your answers at the end of the chapter.

For more practice, see Short Exercises S-5 through S-12. MyAccountingLab

WHAT IS THE PURPOSE OF THE ADJUSTED TRIAL BALANCE AND HOW DO WE PREPARE IT?

Learning Objective 4

Explain the purpose of and prepare an adjusted trial balance

Adjusted Trial Balance
A list of all the accounts with their adjusted balances.

This chapter began with the *unadjusted* trial balance. After the adjustments have been journalized and posted, the account balances are updated and an adjusted trial balance can be prepared by listing all the accounts with their adjusted balances. Remember, the purpose of a trial balance is to ensure that total debits equal total credits. Even if the trial balance balances, it does not guarantee that a mistake has not been made. For example, an adjusting entry could have been recorded for the incorrect amount or could have been omitted entirely. The equality of the trial balance only ensures that each posted transaction had an equal debit and credit amount.

The adjusted trial balance for Smart Touch Learning is shown in Exhibit 5.

Exhibit 5 | **Adjusted Trial Balance**

	SMART TOUCH LEARNING Adjusted Trial Balance December 31, 2014	
	Balance	
Account Title	**Debit**	**Credit**
Cash	$ 12,200	
Accounts Receivable	1,800	
Office Supplies	100	
Prepaid Rent	2,000	
Furniture	18,000	
Accumulated Depreciation—Furniture		$ 300
Building	60,000	
Accumulated Depreciation—Building		250
Land	20,000	
Accounts Payable		200
Utilities Payable		100
Salaries Payable		1,200
Interest Payable		100
Unearned Revenue		400
Notes Payable		60,000
Bright, Capital		48,000
Bright, Withdrawals	5,000	
Service Revenue		17,500
Rent Expense	3,000	
Salaries Expense	4,800	
Supplies Expense	400	
Utilities Expense	100	
Depreciation Expense—Furniture	300	
Depreciation Expense—Building	250	
Interest Expense	100	
Total	$ 128,050	$ 128,050

> Try It!

8. Hooten Carpentry had the following accounts and account balances after adjusting entries. Assume all accounts have normal balances. Prepare the adjusted trial balance for Hooten Carpentry as of December 31, 2015.

Cash	$ 4,025	Hooten, Capital	$?
Land	5,000	Accounts Receivable	660
Utilities Expense	400	Office Supplies	120
Accounts Payable	225	Utilities Payable	210
Accumulated Depreciation—Equipment	1,000	Service Revenue	12,000
Salaries Expense	550	Unearned Revenue	300
Supplies Expense	80	Depreciation Expense—Equipment	800
Equipment	10,000	Hooten, Withdrawals	500

Check your answers at the end of the chapter.

For more practice, see Short Exercise S-13. MyAccountingLab

WHAT IS THE IMPACT OF ADJUSTING ENTRIES ON THE FINANCIAL STATEMENTS?

Learning Objective 5

Identify the impact of adjusting entries on the financial statements

The adjusted trial balance is used to prepare the financial statements. If adjusting entries are not recorded, the ledger accounts will not reflect the correct balances and the adjusted trial balance will be incorrect. Remember adjusting entries are completed to ensure that all revenues and expenses for the accounting period examined have been recorded. In addition, adjusting entries update the balance sheet accounts so that all accounts are properly valued. Exhibit 6 summarizes the impact on the financial statements had the adjusting entries not been recorded.

Exhibit 6 | Impact of Adjusting Entries on Financial Statements

Type of Adjusting Entry	Description	Adjusting Entry		Impact on Financial Statement if Adjusting Entries Are Not Made
Prepaid Expenses	Advance cash payments of future expenses.	Expense Asset*	DR CR	Income Statement: expenses understated net income overstated Balance Sheet: assets overstated equity overstated
Unearned Revenues	Advance cash receipts of future revenues.	Liability Revenue	DR CR	Income Statement: revenues understated net income understated Balance Sheet: liabilities overstated equity understated
Accrued Expenses	An expense that has been incurred but not paid.	Expense Liability	DR CR	Income Statement: expenses understated net income overstated Balance Sheet: liabilities understated equity overstated
Accrued Revenues	A revenue that has been earned but cash has not yet been collected.	Asset Revenue	DR CR	Income Statement: revenues understated net income understated Balance Sheet: assets understated equity understated

* If recording depreciation: the contra asset, Accumulated Depreciation, is credited.

> **Try It!**

9. Identify the impact on the income statement and balance sheet if adjusting entries for the following situations were not recorded.

   a. Office Supplies used, $800.
   b. Accrued service revenue, $4,000.
   c. Depreciation on building, $3,500.
   d. Prepaid Insurance expired, $650.
   e. Accrued salaries expense, $2,750.
   f. Service revenue that was collected in advance has now been earned, $130.

   Check your answers at the end of the chapter.

For more practice, see Short Exercise S-14. MyAccountingLab

HOW COULD A WORKSHEET HELP IN PREPARING ADJUSTING ENTRIES AND THE ADJUSTED TRIAL BALANCE?

A useful step in preparing adjusting entries and the adjusted trial balance is to create a worksheet. A worksheet is an internal document that helps summarize data for the preparation of the financial statements. The worksheet is not a journal, a ledger, or a financial statement. It is merely a summary device that helps identify the accounts that need adjustments. Most worksheets are completed using Microsoft Excel.

Exhibit 7 shows the partially completed worksheet for Smart Touch Learning.

Learning Objective 6

Explain the purpose of a worksheet and use it to prepare adjusting entries and the adjusted trial balance

Worksheet

An internal document that helps summarize data for the preparation of financial statements.

Exhibit 7 | Partially Completed Worksheet

	A	B	C	D	E	F	G	H	I	J	K	L	M
1						SMART TOUCH LEARNING							
2						Worksheet							
3						December 31, 2014							
4													
5	Account Names	Unadjusted Trial Balance			Adjustments			Adjusted Trial Balance		Income Statement		Balance Sheet	
6		Debit	Credit		Debit	Credit		Debit	Credit	Debit	Credit	Debit	Credit
7	Cash	$ 12,200						$ 12,200					
8	Accounts Receivable	1,000		(h)	$ 800			1,800					
9	Office Supplies	500				$ 400	(b)	100					
10	Prepaid Rent	3,000				1,000	(a)	2,000					
11	Furniture	18,000						18,000					
12	Accumulated Depreciation—Furniture					300	(c)		$ 300				
13	Building	60,000						60,000					
14	Accumulated Depreciation—Building					250	(d)		250				
15	Land	20,000						20,000					
16	Accounts Payable		$ 200						200				
17	Utilities Payable		100						100				
18	Salaries Payable					1,200	(f)		1,200				
19	Interest Payable					100	(g)		100				
20	Unearned Revenue		600	(e)	200				400				
21	Notes Payable		60,000						60,000				
22	Bright, Capital		48,000						48,000				
23	Bright, Withdrawals	5,000						5,000					
24	Service Revenue		16,500			1,000	(e,h)		17,500				
25	Rent Expense	2,000		(a)	1,000			3,000					
26	Salaries Expense	3,600		(f)	1,200			4,800					
27	Supplies Expense			(b)	400			400					
28	Utilities Expense	100						100					
29	Depreciation Expense—Furniture			(c)	300			300					
30	Depreciation Expense—Building			(d)	250			250					
31	Interest Expense			(g)	100			100					
32	Total	$ 125,400	$ 125,400		$ 4,250	$ 4,250		$ 128,050	$ 128,050				
33													

In this chapter, we complete a part of the worksheet. For now, we will concern ourselves with the first four sections.

Section 1. Account names: The account names are taken from and listed in the same order as the chart of accounts. (Cash first, Accounts Receivable second, and so on).

Section 2. Unadjusted trial balance: The account balances are copied directly from the ledger before any adjustments. Total debits must equal total credits.

Section 3. Adjustments: Enter the adjusting journal entries that were made on December 31.

Section 4. Adjusted trial balance: Gives the account balances after adjustments. Each amount in these columns is computed by combining the unadjusted trial balance amounts plus or minus the adjustments. For example, Accounts Receivable starts with a debit balance of $1,000. Adding the $800 debit from the adjustment gives Accounts Receivable an adjusted balance of $1,800. Service Revenue starts with a $16,500 credit balance. Adding the $1,000 credit from the adjustments gives Service Revenue an adjusted balance of $17,500. As with the unadjusted trial balance, total debits must equal total credits.

The income statement and balance sheet sections of the worksheet remain to be completed.

> Try It!

10. The partial worksheet for Sam's Delivery Service follows. Complete the adjusted trial balance columns.

	A	B	C	D	E	F	G	H	I	J	K	L	M
1					SAM'S DELIVERY SERVICE								
2					Worksheet								
3					December 31, 2014								
4													
5	Account Names	Unadjusted Trial Balance			Adjustments			Adjusted Trial Balance		Income Statement		Balance Sheet	
6		Debit	Credit		Debit	Credit		Debit	Credit	Debit	Credit	Debit	Credit
7	Cash	$ 6,500											
8	Accounts Receivable	800		(g)	$ 225								
9	Office Supplies	250				$ 80	(b)						
10	Prepaid Rent	1,000				800	(a)						
11	Delivery Van	23,000											
12	Accumulated Depreciation—Delivery Van					750	(c)						
13	Equipment	15,000											
14	Accumulated Depreciation—Equipment					300	(d)						
15	Accounts Payable		$ 800										
16	Utilities Payable		230										
17	Salaries Payable					875	(f)						
18	Unearned Revenue		400	(e)	130								
19	Sam, Capital		37,800										
20	Sam, Withdrawals	8,000											
21	Delivery Revenue		23,000			355	(e,g)						
22	Rent Expense	3,000		(a)	800								
23	Salaries Expense	4,500		(f)	875								
24	Supplies Expense			(b)	80								
25	Utilities Expense	180											
26	Depreciation Expense—Delivery Van			(c)	750								
27	Depreciation Expense—Equipment			(d)	300								
28	**Total**	$ 62,230	$ 62,230		$ 3,160	$ 3,160							
29													

Check your answer at the end of the chapter.

For more practice, see Short Exercise S-15. MyAccountingLab

APPENDIX A: Alternative Treatment of Recording Prepaid Expenses and Unearned Revenues

This text illustrates the most popular way to account for prepaid expenses and unearned revenues. This appendix illustrates an alternative approach.

Learning Objective 7

Understand the alternative treatment of recording prepaid expenses and unearned revenues

WHAT IS AN ALTERNATIVE TREATMENT OF RECORDING PREPAID EXPENSES AND UNEARNED REVENUES?

Prepaid Expenses

Recall that prepaid expenses are advance payments of future expenses such as insurance, rent, and advertising. Office supplies are also accounted for as prepaid expenses.

When a business prepays an expense—rent, for example—it can debit an *asset* account (Prepaid Rent). For example, Smart Touch Learning prepaid three months of office rent totaling $3,000 on December 1, 2014. The journal entry can be recorded as:

$$\left. \frac{\text{A} \uparrow \downarrow}{\substack{\text{Prepaid} \\ \text{Rent} \uparrow \\ \text{Cash} \downarrow}} \right\} = \left\{ \frac{\text{L}}{} + \frac{\text{E}}{} \right.$$

Date	Accounts and Explanation	Debit	Credit
Dec. 1	Prepaid Rent	3,000	
	Cash		3,000
	Paid rent in advance.		

Prepaid Expense Recorded Initially as an Expense

Prepaying an expense creates an asset. However, the asset may be so short-lived that it will expire in the current accounting period—within one year or less. Thus, the accountant may decide to debit the prepayment to an expense account at the time of payment. The entry could, alternatively, be recorded as follows:

$$\left. \frac{\text{A} \downarrow}{\text{Cash} \downarrow} \right\} = \left\{ \frac{\text{L}}{} + \frac{\text{E} \downarrow}{\substack{\text{Rent} \\ \text{Expense} \uparrow}} \right.$$

Date	Accounts and Explanation	Debit	Credit
Dec. 1	Rent Expense	3,000	
	Cash		3,000
	Paid rent in advance.		

As of December 31, only one month's prepayment has expired, leaving two months of rent still prepaid. In this case, the accountant must transfer 2/3 of the original prepayment of $3,000, or $2,000, to the asset account Prepaid Rent. At December 31, 2014, the business still has the benefit of prepayment for January 1 through February 28 of 2015. The adjusting entry at December 31 is as follows:

$$\left. \frac{\text{A} \uparrow}{\substack{\text{Prepaid} \\ \text{Rent} \uparrow}} \right\} = \left\{ \frac{\text{L}}{} + \frac{\text{E} \uparrow}{\substack{\text{Rent} \\ \text{Expense} \downarrow}} \right.$$

Date	Accounts and Explanation	Debit	Credit
Dec. 31	Prepaid Rent	2,000	
	Rent Expense		2,000
	To record prepaid rent.		

After posting, the two accounts appear as follows:

Prepaid Rent			Rent Expense			
Dec. 31	2,000		Dec. 1	3,000	2,000	Dec. 31
Bal.	2,000		Bal.	1,000		

At December 31, the $3,000 prepayment is correctly divided as $2,000 of Prepaid Rent and $1,000 of Rent Expense, regardless of whether the business initially debits the prepayment to an asset or to an expense account.

Unearned Revenues

Unearned revenues arise when a business collects cash before earning the revenue. Unearned revenues are liabilities because the business that receives the cash owes the customer goods or services to be delivered later.

When a business receives cash in advance of providing services, a *liability* can be created. As an example, a law firm engages Smart Touch Learning to provide monthly e-learning services, agreeing to pay $600 in advance. Smart Touch Learning received the $600 on December 21. Smart Touch Learning records the following entry.

Date	Accounts and Explanation	Debit	Credit
Dec. 21	Cash	600	
	Unearned Revenue		600
	Collected cash for future services.		

$$A\uparrow \left\} = \left\{ \begin{array}{l} L\uparrow \quad + \quad E \\ \text{Unearned} \\ \text{Revenue}\uparrow \end{array} \right.$$
Cash↑

Unearned Revenues Recorded Initially as a Revenue

Another way to account for the receipt of cash is to credit a *revenue* account when the business receives cash.

Date	Accounts and Explanation	Debit	Credit
Dec. 21	Cash	600	
	Service Revenue		600
	Collected cash for future services.		

$$A\uparrow \left\} = \left\{ \begin{array}{l} L \quad + \quad E\uparrow \\ \text{Service} \\ \text{Revenue}\uparrow \end{array} \right.$$
Cash↑

If the business then earns all the revenue within the same accounting period, no adjusting entry is needed at the end. However, if the business earns only part of the revenue in that period, it must make an adjusting entry. In our example, Smart Touch Learning has earned only 1/3 of the $600, or $200, by December 31, 2014. Accordingly, Smart Touch

Learning must make an adjusting entry to transfer the unearned portion (2/3 of $600, or $400) from the revenue account to a liability, as follows:

Date	Accounts and Explanation	Debit	Credit
Dec. 31	Service Revenue	400	
	Unearned Revenue		400
	To record unearned revenue.		

The adjusting entry transfers the unearned portion of service revenue to the liability account because Smart Touch Learning still owes e-learning services next year. After posting, the total amount, $600, is properly divided between the liability account—$400, and the revenue account—$200, as follows:

Unearned Revenue		Service Revenue		
	400 Dec. 31 ◄——— Dec. 31	400	600	Dec. 21
	400 Bal.		200	Bal.

At December 31, the $600 cash receipt is correctly divided: $400 of Unearned Revenue and $200 of Service Revenue, regardless of whether the business initially credits the cash receipt to a liability or to a revenue account.

> ## Try It!

11A. Iron Horse Printing Services purchased $1,000 of printing supplies for cash, recording the transaction using the alternative treatment for prepaid expenses. At the end of the year, Iron Horse had $300 of printing supplies remaining. Record the journal entry for the purchase of printing supplies and the adjusting entry for printing supplies not used.

Check your answer at the end of the chapter.

For more practice, see Short Exercises SA-16 and SA-17. MyAccountingLab

REVIEW

> ## Things You Should Know

1. **What is the difference between cash basis accounting and accrual basis accounting?**

    - Cash basis accounting: Revenue is recorded only when cash is received, and expenses are recorded only when cash is paid.
      - Not GAAP
      - Often used by small businesses
    - Accrual basis accounting: Revenue is recorded when earned, and expenses are recorded when incurred.

2. **What concepts and principles apply to accrual basis accounting?**

    - The time period concept assumes that a business's activities can be sliced into small time segments and that financial statements can be prepared for specific periods, such as a month, quarter, or year.
    - The revenue recognition principle requires companies to record revenue when it has been earned and determines the amount of revenue to record.
    - The matching principle guides accounting for expenses and ensures that all expenses are recorded when they are incurred during the period. It then matches those expenses against the revenues of the period.

3. **What are adjusting entries and how do we record them?**

    - Adjusting entries are completed at the end of the accounting period and record revenues to the period in which they are earned and expenses to the period in which they occur.
    - Adjusting entries also update the asset and liability accounts.
    - Four types of adjusting entries:
      - Prepaid expenses: advance payment of future expenses adjusted for amount used

Date	Accounts and Explanation	Debit	Credit
	Expense	DR	
	Asset		CR

      - Unearned revenues: advance receipts of future revenues adjusted for amount earned

Date	Accounts and Explanation	Debit	Credit
	Liability	DR	
	Revenue		CR

- Accrued expenses: expenses that have been incurred but not paid

Date	Accounts and Explanation	Debit	Credit
	Expense	DR	
	Liability		CR

- Accrued revenues: revenues that have been earned but not collected

Date	Accounts and Explanation	Debit	Credit
	Asset	DR	
	Revenue		CR

4. What is the purpose of the adjusted trial balance and how do we prepare it?

- An adjusted trial balance is a list of all the accounts with their adjusted balances.

- It ensures that total debits equal total credits.

5. What is the impact of adjusting entries on the financial statements?

- If adjusting entries are not recorded, the balance sheet and income statement accounts will either be overstated or understated.

- Overstating or understating accounts causes the financial statements to be incorrect.

6. How could a worksheet help in preparing adjusting entries and the adjusted trial balance?

- A worksheet is an internal document that helps identify the accounts that need adjustments.

- In addition, a worksheet helps summarize data for the preparation of the financial statements.

7. What is an alternative treatment of recording prepaid expenses and unearned revenues? (Appendix A)

- Prepaid expenses can be recorded to an expense account at the time of payment. The adjusting entry would transfer any remaining prepayment to the asset account, Prepaid Expenses.

- Unearned revenues can be recorded to a revenue account at the time of cash receipt. The adjusting entry would transfer any remaining liability to the liability account, Unearned Revenue.

> Summary Problem 1

The unadjusted trial balance as of December 31, 2014, the end of the annual accounting period for Super Employment Services, follows:

SUPER EMPLOYMENT SERVICES Unadjusted Trial Balance December 31, 2014		
	Balance	
Account Title	Debit	Credit
Cash	$ 6,000	
Accounts Receivable	5,000	
Office Supplies	1,000	
Furniture	10,000	
Accumulated Depreciation—Furniture		$ 4,000
Building	40,000	
Accumulated Depreciation—Building		30,000
Land	10,000	
Accounts Payable		2,000
Salaries Payable		
Unearned Revenue		8,000
Mudge, Capital		12,000
Mudge, Withdrawals	25,000	
Service Revenue		60,000
Salaries Expense	16,000	
Supplies Expense		
Depreciation Expense—Furniture		
Depreciation Expense—Building		
Advertising Expense	3,000	
Total	$ 116,000	$ 116,000

Data needed for the adjusting entries include the following:

a. Office Supplies on hand at year-end, $200.

b. Depreciation on furniture, $2,000.

c. Depreciation on building, $1,000.

d. Salaries owed but not yet paid, $500.

e. Accrued service revenue, $1,300.

f. $3,000 of the unearned revenue has been earned.

Requirements

1. Open the ledger accounts in T-account form with their unadjusted balances as shown on the unadjusted trial balance.

2. Journalize Super's adjusting entries at December 31, 2014. Use the letter (a, b, and so on) as the date.

3. Post the adjusting entries to T-accounts. Determine the ending balances in the T-accounts on December 31, 2014.

4. Prepare an adjusted trial balance.

5. Prepare a partial worksheet including the account names, unadjusted trial balance, adjustments, and adjusted trial balance.

> Solution

Requirements 1 and 3

Assets

Cash

Bal. 6,000	

Accounts Receivable

Bal. 5,000	
(e) 1,300	
Bal. 6,300	

Office Supplies

Bal. 1,000	800 (a)
Bal. 200	

Furniture

Bal. 10,000	

Accumulated Depreciation—Furniture

	4,000 Bal.
	2,000 (b)
	6,000 Bal.

Building

Bal. 40,000	

Accumulated Depreciation—Building

	30,000 Bal.
	1,000 (c)
	31,000 Bal.

Land

Bal. 10,000	

Liabilities

Accounts Payable

	2,000 Bal.

Salaries Payable

	500 (d)
	500 Bal.

Unearned Revenue

(f) 3,000	8,000 Bal.
	5,000 Bal.

Equity

Mudge, Capital

	12,000 Bal.

Mudge, Withdrawals

Bal. 25,000	

Revenue

Service Revenue

	60,000 Bal.
	1,300 (e)
	3,000 (f)
	64,300 Bal.

Expenses

Salaries Expense

Bal. 16,000	
(d) 500	
Bal. 16,500	

Supplies Expense

(a) 800	
Bal. 800	

Depreciation Expense—Furniture

(b) 2,000	
Bal. 2,000	

Depreciation Expense—Building

(c) 1,000	
Bal. 1,000	

Advertising Expense

Bal. 3,000	

Requirement 2

Date	Accounts and Explanations	Debit	Credit
2014			
(a) Dec. 31	Supplies Expense ($1,000 – $200)	800	
	Office Supplies		800
	To record office supplies used.		
(b) 31	Depreciation Expense—Furniture	2,000	
	Accumulated Depreciation—Furniture		2,000
	To record depreciation expense on furniture.		
(c) 31	Depreciation Expense—Building	1,000	
	Accumulated Depreciation—Building		1,000
	To record depreciation expense on building.		
(d) 31	Salaries Expense	500	
	Salaries Payable		500
	To accrue salaries expense.		
(e) 31	Accounts Receivable	1,300	
	Service Revenue		1,300
	To accrue service revenue.		
(f) 31	Unearned Revenue	3,000	
	Service Revenue		3,000
	To record service revenue earned that was collected in advance.		

Requirement 4

SUPER EMPLOYMENT SERVICES Adjusted Trial Balance December 31, 2014		
	Balance	
Account Title	**Debit**	**Credit**
Cash	$ 6,000	
Accounts Receivable	6,300	
Office Supplies	200	
Furniture	10,000	
Accumulated Depreciation—Furniture		$ 6,000
Building	40,000	
Accumulated Depreciation—Building		31,000
Land	10,000	
Accounts Payable		2,000
Salaries Payable		500
Unearned Revenue		5,000
Mudge, Capital		12,000
Mudge, Withdrawals	25,000	
Service Revenue		64,300
Salaries Expense	16,500	
Supplies Expense	800	
Depreciation Expense—Furniture	2,000	
Depreciation Expense—Building	1,000	
Advertising Expense	3,000	
Total	**$ 120,800**	**$ 120,800**

Requirement 5

	A	B	C	D		E		F	G
1	SUPER EMPLOYMENT SERVICES								
2	Worksheet								
3	December 31, 2014								
4									
5	**Account Names**	**Unadjusted Trial Balance**		**Adjustments**				**Adjusted Trial Balance**	
6		Debit	Credit	Debit		Credit		Debit	Credit
7	Cash	$ 6,000						$ 6,000	
8	Accounts Receivable	5,000		(e) $ 1,300				6,300	
9	Office Supplies	1,000			(a)	$ 800		200	
10	Furniture	10,000						10,000	
11	Accumulated Depreciation—Furniture		$ 4,000		(b)	2,000			$ 6,000
12	Building	40,000						40,000	
13	Accumulated Depreciation—Building		30,000		(c)	1,000			31,000
14	Land	10,000						10,000	
15	Accounts Payable		2,000						2,000
16	Salaries Payable				(d)	500			500
17	Unearned Revenue		8,000	(f)	3,000				5,000
18	Mudge, Capital		12,000						12,000
19	Mudge, Withdrawals	25,000						25,000	
20	Service Revenue		60,000		(e)	1,300			
21					(f)	3,000			64,300
22	Salaries Expense	16,000		(d)	500			16,500	
23	Supplies Expense			(a)	800			800	
24	Depreciation Expense—Furniture			(b)	2,000			2,000	
25	Depreciation Expense—Building			(c)	1,000			1,000	
26	Advertising Expense	3,000						3,000	
27	**Total**	**$ 116,000**	**$ 116,000**	**$ 8,600**		**$ 8,600**		**$ 120,800**	**$ 120,800**
28									

> Key Terms

Accrual Basis Accounting
Accounting method that records revenues when earned and expenses when incurred.

Accrued Expense
An expense that the business has incurred but has not yet paid.

Accrued Revenue
A revenue that has been earned but for which the cash has not yet been collected.

Accumulated Depreciation
The sum of all the depreciation expense recorded to date for a depreciable asset.

Adjusted Trial Balance
A list of all the accounts with their adjusted balances.

Adjusting Entry
An entry made at the end of the accounting period that is used to record revenues to the period in

which they are earned and expenses to the period in which they occur.

Book Value
A depreciable asset's cost minus accumulated depreciation.

Cash Basis Accounting
Accounting method that records revenue only when cash is received and expenses only when cash is paid.

Contra Account

An account that is paired with, and is listed immediately after, its related account in the chart of accounts and associated financial statement, and whose normal balance is the opposite of the normal balance of the related account.

Deferred Revenue

A liability created when a business collects cash from customers in advance of completing a service or delivering a product.

Depreciation

The process by which businesses spread the allocation of a plant asset's cost over its useful life.

Fiscal Year

An accounting year of any twelve consecutive months that may or may not coincide with the calendar year.

Matching Principle

Guides accounting for expenses, ensures that all expenses are recorded when they are incurred during the period, and matches those expenses against the revenues of the period.

Plant Assets

Long-lived, tangible assets, such as land, buildings, and equipment, used in the operation of a business.

Residual Value

The value of a depreciable asset at the end of its useful life.

Revenue Recognition Principle

Requires companies to record revenue when it has been earned and determines the amount of revenue to record.

Straight-line Method

A depreciation method that allocates an equal amount of depreciation each year. (Cost – Residual value) / Useful life.

Time Period Concept

Assumes that a business's activities can be sliced into small time segments and that financial statements can be prepared for specific periods, such as a month, quarter, or year.

Worksheet

An internal document that helps summarize data for the preparation of financial statements.

> Quick Check

1. Which of the following is true of accrual basis accounting and cash basis accounting?

   a. Accrual accounting records revenue only when it is earned.

   b. Accrual accounting is not allowed under GAAP.

   c. Cash basis accounting records all transactions.

   d. All the above are true.

   Learning Objective 1

2. Get Fit Now gains a client who prepays $540 for a package of six physical training sessions. Get Fit Now collects the $540 in advance and will provide the training later. After four training sessions, what should Get Fit Now report on its income statement assuming it uses the accrual basis accounting method?

   a. Service revenue of $360

   b. Service revenue of $540

   c. Unearned service revenue of $360

   d. Cash of $180

   Learning Objective 1

3. The revenue recognition principle requires

   a. time to be divided into annual periods to measure revenue properly.

   b. revenue to be recorded only after the business has earned it.

   c. expenses to be matched with revenue of the period.

   d. revenue to be recorded only after the cash is received.

   Learning Objective 2

Learning Objective 3

4. Adjusting the accounts is the process of
   a. subtracting expenses from revenues to measure net income.
   b. recording transactions as they occur during the period.
   c. updating the accounts at the end of the period.
   d. zeroing out account balances to prepare for the next period.

Learning Objective 3

5. Which of the following is an example of a prepaid adjusting entry?
   a. Recording the usage of office supplies during the period.
   b. Recording salaries expense for employees not yet paid.
   c. Recording revenue that has been earned but not yet received.
   d. Recording interest expense incurred on a notes payable not due until next year.

Learning Objective 3

6. Assume that the weekly payroll of In the Woods Camping Supplies is $300. December 31, end of the year, falls on Tuesday, and In the Woods will pay its employee on Friday for the full week. What adjusting entry will In the Woods make on Tuesday, December 31? (Use five days as a full workweek.)

   a.

Salaries Expense	120	
Salaries Payable		120

   b.

Salaries Payable	300	
Salaries Expense		300

   c.

Salaries Expense	120	
Cash		120

   d. No adjustment is needed because the company will pay the payroll on Friday.

Learning Objective 4

7. The adjusted trial balance shows
   a. amounts that may be out of balance.
   b. account balances after adjustments.
   c. assets and liabilities only.
   d. revenues and expenses only.

Learning Objective 5

8. A & D Window Cleaning performed $450 of services but has not yet billed customers for the month. If A & D fails to record the adjusting entry, what is the impact on the financial statements?
   a. balance sheet: assets understated; equity overstated
      income statement: expense understated
   b. balance sheet: liabilities overstated; equity understated
      income statement: revenues understated
   c. balance sheet: assets overstated, equity understated
      income statement: expenses understated
   d. balance sheet: assets understated, equity understated
      income statement: revenues understated

9. A worksheet

Learning Objective 6

 a. is a journal used to record transactions.

 b. is a financial statement that reports net income during the period.

 c. is an internal document that helps summarize data for the preparation of financial statements.

 d. is a ledger listing the account balances and changes in those accounts.

10A. On February 1, Clovis Wilson, attorney, contracted to provide $3,000 of legal services for the next three months and received $3,000 cash from the client. Assuming Wilson records unearned revenues using the alternative treatment, what would be the adjusting entry recorded on February 28?

**Learning Objective 7
Appendix A**

a.

Cash	3,000	
Unearned Revenue		3,000

b.

Service Revenue	2,000	
Unearned Revenue		2,000

c.

Unearned Revenue	1,000	
Service Revenue		1,000

d.

Cash	3,000	
Service Revenue		3,000

Check your answers at the end of the chapter.

ASSESS YOUR PROGRESS

> Review Questions

1. What is the difference between cash basis accounting versus accrual basis accounting?

2. Which method of accounting (cash or accrual basis) is consistent with generally accepted accounting principles?

3. Which accounting concept or principle requires companies to divide their activities into small time segments such as months, quarters, or years?

4. What is a fiscal year? Why might companies choose to use a fiscal year that is not a calendar year?

5. Under the revenue recognition principle, when is revenue recorded?

6. Under the matching principle, when are expenses recorded?

7. When are adjusting entries completed, and what is their purpose?

8. What are the two basic categories of adjusting entries? Provide two examples of each.

9. What is a prepaid expense?

10. What is the process of allocating the cost of a plant asset over its useful life called?

11. What is a contra account?

12. In the recording of depreciation expense, which account is credited?

13. What does accumulated depreciation represent?

14. How is book value calculated, and what does it represent?

15. What is a deferred revenue? Provide an example.

16. What is an accrued expense? Provide an example.

17. What is an accrued revenue? Provide an example.

18. What are the two rules to remember about adjusting entries?

19. When is an adjusted trial balance prepared, and what is its purpose?

20. If an accrued expense is not recorded at the end of the year, what is the impact on the financial statements?

21. What is a worksheet, and how is it used to help prepare an adjusted trial balance?

22A. If a payment of a prepaid expense was recorded under the alternative treatment, what account would be debited at the time of payment?

23A. If a payment of a prepaid expense was recorded under the alternative treatment, what account would be debited in the adjusting entry?

> Short Exercises

S-1 **Comparing cash and accrual basis accounting for expenses**

Learning Objective 1

The Johnny Flowers Law Firm prepays for advertising in the local newspaper. On January 1, Johnny Flowers paid $900 for six months of advertising.

How much advertising expense should Johnny Flowers Law Firm record for the two months ending February 28 under the

a. cash basis?

b. accrual basis?

S-2 **Comparing cash and accrual basis accounting for revenues**

Learning Objective 1

Safe Home provides house-sitting for people while they are away on vacation. Some of its customers pay immediately after the job is finished. Some customers ask that the business send them a bill. As of the end of the year, Safe Home has collected $900 from cash-paying customers. Safe Home's remaining customers owe the business $1,300.

How much service revenue would Safe Home have for the year under the

a. cash basis?

b. accrual basis?

S-3 **Applying the revenue recognition principle**

Learning Objective 2

Northwest Magazine sells subscriptions for $36 for 12 issues. The company collects cash in advance and then mails out the magazines to subscribers each month.

Apply the revenue recognition principle to determine

a. when *Northwest Magazine* should record revenue for this situation.

b. the amount of revenue *Northwest Magazine* should record for three issues.

S-4 **Applying the matching principle**

Learning Objective 2

Suppose on January 1 Ace's Tavern prepaid rent of $18,000 for the full year.

At July 31, how much rent expense should be recorded for the period January 1 through July 31?

S-5 **Identifying types of adjusting entries**

Learning Objective 3

A select list of transactions for Anuradha's Goals follows:

Apr.	1	Paid six months of rent, $4,800.
	10	Received $1,200 from customer for six-month service contract that began April 1.
	15	Purchased a computer for $1,000.
	18	Purchased $300 of office supplies on account.
	30	Work performed but not yet billed to customer, $500.
	30	Employees earned $600 in salaries that will be paid May 2.

For each transaction, identify what type of adjusting entry would be needed. Select from the following four types of adjusting entries: prepaid expense, unearned revenue, accrued expense, accrued revenue.

S-6 Journalizing and posting adjusting entries for prepaid rent

On April 1, Sport Courts of Toledo prepaid six months of rent, $4,800.

Requirements

1. Record the journal entry for the April 1 payment.

2. Record the adjusting entry required at April 30.

3. Using T-accounts, post the journal entry and adjusting entry to the accounts involved and show their balances at April 30. (Ignore the Cash account.)

S-7 Journalizing and posting an adjusting entry for office supplies

On November 1, Channel Equipment had a beginning balance in the Office Supplies account of $800. During the month, Channel purchased $1,000 of office supplies. At November 30, Channel Equipment had $400 of office supplies on hand.

Requirements

1. Open the Office Supplies T-account and enter the beginning balance and purchase of office supplies.

2. Record the adjusting entry required at November 30.

3. Post the adjusting entry to the two accounts involved and show their balances at November 30.

S-8 Journalizing and posting an adjusting entry for depreciation and determining book value

On May 1, American Gold Exchange paid cash of $54,000 for computers that are expected to remain useful for three years. At the end of three years, the value of the computers is expected to be zero.

Requirements

1. Calculate the amount of depreciation for the month of May using the straight-line depreciation method.

2. Record the adjusting entry for depreciation on May 31.

3. Post the purchase of May 1 and the depreciation on May 31 to T-accounts for the following accounts: Computer Equipment, Accumulated Depreciation—Computer Equipment, and Depreciation Expense—Computer Equipment. Show their balances at May 31.

4. What is the computer equipment's book value on May 31?

S-9 Journalizing and posting an adjusting entry for unearned revenue

Metro Magazine collects cash from subscribers in advance and then mails the magazines to subscribers over a one-year period.

Requirements

1. Record the journal entry to record the original receipt of $170,000 cash.

2. Record the adjusting entry that *Metro Magazine* makes to record earning $12,000 in subscription revenue that was collected in advance.

3. Using T-accounts, post the journal entry and adjusting entry to the accounts involved and show their balances after adjustments. (Ignore the Cash account.)

S-10 Journalizing and posting an adjusting entry for accrued salaries expense

Learning Objective 3

Cedar Park Senior Center has a weekly payroll of $10,000. December 31 falls on Thursday, and Cedar Park Senior Center will pay its employees the following Monday (January 4) for the previous full week. Assume Cedar Park Senior Center has a five-day workweek and has an unadjusted balance in Salaries Expense of $510,000.

Requirements

1. Record the adjusting entry for accrued salaries on December 31.

2. Post the adjusting entry to the accounts involved and show their balances after adjustments.

3. Record the journal entry for payment of salaries made on January 4.

S-11 Journalizing and posting an adjusting entry for accrued interest expense

Learning Objective 3

Thompson Travel borrowed $68,000 on October 1, 2014, by signing a one-year note payable to Metro One Bank. Thompson's interest expense on the note payable for the remainder of the fiscal year (October through December) is $884.

Requirements

1. Record the adjusting entry to accrue interest expense at December 31, 2014.

2. Post the adjusting entry to the T-accounts of the two accounts affected by the adjustment.

S-12 Journalizing an adjusting entry for accrued revenue

Learning Objective 3

At the end of June, Goldenburg Dental had performed $3,000 of dental services but has not yet billed customers.

Record the adjusting entry for accrued revenue.

S-13 Preparing an adjusted trial balance

Learning Objective 4

Scott Tax Services had the following accounts and account balances after adjusting entries. Assume all accounts have normal balances.

Cash	$?	Equipment	$ 15,000
Land	20,000	Accounts Receivable	2,250
Utilities Payable	350	Office Supplies	200
Accounts Payable	3,100	Scott, Capital	18,400
Accumulated Depreciation—Equipment	2,400	Utilities Expense	750
Service Revenue	60,000	Unearned Revenue	600
Supplies Expense	800	Depreciation Expense—Equipment	1,200
Scott, Withdrawals	22,000	Salaries Expense	4,500

Prepare the adjusted trial balance for Scott Tax Services as of December 31, 2015.

The Adjusting Process

Learning Objective 5

S-14 Determining the effects on financial statements

In recording adjusting entries, Reagan Financial Advisors failed to record the adjusting entries for the following situations.

a. Office supplies on hand, $100.

b. Accrued revenues, $5,000.

c. Accrued interest expense, $250.

d. Depreciation, $800.

e. Unearned revenue that has been earned, $550.

Determine the effects on the income statement and balance sheet by identifying whether assets, liabilities, equity, revenue, and expenses are either overstated or understated. Use the following table. Adjustment *a* has been provided as an example.

Adjustment	Balance Sheet			Income Statement	
Not Recorded	Assets	Liabilities	Equity	Revenue	Expenses
(a)	Overstated		Overstated		Understated

Learning Objective 6

S-15 Preparing a partial worksheet

Famous Cut Hair Stylists has begun the preparation of its worksheet as follows:

	A	B	C	D	E	F	G
1	FAMOUS CUT HAIR STYLISTS						
2	Worksheet						
3	December 31, 2014						
4							
5	Account Names	Unadjusted Trial Balance		Adjustments		Adjusted Trial Balance	
6		Debit	Credit	Debit	Credit	Debit	Credit
7	Cash	$ 800					
8	Office Supplies	900					
9	Equipment	19,100					
10	Accumulated Depreciation—Equipment		$ 1,000				
11	Accounts Payable		200				
12	Interest Payable						
13	Note Payable		2,500				
14	Fabio, Capital		7,400				
15	Service Revenue		14,800				
16	Rent Expense	4,500					
17	Supplies Expense						
18	Depreciation Expense—Equipment						
19	Interest Expense	600					
20	Total	$ 25,900	$ 25,900				
21							

Year-end data include the following:

a. Office supplies on hand, $300.

b. Depreciation, $1,000.

c. Accrued interest expense, $600.

Complete Famous Cut's worksheet through the adjusted trial balance section. In the adjustments section, mark each adjustment by letter.

SA-16 Journalizing the alternative treatment of prepaid expenses

Learning Objective 7 Appendix A

On December 1, 2014, Design Security Systems paid $9,000 for store rent covering the three-month period ending February 28, 2015.

Requirements

1. Journalize the entry on December 1 by using the alternative treatment of prepaid expenses.

2. Record the December 31 adjusting entry.

SA-17 Journalizing the alternative treatment of unearned revenues

Learning Objective 7 Appendix A

On December 1, 2014, Great Hills Landscaping collected $4,500 in advance from customers for landscaping services. The service revenue will be earned monthly over the six-month period ending May 31, 2015.

Requirements

1. Journalize the entry on December 1 by using the alternative treatment of unearned revenues.

2. Record the December 31 adjusting entry.

> ## Exercises

Learning Objectives 1, 2

E-18 Comparing cash and accrual basis accounting and applying the revenue recognition principle

Momentous Occasions is a photography business that shoots videos at college parties. The freshman class pays $1,000 in advance on March 3 to guarantee services for its party to be held April 2. The sophomore class promises a minimum of $2,800 for filming its formal dance and actually pays cash of $4,100 on February 28 at the dance.

Answer the following questions about the correct way to account for revenue under the accrual basis.

a. Considering the $1,000 paid by the freshman class, on what date was revenue earned? Did the earnings occur on the same date cash was received?

b. Considering the $4,100 paid by the sophomore class, on what date was revenue earned? Did the earnings occur on the same date cash was received?

Learning Objectives 1, 2

2. Cash basis, $(1,700)

E-19 Comparing cash and accrual basis accounting and applying the revenue recognition principle and the matching principle

Sweet Catering completed the following selected transactions during May 2014:

May	1	Prepaid rent for three months, $1,500.
	5	Received and paid electricity bill, $400.
	9	Received cash for meals served to customers, $2,600.
	14	Paid cash for kitchen equipment, $2,400.
	23	Served a banquet on account, $3,000.
	31	Made the adjusting entry for rent (from May 1).
	31	Accrued salary expense, $1,400.
	31	Recorded depreciation for May on kitchen equipment, $40.

Requirements

1. Show whether each transaction would be handled as a revenue or an expense using both the cash basis and accrual basis accounting systems by completing the following table. (Expenses should be shown in parentheses.) Also, indicate the dollar amount of the revenue or expense. The May 1 transaction has been completed as an example.

Amount of Revenue (Expense) for May		
Date	Cash Basis Amount of Revenue (Expense)	Accrual Basis Amount of Revenue (Expense)
May 1	$(1,500)	$0

2. After completing the table, calculate the amount of net income or net loss for Sweet Catering under the accrual basis and cash basis accounting systems for May.

3. Considering your results from Requirement 2, which method gives the best picture of the true earnings of Sweet Catering? Why?

E-20 Determining the amount of prepaid expenses

Learning Objective 3

Situation A. Rent Expense, $2,000

Consider the facts presented in the following table for Tropical View:

	Situation			
	A	B	C	D
Beginning Prepaid Rent	$1,200	$ 900	$ 200	$ 700
Payments for Prepaid Rent during the year	1,400	b	1,800	f
Total amount to account for	2,600	1,400	c	e
Subtract: Ending Prepaid Rent	600	500	d	400
Rent Expense	$ a	$ 900	$1,900	$1,100

Complete the table by filling in the missing values.

E-21 Journalizing adjusting entries

Learning Objective 3

b. DR Salaries Expense, $1,500

Consider the following situations:

a. Business receives $2,000 on January 1 for 10-month service contract for the period January 1 through October 31.

b. Total salaries for all employees is $3,000 per month. Employees are paid on the 1st and 15th of the month.

c. Work performed but not yet billed to customers for the month is $900.

d. The company pays interest on its $10,000, 6% note payable of $50 on the first day of each month.

Assume the company records adjusting entries monthly. Journalize the adjusting entries needed as of January 31.

E-22 Journalizing adjusting entries

Learning Objective 3

e. DR Insurance Expense, $250

Consider the following independent situations at December 31.

a. On August 1, a business collected $3,300 rent in advance, debiting Cash and crediting Unearned Revenue. The tenant was paying one year's rent in advance. On December 31, the business must account for the amount of rent it has earned.

b. Salaries expense is $1,700 per day—Monday through Friday—and the business pays employees each Friday. This year December 31 falls on a Thursday.

c. The unadjusted balance of the Office Supplies account is $3,500. Office supplies on hand total $1,700.

d. Equipment depreciation was $300.

e. On March 1, when the business prepaid $600 for a two-year insurance policy, the business debited Prepaid Insurance and credited Cash.

Journalize the adjusting entry needed on December 31 for each situation. Use the letters to label the journal entries.

E-23 Journalizing adjusting entries

Consider the following situations for College Park Welding Services.

a. Depreciation for the current year includes Equipment, $2,400.

b. Each Monday, College Park pays employees for the previous week's work. The amount of weekly payroll is $5,600 for a seven-day workweek (Monday to Sunday). This year December 31 falls on Thursday.

c. The beginning balance of Office Supplies was $2,500. During the year, College Park purchased office supplies for $3,000, and at December 31 the office supplies on hand totaled $1,700.

d. College Park prepaid a two full years' insurance on August 1 of the current year, $5,280. Record insurance expense for the year ended December 31.

e. College Park had earned $3,200 of unearned revenue.

f. College Park had incurred (but not recorded) $150 of interest expense on a note payable. The interest will not be paid until February 28.

g. College Park billed customers, $6,000, for welding services performed.

Journalize the adjusting entry needed on December 31 for each situation. Use the letters to label the journal entries.

E-24 Journalizing adjusting entries and posting to T-accounts

The accounting records of Maura Grayson Architect include the following selected, unadjusted balances at March 31: Accounts Receivable, $1,400; Office Supplies, $1,100; Prepaid Rent, $2,400; Equipment, $10,000; Accumulated Depreciation—Equipment, $0; Salaries Payable, $0; Unearned Revenue, $600; Service Revenue, $4,200; Salaries Expense, $1,300; Supplies Expense, $0; Rent Expense, $0; Depreciation Expense—Equipment, $0. The data developed for the March 31 adjusting entries are as follows:

a. Service revenue accrued, $900.

b. Unearned revenue that has been earned, $200.

c. Office Supplies on hand, $600.

d. Salaries owed to employees, $400.

e. One month of prepaid rent has expired, $800.

f. Depreciation on equipment, $150.

Requirements

1. Open a T-account for each account using the unadjusted balances given.

2. Journalize the adjusting entries using the letter and March 31 date in the date column.

3. Post the adjustments to the T-accounts, entering each adjustment by letter. Show each account's adjusted balance.

E-25 Journalizing adjusting entries and posting to T-accounts

The unadjusted trial balance for First Class Maids Company, the cleaning service, is as follows:

3. Office Supplies bal., $1,200 DR

FIRST CLASS MAIDS COMPANY		
Unadjusted Trial Balance		
December 31, 2014		
	Balance	
Account Title	**Debit**	**Credit**
Cash	$ 700	
Office Supplies	3,000	
Prepaid Insurance	800	
Equipment	29,000	
Accumulated Depreciation—Equipment		$ 7,000
Accounts Payable		2,800
Salaries Payable		
Unearned Revenue		500
Molly, Capital		7,200
Molly, Withdrawals	3,000	
Service Revenue		25,000
Salaries Expense	6,000	
Supplies Expense		
Depreciation Expense—Equipment		
Insurance Expense		
Total	$ 42,500	$ 42,500

During the 12 months ended December 31, 2014, First Class Maids:

a. used office supplies of $1,800.

b. used prepaid insurance of $620.

c. depreciated equipment, $460.

d. accrued salaries expense of $310 that hasn't been paid yet.

e. earned $360 of unearned revenue.

Requirements

1. Open a T-account for each account using the unadjusted balances.

2. Journalize the adjusting entries using the letter and December 31 date in the date column.

3. Post the adjustments to the T-accounts, entering each adjustment by letter. Show each account's adjusted balance.

Note: Exercise E-26 should be used only in conjunction with Exercise E-25.

Learning Objective 4

Adjusted trial balance, $43,270 total

E-26 Preparing an adjusted trial balance

Refer to the data in Exercise E-25 and prepare an adjusted trial balance.

Learning Objective 5

E-27 Identifying the impact of adjusting entries on the financial statements

Ausley Acoustics recorded the following transactions during October 2014.

a. Received $1,500 cash from customer for three months of service beginning October 1, 2014, and ending December 31, 2014. The company recorded a $1,500 debit to Cash and a $1,500 credit to Unearned Revenue.

b. Employees are paid $1,000 on Monday following the five-day work week. October 31, 2014, is on Friday.

c. The company pays $240 on October 1 for their six-month auto insurance policy. The company recorded a $240 debit to Prepaid Insurance and a $240 credit to Cash.

d. The company purchased office furniture for $6,300 on January 2, 2014. The company recorded a $6,300 debit to Office Furniture and a $6,300 credit to Accounts Payable. Annual depreciation for the furniture is $900.

e. The company began October with $50 of office supplies on hand. On October 10, the company purchased office supplies on account of $100. The company recorded a $100 debit to Office Supplies and a $100 credit to Accounts Payable. The company used $120 of office supplies during October.

f. The company received its electric bill on October 30 for $125 but did not pay it until November 10.

g. The company paid November's rent of $800 on October 30. On October 30, the company recorded an $800 debit to Rent Expense and an $800 credit to Cash.

Indicate if an adjusting entry is needed for each item on October 31 for the month of October. Assuming the adjusting entry is not made, indicate which specific category or categories of accounts on the financial statements are misstated and if they are overstated or understated. Use the following table as a guide. Item *a* is completed as an example:

Item	Adjusting Entry Needed?	Specific Category of Accounts on the Balance Sheet	Over / Understated	Specific Category of Accounts on the Income Statement	Over / Understated
(a)	Yes	*Liability* *Equity*	*Over* *Under*	*Revenue*	*Under*

E-28 Journalizing adjusting entries and analyzing their effect on the income statement

Learning Objectives 3, 5

1. d. DR Salaries Expense, $10,400

The following data at July 31, 2014, are given for EBM.

a. Depreciation, $500.

b. Prepaid rent expires, $600.

c. Interest expense accrued, $300.

d. Employee salaries owed for Monday through Thursday of a five-day workweek; weekly payroll, $13,000.

e. Unearned revenue earned, $1,300.

f. Office supplies used, $250.

Requirements

1. Journalize the adjusting entries needed on July 31, 2014.

2. Suppose the adjustments made in Requirement 1 were not made. Compute the overall overstatement or understatement of net income as a result of the omission of these adjustments.

E-29 Using the worksheet to record the adjusting journal entries

Learning Objective 6

1. Adjustments, $4,200 total

The worksheet of Jobs–4–U Employment Service follows but is incomplete.

	A	B	C	D	E	F	G
1		JOBS–4–U EMPLOYMENT SERVICE					
2		Worksheet					
3		April 30, 2014					
4							
5	Account Names	Unadjusted Trial Balance		Adjustments		Adjusted Trial Balance	
6		Debit	Credit	Debit	Credit	Debit	Credit
7	Cash	$ 900				$ 900	
8	Accounts Receivable	4,100				5,600	
9	Office Supplies	1,000				500	
10	Equipment	32,500				32,500	
11	Accumulated Depreciation—Equipment		$ 14,400				$ 15,400
12	Salaries Payable						1,200
13	Yost, Capital		23,300				23,300
14	Yost, Withdrawals	4,800				4,800	
15	Service Revenue		9,100				10,600
16	Salaries Expense	2,500				3,700	
17	Rent Expense	1,000				1,000	
18	Depreciation Expense—Equipment					1,000	
19	Supplies Expense					500	
20	Total	$ 46,800	$ 46,800			$ 50,500	$ 50,500
21							

Requirements

1. Calculate and enter the adjustment amounts directly in the Adjustments columns. Use letters *a* through *d* to label the four adjustments.

2. Prepare each adjusting journal entry calculated in Requirement 1. Date the entries and include explanations.

E-30 Using the worksheet to prepare the adjusted trial balance

The worksheet of Miller's Landscaping Services follows but is incomplete.

Adjusted trial balance, $256,780 total

	A	B	C	D	E	F	G
1		MILLER'S LANDSCAPING SERVICES					
2		Worksheet					
3		December 31, 2014					
4							
5	**Account Names**	**Unadjusted Trial Balance**		**Adjustments**		**Adjusted Trial Balance**	
6		Debit	Credit	Debit	Credit	Debit	Credit
7	Cash	$ 25,400					
8	Accounts Receivable	6,500		(h) $ 2,000			
9	Office Supplies	430			(b) $ 170		
10	Prepaid Insurance	2,500			(a) 1,250		
11	Equipment	65,000					
12	Accumulated Depreciation—Equipment				(c) 1,000		
13	Trucks	90,000					
14	Accumulated Depreciation—Trucks				(d) 1,500		
15	Accounts Payable		$ 4,600				
16	Utilities Payable		500				
17	Salaries Payable				(f) 7,300		
18	Interest Payable				(g) 100		
19	Unearned Revenue		3,600	(e) 2,400			
20	Notes Payable		35,000				
21	Miller, Capital		120,680				
22	Miller, Withdrawals	15,000					
23	Service Revenue		80,500		(e, h) 4,400		
24	Rent Expense	10,500		(a) 1,250			
25	Salaries Expense	24,150		(f) 7,300			
26	Supplies Expense			(b) 170			
27	Utilities Expense	5,400					
28	Depreciation Expense—Equipment			(c) 1,000			
29	Depreciation Expense—Trucks			(d) 1,500			
30	Interest Expense			(g) 100			
31	**Total**	**$ 244,880**	**$ 244,880**	**$ 15,720**	**$ 15,720**		
32							

Calculate and enter the adjusted account balances in the Adjusted Trial Balance columns.

EA-31 Understanding the alternative treatment of prepaid expenses

At the beginning of the year, office supplies of $1,100 were on hand. During the year, Dash Air Conditioning Service paid $5,000 for more office supplies. At the end of the year, Dash has $700 of office supplies on hand.

Requirements

1. Record the adjusting entry assuming that Dash records the purchase of office supplies by initially debiting an asset account. Post the adjusting entry to the Office Supplies and Supplies Expense T-accounts. Make sure to include the beginning balance and purchase of office supplies in the Office Supplies T-account.

2. Record the adjusting entry assuming that Dash records the purchase of office supplies by initially debiting an expense account. Post the adjusting entry to the Office Supplies and Supplies Expense T-accounts. Make sure to include the beginning balance in the Office Supplies T-account, and the purchase of office supplies in the Supplies Expense T-account.

3. Compare the ending balances of the T-accounts under both approaches. Are they the same?

Learning Objectives 3, 7
Appendix A

2. CR Office Supplies, $400

EA-32 Understanding the alternative treatment of unearned revenues

At the beginning of the year, Posh Advertising owed customers $2,700 for unearned revenue collected in advance. During the year, Posh received advance cash receipts of $7,300 and earned $30,000 of service revenue (exclusive of any amount earned from advance payments). At year-end, the liability for unearned revenue is $3,500 and unadjusted service revenue is $30,000.

Requirements

1. Record the adjusting entry assuming that Posh records the cash receipt of unearned revenue by initially crediting a liability account. Post the adjusting entry to the Unearned Revenue and Service Revenue T-accounts. Make sure to include the beginning balance and additional unearned revenue in the Unearned Revenue T-account.

2. Record the adjusting entry assuming that Posh records the cash receipt of unearned revenue by initially crediting a revenue account. Post the adjusting entry to the Unearned Revenue and Service Revenue T-accounts. Make sure to include the beginning balance in the Unearned Revenue T-account and the additional unearned revenue in the Service Revenue T-account.

3. Compare the ending balances of the T-accounts under both approaches. Are they the same?

Learning Objectives 3, 7
Appendix A

2. DR Service Revenue, $800

> Problems **Group A**

Learning Objective 3

1. b. DR Insurance Expense, $4,500

P-33A Journalizing adjusting entries and subsequent journal entries

Laughter Landscaping has collected the following data for the December 31 adjusting entries:

a. Each Friday, Laughter pays employees for the current week's work. The amount of the weekly payroll is $7,000 for a five-day workweek. This year December 31 falls on a Wednesday. Laughter will pay its employees on January 2.

b. On January 1 of the current year, Laughter purchases an insurance policy that covers two years, $9,000.

c. The beginning balance of Office Supplies was $4,000. During the year, Laughter purchased office supplies for $5,200, and at December 31 the office supplies on hand total $2,400.

d. During December, Laughter designed a landscape plan and the client prepaid $7,000. Laughter recorded this amount as Unearned Revenue. The job will take several months to complete, and Laughter estimates that the company has earned 40% of the total revenue during the current year.

e. At December 31, Laughter had earned $3,500 for landscape services completed for Turnkey Appliances. Turnkey has stated that they will pay Laughter on January 10.

f. Depreciation for the current year includes Equipment, $3,700; and Trucks, $1,300.

g. Laughter has incurred $300 of interest expense on a $450 interest payment due on January 15.

Requirements

1. Journalize the adjusting entry needed on December 31, for each of the previous items affecting Laughter Landscaping. Assume Laughter records adjusting entries only at the end of the year.

2. Journalize the subsequent journal entries for adjusting entries *a*, *d*, and *g*.

Learning Objectives 3, 5

1. d. DR Depreciation Expense, $11,000

P-34A Journalizing adjusting entries and identifying the impact on financial statements

Dillon Fishing Charters has collected the following data for the December 31 adjusting entries:

a. The company received its electric bill on December 20 for $230 but will not pay it until January 5. (Use the Utilities Payable account.)

b. Dillon purchased a six-month boat insurance policy on November 1 for $4,800. Dillon recorded a debit to Prepaid Insurance.

c. As of December 31, Dillon had earned $2,500 of charter revenue that has not been recorded or received.

d. Dillon's fishing boat was purchased on January 1 at a cost of $60,000. Dillon expects to use the boat for five years and that it will have a residual value of $5,000. Determine annual depreciation assuming the straight-line depreciation method is used.

e. On October 1, Dillon received $8,000 prepayment for a deep-sea fishing charter that will take place in December. As of December 31, Dillon has completed the charter.

Requirements

1. Journalize the adjusting entries needed on December 31 for Dillon Fishing Charters. Assume Dillon records adjusting entries only at the end of the year.

2. If Dillon had not recorded the adjusting entries, indicate which specific category of accounts on the financial statements would be misstated and if the misstatement is overstated or understated. Use the following table as a guide.

Adjusting Entry	Specific Category of Accounts on the Balance Sheet	Over / Understated	Specific Category of Accounts on the Income Statement	Over / Understated

P-35A **Journalizing and posting adjustments to the T-accounts and preparing an adjusted trial balance**

Learning Objectives 3, 4

The unadjusted trial balance of Arlington Air Purification System at December 31, 2014, and the data needed for the adjustments follow.

3. Adjusted trial balance, $70,500 total

ARLINGTON AIR PURIFICATION SYSTEM Unadjusted Trial Balance December 31, 2014		
	Balance	
Account Title	**Debit**	**Credit**
Cash	$ 7,700	
Accounts Receivable	19,200	
Prepaid Rent	2,400	
Office Supplies	1,300	
Equipment	19,900	
Accumulated Depreciation—Equipment		$ 4,300
Accounts Payable		3,600
Salaries Payable		
Unearned Revenue		2,600
Arlington, Capital		39,500
Arlington, Withdrawals	9,500	
Service Revenue		15,400
Salaries Expense	3,500	
Rent Expense		
Depreciation Expense—Equipment		
Advertising Expense	1,900	
Supplies Expense		
Total	$ 65,400	$ 65,400

Adjustment data at December 31 follow:

a. On December 15, Arlington contracted to perform services for a client receiving $2,600 in advance. Arlington recorded this receipt of cash as Unearned Revenue. As of December 31, Arlington has completed $1,100 of the services.

b. Arlington prepaid two months of rent on December 1.

c. Arlington used $600 of office supplies.

d. Depreciation for the equipment is $900.

e. Arlington received a bill for December's online advertising, $900. Arlington will not pay the bill until January. (Use Accounts Payable.)

f. Arlington pays its employees on Monday for the previous weekly wages. Its employees earn $1,500 for a five-day workweek. December 31 falls on Wednesday this year.

g. On October 1, Arlington agreed to provide a four-month air system check (beginning October 1) for a customer for $3,200. Arlington has completed the system check every month, but payment has not yet been received and no entries have been made.

Requirements

1. Journalize the adjusting entries on December 31.

2. Using the unadjusted trial balance, open the T-accounts with the unadjusted balances. Post the adjusting entries to the T-accounts.

3. Prepare the adjusted trial balance.

4. How will Arlington Air Purification System use the adjusted trial balance?

Learning Objectives 3, 4

3. Adjusted trial balance, $449,990 total

P-36A Journalizing and posting adjustments to the four-column accounts and preparing an adjusted trial balance

The unadjusted trial balance of Lexington Inn Company at December 31, 2014, and the data needed for the adjustments follow.

LEXINGTON INN COMPANY Unadjusted Trial Balance December 31, 2014		
	Balance	
Account Title	**Debit**	**Credit**
Cash	$ 12,100	
Accounts Receivable	14,300	
Prepaid Insurance	2,300	
Office Supplies	1,100	
Building	411,000	
Accumulated Depreciation—Building		$ 312,500
Accounts Payable		1,950
Salaries Payable		
Unearned Revenue		2,400
Calvasina, Capital		114,740
Calvasina, Withdrawals	2,860	
Service Revenue		15,600
Salaries Expense	2,700	
Insurance Expense		
Depreciation Expense—Building		
Advertising Expense	830	
Supplies Expense		
Total	$ 447,190	$ 447,190

Adjustment data at December 31 follow:

a. As of December 31, Lexington had $700 of Prepaid Insurance remaining.

b. At the end of the month, Lexington had $600 of office supplies remaining.

c. Depreciation on the building is $1,600.

d. Lexington pays its employees weekly on Friday. Its employees earn $2,000 for a five-day workweek. December 31 falls on Wednesday this year.

e. On November 20, Lexington contracted to perform services for a client receiving $2,400 in advance. Lexington recorded this receipt of cash as Unearned Revenue. As of December 31, Lexington has $1,400 still unearned.

Requirements

1. Journalize the adjusting entries on December 31.

2. Using the unadjusted trial balance, open the accounts (use a four-column ledger) with the unadjusted balances. Post the adjusting entries to the ledger accounts.

3. Prepare the adjusted trial balance.

4. Assuming the adjusted trial balance has total debits equal to total credits, does this mean that the adjusting entries have been recorded correctly? Explain.

P-37A Using the worksheet to record the adjusting journal entries

Galant Theater Production Company's partially completed worksheet as of December 31, 2014, follows.

Learning Objective 6

2. d. CR Accumulated Depreciation, $4,400

	A	B	C	D	E	F	G
1		GALANT THEATER PRODUCTION COMPANY						
2		Worksheet						
3		December 31, 2014						
4								
5	Account Names	Unadjusted Trial Balance		Adjustments		Adjusted Trial Balance	
6		Debit	Credit	Debit	Credit	Debit	Credit
7	Cash	$ 3,900				$ 3,900	
8	Accounts Receivable	6,100				6,900	
9	Office Supplies	1,700				300	
10	Prepaid Insurance	2,700				2,100	
11	Equipment	25,000				25,000	
12	Accumulated Depreciation—Equipment		$ 8,800				$ 13,200
13	Accounts Payable		4,000				4,000
14	Salaries Payable						300
15	Galant, Capital		20,300				20,300
16	Galant, Withdrawals	30,500				30,500	
17	Service Revenue		71,000				71,800
18	Depreciation Expense—Equipment					4,400	
19	Supplies Expense					1,400	
20	Utilities Expense	4,700				4,700	
21	Salaries Expense	29,500				29,800	
22	Insurance Expense					600	
23	Total	$ 104,100	$ 104,100			$ 109,600	$ 109,600
24							

Requirements

1. Analyze the worksheet to determine the adjusting entries that account for the differences between the unadjusted trial balance and the adjusted trial balance. Complete the worksheet. Use letters *a* through *e* to label the five adjustments.

2. Journalize the adjusting entries.

4. Dec 31, CR Insurance Expense,
$3,000

PA-38A Understanding the alternative treatment of prepaid expenses and unearned revenues

Easy Pages Pack'n Mail completed the following transactions during 2014:

Nov. 1	Paid $6,000 store rent covering the three-month period ending January 31, 2015.
Nov. 1	Paid $6,000 insurance covering the four-month period ending February 28, 2015.
Dec. 1	Collected $5,200 cash in advance from customers. The service revenue will be earned $1,300 monthly over the four-month period ending March 31, 2015.
Dec. 1	Collected $4,500 cash in advance from customers. The service revenue will be earned $1,500 monthly over the three-month period ending February 28, 2015.

Requirements

1. Journalize the transactions assuming that Easy Pages debits an asset account for prepaid expenses and credits a liability account for unearned revenues.

2. Journalize the related adjusting entries at December 31, 2014.

3. Post the journal and adjusting entries to the T-accounts, and show their balances at December 31, 2014. (Ignore the Cash account.)

4. Repeat Requirements 1–3. This time debit an expense account for prepaid expenses and credit a revenue account for unearned revenues.

5. Compare the account balances in Requirements 3 and 4. They should be equal.

> Problems **Group B**

P-39B Journalizing adjusting entries and subsequent journal entries

Learning Objective 3

1. b. DR Insurance Expense, $2,750

Lindsey Landscaping has the following data for the December 31 adjusting entries:

a. Each Friday, Lindsey pays employees for the current week's work. The amount of the weekly payroll is $6,500 for a five-day workweek. This year December 31 falls on a Wednesday. Lindsey will pay its employees on January 2.

b. On January 1 of the current year, Lindsey purchases an insurance policy that covers two years, $5,500.

c. The beginning balance of Office Supplies was $4,200. During the year, Lindsey purchased office supplies for $5,100, and at December 31 the office supplies on hand total $2,400.

d. During December, Lindsey designed a landscape plan and the client prepaid $9,000. Lindsey recorded this amount as Unearned Revenue. The job will take several months to complete, and Lindsey estimates that the company has earned 70% of the total revenue during the current year.

e. At December 31, Lindsey had earned $4,000 for landscape services completed for Tomball Appliances. Tomball has stated that they will pay Lindsey on January 10.

f. Depreciation for the current year includes Equipment, $3,600; and Trucks, $1,400.

g. Lindsey has incurred $200 of interest expense on a $500 interest payment due on January 15.

Requirements

1. Journalize the adjusting entry needed on December 31, for each of the previous items affecting Lindsey Landscaping. Assume Lindsey records adjusting entries only at the end of the year.

2. Journalize the subsequent journal entries for adjusting entries *a, d,* and *g.*

P-40B Journalizing adjusting entries and identifying the impact on financial statements

Learning Objectives 3, 5

1. d. DR Depreciation Expense, $9,000

Donald Fishing Charters has collected the following data for the December 31 adjusting entries:

a. The company received its electric bill on December 20 for $400 but will not pay it until January 5. (Use the Utilities Payable account.)

b. Donald purchased a six-month boat insurance policy on November 1 for $1,800. Donald recorded a debit to Prepaid Insurance.

c. As of December 31, Donald had earned $2,300 of charter revenue that has not been recorded or received.

d. Donald's fishing boat was purchased on January 1 at a cost of $50,000. Donald expects to use the boat for five years and that it will have a residual value of $5,000. Determine annual depreciation assuming the straight-line depreciation method is used.

e. On October 1, Donald received $6,000 prepayment for a deep-sea fishing charter that will take place in December. As of December 31, Donald has completed the charter.

The Adjusting Process

Requirements

1. Journalize the adjusting entries needed on December 31 for Donald Fishing Charters. Assume Donald records adjusting entries only at the end of the year.

2. If Donald had not recorded the adjusting entries, indicate which specific category of accounts on the financial statements would be misstated and if the misstatement is overstated or understated. Use the following table as a guide.

Adjusting Entry	Specific Category of Accounts on the Balance Sheet	Over / Understated	Specific Category of Accounts on the Income Statement	Over / Understated

Learning Objectives 3, 4

3. Adjusted trial balance, $68,430 total

P-41B Journalizing and posting adjustments to the T-accounts and preparing an adjusted trial balance

The unadjusted trial balance of Canton Air Purification System at December 31, 2014, and the data needed for the adjustments follow.

CANTON AIR PURIFICATION SYSTEM
Unadjusted Trial Balance
December 31, 2014

	Balance	
Account Title	**Debit**	**Credit**
Cash	$ 7,200	
Accounts Receivable	19,400	
Prepaid Rent	2,200	
Office Supplies	1,600	
Equipment	20,000	
Accumulated Depreciation—Equipment		$ 3,700
Accounts Payable		3,400
Salaries Payable		
Unearned Revenue		2,600
Canton, Capital		39,000
Canton, Withdrawals	9,600	
Service Revenue		15,900
Salaries Expense	3,300	
Rent Expense		
Depreciation Expense—Equipment		
Advertising Expense	1,300	
Supplies Expense		
Total	$ 64,600	$ 64,600

Adjustment data at December 31 follow:

a. On December 15, Canton contracted to perform services for a client receiving $2,000 in advance. Canton recorded this receipt of cash as Unearned Revenue. As of December 31, Canton has completed $1,800 of the services.

b. Canton prepaid two months of rent on December 1.

c. Canton used $400 of office supplies during the month.

d. Depreciation for the equipment is $700.

e. Canton received a bill for December's online advertising, $400. Canton will not pay the bill until January. (Use Accounts Payable.)

f. Canton pays its employees weekly on Monday for the previous week's wages. Its employees earn $2,000 for a five-day workweek. December 31 falls on Wednesday this year.

g. On October 1, Canton agreed to provide a four-month air system check (beginning October 1) for a customer for $2,040. Canton has completed the system check every month, but payment has not yet been received and no entries have been made.

Requirements

1. Journalize the adjusting entries on December 31.

2. Using the unadjusted trial balance, open the T-accounts with the unadjusted balances. Post the adjusting entries to the T-accounts.

3. Prepare the adjusted trial balance.

4. How will Canton Air Purification System use the adjusted trial balance?

P-42B Journalizing and posting adjustments to the four-column accounts and preparing an adjusted trial balance

Learning Objectives 3, 4

The unadjusted trial balance of Concord Bed and Breakfast Company at December 31, 2014, and the data needed for the adjustments follow.

3. Adjusted trial balance, $474,090 total

CONCORD BED AND BREAKFAST COMPANY Unadjusted Trial Balance December 31, 2014		
	Balance	
Account Title	**Debit**	**Credit**
Cash	$ 12,000	
Accounts Receivable	14,400	
Prepaid Insurance	2,800	
Office Supplies	1,400	
Building	435,000	
Accumulated Depreciation—Building		$ 310,500
Accounts Payable		1,930
Salaries Payable		
Unearned Revenue		3,000
Calvasina, Capital		141,060
Calvasina, Withdrawals	2,940	
Service Revenue		15,700
Salaries Expense	2,800	
Insurance Expense		
Depreciation Expense—Building		
Advertising Expense	850	
Supplies Expense		
Total	$ 472,190	$ 472,190

The Adjusting Process

Adjustment data at December 31 follow:

a. As of December 31, Concord had $900 of Prepaid Insurance remaining.

b. At the end of the month, Concord had $900 of office supplies remaining.

c. Depreciation on the building is $1,000.

d. Concord pays its employees on Friday for the weekly salaries. Its employees earn $1,500 for a five-day workweek. December 31 falls on Wednesday this year.

e. On November 20, Concord contracted to perform services for a client receiving $3,000 in advance. Concord recorded this receipt of cash as Unearned Revenue. As of December 31, Concord has $2,200 still unearned.

Requirements

1. Journalize the adjusting entries on December 31.

2. Using the unadjusted trial balance, open the accounts (use a four-column ledger) with the unadjusted balances. Post the adjusting entries to the ledger accounts.

3. Prepare the adjusted trial balance.

4. Assuming the adjusted trial balance has total debits equal to total credits, does this mean that the adjusting entries have been recorded correctly? Explain.

Learning Objective 6

2. d. CR Accumulated Depreciation, $3,500

P-43B Using the worksheet to record the adjusting journal entries

Showtime Theater Production Company's partially completed worksheet as of December 31, 2014, follows.

Account Names	Unadjusted Trial Balance		Adjustments		Adjusted Trial Balance	
	Debit	Credit	Debit	Credit	Debit	Credit
SHOWTIME THEATER PRODUCTION COMPANY						
Worksheet						
December 31, 2014						
Cash	$ 3,500				$ 3,500	
Accounts Receivable	6,000				6,900	
Office Supplies	1,300				500	
Prepaid Insurance	2,100				1,300	
Equipment	23,000				23,000	
Accumulated Depreciation—Equipment		$ 8,100				$ 11,600
Accounts Payable		5,000				5,000
Salaries Payable						500
Webber, Capital		21,100				21,100
Webber, Withdrawals	28,500				28,500	
Service Revenue		59,600				60,500
Depreciation Expense—Equipment					3,500	
Supplies Expense					800	
Utilities Expense	5,400				5,400	
Salaries Expense	24,000				24,500	
Insurance Expense					800	
Total	**$ 93,800**	**$ 93,800**			**$ 98,700**	**$ 98,700**

Requirements

1. Analyze the worksheet to determine the adjusting entries that account for the differences between the unadjusted trial balance and the adjusted trial balance. Complete the worksheet. Use letters *a* through *e* to label the five adjustments.

2. Journalize the adjusting entries.

PA-44B Understanding the alternative treatment of prepaid expenses and unearned revenues

Quick Mail completed the following transactions during 2014:

**Learning Objectives 3, 7
Appendix A**

4. Dec 31, CR Insurance Expense, $1,600

Nov. 1	Paid $4,500 store rent covering the three-month period ending January 31, 2015.
1	Paid $3,200 insurance covering the four-month period ending February 28, 2015.
Dec. 1	Collected $4,800 cash in advance from customers. The service revenue will be earned $1,200 monthly over the four-month period ending March 31, 2015.
1	Collected $5,400 cash in advance from customers. The service revenue will be earned $1,800 monthly over the three-month period ending February 28, 2015.

Requirements

1. Journalize the transactions assuming that Quick Mail debits an asset account for prepaid expenses and credits a liability account for unearned revenues.

2. Journalize the related adjusting entries at December 31, 2014.

3. Post the journal and adjusting entries to the T-accounts, and show their balances at December 31, 2014. (Ignore the Cash account.)

4. Repeat Requirements 1–3. This time debit an expense account for prepaid expenses and credit a revenue account for unearned revenues.

5. Compare the account balances in Requirements 3 and 4. They should be equal.

> Continuing Problem

P-45 Preparing adjusting entries and preparing an adjusted trial balance

This problem uses the example of Davis Consulting. You will need to use the unadjusted trial balance and posted T-accounts that you prepared in Problem P2-43. The unadjusted trial balance at December 31, 2014 is duplicated below:

GL

DAVIS CONSULTING Unadjusted Trial Balance December 31, 2014		
	Balance	
Account Title	**Debit**	**Credit**
Cash	$ 16,400	
Accounts Receivable	1,200	
Office Supplies	900	
Equipment	1,800	
Furniture	4,200	
Accounts Payable		$ 4,700
Unearned Revenue		1,400
Davis, Capital		18,000
Davis, Withdrawals	1,400	
Service Revenue		2,600
Rent Expense	550	
Utilities Expense	250	
Total	$ 26,700	$ 26,700

At December 31, the business gathers the following information for the adjusting entries:

a. Accrued service revenue, $550.

b. Earned $700 of the service revenue collected in advance on December 21.

c. Office supplies on hand, $200.

d. Depreciation on equipment, $30; Depreciation on furniture, $70.

e. Accrued $685 expense for administrative assistant's salary.

Requirements

1. Journalize and post the adjusting entries using the T-accounts that you completed in Problem P2-43. In the T-accounts, denote each adjusting amount as *Adj.* and an account balance as *Balance*.

2. Prepare an adjusted trial balance as of December 31, 2014.

> Practice Set

P-46 Preparing adjusting entries and preparing an adjusted trial balance

This problem uses the example of Shine King Cleaning. Start from the unadjusted trial balance that Shine King Cleaning prepared at November 30, 2015, as follows:

		SHINE KING CLEANING Unadjusted Trial Balance November 30, 2015	
		Balance	
Account Title		**Debit**	**Credit**
Cash		$ 73,100	
Accounts Receivable		2,000	
Cleaning Supplies		270	
Prepaid Rent		2,000	
Prepaid Insurance		2,400	
Equipment		2,200	
Truck		8,000	
Accounts Payable			$ 945
Unearned Revenue			3,600
Notes Payable			40,000
Hudson, Capital			43,000
Hudson, Withdrawals		600	
Service Revenue			3,800
Salaries Expense		500	
Advertising Expense		100	
Utilities Expense		175	
Total		$ 91,345	$ 91,345

Consider the following adjustment data:

a. Cleaning supplies on hand at the end of November were $50.

b. One month's combined depreciation on all depreciable assets was estimated to be $170.

c. One month's interest expense is $100.

Requirements

1. Using the data provided from the trial balance and the previous adjustment information, (P2-44) prepare all required adjusting journal entries at November 30.

2. Prepare an adjusted trial balance as of November 30 for Shine King Cleaning.

CRITICAL THINKING

> Decision Cases

Decision Case 1

Lee Nicholas has been the owner and operator of World.com Advertising since its beginning 10 years ago. The company has prospered. Recently, Nicholas mentioned that he would sell the business for the right price.

Assume that you are interested in buying World.com Advertising. You obtain the most recent monthly trial balance, which follows. Revenues and expenses vary little from month to month, and January is a typical month. The trial balance shown is a preliminary or unadjusted trial balance. The controller informs you that the necessary accrual adjustments should include revenues of $3,800 and expenses of $1,100. Also, if you were to buy World.com Advertising, you would hire a manager so you could devote your time to other duties. Assume that this person would require a monthly salary of $5,000.

WORLD.COM ADVERTISING
Trial Balance
January 31, 2015

Account Title	Debit	Credit
	Balance	
Cash	$ 9,700	
Accounts Receivable	14,100	
Prepaid Expenses	2,600	
Building	221,300	
Accumulated Depreciation—Building		$ 68,600
Accounts Payable		13,000
Salaries Payable		
Unearned Revenue		56,700
Nicholas, Capital		110,400
Nicholas, Withdrawals	9,000	
Service Revenue		12,300
Rent Expense		
Salaries Expense	3,400	
Utilities Expense	900	
Depreciation Expense—Building		
Supplies Expense		
Total	$ 261,000	$ 261,000

Requirements

1. Assume that the most you would pay for the business is 20 times the monthly net income *you could expect to earn* from it. Compute this possible price.

2. Nicholas states the least he will take for the business is an amount equal to the business's owner's equity balance on January 31. Compute this amount.

3. Under these conditions, how much should you offer Nicholas? Give your reason.

Decision Case 2

One year ago, Tyler Stasney founded Swift Classified Ads. Stasney remembers that you took an accounting course while in college and comes to you for advice. He wishes to know how much net income his business earned during the past year in order to decide whether to keep the company going. His accounting records consist of the T-accounts from his ledger, which were prepared by an accountant who moved to another city. The ledger at December 31 follows. The accounts have *not* been adjusted.

Cash		Accounts Receivable		Prepaid Rent		Office Supplies	
Dec. 31 5,800		Dec. 31 12,000		Jan. 2 2,800		Jan. 2 2,600	

Equipment		Accumulated Depreciation—Equipment				Accounts Payable	
Jan. 2 36,000							21,500 Dec. 31

Unearned Revenue		Salaries Payable					
	4,000 Dec. 31						

		Stasney, Capital		Stasney, Withdrawals		Service Revenue	
			20,000 Dec. 31	Dec. 31 28,000			59,500 Dec. 31

Salaries Expense		Depreciation Expense—Equipment		Rent Expense		Utilities Expense	
Dec. 31 17,000						Dec. 31 800	

Supplies Expense	

Stasney indicates that at year-end, customers owe him $1,600 for accrued service revenue. These revenues have not been recorded. During the year, Stasney collected $4,000 service revenue in advance from customers, but he earned only $900 of that amount. Rent expense for the year was $2,400, and he used up $1,700 of the supplies. Stasney determines that depreciation on his equipment was $5,000 for the year. At December 31, he owes his employee $1,200 accrued salary.

Help Stasney compute his net income for the year. Advise him whether to continue operating Swift Classified Ads.

> Ethical Issue 1

The net income of Steinbach & Sons, a landscaping company, decreased sharply during 2015. Mort Steinbach, manager of the company, anticipates the need for a bank loan in 2016. Late in 2015, Steinbach instructs the company's accountant to record $2,000 service revenue for landscape services for the Steinbach family, even though the services will not be performed until January 2016. Steinbach also tells the accountant *not* to make the following December 31, 2015, adjusting entries:

Salaries owed to employees	$900
Prepaid insurance that has expired	400

Requirements

1. Compute the overall effects of these transactions on the company's reported net income for 2015.

2. Why is Steinbach taking this action? Is his action ethical? Give your reason, identifying the parties helped and the parties harmed by Steinbach's action.

3. As a personal friend, what advice would you give the accountant?

> Fraud Case 1

XM, Ltd. was a small engineering firm that built high-tech robotic devices for electronics manufacturers. One very complex device was partially completed at the end of 2015. Barb McLauren, head engineer and owner, knew the experimental technology was a failure and XM would not be able to complete the $20,000,000 contract next year. However, she was getting ready to sell the company and retire in January. She told the controller that the device was 80% complete at year-end and on track for successful completion the following spring; the controller accrued 80% of the contract revenue at December 31, 2015. McLauren sold the company in January 2016 and retired. By mid-year, it became apparent that XM would not be able to complete the project successfully and the new owner would never recoup his investment.

Requirements

1. For complex, high-tech contracts, how does a company determine the percentage of completion and the amount of revenue to accrue?

2. What action do you think was taken by XM in 2016 with regard to the revenue that had been accrued the previous year?

> Financial Statement Case 1

Starbucks Corporation—like all other businesses—makes adjusting entries at year-end in order to measure assets, liabilities, revenues, and expenses properly. Examine Starbucks Corporation's Balance Sheet and Income Statement. Visit **www.pearsonhighered.com/Horngren** to view a link to Starbucks Corporation's Fiscal 2011 Annual Report.

Requirements

1. Which asset accounts might Starbucks record adjusting entries for?

2. Which liability accounts might Starbucks record adjusting entries for?

3. Review Note 1 (Property, Plant and Equipment) in the Notes to Consolidated Financial Statements. How are property, plant, and equipment carried on the balance sheet? How is depreciation of these assets calculated? What is the range of useful lives used when depreciating these assets?

> Team Project 1

It's Just Lunch is a nationwide service company that arranges lunch dates for clients. It's Just Lunch collects cash up front for a package of dates. Suppose your group is opening an It's Just Lunch office in your area. You must make some important decisions—where to locate, how to advertise, and so on—and you must also make some accounting decisions. For example, what will be the end of your business's accounting year? How often will you need financial statements to evaluate operating performance and financial position? Will you use the cash basis or the accrual basis? When will you account for the revenue that the business earns? How will you account for the expenses?

Requirements

Write a report (or prepare an oral presentation, as directed by your professor) to address the following considerations:

1. Will the business use the cash basis or the accrual basis of accounting? Give a complete explanation of your reasoning.

2. How often will financial statements be prepared? Why? Discuss how the business will use each financial statement.

3. What kind of revenue will the business earn? When will the business record it as revenue?

4. What kind of expenses will the business incur? When will expenses be recorded?

> Communication Activity 1

In 75 words or fewer, explain adjusting journal entries.

Try It! Solutions

1. Service Revenue = cash received = $105,000

   Expenses = cash paid = $85,000 − $10,000 + $5,000 = $80,000

2. Service Revenue = revenue earned = $130,000

   Expenses = expense incurred = $85,000

3. b

4. a

5. c

6. **a.** prepaid

   b. accrual

   c. prepaid

   d. accrual

   e. prepaid

7.

Date	Accounts and Explanation	Debit	Credit
(a)	Depreciation Expense—Equipment	1,500	
	Accumulated Depreciation—Equipment		1,500
	To record depreciation on equipment.		
(b)	Advertising Expense	700	
	Advertising Payable		700
	To accrue advertising expense.		
(c)	Supplies Expense	350	
	Office Supplies		350
	To record office supplies used. ($600–$250)		
(d)	Accounts Receivable	1,200	
	Rent Revenue		1,200
	To accrue rent revenue.		
(e)	Unearned Revenue	3,000	
	Service Revenue		3,000
	To record service revenue earned that was collected in advance.		

8.

HOOTEN CARPENTRY		
Adjusted Trial Balance		
December 31, 2015		
	Balance	
Account Title	**Debit**	**Credit**
Cash	$ 4,025	
Accounts Receivable	660	
Office Supplies	120	
Equipment	10,000	
Accumulated Depreciation—Equipment		$ 1,000
Land	5,000	
Accounts Payable		225
Utilities Payable		210
Unearned Revenue		300
Hooten, Capital		8,400
Hooten, Withdrawals	500	
Service Revenue		12,000
Salaries Expense	550	
Depreciation Expense—Equipment	800	
Supplies Expense	80	
Utilities Expense	400	
Total	$ 22,135	$ 22,135

9.

a. income statement: Supplies Expense understated, Net income overstated; balance sheet: Office Supplies overstated, Equity overstated

b. income statement: Service Revenue understated, Net income understated; balance sheet: Accounts Receivable understated, Equity understated

c. income statement: Depreciation Expense understated, Net income overstated; balance sheet: Accumulated Depreciation understated making total assets overstated, Equity overstated

d. income statement: Insurance Expense understated, Net income overstated; balance sheet: Prepaid Insurance overstated, Equity overstated

e. income statement: Salaries Expense understated, Net income overstated; balance sheet: Salaries Payable understated, equity overstated

f. income statement: Service Revenue understated, Net income understated; balance sheet: Unearned Revenue overstated, Equity understated

10.

	Unadjusted Trial Balance			Adjustments			Adjusted Trial Balance			Income Statement		Balance Sheet	

SAM'S DELIVERY SERVICE
Worksheet
December 31, 2014

Account Names	Unadjusted Trial Balance			Adjustments			Adjusted Trial Balance		Income Statement		Balance Sheet	
	Debit	Credit		Debit	Credit		Debit	Credit	Debit	Credit	Debit	Credit
Cash	$ 6,500						$ 6,500					
Accounts Receivable	800		(g)	$ 225			1,025					
Office Supplies	250				$ 80	(b)	170					
Prepaid Rent	1,000				800	(a)	200					
Delivery Van	23,000						23,000					
Accumulated Depreciation—Delivery Van					750	(c)		$ 750				
Equipment	15,000						15,000					
Accumulated Depreciation—Equipment					300	(d)		300				
Accounts Payable		$ 800						800				
Utilities Payable		230						230				
Salaries Payable					875	(f)		875				
Unearned Revenue		400	(e)	130				270				
Sam, Capital		37,800						37,800				
Sam, Withdrawals	8,000						8,000					
Delivery Revenue		23,000			355	(e, g)		23,355				
Rent Expense	3,000		(a)	800			3,800					
Salaries Expense	4,500		(f)	875			5,375					
Supplies Expense			(b)	80			80					
Utilities Expense	180						180					
Depreciation Expense—Delivery Van			(c)	750			750					
Depreciation Expense—Equipment			(d)	300			300					
Total	**$ 62,230**	**$ 62,230**		**$ 3,160**	**$ 3,160**		**$ 64,380**	**$ 64,380**				

11A.

Date	Accounts and Explanation	Debit	Credit
	Supplies Expense	1,000	
	Cash		1,000
	To record the purchase of printing supplies.		
	Printing Supplies	300	
	Supplies Expense		300
	To record printing supplies remaining.		

> Quick Check Answers

1. a **2.** a **3.** b **4.** c **5.** a **6.** a **7.** b **8.** d **9.** c **10A.** b

Glossary

Accrual Basis Accounting. Accounting method that records revenues when earned and expenses when incurred.

Accrued Expense. An expense that the business has incurred but has not yet paid.

Accrued Revenue. A revenue that has been earned but for which the cash has not yet been collected.

Accumulated Depreciation. The sum of all the depreciation expense recorded to date for a depreciable asset.

Adjusted Trial Balance. A list of all the accounts with their adjusted balances.

Adjusting Entry. An entry made at the end of the accounting period that is used to record revenues to the period in which they are earned and expenses to the period in which they occur.

Book Value. A depreciable asset's cost minus accumulated depreciation.

Cash Basis Accounting. Accounting method that records revenue only when cash is received and expenses only when cash is paid.

Contra Account. An account that is paired with, and is listed immediately after, its related account in the chart of accounts and associated financial statement, and whose normal balance is the opposite of the normal balance of the related account.

Deferred Revenue. A liability created when a business collects cash from customers in advance of completing a service or delivering a product.

Depreciation. The process by which businesses spread the allocation of a plant asset's cost over its useful life.

Fiscal Year. An accounting year of any twelve consecutive months that may or may not coincide with the calendar year.

Matching Principle. Guides accounting for expenses, ensures that all expenses are recorded when they are incurred during the period, and matches those expenses against the revenues of the period.

Plant Assets. Long-lived, tangible assets, such as land, buildings, and equipment, used in the operation of a business.

Residual Value. The value of a depreciable asset at the end of its useful life.

Revenue Recognition Principle. Requires companies to record revenue when it has been earned and determines the amount of revenue to record.

Straight-Line Method. A depreciation method that allocates an equal amount of depreciation each year. (Cost − Residual value) / Useful life.

Time Period Concept. Assumes that a business's activities can be sliced into small time segments and that financial statements can be prepared for specific periods, such as a month, quarter, or year.

Worksheet. An internal document that helps summarize data for the preparation of financial statements.

Photo Credits

Completing the Accounting Cycle

From Chapter 4 of *Horngren's Accounting*, Tenth edition. Tracie Nobles, Brenda Mattison, Ella Mae Matsumura. Copyright © 2014 by Pearson Education, Inc. All rights reserved.

Completing the Accounting Cycle

It's the End of the Year, Now What?

Christina Merthieu, owner of Bear Paw Inn, just celebrated her business's one-year anniversary. Christina is excited that she has one year of experience running a successful business under her belt. Although her previous job of working as a resort manager has helped her in dealing with customers, she has had to learn a lot about the accounting side of the business. Christina attributes her first-year success to always offering exceptional quality and personal service to her customers. In addition, Christina found a great accountant who has been helping her with the books.

From the beginning, Christina relied on her accountant to provide advice about recording transactions throughout the year. Now that she has completed her first year of business, she is ready to complete the final accounting tasks of the year. Christina's accountant has told her that she can now prepare financial statements to help her evaluate the inn's profit for the year and its financial position. Christina will use those financial statements to assess her business's performance over the past year. Christina is also ready to start her next year of business, and in order to do this, she must get the books ready for next year by recording closing entries.

What Happens at Year End?

As we saw with Christina and the Bear Paw Inn, businesses have special tasks that have to be completed at the end of the accounting cycle. These tasks help the business in evaluating the past year's operations and also prepare the business to start a new year. For example, Four Seasons Hotels and Resorts must prepare annual financial statements that report on the business's profit or loss for the year and its financial position at the end of the year. In addition, Four Seasons must prepare its books for next year—a process that is called closing the books, which consists of journalizing closing entries and updating the capital account for the year. These final tasks in the accounting cycle are what you learn about in this chapter.

chapter outline

How do we prepare financial statements?

How could a worksheet help in preparing financial statements?

What is the closing process, and how do we close the accounts?

How do we prepare a post-closing trial balance?

What is the accounting cycle?

How do we use the current ratio to evaluate business performance?

What are reversing entries? (Appendix A)

Learning Objectives

1   Prepare the financial statements including the classified balance sheet

2   Use the worksheet to prepare financial statements

3   Explain the purpose of, journalize, and post closing entries

4   Prepare the post-closing trial balance

5   Describe the accounting cycle

6   Use the current ratio to evaluate business performance

7   Explain the purpose of and journalize reversing entries (Appendix A)

Our fictitious company, Smart Touch Learning, has completed the adjusting entries necessary to properly measure net income on the income statement and assets and liabilities on the balance sheet. Now that its accounts are up to date, Smart Touch Learning is ready to take the next step in the accounting cycle—preparing the financial statements. In this chapter, you review financial statements and learn how to prepare a more complete version of the balance sheet. In addition, you complete the accounting cycle by learning how to close the books.

HOW DO WE PREPARE FINANCIAL STATEMENTS?

Learning Objective 1

Prepare the financial statements including the classified balance sheet

The financial statements of Smart Touch Learning are prepared from the adjusted trial balance. Exhibit 1 shows the adjusted trial balance for Smart Touch Learning. In the right margin of the exhibit, we see how the accounts are distributed to the financial statements.

As always, the financial statements should be prepared in the following order:

1. **Income statement**—reports revenues and expenses and calculates net income or net loss for the time period.
2. **Statement of owner's equity**—shows how capital changed during the period due to owner contributions, net income (or net loss), and owner withdrawals.
3. **Balance sheet**—reports assets, liabilities, and owner's equity as of the last day of the period.

IFRS

Internationally, companies must present an income statement, a statement of owners' equity and a classified balance sheet— the same as U.S. companies. Yet, the statements may look quite different. Revenue may be called "Turnover" and Net Income may be called "Profit." On the Balance Sheet, assets and liabilities are presented in different order. Cash is often one of the last assets listed.

Exhibit 1 | **Adjusted Trial Balance**

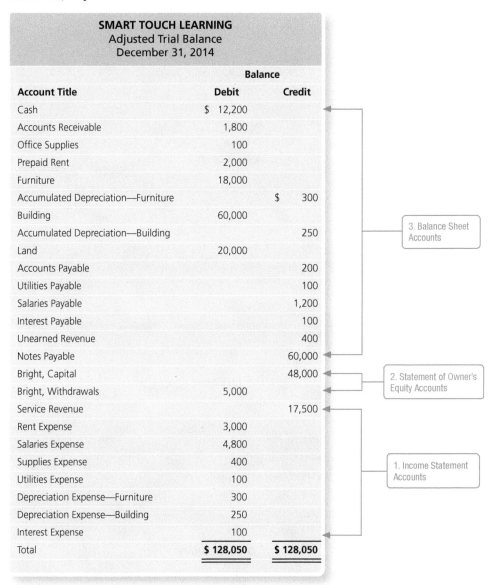

Account Title	Debit	Credit
Cash	$ 12,200	
Accounts Receivable	1,800	
Office Supplies	100	
Prepaid Rent	2,000	
Furniture	18,000	
Accumulated Depreciation—Furniture		$ 300
Building	60,000	
Accumulated Depreciation—Building		250
Land	20,000	
Accounts Payable		200
Utilities Payable		100
Salaries Payable		1,200
Interest Payable		100
Unearned Revenue		400
Notes Payable		60,000
Bright, Capital		48,000
Bright, Withdrawals	5,000	
Service Revenue		17,500
Rent Expense	3,000	
Salaries Expense	4,800	
Supplies Expense	400	
Utilities Expense	100	
Depreciation Expense—Furniture	300	
Depreciation Expense—Building	250	
Interest Expense	100	
Total	$ 128,050	$ 128,050

SMART TOUCH LEARNING
Adjusted Trial Balance
December 31, 2014
Balance

3. Balance Sheet Accounts

2. Statement of Owner's Equity Accounts

1. Income Statement Accounts

The financial statements for Smart Touch Learning are presented in Exhibit 2.

Relationships Among the Financial Statements

The arrows in Exhibit 2 show how the financial statements relate to each other.

1. Net income from the income statement increases capital. A net loss decreases capital.
2. Ending capital from the statement of owner's equity goes to the balance sheet and makes total liabilities plus owner's equity equal total assets, satisfying the accounting equation.

To solidify your understanding of these relationships, trace net income from the income statement to the statement of owner's equity. Then trace ending Bright, Capital to the balance sheet. The statements are always prepared in this order: income statement, then statement of owner's equity, and then balance sheet.

Exhibit 2 | Smart Touch Learning Financial Statements

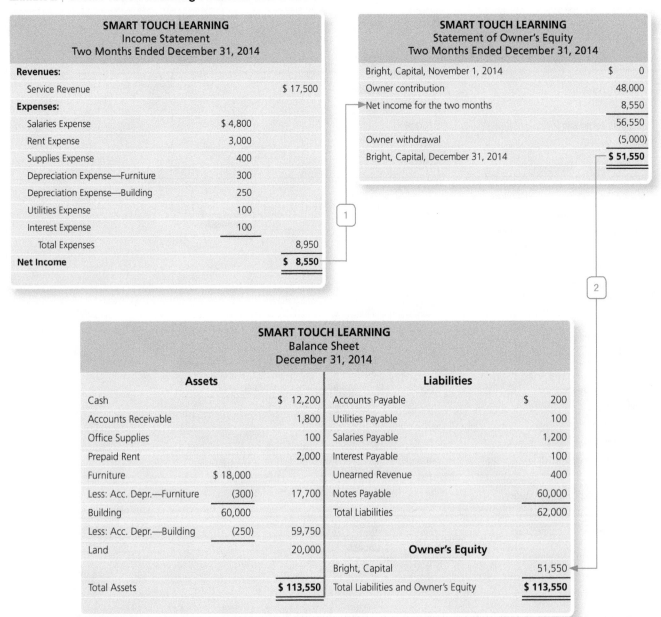

SMART TOUCH LEARNING
Income Statement
Two Months Ended December 31, 2014

Revenues:		
Service Revenue		$ 17,500
Expenses:		
Salaries Expense	$ 4,800	
Rent Expense	3,000	
Supplies Expense	400	
Depreciation Expense—Furniture	300	
Depreciation Expense—Building	250	
Utilities Expense	100	
Interest Expense	100	
Total Expenses		8,950
Net Income		**$ 8,550**

SMART TOUCH LEARNING
Statement of Owner's Equity
Two Months Ended December 31, 2014

Bright, Capital, November 1, 2014	$ 0
Owner contribution	48,000
Net income for the two months	8,550
	56,550
Owner withdrawal	(5,000)
Bright, Capital, December 31, 2014	**$ 51,550**

SMART TOUCH LEARNING
Balance Sheet
December 31, 2014

Assets			Liabilities		
Cash		$ 12,200	Accounts Payable	$	200
Accounts Receivable		1,800	Utilities Payable		100
Office Supplies		100	Salaries Payable		1,200
Prepaid Rent		2,000	Interest Payable		100
Furniture	$ 18,000		Unearned Revenue		400
Less: Acc. Depr.—Furniture	(300)	17,700	Notes Payable		60,000
Building	60,000		Total Liabilities		62,000
Less: Acc. Depr.—Building	(250)	59,750			
Land		20,000	**Owner's Equity**		
			Bright, Capital		51,550
Total Assets		**$ 113,550**	Total Liabilities and Owner's Equity		**$ 113,550**

Classified Balance Sheet

Classified Balance Sheet
A balance sheet that places each asset and each liability into a specific category.

Liquidity
A measure of how quickly an item can be converted to cash.

So far we have presented the *unclassified* balance sheet of Smart Touch Learning. We are now ready for the balance sheet that is actually used in practice—called a classified balance sheet. In a classified balance sheet, each asset and each liability are placed into a specific category.

In a classified balance sheet, assets and liabilities are classified as either *current* (within one year) or *long-term* (more than one year) to show their relative liquidity. Liquidity measures how quickly and easily an account can be converted to cash (because cash is the most liquid asset). Accounts Receivable are relatively liquid because receivables are collected quickly. Office Supplies are less liquid, and Furniture and Buildings are even less so because they take longer to convert to cash or to be used up.

Assets

The balance sheet lists assets in order of liquidity. A classified balance sheet reports two asset categories: *current assets* and *long-term assets*.

Current assets will be converted to cash, sold, or used up during the next 12 months, or within the business's operating cycle if the cycle is longer than a year. The operating cycle is the time span when

1. Cash is used to acquire goods and services.
2. These goods and services are sold to customers.
3. The business collects cash from customers.

For most businesses, the operating cycle is a few months. Cash, Accounts Receivable, Office Supplies, and Prepaid Expenses are examples of current assets.

Long-term assets are all the assets that will not be converted to cash or used up within the business's operating cycle or one year, whichever is greater. Long-term assets are typically made up of three categories: long-term investments, plant assets, and intangible assets.

Long-term Investments Notes Receivable and other investments that are held long-term are considered long-term investments and include investments in bonds or stocks in which the company intends to hold the investment for longer than one year.

Plant Assets Another category of long-term assets is plant assets (also called *fixed assets* or *property, plant, and equipment*). Land, Buildings, Furniture, and Equipment are plant assets. Plant assets are also presented in order of liquidity, with assets such as Furniture and Equipment being presented first and Land presented last.

Intangible Assets Assets with no physical form are intangible assets. Examples of intangible assets include patents, copyrights, and trademarks. Intangible assets are long-term assets that convey special rights, such as the exclusive right to produce or sell an invention or book (patent and copyright) or the representation of a distinctive brand (trademark).

Liabilities

The balance sheet lists liabilities in the order in which they must be paid. The two liability categories reported on the balance sheet are *current liabilities* and *long-term liabilities*.

Current liabilities must be paid either with cash or with goods and services within one year, or within the entity's operating cycle if the cycle is longer than a year. Accounts Payable, Notes Payable due within one year, Salaries Payable, Interest Payable, and Unearned Revenue are all current liabilities. Any portion of a long-term liability that is due within the next year is also reported as a current liability. Current liabilities are listed in the order that they are due.

Long-term liabilities are all liabilities that do not need to be paid within one year or within the entity's operating cycle, whichever is longer. Many Notes Payable are long-term, such as a mortgage on a building.

Owner's Equity

Owner's equity represents the owner's claim to the assets of the business. The owner's equity reported on the balance sheet is transferred from the ending balance on the statement of owner's equity. The equity balance reflects the owner's contributions, net income or net loss of the business, and owner's withdrawals. It represents the amount of assets that is left over after the company has paid its liabilities.

Exhibit 3 presents Smart Touch Learning's classified balance sheet. Notice that the company classifies each asset and each liability as either current or long-term and

Current Assets
Assets that are expected to be converted to cash, sold, or used up during the next 12 months, or within the business's normal operating cycle if the cycle is longer than a year.

Operating Cycle
The time span during which cash is paid for goods and services, which are then sold to customers from whom the business collects cash.

Long-Term Assets
All assets that will not be converted to cash or used up within the business's operating cycle or one year, whichever is greater.

Long-Term Investments
A long-term asset category that includes investments in bonds or stocks in which the company intends to hold the investment for longer than one year.

Plant Assets
A long-term asset category that includes property, plant, and equipment.

Intangible Assets
A long-term asset category that includes assets with no physical form, such as patents, copyrights, and trademarks.

Current Liabilities
Liabilities that must be paid with cash or with goods and services within one year, or within the entity's operating cycle if the cycle is longer than a year.

Long-Term Liabilities
Liabilities that do not need to be paid within one year or within the entity's operating cycle, whichever is longer.

Exhibit 3 | **Classified Balance Sheet**

SMART TOUCH LEARNING Balance Sheet December 31, 2014			
Assets			
Current Assets:			
Cash		$ 12,200	
Accounts Receivable		1,800	
Office Supplies		100	
Prepaid Rent		2,000	
Total Current Assets			$ 16,100
Plant Assets:			
Furniture	$ 18,000		
Less: Accumulated Depreciation—Furniture	(300)	17,700	
Building	60,000		
Less: Accumulated Depreciation—Building	(250)	59,750	
Land		20,000	
Total Plant Assets			97,450
Total Assets			**$ 113,550**
Liabilities			
Current Liabilities:			
Accounts Payable		$ 200	
Utilities Payable		100	
Salaries Payable		1,200	
Interest Payable		100	
Unearned Revenue		400	
Total Current Liabilities			$ 2,000
Long-term Liabilities:			
Notes Payable			60,000
Total Liabilities			62,000
Owner's Equity			
Bright, Capital			51,550
Total Liabilities and Owner's Equity			**$ 113,550**

that the total assets of $113,550 is the same as the total assets on the unclassified balance sheet in Exhibit 2.

Compare the balance sheet in Exhibit 3 with the balance sheet in Exhibit 2. You'll notice two differences. Exhibit 3 is a classified balance sheet, but it is also in a different format than Exhibit 2. The balance sheet in Exhibit 3 is being presented in the *report form*, which lists the assets at the top and liabilities and owner's equity below. Smart Touch Learning's balance sheet in Exhibit 2 lists the assets on the left and the liabilities and the equity on the right in an arrangement known as the *account form*. Although either form is acceptable, the *report form* is more popular.

> **Try It!**

For each account listed, identify the category in which it would appear on a classified balance sheet.

1. Patents
2. Mortgage Payable (due in 5 years)
3. Land
4. Office Supplies
5. Unearned Revenue
6. Investments in stock of another company held long-term
7. Accumulated Depreciation—Furniture

Check your answers at the end of the chapter.

For more practice, see Short Exercises S-1 through S-4. MyAccountingLab

HOW COULD A WORKSHEET HELP IN PREPARING FINANCIAL STATEMENTS?

A worksheet can be used to help prepare adjusting entries. Now you'll learn how the worksheet can be used to help in the preparation of financial statements. Exhibit 4 shows the completed worksheet for Smart Touch Learning. Sections 1 through 4 of the worksheet, shown with a blue background, are already complete. You are now ready to complete the remaining sections that will help in preparing the financial statements.

Learning Objective 2

Use the worksheet to prepare financial statements

Section 5—Income Statement

The income statement section includes only revenue and expense accounts. The revenues and expenses from the adjusted trial balance section will be transferred into the appropriate column in the income statement section. For example, the $17,500 credit balance for Service Revenue in the adjusted trial balance section will be carried over into the credit column in the income statement section. Each column will then be totaled.

Section 6—Balance Sheet

The balance sheet section includes the asset, liability, and equity accounts. The balance of each of these accounts will be transferred from the adjusted trial balance section of the worksheet to the appropriate column in the balance sheet section. For example, Accumulated Depreciation—Furniture, a contra-asset, has a $300 credit balance in the adjusted trial balance section. This amount will be reported as a credit of $300 in the balance sheet section. Each column will then be totaled.

Section 7—Determine Net Income or Net Loss

Compute net income or net loss as total revenues minus total expenses ($17,500 − $8,950). Enter net income (loss) as the balancing amount in the income statement and balance sheet sections. If net income exists, the balance will be entered in the *debit* column of the income

Exhibit 4 | Completed Worksheet

	A	B	C	D	E	F	G	H	I	J	K	L	M
1		SMART TOUCH LEARNING											
2		Worksheet								Section 5		Section 6	
3		December 31, 2014											
4													
5	**Account Names**	**Unadjusted Trial Balance**			**Adjustments**			**Adjusted Trial Balance**		**Income Statement**		**Balance Sheet**	
6		Debit	Credit		Debit	Credit		Debit	Credit	Debit	Credit	Debit	Credit
7	Cash	$ 12,200						$ 12,200				$ 12,200	
8	Accounts Receivable	1,000		(h)	$ 800			1,800				1,800	
9	Office Supplies	500				$ 400	(b)	100				100	
10	Prepaid Rent	3,000				1,000	(a)	2,000				2,000	
11	Furniture	18,000						18,000				18,000	
12	Accumulated Depreciation—Furniture					300	(c)		$ 300				$ 300
13	Building	60,000						60,000				60,000	
14	Accumulated Depreciation—Building					250	(d)		250				250
15	Land	20,000						20,000				20,000	
16	Accounts Payable		$ 200						200				200
17	Utilities Payable		100						100				100
18	Salaries Payable					1,200	(f)		1,200				1,200
19	Interest Payable					100	(g)		100				100
20	Unearned Revenue		600	(e)	200				400				400
21	Notes Payable		60,000						60,000				60,000
22	Bright, Capital		48,000						48,000				48,000
23	Bright, Withdrawals	5,000						5,000				5,000	
24	Service Revenue		16,500			1,000	(e,h)		17,500		$ 17,500		
25	Rent Expense	2,000		(a)	1,000			3,000		$ 3,000			
26	Salaries Expense	3,600		(f)	1,200			4,800		4,800			
27	Supplies Expense			(b)	400			400		400			
28	Utilities Expense	100						100		100			
29	Depreciation Expense—Furniture			(c)	300			300		300			
30	Depreciation Expense—Building			(d)	250			250		250			
31	Interest Expense			(g)	100			100		100			
32	**Total**	$ 125,400	$ 125,400		$ 4,250	$ 4,250		$ 128,050	$ 128,050	$ 8,950	$ 17,500	$ 119,100	$ 110,550
33									Net Income	8,550			8,550
34	**Total**									$ 17,500	$ 17,500	$ 119,100	$ 119,100
35													

Section 7

Section 1-4

Net Income = $17,500 − $8,950

statement section and the *credit* column of the balance sheet section. For example, Smart Touch Learning has net income of $8,550. This amount should be reported as a debit in the income statement section and a credit in the balance sheet section.

If expenses exceed revenues, the result is a net loss. In that event, print Net Loss on the worksheet next to the result. The net loss amount should be entered in the *credit* column of the income statement (to balance out) and in the *debit* column of the balance sheet (to balance out). The main thing to remember is that the net income or net loss is the balancing amount on the worksheet. It should always be recorded on the side that makes the debit and credit columns balance.

Smart Touch Learning has now completed the worksheet as of December 31. Remember that the worksheet is an internal tool that can be used to help in recording adjusting entries and preparing financial statements. The adjusting entries still need to be recorded in the journal and posted to the ledger and the financial statements must still be prepared (as shown in Exhibit 2).

> **Try It!**

For each account listed, identify whether the account would appear in either the income statement section or the balance sheet section of the worksheet. Assuming normal balances, identify if the account would be recorded in the debit (DR) or credit (CR) column.

8. Service Revenue
9. Accounts Payable
10. Cash
11. Depreciation Expense—Building
12. Sandy, Withdrawals
13. Accumulated Depreciation—Building

Check your answers at the end of the chapter.

For more practice, see Short Exercises S-5 through S-7. MyAccountingLab

WHAT IS THE CLOSING PROCESS, AND HOW DO WE CLOSE THE ACCOUNTS?

At the end of the accounting cycle, after the financial statements have been prepared, Smart Touch Learning is ready to close the books. Often referred to as the closing process, this consists of journalizing and posting the closing entries in order to get the accounts ready for the next period. The closing process zeroes out all revenue accounts and all expense accounts in order to measure each period's net income separately from all other periods. It also updates the Capital account balance for net income or loss during the period and any withdrawals made by the owner. The closing process prepares the accounts for the next time period by setting the balances of revenues, expenses, and withdrawals to zero. By completing the closing process, the business is following the time period concept in that it is slicing its activities into small time segments and preparing financial statements for only those specific periods.

Recall that the income statement reports net income for a specific period. For example, the business's net income for the two months ended December 31, 2014 relates exclusively to November and December of 2014. At December 31, 2014, Smart Touch Learning closes its revenue and expense accounts for the last two months of the year. For this reason, revenues and expenses are called temporary accounts (also known as *nominal accounts*). For example, Smart Touch Learning's balance of Service Revenue at December 31, 2014, is $17,500. This balance relates exclusively to the last two months of 2014 and must be zeroed out before the company records revenue for the next year. Similarly, the various expense account balances are for 2014 only and must also be zeroed out at the end of the year.

The Bright, Withdrawals account is also temporary and must be closed at the end of the period because it measures the owner withdrawals for only that one period. All temporary accounts (withdrawals, revenues, and expenses) are closed (zeroed). The balances of temporary accounts do not carry forward into the next time period. Instead, the business starts the new time period with a zero beginning balance in the temporary accounts.

Learning Objective 3
Explain the purpose of, journalize, and post closing entries

Closing Process
A step in the accounting cycle that occurs at the end of the period. The closing process consists of journalizing and posting the closing entries to set the balances of the revenue, expense, and withdrawal accounts to zero for the next period.

Temporary Account
An account that relates to a particular accounting period and is closed at the end of that period—the revenues, expenses, and withdrawal accounts.

Permanent Account

An account that is *not* closed at the end of the period—the asset, liability, and capital accounts.

Closing Entries

Entries that transfer the revenue, expense, and withdrawal balances to the Capital account to prepare the company's books for the next period.

Income Summary

A temporary account into which revenues and expenses are transferred prior to their final transfer into the Capital account. Summarizes net income (or net loss) for the period.

By contrast, the **permanent accounts** (also known as *real accounts*)—the assets, liabilities, and capital—are not closed at the end of the period. Permanent account balances are carried forward into the next time period. All accounts on the balance sheet are permanent accounts.

Closing entries transfer the revenue, expense, and withdrawal balances to the Capital account to prepare the company's books for the next period.

As an intermediate step, the revenues and the expenses may be transferred first to an account titled **Income Summary**. The Income Summary account *summarizes* the net income (or net loss) for the period by collecting the sum of all the expenses (a debit) and the sum of all the revenues (a credit). The Income Summary account is like a temporary "holding tank" that shows the amount of net income or net loss of the current period. Its balance—net income or net loss—is then transferred (closed) to the Capital account (the final account in the closing process). Exhibit 5 summarizes the closing process.

Exhibit 5 | **The Closing Process**

When thinking about which accounts to close, consider your grades in this class as an example. If you made a failing grade on an exam in this class, would you want your exam grade for this class to carry forward to your next accounting class? Your answer would probably be no, because your exam grade in this class does not necessarily represent your knowledge in your next class. In this example, your exam grades are temporary and should not carry forward to your next accounting class. In the same sense, a business's revenues, expenses, and withdrawals for a specific time period should not be carried forward to the next time period because doing so does not accurately reflect that future period.

Shane Wilson is the owner of Dream Builder, a business that specializes in building custom homes, remodeling existing homes, and creating backyard paradises. Shane has just completed his first year of business, and he has been very pleased with his first year of operations. His business is growing and even earned a profit. Shane has just met with his accountant, Felicia Turner, to go over his books for the year and to get ready for next year. Felicia has told him that he will need to close the books for the current year before he can begin recording transactions for next year. Shane is very confused. He doesn't understand and tells Felicia, "I'm not planning on closing my business. It's doing great. Why would I need to close the books?" What should Felicia tell Shane?

Solution

Many new businesses don't realize that they have to close their books each year. Felicia should explain to Shane that closing the books does not imply that the business is closing. Instead, it simply closes the books for the year that has just been completed and prepares the books for a new year. Felicia should explain to Shane that the process of closing the books updates his capital account for the net income and any withdrawals during the year. It allows the business to allocate net income to a specific time period (following the time period concept) and begin the new year with zero balances in all temporary accounts (revenues, expenses, and withdrawals).

Closing Temporary Accounts—Net Income

As stated previously, all temporary accounts are closed (zeroed out) during the closing process. Temporary accounts are not permanent. Only the balance sheet accounts are permanent. The four steps in closing the books follow (and are illustrated in Exhibit 6).

Step 1: Make the revenue accounts equal zero via the Income Summary account. This closing entry transfers total revenues to the *credit* side of the Income Summary account.

For example, Smart Touch Learning has a $17,500 credit balance in Service Revenue. To close this account, we *debit* Service Revenue and *credit* Income Summary.

Service Revenue		Income Summary	
	17,500 Adj. Bal.		17,500 Clos. 1
Clos. 1 17,500			
	0 Bal.		

Date	Accounts and Explanation	Debit	Credit
Dec. 31	Service Revenue	17,500	
	Income Summary		17,500
	To close revenue.		

$$A = \Big\{ L + E\uparrow\downarrow$$

Service Revenue↓
Income Summary↑

Step 2: Make expense accounts equal zero via the Income Summary account. This closing entry transfers total expenses to the *debit* side of the Income Summary account.

As an example, we will review the Rent Expense account for Smart Touch Learning, which has a $3,000 debit balance. This account will be closed with a *credit* to Rent Expense.

Rent Expense	
Adj. Bal. 3,000	
	3,000 Clos. 2
Bal. 0	

Smart Touch Learning will close all expense accounts in the same manner. This will most likely be done with a compound closing entry. Each individual expense account will be *credited* and the Income Summary account will be *debited* for the total amount of expenses.

Date	Accounts and Explanation	Debit	Credit
Dec. 31	Income Summary	8,950	
	Rent Expense		3,000
	Salaries Expense		4,800
	Supplies Expense		400
	Utilities Expense		100
	Depreciation Expense—Furniture		300
	Depreciation Expense—Building		250
	Interest Expense		100
	To close expenses.		

The Income Summary account now holds the net income of $8,550 for the period. The Income Summary T-account after closing revenues and expenses is:

Income Summary

Clos. 2	8,950	17,500	Clos. 1
		8,550	Bal.

Step 3: Make the Income Summary account equal zero via the Capital account. This closing entry transfers net income (or net loss) to the Capital account.

Smart Touch Learning has an $8,550 credit balance in the Income Summary account. This represents net income for the period. Net income will now be transferred to the Capital account. We will *debit* Income Summary and *credit* Bright, Capital. Notice that this closing entry, in effect, increases the Capital account for the net income of the period.

Income Summary

Clos. 2	8,950	17,500	Clos. 1
		8,550	Bal.
Clos. 3	8,550		
		0	Bal.

Bright, Capital

		48,000	Adj. Bal.
		8,550	Clos. 3

Date	Accounts and Explanation	Debit	Credit
Dec. 31	Income Summary	8,550	
	Bright, Capital		8,550
	To close Income Summary.		

Step 4: Make the Withdrawals account equal zero via the Capital account. This entry transfers the withdrawals to the *debit* side of the Capital account.

Completing the Accounting Cycle

Smart Touch Learning has a $5,000 debit balance in the Bright, Withdrawals account. This account will be closed with a *debit* to Bright, Capital and a *credit* to Bright, Withdrawals.

Bright, Capital					Bright, Withdrawals				
		48,000	Adj. Bal.		Adj. Bal.	5,000			
Clos. 4	5,000	8,550	Clos. 3				5,000	Clos. 4	
		51,550	Bal.		Bal.	0			

Date	Accounts and Explanation	Debit	Credit
Dec. 31	Bright, Capital	5,000	
	Bright, Withdrawals		5,000
	To close withdrawals.		

$$A = \left\{ L + E\uparrow\downarrow \right.$$

Bright, Capital↓
Bright, Withdrawals↓

Closing Temporary Accounts—Net Loss

If a business had a net loss for the period, closing entries 1, 2, and 4 would be similar to those completed for net income. However, the closing entry to close the Income Summary account would be different. Consider this example. Suppose a business had a net loss of $2,000. The Income Summary T-account would hold a *debit* balance instead of a *credit* balance. Therefore, the closing entry to close Income Summary, would be a *debit* to Owner, Capital and a *credit* to Income Summary.

> What if a business had a net loss for the period? Would the closing entries be the same?

Income Summary					Owner, Capital				
Clos. 2	5,000	3,000	Clos. 1		Clos. 3	2,000	48,000	Adj. Bal.	
Bal.	2,000								
Net Loss		2,000	Clos. 3						
		0	Bal.						

Date	Accounts and Explanation	Debit	Credit
Dec. 31	Owner, Capital	2,000	
	Income Summary		2,000
	To close Income Summary.		

$$A = \left\{ L + E\uparrow\downarrow \right.$$

Owner, Capital↓
Income Summary↑

Notice that the effect of this closing entry decreases Owner, Capital. This is because a net loss decreases the Capital account.

Exhibit 6 shows the complete closing process for Smart Touch Learning. Panel A gives the closing entries, and Panel B shows the accounts after posting. After the closing entries, Bright, Capital ends with a balance of $51,550. Trace this balance to the statement of owner's equity and then to the balance sheet in Exhibit 2.

Exhibit 6 | Journalizing and Posting Closing Entries

Panel A: Journalizing

Date	Accounts and Explanation	Debit	Credit
Dec. 31	Service Revenue	17,500	
	Income Summary		17,500
	To close revenue.		
31	Income Summary	8,950	
	Rent Expense		3,000
	Salaries Expense		4,800
	Supplies Expense		400
	Utilities Expense		100
	Depreciation Expense—Furniture		300
	Depreciation Expense—Building		250
	Interest Expense		100
	To close expenses		
31	Income Summary	8,550	
	Bright, Capital		8,550
	To close Income Summary.		
31	Bright, Capital	5,000	
	Bright, Withdrawals		5,000
	To close withdrawals.		

When a business uses a computerized accounting system, the software automatically closes the books. The software identifies the temporary accounts, records the closing entries, and posts to the ledger accounts. The closing entries are completed in a matter of seconds.

Panel B: Posting

> Try It!

Benson Auto Repair had the following account balances after adjustments. Assume all accounts had normal balances.

Cash	$ 4,000	Benson, Capital	$ 35,700
Accounts Receivable	3,200	Benson, Withdrawals	2,100
Prepaid Rent	1,900	Service Revenue	1,600
Office Supplies	3,000	Depreciation Expense—Equipment	300
Equipment	34,800	Salaries Expense	800
Accumulated Depreciation—Equipment	1,600	Rent Expense	500
Accounts Payable	5,400	Utilities Expense	600
Notes Payable (long-term)	7,000	Supplies Expense	100

14. Prepare the closing entries for Benson at December 31.
15. What is the balance of Benson, Capital after closing entries have been recorded? (Use a T-account to determine the balance.)

Check your answers at the end of the chapter.

For more practice, see Short Exercises S-8 and S-9. MyAccountingLab

HOW DO WE PREPARE A POST-CLOSING TRIAL BALANCE?

After closing entries are recorded and posted, the accounting cycle ends with a post-closing trial balance (see Exhibit 7). This step lists the accounts and their balances after closing.

Only assets, liabilities, and capital accounts (permanent accounts) appear on the post-closing trial balance. No temporary accounts—revenues, expenses, or withdrawals—are included because they have been closed (their balances are zero). Also notice that the Capital account has been updated to reflect the period's net income (or net loss) and any withdrawals. The ledger is now up to date and ready for the next period.

Learning Objective 4
Prepare the post-closing trial balance

Post-Closing Trial Balance
A list of the accounts and their balances at the end of the period after journalizing and posting the closing entries. It should include only permanent accounts.

Exhibit 7 | Post-Closing Trial Balance

SMART TOUCH LEARNING Post-Closing Trial Balance December 31, 2014		
	Balance	
Account Title	**Debit**	**Credit**
Cash	$ 12,200	
Accounts Receivable	1,800	
Office Supplies	100	
Prepaid Rent	2,000	
Furniture	18,000	
Accumulated Depreciation—Furniture		$ 300
Building	60,000	
Accumulated Depreciation—Building		250
Land	20,000	
Accounts Payable		200
Utilities Payable		100
Salaries Payable		1,200
Interest Payable		100
Unearned Revenue		400
Notes Payable		60,000
Bright, Capital		51,550
Total	$ 114,100	$ 114,100

Permanent Accounts

> **Try It!**

For each account listed, identify whether the account would appear on the post-closing trial balance. Indicate either yes or no.

16. Evans, Withdrawals
17. Service Revenue
18. Cash
19. Advertising Expense
20. Evans, Capital

Check your answers at the end of the chapter.

For more practice, see Short Exercise S-10. MyAccountingLab

WHAT IS THE ACCOUNTING CYCLE?

We have now completed the accounting cycle for Smart Touch Learning. The **accounting cycle** is the process by which companies produce their financial statements for a specific period. It is the steps that are followed throughout the time period. The accounting cycle starts with the beginning asset, liability, and owner's equity account balances left over from the preceding period. Exhibit 8 outlines the complete accounting cycle of Smart Touch Learning and every other business. Start with Step 1 and move clockwise.

Accounting takes place at two different times:

- During the period (Steps 1 through 3)—Journalizing transactions and posting to the accounts
- End of the period (Steps 4 through 10)—Adjusting the accounts, preparing the financial statements, and closing the accounts

Learning Objective 5
Describe the accounting cycle

Accounting Cycle
The process by which companies produce their financial statements for a specific period.

Exhibit 8 | The Accounting Cycle

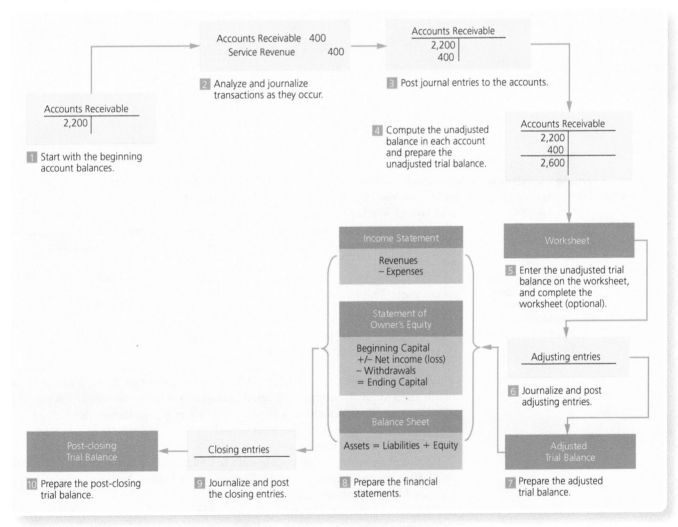

231

> Try It!

21. The steps of the accounting cycle are presented below. Identify the correct order of the steps.

   a. Journalize and post the closing entries.
   b. Start with beginning account balances.
   c. Prepare the financial statements.
   d. Compute the unadjusted balance in each account and prepare the unadjusted trial balance.
   e. Journalize and post adjusting entries.
   f. Enter the unadjusted trial balance on the worksheet and complete the worksheet (optional).
   g. Prepare the adjusted trial balance.
   h. Analyze and journalize transactions as they occur.
   i. Post journal entries to the accounts.
   j. Prepare the post-closing trial balance.

Check your answer at the end of the chapter.

For more practice, see Short Exercise S-11. MyAccountingLab

HOW DO WE USE THE CURRENT RATIO TO EVALUATE BUSINESS PERFORMANCE?

Learning Objective 6
Use the current ratio to evaluate business performance

Current Ratio
Measures the company's ability to pay current liabilities from current assets. Total current assets / Total current liabilities.

Accounting is designed to provide information that business owners, managers, and lenders can use to make decisions. A bank considering lending money to a business must predict whether that business can repay the loan. If a business already has a lot of debt, repayment is less certain than if it does not owe much money. In this chapter, we will introduce another ratio that can be used to measure the business's financial position, the current ratio.

The current ratio measures a company's ability to pay its current liabilities with its current assets. This ratio is computed as follows:

Current ratio = Total current assets / Total current liabilities

A company prefers to have a high current ratio because that means it has plenty of current assets to pay its current liabilities. A current ratio that has increased from the prior period indicates improvement in a company's ability to pay its current debts. A current ratio that has decreased from the prior period signals deterioration in the company's ability to pay its current liabilities.

A rule of thumb: A strong current ratio is 1.50, which indicates that the company has $1.50 in current assets for every $1.00 in current liabilities. A current ratio of 1.00 is considered low and somewhat risky.

We can now evaluate Green Mountain's current ratio. Green Mountain had the following total current assets and current liabilities at the back of the book.

	As of Sep. 24, 2011	As of Sep. 25, 2010
Total current assets (in thousands)	$ 1,131,527	$ 495,269
Total current liabilities (in thousands)	471,374	238,055

The current ratio for Green Mountain as of September 24, 2011, follows:

Current ratio = $1,131,527 / $471,374 = 2.40

In comparison, the current ratio as of September 25, 2010, for Green Mountain was

Current ratio = $495,269 / $238,055 = 2.08

The current ratio has increased slightly from 2010 to 2011. This indicates an increased ability for Green Mountain to pay its current debts. Given that the current ratio is above 1.5 for both years, Green Mountain would be considered a less risky investment than another business with a lower current ratio.

>Ethics   Should revenue be recorded early?

Carnival Custom Painting's owner, Kristi Seay, is hoping to get a loan from her local bank. The business's van engine has just died, and she has no extra cash to replace the engine. Kristi needs a short-term loan of $3,000. Her friend, Brian, is a teller at the bank and has told Kristi that the bank will only approve her for the loan if the business has a current ratio that is above 1.2. Currently, Carnival's current ratio is 1.1. Brian is aware that Kristi has just received a contract for painting a new commercial building. Kristi has told Brian that she expects revenue of $15,000 from the contract but won't receive payment until she completes the job. She plans on starting the job next week, but she won't be finished for another two months, not soon enough to use the cash to replace the engine in the van. Brian has suggested to Kristi that she go ahead and record the revenue and cash receipt of the painting contract even though she hasn't completed it. This, he tells her, will increase her current assets and thereby increase her current ratio to 1.4, well above the bank minimum. What should Kristi do? What would you do?

Solution

Kristi should not record the revenue and cash receipt early. The revenue recognition principle requires that businesses record revenue only when it has been earned. Given that Kristi has not yet started the job, no revenue has been earned. Kristi should look for alternative sources of financing instead of trying to manipulate the current ratio to meet the minimum required by the bank. Another possibility would be for Kristi to renegotiate the contract with the new client to receive $3,000 in advance instead of after the completion of the job. This would allow Kristi to make the repairs on the van and not have to borrow the money from the bank.

> Try It!

22. Benson Auto Repair has the following account balances at December 31, 2015, from its adjusted trial balance. Compute Benson's current ratio.

Cash	$ 4,000	Benson, Capital	$ 35,700
Accounts Receivable	3,200	Benson, Withdrawals	2,100
Prepaid Rent	1,900	Service Revenue	1,600
Office Supplies	3,000	Depreciation Expense—Equipment	300
Equipment	34,800	Salaries Expense	800
Accumulated Depreciation—Equipment	1,600	Rent Expense	500
Accounts Payable	5,400	Utilities Expense	600
Notes Payable (long-term)	7,000	Supplies Expense	100

Check your answer at the end of the chapter.

For more practice, see Short Exercise S-12. MyAccountingLab

APPENDIX A: Reversing Entries: An Optional Step

WHAT ARE REVERSING ENTRIES?

Learning Objective 7

Explain the purpose of and journalize reversing entries

Reversing entries are special journal entries that ease the burden of accounting for transactions in a later period. Reversing entries are the exact opposites of certain adjusting entries. Reversing entries are used in conjunction with accrual-type adjustments, such as accrued salaries expense and accrued service revenue. Generally Accepted Accounting Principles do not require reversing entries. They are used only for convenience and to save time.

Accounting for Accrued Expenses

To see how reversing entries work, let's return to Smart Touch Learning. In the unadjusted trial balance, Salaries Expense has a debit balance of $3,600 for salaries paid during November and December. At December 31, the business still owes it employees an additional $1,200 for the last half of the month, so the business makes the following adjusting entry:

$$A = \left\{ \begin{array}{c} L\uparrow \\ \text{Salaries} \\ \text{Payable}\uparrow \end{array} + \begin{array}{c} E\downarrow \\ \text{Salaries} \\ \text{Expense}\uparrow \end{array} \right.$$

Date	Accounts and Explanation	Debit	Credit
Dec. 31	Salaries Expense	1,200	
	Salaries Payable		1,200
	To accrue salaries expense.		

After posting, the accounts are updated as of December 31:

Salaries Payable			Salaries Expense		
	1,200	Adj.	Nov. 15	1,200	
	1,200	Adj. Bal.	Dec. 1	1,200	
			Dec. 15	1,200	
			Adj.	1,200	
			Adj. Bal.	4,800	

After the adjusting entry, the following are noted:

- The income statement reports Salaries Expense of $4,800.
- The balance sheet reports Salaries Payable of $1,200.

The $4,800 debit balance of Salaries Expense is closed at December 31, 2014, with the following closing entry:

Date	Accounts and Explanation	Debit	Credit
Dec. 31	Income Summary	4,800	
	Salaries Expense		4,800
	To close expense.		

$$A \quad \Big\} = \Big\{ \quad L \quad + \quad E\uparrow\downarrow$$

Income Summary↓
Salaries Expense↓

After posting the closing entry, Salaries Expense has a zero balance as follows:

Salaries Expense			
Nov. 15	1,200		
Dec. 1	1,200		
Dec. 15	1,200		
Adj.	1,200		
Adj. Bal.	4,800		
		4,800	Clos.
Bal.	0		

Accounting Without a Reversing Entry

Assume that Smart Touch Learning will pay its employees the second half of December's salaries along with the first half of January on January 15, 2015. On January 15, the company would record the following journal entry:

Date	Accounts and Explanation	Debit	Credit
2015			
Jan. 15	Salaries Payable	1,200	
	Salaries Expense	1,200	
	Cash		2,400
	To record payment of salaries.		

$$A\downarrow \quad \Big\} = \Big\{ \quad L\downarrow \quad + \quad E\downarrow$$

Cash↓ | Salaries Payable↓ | Salaries Expenses↑

After posting the cash payment, the Salaries Payable and Salaries Expense accounts are as follows:

Salaries Payable			Salaries Expense	
	1,200 Bal. 1/1/15		Jan. 15	1,200
Jan. 15 1,200				
	0 Bal.			

This method of recording the cash payment is correct. However, it wastes time because the business must refer back to the December 31 adjustments. Otherwise, the business does not know the amount of the debit to Salaries Payable (in this example $1,200). Searching December's adjusting entries wastes time and money. To save time, accountants can use reversing entries.

Accounting With a Reversing Entry

A reversing entry switches the debit and the credit of a previous entry. A reversing entry, then, is the exact opposite of a prior adjustment entry. The reversing entry is dated the first day of the new period.

To illustrate reversing entries, recall that on December 31, Smart Touch Learning made the following adjusting entry to accrue Salaries Expense:

$$\left. A \right\} = \left\{ \begin{array}{ccc} L\uparrow & + & E\downarrow \\ \text{Salaries} & & \text{Salaries} \\ \text{Payable}\uparrow & & \text{Expense}\uparrow \end{array} \right.$$

Date	Accounts and Explanation	Debit	Credit
Dec. 31	Salaries Expense	1,200	
	Salaries Payable		1,200
	To accrue salaries expense.		

The reversing entry just reverses the debit and the credit of the adjustment:

$$\left. A \right\} = \left\{ \begin{array}{ccc} L\downarrow & + & E\uparrow \\ \text{Salaries} & & \text{Salaries} \\ \text{Payable}\downarrow & & \text{Expense}\downarrow \end{array} \right.$$

Date	Accounts and Explanation	Debit	Credit
2015			
Jan. 1	Salaries Payable	1,200	
	Salaries Expense		1,200
	To reverse the salaries adjusting entry.		

Observe that the reversing entry is dated the first day of the new period. It is the exact opposite of the adjusting entry. Ordinarily, the accountant who makes the adjusting entries will also prepare reversing entries at the same time. Smart Touch Learning dates the reversing entry as of January 1 so that it affects only the new period. Note how the accounts appear after the accounting clerk posts the reversing entry:

Salaries Payable			Salaries Expense	
	1,200 Adj.		Bal. 1/1/15 0	
	1,200 Bal. 1/1/15			1,200 Rev.
Rev. 1,200				
	0 Bal.			

The arrow between the T-accounts shows the transfer of the $1,200 from Salaries Payable to Salaries Expense. This credit in Salaries Expense does not mean that the entity has negative salaries expense, as you might think. Instead, the odd credit balance in the Salaries Expense account is merely a temporary result of the reversing entry. The credit balance is eliminated on January 15, when Smart Touch Learning pays the payroll and debits Salaries Expense:

Date	Accounts and Explanation	Debit	Credit
Jan. 15	Salaries Expense	2,400	
	Cash		2,400
	To record payment of salaries.		

$$\frac{A\downarrow}{\text{Cash}\downarrow} \Big\} = \Big\{ \frac{L}{} + \frac{E\downarrow}{\substack{\text{Salaries} \\ \text{Expense}\uparrow}}$$

This payment is posted to the Salaries Expense account as follows:

Salaries Expense

Bal. 1/1/15	0		
Jan. 15	2,400	1,200	Rev.
Bal.	1,200		

Now Salaries Expense has a debit balance of $1,200, which is correct and represents only the January salaries. The payment of salaries covered two periods: $1,200 related to last period and $1,200 related to this period. The Salaries Expense account should only contain the amount that relates to this period.

Winters Landscape Services accrued $4,000 of Salaries Expense at December 31. Winters paid the next payroll at January 10 of $6,000. This payment included the accrued amount at December 31, plus $2,000 for the first few days of January.

23A. Record the adjusting journal entry to accrue Salaries Expense.
24A. Record the reversing entry.
25A. Journalize the cash payment.

Check your answers at the end of the chapter.

For more practice, see Short Exercise SA-13. MyAccountingLab

REVIEW

> Things You Should Know

1. How do we prepare financial statements?

- Financial statements are prepared from the adjusted trial balance in the following order:
  1. Income statement—reports revenues and expenses and calculates net income or net loss during the period
  2. Statement of owner's equity—shows how capital changed during the period due to owner contributions, net income or net loss, and owner withdrawals
  3. Balance sheet—reports assets, liabilities, and owner's equity as of the last day of the period
- A classified balance sheet classifies each asset and each liability into a specific categories.

2. How could a worksheet help in preparing financial statements?

- The columns of a worksheet can be extended to help in preparing the financial statements.
- The income statement section will include only revenue and expense accounts.
- The balance sheet section will include assets, liabilities, and equity accounts.

3. What is the closing process, and how do we close the accounts?

- The closing process consists of zeroing out all temporary accounts (revenues, expenses, and withdrawals) in order to get the accounts ready for the next period.
- The closing process also updates the Capital account balance for net income or net loss during the period and any withdrawals made by the owner.
- There are four steps in the closing process:
  1. Make the revenue accounts equal zero via the Income Summary account.
  2. Make the expense accounts equal zero via the Income Summary account.
  3. Make the Income Summary account equal zero via the Capital account.
  4. Make the Withdrawals account equal zero via the Capital account.

4. How do we prepare a post-closing trial balance?

- A post-closing trial balance is prepared after the closing entries are recorded and posted to the ledger.
- It contains only assets, liabilities, and capital accounts (permanent accounts).

5. What is the accounting cycle?

- The accounting cycle is the process by which companies produce their financial statements for a specific period.
    1. Start with beginning account balances.
    2. Analyze and journalize transactions as they occur.
    3. Post journal entries to the accounts.
    4. Compute the unadjusted balance in each account and prepare the unadjusted trial balance.
    5. Enter the unadjusted trial balance on the worksheet and complete the worksheet (optional).
    6. Journalize and post adjusting entries.
    7. Prepare the adjusted trial balance.
    8. Prepare the financial statements.
    9. Journalize and post the closing entries.
    10. Prepare the post-closing trial balance.

6. How do we use the current ratio to evaluate business performance?

- The current ratio measures a company's ability to pay its current liabilities with its current assets.
- Current ratio = Total current assets / Total current liabilities

7. What are reversing entries? (Appendix A)

- Reversing entries are special journal entries that ease the burden of accounting for transactions in a later period.
- Reversing entries are the exact opposites of certain adjusting entries and are used only for accrual adjusting entries.

> Summary Problem

The adjusted trial balance of Martinez Advertising Services, at December 31, 2016, follows.

MARTINEZ ADVERTISING SERVICES Adjusted Trial Balance December 31, 2016		
	Balance	
Account Title	Debit	Credit
Cash	$ 6,000	
Accounts Receivable	6,300	
Office Supplies	200	
Furniture	8,000	
Accumulated Depreciation—Furniture		$ 6,000
Building	42,000	
Accumulated Depreciation—Building		24,000
Land	10,000	
Accounts Payable		2,000
Salaries Payable		500
Unearned Revenue		5,000
Notes Payable (long-term)		7,000
Martinez, Capital		12,000
Martinez, Withdrawals	25,000	
Service Revenue		64,300
Salaries Expense	16,500	
Supplies Expense	800	
Depreciation Expense—Furniture	2,000	
Depreciation Expense—Building	1,000	
Advertising Expense	3,000	
Total	$ 120,800	$ 120,800

Requirements

1. Prepare the income statement for the year ended December 31, 2016.
2. Prepare the statement of owner's equity for the year ended December 31, 2016. Assume the owner had no additional contributions during the year.
3. Prepare the classified balance sheet at December, 31, 2016. Use the report form.
4. Calculate the current ratio at December 31, 2016.
5. Journalize and post the closing entries. Indicate the balance of the Martinez, Capital account after the closing entries are posted.
6. Prepare a post-closing trial balance at December 31, 2016.

> Solution

Requirement 1

MARTINEZ ADVERTISING SERVICES Income Statement Year Ended December 31, 2016		
Revenues:		
Service Revenue		$ 64,300
Expenses:		
Salaries Expense	$ 16,500	
Advertising Expense	3,000	
Depreciation Expense—Furniture	2,000	
Depreciation Expense—Building	1,000	
Supplies Expense	800	
Total Expenses		23,300
Net Income		**$ 41,000**

Requirement 2

MARTINEZ ADVERTISING SERVICES Statement of Owner's Equity Year Ended December 31, 2016	
Martinez, Capital, January 1, 2016	$ 12,000
Owner contribution	0
Net income for the year	41,000
	53,000
Owner withdrawal	(25,000)
Martinez, Capital, December 31, 2016	**$ 28,000**

Requirement 3

MARTINEZ ADVERTISING SERVICES Balance Sheet December 31, 2016			
Assets			
Current Assets:			
Cash		$ 6,000	
Accounts Receivable		6,300	
Office Supplies		200	
Total Current Assets			$ 12,500
Plant Assets:			
Furniture	$ 8,000		
Less: Accumulated Depreciation—Furniture	(6,000)	2,000	
Building	42,000		
Less: Accumulated Depreciation—Building	(24,000)	18,000	
Land		10,000	
Total Plant Assets			30,000
Total Assets			$ 42,500
Liabilities			
Current Liabilities:			
Accounts Payable		$ 2,000	
Salaries Payable		500	
Unearned Revenue		5,000	
Total Current Liabilities			$ 7,500
Long-term Liabilities:			
Notes Payable			7,000
Total Liabilities			14,500
Owner's Equity			
Martinez, Capital			28,000
Total Liabilities and Owner's Equity			$ 42,500

Requirement 4

Current ratio = Total current assets / Total current liabilities = $12,500 / $7,500 = 1.67*

*rounded

Requirement 5

Date	Accounts and Explanation	Debit	Credit
Dec. 31	Service Revenue	64,300	
	Income Summary		64,300
	To close revenue.		
31	Income Summary	23,300	
	Salaries Expense		16,500
	Supplies Expense		800
	Depreciation Expense—Furniture		2,000
	Depreciation Expense—Building		1,000
	Advertising Expense		3,000
	To close expenses.		
31	Income Summary	41,000	
	Martinez, Capital		41,000
	To close Income Summary.		
31	Martinez, Capital	25,000	
	Martinez, Withdrawals		25,000
	To close withdrawals.		

Martinez, Capital

	12,000	Adj. Bal.
Dec. 31 25,000	41,000	Dec. 31
	28,000	Bal.

Martinez, Withdrawals

Adj. Bal. 25,000	25,000	Dec. 31
Bal. 0		

Service Revenue

Dec. 31 64,300	64,300	Adj. Bal.
	0	Bal.

Salaries Expense

Adj. Bal.16,500	16,500	Dec. 31
Bal. 0		

Supplies Expense

Adj. Bal. 800	800	Dec. 31
Bal. 0		

Depreciation Expense—Furniture

Adj. Bal. 2,000	2,000	Dec. 31
Bal. 0		

Depreciation Expense—Building

Adj. Bal. 1,000	1,000	Dec. 31
Bal. 0		

Income Summary

Dec. 31 23,300	64,300	Dec. 31
Dec. 31 41,000	41,000	Bal.
	0	Bal.

Advertising Expense

Adj. Bal. 3,000	3,000	Dec. 31
Bal. 0		

Requirement 6

MARTINEZ ADVERTISING SERVICES		
Post-Closing Trial Balance		
December 31, 2016		
	Balance	
Account Title	**Debit**	**Credit**
Cash	$ 6,000	
Accounts Receivable	6,300	
Office Supplies	200	
Furniture	8,000	
Accumulated Depreciation—Furniture		$ 6,000
Building	42,000	
Accumulated Depreciation—Building		24,000
Land	10,000	
Accounts Payable		2,000
Salaries Payable		500
Unearned Revenue		5,000
Notes Payable (long-term)		7,000
Martinez, Capital		28,000
Total	**$ 72,500**	**$ 72,500**

> Key Terms

Accounting Cycle
The process by which companies produce their financial statements for a specific period.

Classified Balance Sheet
A balance sheet that places each asset and each liability into a specific category.

Closing Entries
Entries that transfer the revenue, expense, and withdrawal balances to the Capital account to prepare the company's books for the next period.

Closing Process
A step in the accounting cycle that occurs at the end of the period. The closing process consists of journalizing and posting the closing entries to set the balances of the revenue, expense, and withdrawal accounts to zero for the next period.

Current Assets
Assets that are expected to be converted to cash, sold, or used up during the next 12 months, or within the business's normal operating cycle if the cycle is longer than a year.

Current Liabilities
Liabilities that must be paid with cash or with goods and services within one year, or within the entity's operating cycle if the cycle is longer than a year.

Current Ratio
Measures the company's ability to pay current liabilities from current assets. Total current assets / Total current liabilities.

Income Summary
A temporary account into which revenues and expenses are transferred prior to their final transfer into the Capital account. Summarizes net income (or net loss) for the period.

Intangible Assets
A long-term asset category that includes assets with no physical form, such as patents, copyrights, and trademarks.

Liquidity
A measure of how quickly an item can be converted to cash.

Long-Term Assets
All assets that will not be converted to cash or used up within the business's operating cycle or one year, whichever is greater.

Long-Term Investments

A long-term asset category that includes investments in bonds or stocks in which the company intends to hold the investment for longer than one year.

Long-Term Liabilities

Liabilities that do not need to be paid within one year or within the entity's operating cycle, whichever is longer.

Operating Cycle

The time span during which cash is paid for goods and services, which are then sold to customers from whom the business collects cash.

Permanent Account

An account that is *not* closed at the end of the period—the asset, liability, and capital accounts.

Plant Assets

A long-term asset category that includes property, plant, and equipment.

Post-Closing Trial Balance

A list of the accounts and their balances at the end of the period after journalizing and posting the closing entries. It should include only permanent accounts.

Reversing Entry (Appendix A)

A special journal entry that eases the burden of accounting for transactions in the next period. Such entries are the exact opposite of a prior adjusting entry.

Temporary Account

An account that relates to a particular accounting period and is closed at the end of that period—the revenues, expenses, and withdrawal accounts.

> Quick Check

1. Assets and liabilities are listed on the balance sheet in order of their

    Learning Objective 1

    a. purchase date.
    b. adjustments.
    c. liquidity.
    d. balance.

2. Which of the following accounts would be included in the plant assets category of the classified balance sheet?

    Learning Objective 1

    a. Land held for investment
    b. Accumulated Depreciation
    c. Office Supplies
    d. Mortgage Payable

3. Which situation indicates a net loss within the Income Statement section of the worksheet?

    Learning Objective 2

    a. Total credits exceed total debits
    b. Total debits exceed total credits
    c. Total debits equal total credits
    d. None of the above

4. Which of the following accounts is *not* closed?

    Learning Objective 3

    a. Depreciation Expense
    b. Withdrawals
    c. Service Revenue
    d. Accumulated Depreciation

Completing the Accounting Cycle

5. What do closing entries accomplish?
   a. Zero out the revenues, expenses, and withdrawals
   b. Transfer revenues, expenses, and withdrawals to the Capital account
   c. Bring the Capital account to its correct ending balance
   d. All of the above

6. Which of the following is *not* a closing entry?

a.

Capital		xxx	
Withdrawals			xxx

b.

Service Revenue		xxx	
Income Summary			xxx

c.

Salaries Payable		xxx	
Income Summary			xxx

d.

Income Summary		xxx	
Rent Expense			xxx

7. Which of the following accounts may appear on a post-closing trial balance?
   a. Cash, Salaries Payable, and Capital
   b. Cash, Salaries Payable, and Service Revenue
   c. Cash, Service Revenue, and Salaries Expense
   d. Cash, Salaries Payable, and Salaries Expense

8. Which of the following steps of the accounting cycle is not completed at the end of the period?

    a. Journalize transactions as they occur.

    b. Journalize and post the closing entries.

    c. Prepare the post-closing trial balance.

    d. Prepare the financial statements.

Learning Objective 5

9. Clean Water Softener Systems has Cash of $600, Accounts Receivable of $900, and Office Supplies of $400. Clean owes $500 on Accounts Payable and Salaries Payable of $200. Clean's current ratio is

    a. 2.71

    b. 2.50

    c. 0.63

    d. 0.37

Learning Objective 6

10A. Which of the following statements concerning reversing entries is true?

    a. Reversing entries are required by Generally Accepted Accounting Principles.

    b. Reversing entries are most often used with accrual-type adjustments.

    c. Reversing entries are dated December 31.

    d. Reversing entries are recorded before adjusting entries.

Learning Objective 7
Appendix A

Check your answers at the end of the chapter.

ASSESS YOUR PROGRESS

> Review Questions

1. What document are financial statements prepared from?

2. What does the income statement report?

3. What does the statement of owner's equity show?

4. What does the balance sheet report?

5. Why are financial statements prepared in a specific order? What is that order?

6. What is a classified balance sheet?

7. Identify two asset categories on the classified balance sheet, and give examples of each category.

8. Identify two liability categories on the classified balance sheet, and give examples of each category.

9. What does liquidity mean?

10. How could a worksheet help in preparing financial statements?

11. If a business had a net loss for the year, where would the net loss be reported on the worksheet?

12. What is the closing process?

13. What are temporary accounts? Are temporary accounts closed in the closing process?

14. What are permanent accounts? Are permanent accounts closed in the closing process?

15. How is the Income Summary account used? Is it a temporary or permanent account?

16. What are the steps in the closing process?

17. If a business had a net loss for the year, what would be the closing entry to close Income Summary and transfer the net loss to the Capital account?

18. What types of accounts are listed on the post-closing trial balance?

19. List the steps of the accounting cycle.

20. What is the current ratio and how is it calculated?

21A. What are reversing entries? Are they required by GAAP?

> Short Exercises

S-1 Preparing an income statement

Learning Objective 1

Dave Hair Stylists' adjusted trial balance follows. Prepare Dave's income statement for the year ended December 31, 2015.

DAVE HAIR STYLISTS Adjusted Trial Balance December 31, 2015		
	Balance	
Account Title	**Debit**	**Credit**
Cash	$ 800	
Accounts Receivable	500	
Office Supplies	900	
Equipment	19,100	
Accumulated Depreciation—Equipment		$ 1,000
Accounts Payable		200
Interest Payable		100
Notes Payable		2,500
Dave, Capital		10,500
Dave, Withdrawals	800	
Service Revenue		14,800
Rent Expense	4,500	
Supplies Expense	300	
Depreciation Expense—Equipment	1,000	
Interest Expense	1,200	
Total	**$ 29,100**	**$ 29,100**

S-2 Preparing a statement of owner's equity

Learning Objective 1

Refer to the data in Short Exercise S-1. Prepare Dave's statement of owner's equity for the year ended December 31, 2015. Assume the owner made no additional contributions during the year.

S-3 Preparing a balance sheet (unclassified, account form)

Learning Objective 1

Refer to the data in Short Exercise S-1. Prepare Dave's unclassified balance sheet at December 31, 2015. Use the account form.

Learning Objective 1

S-4 Classifying balance sheet accounts

For each account listed, identify the category in which it would appear on a classified balance sheet.

a. Office Supplies

b. Interest Payable

c. Kay, Capital

d. Copyrights

e. Land

f. Accumulated Depreciation—Furniture

g. Land (held for long-term investment purposes)

h. Unearned Revenue

i. Notes Payable (due in six years)

Learning Objective 2

S-5 Using the worksheet to prepare financial statements

Answer the following questions:

Requirements

1. What type of normal balance does the Capital account have—debit or credit?

2. Which type of income statement account has the same type of balance as the Capital account?

3. Which type of income statement account has the opposite type of balance as the Capital account?

4. What do we call the difference between total debits and total credits on the income statement section of the worksheet?

Learning Objective 2

S-6 Determining net income using a worksheet

A partial worksheet for Robson Law Firm is presented below. Solve for the missing information.

	A	J	K	L	M
		\multicolumn{2}{c}{Income Statement}		Balance Sheet	
5		Income Statement		Balance Sheet	
6		Debit	Credit	Debit	Credit
32	Total	(a)	$ 20,450	$ 205,400	$ 200,175
33	Net (b)	5,225			(c)
34	Total	(d)	$ 20,450	(e)	(f)
35					

S-7 Determining net loss using a worksheet

Learning Objective 2

A partial worksheet for Ace Adjusters is presented below. Solve for the missing information.

	A	J	K	L	M
		Income Statement		Balance Sheet	
		Debit	Credit	Debit	Credit
5					
6					
32	Total	$ 20,600	(a)	(b)	$ 60,100
33	Net (c)		4,200	(d)	
34	Total	(e)	(f)	(g)	$ 60,100
35					

S-8 Journalizing closing entries

Learning Objective 3

Brett Tilman Enterprises had the following accounts and normal balances listed on its adjusted trial balance: Service Revenue, $20,600; Salaries Expense, $7,200; Rent Expense, $4,500; Advertising Expense, $3,400; Tilman, Withdrawals, $3,800.

Journalize the closing entries for Tilman Enterprises.

S-9 Posting closing entries directly to T-accounts

Learning Objective 3

The following balances appear on the books of Sarah Simon Enterprises: Simon, Capital, $26,100; Simon, Withdrawals, $8,500; Service Revenue, $23,700; Salaries Expense, $6,100; Rent Expense $4,000; Advertising Expense, $3,300. All accounts have normal balances.

Requirements

1. Open a T-account for each account and insert its adjusted balance as given (denote as *Adj. Bal.*) at December 31.

2. Post the closing entries to the accounts, denoting posted amounts as *Clos.*

3. Compute the ending balance of Simon, Capital.

S-10 Identifying accounts included on a post-closing trial balance

Learning Objective 4

For each account listed, identify whether the account would be included on a post-closing trial balance. Signify either Yes (Y) or No (N).

a. Office Supplies

b. Interest Expense

c. Nelson, Capital

d. Nelson, Withdrawals

e. Service Revenue

f. Accumulated Depreciation—Furniture

g. Rent Expense

h. Unearned Revenue

i. Accounts Payable

Learning Objective 5

S-11 Identifying steps in the accounting cycle

Review the steps in the accounting cycle and answer the following questions:

1. What is the first step?
2. Are any steps optional?
3. Which steps are completed throughout the period?
4. Which steps are completed only at the end of the period?
5. What is the last step in the accounting cycle?

Learning Objective 6

S-12 Calculating the current ratio

Heart of Texas Telecom has these account balances at December 31, 2014:

Notes Payable, long-term	$ 7,800	Accounts Payable	$ 3,700
Prepaid Rent	2,300	Accounts Receivable	5,700
Salaries Payable	3,000	Cash	3,500
Service Revenue	10,400	Depreciation Expense—Equip.	1,000
Office Supplies	500	Equipment	15,000
Accumulated Depreciation—Equip.	2,000	Tex, Capital	3,100
Advertising Expense	800	Rent Expense	1,200

Requirements

1. Calculate Heart of Texas Telecom's current ratio.
2. How much in *current* assets does Heart of Texas Telecom have for every dollar of *current* liabilities that it owes?

Learning Objective 7
Appendix A

SA-13 Journalizing reversing entries

Adoption Associates accrued $6,000 of Service Revenue at December 31. Adoption Associates received $10,500 on January 15, including the accrued revenue recorded on December 31.

Requirements

1. Record the adjusting journal entry to accrue Service Revenue.
2. Record the reversing entry.
3. Journalize the cash receipt.

> Exercises

E-14 Preparing the financial statements

The adjusted trial balance for Online Advertising Services is presented below.

Learning Objective 1

Ending Capital $35,500

ONLINE ADVERTISING SERVICES
Adjusted Trial Balance
December 31, 2016

Account Title	Balance	
	Debit	Credit
Cash	$ 13,500	
Accounts Receivable	13,800	
Office Supplies	7,700	
Furniture	17,500	
Accumulated Depreciation—Furniture		$ 13,500
Building	47,500	
Accumulated Depreciation—Building		38,500
Land	17,500	
Accounts Payable		9,500
Salaries Payable		8,000
Unearned Revenue		12,500
Cohen, Capital		59,500
Cohen, Withdrawals	15,500	
Service Revenue		37,900
Salaries Expense	24,000	
Supplies Expense	8,300	
Depreciation Expense—Furniture	1,500	
Depreciation Expense—Building	2,100	
Advertising Expense	10,500	
Total	$ 179,400	$ 179,400

Requirements

1. Prepare the income statement for the year ending December 31, 2016.

2. Prepare the statement of owner's equity for the year ending December 31, 2016. Assume that there were no contributions made by the owner during the year.

3. Prepare the *unclassified* balance sheet as of December 31, 2016. Use the account form.

Completing the Accounting Cycle

E-15 Classifying balance sheet accounts

For each account listed, identify the category that it would appear on a classified balance sheet. Use the following categories: Current Assets, Long-term Investments, Plant Assets, Intangible Assets, Current Liabilities, Long-term Liabilities, and Owner's Equity. If the item does not belong on the classified balance sheet, put an X.

a. Land (used in operations)

b. Accumulated Depreciation—Equipment

c. Taylor, Capital

d. Service Revenue

e. Investment in Starbucks Corporation (to be held long-term)

f. Accounts Receivable

g. Equipment

h. Buildings

i. Notes Payable (due in 10 years)

j. Unearned Revenue

k. Cash

l. Accounts Payable

m. Prepaid Rent

n. Taylor, Withdrawals

o. Land (held for investment purposes)

p. Depreciation Expense

E-16 Preparing a classified balance sheet and calculating the current ratio

The adjusted trial balance of Brian O'Brion Dance Studio Company follows:

BRIAN O'BRION DANCE STUDIO COMPANY Trial Balance August 31, 2014		
	Balance	
Account Title	**Debit**	**Credit**
Cash	$ 15,800	
Office Supplies	2,000	
Prepaid Rent	900	
Equipment	49,000	
Accumulated Depreciation—Equipment		$ 5,500
Accounts Payable		4,500
Salaries Payable		500
Unearned Revenue		5,100
Notes Payable (long-term)		4,400
O'Brion, Capital		36,500
O'Brion, Withdrawals	1,100	
Service Revenue		18,100
Salaries Expense	3,000	
Rent Expense	1,500	
Depreciation Expense—Equipment	300	
Supplies Expense	400	
Utilities Expense	600	
Total	**$ 74,600**	**$ 74,600**

Requirements

1. Prepare the classified balance sheet of Brian O'Brion Dance Studio Company at August 31, 2014. Use the report form. You must compute the ending balance of O'Brion, Capital.

2. Compute O'Brion's current ratio at August 31, 2014. One year ago, the current ratio was 1.49. Indicate whether O'Brion's ability to pay current debts has improved, deteriorated, or remained the same.

E-17 Preparing a worksheet

Learning Objective 2

Net Income $5,200

The trial balance of Telegraphic Link at November 30, follows:

TELEGRAPHIC LINK
Trial Balance
November 30, 2014

Account Title	Balance	
	Debit	Credit
Cash	$ 4,000	
Accounts Receivable	3,200	
Prepaid Rent	1,900	
Office Supplies	3,000	
Equipment	34,800	
Accumulated Depreciation—Equipment		$ 1,600
Accounts Payable		5,400
Salaries Payable		
Thomas, Capital		35,700
Thomas, Withdrawals	2,100	
Service Revenue		8,600
Depreciation Expense—Equipment		
Salaries Expense	1,700	
Rent Expense		
Utilities Expense	600	
Supplies Expense		
Total	$ 51,300	$ 51,300

Additional information at November 30, 2014:

a. Accrued service revenue, $600.

b. Depreciation, $300.

c. Accrued salaries expense, $800.

d. Prepaid rent expired, $500.

e. Office Supplies used, $100.

Requirements

1. Complete Telegraphic Link's worksheet for the month ended November 30, 2014.

2. How much was net income for November?

Note: Exercise E-18 should be used only after completing Exercise E-17.

Learning Objectives 1, 2

Ending Capital $38,800

E-18 Preparing financial statements from the completed worksheet

Use your answer from Exercise E-17 to prepare Telegraphic Link's financial statements.

Requirements

1. Complete the income statement for the month ended November 30, 2014.

2. Complete the statement of owner's equity for the month ended November 30, 2014. Assume that there were no contributions made by the owner during the month.

3. Complete the *unclassified* balance sheet as of November 30, 2014. Use the account form.

Learning Objective 3

E-19 Preparing closing entries from an adjusted trial balance

The adjusted trial balance of Silver Sign Company follows:

	Balance	
SILVER SIGN COMPANY Adjusted Trial Balance January 31, 2014		
Account Title	**Debit**	**Credit**
Cash	$ 14,300	
Office Supplies	2,400	
Prepaid Rent	1,400	
Equipment	45,000	
Accumulated Depreciation—Equipment		$ 6,100
Accounts Payable		4,500
Salaries Payable		300
Unearned Revenue		4,500
Notes Payable (long-term)		5,300
Silver, Capital		32,600
Silver, Withdrawals	800	
Service Revenue		16,800
Salaries Expense	3,600	
Rent Expense	1,400	
Depreciation Expense—Equipment	400	
Supplies Expense	200	
Utilities Expense	600	
Total	$ 70,100	$ 70,100

Requirements

1. Assume Silver Sign Company has a January 31 year end. Journalize Silver's closing entries at January 31.

2. How much net income or net loss did Silver earn for the year ended January 31? How can you tell?

E-20 Preparing closing entries from T-accounts

Learning Objective 3

Ending Capital $26,500

Selected accounts for Klein Photography at December 31, 2014 follow.

Klein, Capital

	47,000

Klein, Withdrawals

17,000	

Service Revenue

	30,000
	2,000

Salaries Expense

25,400	
700	

Supplies Expense

2,400	

Depreciation Expense—Furniture

800	

Depreciation Expense—Building

6,200	

Requirements

1. Journalize Klein Photography's closing entries at December 31, 2014.

2. Determine Klein Photography's ending Klein, Capital balance at December 31, 2014.

E-21 Determining the effects of closing entries on the Capital account

Learning Objective 3

Ewan Insurance Agency started the year with a beginning capital balance of $25,000. During the year, Ewan earned $40,000 of Service Revenue and incurred $21,000 of various expenses. William Ewan withdrew $8,000 from the business. After the closing entries are recorded and posted, what will be the balance of Ewan, Capital?

Learning Objectives 2, 3

Net Income $19,280

E-22 Preparing a worksheet and closing entries

Cynthia Ebersole, CPA had the following partial worksheet as follows:

	A	B	C	D	E	F	G	H	I	J	K	L	M
1						CYNTHIA EBERSOLE, CPA							
2						Worksheet							
3						December 31, 2014							
4													
5	Account Names	Unadjusted Trial Balance			Adjustments			Adjusted Trial Balance		Income Statement		Balance Sheet	
6		Debit	Credit		Debit	Credit		Debit	Credit	Debit	Credit	Debit	Credit
7	Cash	$ 45,200						$ 45,200					
8	Accounts Receivable	8,430		(h)	$ 4,030			12,460					
9	Office Supplies	600				$ 100	(b)	500					
10	Prepaid Rent	5,000				2,500	(a)	2,500					
11	Furniture	25,000						25,000					
12	Accumulated Depreciation—Furniture					1,500	(c)		$ 1,500				
13	Building	100,000						100,000					
14	Accumulated Depreciation—Building					750	(d)		750				
15	Land	10,000						10,000					
16	Accounts Payable		$ 3,400						3,400				
17	Utilities Payable		430						430				
18	Salaries Payable					4,300	(f)		4,300				
19	Interest Payable					200	(g)		200				
20	Unearned Revenue		1,500	(e)	600				900				
21	Notes Payable		20,000						20,000				
22	Ebersole, Capital		174,900						174,900				
23	Ebersole, Withdrawals	30,000						30,000					
24	Service Revenue		105,000			4,630	(e,h)		109,630				
25	Rent Expense	40,000		(a)	2,500			42,500					
26	Salaries Expense	23,000		(f)	4,300			27,300					
27	Supplies Expense			(b)	100			100					
28	Utilities Expense	18,000						18,000					
29	Depreciation Expense—Furniture			(c)	1,500			1,500					
30	Depreciation Expense—Building			(d)	750			750					
31	Interest Expense			(g)	200			200					
32	Total	$ 305,230	$ 305,230		$ 13,980	$ 13,980		$ 316,010	$ 316,010				
33													
34													
35													

Requirements

1. Complete the worksheet.
2. Prepare the closing entries for Cynthia Ebersole, CPA.

E-23 Preparing closing entries from an adjusted trial balance; preparing a post-closing trial balance; and calculating the current ratio

Learning Objectives 3, 4, 6

Mel's Bowling Alley's adjusted trial balance as of December 31, 2014 is presented below.

MEL'S BOWLING ALLEY Adjusted Trial Balance December 31, 2014		
	Balance	
Account Title	Debit	Credit
Cash	$ 15,400	
Accounts Receivable	2,310	
Office Supplies	450	
Prepaid Insurance	2,300	
Equipment	40,000	
Accumulated Depreciation—Equipment		$ 12,000
Building	75,000	
Accumulated Depreciation—Building		4,500
Land	15,000	
Accounts Payable		3,400
Utilities Payable		620
Salaries Payable		2,840
Unearned Revenue		1,300
Turner, Capital		130,325
Turner, Withdrawals	28,000	
Service Revenue		94,000
Insurance Expense	20,000	
Salaries Expense	36,000	
Supplies Expense	800	
Utilities Expense	12,000	
Depreciation Expense—Equipment	1,500	
Depreciation Expense—Building	225	
Total	$ 248,985	$ 248,985

Requirements

1. Prepare the closing entries for Mel's Bowling Alley.
2. Prepare a post-closing trial balance.
3. Compute the current ratio for Mel's Bowling Alley.

Learning Objectives 2, 3, 4

Net Loss $(1,925)

E-24 Preparing a worksheet, closing entries, and a post-closing trial balance

San Marcos Veterinary Hospital completed the following worksheet as of December 31, 2014.

Account Names	Unadjusted Trial Balance Debit	Unadjusted Trial Balance Credit		Adjustments Debit	Adjustments Credit		Adjusted Trial Balance Debit	Adjusted Trial Balance Credit	Income Statement Debit	Income Statement Credit	Balance Sheet Debit	Balance Sheet Credit
	SAN MARCOS VETERINARY HOSPITAL											
	Worksheet											
	December 31, 2014											
Cash	$ 23,100						$ 23,100					
Accounts Receivable	6,210		(f)	$ 1,000			7,210					
Office Supplies	200				$ 150	(b)	50					
Prepaid Rent	2,300				750	(a)	1,550					
Equipment	30,000						30,000					
Accumulated Depreciation—Equipment					900	(c)		$ 900				
Accounts Payable		$ 2,500						2,500				
Utilities Payable		210						210				
Salaries Payable					1,375	(e)		1,375				
Unearned Revenue		3,750	(d)	2,250				1,500				
Kellerman, Capital		72,350						72,350				
Kellerman, Withdrawals	15,000						15,000					
Service Revenue		32,000			3,250	(d,f)		35,250				
Rent Expense	12,000		(a)	750			12,750					
Salaries Expense	15,000		(e)	1,375			16,375					
Supplies Expense			(b)	150			150					
Utilities Expense	7,000						7,000					
Depreciation Expense—Equipment			(c)	900			900					
Total	**$ 110,810**	**$ 110,810**		**$ 6,425**	**$ 6,425**		**$ 114,085**	**$ 114,085**				

Requirements

1. Complete the worksheet for San Marcos Veterinary Hospital.
2. Prepare the closing entries.
3. Prepare a post-closing trial balance.

Learning Objective 7
Appendix A

EA-25 Journalizing reversing entries

Femi Architects recorded the following adjusting entries as of December 31:

a. Service Revenue accrued, $1,000

b. Unearned Revenue that has been earned, $300.

c. Office Supplies on hand, $600. The balance of the Office Supplies account was $800.

d. Salaries owed to employees, $400.

e. One month of Prepaid Rent has expired, $2,000.

f. Depreciation on equipment, $1,000.

Journalize any necessary reversing entries for Femi Architects.

EA-26 Journalizing reversing entries

Learning Objective 7
Appendix A

Home Inspection Services had the following unadjusted balances at December 31, 2014: Salaries Payable, $0; Salaries Expense, $1,000. The following transactions have taken place during the end of 2014 and beginning of 2015:

2014		
Dec. 31	Accrued Salaries Expense at December 31, $3,000.
31	Closed the Salaries Expense account.
2015		
Jan. 1	Reversed the accrued salaries. (Requirement 3 only)
4	Paid salaries of $4,500. This payment included the Salaries Payable amount, plus $1,500 for the first few days of January.

Requirements

1. Open T-accounts for Salaries Payable and Salaries Expense using their unadjusted balances at December 31, 2014.

2. Journalize the entries assuming Home Inspection Services does not use reversing entries. **Do not record the reversing entry on Jan. 1.** Post to the accounts.

3. Open new T-accounts for Salaries Payable and Salaries Expense using their unadjusted balances at December 31, 2014. Journalize the entries assuming Home Inspection Services uses reversing entries. **Don't forget to record the reversing entry on Jan. 1.** Post to the accounts. Compare the balances with Requirement 2 balances.

> Problems **Group A**

P-27A **Preparing financial statements including a classified balance sheet in report form, preparing and posting closing entries, and preparing a post-closing trial balance**

The adjusted trial balance of Elias Real Estate Appraisal at June 30, 2014, follows:

ELIAS REAL ESTATE APPRAISAL Adjusted Trial Balance June 30, 2014		
	Balance	
Account Title	**Debit**	**Credit**
Cash	$ 4,900	
Accounts Receivable	5,300	
Office Supplies	2,400	
Prepaid Insurance	1,800	
Building	74,400	
Accumulated Depreciation—Building		$ 26,700
Land	13,600	
Accounts Payable		19,500
Interest Payable		8,800
Salaries Payable		2,200
Unearned Revenue		1,300
Notes Payable (long-term)		40,000
Elias, Capital		40,500
Elias, Withdrawals	27,900	
Service Revenue		48,200
Insurance Expense	4,500	
Salaries Expense	33,300	
Supplies Expense	600	
Interest Expense	8,800	
Utilities Expense	2,200	
Depreciation Expense—Building	7,500	
Total	**$ 187,200**	**$ 187,200**

Requirements

1. Prepare the company's income statement for the year ended June 30, 2014.

2. Prepare the company's statement of owner's equity for the year ended June 30, 2014. Assume that there were no contributions made by the owner during the year.

3. Prepare the company's classified balance sheet in report form at June 30, 2014.

4. Journalize the closing entries.

5. Open the T-accounts using the balances from the adjusted trial balance and post the closing entries to the T-accounts.

6. Prepare the company's post-closing trial balance at June 30, 2014.

P-28A **Preparing financial statements including a classified balance sheet in report form, preparing closing entries, and using the current ratio to evaluate a company**

Learning Objectives 1, 3, 6

Ending Capital $74,900

The adjusted trial balance of Blume Irrigation System at December 31, 2014, follows:

BLUME IRRIGATION SYSTEM		
Adjusted Trial Balance		
December 31, 2014		
	Balance	
Account Title	**Debit**	**Credit**
Cash	$ 11,000	
Accounts Receivable	43,100	
Office Supplies	3,300	
Prepaid Insurance	4,000	
Equipment	23,000	
Accumulated Depreciation—Equipment		$ 7,900
Building	55,800	
Accumulated Depreciation—Building		24,000
Accounts Payable		24,700
Interest Payable		400
Salaries Payable		3,900
Unearned Revenue		1,600
Notes Payable (long-term)		2,800
Blume, Capital		25,000
Blume, Withdrawals	2,000	
Service Revenue		74,800
Insurance Expense	900	
Salaries Expense	16,300	
Supplies Expense	1,500	
Interest Expense	400	
Depreciation Expense—Equipment	2,000	
Depreciation Expense—Building	1,800	
Total	$ 165,100	$ 165,100

Requirements

1. Prepare the company's income statement for the year ended December 31, 2014.

2. Prepare the company's statement of owner's equity for the year ended December 31, 2014. Assume that there were no contributions made by the owner during the year.

3. Prepare the company's classified balance sheet in report form at December 31, 2014.

4. Journalize the closing entries for Blume Irrigation System.

5. Compute the company's current ratio at December 31, 2014. At December 31, 2013, the current ratio was 1.81. Did the company's ability to pay debts improve or deteriorate, or did it remain the same?

P-29A Preparing a worksheet, financial statements, and closing entries

The *unadjusted* trial balance of Fugazy Investment Advisers at December 31, 2014, follows:

FUGAZY INVESTMENT ADVISERS Unadjusted Trial Balance December 31, 2014		
	Balance	
Account Title	**Debit**	**Credit**
Cash	$ 32,000	
Accounts Receivable	46,000	
Office Supplies	3,000	
Equipment	25,000	
Accumulated Depreciation—Equipment		$ 11,000
Accounts Payable		15,000
Salaries Payable		
Unearned Revenue		2,000
Notes Payable (long-term)		19,000
Fugazy, Capital		38,000
Fugazy, Withdrawals	30,000	
Service Revenue		97,000
Insurance Expense	2,000	
Salaries Expense	32,000	
Supplies Expense		
Interest Expense	3,000	
Rent Expense	9,000	
Depreciation Expense—Equipment		
Total	$ 182,000	$ 182,000

Adjustment data at December 31, 2014:

a. Unearned Revenue earned during the year, $500.

b. Office Supplies on hand, $1,000.

c. Depreciation for the year, $6,000.

d. Accrued Salaries Expense, $1,000.

e. Accrued Service Revenue, $4,000.

Requirements

1. Prepare a worksheet for Fugazy Investment Advisers at December 31, 2014.

2. Prepare the income statement, the statement of owner's equity, and the classified balance sheet in account format. Assume that there were no contributions made by the owner during the year.

3. Prepare closing journal entries.

P-30A Completing the accounting cycle from adjusting entries to post-closing trial balance with an optional worksheet

Learning Objectives 1, 2, 3, 4, 5, 6

Net Income $18,900

The *unadjusted* trial balance of Wolfe Anvils at December 31, 2014, and the data for the adjustments follow:

WOLFE ANVILS
Unadjusted Trial Balance
December 31, 2014

Account Title	Debit	Credit
Cash	$ 4,300	
Accounts Receivable	15,000	
Prepaid Rent	2,700	
Office Supplies	1,600	
Equipment	31,200	
Accumulated Depreciation—Equipment		$ 3,000
Accounts Payable		6,900
Salaries Payable		
Unearned Revenue		5,400
Wolfe, Capital		26,600
Wolfe, Withdrawals	3,500	
Service Revenue		18,900
Salaries Expense	2,500	
Rent Expense		
Depreciation Expense—Equipment		
Supplies Expense		
Total	$ 60,800	$ 60,800

Adjustment data:

a. Unearned Revenue still unearned at December 31, $1,200.

b. Prepaid Rent still in force at December 31, $2,500.

c. Office Supplies used, $1,000.

d. Depreciation, $300.

e. Accrued Salaries Expense at December 31, $200.

Requirements

1. Open the T-accounts using the balances in the unadjusted trial balance.

2. Prepare the adjusting entries and post to the accounts.

3. Prepare an adjusted trial balance.

4. Complete the worksheet for the year ended December 31, 2014. (optional)

5. Prepare the income statement, the statement of owner's equity, and the *classified* balance sheet in report form. Assume that there were no contributions made by the owner during the year.

6. Prepare the closing entries and post to the accounts.

7. Prepare a post-closing trial balance.

8. Calculate the current ratio for the company.

Learning Objectives 1, 2, 3, 4, 5

Ending Capital $54,780

P-31A Completing the accounting cycle from journal entries to post-closing trial balance with an optional worksheet

On December 1, Tim Walker began an auto repair shop, Walker's Quality Automotive. The following transactions occurred during December:

Dec. 1	Walker contributed $48,000 cash to the business in exchange for capital.
1	Purchased $10,000 of equipment paying cash.
1	Paid $1,600 for a 4-month insurance policy starting on December 1.
9	Paid $20,000 cash to purchase land to be used in operations.
10	Purchased office supplies on account, $2,400.
19	Borrowed $15,000 from the bank for business use. Walker signed a note payable to the bank in the name of the business.
22	Paid $1,300 for advertising expenses.
26	Paid $600 on account.
28	The business received a bill for utilities to be paid in January, $240.
31	Revenues earned during the month included $16,500 cash and $2,800 on account.
31	Paid employees' salaries $3,500 and building rent $1,000. Record as a compound entry.
31	The business received $1,140 for auto screening services to be performed next month.
31	Walker withdrew cash of $5,000.

The business uses the following accounts: Cash; Accounts Receivable; Office Supplies; Prepaid Insurance; Equipment; Accumulated Depreciation—Equipment; Land; Accounts Payable; Utilities Payable; Interest Payable; Unearned Revenue; Notes Payable; Walker, Capital; Walker, Withdrawals; Service Revenue; Salaries Expense; Rent Expense; Utilities Expense; Advertising Expense; Supplies Expense; Insurance Expense; Interest Expense; and Depreciation Expense—Equipment.

Adjustment data:

a. Office Supplies used during the month, $800.

b. Depreciation for the month, $200.

c. One month insurance has expired.

d. Accrued Interest Expense, $80.

Requirements

1. Prepare the journal entries and post to the T-accounts.

2. Prepare an unadjusted trial balance.

3. Prepare the adjusting entries and post to the T-accounts.

4. Prepare an adjusted trial balance.

5. Complete the worksheet for the month ended December 31, 2014. (optional)

6. Prepare the income statement, the statement of owner's equity, and the *unclassified* balance sheet in account form.

7. Prepare the closing entries and post to the T-accounts.

8. Prepare a post-closing trial balance.

Learning Objective 7
Appendix A

PA-32A Preparing adjusting entries and reversing entries.

The unadjusted trial balance and adjustment data of Myla's Motors at December 31, 2014, follow:

MYLA'S MOTORS
Unadjusted Trial Balance
December 31, 2014

Account Title	Balance Debit	Balance Credit
Cash	$ 4,300	
Accounts Receivable	26,600	
Office Supplies	500	
Prepaid Insurance	1,700	
Equipment	53,500	
Accumulated Depreciation—Equipment		$ 36,400
Accounts Payable		13,400
Wages Payable		
Unearned Revenue		8,000
Myla, Capital		19,700
Myla, Withdrawals	3,800	
Service Revenue		16,000
Depreciation Expense—Equipment		
Wages Expense	1,600	
Insurance Expense		
Utilities Expense	1,500	
Supplies Expense		
Total	$ 93,500	$ 93,500

Adjusting data at December 31, 2014:

a. Depreciation on equipment, $1,100.

b. Accrued Wages Expense, $600.

c. Office Supplies on hand, $200.

d. Prepaid Insurance expired during December, $200.

e. Unearned Revenue earned during December, $4,000.

f. Accrued Service Revenue, $800.

2015 transactions:

a. On January 4, Myla's Motors paid wages of $1,000. Of this, $600 related to the accrued wages recorded on December 31.

b. On January 10, Myla's Motors received $1,000 for Service Revenue. Of this, $800 is related to the accrued Service Revenue recorded on December 31.

Requirements

1. Journalize adjusting journal entries.

2. Journalize reversing entries for the appropriate adjusting entries.

3. Refer to the 2015 data. Journalize the cash payment and the cash receipt that occurred in 2015.

> Problems Group B

P-33B Preparing financial statements including a classified balance sheet in report form, preparing and posting closing entries, and preparing a post-closing trial balance

Learning Objectives 1, 3, 4

Net Income $58,020

The adjusted trial balance of Smith Real Estate Appraisal at June 30, 2014, follow:

SMITH REAL ESTATE APPRAISAL Adjusted Trial Balance June 30, 2014		
	Balance	
Account Title	**Debit**	**Credit**
Cash	$ 4,600	
Accounts Receivable	4,600	
Office Supplies	2,900	
Prepaid Insurance	1,700	
Building	74,700	
Accumulated Depreciation—Building		$ 8,600
Land	14,000	
Accounts Payable		8,900
Interest Payable		80
Salaries Payable		1,300
Unearned Revenue		2,000
Notes Payable (long-term)		20,000
Smith, Capital		20,600
Smith, Withdrawals	17,000	
Service Revenue		98,600
Insurance Expense	5,500	
Salaries Expense	22,800	
Supplies Expense	100	
Interest Expense	80	
Utilities Expense	3,600	
Depreciation Expense—Building	8,500	
Total	$ 160,080	$ 160,080

Requirements

1. Prepare the company's income statement for the year ended June 30, 2014.

2. Prepare the company's statement of owner's equity for the year ended June 30, 2014. Assume that there were no contributions made by the owner during the year.

3. Prepare the company's classified balance sheet in report form at June 30, 2014.

4. Journalize the closing entries.

5. Open the T-accounts using the balances from the adjusted trial balance and post the closing entries to the T-accounts.

6. Prepare the company's post-closing trial balance at June 30, 2014.

Learning Objectives 1, 3, 6

Ending Capital $77,100

P-34B Preparing financial statements including a classified balance sheet in report form, preparing closing entries, and using the current ratio to evaluate a company

The adjusted trial balance of Browne Irrigation System at December 31, 2014, follows:

	BROWNE IRRIGATION SYSTEM Adjusted Trial Balance December 31, 2014	
	Balance	
Account Title	**Debit**	**Credit**
Cash	$ 6,500	
Accounts Receivable	43,600	
Office Supplies	3,300	
Prepaid Insurance	4,800	
Equipment	23,000	
Accumulated Depreciation—Equipment		$ 6,900
Building	58,200	
Accumulated Depreciation—Building		24,200
Accounts Payable		22,300
Interest Payable		100
Salaries Payable		2,800
Unearned Revenue		1,800
Notes Payable (long-term)		4,200
Browne, Capital		87,000
Browne, Withdrawals	5,000	
Service Revenue		40,000
Insurance Expense	500	
Salaries Expense	17,700	
Supplies Expense	1,600	
Interest Expense	100	
Depreciation Expense—Equipment	5,000	
Depreciation Expense—Building	20,000	
Total	$ 189,300	$ 189,300

Requirements

1. Prepare the company's income statement for the year ended December 31, 2014.

2. Prepare the company's statement of owner's equity for the year ended December 31, 2014. Assume that there were no contributions made by the owner during the year.

3. Prepare the company's classified balance sheet in report form at December 31, 2014.

4. Journalize the closing entries for Browne Irrigation System.

5. Compute the company's current ratio at December 31, 2014. At December 31, 2013, the current ratio was 2.20. Did the company's ability to pay debts improve or deteriorate, or did it remain the same?

P-35B Preparing a worksheet, financial statements, and closing entries

The *unadjusted* trial balance of Giambi Investment Advisers at December 31, 2014, follows:

Learning Objectives 1, 2, 3

Total Assets $92,000

GIAMBI INVESTMENT ADVISERS Unadjusted Trial Balance December 31, 2014		
	Balance	
Account Title	**Debit**	**Credit**
Cash	$ 28,000	
Accounts Receivable	50,000	
Office Supplies	8,000	
Equipment	26,000	
Accumulated Depreciation—Equipment		$ 16,000
Accounts Payable		14,000
Salaries Payable		
Unearned Revenue		1,000
Notes Payable (long-term)		44,000
Giambi, Capital		40,000
Giambi, Withdrawals	50,000	
Service Revenue		97,000
Insurance Expense	4,000	
Salaries Expense	32,000	
Supplies Expense		
Interest Expense	7,000	
Rent Expense	7,000	
Depreciation Expense—Equipment		
Total	$ 212,000	$ 212,000

Adjustment data at December 31, 2014:

a. Unearned Revenue earned during the year, $400.

b. Office Supplies on hand, $5,000.

c. Depreciation for the year, $4,000.

d. Accrued Salaries Expense, $2,000.

e. Accrued Service Revenue, $3,000.

Requirements

1. Prepare a worksheet for Giambi Investment Advisers at December 31, 2014.

2. Prepare the income statement, the statement of owner's equity, and the classified balance sheet in account format. Assume that there were no contributions made by the owner during the year.

3. Prepare closing journal entries.

Learning Objectives 1, 2, 3, 4, 5, 6

Net Income $17,200

P-36B Completing the accounting cycle from adjusting entries to post-closing trial balance with an optional worksheet

The *unadjusted* trial balance of Leopard Anvils at December 31, 2014, and the data for the adjustments follow:

LEOPARD ANVILS Unadjusted Trial Balance December 31, 2014		
	Balance	
Account Title	**Debit**	**Credit**
Cash	$ 4,400	
Accounts Receivable	14,800	
Prepaid Rent	2,300	
Office Supplies	1,200	
Equiment	30,100	
Accumulated Depreciation—Equipment		$ 4,600
Accounts Payable		7,500
Salaries Payable		
Unearned Revenue		4,900
Leopard, Capital		25,700
Leopard, Withdrawals	4,800	
Service Revenue		17,400
Salaries Expense	2,500	
Rent Expense		
Depreciation Expense—Equipment		
Supplies Expense		
Total	$ 60,100	$ 60,100

Adjustment data:

a. Unearned Revenue still unearned at December 31, $400.

b. Prepaid Rent still in force at December 31, $1,800.

c. Office Supplies used, $800.

d. Depreciation, $400.

e. Accrued Salaries Expense at December 31, $500.

Requirements

1. Open the T-accounts using the balances in the unadjusted trial balance.

2. Prepare the adjusting entries and post to the accounts.

3. Prepare an adjusted trial balance.

4. Complete the worksheet for the year ended December 31, 2014. (optional)

5. Prepare the income statement, the statement of owner's equity, and the *classified* balance sheet in report form. Assume that there were no contributions made by the owner during the year.

6. Prepare the closing entries and post to the accounts.

7. Prepare a post-closing trial balance.

8. Calculate the current ratio for the company.

P-37B Completing the accounting cycle from journal entries to post-closing trial balance with an optional worksheet

Learning Objectives 1, 2, 3, 4, 5

Ending Capital $58,030

On December 1, Michael Dosler began an auto repair shop, Dosler's Quality Automotive. The following transactions occurred during December:

Dec. 1	Dosler contributed $60,000 cash to the business in exchange for capital.
1	Purchased $12,000 of equipment paying cash.
1	Paid $2,000 for a 4-month insurance policy starting on December 1.
9	Paid $22,000 cash to purchase land to be used in operations.
10	Purchased office supplies on account, $3,300.
19	Borrowed $25,000 from the bank for business use. Dosler signed a notes payable to the bank in the name of the business.
22	Paid $800 for advertising expenses.
26	Paid $1,000 on account.
28	The business received a bill for utilities to be paid in January, $320.
31	Revenues earned during the month included $10,000 cash and $1,200 on account.
31	Paid employees' salaries $2,100 and building rent $950. Record as a compound entry.
31	The business received $2,400 for auto screening services to be performed next month.
31	Dosler withdrew cash of $7,000.

The business uses the following accounts: Cash; Accounts Receivable; Office Supplies; Prepaid Insurance; Equipment; Accumulated Depreciation—Equipment; Land; Accounts Payable; Utilities Payable; Interest Payable; Unearned Revenue; Notes Payable; Dosler, Capital; Dosler, Withdrawals; Service Revenue; Salaries Expense; Rent Expense; Utilities Expense; Advertising Expense; Supplies Expense; Insurance Expense; Interest Expense; and Depreciation Expense—Equipment.

Adjustment data:

a. Office Supplies used during the month, $1,000.

b. Depreciation for the month, $400.

c. One month insurance has expired.

d. Accrued Interest Expense, $100.

Requirements

1. Prepare the journal entries and post to the T-accounts.

2. Prepare an unadjusted trial balance.

3. Prepare the adjusting entries and post to the T-accounts.

4. Prepare an adjusted trial balance.

5. Complete the worksheet for the month ended December 31, 2014. (optional)

6. Prepare the income statement, the statement of owner's equity, and the *unclassified* balance sheet in account form.

7. Prepare the closing entries and post to the T-accounts.

8. Prepare a post-closing trial balance.

PA-38B Preparing adjusting entries and reversing entries.

The unadjusted trial balance of and adjustment data of Brooke's Motors at December 31, 2014, follow:

BROOKE'S MOTORS
Unadjusted Trial Balance
December 31, 2014

Account Title	Debit	Credit
	Balance	
Cash	$ 4,200	
Accounts Receivable	26,500	
Office Supplies	800	
Prepaid Insurance	1,800	
Equiment	53,500	
Accumulated Depreciation—Equipment		$ 36,300
Accounts Payable		13,300
Wages Payable		
Unearned Revenue		8,500
Brooke, Capital		19,000
Brooke, Withdrawals	3,500	
Service Revenue		16,500
Depreciation Expense—Equipment		
Wages Expense	2,100	
Insurance Expense		
Utilities Expense	1,200	
Supplies Expense		
Total	$ 93,600	$ 93,600

Adjusting data at December 31, 2014:

a. Depreciation on equipment, $1,400.

b. Accrued Wages Expense, $500.

c. Office Supplies on hand, $400.

d. Prepaid Insurance expired during December, $300.

e. Unearned Revenue earned during December, $3,500.

f. Accrued Service Revenue, $900.

2015 transactions:

a. On January 4, Brooke's Motors paid wages of $950. Of this, $500 related to the accrued wages recorded on December 31.

b. On January 10, Brooke's Motors received $1,300 for Service Revenue. Of this, $900 related to the accrued Service Revenue recorded on December 31.

Requirements

1. Journalize adjusting journal entries.

2. Journalize reversing entries for the appropriate adjusting entries.

3. Refer to the 2015 data. Journalize the cash payment and the cash receipt that occurred in 2015.

> Continuing Problem

This problem deals with a company named Davis Consulting.

P-39 Completing the accounting cycle from adjusted trial balance to post-closing trial balance with an optional worksheet

Start from the posted T-accounts and the adjusted trial balance that Davis Consulting prepared for the company at December 31.

Requirements

1. Complete the worksheet at December 31. (optional)

2. Prepare an income statement for the month ended December 31.

3. Prepare a statement of owner's equity for the month ended December 31.

4. Prepare a classified balance sheet (report form) at December 31.

5. Journalize and post the closing entries at December 31. Denote each closing amount as *Clo.* and each account balance as *Balance*.

6. Prepare a post-closing trial balance.

> Practice Set

P-40 Completing the accounting cycle from adjusted trial balance to post-closing trial balance with an optional worksheet

Requirements

1. Prepare an accounting worksheet. (optional)

2. Prepare an income statement, statement of owner's equity, and *classified* balance sheet using the report format. Assume the Notes Payable is long-term.

3. Prepare closing entries for the month and post to the accounts.

4. Prepare a post-closing trial balance.

CRITICAL THINKING

> Decision Case 1

One year ago, Ralph Collins founded Collins Consignment Sales Company, and the business has prospered. Collins comes to you for advice. He wishes to know how much net income the business earned during the past year. The accounting records consist of the T-accounts in the ledger, which were prepared by an accountant who has moved. The accounts at December 31, 2014 follow:

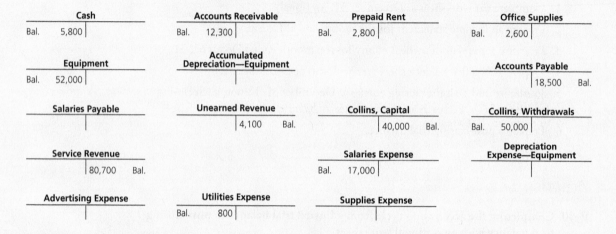

Collins indicates that, at year-end, customers owe him $1,000 accrued service revenue, which he expects to collect early next year. These revenues have not been recorded. During the year, he collected $4,100 service revenue in advance from customers, but the business has earned only $800 of that amount. During the year he has incurred $2,400 of advertising expense, but he has not yet paid for it. In addition, he has used up $2,100 of the office supplies. Collins determines that depreciation on equipment was $7,000 for the year. At December 31, 2014, he owes his employee $1,200 accrued salary.

Collins expresses concern that withdrawals during the year might have exceeded the business's net income. To get a loan to expand the business, Collins must show the bank that the business's owner's equity has grown from its original $40,000 balance. Has it? You and Collins agree that you will meet again in one week.

Requirements

1. Prepare the financial statement that helps address the first issue concerning Collins.

2. Can Collins expect to get the loan? Give your reason(s).

> Ethical Issue 1

Grant Film Productions wishes to expand and has borrowed $100,000. As a condition for making this loan, the bank requires that the business maintain a current ratio of at least 1.50.

Business has been good but not great. Expansion costs have brought the current ratio down to 1.40 on December 15. Rita Grant, owner of the business, is considering what might happen if she reports a current ratio of 1.40 to the bank. One course of action for Grant is to record in December $10,000 of revenue that the business will earn in January of next year. The contract for this job has been signed.

Requirements

1. Journalize the revenue transaction, and indicate how recording this revenue in December would affect the current ratio.

2. Discuss whether it is ethical to record the revenue transaction in December. Identify the accounting principle relevant to this situation, and give the reasons underlying your conclusion.

> Fraud Case 1

Arthur Chen, a newly minted CPA, was on his second audit job in the Midwest with a new client called Parson Farm Products. He was looking through the past four years of financials and doing a few ratios when he noticed something odd. The current ratio went from 1.9 in 2011 down to 0.3 in 2012, despite the fact that 2012 had record income. He decided to sample a few transactions from December 2012. He found that many of Parson's customers had returned products to the company because of substandard quality. Chen discovered that the company was clearing the receivables (i.e., crediting accounts receivable) but "stashing" the debits in an obscure long-term asset account called "grain reserves" to keep the company's income "in the black" (i.e., positive income).

Requirements

1. How did the fraudulent accounting just described affect the current ratio?

2. Can you think of any reasons why someone in the company would want to take this kind of action?

> Financial Statement Case 1

This case, based on the balance sheet of **Starbucks Corporation**, will familiarize you with some of the assets and liabilities of that company. Visit **www.pearsonhighered.com/Horngren** to view a link to the Starbucks Corporation Fiscal 2011 Annual Report. Use the Starbucks Corporation balance sheet to answer the following questions.

Completing the Accounting Cycle

Requirements

1. Which balance sheet format does Starbucks use?

2. Name the company's largest current asset and largest current liability at October 2, 2011.

3. Compute Starbucks' current ratios at October 2, 2011, and October 3, 2010. Did the current ratio improve, worsen, or hold steady?

4. Under what category does Starbucks report furniture, fixtures, and equipment?

5. What was the cost of the company's fixed assets at October 2, 2011? What was the amount of accumulated depreciation? What was the book value of the fixed assets? See Note 6 for the data.

> Team Project 1

Kathy Wintz formed a lawn service business as a summer job. To start the business on May 1, 2014, she deposited $1,000 in a new bank account in the name of the business. The $1,000 consisted of a $600 loan from Bank One to her company, Wintz Lawn Service, and $400 of her own money. The company gave $400 of capital to Wintz. Wintz rented lawn equipment, purchased supplies, and hired other students to mow and trim customers' lawns.

At the end of each month, Wintz mailed bills to the customers. On August 31, she was ready to dissolve the business and return to college. Because she was so busy, she kept few records other than the checkbook and a list of receivables from customers.

At August 31, the business's checkbook shows a balance of $2,000, and customers still owe $750. During the summer, the business collected $5,500 from customers. The business checkbook lists payments for supplies totaling $400, and it still has gasoline, weed trimmer cord, and other supplies that cost a total of $50. The business paid employees $1,800 and still owes them $300 for the final week of the summer.

Wintz rented some equipment from Ludwig's Machine Shop. On May 1, the business signed a six-month rental agreement on mowers and paid $600 for the full rental period in advance. Ludwig's will refund the unused portion of the prepayment if the equipment is returned in good shape. In order to get the refund, Wintz has kept the mowers in excellent condition. In fact, the business had to pay $300 to repair a mower.

To transport employees and equipment to jobs, Wintz used a trailer that the business bought for $300. The business estimates that the summer's work used up one-third of the trailer's service potential. The business checkbook lists a payment of $500 for cash withdrawals during the summer. The business paid the loan back during August. (For simplicity, ignore any interest expense associated with the loan.)

Requirements

1. As a team, prepare the income statement and the statement of owner's equity of Wintz Lawn Service for the four months May 1 through August 31, 2014.

2. Prepare the classified balance sheet (report form) of Wintz Lawn Service at August 31, 2014.

3. Was Wintz's summer work successful? Give your team's reason for your answer.

> Communication Activity 1

In 25 words or fewer, explain the rationale for closing the temporary accounts.

Try It! Solutions

1. Intangible assets
2. Long-term liabilities
3. Plant assets
4. Current assets
5. Current liabilities
6. Long-term investments
7. Plant assets

8. Income statement, CR
9. Balance sheet, CR
10. Balance sheet, DR
11. Income statement, DR
12. Balance sheet, DR
13. Balance sheet, CR

14.

Date	Accounts and Explanation	Debit	Credit
Dec. 31	Service Revenue	1,600	
	Income Summary		1,600
	To close revenue.		
31	Income Summary	2,300	
	Depreciation Expense—Equipment		300
	Salaries Expense		800
	Rent Expense		500
	Utilities Expense		600
	Supplies Expense		100
	To close expenses.		
31	Benson, Capital	700	
	Income Summary		700
	To close Income Summary.		
31	Benson, Capital	2,100	
	Benson, Withdrawals		2,100
	To close withdrawals.		

15.

Benson, Capital			
		35,700	Adj. Bal.
Clos. 3	700		
Clos. 4	2,100		
		32,900	Bal.

16. No

17. No

18. Yes

19. No

20. Yes

21. b, h, i, d, f, e, g, c, a, j

22. Current ratio = Total current assets / Total current liabilities
    = ($4,000 + $3,200 + $1,900 + $3,000) / $5,400
    = $12,100 / $5,400 = 2.24 (rounded)

23A.

Date	Accounts and Explanation	Debit	Credit
Dec. 31	Salaries Expense	4,000	
	Salaries Payable		4,000
	To accrue salaries expense		

24A.

Date	Accounts and Explanation	Debit	Credit
Jan. 1	Salaries Payable	4,000	
	Salaries Expense		4,000
	To reverse the salaries adjusting entry.		

25A.

Date	Accounts and Explanation	Debit	Credit
Jan. 10	Salaries Expense	6,000	
	Cash		6,000
	To record payment of salaries.		

> Quick Check Answers

1. c **2.** b **3.** b **4.** d **5.** d **6.** c **7.** a **8.** a **9.** a **10A.** b

Glossary

Accounting Cycle. The process by which companies produce their financial statements for a specific period.

Classified Balance Sheet. A balance sheet that places each asset and each liability into a specific category.

Closing Entries. Entries that transfer the revenue, expense, and withdrawal balances to the Capital account to prepare the company's books for the next period.

Closing Process. A step in the accounting cycle that occurs at the end of the period. The closing process consists of journalizing and posting the closing entries to set the balances of the revenue, expense, and withdrawal accounts to zero for the next period.

Current Assets. Assets that are expected to be converted to cash, sold, or used up during the next 12 months, or within the business's normal operating cycle if the cycle is longer than a year.

Current Liabilities. Liabilities that must be paid with cash or with goods and services within one year, or within the entity's operating cycle if the cycle is longer than a year.

Current Ratio. Measures the company's ability to pay current liabilities from current assets. Total current assets / Total current liabilities.

Income Summary. A temporary account into which revenues and expenses are transferred prior to their final transfer into the Capital account. Summarizes net income (or net loss) for the period.

Intangible Assets. A long-term asset category that includes assets with no physical form, such as patents, copyrights, and trademarks. An asset with no physical form that is valuable because of the special rights it carries.

Liquidity. A measure of how quickly an item can be converted to cash.

Long-Term Assets. All assets that will not be converted to cash or used up within the business's operating cycle or one year, whichever is greater.

Long-Term Investments. A long-term asset category that includes investments in bonds or stocks in which the company intends to hold the investment for longer than one year. Investments in debt and equity securities that are highly liquid and that the investor intends to sell in one year or less.

Long-Term Liabilities. Liabilities that do not need to be paid within one year or within the entity's operating cycle, whichever is longer.

Operating Cycle. The time span during which cash is paid for goods and services, which are then sold to customers from whom the business collects cash.

Permanent Account. An account that is *not* closed at the end of the period—the asset, liability, and capital accounts.

Plant Assets. Long-lived, tangible assets, such as land, buildings, and equipment, used in the operation of a business.

Post-Closing Trial Balance. A list of the accounts and their balances at the end of the period after journalizing and posting the closing entries. It should include only permanent accounts.

Reversing Entry. A special journal entry that eases the burden of accounting for transactions in the next period. Such entries are the exact opposite of a prior adjusting entry. (Appendix A)

Temporary Account. An account that relates to a particular accounting period and is closed at the end of that period—the revenues, expenses, and withdrawal accounts.

Photo Credits

Merchandising Operations

From Chapter 5 of *Horngren's Accounting*, Tenth edition. Tracie Nobles, Brenda Mattison, Ella Mae Matsumura. Copyright © 2014 by Pearson Education, Inc. All rights reserved.

Merchandising Operations

Will They Buy It?

Julie Ryski studied the model on the catwalk who was wearing the latest spring fashion. As a retail buyer for a nationwide high-end department store, Julie is responsible for selecting merchandise that will be sold in stores across America. Not only must Julie have a keen eye for the latest fashion designs and seasonal variations, but she must also understand the needs of the department store's customers. Julie enjoys attending fashion shows and other fashion-oriented promotions, but she knows that there is more to her responsibilities than simply selecting the newest spring outfits.

As Julie contemplates the model and whether she should purchase this merchandise for the department store's spring line, she knows that she has to always keep the department store's gross profit in mind. She is responsible for ensuring that the merchandise she buys will be purchased by customers and that it is priced effectively to ensure the highest profit maximization possible. In addition, she must ensure that this merchandise can meet the department store's sales goals and ultimate financial objectives. In the long run, Julie is responsible for all aspects of the merchandise that is sold in the store. She must understand how merchandise is reported on the financial statements, how it is recorded in the accounting records, and how the department store determines gross profit (the difference between the original cost and the retail price). Julie's buying decisions and expertise play a major role in the company's profits. Her pricing decisions ultimately affect the net income of the department store and are a major component of the department store's bottom line.

How Do Businesses Account for Merchandise Inventory?

In this chapter, we begin our exploration of companies that sell goods (called merchandise inventory) to customers. Although many accounting concepts concerning service businesses apply, merchandisers (businesses that sell inventory) have some unique characteristics you must learn how to account for. For example, Macy's, Inc., a nationally known premier retailer with more than 800 department stores and furniture galleries in 45 states, must have a way of accurately tracking the purchase and sale of its inventory. In addition, Macy's needs to determine if it is selling its merchandise at the right sales prices in order to ensure maximum profit. This chapter explores merchandising operations and how such businesses account for merchandise inventory.

chapter outline

What are merchandising operations?

How are purchases of merchandise inventory recorded in a perpetual inventory system?

How are sales of merchandise inventory recorded in a perpetual inventory system?

What are the adjusting and closing entries for a merchandiser?

How are a merchandiser's financial statements prepared?

How do we use the gross profit percentage to evaluate business performance?

How are merchandise inventory transactions recorded in a periodic inventory system? (Appendix A)

Learning Objectives

1. Describe merchandising operations and the two types of merchandise inventory systems

2. Account for the purchase of merchandise inventory using a perpetual inventory system

3. Account for the sale of merchandise inventory using a perpetual inventory system

4. Adjust and close the accounts of a merchandising business

5. Prepare a merchandiser's financial statements

6. Use the gross profit percentage to evaluate business performance

7. Account for the purchase and sale of merchandise inventory using a periodic inventory system (Appendix A)

WHAT ARE MERCHANDISING OPERATIONS?

Learning Objective 1

Describe merchandising operations and the two types of merchandise inventory systems

Merchandiser
A business that sells merchandise, or goods, to customers.

Merchandise Inventory
The merchandise that a business sells to customers.

Wholesaler
A type of merchandiser that buys goods from manufacturers and then sells them to retailers.

Retailer
A type of merchandiser that buys merchandise either from a manufacturer or a wholesaler and then sells those goods to consumers.

In this chapter, you learn about accounting for merchandisers. A merchandiser is a business that sells merchandise, or goods, to customers. The merchandise that this type of business sells is called merchandise inventory. Merchandisers are often identified as either wholesalers or retailers. A wholesaler is a merchandiser that buys goods from a manufacturer and then sells them to retailers. A retailer buys merchandise either from a manufacturer or a wholesaler and then sells those goods to consumers.

The Operating Cycle of a Merchandising Business

The operating cycle of a merchandiser is as follows (see Exhibit 1):

Exhibit 1 | Operating Cycle of a Merchandiser

1. It begins when the company purchases inventory from an individual or business, called a **vendor**.
2. The company then sells the inventory to a customer.
3. Finally, the company collects cash from customers.

Because the operating cycle of a merchandiser is different than that of a service company, the financial statements differ. Exhibit 2 shows how a service entity's financial statements (on the left) differ from a merchandiser's financial statements (on the right). As you can see, merchandisers have some new balance sheet and income statement items.

On the income statement, a merchandising company reports the cost of merchandise inventory that has been sold to customers, or **Cost of Goods Sold (COGS)**. Cost of Goods Sold is also called *Cost of Sales*. Because COGS is usually a merchandiser's main expense, an intermediary calculation, gross profit, is determined before

Vendor
The individual or business from whom a company purchases goods.

Cost of Goods Sold (COGS)
The cost of the merchandise inventory that the business has sold to customers.

Exhibit 2 | Financial Statements of a Service Company and a Merchandising Company

SERVICE COMPANY Income Statement Year Ended December 31, 2015			MERCHANDISING COMPANY Income Statement Year Ended December 31, 2015		
Service Revenue		$ 230,000	Sales Revenue		$ 230,000
Operating Expenses:			Cost of Goods Sold		100,000
Salaries Expense	$ 80,000		Gross Profit		130,000
Rent Expense	24,000		Operating Expenses:		
Depreciation Expense—Furniture	9,000		Salaries Expense	$ 80,000	
Utilities Expense	3,000		Rent Expense	24,000	
Total Operating Expenses		116,000	Depreciation Expense—Furniture	9,000	
Net Income		$ 114,000	Utilities Expense	3,000	
			Total Operating Expenses		116,000
			Net Income		$ 14,000

Sales Revenue − Cost of Goods Sold = Gross Profit

Service Revenue − Operating Expenses = Net Income

Gross Profit − Operating Expenses = Net Income

SERVICE COMPANY Balance Sheet (Partial) December 31, 2015			MERCHANDISING COMPANY Balance Sheet (Partial) December 31, 2015		
Assets			**Assets**		
Current Assets:			Current Assets:		
Cash	$ 34,000		Cash	$ 34,000	
Accounts Receivable	10,800		Accounts Receivable	10,800	
Office Supplies	800		Merchandise Inventory	60,000	
Prepaid Rent	2,100		Office Supplies	800	
Total Current Assets		$ 47,700	Prepaid Rent	2,100	
			Total Current Assets		$ 107,700

Merchandise Inventory is included in a merchandising company's current assets.

Gross Profit
Excess of net Sales Revenue over Cost of Goods Sold.

calculating net income. **Gross profit** (also called *gross margin*) is calculated as net Sales Revenue minus Cost of Goods Sold and represents the mark-up on the merchandise inventory. Gross profit is the extra amount the company receives from the customer (for the merchandise sold) over what the company paid to the vendor. After calculating gross profit, operating expenses are then deducted to determine net income. **Operating expenses** are expenses (other than Cost of Goods Sold) that occur in the entity's major line of business.

Operating Expenses
Expenses, other than Cost of Goods Sold, that are incurred in the entity's major line of business.

On the balance sheet, a merchandiser includes Merchandise Inventory in the current assets section representing the value of inventory that the business has on hand to sell to customers. Assets in the current asset section are listed in the order of liquidity; therefore, Merchandise Inventory is usually listed below Accounts Receivable but before the prepaid assets.

Merchandise Inventory Systems: Perpetual and Periodic Inventory Systems

Businesses must have a way to determine the value of merchandise inventory on hand and also the value sold. There are two main types of inventory accounting systems that are used:

- Periodic inventory system
- Perpetual inventory system

Periodic Inventory System
An inventory system that requires businesses to obtain a physical count of inventory to determine quantities on hand.

The **periodic inventory system** requires businesses to obtain a physical count of inventory to determine the quantities on hand. The system is normally used for relatively inexpensive goods, such as in a small, local store without optical-scanning cash registers that does not keep a running record of every loaf of bread and every key chain that it sells. Restaurants and small retail stores often use the periodic inventory system. Appendix A covers the periodic inventory system, which is becoming less and less popular because most accounting is done using computerized methods.

Perpetual Inventory System
An inventory system that keeps a running computerized record of merchandise inventory.

The **perpetual inventory system** keeps a running computerized record of merchandise inventory—that is, the number of inventory units and the dollar amounts associated with the inventory are perpetually (constantly) updated. This system achieves better control over the inventory. A modern perpetual inventory system records the following:

- Units purchased and cost amounts.
- Units sold and sales and cost amounts.
- The quantity of merchandise inventory on hand and its cost.

In a perpetual inventory system, merchandise inventory and purchasing systems are integrated with the records for Accounts Receivable and Sales Revenue. For example, major department stores' computers use bar codes to keep up-to-the-minute records and show the current inventory at any time.

In a perpetual inventory system, the "cash register" at the store is a computer terminal that records sales and updates inventory records. Bar codes are scanned by a laser. The bar coding represents merchandise inventory and cost data that are used to keep track of each unique inventory item. However, note that even in a perpetual inventory system, the business must count inventory at least once a year. The physical count captures inventory transactions that are not recorded by the electronic system (such as misplaced, stolen, or damaged inventory). The count establishes the correct amount of ending inventory for the financial statements and also serves as a check on the perpetual records.

Are the bar codes < I see on goods I purchase used to track inventory in the accounting system?

> Try It!

Match the accounting terminology to the definitions.

1. Cost of Goods Sold		a. An inventory system that requires businesses to obtain a physical count of inventory to determine quantities on hand.
2. Perpetual inventory system		b. Expenses, other than Cost of Goods Sold, that are incurred in the entity's major line of business.
3. Vendor		c. Excess of net Sales Revenue over Cost of Goods Sold.
4. Periodic inventory system		d. The cost of merchandise inventory that the business has sold to customers.
5. Operating expenses		e. The individual or business from whom a company purchases goods.
6. Gross profit		f. An inventory system that keeps a running computerized record of merchandise inventory.

Check your answers at the end of the chapter.

For more practice, see Short Exercise S-1. MyAccountingLab

HOW ARE PURCHASES OF MERCHANDISE INVENTORY RECORDED IN A PERPETUAL INVENTORY SYSTEM?

As noted previously, the cycle of a merchandising entity begins with the purchase of merchandise inventory. We will use a fictitious company, Smart Touch Learning, which has decided to sell touch screen tablet computers that are preloaded with its e-learning software programs. Smart Touch Learning will purchase these tablets from a vendor.

The vendor (Southwest Electronics Direct) ships the tablet computers to Smart Touch Learning and sends an invoice the same day. The **invoice** is the seller's (Southwest Electronics Direct) request for payment from the buyer (Smart Touch Learning). An invoice is also called a *bill*. Exhibit 3 (on the next page) is the bill that Smart Touch Learning receives from Southwest Electronics Direct. After the merchandise inventory is received, Smart Touch Learning pays the vendor.

Learning Objective 2

Account for the purchase of merchandise inventory using a perpetual inventory system

Invoice

A seller's request for payment from the purchaser.

Exhibit 3 | Purchase Invoice

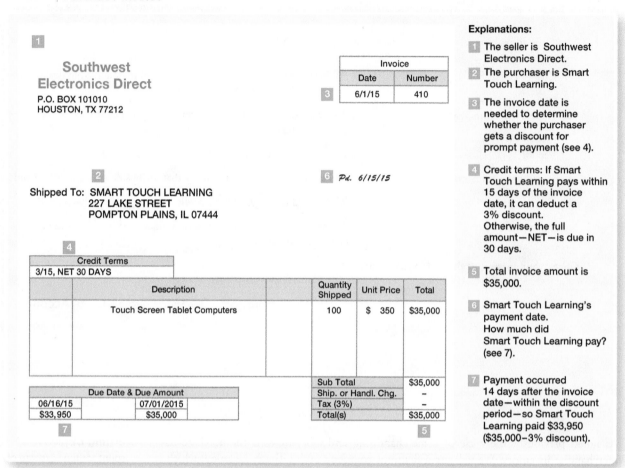

	Invoice	
	Date	**Number**
3	6/1/15	410

Southwest Electronics Direct
P.O. BOX 101010
HOUSTON, TX 77212

6 *Pd. 6/15/15*

Shipped To: SMART TOUCH LEARNING
227 LAKE STREET
POMPTON PLAINS, IL 07444

Credit Terms
3/15, NET 30 DAYS

Description		Quantity Shipped	Unit Price	Total
Touch Screen Tablet Computers		100	$ 350	$35,000

Due Date & Due Amount		
06/16/15		07/01/2015
$33,950		$35,000

	Total
Sub Total	$35,000
Ship. or Handl. Chg.	–
Tax (3%)	–
Total(s)	$35,000

Explanations:

1. The seller is Southwest Electronics Direct.
2. The purchaser is Smart Touch Learning.
3. The invoice date is needed to determine whether the purchaser gets a discount for prompt payment (see 4).
4. Credit terms: If Smart Touch Learning pays within 15 days of the invoice date, it can deduct a 3% discount. Otherwise, the full amount—NET—is due in 30 days.
5. Total invoice amount is $35,000.
6. Smart Touch Learning's payment date. How much did Smart Touch Learning pay? (see 7).
7. Payment occurred 14 days after the invoice date—within the discount period—so Smart Touch Learning paid $33,950 ($35,000–3% discount).

Purchase of Merchandise Inventory

Here we use the actual invoice in Exhibit 3 to illustrate the purchasing process. Suppose Smart Touch Learning receives the goods on June 3, 2015 and makes payment on that date (ignore the credit terms on the invoice at this point). Smart Touch Learning records this purchase as follows:

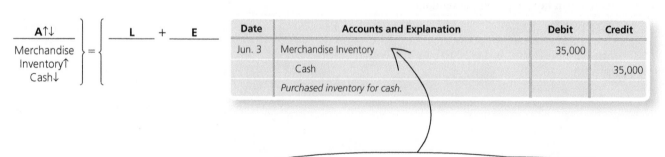

$$\underline{\quad A\uparrow\downarrow \quad} \Big\} = \Big\{ \underline{\quad L \quad} + \underline{\quad E \quad}$$
Merchandise
Inventory↑
Cash↓

Date	Accounts and Explanation	Debit	Credit
Jun. 3	Merchandise Inventory	35,000	
	Cash		35,000
	Purchased inventory for cash.		

The Merchandise Inventory account, an asset, is used only for goods purchased that the business owns and intends to resell to customers. Office Supplies, Equipment, and other assets are recorded in their own accounts.

Assume that on June 3, instead of paying cash, Smart Touch Learning receives the merchandise inventory on account. The purchase of inventory on account is recorded as follows:

Date	Accounts and Explanation	Debit	Credit
Jun. 3	Merchandise Inventory	35,000	
	Accounts Payable		35,000
	Purchased inventory on account.		

$$\underset{\substack{\text{Merchandise} \\ \text{Inventory}\uparrow}}{\underline{\quad A\uparrow \quad}} \Big\} = \Big\{ \underset{\substack{\text{Accounts} \\ \text{Payable}\uparrow}}{\underline{\quad L\uparrow \quad}} + \underline{\quad E \quad}$$

Purchase Discounts

Many businesses offer purchasers a discount for early payment. This is called a **purchase discount**. Southwest Electronics Direct's **credit terms** of "3/15, NET 30 DAYS" mean that Smart Touch Learning can deduct 3% from the total bill (excluding freight charges, if any) if the company pays within 15 days of the invoice date. Otherwise, the full amount—NET—is due in 30 days. These credit terms can also be expressed as "3/15, n/30."

Terms of "n/30" mean that no discount is offered and payment is due 30 days after the invoice date. Most credit terms express the discount, the discount time period, and the final due date. Occasionally, the credit terms are expressed as EOM, which means payment is due at the end of the current month.

If Smart Touch Learning pays on June 15, 2015, which is within the discount period, the cash payment entry would be as follows:

Purchase Discount
A discount that businesses offer to purchasers as an incentive for early payment.

Credit Terms
The payment terms of purchase or sale as stated on the invoice.

Date	Accounts and Explanation	Debit	Credit
Jun. 15	Accounts Payable	35,000	
	Cash ($35,000 − $1,050)		33,950
	Merchandise Inventory ($35,000 × 0.03)		1,050
	Paid within discount period.		

$$\underset{\substack{\text{Cash}\downarrow \\ \text{Merchandise} \\ \text{Inventory}\downarrow}}{\underline{\quad A\downarrow \quad}} \Big\} = \Big\{ \underset{\substack{\text{Accounts} \\ \text{Payable}\downarrow}}{\underline{\quad L\downarrow \quad}} + \underline{\quad E \quad}$$

> *When making payment within a discount period, always debit Accounts Payable for the full amount of the invoice; otherwise there will be a balance remaining in the payable account even though the invoice has been paid in full.*

The purchase discount is credited to the Merchandise Inventory account because the discount for early payment decreases the actual cost paid for Merchandise Inventory, as shown in the T-account:

Merchandise Inventory					Accounts Payable			
June 3	35,000	1,050	June 15		June 15	35,000	35,000	June 3
Bal.	**33,950**				**Bal.**	**0**		

Notice that the balance in the Merchandise Inventory account, $33,950, is exactly what was paid for the Merchandise Inventory on June 15, 2015. Also notice that the Accounts Payable account shows that the invoice was paid in full with no remaining balance.

>Ethics How should you handle gifts from vendors?

Anthony Jackson works as a buyer for a large department store that has decided to expand into selling seasonal home decor. Anthony has been charged with the responsibility of selecting the vendor for the new inventory that the store will sell. His purchasing manager has provided him with two possible vendors to choose from. One vendor, Abbey's Wholesalers, has a long-standing relationship with the department store and can be counted on to provide high-quality goods on a timely basis. The other vendor, Zeta Wholesalers, is a new company that doesn't have much of a track record and is just getting established as a home decor wholesaler. Anthony has contacted both vendors to set up meetings to discuss the new inventory and possible credit terms available. The day before the meeting with the potential vendors, Anthony receives a pair of football tickets to a major NFL game in the mail from Abbey's Wholesalers thanking him for his continued relationship with the wholesaler. What should Anthony do?

Solution

Anthony should contact his purchasing manager and explain the situation to him or her. By accepting the football tickets, Anthony might unknowingly be violating the code of ethics of the business. Most businesses have a code of ethics that relates to inventory management and purchasing specifically discussing conflicts of interest. Conflicts of interest occur when a vendor is selected above another vendor because of possible personal financial gain such as receiving gifts or entertainment from the selected vendor. Anthony should carefully discuss the situation with his manager before accepting the tickets.

What if a < purchaser does not pay for the invoice within the discount period?

What if Smart Touch Learning pays this invoice on June 24, 2015, after the discount period ends? Smart Touch Learning must pay the full $35,000. In that case, the payment entry is as follows:

$$\left.\begin{array}{c} \underline{\text{A}\downarrow} \\ \text{Cash}\downarrow \end{array}\right\} = \left\{\begin{array}{c} \underline{\text{L}\downarrow} \\ \text{Accounts} \\ \text{Payable}\downarrow \end{array} + \underline{\quad\text{E}\quad} \right.$$

Date	Accounts and Explanation	Debit	Credit
Jun. 24	Accounts Payable	35,000	
	Cash		35,000
	Paid after discount period.		

Purchase Returns and Allowances

Sellers allow purchasers to return merchandise that is defective, damaged, or otherwise unsuitable. This is called a **purchase return** from the purchaser's perspective. Alternately, the seller may deduct an allowance from the amount the buyer owes. **Purchase allowances** are granted to the purchaser as an incentive to *keep* goods that are not "as ordered." Together, purchase returns and allowances decrease the buyer's cost of the merchandise inventory.

Assume that Smart Touch Learning has not yet paid the original bill of June 1. Suppose 20 of the tablets purchased on that invoice (Exhibit 3) were damaged in shipment. On June 4, Smart Touch Learning returns the goods (tablets, in this case) valued at $7,000 to the vendor and records the purchase return as follows:

Purchase Return

A situation in which sellers allow purchasers to return merchandise that is defective, damaged, or otherwise unsuitable.

Purchase Allowance

An amount granted to the purchaser as an incentive to keep goods that are not "as ordered."

Date	Accounts and Explanation	Debit	Credit
Jun. 4	Accounts Payable	7,000	
	Merchandise Inventory (20 tablets × $350 per tablet)		7,000
	Returned inventory to seller (vendor).		

$$A\downarrow \left.\begin{array}{c} \\ \text{Merchandise} \\ \text{Inventory}\downarrow \end{array}\right\} = \left\{\begin{array}{c} L\downarrow \quad + \quad E \\ \text{Accounts} \\ \text{Payable}\downarrow \end{array}\right.$$

The exact same entry is made for a purchase allowance granted to the buyer from the seller (vendor). The only difference between a purchase return and a purchase allowance is that, in the case of the allowance, Smart Touch Learning keeps the inventory.

Occasionally a business will return merchandise inventory or receive an allowance before payment has been made. In this scenario, if the payment of the invoice is made within the discount period, the discount should be calculated net of the return. Let's look at another example. Suppose that on June 10, Smart Touch Learning purchased 15 tablets from Southwest Electronics Direct on account with credit terms of 3/15, n/30 at a cost of $5,250. Five days later, Smart Touch Learning returned five tablets to the vendor because of damages and received a purchase return of $1,750. When Smart Touch Learning makes payment on June 20 (within the discount period), it will calculate the discount on the amount due less the return or $3,500 ($5,250 − $1,750). Smart Touch Learning's discount will be $105 ($3,500 × 0.03). The entries that Smart Touch Learning would record for these transactions follow:

Date	Accounts and Explanation	Debit	Credit
Jun. 10	Merchandise Inventory	5,250	
	Accounts Payable		5,250
	Purchased inventory on account.		
15	Accounts Payable	1,750	
	Merchandise Inventory		1,750
	Returned inventory to the seller (vendor).		
20	Accounts Payable ($5,250 − $1,750)	3,500	
	Cash ($3,500 − $105)		3,395
	Merchandise Inventory ($3,500 × 0.03)		105
	Paid within discount period net of return.		

$$A\uparrow \left.\begin{array}{c} \\ \text{Merchandise} \\ \text{Inventory}\uparrow \end{array}\right\} = \left\{\begin{array}{c} L\uparrow \quad + \quad E \\ \text{Accounts} \\ \text{Payable}\uparrow \end{array}\right.$$

$$A\downarrow \left.\begin{array}{c} \\ \text{Merchandise} \\ \text{Inventory}\downarrow \end{array}\right\} = \left\{\begin{array}{c} L\downarrow \quad + \quad E \\ \text{Accounts} \\ \text{Payable}\downarrow \end{array}\right.$$

$$A\downarrow \left.\begin{array}{c} \\ \text{Cash}\downarrow \\ \text{Merchandise} \\ \text{Inventory}\downarrow \end{array}\right\} = \left\{\begin{array}{c} L\downarrow \quad + \quad E \\ \text{Accounts} \\ \text{Payable}\downarrow \end{array}\right.$$

> Decisions

Should the business borrow money to make payment within the discount period?

D&B Grocers recently made a large purchase of merchandise inventory on account with credit terms of 5/10, n/30. D&B does not have the cash flow to pay the invoice within the discount period but will have the necessary funds to make payment by the invoice due date. The grocer is considering borrowing money on its line of credit in order to take advantage of the 5% discount. Should D&B borrow the money to make payment within the discount period?

Solution

D&B should only borrow the money if the amount of interest expense paid on the loan will be less than the discount received. It does not make sense for the grocer to borrow money to make an early payment if in the long run it will end up paying more in interest expense than the discount received.

FOB Shipping Point
Situation in which the buyer takes ownership (title) to the goods after the goods leave the seller's place of business (shipping point) and the buyer typically pays the freight.

FOB Destination
Situation in which the buyer takes ownership (title) to the goods at the delivery destination point and the seller typically pays the freight.

Freight In
The transportation cost to ship goods into the purchaser's warehouse; therefore, it is freight on purchased goods.

Freight Out
The transportation cost to ship goods out of the seller's warehouse; therefore, it is freight on goods sold to a customer.

Transportation Costs

Either the seller or the buyer must pay the transportation cost of shipping merchandise inventory. The purchase agreement specifies FOB (free on board) terms to determine when title to the goods transfers to the purchaser and who pays the freight. Exhibit 4 shows that

- **FOB shipping point** means the buyer takes ownership (title) to the goods after the goods leave the seller's place of business (shipping point). In most cases, the buyer (owner of the goods while in transit) also pays the freight.
- **FOB destination** means the buyer takes ownership (title) to the goods at the delivery destination point. In most cases, the seller (owner of the goods while in transit) usually pays the freight.

Freight costs are either freight in or freight out.

- **Freight in** is the transportation cost to ship goods into the purchaser's warehouse; thus, it is freight on purchased goods.
- **Freight out** is the transportation cost to ship goods out of the seller's warehouse and to the customer; thus, it is freight on goods sold.

Exhibit 4 | FOB Terms Determine Who Pays the Freight

Freight In

With the terms FOB shipping point, the buyer owns the goods while they are in transit, so the buyer pays the freight. Because the freight is a cost that must be paid to acquire the inventory, freight in becomes part of the cost of merchandise inventory. As a result, freight in costs are debited to the Merchandise Inventory account. Suppose Smart Touch Learning pays a $60 freight charge on June 3 and makes the following entry:

Date	Accounts and Explanation	Debit	Credit
Jun. 3	Merchandise Inventory	60	
	Cash		60
	Paid a freight bill.		

$$\frac{A\uparrow\downarrow}{\text{Merchandise Inventory}\uparrow \atop \text{Cash}\downarrow} = \frac{L}{} + \frac{E}{}$$

Freight In Within Discount Period

Discounts are computed only on the merchandise purchased from the seller. Discounts are not computed on the transportation costs because there is no discount on freight.

Under FOB shipping point, the seller sometimes prepays the transportation cost as a convenience and lists this cost on the invoice. Assume, for example, Smart Touch Learning makes a $5,000 purchase of goods, coupled with a related freight charge of $400, on June 20 on account with terms of 3/5, n/30. The seller prepays the freight charge. The purchase would be recorded as follows:

Date	Accounts and Explanation	Debit	Credit
Jun. 20	Merchandise Inventory ($5,000 + $400)	5,400	
	Accounts Payable		5,400
	Purchased inventory on account, including freight.		

$$\frac{A\uparrow}{\text{Merchandise Inventory}\uparrow} = \frac{L\uparrow}{\text{Accounts Payable}\uparrow} + \frac{E}{}$$

If Smart Touch Learning pays within the discount period, the discount will be computed only on the $5,000 merchandise cost, not on the total invoice of $5,400. The $400 freight is not eligible for the discount. So, the 3% discount would be $150 ($5,000 × 0.03). The entry to record the early payment on June 25 follows:

Date	Accounts and Explanation	Debit	Credit
Jun. 25	Accounts Payable	5,400	
	Cash ($5,400 − $150)		5,250
	Merchandise Inventory ($5,000 × 0.03)		150
	Paid within discount period, including freight.		

$$\frac{A\downarrow}{\text{Cash}\downarrow \atop \text{Merchandise Inventory}\downarrow} = \frac{L\downarrow}{\text{Accounts Payable}\downarrow} + \frac{E}{}$$

Cost of Inventory Purchased

The net cost of merchandise inventory purchased includes the purchase cost of inventory, less purchase returns and allowances, less purchase discounts, plus freight in. Knowing the net cost of inventory allows a business to determine the actual cost of the merchandise purchased and is calculated as follows:

Net Cost of Inventory Purchased = Purchase cost of inventory − Purchase returns and allowances − Purchase discounts + Freight in

Suppose that during the year, Smart Touch Learning buys $281,750 of inventory, returns $61,250 of the goods, and takes a $4,410 early payment discount. The company also pays $14,700 of freight in. The following summary shows Smart Touch Learning's net cost of this merchandise inventory purchased.

Purchases	$ 281,750
Less: Purchase Returns and Allowances	61,250
Purchase Discounts	4,410
Plus: Freight In	14,700
Net Cost of Inventory Purchased	$ 230,790

> **Try It!**

7. Click Computers has the following transactions in July related to the purchase of merchandise inventory.

July 1	Purchase of $20,500 worth of computers on account, terms of 2/10, n/30.
3	Return of $4,000 of the computers to the vendor.
9	Payment made on account.

Journalize the purchase transactions for Click Computers.

Check your answer at the end of the chapter.

For more practice, see Short Exercises S-2 and S-3. MyAccountingLab

HOW ARE SALES OF MERCHANDISE INVENTORY RECORDED IN A PERPETUAL INVENTORY SYSTEM?

Learning Objective 3

Account for the sale of merchandise inventory using a perpetual inventory system

After a company buys merchandise inventory, the next step is to sell the goods. We shift now to the selling side and follow Smart Touch Learning through a sequence of selling transactions.

Sale of Merchandise Inventory

Sales of retailers, such as Smart Touch Learning, are often made for cash. Suppose Smart Touch Learning sold two tablets for cash on June 19, 2015, to a customer and issued the sales invoice in Exhibit 5. To the seller, a sales invoice is a bill showing what amount the customer must pay.

Sales Revenue
The amount that a merchandiser earns from selling its inventory.

The amount a business earns from selling merchandise inventory is called **Sales Revenue** (also called *Sales*). At the time of the sale, two entries must be recorded in the perpetual inventory system: One entry records the Sales Revenue and the Cash (or Accounts Receivable) at the time of the sale. The second entry records Cost of Goods Sold (debit the expense) and reduces the Merchandise Inventory (credit the asset).

Exhibit 5 | Sales Invoice

Date: June 19, 2015   Invoice #582

SMART TOUCH LEARNING
227 LAKE STREET
POMPTON PLAINS, IL 07444

Quantity	Item	Unit Price	Total
2	Touch Screen Tablet Computers	$500	$1,000
Total			$1,000

Remember, Cost of Goods Sold (COGS) is an expense account and represents the cost of inventory that has been sold to customers.

To record the sale by Smart Touch Learning, two journal entries must be recorded. The first journal entry records the cash sale of $1,000 by debiting Cash and crediting Sales Revenue. A second journal entry must also be made to record the expense and decrease the Merchandise Inventory balance. Suppose these goods sold by Smart Touch Learning cost $700. The second journal entry would transfer the $700 from the Merchandise Inventory account to the Cost of Goods Sold account, as follows:

	Date	Accounts and Explanation	Debit	Credit
This entry records the sales revenue.	Jun. 19	Cash	1,000	
		Sales Revenue		1,000
		Cash sale.		
This entry records the expense and the reduction of merchandise inventory.	19	Cost of Goods Sold	700	
		Merchandise Inventory		700
		Recorded the cost of goods sold.		

$$\underset{\text{Cash}\uparrow}{\text{A}\uparrow} \Big\} = \Big\{ \text{L} \quad + \quad \underset{\substack{\text{Sales}\\\text{Revenue}\uparrow}}{\text{E}\uparrow}$$

$$\underset{\substack{\text{Merchandise}\\\text{Inventory}\downarrow}}{\text{A}\downarrow} \Big\} = \Big\{ \text{L} \quad + \quad \underset{\substack{\text{Cost of Goods}\\\text{Sold}\uparrow}}{\text{E}\downarrow}$$

The Cost of Goods Sold account keeps a current balance throughout the period in a perpetual inventory system of the cost of merchandise inventory sold. In this example, Cost of Goods Sold is $700 (the cost to Smart Touch Learning) rather than $1,000, the selling price (retail) of the goods. Cost of Goods Sold is always based on the company's cost, not the retail price.

Merchandise Inventory			Cost of Goods Sold	
Bal. xx,xxx	700 June 19 ⟶	June 19	700	

Many sales are made on account (on credit) instead of with cash. Now let's assume that Smart Touch Learning sold 10 tablets for $500 each, making a $5,000 (10 tablets × $500 per tablet) sale on account with terms of 2/10, n/30 for goods that cost $3,500 on June 21. The entries to record the sale and cost of goods sold follow:

A↑ = L + E↑
Accounts Receivable↑ = Sales Revenue↑

A↓ = L + E↓
Merchandise Inventory↓ = Cost of Goods Sold↑

Date	Accounts and Explanation	Debit	Credit
Jun. 21	Accounts Receivable	5,000	
	Sales Revenue		5,000
	Sale on account.		
21	Cost of Goods Sold	3,500	
	Merchandise Inventory		3,500
	Recorded the cost of goods sold.		

Sales Discounts

Sales Discounts
Reduction in the amount of cash received from a customer for early payment.

Many sellers offer customers a discount for early payment. We saw that purchase discounts decrease the cost of inventory purchases. In the same way, sales discounts decrease the net amount of revenue earned on sales. The Sales Discounts account is a contra account to Sales Revenue. Contra account has the opposite normal balance of its companion account. So, Sales Discounts is a contra revenue account and has a normal debit balance.

Assume the customer that purchased the tablets on June 21 made payment on June 30, within the discount period. Smart Touch Learning will collect $4,900—the $5,000 amount owed less the 2 percent discount, $100 ($5,000 × 0.02). Smart Touch Learning will record the collection of cash on the receivable and the corresponding sales discount as follows:

A↓ = L + E↓
Cash↑
Accounts Receivable↓ = Sales Discounts↑

Date	Accounts and Explanation	Debit	Credit
Jun. 30	Cash ($5,000 − $100)	4,900	
	Sales Discounts ($5,000 × 0.02)	100	
	Accounts Receivable		5,000
	Cash collection within the discount period.		

An increase in the Sales Discount contra account is recorded as a debit. This increase reduces the overall Sales Revenue of the company.

Notice that Smart Touch Learning credited Accounts Receivable for the full amount of the invoice. As shown in the following T-account, by doing this, Smart Touch Learning has accurately shown that the invoice was paid in full with no remaining balance.

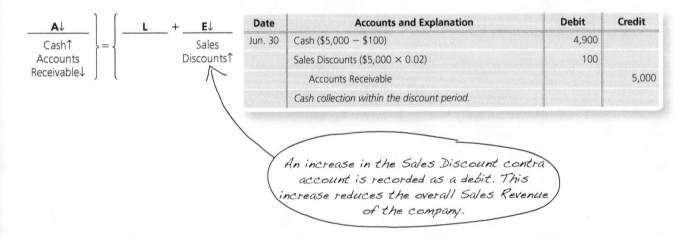

Accounts Receivable		
June 21 5,000	5,000 June 30	
Bal. **0**		

Assume instead that the customer did not pay the invoice within the discount period, but paid on July 15. The customer would instead pay the full amount of $5,000 and Smart Touch Learning would record the collection of cash as follows:

Date	Accounts and Explanation	Debit	Credit
Jul. 15	Cash	5,000	
	Accounts Receivable		5,000
	Cash collection after the discount period.		

$$A\uparrow\downarrow \Big\} = \Big\{ \underline{\quad L \quad} + \underline{\quad E \quad}$$

Cash↑
Accounts
Receivable↓

Sales Returns and Allowances

After making a sale, Smart Touch Learning may have customers that return goods, asking for a refund or credit to the customer's account. Or the company may instead grant a sales allowance to encourage the customer to accept the non-standard goods. Such an allowance reduces the future cash collected from the customer. The return of goods or granting of an allowance is called Sales Returns and Allowances. Similar to Sales Discounts, the Sales Returns and Allowances account is a contra account to Sales Revenue and has a normal debit balance.

Sales Returns and Allowances
Decreases in the seller's receivable from a customer's return of merchandise or from granting the customer an allowance from the amount owed to the seller.

Sales Return

Assume that the customer has not yet paid the original bill of June 21. Suppose, on June 25, the customer returns three of the tablets that were sold for $1,500, with a cost of goods sold of $1,050. When recording a return of merchandise, the seller must record two journal entries: one to record the sales return and decrease the receivable ($1,500) and the other to update the Merchandise Inventory account for the cost of the returned merchandise ($1,050). Smart Touch Learning will record the following two journal entries when the merchandise is returned:

	Date	Accounts and Explanation	Debit	Credit
This entry records the sales returns and allowances.	Jun. 25	Sales Returns and Allowances	1,500	
		Accounts Receivable		1,500
		Received returned goods.		
This entry records the return of the merchandise.	25	Merchandise Inventory	1,050	
		Cost of Goods Sold		1,050
		Placed goods back in inventory.		

$$A\downarrow \Big\} = \Big\{ \underline{\quad L \quad} + \underline{\quad E\downarrow \quad}$$

Accounts
Receivable↓

Sales
Returns and
Allowances↑

$$A\uparrow \Big\} = \Big\{ \underline{\quad L \quad} + \underline{\quad E\uparrow \quad}$$

Merchandise
Inventory↑

Cost of Goods
Sold↓

By recording the above journal entry, the Sales Returns and Allowances account increases and the Accounts Receivable decreases. The seller will not collect cash for the returned goods. In addition, the Merchandise Inventory account increases to reflect the returned goods, but the Cost of Goods Sold must be decreased because the goods are no longer considered sold.

Sales Allowance

When a seller grants a sales allowance, there are no returned goods from the customer. Therefore, there is no second entry to adjust the Merchandise Inventory account. Suppose that on June 28 Smart Touch Learning grants a $100 sales allowance for goods damaged in transit. A sales allowance is recorded as follows:

$$A\downarrow = L + E\downarrow$$

Accounts Receivable↓ = L + Sales Returns and Allowances↑

Date	Accounts and Explanation	Debit	Credit
Jun. 28	Sales Returns and Allowances	100	
	Accounts Receivable		100
	Granted a sales allowance for damaged goods.		

After the return and allowance have been posted, the Accounts Receivable balance related to the June 21 sale is $3,400, as follows:

Accounts Receivable

June 21	5,000	1,500	June 25
		100	June 28
Bal.	**3,400**		

Sales Returns and Allowances Within Discount Period

If sales returns and allowances occur before the discount period has expired, any discount allowed would be calculated net of the returns and allowances. For example, suppose that on June 30, Smart Touch Learning receives payment on the receivable. The company's cash receipt is $3,332, and the entry recorded is as follows:

$$A\downarrow = L + E\downarrow$$

Cash↑ Accounts Receivable↓ = L + Sales Discounts↑

Date	Accounts and Explanation	Debit	Credit
Jun. 30	Cash ($3,400 − $68)	3,332	
	Sales Discounts ($3,400 × 0.02)	68	
	Accounts Receivable		3,400
	Cash collection within discount period net of return		
	and allowance.		

Transportation Costs—Freight Out

Remember that a freight out expense is one in which the seller pays freight charges to ship goods to customers. Freight out is a delivery expense to the seller. Delivery expense is an operating expense and is debited to the Delivery Expense account. For example, assume Smart Touch Learning paid $30 to ship goods to a customer on June 21. The entry to record that payment is as follows:

$$A\downarrow = L + E\downarrow$$

Cash↓ = L + Delivery Expense↑

Date	Accounts and Explanation	Debit	Credit
Jun. 21	Delivery Expense	30	
	Cash		30
	Paid a freight bill.		

Net Sales Revenue and Gross Profit

Net Sales Revenue is calculated as Sales Revenue less Sales Returns and Allowances and Sales Discounts. Net Sales Revenue is the amount a company has made on sales of merchandise inventory after returns and allowances and discounts have been taken out.

Net Sales Revenue
The amount a company has made on sales of merchandise inventory after returns, allowances, and discounts have been taken out. Sales Revenue less Sales Returns and Allowances and Sales Discounts.

Net Sales Revenue = Sales Revenue − Sales Returns and Allowances − Sales Discounts

Suppose during the year Smart Touch Learning sells $297,500 of merchandise inventory, receives $11,200 of sales returns and allowances, and accepts $5,600 of early payment discounts. The following summary shows Smart Touch Learning's net sales revenue.

Sales Revenue	$ 297,500
Less: Sales Returns and Allowances	11,200
Sales Discounts	5,600
Net Sales Revenue	$ 280,700

After determining net sales revenue, Smart Touch Learning can then calculate its gross profit. Remember, gross profit is the markup on the merchandise inventory and is calculated as net sales revenue minus cost of goods sold. For this example, assume Smart Touch Learning's Cost of Goods Sold is $199,500; its gross profit is calculated as follows:

Net Sales Revenue	$ 280,700
Less: Cost of Goods Sold	199,500
Gross Profit	$ 81,200

Gross profit, along with net income, is a measure of business success. A sufficiently high gross profit is vital to a merchandiser. The gross profit is reported on the merchandiser's income statement and is the sum of the gross profits on all merchandise sold. The gross profit must cover the company's operating expenses for the company to survive.

> Try It!

8. Click Computers has the following transactions in July related to the sale of merchandise inventory.

July 12	Sold computers on account for $8,000 to customers, terms 3/15, n/30. The cost of the computers is $4,800.
21	Accepted a $1,000 return from a customer. The computer returned had a cost of $600.
26	Received payment from customer on balance due.

Journalize the sales transactions for Click Computers.

Check your answer at the end of the chapter.

For more practice, see Short Exercises S-4 and S-5. MyAccountingLab

WHAT ARE THE ADJUSTING AND CLOSING ENTRIES FOR A MERCHANDISER?

Learning Objective 4

Adjust and close the accounts of a merchandising business

A merchandiser adjusts and closes accounts the same way a service entity does. If a work-sheet is used, the unadjusted trial balance is entered, and the worksheet is completed to determine net income or net loss.

Adjusting Merchandise Inventory Based on a Physical Count

Inventory Shrinkage

The loss of inventory that occurs because of theft, damage, and errors.

The Merchandise Inventory account should stay current at all times in a perpetual inventory system. However, the actual amount of inventory on hand may differ from what the books show. This difference can occur because of theft, damage, and errors and is referred to as **inventory shrinkage**. For this reason, businesses take a physical count of inventory *at least* once a year. The most common time to count inventory is at the end of the fiscal year. The business then adjusts the Merchandise Inventory account based on the physical count. Smart Touch Learning must record an adjusting entry to account for this lost inventory.

Smart Touch Learning's Merchandise Inventory account shows an unadjusted balance of $31,530. With no shrinkage—due to theft or error—the business should have inventory costing $31,530. But on December 31, Smart Touch Learning counts the inventory on hand, and the total cost comes to only $31,290.

Adjusting entry = Merchandise inventory balance before adjustment − Actual merchandise inventory on hand = $31,530 − $31,290 = $240

Smart Touch Learning records this adjusting entry for inventory shrinkage:

Date	Accounts and Explanation	Debit	Credit
Dec. 31	Cost of Goods Sold	240	
	Merchandise Inventory		240
	Adjustment for inventory shrinkage.		

$$A\downarrow \quad\Big\}= \Big\{\quad L \quad + \quad E\downarrow$$

Merchandise Inventory↓ = Cost of Goods Sold↑

This entry brings Merchandise Inventory to its correct balance.

Merchandise Inventory

Unadj. Bal.	31,530	240	Adj.	Dec. 31
Bal.	**31,290**			

Closing the Accounts of a Merchandiser

Exhibit 6 (on the next page) presents Smart Touch Learning's adjusted trial balance and closing entries for the year, with the new accounts (highlighted in blue). Closing still means to zero out all temporary accounts (accounts that aren't on the balance sheet).

The four-step closing process for a merchandising company follows:

Step 1: Make the revenue accounts equal zero via the Income Summary account.

Step 2: Make expense accounts and other temporary accounts with a debit balance (Sales Returns and Allowances and Sales Discounts) equal zero via the Income Summary account.

Step 3: Make the Income Summary account equal zero via the Capital account. This closing entry transfers net income (or net loss) to Capital.

Step 4: Make the Withdrawals account equal zero via the Capital account.

Worksheet for a Merchandising Business—Perpetual Inventory System

The worksheet of a merchandiser is similar to the worksheet for a service business. The main new account is the Merchandise Inventory account, which must be adjusted based on a physical count due to inventory shrinkage. Also, the merchandiser's worksheet carries the other new merchandising accounts (Sales Revenue, Sales Returns and Allowances, Sales Discounts, and Cost of Goods Sold). Worksheet procedures are the same as for a service business. The sum of the unadjusted trial balance amounts, plus or minus the adjustments, equals the adjusted trial balance amounts. The revenue and expenses are then moved to the income statement and the assets, liabilities, and equity amounts are moved to the balance sheet.

Exhibit 6 | **Adjusted Trial Balance and Closing Entries**

	Balance	
SMART TOUCH LEARNING Adjusted Trial Balance December 31, 2015		
Account Title	**Debit**	**Credit**
Cash	$ 8,810	
Accounts Receivable	4,400	
Merchandise Inventory	31,290	
Office Supplies	100	
Prepaid Rent	4,000	
Furniture	18,000	
Accumulated Depreciation—Furniture		$ 2,100
Building	60,000	
Accumulated Depreciation—Building		1,750
Land	20,000	
Accounts Payable		10,800
Utilities Payable		2,500
Salaries Payable		1,500
Interest Payable		300
Unearned Revenue		900
Notes Payable		60,000
Bright, Capital		51,550
Bright, Withdrawals	10,000	
Sales Revenue		297,500
Sales Returns and Allowances	11,200	
Sales Discounts	5,600	
Cost of Goods Sold	199,500	
Salaries Expense	15,000	
Rent Expense	13,000	
Utilities Expense	11,300	
Insurance Expense	6,500	
Depreciation Expense—Furniture	1,800	
Depreciation Expense—Building	1,500	
Advertising Expense	2,400	
Interest Expense	2,300	
Delivery Expense	1,600	
Supplies Expense	600	
Total	**$ 428,900**	**$ 428,900**

Temporary accounts that are closed.

Exhibit 6 | **(Continued)**

Date	Accounts and Explanation	Debit	Credit
Dec. 31	Sales Revenue	297,500	
	Income Summary		297,500
	To close revenue.		
31	Income Summary	272,300	
	Sales Returns and Allowances		11,200
	Sales Discounts		5,600
	Cost of Goods Sold		199,500
	Salaries Expense		15,000
	Rent Expense		13,000
	Utilities Expense		11,300
	Insurance Expense		6,500
	Depreciation Expense—Furniture		1,800
	Depreciation Expense—Building		1,500
	Advertising Expense		2,400
	Interest Expense		2,300
	Delivery Expense		1,600
	Supplies Expense		600
	To close expenses and other debit accounts.		
31	Income Summary	25,200	
	Bright, Capital		25,200
	To close Income Summary.		
31	Bright, Capital	10,000	
	Bright, Withdrawals		10,000
	To close withdrawals.		

A		L	+	E↑↓
	= {			Sales Revenue↓ Income Summary↑

A		L	+	E↑↓
	= {			Income Summary↓ Sales Returns and Allowances↓ Sales Discounts↓ Expenses↓

A		L	+	E↑↓
	= {			Income Summary↓ Bright, Capital↑

A		L	+	E↑↓
	= {			Bright, Capital↓ Bright, Withdrawals↓

Income Summary

Clos. 2	272,300	297,500	Clos. 1
		25,200	Bal.
Clos. 3	25,200		
		0	**Bal.**

Bright, Capital

		51,550	Adj. Bal.
Clos. 4	10,000	25,200	Clos. 3
		66,750	**Bal.**

Bright, Withdrawals

Adj. Bal.	10,000		
		10,000	Clos. 4
Bal.	**0**		

▷ Try It!

9. Click Computers' Merchandise Inventory account at year-end is showing a balance of $43,000. The physical count of inventory came up with $42,500. Journalize the adjusting entry needed to account for the inventory shrinkage.

Check your answer at the end of the chapter.

For more practice, see Short Exercises S-6 and S-7. MyAccountingLab

HOW ARE A MERCHANDISER'S FINANCIAL STATEMENTS PREPARED?

Learning Objective 5

Prepare a merchandiser's financial statements

The financial statements that you have learned for a service business are also used by a merchandiser. However, the merchandiser's financial statements will contain the new accounts that have been introduced in this chapter. Let's take a look at some of the differences for a merchandising business.

Income Statement

As you have learned, the balance sheet can appear in two formats:

- The report format (assets at top, liabilities and owner's equity at bottom).
- The account format (assets at left, liabilities and owner's equity at right).

There are also two formats for the income statement:

- The single-step format.
- The multi-step format.

Single-Step Income Statement

Single-Step Income Statement

Income statement format that groups all revenues together and then lists and deducts all expenses together without calculating any subtotals.

The single-step income statement is the income statement format that you first learned. It groups all revenues together and all expenses together without calculating other subtotals. Many companies use this format. The single-step format clearly distinguishes revenues from expenses and works well for service entities because they have no gross profit to report. Exhibit 7 shows a single-step income statement for Smart Touch Learning.

Multi-Step Income Statement

Multi-Step Income Statement

Income statement format that contains subtotals to highlight significant relationships. In addition to net income, it reports gross profit and operating income.

A multi-step income statement lists several important subtotals. In addition to net income (the bottom line), it also reports subtotals for gross profit and operating income (income from operations). The multi-step income statement for Smart Touch Learning appears in Exhibit 8 (on the next page).

Exhibit 7 | **Single-Step Income Statement**

Cost of Goods Sold represents a _functional_ expense. Such expenses explain the purpose of the cost incurred. IFRS allows companies to present expenses according to their function or nature. By nature, expenses are described as salaries, utilities, or advertising expenses.

SMART TOUCH LEARNING Income Statement Year Ended December 31, 2015		
Revenues:		
Net Sales Revenue		$ 280,700
Expenses:		
Cost of Goods Sold	$ 199,500	
Salaries Expense	15,000	
Rent Expense	13,000	
Utilities Expense	11,300	
Insurance Expense	6,500	
Depreciation Expense—Furniture	1,800	
Depreciation Expense—Building	1,500	
Advertising Expense	2,400	
Interest Expense	2,300	
Delivery Expense	1,600	
Supplies Expense	600	
Total Expenses		255,500
Net Income		$ 25,200

Exhibit 8 | **Multi-Step Income Statement**

SMART TOUCH LEARNING
Income Statement
Year Ended December 31, 2015

Sales Revenue	$ 297,500	
Less: Sales Returns and Allowances	11,200	
Sales Discounts	5,600	
Net Sales Revenue		$ 280,700
Cost of Goods Sold		199,500
Gross Profit		81,200
Operating Expenses:		
Selling Expenses:		
Salaries Expense	8,100	
Rent Expense	7,300	
Advertising Expense	2,400	
Depreciation Expense	2,200	
Delivery Expense	1,600	
Total Selling Expenses	21,600	
Administrative Expenses:		
Utilities Expense	11,300	
Salaries Expense	6,900	
Insurance Expense	6,500	
Rent Expense	5,700	
Depreciation Expense	1,100	
Supplies Expense	600	
Total Administrative Expenses	32,100	
Total Operating Expenses		53,700
Operating Income		27,500
Other Revenues and (Expenses):		
Interest Expense	(2,300)	
Total Other Revenues and (Expenses)		(2,300)
Net Income		$ 25,200

Brackets at left: Gross Profit; Operating Income; Other Revenues and (Expenses) and Net Income

The income statement begins with net sales revenue, cost of goods sold, and gross profit. Next, the operating expenses, those expenses other than cost of goods sold, are listed. Both merchandisers and service companies report operating expenses in two categories:

- **Selling expenses** are expenses related to marketing and selling the company's products. These include sales salaries, sales commissions, advertising, depreciation on store buildings and equipment, store rent, utilities on store buildings, property taxes on store buildings, and delivery expense.

- **Administrative expenses** include expenses *not* related to marketing the company's products. These include office expenses, such as the salaries of the executives and office employees; depreciation on office buildings and equipment; rent other than on stores (for example, rent on the administrative office); utilities other than on stores (for example, utilities on the administrative office); and property taxes on the administrative office building.

Selling Expenses
Expenses related to marketing and selling the company's products.

Administrative Expenses
Expenses incurred that are not related to marketing the company's products.

Operating Income
Measures the results of the entity's major ongoing activities. Gross profit minus operating expenses.

Gross profit minus operating expenses equals operating income (also called *income from operations*). Operating income measures the results of the entity's major ongoing activities (normal operations).

Other Revenues and Expenses
Revenues or expenses that are outside the normal, day-to-day operations of a business, such as a gain or loss on the sale of plant assets or interest expense.

The last section of the income statement is other revenues and expenses. This category reports revenues and expenses that fall outside the business's main, day-to-day, regular operations. Examples include interest revenue, interest expense, and gains and losses on the sale of plant assets. These examples have nothing to do with the business's "normal" business. As a result, they are classified as "other" items.

Statement of Owner's Equity and the Balance Sheet

A merchandiser's statement of owner's equity looks exactly like that of a service business. The balance sheet will also look the same as for a service business, except merchandisers have an additional current asset, Merchandise Inventory. Service businesses do not have merchandise inventory.

> Try It!

10. Capital City Motorcycle's selected accounts as of December 31, 2015 follow:

Selling Expenses	$ 10,500
Interest Revenue	1,000
Sales Returns and Allowances	4,500
Sales Revenue	120,000
Cost of Goods Sold	85,000
Sales Discounts	2,000
Administrative Expenses	8,000

Prepare the multi-step income statement for the year ended December 31, 2015.
Check your answer at the end of the chapter.

For more practice, see Short Exercises S-8 and S-9. MyAccountingLab

HOW DO WE USE THE GROSS PROFIT PERCENTAGE TO EVALUATE BUSINESS PERFORMANCE?

Learning Objective 6
Use the gross profit percentage to evaluate business performance

Merchandisers use several ratios to evaluate their operations, and among them is the gross profit percentage. The gross profit percentage measures the profitability of each sales dollar above the cost of goods sold and is computed as follows:

Gross Profit Percentage
Measures the profitability of each sales dollar above the cost of goods sold. Gross profit / Net sales revenue.

Gross profit percentage = Gross profit / Net sales revenue

The gross profit percentage is one of the most carefully watched measures of profitability. It reflects a business's ability to earn a profit on its merchandise inventory. The gross profit earned on merchandise inventory must be high enough to cover the remaining operating expenses and to earn net income. A small increase in the gross profit percentage from last year to this year may signal an important rise in income. Conversely, a small decrease from last year to this year may signal trouble. Gross profit percentages vary among industries, but in general, a high gross profit percentage is desired.

Using the example of **Green Mountain Coffee Roasters, Inc.,** we can now calculate the gross profit percentage. Green Mountain had the following total net sales and cost of sales (cost of goods sold).

	For year ended Sep. 24, 2011 (in thousands)	For year ended Sep. 25, 2010 (in thousands)
Net sales	$ 2,650,899	$ 1,356,775
Cost of sales	1,746,274	931,017

Gross profit is calculated as total net sales less cost of sales. To determine the gross profit percentage, the gross profit is then divided by total net sales. The gross profit percentage for the year ending September 24, 2011, follows:

Gross profit percentage = ($2,650,899 − $1,746,274) / $2,650,899 = 0.341 = 34.1%

In comparison, the gross profit percentage for the year ending September 25, 2010, was

Gross profit percentage = ($1,356,775 − $931,017) / $1,356,775 = 0.314 = 31.4%

The gross profit percentage has stayed relatively stable from 2010 to 2011 signifying that Green Mountain is maintaining a steady gross profit on its cost of sales even given the significant increase in net sales. However, when comparing with the industry average for gross profit percentage, 56.83%, Green Mountain is significantly lower than average. Green Mountain should consider the amount of profit it is earning on its merchandise inventory.

 Try It!

11. Capital City Motorcycle's selected accounts as of December 31, 2015 follow:

Selling Expenses	$ 10,500
Interest Revenue	1,000
Sales Returns and Allowances	4,500
Sales Revenue	120,000
Cost of Goods Sold	85,000
Sales Discounts	2,000
Administrative Expenses	8,000

Determine the gross profit percentage for the year ended December 31, 2015.
Check your answer at the end of the chapter.

For more practice, see Short Exercise S-10. MyAccountingLab

APPENDIX A: Accounting for Merchandise Inventory in a Periodic Inventory System

HOW ARE MERCHANDISE INVENTORY TRANSACTIONS RECORDED IN A PERIODIC INVENTORY SYSTEM?

Learning Objective 7

Account for the purchase and sale of merchandise inventory using a periodic inventory system

Some smaller businesses find it too expensive to invest in a perpetual inventory system. These businesses use a periodic inventory system. In a periodic inventory system, businesses must obtain a physical count of inventory to determine quantities on hand.

Purchases of Merchandise Inventory

All inventory systems use the Merchandise Inventory account. But in a periodic inventory system, purchases, purchase discounts, purchase returns and allowances, and freight in costs are recorded in separate accounts during the year and then the Merchandise Inventory account is updated in the closing process. Let's account for Smart Touch Learning's purchase of the tablet computers from Southwest Electronics Direct shown in Exhibit A-1.

Exhibit A-1 | Purchase Invoice

Explanations:

1. The seller is Southwest Electronics Direct.
2. The purchaser is Smart Touch Learning.
3. The invoice date is needed to determine whether the purchaser gets a discount for prompt payment (see 4).
4. Credit terms: If Smart Touch Learning pays within 15 days of the invoice date, it can deduct a 3% discount. Otherwise, the full amount—NET—is due in 30 days.
5. Total invoice amount is $35,000
6. Smart Touch Learning's payment date. How much did Smart Touch Learning pay? (see 7).
7. Payment occurred 14 days after the invoice date—within the discount period—so Smart Touch Learning paid $33,950 ($35,000 - 3% discount).

1

Southwest Electronics Direct
P.O. BOX 101010
HOUSTON, TX 77212

	Invoice	
	Date	Number
3	6/1/15	410

6 *Pd. 6/15/15*

2

Shipped To: SMART TOUCH LEARNING
227 LAKE STREET
POMPTON PLAINS, IL 07444

4

Credit Terms					
3/15, NET 30 DAYS					
	Description		Quantity Shipped	Unit Price	Total
	Touch Screen Tablet Computers		100	$ 350	$35,000

Due Date & Due Amount			Sub Total	$35,000
06/16/15		07/01/2015	Ship. or Handl. Chg.	–
$33,950		$35,000	Tax (3%)	–
7			Total(s)	$35,000
				5

Merchandising Operations

The following entries record the receipt of goods on account on June 3 and payment on June 15 (within the discount period) using the periodic inventory system.

Date	Accounts and Explanation	Debit	Credit
Jun. 3	Purchases	35,000	
	Accounts Payable		35,000
	Purchased inventory on account.		
15	Accounts Payable	35,000	
	Cash ($35,000 − $1,050)		33,950
	Purchase Discounts ($35,000 × 0.03)		1,050
	Paid within discount period.		

A | = { | L↑ | + | E↓ |
| | Accounts Payable↑ | | Purchases↑ |

A↓ Cash↓ | = { | L↓ Accounts Payable↓ | + | E↑ Purchase Discounts↑ |

When using the periodic inventory system, the Merchandise Inventory account is not updated during the period. Therefore, it will never be used when recording purchases, discounts, returns, or sales of inventory.

Notice that the purchase of merchandise inventory is not recorded directly into the Merchandise Inventory account. Instead, it is recorded in a separate account called Purchases (an expense account). Likewise, when Smart Touch Learning makes payment for the merchandise, the purchase discount is recorded in a separate account called Purchase Discounts (a contra expense account).

Recording Purchase Returns and Allowances

Suppose that, prior to payment, on June 4, Smart Touch Learning returned 20 tablets to the vendor costing $7,000. The company would record this return as follows:

Date	Accounts and Explanation	Debit	Credit
Jun. 4	Accounts Payable	7,000	
	Purchase Returns and Allowances		7,000
	Returned inventory to seller (vendor).		

A | = { | L↓ Accounts Payable↓ | + | E↑ Purchase Returns and Allowances↑ |

In the periodic inventory system, instead of recording the return to Merchandise Inventory, a separate account, Purchase Returns and Allowances, is used. Both Purchase Discounts and Purchase Returns and Allowances are contra expense accounts. They are related to the Purchases account.

During the period, the business records the cost of all inventory bought in the Purchases account. The balance of Purchases is a *gross* amount because it does not include subtractions for discounts, returns, or allowances. **Net purchases** is the remainder after subtracting the contra accounts from Purchases:

Net Purchases
Purchases less purchase returns and allowances less purchase discounts.

Purchases
− Purchase Returns and Allowances
− Purchase Discounts
= Net Purchases

Recording Transportation Costs

Under the periodic inventory system, freight in is debited to a separate Freight In account (an expense account) as opposed to debiting the Merchandise Inventory account. For example, suppose Smart Touch Learning pays a $60 freight charge on June 3. The company would make the following entry:

Date	Accounts and Explanation	Debit	Credit
Jun. 3	Freight In	60	
	Cash		60
	Paid a freight bill.		

Sale of Merchandise Inventory

Recording sales of merchandise inventory is streamlined in the periodic inventory system. With no running record of merchandise inventory to maintain, there is no need to record an entry to Merchandise Inventory and Cost of Goods Sold. Instead, a sale of inventory only involves recording the Sales Revenue portion. Suppose that on June 19, Smart Touch Learning sold 10 tablets for a total sale of $5,000 on account. The company would record the sale as follows:

$$\frac{A\uparrow}{\text{Accounts Receivable}\uparrow} \left.\right\} = \left\{ \frac{L}{} + \frac{E\uparrow}{\text{Sales Revenue}\uparrow} \right.$$

Date	Accounts and Explanation	Debit	Credit
Jun. 19	Accounts Receivable	5,000	
	Sales Revenue		5,000
	Sale on account.		

Accounting for sales discounts and sales returns and allowances is the same as in a perpetual inventory system, except that there are no entries to Merchandise Inventory or Cost of Goods Sold.

Adjusting and Closing Entries

When using the periodic inventory system, there is no need to record an adjusting entry for inventory shrinkage. This is because there is no perpetual running balance of the Merchandise Inventory account. Instead, the business determines the ending Merchandise Inventory amount by taking a physical count of inventory. The amount of this physical count is the amount that is recorded as ending Merchandise Inventory ($31,290 for Smart Touch Learning).

The process of recording the ending Merchandise Inventory is completed through the closing entry process. Let's take a look at Smart Touch Learning's adjusted trial balance and closing entries for the year under the periodic inventory system shown in Exhibit A-2 (on the next page). The accounts that are used in the periodic inventory system are highlighted in blue.

Exhibit A-2 | Adjusted Trial Balance and Closing Entries

SMART TOUCH LEARNING
Adjusted Trial Balance
December 31, 2015

Account Title	Balance Debit	Balance Credit
Cash	$ 8,810	
Accounts Receivable	4,400	
Merchandise Inventory (beginning)	0	
Office Supplies	100	
Prepaid Rent	4,000	
Furniture	18,000	
Accumulated Depreciation—Furniture		$ 2,100
Building	60,000	
Accumulated Depreciation—Building		1,750
Land	20,000	
Accounts Payable		10,800
Utilities Payable		2,500
Salaries Payable		1,500
Interest Payable		300
Unearned Revenue		900
Notes Payable		60,000
Bright, Capital		51,550
Bright, Withdrawals	10,000	
Sales Revenue		297,500
Sales Returns and Allowances	11,200	
Sales Discounts	5,600	
Purchases	281,750	
Purchase Returns and Allowances		61,250
Purchase Discounts		4,410
Freight In	14,700	
Salaries Expense	15,000	
Rent Expense	13,000	
Utilities Expense	11,300	
Insurance Expense	6,500	
Depreciation Expense—Furniture	1,800	
Depreciation Expense—Building	1,500	
Advertising Expense	2,400	
Interest Expense	2,300	
Delivery Expense	1,600	
Supplies Expense	600	
Total	$ 494,560	$ 494,560

Temporary accounts that are closed.

Exhibit A-2 | **(Continued)**

Date	Accounts and Explanation	Debit	Credit
Dec. 31	Sales Revenue	297,500	
	Purchase Returns and Allowances	61,250	
	Purchase Discounts	4,410	
	Merchandise Inventory (ending)	31,290	
	Income Summary		394,450
	To close revenue and other credit accounts		
	and record ending merchandise inventory.		
31	Income Summary	369,250	
	Sales Returns and Allowances		11,200
	Sales Discounts		5,600
	Purchases		281,750
	Freight In		14,700
	Merchandise Inventory (beginning)		0
	Salaries Expense		15,000
	Rent Expense		13,000
	Utilities Expense		11,300
	Insurance Expense		6,500
	Depreciation Expense—Furniture		1,800
	Depreciation Expense—Building		1,500
	Advertising Expense		2,400
	Interest Expense		2,300
	Delivery Expense		1,600
	Supplies Expense		600
	To close expenses and other debit accounts		
	and remove beginning merchandise inventory.		
31	Income Summary	25,200	
	Bright, Capital		25,200
	To close Income Summary.		
31	Bright, Capital	10,000	
	Bright, Withdrawals		10,000
	To close withdrawals.		

A↑ } = { L + E↑
Merchandise Inventory↑
Sales Revenue↓
Purchase Returns and Allowances↓
Purchase Discounts↓
Income Summary↑

A↓ } = { L + E↓
Merchandise Inventory↓
Income Summary↓
Sales Returns and Allowances↓
Sales Discounts↓
Expenses↓

A } = { L + E↑↓
Income Summary↓
Bright, Capital↑

A } = { L + E↑↓
Bright, Capital↓
Bright, Withdrawals↓

Income Summary

Clos. 2	369,250	394,450	Clos. 1
		25,200	Bal.
Clos. 3	25,200		
		0	**Bal.**

Bright, Capital

		51,550	Adj. Bal.
Clos. 4	10,000	25,200	Clos. 3
		66,750	**Bal.**

Bright, Withdrawals

Adj. Bal.	10,000		
		10,000	Clos. 4
Bal.	**0**		

The four-step closing process under the periodic inventory system is similar to the perpetual inventory system, but let's take a moment to highlight the differences:

Step 1: Using the periodic inventory system, Sales Revenue is still closed with a debit via the Income Summary Account; but in addition, all other temporary accounts with credit balances (Purchase Returns and Allowances and Purchase Discounts) are also closed. The ending Merchandise Inventory (determined from the physical count) is recorded as a debit.

Step 2: Expense accounts and other temporary accounts with debit balances are still closed via the Income Summary account. In addition, the beginning Merchandise Inventory, Purchases, and Freight In are also closed via the Income Summary account.

Step 3 and Step 4: These steps, closing the Income Summary account and owner withdrawals, are the same under both methods.

> *The key difference in the closing process under the periodic inventory system is how merchandise inventory is handled. In the periodic inventory system, the ending merchandise inventory balance must be recorded as a debit during closing and the beginning merchandise inventory balance must be recorded as a credit during closing. The additional Purchases and related contra accounts must also be closed.*

Preparing Financial Statements

The financial statements under the perpetual and periodic inventory systems are similar. However, the periodic inventory system requires an additional calculation—the cost of goods sold. As we have seen under the perpetual inventory system, cost of goods sold is simply the sum of the amounts posted to that account. Cost of goods sold must be computed separately under the periodic inventory system. At the end of each period, the company combines a number of accounts to compute cost of goods sold for the period, and this calculation is shown on the income statement. Cost of goods sold is calculated as follows for Smart Touch Learning:

Beginning Merchandise Inventory		$ 0
Purchases	$ 281,750	
Less: Purchase Returns and Allowances	61,250	
Purchase Discounts	4,410	
Net Purchases	216,090	
Plus: Freight In:	14,700	
Net Cost of Purchases		230,790
Cost of Goods Available for Sale		230,790
Less: Ending Inventory		31,290
Cost of Goods Sold		$ 199,500

The multi-step income statement for Smart Touch Learning is presented in Exhibit A-3. Notice that the net income is the same under both methods.

Exhibit A-3 | Multi-Step Income Statement

SMART TOUCH LEARNING			
Income Statement			
Year Ended December 31, 2015			
Sales Revenue		$ 297,500	
Less: Sales Returns and Allowances		11,200	
Sales Discounts		5,600	
Net Sales Revenue			$ 280,700
Cost of Goods Sold:			
Beginning Merchandise Inventory		0	
Purchases	$ 281,750		
Less: Purchase Returns and Allowances	61,250		
Purchase Discounts	4,410		
Net Purchases	216,090		
Plus: Freight In:	14,700		
Net Cost of Purchases		230,790	
Cost of Goods Available for Sale		230,790	
Less: Ending Merchandise Inventory		31,290	
Cost of Goods Sold			199,500
Gross Profit			81,200
Operating Expenses:			
Selling Expenses:			
Salaries Expense		8,100	
Rent Expense		7,300	
Advertising Expense		2,400	
Depreciation Expense		2,200	
Delivery Expense		1,600	
Total Selling Expenses		21,600	
Administrative Expenses:			
Utilities Expense		11,300	
Salaries Expense		6,900	
Insurance Expense		6,500	
Rent Expense		5,700	
Depreciation Expense		1,100	
Supplies Expense		600	
Total Administrative Expenses		32,100	
Total Operating Expenses			53,700
Operating Income			27,500
Other Revenues and (Expenses):			
Interest Expense		(2,300)	
Total Other Revenues and (Expenses)			(2,300)
Net Income			$ 25,200

Gross Profit

Operating Income

Other Revenues and (Expenses) and Net Income

Exhibit A-4 provides a side-by-side comparison of periodic and perpetual inventory system journal entries for the same company's transactions.

Exhibit A-4 | **Perpetual Versus Periodic Inventory System**

PERPETUAL INVENTORY SYSTEM

Purchased inventory on account:

Date	Accounts and Explanation	Debit	Credit
	Merchandise Inventory	5,250	
	Accounts Payable		5,250
	Purchased inventory on account.		

Returned inventory to seller (vendor):

Date	Accounts and Explanation	Debit	Credit
	Accounts Payable	1,750	
	Merchandise Inventory		1,750
	Returned inventory to seller (vendor).		

Paid a freight bill on a purchase:

Date	Accounts and Explanation	Debit	Credit
	Merchandise Inventory	60	
	Cash		60
	Paid a freight bill.		

Paid merchandise invoice within discount period:

Date	Accounts and Explanation	Debit	Credit
	Accounts Payable	3,500	
	Cash		3,395
	Merchandise Inventory		105
	Paid within discount period.		

Paid merchandise invoice after discount period:

Date	Accounts and Explanation	Debit	Credit
	Accounts Payable	3,500	
	Cash		3,500
	Paid after discount period.		

Sale on account:

Date	Accounts and Explanation	Debit	Credit
	Accounts Receivable	5,000	
	Sales Revenue		5,000
	Sale on account.		
	Cost of Goods Sold	3,500	
	Merchandise Inventory		3,500
	Recorded the cost of goods sold.		

PERIODIC INVENTORY SYSTEM

Purchased inventory on account:

Date	Accounts and Explanation	Debit	Credit
	Purchases	5,250	
	Accounts Payable		5,250
	Purchased inventory on account.		

Returned inventory to seller (vendor):

Date	Accounts and Explanation	Debit	Credit
	Accounts Payable	1,750	
	Purchase Returns and Allowances		1,750
	Returned inventory to seller (vendor).		

Paid a freight bill on a purchase:

Date	Accounts and Explanation	Debit	Credit
	Freight In	60	
	Cash		60
	Paid a freight bill.		

Paid merchandise invoice within discount period:

Date	Accounts and Explanation	Debit	Credit
	Accounts Payable	3,500	
	Cash		3,395
	Purchase Discounts		105
	Paid within discount period.		

Paid merchandise invoice after discount period:

Date	Accounts and Explanation	Debit	Credit
	Accounts Payable	3,500	
	Cash		3,500
	Paid after discount period.		

Sale on account:

Date	Accounts and Explanation	Debit	Credit
	Accounts Receivable	5,000	
	Sales Revenue		5,000
	Sale on account.		

Exhibit A-4 | **(Continued)**

PERPETUAL INVENTORY SYSTEM	PERIODIC INVENTORY SYSTEM

Paid a freight bill on a sale:

Date	Accounts and Explanation	Debit	Credit
	Delivery Expense	30	
	Cash		30
	Paid a freight bill.		

Date	Accounts and Explanation	Debit	Credit
	Delivery Expense	30	
	Cash		30
	Paid a freight bill.		

Received returned goods:

Date	Accounts and Explanation	Debit	Credit
	Sales Returns and Allowances	1,500	
	Accounts Receivable		1,500
	Received returned goods.		
	Merchandise Inventory	1,050	
	Cost of Goods Sold		1,050
	Placed goods back in inventory.		

Date	Accounts and Explanation	Debit	Credit
	Sales Returns and Allowances	1,500	
	Accounts Receivable		1,500
	Received returned goods.		

Granted a sales allowance:

Date	Accounts and Explanation	Debit	Credit
	Sales Returns and Allowances	100	
	Accounts Receivable		100
	Granted a sales allowance for damaged goods.		

Date	Accounts and Explanation	Debit	Credit
	Sales Returns and Allowances	100	
	Accounts Receivable		100
	Granted a sales allowance for damaged goods.		

Collected cash within the discount period:

Date	Accounts and Explanation	Debit	Credit
	Cash	3,332	
	Sales Discounts	68	
	Accounts Receivable		3,400
	Cash collection within the discount period.		

Date	Accounts and Explanation	Debit	Credit
	Cash	3,332	
	Sales Discounts	68	
	Accounts Receivable		3,400
	Cash collection within the discount period.		

Collected cash after the discount period:

Date	Accounts and Explanation	Debit	Credit
	Cash	3,400	
	Accounts Receivable		3,400
	Cash collection after the discount period.		

Date	Accounts and Explanation	Debit	Credit
	Cash	3,400	
	Accounts Receivable		3,400
	Cash collection after the discount period.		

Adjusted for inventory shrinkage:

Date	Accounts and Explanation	Debit	Credit
	Cost of Goods Sold	240	
	Merchandise Inventory		240
	Adjustment for inventory shrinkage.		

Exhibit A-4 | **(Continued)**

PERPETUAL INVENTORY SYSTEM				PERIODIC INVENTORY SYSTEM			

Closing entries:

Date	Accounts and Explanation	Debit	Credit	Date	Accounts and Explanation	Debit	Credit
	Sales Revenue	297,500			Sales Revenue	297,500	
	Income Summary		297,500		Purchase Returns and Allowances	61,250	
	To close revenue account.				Purchase Discounts	4,410	
					Merchandise Inventory (ending)	31,290	
					Income Summary		394,450
					To close revenue and other credit accounts		
					and record ending merchandise inventory.		
	Income Summary	272,300			Income Summary	369,250	
	Sales Returns and Allowances		11,200		Sales Returns and Allowances		11,200
	Sales Discounts		5,600		Sales Discounts		5,600
	Cost of Goods Sold		199,500		Purchases		281,750
	Salaries Expense		15,000		Freight In		14,700
	Rent Expense		13,000		Merchandise Inventory (beginning)		0
	Utilities Expense		11,300		Salaries Expense		15,000
	Insurance Expense		6,500		Rent Expense		13,000
	Depreciation Expense—Furniture		1,800		Utilities Expense		11,300
	Depreciation Expense—Building		1,500		Insurance Expense		6,500
	Advertising Expense		2,400		Depreciation Expense—Furniture		1,800
	Interest Expense		2,300		Depreciation Expense—Building		1,500
	Delivery Expense		1,600		Advertising Expense		2,400
	Supplies Expense		600		Interest Expense		2,300
	To close expenses and other debit accounts.				Delivery Expense		1,600
					Supplies Expense		600
					To close expenses and other debit accounts		
					and remove beginning merchandise inventory.		
	Income Summary	25,200			Income Summary	25,200	
	Bright, Capital		25,200		Bright, Capital		25,200
	To close Income Summary.				*To close Income Summary.*		
	Bright, Capital	10,000			Bright, Capital	10,000	
	Bright, Withdrawals		10,000		Bright, Withdrawals		10,000
	To close withdrawals.				*To close withdrawals.*		

> ## Try It!

12. Click Computers has the following transactions in July related to purchase and sale of merchandise inventory.

July 1	Purchase of $20,500 worth of computers on account, terms of 2/10, n/30.
3	Return of $4,000 of the computers to the vender.
9	Payment made on account.
12	Sold computers on account for $8,000 to customers, terms 3/15, n/30. The cost of the computers is $4,800.
21	Accepted a $1,000 return from a customer. The computer returned had a cost of $600.
26	Received payment from customer on balance due.

Journalize the transactions for Click Computers assuming that the company uses the periodic inventory system.
Check your answers at the end of the chapter.

For more practice, see Short Exercises SA-11, SA-12, SA-13, and SA-14. MyAccountingLab

REVIEW

1. What are merchandising operations?

- A merchandiser is a business that sells merchandise, or goods, to customers.
- There are two main types of inventory accounting systems that are used by merchandisers:
  - Periodic inventory system—requires businesses to obtain a physical count of inventory to determine quantities on hand
  - Perpetual inventory system—keeps a running computerized record of merchandise inventory

2. How are purchases of merchandise inventory recorded in a perpetual inventory system?

- Purchase of merchandise inventory

Merchandise Inventory	DR	
Cash or Accounts Payable		CR

- Purchase return

Cash or Accounts Payable	DR	
Merchandise Inventory		CR

- Payment of freight in

Merchandise Inventory	DR	
Cash		CR

- Payment within discount period

Accounts Payable	DR	
Cash		CR
Merchandise Inventory		CR

- Payment after discount period

Accounts Payable	DR	
Cash		CR

3. How are sales of merchandise inventory recorded in a perpetual inventory system?

- Sale of merchandise inventory

Cash or Accounts Receivable	DR	
Sales Revenue		CR
Cost of Goods Sold	DR	
Merchandise Inventory		CR

- Sales return

Sales Returns and Allowances	DR	
Cash or Accounts Receivable		CR
Merchandise Inventory	DR	
Cost of Goods Sold		CR

- Sales allowance

Sales Returns and Allowances	DR	
Cash or Accounts Receivable		CR

- Payment of freight out

Delivery Expense	DR	
Cash		CR

- Collection of cash during discount period

Cash	DR	
Sales Discounts	DR	
Accounts Receivable		CR

- Collection of cash after discount period

Cash	DR	
Accounts Receivable		CR

4. What are the adjusting and closing entries for a merchandiser?

- An adjusting entry must be made for inventory shrinkage, the loss of inventory that occurs because of theft, damage, and errors.
- The closing entries are similar to those already learned, except for including the new accounts (Sales Revenue, Sales Returns and Allowances, Sales Discounts, and Cost of Goods Sold).

Merchandising Operations

5. How are a merchandiser's financial statements prepared?

- There are two formats for the income statement:
  - Single-step income statement—groups all revenues together and all expenses together without calculating other subtotals
  - Multi-step income statement—lists several important subtotals including gross profit, operating income, and net income
- A merchandiser's statement of owner's equity looks exactly like that of a service business.
- The balance sheet will also look the same, except merchandisers have an additional current asset, Merchandise Inventory.

6. How do we use the gross profit percentage to evaluate business performance?

- The gross profit percentage measures the profitability of each sales dollar above the cost of goods sold.
- Gross profit percentage = Gross profit / Net sales revenue.

7. How are merchandise inventory transactions recorded in a periodic inventory system? (Appendix A)

- The Merchandise Inventory account is not used when recording purchase transactions. Instead Purchases, Purchase Discounts, Purchase Returns and Allowances, and Freight In are used.
- Sales transactions only involve recording the Sales Revenue. The Merchandise Inventory account is not used.
- An adjustment for inventory shrinkage is not needed.
- Closing entries are similar to the perpetual inventory system with the addition of closing the new accounts discussed. Ending Merchandise Inventory must be recorded and beginning Merchandise Inventory must be removed.

> Summary Problem 1

Suppose Heat Miser Air Conditioner Company engaged in the following transactions during June of the current year:

Jun. 3	Purchased inventory on account with credit terms of 1/10, n/EOM, $1,600.
9	Returned 40% of the inventory purchased on June 3. It was defective.
12	Sold goods for cash, $920 (cost, $550).
15	Purchased goods for $5,000 on account. Credit terms were 3/15, n/30.
16	Paid a $260 freight bill on goods purchased.
18	Sold inventory for $2,000 on account with credit terms of 2/10, n/30 (cost, $1,180).
22	Received returned goods from the customer of the June 18 sale, $800 (cost, $480).
24	Paid supplier for goods purchased on June 15.
28	Receive cash in full settlement of the account from the customer who purchased inventory on June 18.
29	Paid the amount owed on account from the purchase of June 3.

Requirements

1. Journalize the preceding transactions. Assume Heat Miser uses a perpetual inventory system.

2. Set up T-accounts and post the journal entries to show the ending balances in the Merchandise Inventory and the Cost of Goods Sold accounts only.

> Solution

Requirement 1

Date	Accounts and Explanation	Debit	Credit
Jun. 3	Merchandise Inventory	1,600	
	Accounts Payable		1,600
	Purchased inventory on account.		
9	Accounts Payable ($1,600 × 0.40)	640	
	Merchandise Inventory		640
	Returned inventory to seller (vendor).		
12	Cash	920	
	Sales Revenue		920
	Cash sale.		
12	Cost of Goods Sold	550	
	Merchandise Inventory		550
	Recorded the cost of goods sold.		
15	Merchandise Inventory	5,000	
	Accounts Payable		5,000
	Purchased inventory on account.		
16	Merchandise Inventory	260	
	Cash		260
	Paid a freight bill.		

Jun. 18	Accounts Receivable	2,000	
	Sales Revenue		2,000
	Sale on account.		
18	Cost of Goods Sold	1,180	
	Merchandise Inventory		1,180
	Recorded the cost of goods sold.		
22	Sales Returns and Allowances	800	
	Accounts Receivable		800
	Received returned goods.		
22	Merchandise Inventory	480	
	Cost of Goods Sold		480
	Placed goods back in inventory.		
24	Accounts Payable	5,000	
	Cash ($5,000 − $150)		4,850
	Merchandise Inventory ($5,000 × 0.03)		150
	Paid within discount period.		
28	Cash ($1,200 − $24)	1,176	
	Sales Discounts ($1,200 × 0.02)	24	
	Accounts Receivable ($2,000 − $800)		1,200
	Cash collection within discount period net of		
	return.		
29	Accounts Payable ($1,600 − $640)	960	
	Cash		960
	Paid after discount period net of return.		

Requirement 2

Merchandise Inventory				Cost of Goods Sold			
Jun. 3	1,600	640	Jun. 9	Jun. 12	550	480	Jun. 22
Jun. 15	5,000	550	Jun. 12	Jun. 18	1,180		
Jun. 16	260	1,180	Jun. 18	**Bal.**	**1,250**		
Jun. 22	480	150	Jun. 24				
Bal.	**4,820**						

> Summary Problem 2

King Cornelius Company uses a perpetual inventory system. The adjusted trial balance of King Cornelius Company follows:

KING CORNELIUS COMPANY Adjusted Trial Balance December 31, 2015		
	Balance	
Account Title	**Debit**	**Credit**
Cash	$ 5,600	
Accounts Receivable	37,100	
Merchandise Inventory	25,800	
Office Supplies	1,300	
Prepaid Rent	1,000	
Furniture	26,500	
Accumulated Depreciation—Furniture		$ 23,800
Accounts Payable		6,300
Salaries Payable		2,000
Interest Payable		600
Unearned Revenue		2,400
Notes Payable, long-term		35,000
Cornelius, Capital		22,200
Cornelius, Withdrawals	48,000	
Sales Revenue		244,000
Sales Returns and Allowances	10,000	
Sales Discounts	8,000	
Interest Revenue		2,000
Cost of Goods Sold	81,000	
Salaries Expense	72,700	
Rent Expense	7,700	
Utilities Expense	5,800	
Depreciation Expense—Furniture	2,700	
Supplies Expense	2,200	
Interest Expense	2,900	
Total	$ 338,300	$ 338,300

Requirements

1. Journalize the closing entries at December 31. Post to the Income Summary account as an accuracy check on net income. Recall that the credit balance closed out of Income Summary should equal net income as computed on the income statement. Also post to Cornelius, Capital, whose balance should agree with the amount reported on the balance sheet.

2. Prepare the company's multi-step income statement, statement of owner's equity, and balance sheet in report form for year ended December 31, 2015. Note: King Cornelius doesn't separate its operating expenses as either selling or administrative.

3. Compute the gross profit percentage for 2015.

Requirement 1

Date	Accounts and Explanation	Debit	Credit
Dec. 31	Sales Revenue	244,000	
	Interest Revenue	2,000	
	Income Summary		246,000
	To close revenue accounts.		
31	Income Summary	193,000	
	Sales Returns and Allowances		10,000
	Sales Discounts		8,000
	Cost of Goods Sold		81,000
	Salaries Expense		72,700
	Rent Expense		7,700
	Utilities Expense		5,800
	Depreciation Expense—Furniture		2,700
	Supplies Expense		2,200
	Interest Expense		2,900
	To close expenses and other debit accounts.		
31	Income Summary	53,000	
	Cornelius, Capital		53,000
	To close Income Summary.		
31	Cornelius, Capital	48,000	
	Cornelius, Withdrawals		48,000
	To close withdrawals.		

	Income Summary			
Clos. 2	193,000	246,000	Clos. 1
		53,000	Bal.
Clos. 3	53,000		
		0	**Bal.**

	Cornelius, Capital			
		22,200	Adj. Bal.
Clos. 4	48,000	53,000	Clos. 3
		27,200	**Bal.**

	Cornelius, Withdrawals			
Adj. Bal.	48,000		
		48,000	Clos. 4
Bal.	**0**		

Requirement 2

KING CORNELIUS COMPANY Income Statement Year Ended December 31, 2015		
Sales Revenue	$ 244,000	
Less: Sales Discounts	8,000	
Sales Returns and Allowances	10,000	
Net Sales Revenue		$ 226,000
Cost of Goods Sold		81,000
Gross Profit		145,000
Operating Expenses:		
Salaries Expense	72,700	
Rent Expense	7,700	
Utilities Expense	5,800	
Depreciation Expense—Furniture	2,700	
Supplies Expense	2,200	
Total Operating Expenses		91,100
Operating Income		53,900
Other Revenues and (Expenses):		
Interest Revenue	2,000	
Interest Expense	(2,900)	
Total Other Revenues and (Expenses)		(900)
Net Income		$ 53,000

KING CORNELIUS COMPANY Statement of Owner's Equity Year Ended December 31, 2015	
Cornelius, Capital, January 1, 2015	$ 22,200
Owner contribution	0
Net income for the year	53,000
	$ 75,200
Owner withdrawal	(48,000)
Cornelius, Capital, December 31, 2015	$ 27,200

KING CORNELIUS COMPANY
Balance Sheet
December 31, 2015

Assets

Current Assets:

Cash	$ 5,600	
Accounts Receivable	37,100	
Merchandise Inventory	25,800	
Office Supplies	1,300	
Prepaid Rent	1,000	
Total Current Assets		$ 70,800

Plant Assets:

Furniture	26,500	
Less: Accumulated Depreciation—Furniture	(23,800)	
Total Plant Assets		2,700
Total Assets		**$ 73,500**

Liabilities

Current Liabilities:

Accounts Payable	$ 6,300	
Salaries Payable	2,000	
Interest Payable	600	
Unearned Revenue	2,400	
Total Current Liabilities		$ 11,300

Long-term Liabilities:

Notes Payable		35,000
Total Liabilities		46,300

Owner's Equity

Cornelius, Capital		27,200
Total Liabilities and Owner's Equity		**$ 73,500**

Requirement 3

Gross profit percentage = Gross profit / Net sales revenue = $145,000 / $226,000 = 0.62 = 64.2%

> Key Terms

Administrative Expenses
Expenses incurred that are not related to marketing the company's products.

Cost of Goods Sold (COGS)
The cost of the merchandise inventory that the business has sold to customers.

Credit Terms
The payment terms of purchase or sale as stated on the invoice.

FOB Destination
Situation in which the buyer takes ownership (title) to the goods at the delivery destination point and the seller typically pays the freight.

FOB Shipping Point
Situation in which the buyer takes ownership (title) to the goods after the goods leave the seller's place of business (shipping point) and the buyer typically pays the freight.

Freight In
The transportation cost to ship goods into the purchaser's warehouse; therefore, it is freight on purchased goods.

Freight Out
The transportation cost to ship goods out of the seller's warehouse;

therefore, it is freight on goods sold to a customer.

Gross Profit
Excess of net Sales Revenue over Cost of Goods Sold.

Gross Profit Percentage
Measures the profitability of each sales dollar above the cost of goods sold. Gross profit / Net sales revenue.

Inventory Shrinkage
The loss of inventory that occurs because of theft, damage, and errors.

Invoice
A seller's request for payment from the purchaser.

Merchandise Inventory
The merchandise that a business sells to customers.

Merchandiser
A business that sells merchandise, or goods, to customers.

Multi-Step Income Statement
Income statement format that contains subtotals to highlight significant relationships. In addition to net income, it reports gross profit and operating income.

Net Purchases (Appendix A)
Purchases less purchase returns and allowances less purchase discounts.

Net Sales Revenue
The amount a company has made on sales of merchandise inventory after returns, allowances, and discounts have

been taken out. Sales Revenue less Sales Returns and Allowances and Sales Discounts.

Operating Expenses
Expenses, other than Cost of Goods Sold, that are incurred in the entity's major line of business.

Operating Income
Measures the results of the entity's major ongoing activities. Gross profit minus operating expenses.

Other Revenues and Expenses
Revenues or expenses that are outside the normal, day-to-day operations of a business, such as a gain or loss on the sale of plant assets or interest expense.

Periodic Inventory System
An inventory system that requires businesses to obtain a physical count of inventory to determine quantities on hand.

Perpetual Inventory System
An inventory system that keeps a running computerized record of merchandise inventory.

Purchase Allowance
An amount granted to the purchaser as an incentive to keep goods that are not "as ordered."

Purchase Discount
A discount that businesses offer to purchasers as an incentive for early payment.

Purchase Return
A situation in which sellers allow purchasers to return merchandise that is defective, damaged, or otherwise unsuitable.

Retailer
A type of merchandiser that buys merchandise either from a manufacturer or a wholesaler and then sells those goods to consumers.

Sales Discounts
Reduction in the amount of cash received from a customer for early payment.

Sales Returns and Allowances
Decreases in the seller's receivable from a customer's return of merchandise or from granting the customer an allowance from the amount owed to the seller.

Sales Revenue
The amount that a merchandiser earns from selling its inventory.

Selling Expenses
Expenses related to marketing and selling the company's products.

Single-Step Income Statement
Income statement format that groups all revenues together and then lists and deducts all expenses together without calculating any subtotals.

Vendor
The individual or business from whom a company purchases goods.

Wholesaler
A type of merchandiser that buys goods from manufacturers and then sells them to retailers.

> Quick Check

1. Which account does a merchandiser use that a service company does not use?
   - **a.** Cost of Goods Sold
   - **b.** Merchandise Inventory
   - **c.** Sales Revenue
   - **d.** All of the above

   Learning Objective 1

2. The two main inventory accounting systems are the
   - **a.** perpetual and periodic.
   - **b.** purchase and sale.
   - **c.** returns and allowances.
   - **d.** cash and accrual.

   Learning Objective 1

3. The journal entry for the purchase of inventory on account *using the perpetual inventory system* is

a.

Merchandise Inventory	DR	
Accounts Receivable		CR

b.

Accounts Payable	DR	
Merchandise Inventory		CR

c.

Merchandise Inventory	DR	
Accounts Payable		CR

d.

Merchandise Inventory	DR	
Cash		CR

4. JC Manufacturing purchased inventory for $5,300 and also paid a $260 freight bill. JC Manufacturing returned 45% of the goods to the seller and later took a 2% purchase discount. Assume JC Manufacturing uses a perpetual inventory system. What is JC Manufacturing's final cost of the inventory that it kept? (Round your answer to the nearest whole number.)

a. $2,997   c. $3,117
b. $2,337   d. $2,857

5. Suppose Austin Sound had sales of $300,000 and sales returns of $45,000. Cost of goods sold was $152,000. How much gross profit did Austin Sound report?

a. $148,000   c. $255,000
b. $103,000   d. $88,000

6. Suppose Dave's Discount's Merchandise Inventory account showed a balance of $8,000 before the year-end adjustments. The physical count of goods on hand totaled $7,400. Dave uses a perpetual inventory system. To adjust the accounts, which entry would the company make?

a.

Cost of Goods Sold	600	
Merchandise Inventory		600

b.

Merchandise Inventory	600	
Accounts Receivable		600

c.

Accounts Payable	600	
Merchandise Inventory		600

d.

Merchandise Inventory	600	
Cost of Goods Sold		600

7. Which of the following accounts would be closed at the end of the year *using the perpetual inventory system*?

Learning Objective 4

   a. Cost of Goods Sold
   b. Merchandise Inventory
   c. Accounts Receivable
   d. Accounts Payable

8. What is the order of the subtotals that appear on a multi-step income statement?

Learning Objective 5

   a. Gross Profit, Operating Income, Net Income, Other Revenues and Expenses
   b. Operating Income, Gross Profit, Net Income, Other Revenues and Expenses
   c. Other Revenues and Expenses, Operating Income, Gross Profit, Net Income
   d. Gross Profit, Operating Income, Other Revenues and Expenses, Net Income

9. Assume Juniper Natural Dyes made Net Sales Revenue of $90,000 and Cost of Goods Sold totaled $58,000. What was Juniper Natural Dyes' gross profit percentage for this period? (Round your answer to the nearest whole percent.)

Learning Objective 6

   a. 36%
   b. 3.4 times
   c. 64%
   d. 17%

10A. The journal entry for the purchase of inventory on account *using the periodic inventory system* is

Learning Objective 7
Appendix A

   a.

Purchases	DR	
Accounts Receivable		CR

   b.

Accounts Payable	DR	
Merchandise Inventory		CR

   c.

Merchandise Inventory	DR	
Accounts Payable		CR

   d.

Purchases	DR	
Accounts Payable		CR

Check your answers at the end of the chapter.

ASSESS YOUR PROGRESS

> Review Questions

1. What is a merchandiser, and what is the name of the merchandise that it sells?
2. What are the two types of merchandisers? How do they differ?
3. Describe the operating cycle of a merchandiser.
4. What is Cost of Goods Sold (COGS) and where is it reported?
5. How is gross profit calculated and what does it represent?
6. What are the two types of inventory accounting systems? Briefly describe each.
7. What is an invoice?
8. What account is debited when recording a purchase of inventory when using the perpetual inventory system?
9. What would the credit terms of "2/10, n/EOM" mean?
10. What is a purchase return? How does a purchase allowance differ from a purchase return?
11. Describe FOB shipping point and FOB destination. When does the buyer take ownership of the goods and who typically pays the freight?
12. How is the net cost of inventory calculated?
13. What are the two journal entries involved when recording the sale of inventory when using the perpetual inventory system?
14. When granting a sales allowance, is there a return of merchandise inventory from the customer? Describe the journal entry(ies) that would be recorded.
15. What is freight out and how is it recorded by the seller?
16. How is net sales revenue calculated?
17. What is inventory shrinkage? Describe the adjusting entry that would be recorded to account for inventory shrinkage.
18. What are the four steps involved in the closing process for a merchandising company?
19. Describe the single-step income statement.
20. Describe the multi-step income statement.
21. What financial statement is merchandise inventory reported on and in what section?
22. What does the gross profit percentage measure and how is it calculated?
23A. What account is debited when recording a purchase of inventory when using a periodic inventory system?
24A. When recording purchase returns and purchase allowances under the periodic inventory system, what account is used?
25A. What account is debited when recording the payment of freight in when using the periodic inventory system?
26A. Describe the journal entry(ies) when recording a sale of inventory using the periodic inventory system.

27A. Is an adjusting entry needed for inventory shrinkage when using the periodic inventory system? Explain.

28A. Highlight the differences in the closing process when using the periodic inventory system rather than the perpetual inventory system.

29A. Describe the calculation of cost of goods sold when using the periodic inventory system.

> Short Exercises

For all short exercises, assume the perpetual inventory system is used unless stated otherwise. Round all numbers to the nearest whole dollar unless stated otherwise.

S-1 Comparing periodic and perpetual inventory systems

For each statement below, identify whether the statement applies to the periodic inventory system or perpetual inventory system.

  a. Normally used for relatively inexpensive goods.

  b. Keeps a running computerized record of merchandise inventory.

  c. Achieves better control over merchandise inventory.

  d. Requires a physical count of inventory to determine the quantities on hand.

  e. Uses bar codes to keep up-to-the-minute records of inventory.

S-2 Journalizing purchase transactions

Consider the following transactions for KC Toys:

Jul. 8	KC Toys buys $185,800 worth of MegoBlock toys on account with credit terms of 2/10, n/30.
12	KC Toys returns $18,500 of the merchandise to MegoBlock due to damage during shipment.
15	KC Toys paid the amount due, less the return and discount.

Requirements

1. Journalize the purchase transactions. Explanations are not required.
2. In the final analysis, how much did the inventory cost KC Toys?

S-3 Journalizing purchase transactions

Consider the following transactions for Dady Drug Store:

Mar. 2	Dady buys $20,250 worth of inventory on account with credit terms of 3/15, n/30, FOB shipping point.
3	Dady pays a $90 freight charge.
8	Dady returns $5,000 of the merchandise due to damage during shipment.
14	Dady paid the amount due, less return and discount.

Requirements

1. Journalize the purchase transactions. Explanations are not required.
2. In the final analysis, how much did the inventory cost Dady?

Learning Objective 1

Learning Objective 2

Learning Objective 2

Learning Objective 3

S-4 Journalizing sales transactions

Journalize the following sales transactions for Tomas Sportswear. Explanations are not required.

Jul. 1	Tomas sold $61,000 of women's sportswear on account, credit terms are 2/10, n/45. Cost of goods is $32,000.
5	Tomas received a $2,000 sales return on damaged goods from the customer. Cost of goods damaged is $1,050.
10	Tomas receives payment from the customer on the amount due, less the return and discount.

Learning Objectives 2, 3

S-5 Journalizing purchase and sales transactions

Suppose Piranha.com sells 2,500 books on account for $15 each (cost of these books is $22,500), credit terms 2/15, n/60 on October 10, 2015, to The Textbook Store. One hundred of these books (cost $900) were damaged in shipment, so Piranha.com later received the damaged goods from The Textbook Store as sales returns on October 13, 2015. The Textbook Store paid the balance to Piranha.com on October 22, 2015.

Requirements

1. Journalize The Textbook Store's October 2015 transactions.
2. Journalize Piranha.com's October 2015 transactions.

Learning Objective 4

S-6 Adjusting for inventory shrinkage

Rich's Furniture's unadjusted Merchandise Inventory account at year-end is $63,000. The physical count of inventory came up with a total of $61,900. Journalize the adjusting entry needed to account for inventory shrinkage.

Learning Objective 4

S-7 Journalizing closing entries

Rockwell RV Center's accounting records include the following accounts at December 31, 2015.

Cost of Goods Sold	$ 385,000	Accumulated Depreciation—Building	$ 39,000
Accounts Payable	17,000	Cash	44,600
Rent Expense	21,000	Sales Revenue	696,000
Building	108,000	Depreciation Expense—Building	12,000
Rockwell, Capital	208,800	Rockwell, Withdrawals	61,000
Merchandise Inventory	261,000	Sales Discounts	9,000
Sales Returns and Allowances	39,200	Interest Revenue	5,000
Notes Receivable	26,600		

Requirements

1. Journalize the required closing entries for Rockwell.
2. Determine the ending balance in the Rockwell, Capital account.

Use the following information to answer Short Exercises S-8 and S-9.

Carolina Communications reported the following figures from its adjusted trial balance:

Cash	$ 3,800	Cost of Goods Sold	$ 18,000
Selling Expenses	1,000	Equipment, net	10,200
Accounts Payable	4,100	Accrued Liabilities	1,700
Carolina, Capital	4,230	Sales Revenue	40,000
Notes Payable, long-term	700	Accounts Receivable	2,700
Merchandise Inventory	500	Interest Expense	30
Administrative Expenses	2,500	Sales Discounts	4,800
Sales Returns and Allowances	7,200		

S-8 Preparing a merchandiser's income statement

Prepare Carolina Communications' multi-step income statement for the year ended July 31, 2015.

Learning Objective 5

S-9 Preparing a merchandiser's statement of owner's equity and balance sheet

Learning Objective 5

Requirements

1. Prepare Carolina Communications' statement of owner's equity for the year ended July 31, 2015. Assume that there were no additional contributions or withdrawals during the year.
2. Prepare Carolina Communications' classified balance sheet at July 31, 2015. Use the report format.

S-10 Computing the gross profit percentage

Learning Objective 6

Mantis Landscape Supply's selected accounts as of December 31, 2015 follow. Compute the gross profit percentage for 2015.

Selling Expenses	$ 13,650
Interest Revenue	1,300
Sales Returns and Allowances	5,850
Sales Revenue	132,000
Cost of Goods Sold	110,500
Sales Discounts	2,600
Administrative Expenses	10,400

SA-11 Journalizing purchase transactions—periodic inventory system

**Learning Objective 7
Appendix A**

Consider the following transactions for Gates Packing Supplies:

Apr. 10	Gates Packing Supplies buys $148,600 worth of merchandise inventory on account with credit terms of 2/10, n/30.
12	Gates returns $14,800 of the merchandise to the vendor due to damage during shipment.
19	Gates paid the amount due, less the return and discount.

Requirements

1. Journalize the purchase transactions assuming Gates Packing Supplies uses the periodic inventory system. Explanations are not required.
2. What is the amount of net purchases?

SA-12 Journalizing sales transactions—periodic inventory system

Journalize the following sales transactions for Shelton Camera Store using the periodic inventory system. Explanations are not required.

Dec. 3	Shelton sold $36,600 of camera equipment on account, credit terms are 1/15, n/EOM.
5	Shelton received a $1,200 sales return on damaged goods from the customer.
17	Shelton receives payment from the customer on the amount due, less the return and discount.

SA-13 Journalizing closing entries—periodic inventory system

D & S Printing Supplies' accounting records include the following accounts at December 31, 2015.

Purchases	$ 184,680	Accumulated Depreciation—Building	$ 15,600
Accounts Payable	8,400	Cash	17,200
Rent Expense	8,400	Sales Revenue	278,400
Building	43,200	Depreciation Expense—Building	4,800
Diaz, Capital	83,520	Diaz, Withdrawals	24,400
Merchandise Inventory, Beginning	115,000	Sales Discounts	3,600
Sales Returns and Allowances	15,680	Interest Expense	2,000
Notes Payable	10,640	Merchandise Inventory, Ending	104,400
Purchase Discounts	3,400	Purchase Returns and Allowances	20,600

Requirements

1. Journalize the required closing entries for D & S Printing Supplies assuming that D & S uses the periodic inventory system.
2. Determine the ending balance in the Diaz, Capital account.

SA-14 Computing cost of goods sold in a periodic inventory system

G Wholesale Company began the year with merchandise inventory of $6,000. During the year, G purchased $97,000 of goods and returned $6,200 due to damage. G also paid freight charges of $1,500 on inventory purchases. At year-end, G's ending merchandise inventory balance stood at $17,300. Assume that G uses the periodic inventory system. Compute G's cost of goods sold for the year.

> Exercises

For all exercises, assume the perpetual inventory system is used unless stated otherwise. Round all numbers to the nearest whole dollar unless stated otherwise.

E-15 Using accounting vocabulary

Match the accounting terms with the corresponding definitions.

1. Credit Terms
2. FOB Destination
3. Invoice
4. Cost of Goods Sold
5. Net Sales Revenue
6. Purchase Allowance
7. FOB Shipping Point
8. Wholesaler
9. Purchase Discount
10. Retailer

a. The cost of the merchandise inventory that the business has sold to customers.

b. An amount granted to the purchaser as an incentive to keep goods that are not "as ordered."

c. A type of merchandiser that buys merchandise either from a manufacturer or a wholesaler and then sells those goods to consumers.

d. A situation in which the buyer takes ownership (title) at the delivery destination point.

e. A type of merchandiser that buys goods from manufacturers and then sells them to retailers.

f. A discount that businesses offer to purchasers as an incentive for early payment.

g. A situation in which the buyer takes title to the goods after the goods leave the seller's place of business.

h. The terms of purchase or sale as stated on the invoice.

i. The amount a company has made on sales of merchandise inventory after returns and allowances and discounts have been taken out.

j. A seller's request for cash from the purchaser.

Learning Objective 2

Oct. 1 Cash $769.35

E-16 Journalizing purchase transactions from an invoice

Kingston Tires received the following invoice from a supplier (Fields Distribution, Inc.):

FIELDS DISTRIBUTION, INC.
7290 S. Prospect Street
Ravenna, OH 44266

Invoice date: September 23, 2015

Sold to: Kingston Tires
6678 Diamond Avenue
Ravenna, OH 44266

Payment terms: 1/10, n/30

Description	Quantity Shipped	Price	Amount
D39–X4 Radials	4	$38.12	$152.48
M223 Belted-bias	10	42.84	428.40
Q92 Truck tires	6	58.12	348.72
Total			$929.60

Due date:	Amount:
October 3, 2015	$920.30
October 4 through October 23, 2015	$929.60

Requirements

1. Journalize the transaction required by Kingston Tires on September 23, 2015. Do not round numbers to the nearest whole dollar. Assume tires are purchased on account.

2. Journalize the return on Kingston's books on September 28, 2015, of the D39–X4 Radials, which were ordered by mistake. Do not round numbers to the nearest whole dollar.

3. Journalize the payment on October 1, 2015, to Fields Distribution, Inc. Do not round numbers to the nearest whole dollar.

Learning Objective 2

July 24 Merch. Inv. $60

E-17 Journalizing purchase transactions

Hayes Jewelers had the following purchase transactions. Journalize all necessary transactions. Explanations are not required.

Jun. 20	Purchased inventory of $5,800 on account from Slater Diamonds, a jewelry importer. Terms were 3/15, n/45, FOB shipping point.
20	Paid freight charges, $400.
Jul. 4	Returned $800 of inventory to Slater.
14	Paid Slater Diamonds, less return.
16	Purchased inventory of $3,480 on account from Schmitt Diamonds, a jewelry importer. Terms were 2/10, n/EOM, FOB destination.
18	Received a $480 allowance from Schmitt for damaged but usable goods.
24	Paid Schmitt Diamonds, less allowance and discount.

Merchandising Operations

E-18 Computing missing amounts

Consider the following incomplete table of merchandiser's profit data. Calculate the missing amounts to complete the table.

Sales	$ 89,500	$ 103,600	$ 66,200	$ (f)
Sales Returns and Allowances	936	(b)	1,600	894
Sales Discounts	624	876	400	2,086
Net Sales	87,940	99,200	(d)	(g)
Cost of Goods Sold	60,200	(c)	40,500	75,800
Gross Profit	(a)	34,020	(e)	36,720

Learning Objective 3

E-19 Journalizing sales transactions

Journalize the following sales transactions for Antique Mall. Explanations are not required.

Learning Objective 3

Jan. 13 Sales Discounts $354

Jan. 4   Sold $12,200 of antiques on account, credit terms are 3/15, n/30. Cost of goods is $6,400.

8   Received a $400 sales return on damaged goods from the customer. Cost of goods damaged is $210.

13   Antique Mall receives payment from the customer on the amount due from Jan. 4, less the return and discount.

20   Sold $4,800 of antiques on account, credit terms are 1/10, n/45, FOB destination. Cost of goods is $1,200.

20   Antique Mall paid $100 on freight out.

25   Antique Mall negotiated a $300 allowance on the goods sold on Jan. 20.

29   Receives payment from the customer on the amount due from Jan. 20, less the allowance and discount.

E-20 Journalizing purchase and sales transactions

Journalize the following transactions for Soul Art Gift Shop. Explanations are not required.

Learning Objectives 2, 3

Feb. 23 Cash $3,773

Feb. 3   Purchased $2,700 of merchandise inventory on account under terms 4/10, n/EOM and FOB shipping point.

7   Returned $400 of defective merchandise purchased on February 3.

9   Paid freight bill of $100 on February 3 purchase.

10   Sold merchandise inventory on account for $4,350. Payment terms were 2/15, n/30. These goods cost the company $2,300.

12   Paid amount owed on credit purchase of February 3, less the return and the discount.

16   Granted a sales allowance of $500 on the February 10 sale.

23   Received cash from February 10 customer in full settlement of their debt, less the allowance and the discount.

E-21 Journalizing adjusting entries and computing gross profit

Emerson St. Paul Book Shop's accounts at June 30, 2015, included the following unadjusted balances:

Merchandise Inventory	$ 5,400
Cost of Goods Sold	40,300
Sales Revenue	85,300
Sales Discounts	1,400
Sales Returns and Allowances	2,000

The cost associated with the physical count of inventory on hand on June 30, 2015, was $5,000.

Requirements

1. Journalize the adjustment for inventory shrinkage.
2. Compute the gross profit.

Use the following information to answer Exercises E-22 through E-24.

The adjusted trial balance of Budget Business Systems at March 31, 2015, follows:

BUDGET BUSINESS SYSTEMS Adjusted Trial Balance March 31, 2015		
	Balance	
Account Title	**Debit**	**Credit**
Cash	$ 2,400	
Accounts Receivable	11,400	
Merchandise Inventory	31,700	
Office Supplies	6,400	
Equipment	42,500	
Accumulated Depreciation—Equipment		$ 13,900
Accounts Payable		9,200
Salaries Payable		1,000
Notes Payable, long-term		7,900
Bitzes, Capital		34,000
Bitzes, Withdrawals	43,000	
Sales Revenue		234,500
Sales Returns and Allowances	1,000	
Sales Discounts	1,500	
Cost of Goods Sold	116,300	
Selling Expense	27,200	
Administrative Expense	14,800	
Interest Expense	2,300	
Total	$ 300,500	$ 300,500

E-22 Journalizing closing entries

Requirements

1. Journalize the required closing entries at March 31, 2015.

2. Set up T-accounts for Income Summary; Bitzes, Capital; and Bitzes, Withdrawals. Post the closing entries to the T-accounts and calculate their ending balances.

3. How much was Budget's net income or net loss?

Learning Objective 4

2. Ending Capital Balance $62,400

E-23 Preparing a single-step income statement

Prepare Budget's *single-step* income statement for the year ended March 31, 2015.

Learning Objective 5

Net Income $71,400

E-24 Preparing a multi-step income statement

Prepare Budget's *multi-step* income statement for the year ended March 31, 2015.

Learning Objective 5

Gross Profit $115,700

E-25 Computing the gross profit percentage

LanWan Software earned net sales revenue of $65,000,000 in 2015. Cost of goods sold was $39,000,000, and net income reached $9,000,000, the company's highest ever. Compute the company's gross profit percentage for 2015.

Learning Objective 6

Gross Profit Percentage 40%

EA-26 Journalizing purchase transactions—periodic inventory system

Lopez Appliances had the following purchase transactions. Journalize all necessary transactions using the periodic inventory system. Explanations are not required.

Learning Objective 7 Appendix A

Sep. 17 Cash $5,880

Sep. 4	Purchased inventory of $6,960 on account from Marx Appliance Wholesale, an appliance wholesaler. Terms were 2/15, n/30, FOB shipping point.
4	Paid freight charges, $480.
10	Returned $960 of inventory to Marx.
17	Paid Marx Appliance Wholesale, less return and discount.
20	Purchased inventory of $4,200 on account from MR Appliance, an appliance wholesaler. Terms were 3/10, n/45, FOB destination.
22	Received a $580 allowance from MR Appliance for damaged but usable goods.
29	Paid MR Appliance, less allowance and discount.

EA-27 Journalizing sales transactions—periodic inventory system

Journalize the following sales transactions for Double M Archery using the periodic inventory system. Explanations are not required.

Learning Objective 7 Appendix A

Aug. 24 Sales Discounts $27

Aug. 1	Sold $7,320 of equipment on account, credit terms are 3/10, n/30.
3	Received a $240 sales return on damaged goods from the customer.
8	Double M receives payment from the customer on the amount due from Aug. 1, less the return and discount.
15	Sold $2,880 of equipment on account, credit terms are 1/10, n/45, FOB destination.
15	Double M paid $60 on freight out.
20	Double M negotiated a $180 allowance on the goods sold on Aug. 15.
24	Receives payment from the customer on the amount due from Aug. 15, less the allowance and discount.

EA-28 Journalizing purchase and sales transactions—periodic inventory system

Journalize the following transactions for Moto Bicycles using the periodic inventory system. Explanations are not required.

Nov. 2	Purchased $3,780 of merchandise inventory on account under terms 2/10, n/EOM and FOB shipping point.
6	Returned $560 of defective merchandise purchased on November 2.
8	Paid freight bill of $140 on November 2 purchase.
10	Sold merchandise inventory on account for $6,090. Payment terms were 1/15, n/45.
11	Paid amount owed on credit purchase of November 2, less the return and the discount.
15	Granted a sales allowance of $700 on the November 10 sale.
22	Received cash from November 10 customer in full settlement of their debt, less the allowance and the discount.

EA-29 Journalizing closing entries—periodic inventory system

Cruiser's Boat Supply uses the periodic inventory method. The adjusted trial balance of Cruiser's Boat Supply at December 31, 2015, follows:

CRUISER'S BOAT SUPPLY		
Adjusted Trial Balance		
December 31, 2015		
	Balance	
Account Title	Debit	Credit
Cash	$ 3,360	
Accounts Receivable	15,960	
Merchandise Inventory (beginning)	44,380	
Office Supplies	8,960	
Equipment	59,500	
Accumulated Depreciation—Equipment		$ 19,460
Accounts Payable		12,880
Salaries Payable		1,400
Notes Payable, long-term		11,060
Armstrong, Capital		50,040
Armstrong, Withdrawals	60,200	
Sales Revenue		328,300
Sales Returns and Allowances	1,400	
Sales Discounts	2,100	
Interest Revenue		3,220
Purchases	274,720	
Purchase Returns and Allowances		94,820
Purchase Discounts		8,200
Selling Expense	38,080	
Administrative Expense	20,720	
Total	$ 529,380	$ 529,380

Requirements

1. Journalize the required closing entries at December 31, 2015. Assume ending Merchandise Inventory is $53,260.

2. Set up T-accounts for Income Summary; Armstrong, Capital; and Armstrong, Withdrawals. Post the closing entries to the T-accounts and calculate their ending balances.

3. How much was Cruiser's net income or net loss?

EA-30 Computing cost of goods sold in a periodic inventory system

Delta Electric uses the periodic inventory system. Delta reported the following selected amounts at May 31, 2015:

Learning Objective 7
Appendix A

1b. Cost of Goods Sold $69,000

Merchandise Inventory, June 1, 2014	$ 16,000	Freight In	$ 4,000
Merchandise Inventory, May 31, 2015	23,000	Sales Revenue	174,000
Purchases	84,000	Sales Discounts	6,000
Purchase Discounts	3,000	Sales Returns and Allowances	17,000
Purchase Returns and Allowances	9,000	Delta, Capital	47,000

Compute the following for Delta:

a. Net sales revenue.

b. Cost of goods sold.

c. Gross profit.

> Problems **Group A**

For all problems, assume the perpetual inventory system is used unless stated otherwise. Round all numbers to the nearest whole dollar unless stated otherwise.

Learning Objectives 1, 2, 3

Sep. 10 Cash $4,455

P-31A Journalizing purchase and sale transactions

Journalize the following transactions that occurred in September 2015 for Aquamarines. No explanations are needed. Identify each accounts payable and accounts receivable with the vendor or customer name.

Sep. 3	Purchased merchandise inventory on account from Shallin Wholesalers, $5,000. Terms 1/15, n/EOM, FOB shipping point.
4	Paid freight bill of $80 on September 3 purchase.
4	Purchased merchandise inventory for cash of $1,700.
6	Returned $500 of inventory from September 3 purchase.
8	Sold merchandise inventory to Hermosa Company, $6,000, on account. Terms 2/15, n/35. Cost of goods, $2,640.
9	Purchased merchandise inventory on account from Thomas Wholesalers, $8,000. Terms 2/10, n/30, FOB destination.
10	Made payment to Shallin Wholesalers for goods purchased on September 3, less return and discount.
12	Received payment from Hermosa Company, less discount.
13	After negotiations, received a $200 allowance from Thomas Wholesalers.
15	Sold merchandise inventory to Jordan Company, $2,500, on account. Terms 1/10, n/EOM. Cost of goods, $1,050.
22	Made payment, less allowance, to Thomas Wholesalers for goods purchased on September 9.
23	Jordan Company returned $400 of the merchandise sold on September 15. Cost of goods, $160.
25	Sold merchandise inventory to Smithsons for $1,100 on account that cost $400. Terms of 2/10, n/30 were offered, FOB shipping point. As a courtesy to Smithsons, $75 of freight was added to the invoice for which cash was paid by Aquamarines.
26	After negotiations, granted a $100 allowance to Smithsons for merchandise purchased on September 25.
29	Received payment from Smithsons, less allowance and discount.
30	Received payment from Jordan Company, less return.

P-32A Journalizing purchase and sale transactions

Journalize the following transactions that occurred in November 2015 for Thelma's Amusement. No explanations are needed. Identify each accounts payable and accounts receivable with the vendor or customer name.

Learning Objectives 1, 2, 3

Nov. 14 Merch. Inv. $144

Nov. 4	Purchased merchandise inventory on account from Valencia Company, $9,600. Terms 3/10, n/EOM, FOB shipping point.
6	Paid freight bill of $120 on November 4 purchase.
8	Returned half the inventory purchased on November 4 from Valencia Company.
10	Sold merchandise inventory for cash, $1,200. Cost of goods, $700. FOB destination.
11	Sold merchandise inventory to Gilmore Corporation, $10,250, on account, terms of 1/10, n/EOM. Cost of goods, $5,500. FOB shipping point.
12	Paid freight bill of $40 on November 10 sale.
13	Sold merchandise inventory to Callahan Company, $9,900, on account, terms of 2/15, n/45. Cost of goods, $5,300. FOB shipping point.
14	Paid the amount owed on account from November 4, less return and discount.
16	After negotiations, granted a $250 allowance to Gilmore Corporation on November 11 sale.
17	Received defective inventory as a sales return from the November 13 sale, $600. Cost of goods, $450.
18	Purchased inventory of $4,100 on account from Russo Corporation. Payment terms were 2/10, n/30, FOB destination.
20	Received cash from Gilmore Corporation, less allowance and discount.
26	Paid amount owed on account from November 18, less discount.
28	Received cash from Callahan Company, less return and discount.
29	Purchased inventory from Suarez Corporation for cash, $12,000, FOB shipping point. Freight in paid to shipping company, $200.

P-33A Preparing a multi-step income statement, journalizing closing entries and preparing a post-closing trial balance

The adjusted trial balance of Big Papi Music Company at June 30, 2015, follows:

BIG PAPI MUSIC COMPANY Adjusted Trial Balance June 30, 2015		
	Balance	
Account Title	**Debit**	**Credit**
Cash	$ 3,600	
Accounts Receivable	38,800	
Merchandise Inventory	17,200	
Office Supplies	200	
Furniture	40,000	
Accumulated Depreciation—Furniture		$ 8,400
Accounts Payable		13,300
Salaries Payable		1,200
Unearned Revenue		6,700
Notes Payable, long-term		15,000
Papi, Capital		36,000
Papi, Withdrawals	40,500	
Sales Revenue		180,000
Sales Returns and Allowances	3,000	
Sales Discounts	2,000	
Cost of Goods Sold	82,500	
Selling Expense	19,200	
Administrative Expense	12,000	
Interest Expense	1,600	
Total	$ 260,600	$ 260,600

Requirements

1. Prepare Big Papi's multi-step income statement for the year ended June 30, 2015.
2. Journalize Big Papi's closing entries.
3. Prepare a post-closing trial balance as of June 30, 2015.

P-34A **Journalizing adjusting entries, preparing adjusted trial balance, and preparing financial statements**

Learning Objectives 4, 5

2. Total Credits $469,400

The unadjusted trial balance for Taylor Electronics Company follows:

TAYLOR ELECTRONICS COMPANY Unadjusted Trial Balance March 31, 2015		
	Balance	
Account Title	**Debit**	**Credit**
Cash	$ 3,900	
Accounts Receivable	33,600	
Interest Receivable	0	
Merchandise Inventory	45,100	
Office Supplies	6,000	
Equipment	129,100	
Accumulated Depreciation—Equipment		$ 37,700
Accounts Payable		16,700
Salaries Payable		0
Interest Payable		0
Unearned Revenue		13,800
Notes Payable, long-term		46,000
Taylor, Capital		52,430
Taylor, Withdrawals	20,000	
Sales Revenue		297,000
Sales Returns and Allowances	7,500	
Sales Discounts	2,900	
Interest Revenue		0
Cost of Goods Sold	162,300	
Salaries Expense (Selling)	22,900	
Rent Expense (Selling)	15,300	
Salaries Expense (Administrative)	5,010	
Utilities Expense (Administrative)	10,020	
Depreciation Expense—Equipment (Administrative)	0	
Interest Expense	0	
Total	**$ 463,630**	**$ 463,630**

Requirements

1. Journalize the adjusting entries using the following data:
   a. Interest revenue accrued, $200.
   b. Salaries (Selling) accrued, $2,700.
   c. Depreciation expense—Equipment (Administrative), $1,670.
   d. Interest expense accrued, $1,200.
   e. A physical count of inventory was completed. The ending Merchandise Inventory should have a balance of $44,500.
2. Prepare Taylor Electronics' adjusted trial balance as of March 31, 2015.
3. Prepare Taylor Electronics' *multi-step* income statement for year ended March 31, 2015.
4. Prepare Taylor Electronics' statement of owner's equity for year ended March 31, 2015. Assume Taylor made no additional contributions during the year.
5. Prepare Taylor Electronics' classified balance sheet in *report form* as of March 31, 2015.

Learning Objectives 5, 6

2. Operating Income $71,900

P-35A Preparing a single-step income statement, preparing a multi-step income statement, and computing the gross profit percentage

The records of Grade A Steak Company list the following selected accounts for the quarter ended April 30, 2015:

Interest Revenue	$ 800	Accounts Payable	$ 17,000
Merchandise Inventory	45,100	Accounts Receivable	33,500
Notes Payable, long-term	47,000	Accumulated Depreciation—Equipment	37,600
Salaries Payable	2,400	Angus, Capital, Jan. 31	53,300
Sales Discounts	2,000	Angus, Withdrawals	20,000
Sales Returns and Allowances	7,500	Cash	7,600
Sales Revenue	296,100	Cost of Goods Sold	162,100
Rent Expense (Selling)	21,780	Equipment	130,600
Office Supplies	5,700	Interest Payable	1,200
Unearned Revenue	13,300	Rent Expense (Administrative)	9,780
Interest Expense	2,000	Utilities Expense (Selling)	10,890
Depreciation Expense—Equipment (Administrative)	1,630	Delivery Expense (Selling)	3,630
Utilities Expense (Administrative)	4,890		

Requirements

1. Prepare a single-step income statement.
2. Prepare a multi-step income statement.
3. M. Davidson, manager of the company, strives to earn a gross profit percentage of at least 50%. Did Grade A achieve this goal? Show your calculations.

PA-36A Journalizing purchase and sale transactions—periodic inventory system

Learning Objective 7
Appendix A

Mar. 10 Cash $1,683

Journalize the following transactions that occurred in March 2015 for Durham Company. Assume Durham uses the periodic inventory system. No explanations are needed. Identify each accounts payable and accounts receivable with the vendor or customer name.

Mar. 3	Purchased merchandise inventory on account from Stout Wholesalers, $2,000. Terms 1/15, n/EOM, FOB shipping point.
4	Paid freight bill of $50 on March 3 purchase.
4	Purchased merchandise inventory for cash of $1,020.
6	Returned $300 of inventory from March 3 purchase.
8	Sold merchandise inventory to Herman Company, $3,600, on account. Terms 2/15, n/35.
9	Purchased merchandise inventory on account from Tapia Wholesalers, $4,800. Terms 2/10, n/30, FOB destination.
10	Made payment to Stout Wholesalers for goods purchased on March 3, less return and discount.
12	Received payment from Herman Company, less discount.
13	After negotiations, received a $120 allowance from Tapia Wholesalers.
15	Sold merchandise inventory to Jarvis Company, $1,500, on account. Terms 1/10, n/EOM.
22	Made payment, less allowance, to Tapia Wholesalers for goods purchased on March 9.
23	Jarvis Company returned $240 of the merchandise sold on March 15.
25	Sold merchandise inventory to Stark for $660 on account. Terms of 2/10, n/30 were offered, FOB shipping point.
26	After negotiations, granted a $60 allowance to Stark for merchandise sold on March 25.
29	Received payment from Stark, less allowance and discount.
30	Received payment from Jarvis Company, less return.

Learning Objective 7
Appendix A

1. Gross Profit $203,500

PA-37A Preparing a multi-step income statement and journalizing closing entries

Tucker Department Store uses a periodic inventory system. The adjusted trial balance of Tucker Department Store at December 31, 2015, follows:

TUCKER DEPARTMENT STORE		
Adjusted Trial Balance		
December 31, 2015		

	Balance	
Account Title	**Debit**	**Credit**
Cash	$ 7,920	
Accounts Receivable	85,360	
Merchandise Inventory (beginning)	37,840	
Office Supplies	440	
Furniture	88,000	
Accumulated Depreciation—Furniture		$ 18,480
Accounts Payable		29,260
Salaries Payable		2,640
Unearned Revenue		14,740
Notes Payable, long-term		33,000
Tucker, Capital		77,860
Tucker, Withdrawals	89,100	
Sales Revenue		396,000
Sales Returns and Allowances	6,600	
Sales Discounts	4,400	
Purchases	299,600	
Purchase Returns and Allowances		114,040
Purchase Discounts		6,000
Freight In	600	
Selling Expense	42,240	
Administrative Expense	26,400	
Interest Expense	3,520	
Total	$ 692,020	$ 692,020

Requirements

1. Prepare Tucker Department Store's multi-step income statement for the year ended December 31, 2015. Assume ending Merchandise Inventory is $36,500.

2. Journalize Tucker Department Store's closing entries.

> Problems **Group B**

For all problems, assume the perpetual inventory system is used unless stated otherwise. Round all numbers to the nearest whole dollar unless stated otherwise.

P-38B Journalizing purchase and sale transactions

Journalize the following transactions that occurred in February 2015 for Gems. No explanations are needed. Identify each accounts payable and accounts receivable with the vendor or customer name.

Learning Objectives 1, 2, 3

Feb. 12 Cash $9,408

Feb. 3	Purchased merchandise inventory on account from Smith Wholesalers, $8,000. Terms 1/15, n/EOM, FOB shipping point.
4	Paid freight bill of $130 on February 3 purchase.
4	Purchased merchandise inventory for cash of $2,720.
6	Returned $800 of inventory from February 3 purchase.
8	Sold merchandise inventory to Harger Company, $9,600, on account. Terms 2/15, n/35. Cost of goods, $4,220.
9	Purchased merchandise inventory on account from Taylor Wholesalers, $12,800. Terms 2/10, n/30, FOB destination.
10	Made payment to Smith Wholesalers for goods purchased on February 3, less return and discount.
12	Received payment from Harger Company, less discount.
13	After negotiations, received a $320 allowance from Taylor Wholesalers.
15	Sold merchandise inventory to Jovan Company, $4,000, on account. Terms 1/10, n/EOM. Cost of goods, $1,680.
22	Made payment, less allowance, to Taylor Wholesalers for goods purchased on February 9.
23	Jovan Company returned $640 of the merchandise sold on February 15. Cost of goods, $250.
25	Sold merchandise inventory to Stubbs for $1,760 on account that cost $640. Terms of 2/10, n/30 were offered, FOB shipping point. As a courtesy to Stubbs, $75 of freight was added to the invoice for which cash was paid by Gems.
26	After negotiations, granted a $160 allowance to Stubbs for merchandise purchased on February 25.
27	Received payment from Stubbs, less allowance and discount.
28	Received payment from Jovan Company, less return.

Learning Objectives 1, 2, 3

Jan. 14 Merch. Inv. $173

P-39B Journalizing purchase and sale transactions

Journalize the following transactions that occurred in January 2015 for Trisha's Amusements. No explanations are needed. Identify each accounts payable and accounts receivable with the vendor or customer name.

Jan. 4	Purchased merchandise inventory on account from Villanueva Company, $11,520. Terms 3/10, n/EOM, FOB shipping point.
6	Paid freight bill of $140 on January 4 purchase.
8	Returned half the inventory purchased on January 4 from Villanueva Company.
10	Sold merchandise inventory for cash, $1,440. Cost of goods, $840. FOB destination.
11	Sold merchandise inventory to Gillespie Corporation, $12,300, on account, terms of 1/10, n/EOM. Cost of goods, $6,600. FOB shipping point.
12	Paid freight bill of $50 on January 10 sale.
13	Sold merchandise inventory to Calhoun Company, $11,800, on account, terms of 2/15, n/45. Cost of goods, $6,360. FOB shipping point.
14	Paid the amount owed on account from January 4, less return and discount.
16	After negotiations, granted a $300 allowance to Gillespie Corporation on January 11 sale.
17	Received defective inventory as a sales return from the January 13 sale, $720. Cost of goods, $540.
18	Purchased inventory of $4,920 on account from Rocha Corporation. Payment terms were 2/10, n/30, FOB destination.
20	Received cash from Gillespie Corporation, less allowance and discount.
26	Paid amount owed on account from January 18, less discount.
28	Received cash from Calhoun Company, less return and discount.
29	Purchased inventory from Sexton Corporation for cash, $14,400, FOB shipping point. Freight in paid to shipping company, $240.

P-40B **Preparing a multi-step income statement, journalizing closing entries and preparing a post-closing trial balance**

The adjusted trial balance of Daddy's Music Company at April 30, 2015, follows:

Learning Objectives 4, 5

1. Operating Income $57,000

DADDY'S MUSIC COMPANY Adjusted Trial Balance April 30, 2015		
	Balance	
Account Title	**Debit**	**Credit**
Cash	$ 4,300	
Accounts Receivable	38,200	
Merchandise Inventory	17,800	
Office Supplies	600	
Furniture	39,400	
Accumulated Depreciation—Furniture		$ 9,000
Accounts Payable		13,600
Salaries Payable		1,200
Unearned Revenue		6,600
Notes Payable, long-term		14,000
Otousan, Capital		40,100
Otousan, Withdrawals	40,000	
Sales Revenue		180,000
Sales Returns and Allowances	6,500	
Sales Discounts	1,500	
Cost of Goods Sold	81,800	
Selling Expense	19,200	
Administrative Expense	14,000	
Interest Expense	1,200	
Total	**$ 264,500**	**$ 264,500**

Requirements

1. Prepare Daddy's multi-step income statement for the year ended April 30, 2015.

2. Journalize Daddy's closing entries.

3. Prepare a post-closing trial balance as of April 30, 2015.

Learning Objectives 4, 5

P-41B Journalizing adjusting entries, preparing adjusted trial balance, and preparing financial statements

2. Total Credits $471,520

The unadjusted trial balance for Smith Electronics Company follows:

SMITH ELECTRONICS COMPANY Unadjusted Trial Balance October 31, 2015		
	Balance	
Account Title	**Debit**	**Credit**
Cash	$ 4,320	
Accounts Receivable	33,900	
Interest Receivable	0	
Merchandise Inventory	45,400	
Office Supplies	6,300	
Equipment	130,900	
Accumulated Depreciation—Equipment		$ 38,100
Accounts Payable		16,900
Salaries Payable		0
Interest Payable		0
Unearned Revenue		13,800
Notes Payable, long-term		47,000
Smith, Capital		52,500
Smith, Withdrawals	19,000	
Sales Revenue		296,500
Sales Returns and Allowances	8,100	
Sales Discounts	2,700	
Interest Revenue		0
Cost of Goods Sold	162,100	
Salaries Expense (Selling)	22,500	
Rent Expense (Selling)	15,000	
Salaries Expense (Administrative)	4,860	
Utilities Expense (Administrative)	9,720	
Depreciation Expense—Equipment (Administrative)	0	
Interest Expense	0	
Total	$ 464,800	$ 464,800

Requirements

1. Journalize the adjusting entries using the following data:
   a. Interest revenue accrued, $500.
   b. Salaries (Selling) accrued, $3,400.
   c. Depreciation expense—Equipment (Administrative), $1,620.
   d. Interest expense accrued, $1,200.
   e. A physical count of inventory was completed. The ending Merchandise Inventory should have a balance of $44,800.

2. Prepare Smith Electronics' adjusted trial balance as of October 31, 2015.

3. Prepare Smith Electronics' *multi-step* income statement for year ended October 31, 2015.

4. Prepare Smith Electronics' statement of owner's equity for year ended October 31, 2015. Assume Smith made no additional contributions during the year.

5. Prepare Smith Electronics' classified balance sheet in *report form* as of October 31, 2015.

P-42B **Preparing a single-step income statement, preparing a multi-step income statement, and computing the gross profit percentage**

Learning Objectives 5, 6

2. Operating Income $70,100

The records of Hill Tower Steak Company list the following selected accounts for the quarter ended September 30, 2015:

Interest Revenue	$ 400	Accounts Payable	$ 16,500
Merchandise Inventory	45,700	Accounts Receivable	33,900
Notes Payable, long-term	42,000	Accumulated Depreciation—Equipment	37,500
Salaries Payable	3,400	Holstein, Capital, Jun. 30	54,900
Sales Discounts	2,200	Holstein, Withdrawals	18,500
Sales Returns and Allowances	8,400	Cash	8,100
Sales Revenue	296,700	Cost of Goods Sold	162,400
Rent Expense (Selling)	22,500	Equipment	125,000
Office Supplies	6,000	Interest Payable	1,200
Unearned Revenue	13,200	Rent Expense (Administrative)	9,660
Interest Expense	2,000	Utilities Expense (Selling)	11,250
Depreciation Expense—Equipment (Administrative)	1,610	Delivery Expense (Selling)	3,750
Utilities Expense (Administrative)	4,830		

Requirements

1. Prepare a single-step income statement.

2. Prepare a multi-step income statement.

3. A. Williams, manager of the company, strives to earn a gross profit percentage of at least 50%. Did Hill Tower achieve this goal? Show your calculations.

Learning Objective 7
Appendix A

Jun. 10 Purchase Discount $30

PA-43B Journalizing purchase and sale transactions—periodic inventory system

Journalize the following transactions that occurred in June 2015 for Dorsey Company. Assume Dorsey uses the periodic inventory system. No explanations are needed. Identify each accounts payable and accounts receivable with the vendor or customer name.

Jun. 3	Purchased merchandise inventory on account from Ramos Wholesalers, $3,500. Terms 1/15, n/EOM, FOB shipping point.
4	Paid freight bill of $90 on June 3 purchase.
4	Purchased merchandise inventory for cash of $1,785.
6	Returned $525 of inventory from June 3 purchase.
8	Sold merchandise inventory to Wallace Company, $6,300, on account. Terms 2/15, n/35.
9	Purchased merchandise inventory on account from Griffin Wholesalers, $8,400. Terms 2/10, n/30, FOB destination.
10	Made payment to Ramos Wholesalers for goods purchased on June 3, less return and discount.
12	Received payment from Wallace Company, less discount.
13	After negotiations, received a $210 allowance from Griffin Wholesalers.
15	Sold merchandise inventory to West Company, $2,625, on account. Terms 1/10, n/EOM.
22	Made payment, less allowance, to Griffin Wholesalers for goods purchased on June 9.
23	West Company returned $420 of the merchandise sold on June 15.
25	Sold merchandise inventory to Cole for $1,155 on account. Terms of 2/10, n/30 were offered, FOB shipping point.
26	After negotiations, granted a $105 allowance to Cole for merchandise sold on June 25.
29	Received payment from Cole, less allowance and discount.
30	Received payment from West Company, less return.

PA-44B Preparing a multi-step income statement and journalizing closing entries

Learning Objective 7
Appendix A

1. Gross Profit $162,800

Tran Department Store uses a periodic inventory system. The adjusted trial balance of Tran Department Store at December 31, 2015, follows:

TRAN DEPARTMENT STORE
Adjusted Trial Balance
December 31, 2015

Account Title	Balance	
	Debit	Credit
Cash	$ 6,550	
Accounts Receivable	68,300	
Merchandise Inventory (beginning)	30,200	
Office Supplies	350	
Furniture	70,400	
Accumulated Depreciation—Furniture		$ 14,800
Accounts Payable		23,500
Salaries Payable		2,100
Unearned Revenue		11,800
Notes Payable, long-term		26,400
Tran, Capital		62,300
Tran, Withdrawals	71,200	
Sales Revenue		316,800
Sales Returns and Allowances	5,300	
Sales Discounts	3,500	
Purchases	239,720	
Purchase Returns and Allowances		91,200
Purchase Discounts		4,800
Freight In	480	
Selling Expense	33,800	
Administrative Expense	21,100	
Interest Expense	2,800	
Total	$ 553,700	$ 553,700

Requirements

1. Prepare Tran Department Store's multi-step income statement for the year ended December 31, 2015. Assume ending Merchandise Inventory is $29,200.

2. Journalize Tran Department Store's closing entries.

> Continuing Problem

3. Net Income $9,794

P-45 Journalizing purchase and sale transactions, making closing entries, preparing financial statements, and computing the gross profit percentage

This problem Davis Consulting Davis Consulting performs systems consulting. The company has also begun selling accounting software and uses the perpetual inventory system to account for software inventory. During January, Davis Consulting completed the following transactions:

Jan. 2	Completed a consulting engagement and received cash of $7,800.
2	Prepaid three months office rent, $1,650.
7	Purchased 80 units software inventory on account, $1,680, plus freight in, $80.
18	Sold 40 software units on account, $3,500 (cost $880).
19	Consulted with a client for a fee of $1,000 on account.
20	Paid employee salaries, $2,055, which includes accrued salaries from December.
21	Paid on account, $1,760.
22	Purchased 240 units software inventory on account, $6,240.
24	Paid utilities, $250.
28	Sold 120 units software for cash, $4,680 (cost $2,960).
31	Recorded the following adjusting entries:
	a. Accrued salaries expense, $686
	b. Depreciation, $100 (Equipment, $30; Furniture, $70)
	c. Expiration of prepaid rent, $550
	d. Physical count of software inventory, 145 units, $3,770

Requirements

1. Open the following T-accounts in the ledger: Cash, $16,400; Accounts Receivable, $1,750; Software Inventory, $0; Office Supplies, $200; Prepaid Rent, $0; Equipment, $1,800; Accumulated Depreciation—Equipment, $30; Furniture, $4,200; Accumulated Depreciation—Furniture, $70; Accounts Payable, $4,700; Salaries Payable, $685; Unearned Revenue, $700; Davis, Capital, $18,165; Davis, Withdrawals, $0; Income Summary, $0, Service Revenue, $0; Sales Revenue, $0; Cost of Goods Sold, $0; Salaries Expense, $0; Rent Expense, $0; Utilities Expense, $0; Depreciation Expense—Equipment, $0; and Depreciation Expense—Furniture, $0.

2. Journalize and post the January transactions. Compute each account balance, and denote the balance as *Bal.*

3. Prepare the month ended January 31, 2015 income statement of Davis Consulting. Use the multi-step format. List Service Revenue under gross profit and ignore classifying the expenses as selling and administrative.

4. Journalize and post the closing entries. Denote each closing amount as *Clo.* After posting all closing entries, prove the equality of debits and credits in the ledger.

5. Compute the gross profit percentage of Davis Consulting.

> Practice Set

P-46 Journalizing purchase and sale transactions, making closing entries, preparing financial statements, and computing the gross profit percentage

Shine King Cleaning has decided that, in addition to providing cleaning services, it will sell cleaning products. Shine King uses the perpetual inventory system. During December 2015, Shine King completed the following transactions:

4. Net Income $1,662

Dec. 2	Purchased 600 units of inventory for $3,600 on account from Sparkle, Co. on terms, 3/10, n/20.
5	Purchased 400 units of inventory from Borax on account with terms 4/5, n/30. The total invoice was for $3,200, which included a $200 freight charge.
7	Returned 100 units of inventory to Sparkle from the December 2 purchase (cost $600).
9	Paid Borax.
11	Sold 350 units of goods to Happy Maids for $4,900 on account with terms 5/10, n/30. Shine King's cost of the goods was $2,100.
12	Paid Sparkle.
15	Received 30 units with a retail price of $420 of goods back from customer Happy Maids. The goods cost Shine King $180.
21	Received payment from Happy Maids, settling the amount due in full.
28	Sold 200 units of goods to Bridget, Inc. for cash of $3,000 (cost $1,144).
29	Paid cash for Utilities of $350.
30	Paid cash for Sales Commission Expense of $225.
31	Recorded the following adjusting entries: a. Physical count of inventory on December 31 showed 330 units of goods on hand, $2,541 b. Depreciation, $170 c. Accrued salaries expense of $700 d. Prepared all other adjustments necessary for December

Requirements

1. Open the following T-accounts in the ledger: Cash, $73,100; Accounts Receivable, $2,000; Merchandise Inventory, $0; Cleaning Supplies, $50; Prepaid Rent, $1,500; Prepaid Insurance, $2,200; Equipment, $2,200; Truck, $8,000; Accumulated Depreciation, $170; Accounts Payable, $945; Unearned Revenue, $3,450; Salaries Payable, $0; Interest Payable, $100; Notes Payable (Long-term), $40,000; Hudson, Capital, $44,385; Hudson, Withdrawals, $0; Income Summary, $0; Service Revenue, $0; Sales Revenue, $0; Sales Returns and Allowances, $0; Sales Discounts, $0; Cost of Goods Sold, $0; Sales Commission Expense, $0; Utilities Expense, $0; Depreciation Expense, $0; Salaries Expense, $0; Insurance Expense, $0; Rent Expense, $0; Interest Expense, $0.

2. Journalize and post the December transactions. Compute each account balance, and denote the balance as *Bal.* Identify each accounts payable and accounts receivable with the vendor or customer name.

3. Journalize and post the adjusting entries. Denote each adjusting amount as *Adj.* Compute each account balance and denote the balance as *Bal.* After posting all adjusting entries, prove the equality of debits and credits in the ledger.

4. Prepare the December multi-step income statement, statement of owner's equity, and classified balance sheet for the company. List Service Revenue under gross profit and ignore classifying the expenses as selling and administrative.

5. Journalize the December closing entries for the company.

6. Compute the gross profit percentage for the company.

CRITICAL THINKING

> Decision Cases

Decision Case 1

Jan Lorange is the owner of Poppa Rollo's Pizza, which has prospered during its second year of operation. In order to help her decide whether to open another pizzeria, Lorange has prepared the current income statement of the business. Lorange read in an industry trade journal that a successful two-year-old pizzeria meets the following criteria:

a. Gross profit percentage is at least 60%.

b. Net income is at least $90,000.

Lorange believes the business meets both criteria. She intends to go ahead with the expansion plan and asks your advice on preparing the income statement in accordance with Generally Accepted Accounting Principles. When you point out that the statement includes errors, Lorange assures you that all amounts are correct. But some items are listed in the wrong place.

POPPA ROLLO'S PIZZA Income Statement Year Ended December 31, 2015	
Sales Revenue	$ 195,000
Gain on Sale of Land	24,600
Total Revenue	219,600
Cost of Goods Sold	85,200
Gross Profit	134,400
Operating Expenses:	
Salaries Expense	35,600
Interest Expense	6,000
Depreciation Expense	4,800
Utilities Expense	3,700
Total Operating Expense	50,100
Income from Operations	84,300
Other Revenue:	
Sales Returns	10,700
Net Income	$ 95,000

Prepare a corrected multi-step income statement and make a recommendation about whether Lorange should undertake the expansion. Ignore classifying the expenses as selling or administrative.

Decision Case 2

Bill Hildebrand opened Party-Time T-Shirts to sell T-shirts for parties at his college. The company completed the first year of operations, and the owner is generally pleased with operating results as shown by the following income statement:

PARTY-TIME T-SHIRTS Income Statement Year Ended December 31, 2014	
Net Sales Revenue	$ 350,000
Cost of Goods Sold	210,000
Gross Profit	140,000
Operating Expenses:	
Selling Expense	40,000
Administrative Expense	25,000
Net Income	$ 75,000

Hildebrand is considering how to expand the business. He proposes two ways to increase profits to $100,000 during 2015.

a. Hildebrand believes he should advertise more heavily. He believes additional advertising costing $20,000 will increase net sales by 30% and leave administrative expense unchanged. Assume that Cost of Goods Sold will remain at the same percentage of net sales as in 2014, so if net sales increases in 2015, Cost of Goods Sold will increase proportionately.

b. Hildebrand proposes selling higher-margin merchandise, such as party dresses, in addition to the existing product line. An importer can supply a minimum of 1,000 dresses for $40 each; Party-Time can mark these dresses up 100% and sell them for $80. Hildebrand realizes he will have to advertise the new merchandise, and this advertising will cost $5,000. Party-Time can expect to sell only 80% of these dresses during the coming year.

Help Hildebrand determine which plan to pursue. Prepare a single-step income statement for 2015 to show the expected net income under each plan.

> Ethical Issue 1

Dobbs Wholesale Antiques makes all sales under terms of FOB shipping point. The company usually ships inventory to customers approximately one week after receiving the order. For orders received late in December, Kathy Dobbs, the owner, decides when to ship the goods. If profits are already at an acceptable level, Dobbs delays shipment until January. If profits for the current year are lagging behind expectations, Dobbs ships the goods during December.

Requirements

1. Under Dobbs' FOB policy, when should the company record a sale?

2. Do you approve or disapprove of Dobbs' manner of deciding when to ship goods to customers and record the sales revenue? If you approve, give your reason. If you disapprove, identify a better way to decide when to ship goods. (There is no accounting rule against Dobbs' practice.)

> Fraud Case 1

Rae Philippe was a warehouse manager for Atkins Oilfield Supply, a business that operated across eight Western states. She was an old pro and had known most of the other warehouse managers for many years. Around December each year, auditors would come to do a physical count of the inventory at each warehouse. Recently, Rae's brother started his own drilling company and persuaded Rae to "loan" him 80 joints of 5-inch drill pipe to use for his first well. He promised to have it back to Rae by December, but the well encountered problems and the pipe was still in the ground. Rae knew the auditors were on the way, so she called her friend Andy, who ran another Atkins warehouse. "Send me over 80 joints of 5-inch pipe tomorrow, and I'll get them back to you ASAP," said Rae. When the auditors came, all the pipe on the books was accounted for, and they filed a "no-exception" report.

Requirements

1. Is there anything the company or the auditors could do in the future to detect this kind of fraudulent practice?

2. How would this kind of action affect the financial performance of the company?

> Financial Statement Case 1

This case uses both the income statement (consolidated statement of earnings) and the balance sheet of **Starbucks Corporation**. Visit **www.pearsonhighered.com/ Horngren** to view a link to the Starbucks Corporation Fiscal 2011 Annual Report.

Requirements

1. What was value of the company's inventory at October 2, 2011, and October 3, 2010?

2. Review Note 4 (specifically Inventories) in the Notes to Consolidated Financial Statements. What do Starbucks' inventories consist of?

3. What was the amount of Starbucks' cost of goods sold (cost of sales) for the year ending October 2, 2011, and the year ending October 3, 2010?

4. What income statement format does Starbucks use? Explain.

5. Compute Starbucks' gross profit percentage for the year ending October 2, 2011, and the year ending October 3, 2010. Did the gross profit percentage improve, worsen, or hold steady? Assuming the industry average for gross profit percentage is 56.83%, how does Starbucks compare to the industry?

> Team Project 1

With a small team of classmates, visit one or more merchandising businesses in your area. Interview a responsible manager of the company to learn about its inventory policies and accounting system. Obtain answers to the following questions, write a report, and be prepared to make a presentation to the class if your instructor so directs.

Requirements

1. What merchandise inventory does the business sell?

2. From whom does the business buy its inventory? Is the relationship with the supplier new or longstanding?

3. What are the FOB terms on inventory purchases? Who pays the freight, the buyer or the seller? Is freight a significant amount? What percentage of total inventory cost is the freight?

4. What are the credit terms on inventory purchases—2/10, n/30, or other? Does the business pay early to get purchase discounts? If so, why? If not, why not?

5. How does the business actually pay its suppliers? Does it mail a check or pay electronically? What is the actual payment procedure?

6. Which type of inventory accounting system does the business use—perpetual or periodic? Is this system computerized?

7. How often does the business take a physical count of its inventory? When during the year is the count taken? Describe the count procedures followed by the company.

8. Does the manager use the gross profit percentage to evaluate the business? If not, show the manager how to use this ratio in decision making.

9. Ask any other questions your group considers appropriate.

> Communication Activity 1

In 100 words or fewer, explain the difference between a sales discount and a purchase discount.

MyAccountingLab   **For a wealth of online resources, including exercises, problems, media, and immediate tutorial help, please visit** www.myaccountinglab.com.

Try It! Solutions

1.	d		**4.**	a
2.	f		**5.**	b
3.	e		**6.**	c

7.

Date	Accounts and Explanation	Debit	Credit
Jul. 1	Merchandise Inventory	20,500	
	Accounts Payable		20,500
	Purchased inventory on account.		
3	Accounts Payable	4,000	
	Merchandise Inventory		4,000
	Returned inventory to seller (vendor).		
9	Accounts Payable ($20,500 − $4,000)	16,500	
	Cash ($16,500 − $330)		16,170
	Merchandise Inventory ($16,500 × 0.02)		330
	Paid within discount period net of return.		

8.

Date	Accounts and Explanation	Debit	Credit
Jul. 12	Accounts Receivable	8,000	
	Sales Revenue		8,000
	Sale on account.		
12	Cost of Goods Sold	4,800	
	Merchandise Inventory		4,800
	Recorded the cost of goods sold.		
21	Sales Returns and Allowances	1,000	
	Accounts Receivable		1,000
	Received returned goods.		
21	Merchandise Inventory	600	
	Cost of Goods Sold		600
	Placed goods back in inventory.		
26	Cash ($7,000 − $210)	6,790	
	Sales Discounts ($7,000 × 0.03)	210	
	Accounts Receivable ($8,000 − $1,000)		7,000
	Cash collection within discount period net of return.		

9.

Date	Accounts and Explanation	Debit	Credit
Dec. 31	Cost of Goods Sold	500	
	Merchandise Inventory		500
	Adjustment for inventory shrinkage.		

10.

CAPITAL CITY MOTORCYCLE
Income Statement
Year Ended December 31, 2015

Sales Revenue	$ 120,000	
Less: Sales Returns and Allowances	4,500	
Sales Discounts	2,000	
Net Sales Revenue		$ 113,500
Cost of Goods Sold		85,000
Gross Profit		28,500
Operating Expenses:		
Selling Expenses	10,500	
Administrative Expenses	8,000	
Total Operating Expenses		18,500
Operating Income		10,000
Other Revenues and (Expenses):		
Interest Revenue	1,000	
Total Other Revenues and (Expenses)		1,000
Net Income		$ 11,000

11.

Gross profit percentage = Gross profit / Net sales revenue = ($120,000 − $4,500 − $2,000 − $85,000) / ($120,000 − $4,500 − $2,000) = 0.251 = 25.1%

12.

Date	Accounts and Explanation	Debit	Credit
Jul. 1	Purchases	20,500	
	Accounts Payable		20,500
	Purchased inventory on account.		
3	Accounts Payable	4,000	
	Purchase Returns and Allowances		4,000
	Returned inventory to seller (vendor).		
9	Accounts Payable ($20,500 − $4,000)	16,500	
	Cash ($16,500 − $330)		16,170
	Purchase Discounts ($16,500 × 0.02)		330
	Paid within discount period net of return.		
12	Accounts Receivable	8,000	
	Sales Revenue		8,000
	Sale on account.		
21	Sales Returns and Allowances	1,000	
	Accounts Receivable		1,000
	Received returned goods.		
26	Cash ($7,000 − $210)	6,790	
	Sales Discounts ($7,000 × 0.03)	210	
	Accounts Receivable ($8,000 − $1,000)		7,000
	Cash collection within discount period net of return.		

> Quick Check Answers

1. d **2.** a **3.** c **4.** c **5.** b **6.** a **7.** a **8.** d **9.** a **10A.** d
Completing a Merchandiser's Accounting Cycle

Glossary

Administrative Expenses. Expenses incurred that are not related to marketing the company's products.

Cost of Goods Sold (COGS). The cost of the merchandise inventory that the business has sold to customers.

Credit Terms. The payment terms of purchase or sale as stated on the invoice.

FOB Destination. Situation in which the buyer takes ownership (title) to the goods at the delivery destination point and the seller typically pays the freight.

FOB Shipping Point. Situation in which the buyer takes ownership (title) to the goods after the goods leave the seller's place of business (shipping point) and the buyer typically pays the freight.

Freight In. The transportation cost to ship goods into the purchaser's warehouse; therefore, it is freight on purchased goods.

Freight Out. The transportation cost to ship goods out of the seller's warehouse; therefore, it is freight on goods sold to a customer.

Gross Profit. Excess of net Sales Revenue over Cost of Goods Sold.

Gross Profit Percentage. Measures the profitability of each sales dollar above the cost of goods sold. Gross profit / Net sales revenue.

Inventory Shrinkage. The loss of inventory that occurs because of theft, damage, and errors.

Invoice. A seller's request for payment from the purchaser.

Merchandise Inventory. The merchandise that a business sells to customers.

Merchandiser. A business that sells merchandise, or goods, to customers.

Multi-Step Income Statement. Income statement format that contains subtotals to highlight significant relationships. In addition to net income, it reports gross profit and operating income.

Net Purchases. Purchases less purchase returns and allowances less purchase discounts. (Appendix A)

Net Sales Revenue. The amount a company has made on sales of merchandise inventory after returns, allowances, and discounts have been taken out. Sales Revenue less Sales Returns and Allowances and Sales Discounts.

Operating Expenses. Expenses, other than Cost of Goods Sold, that are incurred in the entity's major line of business.

Operating Income. Measures the results of the entity's major ongoing activities. Gross profit minus operating expenses.

Other Revenues and Expenses. Revenues or expenses that are outside the normal, day-to-day operations of a business, such as a gain or loss on the sale of plant assets or interest expense.

Periodic Inventory System. An inventory system that requires businesses to obtain a physical count of inventory to determine quantities on hand.

Perpetual Inventory System. An inventory system that keeps a running computerized record of merchandise inventory.

Purchase Allowance. An amount granted to the purchaser as an incentive to keep goods that are not "as ordered."

Purchase Discount. A discount that businesses offer to purchasers as an incentive for early payment.

Purchase Return. A situation in which sellers allow purchasers to return merchandise that is defective, damaged, or otherwise unsuitable.

Retailer. A type of merchandiser that buys merchandise either from a manufacturer or a wholesaler and then sells those goods to consumers.

Sales Discounts. Reduction in the amount of cash received from a customer for early payment.

Sales Returns and Allowances. Decreases in the seller's receivable from a customer's return of merchandise or from granting the customer an allowance from the amount owed to the seller.

Sales Revenue. The amount that a merchandiser earns from selling its inventory.

Selling Expenses. Expenses related to marketing and selling the company's products.

Single-Step Income Statement. Income statement format that groups all revenues together and then lists and deducts all expenses together without calculating any subtotals.

Vendor. The individual or business from whom a company purchases goods.

Wholesaler. A type of merchandiser that buys goods from manufacturers and then sells them to retailers.

Photo Credits

Merchandise Inventory

From Chapter 6 of *Horngren's Accounting*, Tenth edition. Tracie Nobles, Brenda Mattison, Ella Mae Matsumura. Copyright © 2014 by Pearson Education, Inc. All rights reserved.

Merchandise Inventory

What Is the Cost of This Merchandise Inventory?

Jorell was excited about the most recent shipment of merchandise inventory that he received today. As the owner of a successful sporting goods store, he has decided to expand his merchandise inventory line by offering outdoor cooking items such as grills, cookers, and accessories. He believes that this new merchandise inventory will draw new customers to his store and eventually bring more profit to the business.

As Jorell prepares the merchandise inventory for sale, he must decide how the business will track the cost of each product sold. For example, if the business sells 500 identical outdoor grills that were purchased at different times and at different costs, how will the business determine the cost of each grill sold? Should the business keep detailed cost records for each specific grill sold? Or should the business use an inventory costing method that will approximate the flow of inventory costs? For example, the business might decide to assign the costs of the first grills purchased to the first grills sold rather than tracking the cost of each grill individually. Or it might decide, instead, to assign the costs of the last grills purchased to the first grills sold.

Jorell understands that he has several options when it comes to selecting an inventory costing method. He wants to select a method that will be relatively easy to implement and maintain. He knows that by selecting the best method for his business, he will be able to easily determine the cost of the goods sold and, ultimately, his gross profit.

What Is the Cost of Merchandise Inventory?

In this chapter, we examine merchandise inventory by learning how to account for the cost of inventory. When Dick's Sporting Goods, Inc., a retail shop that sells sporting goods, apparel, and footwear, purchases and sells inventory, the business must account for the inventory appropriately. Dick's must determine the cost of the inventory that is sold in order to calculate gross profit. If a business only had a small amount of inventory, identifying the cost of one particular item would be simple. However, large businesses, such as Dick's, have millions of items of inventory, which makes tracking costs very difficult. In this chapter, you learn that every business must select an inventory costing method that allows it to track costs and determine the cost of goods sold, gross profit, and value of ending merchandise inventory.

chapter outline

What are the accounting principles and controls that relate to merchandise inventory?

How are merchandise inventory costs determined under a perpetual inventory system?

How are financial statements affected by using different inventory costing methods?

How is merchandise inventory valued when using the lower-of-cost-or-market rule?

What are the effects of merchandise inventory errors on the financial statements?

How do we use inventory turnover and days' sales in inventory to evaluate business performance?

How are merchandise inventory costs determined under a periodic inventory system? (Appendix A)

How can the cost of ending merchandise inventory be estimated? (Appendix B)

Learning Objectives

1. Identify accounting principles and controls related to merchandise inventory

2. Account for merchandise inventory costs under a perpetual inventory system

3. Compare the effects on the financial statements when using the different inventory costing methods

4. Apply the lower-of-cost-or-market rule to merchandise inventory

5. Measure the effects of merchandise inventory errors on the financial statements

6. Use inventory turnover and days' sales in inventory to evaluate business performance

7. Account for merchandise inventory costs under a periodic inventory system (Appendix A)

8. Estimate the cost of ending merchandise inventory using the gross profit method and the retail method (Appendix B)

WHAT ARE THE ACCOUNTING PRINCIPLES AND CONTROLS THAT RELATE TO MERCHANDISE INVENTORY?

Learning Objective 1

Identify accounting principles and controls related to merchandise inventory

Accounting Principles

Let's begin by learning about several accounting principles that affect merchandise inventories. Among them are consistency, disclosure, materiality, and accounting conservatism.

Consistency Principle

Consistency Principle
A business should use the same accounting methods and procedures from period to period.

The **consistency principle** states that businesses should use the same accounting methods and procedures from period to period. Consistency helps investors and creditors compare a company's financial statements from one period to the next.

Suppose you are analyzing a company's net income over a two-year period in which there was an increase in net income from the first year to the second. Analysis of the income statement shows Sales Revenue was almost the same for both years, but Cost of Goods Sold decreased significantly, which resulted in increases in gross profit and operating income. Without further information, you might conclude that the company was able to purchase its inventory at a lower cost in the second year and that profits will continue to increase in future years. However, changing inventory costing methods could have caused this one-time change, in which case, future profits will not be affected. Therefore, companies must be consistent in the accounting methods they use. If changes are made in accounting methods, these changes must be reported. Investors and creditors need this information to make wise decisions about the company.

Disclosure Principle

Disclosure Principle
A business's financial statements must report enough information for outsiders to make knowledgeable decisions about the company.

The **disclosure principle** holds that a company should report enough information for outsiders to make knowledgeable decisions about the company. In short, the company should report information that is relevant and has faithful representation. This includes disclosing the method being used to account for merchandise inventories. All major accounting methods and procedures are described in the footnotes to the financial statements. Suppose a banker is comparing two companies—one using inventory method A and the other using inventory method B. The B company reports higher net income but only because of the inventory method it selected. Without knowledge of these accounting methods, the banker could lend money to the wrong business.

Materiality Concept

The **materiality concept** states that a company must perform strictly proper accounting *only* for significant items. Information is significant—or, in accounting terms, *material*—when it would cause someone to change a decision. The materiality concept frees accountants from having to report every last item in strict accordance with GAAP. For example, $1,000 is material to a small business with annual sales of $100,000. However, $1,000 isn't material to a large company with annual sales of $100,000,000. Therefore, the accounting principles followed for a $1,000 cost in a small company may be different from the accounting principles followed for a $1,000 cost in a large company.

Materiality Concept
A company must perform strictly proper accounting only for items that are significant to the business's financial situation.

Conservatism

Conservatism in accounting means exercising caution in reporting items in the financial statements. Conservatism espouses the following ideas:

- Anticipate no gains, but provide for all probable losses.
- If in doubt, record an asset at the lowest reasonable amount and a liability at the highest reasonable amount.
- When there's a question, record an expense rather than an asset.
- When you are faced with a decision between two possible options, you must choose the option that undervalues, rather than overvalues, your business.

Conservatism
A business should report the least favorable figures in the financial statements when two or more possible options are presented.

The goal of conservatism is to report realistic figures and never overstate assets or net income.

Control Over Merchandise Inventory

Maintaining good controls over merchandise inventory is very important for a merchandiser. Good controls ensure that inventory purchases and sales are properly authorized and accounted for by the accounting system. This can be accomplished by taking the following measures:

- Ensure merchandise inventory is not purchased without proper authorization, including purchasing only from approved vendors and within acceptable dollar ranges.
- After inventory is purchased, the order should be tracked and properly documented when received. At time of delivery, a count of inventory received should be completed and each item should be examined for damage.

- Damaged inventory should be properly recorded and then should either be used, disposed of, or returned to the vendor.
- A physical count of inventory should be completed at least once a year to track inventory shrinkage due to theft, damage, and errors.
- When sales are made, the inventory sold should be properly recorded and removed from the inventory count. This will prevent the company from running out of inventory, often called a stockout.

> Try It!

Match the accounting terminology to the definitions.

1.	Conservatism	**a.** A business should report the least favorable figures in the financial statements when two or more possible options are presented.
2.	Materiality concept	**b.** A business's financial statements must report enough information for outsiders to make knowledgeable decisions about the company.
3.	Disclosure principle	**c.** A business should use the same accounting methods and procedures from period to period.
4.	Consistency principle	**d.** A company must perform strictly proper accounting only for items that are significant to the business's financial situation.

Check your answers at the end of the chapter.

For more practice, see Short Exercise S-1. MyAccountingLab

HOW ARE MERCHANDISE INVENTORY COSTS DETERMINED UNDER A PERPETUAL INVENTORY SYSTEM?

Learning Objective 2

Account for merchandise inventory costs under a perpetual inventory system

Keep in mind these key equations:

Ending Merchandise Inventory = Number of units *on hand* × Unit cost

Cost of Goods Sold = Number of unit *sold* × Unit cost

Companies determine the number of units on hand from perpetual inventory records backed up by a physical count. Exhibit 1 gives the inventory data for TAB0503, one model of tablets that Smart Touch Learning sells.

As shown in this exhibit, Smart Touch Learning began August with 2 TAB0503s in inventory. It purchased 4 more tablets on August 5, bringing the total quantity on hand to 6 (2 + 4). On August 15, it sold 4 tablets, leaving 2 remaining on hand (6 − 4). Smart

Exhibit 1 | **Perpetual Inventory Record**

Item: TAB0503				
Date	Quantity Purchased	Quantity Sold	Cost per Unit	Quantity on Hand
Aug. 1			$350	2
5	4		$350	6 ← 2 + 4
15		4		2 ←
26	12		$350	14 6 − 4
31		10		4
Totals	16	14		4

Touch Learning then purchased 12 more on August 26 and sold 10 on August 31. It had 4 TAB0503s at the end of August (2 + 12 − 10). The company sold each tablet for $500 to its customers.

Measuring inventory cost is easy when prices do not change. For example, looking at Exhibit 1, you can see that Smart Touch Learning's cost per unit remained the same at $350. Therefore ending inventory and cost of goods sold can be calculated easily.

$$
\begin{aligned}
\text{Ending Merchandise Inventory} &= \text{Number of units } \textit{on hand} \times \text{Unit cost} \\
&= 4 \text{ units} \times \$350 \text{ per unit} \\
&= \$1,400 \\
\text{Cost of Goods Sold} &= \text{Number of unit } \textit{sold} \times \text{Unit cost} \\
&= 14 \text{ units} \times \$350 \text{ per unit} \\
&= \$4,900
\end{aligned}
$$

But what if unit cost does change? For example, what if the cost per unit increased to $360 on August 5 and $380 on August 26, as shown in Exhibit 2? When inventory

Exhibit 2 | **Perpetual Inventory Record—Changes in Cost per Unit**

Item: TAB0503				
Date	Quantity Purchased	Quantity Sold	Cost per Unit	Quantity on Hand
Aug. 1			$350	2
5	4		$360	6
15		4		2
26	12		$380	14
31		10		4
Totals	16	14		4

is sold on August 31, how many of the tablets sold cost $350? How many cost $360? And, how many cost $380? To compute ending inventory and cost of goods sold, Smart Touch Learning must assign a unit cost to each inventory item. This is done by using one of four inventory costing methods:

1. Specific identification
2. First-in, first-out (FIFO)
3. Last-in, first-out (LIFO)
4. Weighted-average

With the exception of the specific identification method, each inventory costing method approximates the flow of inventory costs in a business and is used to determine the amount of cost of goods sold and ending merchandise inventory.

Specific Identification Method

The specific identification method uses the specific cost of each unit of inventory to determine ending inventory and to determine cost of goods sold. In the specific identification method, the company knows exactly which item was sold and exactly what the item cost. This costing method is best for businesses that sell unique, easily identified inventory items, such as automobiles (identified by the vehicle identification number [VIN]), jewels (a specific diamond ring), and real estate (identified by address). For instance, assume that of the 4 tablets sold on August 15, 1 had a cost of $350 and 3 had a cost of $360. As of the August 31 sale, 1 had a cost of $350, and 9 had a cost of $380. Cost of goods sold and ending merchandise inventory can be calculated as shown in Exhibit 3.

Inventory Costing Method
A method of approximating the flow of inventory costs in a business that is used to determine the amount of cost of goods sold and ending merchandise inventory.

Specific Identification Method
An inventory costing method based on the specific cost of particular units of inventory.

Exhibit 3 | Perpetual Inventory Record: Specific Identification

Date	Purchases Quantity	Unit Cost	Total Cost	Cost of Goods Sold Quantity	Unit Cost	Total Cost	Inventory on Hand Quantity	Unit Cost	Total Cost
Aug. 1							2 units	× $350	= $700 } $700
5	4 units	× $360	= $1,440				2 units / 4 units	× $350 / × $360	= $700 / = $1,440 } $2,140
15				1 unit / 3 units	× $350 / × $360	= $350 / = $1,080 } $1,430	1 unit / 1 unit	× $350 / × $360	= $350 / = $360 } $710
26	12 units	× $380	= $4,560				1 unit / 1 unit / 12 units	× $350 / × $360 / × $380	= $350 / = $360 / = $4,560 } $5,270
31				1 unit / 9 units	× $350 / × $380	= $350 / = $3,420 } $3,770	1 unit / 3 units	× $360 / × $380	= $360 / = $1,140 } $1,500
Totals	16 units		$6,000	14 units		$5,200	4 units		$1,500

Notice that under the specific identification method, when inventory is sold, a specific cost is assigned to it. For example, on the August 15 sale, Smart Touch Learning knew that it had sold 1 unit costing $350 and 3 units costing $360. This left 1 unit (2 − 1) at $350 and 1 unit (4 − 3) at $360 in ending inventory. This method requires the business to keep detailed records of inventory sales and purchases and to also be able to carefully identify the inventory that is sold.

First-In, First-Out (FIFO) Method

Under the **first-in, first-out (FIFO) method**, the cost of goods sold is based on the oldest purchases—that is, the first units to come in are assumed to be the first units to go out of the warehouse (sold). In Exhibit 4, this is illustrated by the cost of goods sold coming from the *first* goods purchased, which are from the August 1 beginning inventory. FIFO costing is consistent with the physical movement of inventory (for most companies). That is, under the FIFO inventory costing method, companies sell their oldest inventory first.

First-In, First-Out (FIFO) Method
An inventory costing method in which the first costs into inventory are the first costs out to cost of goods sold. Ending inventory is based on the costs of the most recent purchases.

Exhibit 4 | Perpetual Inventory Record: First-In, First-Out (FIFO)

	Purchases			Cost of Goods Sold			Inventory on Hand		
Date	Quantity	Unit Cost	Total Cost	Quantity	Unit Cost	Total Cost	Quantity	Unit Cost	Total Cost
Aug. 1							2 units	× $ 350	= $ 700 } $ 700
5	4 units	× $ 360	= $ 1,440				2 units 4 units	× $ 350 × $ 360	= $ 700 } = $ 1,440 } $ 2,140
15				2 units 2 units	× $ 350 × $ 360	= $ 700 } = $ 720 } $ 1,420	2 units	× $ 360	= $ 720 } $ 720
26	12 units	× $ 380	= $ 4,560				2 units 12 units	× $ 360 × $ 380	= $ 720 } = $ 4,560 } $ 5,280
31				2 units 8 units	× $ 360 × $ 380	= $ 720 } = $ 3,040 } $ 3,760	4 units	× $ 380	= $ 1,520 } $ 1,520
Totals	16 units		$ 6,000	14 units		$ 5,180	4 units		$ 1,520

Smart Touch Learning began August with 2 TAB0503s that cost $350 each. After the August 5 purchase, the inventory on hand consists of 6 units (2 + 4). On August 15, the company sold 4 units. Under FIFO, the first 2 units sold had the oldest cost ($350 per unit). The next 2 units sold cost $360 each. That leaves 2 units in inventory on August 15 at $360 each. The remainder of the inventory record follows the same pattern. Consider the sale on August 31 of 10 units. The oldest cost is from August 5 (2 units @ $360). The next oldest cost is from the August 26 purchase at $380 each (8 units @ $380). This leaves 4 units in inventory on August 31 at $380 each.

The FIFO monthly summary at August 31 is as follows:

- Cost of goods sold: 14 units that cost a total of $5,180.

- Ending inventory: 4 units that cost a total of $1,520.

Notice the total cost of goods sold of $5,180 plus the total ending inventory of $1,520 equals the total cost of goods available for sale during August $6,700 [(2 units @ $350) + (4 units @ $360) + (12 units @ $380)]. Cost of goods available for sale represents the total cost of merchandise inventory that is available for sale during the time period. Smart Touch Learning measures cost of goods sold and ending merchandise inventory in this manner to prepare its financial statements.

Cost of Goods Available for Sale
The total cost spent on inventory that was available to be sold during a period.

Merchandise Inventory

Journal Entries Under FIFO

The journal entries under FIFO are presented below. We assume all purchases and sales of inventory are on account. The amounts unique to FIFO are shown in blue for emphasis. All other amounts are the same for all four inventory methods.

Date	Accounts and Explanation	Debit	Credit
Aug. 5	Merchandise Inventory (4 × $360)	1,440	
	Accounts Payable		1,440
	Purchased inventory on account.		
15	Accounts Receivable (4 × $500)	2,000	
	Sales Revenue		2,000
	Sale on account.		
15	Cost of Goods Sold (2 × $350) + (2 × $360)	1,420	
	Merchandise Inventory		1,420
	Recorded the cost of goods sold.		
26	Merchandise Inventory (12 × $380)	4,560	
	Accounts Payable		4,560
	Purchased inventory on account.		
31	Accounts Receivable (10 × $500)	5,000	
	Sales Revenue		5,000
	Sale on account.		
31	Cost of Goods Sold (2 × $360) + (8 × $380)	3,760	
	Merchandise Inventory		3,760
	Recorded the cost of goods sold.		

Equations left margin:

A↑ Merchandise Inventory↑ = L↑ Accounts Payable↑ + E

A↑ Accounts Receivable↑ = L + E↑ Sales Revenue↑

A↓ Merchandise Inventory↓ = L + E↓ Cost of Goods Sold↑

A↑ Merchandise Inventory↑ = L↑ Accounts Payable↑ + E

A↑ Accounts Receivable↑ = L + E↑ Sales Revenue↑

A↓ Merchandise Inventory↓ = L + E↓ Cost of Goods Sold↑

For example, on August 5, Smart Touch Learning purchased $1,440 of inventory and made the first journal entry. On August 15, the company sold 4 TAB0503s for the sale price of $500 each. Smart Touch Learning recorded the sale, $2,000, and the cost of goods sold, $1,420 (calculated in Exhibit 4 as 2 units @ $350 plus 2 units @ $360). The remaining journal entries (August 26 and 31) follow the inventory data in Exhibit 4.

Last-In, First-Out (LIFO) Method

Last-in, first-out (LIFO) is the opposite of FIFO. Under the last-in, first-out (LIFO) method, ending inventory comes from the oldest costs (beginning inventory and earliest purchases) of the period. The cost of goods sold is based on the most recent

Last-In, First-Out (LIFO) Method
An inventory costing method in which the last costs into inventory are the first costs out to cost of goods sold. The method leaves the oldest costs—those of beginning inventory and the earliest purchases of the period—in ending inventory.

380

purchases (new costs)—that is, the last units in are assumed to be the first units out of the warehouse (sold). This is illustrated by the cost of goods sold for the August 31 sale coming from the *last* goods in the warehouse—the August 26 purchase in Exhibit 5. Under the LIFO inventory costing method, companies sell their newest inventory first.

Exhibit 5 | **Perpetual Inventory Record: Last-In, First-Out (LIFO)**

Date	Purchases			Cost of Goods Sold			Inventory on Hand		
	Quantity	Unit Cost	Total Cost	Quantity	Unit Cost	Total Cost	Quantity	Unit Cost	Total Cost
Aug. 1							2 units	× $ 350	= $ 700 } $ 700
5	4 units	× $ 360	= $ 1,440				2 units 4 units	× $ 350 × $ 360	= $ 700 } = $ 1,440 } $ 2,140
15				4 units	× $ 360	= $ 1,440 } $ 1,440	2 units	× $ 350	= $ 700 } $ 700
26	12 units	× $ 380	= $ 4,560				2 units 12 units	× $ 350 × $ 380	= $ 700 } = $ 4,560 } $ 5,260
31				10 units	× $ 380	= $ 3,800 } $ 3,800	2 units 2 units	× $ 350 × $ 380	= $ 700 } = $ 760 } $ 1,460
Totals	16 units		$ 6,000	14 units		$ 5,240	4 units		$ 1,460

Again, Smart Touch Learning had 2 TAB0503s at the beginning. After the purchase on August 5, the company holds 6 units of inventory (2 units @ $350 plus 4 units @ $360). On August 15, Smart Touch Learning sells 4 units. Under LIFO, the cost of goods sold always comes from the most recent purchase (4 units @ $360). That leaves 2 TAB0503s in inventory on August 15 (2 units @ $350).

The purchase of 12 units on August 26 adds a new $380 layer to inventory. Now inventory holds 14 units.

Then the sale of 10 units on August 31 peels back units in LIFO order (10 units @ $380). The LIFO monthly summary at August 31 is as follows:

- Cost of goods sold: 14 units that cost a total of $5,240.
- Ending inventory: 4 units that cost a total of $1,460.

Under LIFO, Smart Touch Learning could measure cost of goods sold and ending inventory in this manner to prepare its financial statements.

Journal Entries Under LIFO

The journal entries under LIFO follow. We assume all purchases and sales of inventory are on account. Amounts unique to LIFO are shown in blue.

IFRS

LIFO is not permitted under International Financial Reporting Standards (IFRS). Under IFRS, companies may only use the Specific Identification, FIFO, and Weighted-Average methods to cost inventory. If LIFO were eliminated as an acceptable method under GAAP, those U.S. companies currently using the LIFO cost method would experience significant income statement and balance sheet effects. Approximately, one-third of U.S. companies use the LIFO method to cost at least part of their inventory.

		Date	Accounts and Explanation	Debit	Credit
$\dfrac{A\uparrow}{\text{Merchandise Inventory}\uparrow}$ = $\left\{\dfrac{L\uparrow}{\text{Accounts Payable}\uparrow} + \dfrac{E}{}\right.$		Aug. 5	Merchandise Inventory (4 × $360)	1,440	
			Accounts Payable		1,440
			Purchased inventory on account.		
$\dfrac{A\uparrow}{\text{Accounts Receivable}\uparrow}$ = $\left\{\dfrac{L}{} + \dfrac{E\uparrow}{\text{Sales Revenue}\uparrow}\right.$		15	Accounts Receivable (4 × $500)	2,000	
			Sales Revenue		2,000
			Sale on account.		
$\dfrac{A\downarrow}{\text{Merchandise Inventory}\downarrow}$ = $\left\{\dfrac{L}{} + \dfrac{E\downarrow}{\text{Cost of Goods Sold}\uparrow}\right.$		15	Cost of Goods Sold (4 × $360)	1,440	
			Merchandise Inventory		1,440
			Recorded the cost of goods sold.		
$\dfrac{A\uparrow}{\text{Merchandise Inventory}\uparrow}$ = $\left\{\dfrac{L\uparrow}{\text{Accounts Payable}\uparrow} + \dfrac{E}{}\right.$		26	Merchandise Inventory (12 × $380)	4,560	
			Accounts Payable		4,560
			Purchased inventory on account.		
$\dfrac{A\uparrow}{\text{Accounts Receivable}\uparrow}$ = $\left\{\dfrac{L}{} + \dfrac{E\uparrow}{\text{Sales Revenue}\uparrow}\right.$		31	Accounts Receivable (10 × $500)	5,000	
			Sales Revenue		5,000
			Sale on account.		
$\dfrac{A\downarrow}{\text{Merchandise Inventory}\downarrow}$ = $\left\{\dfrac{L}{} + \dfrac{E\downarrow}{\text{Cost of Goods Sold}\uparrow}\right.$		31	Cost of Goods Sold (10 × $380)	3,800	
			Merchandise Inventory		3,800
			Recorded the cost of goods sold.		

On August 5, Smart Touch Learning purchased inventory of $1,440. The August 15 sale brought in sales revenue (4 units @ $500 = $2,000) and cost of goods sold (4 units @ $360 = $1,440). The August 26 and 31 entries also come from the data in Exhibit 5.

Think about going to the grocery store to buy a gallon of milk. Which gallon is in front of the milk cooler: the older milk or the newer milk? The older milk is in front. That's FIFO. Now visualize reaching all the way to the back of the cooler to get the newer milk. That's LIFO. It's important to understand that although this image represents the physical flow of goods, an inventory costing system may or may not match the physical flow. The costing system is only an assumption about how cost flows. The inventory does not have to actually be sold in the FIFO manner in order to record it as FIFO.

Weighted-Average Method

Weighted-Average Method
An inventory costing method based on the weighted average cost per unit of inventory that is calculated after each purchase. Weighted average cost per unit is determined by dividing the cost of goods available for sale by the number of units available.

Under the **weighted-average method**, the business computes a new weighted average cost per unit after each purchase. Ending inventory and cost of goods sold are then based on the same weighted average cost per unit. After the first purchase on August 5, the weighted average cost per unit sold falls somewhere between the beginning inventory cost of $350 and the most recent purchase cost of $360.

Exhibit 6 shows a perpetual inventory record for the weighted-average method. We round average unit cost to the nearest cent and total cost to the nearest dollar.

Exhibit 6 | Perpetual Inventory Record: Weighted-Average

Date	Purchases Quantity	Unit Cost	Total Cost	Cost of Goods Sold Quantity	Unit Cost	Total Cost	Inventory on Hand Quantity	Unit Cost	Total Cost	
Aug. 1							2 units	× $ 350	= $ 700	
5	4 units	× $ 360	= $ 1,440				6 units	× $ 356.67	= $ 2,140	$ 2,140 / 6 units = $ 356.67
15				4 units	× $ 356.67	= $ 1,427	2 units	× $ 356.67	= $ 713	
26	12 units	× $ 380	= $ 4,560				14 units	× $ 376.64	= $ 5,273	$ 5,273 / 14 units = $ 376.64
31				10 units	× $ 376.64	= $ 3,766	4 units	× $ 376.64	= $ 1,507	
Totals	16 units		$ 6,000	14 units		$ 5,193	4 units		$ 1,507	

As noted previously, after each purchase, Smart Touch Learning computes a new weighted average cost per unit. For example, on August 5, the new weighted average unit cost is as follows:

Cost of goods available for sale / Number of units available = ($700 + $1,440) / (2 units + 4 units)
= $2,140 / 6 units
= $356.67 (rounded)

Under the weighted-average method, the cost per unit is a weighted average. You cannot take the average of the two unit costs ($350 and $360) to determine the new unit cost. Instead, you must use the total cost of goods available for sale ($2,140) divided by the number of units available (6 units).

The goods sold on August 15 are then costed out at $356.67 per unit. On August 26 when the next purchase is made, the new weighted average unit cost is as follows:

Cost of goods available for sale / Number of units available = ($713 + $4,560) / (2 units + 12 units)
= $5,273 / 14 units
= $376.64 (rounded)

The weighted-average cost summary at August 31 is as follows:

- Cost of goods sold: 14 units that cost a total of $5,193.
- Ending inventory: 4 units that cost a total of $1,507.

> *With the weighted-average cost method, rounding errors will often occur. However this is not the case in this example. Notice that cost of goods sold and ending inventory total $6,700 ($5,193 + $1,507), which equals the total cost of goods available for sale.*

Under the weighted-average cost method, Smart Touch Learning could use these amounts to prepare its financial statements.

Journal Entries Under Weighted-Average

The journal entries under weighted-average costing follow. We assume all purchases and sales of inventory are on account. Amounts unique to the weighted-average method are shown in blue.

					Date	Accounts and Explanation	Debit	Credit
A↑		**L↑**	+	**E**	Aug. 5	Merchandise Inventory (4 × $360)	1,440	
Merchandise Inventory↑	=	Accounts Payable↑				Accounts Payable		1,440
						Purchased inventory on account.		
A↑		**L**	+	**E↑**	15	Accounts Receivable (4 × $500)	2,000	
Accounts Receivable↑	=			Sales Revenue↑		Sales Revenue		2,000
						Sale on account.		
A↓		**L**	+	**E↓**	15	Cost of Goods Sold (4 × $356.67)	1,427	
Merchandise Inventory↓	=			Cost of Goods Sold↑		Merchandise Inventory		1,427
						Recorded the cost of goods sold.		
A↑		**L↑**	+	**E**	26	Merchandise Inventory (12 × $380)	4,560	
Merchandise Inventory↑	=	Accounts Payable↑				Accounts Payable		4,560
						Purchased inventory on account.		
A↑		**L**	+	**E↑**	31	Accounts Receivable (10 × $500)	5,000	
Accounts Receivable↑	=			Sales Revenue↑		Sales Revenue		5,000
						Sale on account.		
A↓		**L**	+	**E↓**	31	Cost of Goods Sold (10 × $376.64)	3,766	
Merchandise Inventory↓	=			Cost of Goods Sold↑		Merchandise Inventory		3,766
						Recorded the cost of goods sold.		

On August 5, Smart Touch Learning purchased $1,440 of inventory and made the first journal entry. On August 15, Smart Touch Learning sold 4 TAB0503s for $500 each. The company recorded the sale ($2,000) and the cost of goods sold (4 units at $356.67 = $1,427). The remaining journal entries (August 26 and 31) follow the same procedure.

5. Serenity Books has the following transactions in August related to merchandise inventory.

Aug. 1	Beginning merchandise inventory, 10 books @ $15 each
3	Sold 3 books @ $20 each
12	Purchased 8 books @ $18 each
15	Sold 9 books @ $20 each
20	Purchased 4 books @ $20 each
28	Sold 5 books @ $25 each

a. Determine the cost of goods sold and ending merchandise inventory by preparing a perpetual inventory record using the specific identification method. Assume the following costing information for the books sold during the month:

    August 3: 3 books costing $15 each
    August 15: 4 books costing $15 each and 5 books costing $18 each
    August 28: 2 books costing $18 each and 3 books costing $20 each

b. Determine the cost of goods sold and ending merchandise inventory by preparing a perpetual inventory record using the FIFO inventory costing method.
c. Determine the cost of goods sold and ending merchandise inventory by preparing a perpetual inventory record using the LIFO inventory costing method.
d. Determine the cost of goods sold and ending merchandise inventory by preparing a perpetual inventory record using the weighted-average inventory costing method. Round weighted average unit cost to the nearest cent and total cost to the nearest dollar.

Check your answers at the end of the chapter.

For more practice, see Short Exercises S-2 through S-6. MyAccountingLab

HOW ARE FINANCIAL STATEMENTS AFFECTED BY USING DIFFERENT INVENTORY COSTING METHODS?

What leads Smart Touch Learning to select the specific identification, FIFO, LIFO, or weighted-average inventory costing method? The different methods have different benefits.

Learning Objective 3

Compare the effects on the financial statements when using the different inventory costing methods

Income Statement

Exhibit 7 summarizes the results for the four inventory costing methods for Smart Touch Learning. It shows sales revenue, cost of goods sold, and gross profit for specific identification, FIFO, LIFO, and weighted-average.

Exhibit 7 | **Comparative Results for Specific Identification, FIFO, LIFO, and Weighted-Average—Income Statement**

	Specific Identification	FIFO	LIFO	Weighted-Average
Sales Revenue (14 units × $500)	$ 7,000	$ 7,000	$ 7,000	$ 7,000
Less: Cost of Goods Sold	5,200	5,180	5,240	5,193
Gross Profit	$ 1,800	$ 1,820	$ 1,760	$ 1,807

How do businesses < decide which inventory costing method to use?

Exhibit 7 shows that FIFO produces the lowest cost of goods sold and the highest gross profit for Smart Touch Learning. Because operating expenses are the same, regardless of which inventory method a company uses, net income is also the highest under FIFO when inventory costs are rising. Many companies prefer high income in order to attract investors and borrow on favorable terms. FIFO offers this benefit in a period of rising costs.

When inventory costs are rising, LIFO results in the highest cost of goods sold and the lowest gross profit. Lower profits mean lower taxable income; thus, LIFO lets companies pay the lowest income taxes when inventory costs are rising. Low tax payments conserve cash, and that is the main benefit of LIFO. The downside of LIFO is that the company reports low net income.

The weighted-average method generates amounts that fall between the extremes of FIFO and LIFO. Therefore, companies that seek a "middle-ground" solution use the weighted-average method for inventory.

Balance Sheet

Consider again the purchases made by Smart Touch Learning during August. The company had total inventory in August as follows:

Aug. 1	2 units × $350	$ 700
Aug. 5	4 units × $360	1,440
Aug. 26	12 units × $380	4,560
Cost of goods available for sale		$ 6,700

Only one of two things can happen to the tablets—either they remain in the warehouse (ending merchandise inventory) or they are sold (Cost of Goods Sold). Ending merchandise inventory can be calculated by determining first the cost of goods available for sale (beginning merchandise inventory plus inventory purchased) and then subtracting merchandise inventory sold (Cost of Goods Sold). Exhibit 8 shows the results of Smart Touch Learning's ending merchandise inventory for each of the costing methods for August.

Exhibit 8 | Comparative Results for Specific Identification, FIFO, LIFO, and Weighted-Average—Balance Sheet

	Specific Identification	FIFO	LIFO	Weighted-Average
Beginning Merchandise Inventory	$ 700	$ 700	$ 700	$ 700
Plus: Net Cost of Purchases	6,000	6,000	6,000	6,000
Cost of Goods Available for Sale	6,700	6,700	6,700	6,700
Less: Cost of Goods Sold	5,200	5,180	5,240	5,193
Ending Merchandise Inventory	$ 1,500	$ 1,520	$ 1,460	$ 1,507

The weighted-average ending merchandise inventory number shown in Exhibit 6 may be slightly different than that found in Exhibit 8. This is because of rounding. When completing your homework, always read carefully for directions on how to round when using the weighted-average method.

When using the FIFO inventory costing method, ending merchandise inventory will be the highest when costs are increasing. LIFO produces the lowest ending merchandise inventory with weighted-average again in the middle.

So far we have been ignoring the effects on the income statement and balance sheet when using the specific identification method. This is because under specific identification, the results will vary depending on which costs are assigned to the inventory sold. Most companies will not choose to use the specific identification method unless they want to match each inventory item sold with its exact cost.

Merchandise Inventory

We have looked at the effects on the financial statements when inventory costs are rising. When inventory costs are instead declining, the effects on the financial statements will be the opposite of those discussed above. Exhibit 9 summarizes the effects on the financial statements during periods of rising and declining inventory costs.

Exhibit 9 | Effects on the Financial Statements During Periods of Rising and Declining Inventory Costs

Period of Rising Inventory Costs:				
	Specific Identification	FIFO	LIFO	Weighted-Average
Income Statement:				
Cost of Goods Sold	Varies	Lowest	Highest	Middle
Net Income	Varies	Highest	Lowest	Middle
Balance Sheet:				
Ending Merchandise Inventory	Varies	Highest	Lowest	Middle

Period of Declining Inventory Costs:				
	Specific Identification	FIFO	LIFO	Weighted-Average
Income Statement:				
Cost of Goods Sold	Varies	Highest	Lowest	Middle
Net Income	Varies	Lowest	Highest	Middle
Balance Sheet:				
Ending Merchandise Inventory	Varies	Lowest	Highest	Middle

> Try It!

6. Antelope Motors is considering which inventory costing method it should use. The business wants to maximize gross profits during a period of declining costs. Which inventory costing method should Antelope Motors select?

Check your answer at the end of the chapter.

For more practice, see Short Exercise S-7. MyAccountingLab

HOW IS MERCHANDISE INVENTORY VALUED WHEN USING THE LOWER-OF-COST-OR-MARKET RULE?

In addition to the specific identification, FIFO, LIFO, and weighted-average inventory costing methods, accountants face other inventory issues, such as the lower-of-cost-or-market (LCM) rule. LCM shows accounting conservatism in action and requires that merchandise inventory be reported in the financial statements at whichever is lower of the following:

- The historical cost of the inventory
- The market value of the inventory

Computing the Lower-of-Cost-or-Market

For inventories, market value generally means the current replacement cost (that is, the cost to replace the inventory on hand). If the replacement cost of inventory is less than its historical cost, the business must adjust the inventory value. By adjusting the inventory down (crediting Merchandise Inventory), the balance sheet value of the asset, Merchandise Inventory, is at its correct value (market) rather than its overstated value (cost). If the merchandise inventory's market value is greater than cost, then we don't adjust the Merchandise Inventory account because of the conservatism principle.

Recording the Adjusting Journal Entry to Adjust Merchandise Inventory

Suppose Smart Touch Learning paid $3,000 for its TAB0503 inventory. By December 31, the merchandise inventory can now be replaced for $2,200, and the decline in value appears permanent. Market value is below cost, and the entry to write down the inventory to LCM is as follows:

Date	Accounts and Explanation	Debit	Credit
Dec. 31	Cost of Goods Sold	800	
	Merchandise Inventory ($3,000 − $2,200)		800
	To write merchandise inventory down to market value.		

In this case, Smart Touch Learning's balance sheet would report this inventory as follows:

SMART TOUCH LEARNING
Balance Sheet (Partial)
December 31, 2015
Current Assets:
Merchandise Inventory $ 2,200

Learning Objective 4

Apply the lower-of-cost-or-market rule to merchandise inventory

Lower-of-Cost-or-Market (LCM) Rule

Rule that merchandise inventory should be reported in the financial statements at whichever is lower—its historical cost or its market value.

IFRS

Under International Financial Reporting Standards, inventory must be reported at the lower-of-cost-or-market value. Importantly, "market" is defined differently. Under IFRS, the market value of inventory is defined as the "net realizable value," or essentially its selling price. (What will the company "really" get for its inventory?) If the historical cost is higher than the selling price, then inventory must be written down. The IFRS approach results in fewer write-downs on inventory. In some circumstances, if a write-down is necessary, it may be reversed at a later date. Reversing write-downs of inventory never happens under GAAP.

$$\underline{\quad A\downarrow \quad} \Biggr\}=\Biggl\{ \underline{\;L\;}+\underline{\quad E\downarrow \quad}$$

Merchandise Inventory↓	=	Cost of Goods Sold↑

Companies often disclose that the LCM rule is followed in notes to their financial statements, as shown here for Smart Touch Learning:

> NOTE 2: STATEMENT OF SIGNIFICANT ACCOUNTING POLICIES
> *Merchandise Inventories*. Merchandise inventories are carried at the *lower-of-cost-or-market*. Cost is determined using the first-in, first-out method.

> Decisions   Should inventory be marked down?

Haley Richardson works for a large retail electronic store, Electronics 'R Us, and is responsible for handling all aspects of merchandise inventory. Earlier in the year, the store had purchased large quantities of the newest laptop computer, counting on the fact that consumers would be rushing into the store to buy them. What Electronics 'R Us didn't know was that the laptops would be obsolete before they could get them sold. Now, as Haley stares at the laptops sitting on the shelf, she wonders what she should do. What would you do?

Solution

Generally Accepted Accounting Principles require that companies evaluate the cost of inventory annually to determine whether the current market value is less than the cost of the inventory on the balance sheet. Haley should review the business's stock of laptops and determine the market value. It's important that Haley realize that market value does not mean the value at which the laptops can be sold. Instead, market value represents the current replacement cost or the cost that Electronics 'R Us would incur to replace the laptops on hand. If the replacement cost is less than the historical cost of the laptops, then Haley should record an entry to write down the value of the laptops. This ensures that Electronics 'R Us is reporting the value of the laptops accurately on its balance sheet.

> **> Try It!**
>
> 7. T. J. Jackson Supplies had merchandise inventory that cost $1,300. The market value of the merchandise inventory is $750. What value should Jackson Supplies show on the balance sheet for merchandise inventory? Record the adjusting entry, if one is needed.
>
> **Check your answer at the end of the chapter.**
>
> For more practice, see Short Exercise S-8.   MyAccountingLab

WHAT ARE THE EFFECTS OF MERCHANDISE INVENTORY ERRORS ON THE FINANCIAL STATEMENTS?

Learning Objective 5

Measure the effects of merchandise inventory errors on the financial statements

Businesses perform a physical count of their merchandise inventory at the end of the fiscal or accounting period. For the financial statements to be accurate, it is important to get a correct count. This can be difficult for a company with widespread operations.

An error in ending merchandise inventory creates a whole string of errors in other related accounts. To illustrate, suppose Smart Touch Learning accidentally reported $5,000 more ending merchandise inventory than it actually had. In that case, ending merchandise inventory would be overstated by $5,000 on the balance sheet. The following shows how an overstatement of ending inventory affects cost of goods sold, gross profit, and net income:

	Ending Merchandise Inventory Overstated $5,000
Sales Revenue	Correct
Cost of Goods Sold:	
Beginning Merchandise Inventory	Correct
Net Cost of Purchases	Correct
Cost of Goods Available for Sale	Correct
Less: Ending Merchandise Inventory	ERROR: Overstated $5,000
Cost of Goods Sold	Understated $5,000
Gross Profit	Overstated $5,000
Operating Expenses	Correct
Net Income	Overstated $5,000

Understating the ending inventory—reporting the inventory too low—has the opposite effect. If Smart Touch Learning understated the inventory by $1,200, the effect would be as shown here:

	Ending Merchandise Inventory Understated $1,200
Sales Revenue	Correct
Cost of Goods Sold:	
Beginning Merchandise Inventory	Correct
Net Cost of Purchases	Correct
Cost of Goods Available for Sale	Correct
Less: Ending Merchandise Inventory	ERROR: Understated $1,200
Cost of Goods Sold	Overstated $1,200
Gross Profit	Understated $1,200
Operating Expenses	Correct
Net Income	Understated $1,200

Exhibit 10 | Inventory Errors

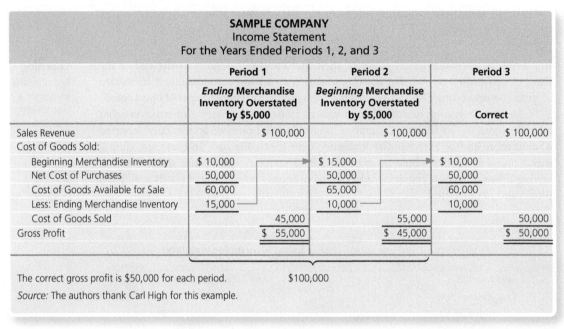

SAMPLE COMPANY
Income Statement
For the Years Ended Periods 1, 2, and 3

	Period 1		Period 2		Period 3	
	Ending Merchandise Inventory Overstated by $5,000		**Beginning** Merchandise Inventory Overstated by $5,000		Correct	
Sales Revenue		$ 100,000		$ 100,000		$ 100,000
Cost of Goods Sold:						
Beginning Merchandise Inventory	$ 10,000		$ 15,000		$ 10,000	
Net Cost of Purchases	50,000		50,000		50,000	
Cost of Goods Available for Sale	60,000		65,000		60,000	
Less: Ending Merchandise Inventory	15,000		10,000		10,000	
Cost of Goods Sold		45,000		55,000		50,000
Gross Profit		$ 55,000		$ 45,000		$ 50,000

The correct gross profit is $50,000 for each period. $100,000

Source: The authors thank Carl High for this example.

Recall that one period's ending merchandise inventory becomes the next period's beginning inventory. As a result, an error in ending merchandise inventory carries over into the next period. Exhibit 10 illustrates the effect of an inventory error, assuming all other items on the income statement are unchanged for the three periods. Period 1's ending merchandise inventory is overstated by $5,000; Period 1's ending merchandise inventory should be $10,000. The error carries over to Period 2. Period 3 is correct. In fact, both Period 1 and Period 2 should look like Period 3.

Ending merchandise inventory is *subtracted* to compute cost of goods sold in one period and the same amount is *added* as beginning merchandise inventory in the next period. Therefore, an inventory error cancels out after two periods. The overstatement of cost of goods sold in Period 2 counterbalances the understatement for Period 1. Thus, total gross profit for the two periods combined is correct. These effects are summarized in Exhibit 11.

Exhibit 11 | Effects of Inventory Errors

SAMPLE COMPANY
Income Statement
For the Years Ended Periods 1 and 2

	Period 1		Period 2	
	Cost of Goods Sold	Gross Profit and Net Income	Cost of Goods Sold	Gross Profit and Net Income
Period 1 Ending Merchandise Inventory *overstated*	Understated	Overstated	Overstated	Understated
Period 1 Ending Merchandise Inventory *understated*	Overstated	Understated	Understated	Overstated

>Ethics — Should the inventory be included?

One of A'isha Sowell's main responsibilities at the end of the fiscal or accounting year is to manage the count of physical inventory for her employer. She knows that it is important that the business get an accurate count of inventory so that its financial statements are reported correctly. In reviewing the inventory count sheet, she realizes that a large crate of inventory that has already been sold but not yet delivered was included in the count of inventory. The crate has left her employer, but is still in transit at fiscal year end. A'isha does not believe that it should be included because the inventory was sold FOB shipping point. When A'isha went to her supervisor with this information, she was told that she shouldn't worry about it because the error would ultimately correct itself. What should A'isha do?

Solution

Companies whose profits are lagging can be tempted to increase reported income to make the business look more successful. One easy way to do this is to overstate ending inventory. A'isha is correct in her assumption that the inventory should not be included in the physical count of inventory. While this error will ultimately correct itself (in two years), in the current year, the business will be overstating gross profit and net income. This overstatement could cause investors to view the business more favorably than they should. A'isha should stand firm in her decision to not include the inventory in the count.

> Try It!

8. The Shirley's Gourmet Foods' merchandise inventory data for the year ended December 31, 2015, follow:

Sales Revenue		$ 48,000
Cost of Goods Sold:		
Beginning Merchandise Inventory	$ 3,360	
Net Cost of Purchases	21,280	
Cost of Goods Available for Sale	24,640	
Less: Ending Merchandise Inventory	4,960	
Cost of Goods Sold		19,680
Gross Profit		$ 28,320

Assume that the ending merchandise inventory was accidentally overstated by $1,920. What are the correct amounts for cost of goods sold and gross profit?

Check your answer at the end of the chapter.

For more practice, see Short Exercise S-9. MyAccountingLab

HOW DO WE USE INVENTORY TURNOVER AND DAYS' SALES IN INVENTORY TO EVALUATE BUSINESS PERFORMANCE?

Learning Objective 6

Use inventory turnover and days' sales in inventory to evaluate business performance

Owners and managers strive to sell merchandise inventory quickly because the merchandise inventory generates no profit until it is sold. Further, fast-selling inventory is less likely to become obsolete (worthless) and does not require the business to pay for high storage and insurance costs often associated with keeping inventory on hand. There are two ratios that help owners and managers monitor their inventory levels: Inventory Turnover and Days' Sales in Inventory.

Inventory Turnover

Inventory Turnover
Measures the number of times a company sells its average level of merchandise inventory during a period. Cost of goods sold / Average merchandise inventory.

Companies try to manage their inventory levels such that they will have just enough inventory to meet customer demand without investing large amounts of money in inventory sitting on the shelves gathering dust. Inventory turnover measures how rapidly merchandise inventory is sold. It is computed as follows:

> Inventory turnover = Cost of goods sold / Average merchandise inventory
> Average merchandise inventory = (Beginning merchandise inventory + Ending merchandise inventory) / 2

A high rate of turnover indicates ease in selling inventory; a low rate indicates difficulty. For example, an inventory value of 4 means that the company sold its average level of inventory four times—once every three months—during the year. Inventory turnover varies widely with the nature of the business and should be evaluated against industry averages.

Days' Sales in Inventory

Days' Sales in Inventory
Measures the average number of days that inventory is held by a company. 365 days / Inventory turnover.

Another key measure is the days' sales in inventory ratio. This ratio measures the average number of days merchandise inventory is held by the company and is calculated as follows:

> Days' sales in inventory = 365 days / Inventory turnover

Days' sales in inventory also varies widely, depending on the business. A lower days' sales in inventory is preferable because it indicates that the company is able to sell its inventory quickly, thereby reducing its inventory storage and insurance costs, as well as reducing the risk of holding obsolete inventory.

Let's turn to **Green Mountain Coffee Roasters, Inc.** and evaluate the company's inventory levels using the two ratios discussed. Presented below are the cost of goods sold and beginning and ending merchandise inventory figures (in thousands) from Green Mountain's income statement and balance sheet on September 24, 2011.

Cost of goods sold (Cost of sales)	$ 1,746,274
Beginning merchandise inventory	262,478
Ending merchandise inventory	672,248

Green Mountain's inventory turnover is 3.74 times per year and is calculated as:

Inventory turnover = Cost of goods sold / Average merchandise inventory
= $1,746,274 / [($262,478 + $672,248) / 2]
= 3.74 times per year

Its days' sales in inventory is 97.6 days and is calculated as:

Days' sales in inventory = 365 days / Inventory turnover
= 365 days / 3.74
= 97.6 days

It appears that Green Mountain sells its average inventory 3.74 times per year. A high turnover rate is desirable, and an increase in the turnover rate usually means higher profits. In addition, the days' sales in inventory of Green Mountain indicates that the company, on average, has 97.6 days' supply of inventory on hand. This seems a little high for a consumer beverage company, but it should be evaluated against the industry average.

9. The Opa's Carving Shop had the following financial data for the year ended December 31, 2015:

Cost of Goods Sold	$ 484,000
Beginning Merchandise Inventory	88,800
Ending Merchandise Inventory	111,200

What is the inventory turnover and days' sales in inventory for the year?

Check your answers at the end of the chapter.

For more practice, see Short Exercise S-10. MyAccountingLab

APPENDIX A: Merchandise Inventory Costs Under a Periodic Inventory System

HOW ARE MERCHANDISE INVENTORY COSTS DETERMINED UNDER A PERIODIC INVENTORY SYSTEM?

Accounting is simpler in a periodic inventory system because the company keeps no daily running record of inventory on hand. The only way to determine the ending merchandise inventory and cost of goods sold in a periodic inventory system is to take a physical

Learning Objective 7
Account for merchandise inventory costs under a periodic inventory system

inventory to count the goods left (on hand)—usually at the end of the fiscal year. The periodic inventory system works well for a small business in which the inventory can be controlled by visual inspection—that is, the inventory usually is not large in size or dollar amount.

The various inventory costing methods (specific identification, FIFO, LIFO, and weighted-average) in a periodic inventory system follow the pattern illustrated earlier for the perpetual inventory system. To show how the periodic inventory system works, we use the same Smart Touch Learning data that we used for the perpetual inventory system (see Exhibit A-1).

Exhibit A-1 | **Perpetual Inventory Record—Changes in Cost per Unit**

Item: TAB0503

Date	Quantity Purchased	Quantity Sold	Cost per Unit	Quantity on Hand
Aug. 1			$350	2
5	4		$360	6
15		4		2
26	12		$380	14
31		10		4
Totals	16	14		4

We use these data to illustrate FIFO, LIFO, and weighted-average cost. We will not illustrate the specific identification inventory costing method because it is calculated the same under both the perpetual and periodic inventory systems.

For all four inventory costing methods, cost of goods available for sale is always the sum of beginning inventory plus net purchases:

Beginning merchandise inventory (2 units × $350)	$ 700
Plus: Net purchases (4 units × $360) + (12 units × $380)	6,000
Cost of goods available for sale	$ 6,700

The different methods—specific identification, FIFO, LIFO, and weighted-average cost—compute different amounts for ending inventory and cost of goods sold. In other words, the $6,700 invested in cost of goods available for sale will be either on the balance sheet in Merchandise Inventory or expensed on the income statement, as Cost of Goods Sold. The amount on the balance sheet will be the cost of the four tablets that were not sold and are still on hand. The amount on the income statement will be the cost of the 14 tablets sold.

First-In, First-Out (FIFO) Method

Under FIFO, the ending inventory comes from the newest—the most recent—purchases, which cost $380 per unit as illustrated below:

Beginning merchandise inventory (2 units × $350)	$ 700
Net cost of purchases (4 units × $360) + (12 units × $380)	6,000
Cost of goods available for sale	$ 6,700
Less: Ending merchandise inventory (4 × $380)	(1,520)
Cost of goods sold	$ 5,180

Notice that the FIFO periodic cost of goods sold is $5,180, exactly the same amount as we calculated using the FIFO perpetual inventory method. The amounts obtained for cost of goods sold and ending merchandise inventory are always the same for FIFO perpetual and FIFO periodic. This occurs because FIFO sells the oldest inventory acquisitions first. Therefore, it does not matter when FIFO is calculated; the earliest purchase will always be the same whether we calculate cost of goods sold on the sale date (perpetual) or at the end of the period (periodic).

Last-In, First-Out (LIFO) Method

Under LIFO, the ending inventory comes from the oldest costs of the period—in this case, the beginning inventory of two units that cost $350 per unit, plus two from the first purchase at $360. LIFO is calculated as follows:

Beginning merchandise inventory (2 units × $350)	$ 700
Net cost purchases (4 units × $360) + (12 units × $380)	6,000
Cost of goods available for sale	$ 6,700
Less: Ending merchandise inventory (2 × $350) + (2 × $360)	(1,420)
Cost of goods sold	$ 5,280

Weighted-Average Method

In the weighted-average inventory costing method, when using the periodic inventory system, we compute a single weighted average cost per unit for the entire period:

Cost of goods available for sale (entire period) / Number of units available = $6,700 / 18 units
= $372.22 (rounded)

Merchandise Inventory

Then apply this weighted average cost to compute ending merchandise inventory (rounded to the nearest dollar) and cost of goods sold, as shown:

Beginning merchandise inventory (2 units × $350)	$ 700
Net cost of purchases (4 units × $360) + (12 units × $380)	6,000
Cost of goods available for sale	$ 6,700
Less: Ending merchandise inventory (4 × $372.22)	(1,489)
Cost of goods sold	$ 5,211

Notice that when using the periodic system with the LIFO and weighted-average periodic methods, the dollar amounts obtained for the ending merchandise inventory and cost of goods sold are different than those obtained with the perpetual inventory system. This is because the perpetual inventory system keeps a running balance of inventory while the periodic inventory system does not. Under the periodic inventory system, the ending merchandise inventory is determined without regards to when the sales dates of inventory occurred.

> Try It!

10A. Serenity Books has the following transactions in August related to merchandise inventory.

Aug. 1	Beginning merchandise inventory, 10 books @ $15 each
3	Sold 3 books @ $20 each
12	Purchased 8 books @ $18 each
15	Sold 9 books @ $20 each
20	Purchased 4 books @ $20 each
28	Sold 5 books @ $25 each

a. Determine the cost of goods sold and ending merchandise inventory using the FIFO inventory costing method assuming Serenity Books uses the periodic inventory system.
b. Determine the cost of goods sold and ending merchandise inventory using the LIFO inventory costing method assuming Serenity Books uses the periodic inventory system.
c. Determine the cost of goods sold and ending merchandise inventory using the weighted-average inventory costing method assuming Serenity Books uses the periodic inventory system.

Check your answers at the end of the chapter.

For more practice, see Short Exercises SA-11 through SA-13. MyAccountingLab

APPENDIX B: Estimating Ending Merchandise Inventory

HOW CAN THE COST OF ENDING MERCHANDISE INVENTORY BE ESTIMATED?

Often a business must *estimate* the value of its ending merchandise inventory because the business suffered a natural catastrophe, such as a fire, and lost all of its inventory. When this happens, the business will only have partial records showing its beginning merchandise inventory, records from vendors showing its net purchases, and sales revenue information.

Gross Profit Method

A company can use the gross profit method, which uses the cost of goods sold formula and the gross profit percentage to determine the cost of ending merchandise inventory. Recall that cost of goods available for sale is either deemed sold (COGS) or accounted for in ending merchandise inventory. Because COGS plus ending merchandise inventory equals cost of goods available for sale, we can rearrange the COGS formula as shown in Exhibit B-1 to determine either cost of goods sold or ending merchandise inventory. The company will use this rearranged formula to estimate the cost of goods sold based on the gross profit percentage (gross profit divided by net sales revenue).

Learning Objective 8

Estimate the cost of ending merchandise inventory using the gross profit method and the retail method

Gross Profit Method

A way to estimate ending merchandise inventory on the basis of the cost of goods sold formula and the gross profit percentage.

Exhibit B-1 | **Cost of Goods Sold Formula**

Original formula:		Rearranged formula:	
Beginning merchandise inventory	$ 14,000	Beginning merchandise inventory	$ 14,000
Net cost of purchases	66,000	Net cost of purchases	66,000
Cost of goods available for sale	80,000	Cost of goods available for sale	80,000
Less: Ending merchandise inventory	20,000	Less: Cost of goods sold	60,000
Cost of goods sold	$ 60,000	Ending merchandise inventory	$ 20,000

For example, suppose Smart Touch Learning suffers a natural catastrophe and its entire merchandise inventory is destroyed. To collect insurance, the company must estimate the cost of the inventory destroyed. Using its normal gross profit percentage (that is, the gross profit percentage from historical records), Smart Touch Learning can estimate cost of goods sold. Then it needs to subtract cost of goods sold from cost of goods available for sale to estimate ending merchandise inventory.

Smart Touch Learning had $14,000 beginning merchandise inventory, and it knows that it had net purchases during the time period of $66,000. In addition, the company had $100,000 of net sales revenue. Smart Touch Learning can use its normal gross profit percentage of 40% to determine an estimated cost of goods sold. Exhibit B-2 illustrates the gross profit method:

Exhibit B-2 | **The Gross Profit Method**

Beginning merchandise inventory		$ 14,000
Net cost of purchases		66,000
Cost of goods available for sale		80,000
Estimated cost of goods sold		
Net Sales revenue	$ 100,000	
Less: Estimated gross profit of 40% ($100,000 × 40%)	40,000	
Estimated cost of goods sold		60,000
Estimated ending merchandise inventory		**$ 20,000**

This method allows Smart Touch Learning to determine an estimate of the cost of ending merchandise inventory by using its normal gross profit percentage.

The Retail Method

Retail Method
A way to estimate the cost of ending merchandise inventory on the basis of the ratio of the goods available for sale at cost to the goods available for sale at retail.

The retail method is another method that can be used to estimate ending merchandise inventory. In the retail method, the business uses its ratio of the goods available for sale at cost to the goods available for sale at retail to determine the cost of estimated ending merchandise inventory.

Assume a business has the following cost and retail pricing on its merchandise inventory. In addition, sales revenue for the time period is $40,000.

	Cost	Retail
Beginning merchandise inventory	$ 20,000	$ 34,000
Net purchases	80,000	136,000
Goods available for sale	$ 100,000	$ 170,000
Cost to retail ratio = $100,000 / $170,000 =		59%

The business will use its ratio of cost to retail to estimate the cost of ending merchandise inventory as shown in Exhibit B-3:

Exhibit B-3 | The Retail Method

	Cost	Retail
Beginning merchandise inventory	$ 20,000	$ 34,000
Net purchases	80,000	136,000
Goods available for sale	$ 100,000	$ 170,000
Less: Net sales revenue		40,000
Ending merchandise inventory at retail		$ 130,000
Estimated ending merchandise inventory at cost ($130,000 × 59%)	$ 76,700	

> **Try It!**

11B. R. E. Bob's Farm Equipment began the year with merchandise inventory of $33,960 and purchased $210,400 of goods during the year. Sales for the year are $400,800, and Bob's gross profit percentage is 40% of sales. Compute the estimated cost of ending merchandise inventory by the gross profit method.

Check your answer at the end of the chapter.

For more practice, see Short Exercises SB-14 and SB-15. MyAccountingLab

REVIEW

> Things You Should Know

1. What are the accounting principles and controls that relate to merchandise inventory?

- Consistency principle: Businesses should use the same accounting methods and procedures from period to period.

- Disclosure principle: A company's financial statements should report enough information for outsiders to make knowledgeable decisions about the company.

- Materiality concept: A company must perform strictly proper accounting only for significant items.

- Conservatism: A company should exercise caution in reporting items in the financial statements.

- Controls over merchandise inventory ensure that inventory purchases and sales are properly authorized and accounted for by the accounting system.

2. How are merchandise inventory costs determined under a perpetual inventory system?

- Four costing methods can be used to determine merchandise inventory costs:

  - Specific identification method—Uses the specific cost of each unit of inventory to determine ending inventory and to determine cost of goods sold.

  - First-in, first-out (FIFO) method—First costs into inventory are the first costs out to cost of goods sold; ending inventory is based on the costs of the most recent purchases.

  - Last-in, first-out (LIFO) method—Last costs into inventory are the first costs out to cost of goods sold; ending inventory is based on the costs of the oldest inventory.

  - Weighted-average method—Method based on the weighted average cost per unit of inventory after each purchase. Weighted average cost per unit is determined by dividing the cost of goods available for sale by the number of units available for sale.

3. How are financial statements affected by using different inventory costing methods?

- The FIFO method results in the lowest cost of goods sold and the highest gross profit when costs are rising.

- The LIFO method results in the highest cost of goods sold and the lowest gross profit when costs are rising.

- The weighted-average method generates amounts for cost of goods sold and gross profit that fall between FIFO and LIFO if costs are consistently increasing or decreasing.

4. How is merchandise inventory valued when using the lower-of-cost-or-market rule?

- Lower-of-cost-or-market requires that merchandise be reported in the financial statements at whichever is lower of the following:
  - The historical cost of the inventory
  - The market value of the inventory
- An adjusting entry must be recorded to write down merchandise inventory if the market value is lower than the historical cost.

5. What are the effects of merchandise inventory errors on the financial statements?

- An error in ending merchandise inventory creates a whole string of errors in other related accounts.
- One period's ending merchandise inventory becomes the next period's beginning merchandise inventory.

6. How do we use inventory turnover and days' sales in inventory to evaluate business performance?

- Inventory turnover measures how rapidly merchandise inventory is sold and is calculated as:

  Cost of goods sold / Average merchandise inventory.

- Days' sales in inventory measures the average number of days merchandise inventory is held by the company and is calculated as follows:

  365 days / Inventory turnover.

7. How are merchandise inventory costs determined under a periodic inventory system? (Appendix A)

- Specific identification, FIFO, LIFO, and weighted-average can be used in a periodic inventory system.
- Specific identification and FIFO will produce the same amounts for ending merchandise inventory and cost of goods sold under both the perpetual and periodic inventory systems.
- LIFO and weighted-average result in different amounts for ending merchandise inventory and cost of goods sold under the perpetual and periodic inventory systems.

8. How can the cost of ending merchandise inventory be estimated? (Appendix B)

- Gross profit method—Estimates the cost of ending merchandise inventory using the cost of goods sold formula and the gross profit percentage.
- Retail method—Estimates the cost of ending merchandise inventory based on the ratio of the goods available for sale at cost to the goods available for sale at retail.

> Summary Problem

Watches R Us specializes in designer watches and leather goods. Watches R Us uses the perpetual inventory system. Assume Watches R Us began June holding 10 wristwatches that cost $50 each. During June, Watches R Us bought and sold inventory as follows:

Jun. 3	Sold 8 units for $100 each.
16	Purchased 10 units at $56 each.
23	Sold 8 units for $100 each.

Requirements

1. Prepare a perpetual inventory record for Watches R Us using the FIFO, LIFO, and weighted-average inventory costing methods.

2. Journalize all of Watches R Us's inventory transactions for June under all three costing methods. Assume all sales and purchases are on account. Explanations are not required.

3. Show the computation of gross profit for each method.

4. Which method maximizes net income? Which method minimizes income taxes?

> Solution

1. Perpetual inventory records:

FIFO:

Date	Purchases Quantity	Purchases Unit Cost	Purchases Total Cost	Cost of Goods Sold Quantity	Cost of Goods Sold Unit Cost	Cost of Goods Sold Total Cost	Inventory on Hand Quantity	Inventory on Hand Unit Cost	Inventory on Hand Total Cost
Jun. 1							10 units	× $ 50	= $ 500 } $ 500
3				8 units	× $ 50	= $ 400 } $ 400	2 units	× $ 50	= $ 100 } $ 100
16	10 units	× $ 56	= $ 560				2 units 10 units	× $ 50 × $ 56	= $ 100 = $ 560 } $ 660
23				2 units 6 units	× $ 50 × $ 56	= $ 100 = $ 336 } $ 436	4 units	× $ 56	= $ 224 } $ 224
Totals	10 units		$ 560	16 units		$ 836	4 units		$ 224

LIFO:

Date	Purchases Quantity	Purchases Unit Cost	Purchases Total Cost	Cost of Goods Sold Quantity	Cost of Goods Sold Unit Cost	Cost of Goods Sold Total Cost	Inventory on Hand Quantity	Inventory on Hand Unit Cost	Inventory on Hand Total Cost
Jun. 1							10 units	× $ 50	= $ 500 } $ 500
3				8 units	× $ 50	= $ 400 } $ 400	2 units	× $ 50	= $ 100 } $ 100
16	10 units	× $ 56	= $ 560				2 units 10 units	× $ 50 × $ 56	= $ 100 = $ 560 } $ 660
23				8 units	× $ 56	= $ 448 } $ 448	2 units 2 units	× $ 50 × $ 56	= $ 100 = $ 112 } $ 212
Totals	10 units		$ 560	16 units		$ 848	4 units		$ 212

Weighted-Average:

Date	Purchases Quantity	Purchases Unit Cost	Purchases Total Cost	Cost of Goods Sold Quantity	Cost of Goods Sold Unit Cost	Cost of Goods Sold Total Cost	Inventory on Hand Quantity	Inventory on Hand Unit Cost	Inventory on Hand Total Cost
Jun. 1							10 units	× $ 50	= $ 500
3				8 units	× $ 50	= $ 400	2 units	× $ 50	= $ 100
16	10 units	× $ 56	= $ 560				12 units	× $ 55	= $ 660 $ 660 / 12 units = $ 55
23				8 units	× $ 55	= $ 440	4 units	× $ 55	= $ 220
Totals	10 units		$ 560	16 units		$ 840	4 units		$ 220

Merchandise Inventory

2. Journal entries:

FIFO:

Date	Accounts and Explanation	Debit	Credit
Jun. 3	Accounts Receivable	800	
	Sales Revenue		800
3	Cost of Goods Sold	400	
	Merchandise Inventory		400
16	Merchandise Inventory	560	
	Accounts Payable		560
23	Accounts Receivable	800	
	Sales Revenue		800
23	Cost of Goods Sold	436	
	Merchandise Inventory		436

LIFO:

Date	Accounts and Explanation	Debit	Credit
Jun. 3	Accounts Receivable	800	
	Sales Revenue		800
3	Cost of Goods Sold	400	
	Merchandise Inventory		400
16	Merchandise Inventory	560	
	Accounts Payable		560
23	Accounts Receivable	800	
	Sales Revenue		800
23	Cost of Goods Sold	448	
	Merchandise Inventory		448

Weighted Average:

Date	Accounts and Explanation	Debit	Credit
Jun. 3	Accounts Receivable	800	
	Sales Revenue		800
3	Cost of Goods Sold	400	
	Merchandise Inventory		400
16	Merchandise Inventory	560	
	Accounts Payable		560
23	Accounts Receivable	800	
	Sales Revenue		800
23	Cost of Goods Sold	440	
	Merchandise Inventory		440

3. Gross profit:

	FIFO	LIFO	Weighted-Average
Sales Revenue ($800 + $800)	$ 1,600	$ 1,600	$ 1,600
Less: Cost of Goods Sold ($400 + $436)	836		
($400 + $448)		848	
($400 + $440)			840
Gross Profit	$ 764	$ 752	$ 760

4. FIFO maximizes net income.

   LIFO minimizes income taxes.

> Key Terms

Conservatism
A business should report the least favorable figures in the financial statements when two or more possible options are presented.

Consistency Principle
A business should use the same accounting methods and procedures from period to period.

Cost of Goods Available for Sale
The total cost spent on inventory that was available to be sold during a period.

Days' Sales in Inventory
Measures the average number of days that inventory is held by a company. 365 days / Inventory turnover.

Disclosure Principle
A business's financial statements must report enough information for outsiders to make knowledgeable decisions about the company.

First-In, First-Out (FIFO) Method
An inventory costing method in which the first costs into inventory are the first costs out to cost of goods sold. Ending inventory is based on the costs of the most recent purchases.

Gross Profit Method (Appendix B)
A way to estimate ending merchandise inventory on the basis of the cost of goods sold formula and the gross profit percentage.

Inventory Costing Method
A method of approximating the flow of inventory costs in a business that is used to determine the amount of cost of goods sold and ending merchandise inventory.

Inventory Turnover
Measures the number of times a company sells its average level of merchandise inventory during a period. Cost of goods sold / Average merchandise inventory.

Last-In, First-Out (LIFO) Method
An inventory costing method in which the last costs into inventory are the first costs out to cost of goods sold. The method leaves the oldest costs—those of beginning inventory and the earliest purchases of the period—in ending inventory.

Lower-of-Cost-or-Market (LCM) Rule
Rule that merchandise inventory should be reported in the financial statements at whichever is lower—its historical cost or its market value.

Materiality Concept
A company must perform strictly proper accounting only for items that are significant to the business's financial situation.

Retail Method (Appendix B)
A way to estimate the cost of ending merchandise inventory on the basis of the ratio of the goods available for sale at cost to the goods available for sale at retail.

Specific Identification Method
An inventory costing method based on the specific cost of particular units of inventory.

Weighted-Average Method
An inventory costing method based on the weighted average cost per unit of inventory that is calculated after each purchase. Weighted average cost per unit is determined by dividing the cost of goods available for sale by the number of units available.

> Quick Check

1. Which principle or concept states that businesses should use the same accounting methods and procedures from period to period?

   a. Disclosure

   b. Conservatism

   c. Consistency

   d. Materiality

   Learning Objective 1

2. Which inventory costing method assigns to ending merchandise inventory the newest—the most recent—costs incurred during the period?

   a. First-in, first-out (FIFO)

   b. Weighted-average

   c. Specific identification

   d. Last-in, first-out (LIFO)

   Learning Objective 2

3. Assume Nile.com began April with 14 units of inventory that cost a total of $266. During April, Nile purchased and sold goods as follows:

   Learning Objective 2

Apr. 8	Purchase	42 units @ $20
14	Sale	35 units @ $40
22	Purchase	28 units @ $22
27	Sale	42 units @ $40

   Under the FIFO inventory costing method and the perpetual inventory system, how much is Nile's cost of goods sold for the sale on April 14?

   a. $1,106

   b. $686

   c. $1,400

   d. $700

4. Suppose Nile.com used the weighted-average inventory costing method and the perpetual inventory system. Use the Nile.com data in Question 3 to compute the weighted average unit cost of the company's inventory on hand at April 8. Round weighted average unit cost to the nearest cent.

   a. $21.00

   b. $19.75

   c. $19.50

   d. Cannot be determined from the data given

   Learning Objective 2

5. Which inventory costing method results in the lowest net income during a period of rising inventory costs?

   a. Weighted-average

   b. Specific identification

   c. First-in, first-out (FIFO)

   d. Last-in, first-out (LIFO)

   Learning Objective 3

Learning Objective 4

6. Which of the following is most closely linked to accounting conservatism?

    a. Lower-of-cost-or-market rule

    b. Materiality concept

    c. Disclosure principle

    d. Consistency principle

Learning Objective 5

7. At December 31, 2015, Stevenson Company overstated ending inventory by $36,000. How does this error affect cost of goods sold and net income for 2015?

    a. Overstates cost of goods sold and understates net income

    b. Understates cost of goods sold and overstates net income

    c. Leaves both cost of goods sold and net income correct because the errors cancel each other

    d. Overstates both cost of goods sold and net income

Learning Objective 6

8. Suppose Maestro's had cost of goods sold during the year of $230,000. Beginning merchandise inventory was $35,000 and ending merchandise inventory was $45,000. Determine Maestro's inventory turnover for the year. Round to the nearest hundredth.

    a. 6.57 times per year

    b. 5.75 times per year

    c. 5.11 times per year

    d. 17.39 times per year

Learning Objective 7
Appendix A

9A. Suppose Nile.com used the LIFO inventory costing method and the periodic inventory system. Use the Nile.com data in Question 3 to determine Nile's cost of goods sold at the end of the month.

    a. $1,568

    b. $133

    c. $1,589

    d. $154

Learning Objective 8
Appendix B

10B. Suppose Supreme Clothing suffered a hurricane loss and needs to estimate the cost of the goods destroyed. Beginning inventory was $94,000, net cost of purchases totaled $564,000, and sales came to $940,000. Supreme's normal gross profit percentage is 55%. Use the gross profit method to estimate the cost of the inventory lost in the hurricane.

    a. $658,000

    b. $235,000

    c. $517,000

    d. $141,000

Check your answers at the end of the chapter.

ASSESS YOUR PROGRESS

> Review Questions

1. Which principle states that businesses should use the same accounting methods and procedures from period to period?

2. What does the disclosure principle require?

3. Discuss the materiality concept. Is the dollar amount that is material the same for a company that has annual sales of $10,000 compared with a company that has annual sales of $1,000,000?

4. What is the goal of conservatism?

5. Discuss some measures that should be taken to maintain control over merchandise inventory.

6. Under a perpetual inventory system, what are the four inventory costing methods and how does each method determine ending merchandise inventory and cost of goods sold?

7. When using a perpetual inventory system and the weighted-average inventory costing method, when does the business compute a new weighted average cost per unit?

8. During periods of rising costs, which inventory costing method produces the highest gross profit?

9. What does the lower-of-cost-or-market (LCM) rule require?

10. What account is debited when recording the adjusting entry to write down merchandise inventory under the LCM rule?

11. What is the effect on cost of goods sold, gross profit, and net income if ending merchandise inventory is understated?

12. When does an inventory error cancel out and why?

13. How is inventory turnover calculated and what does it measure?

14. How is days' sales in inventory calculated and what does it measure?

15A. When using the periodic inventory system, which inventory costing method(s) produces the same result as when using the perpetual inventory system?

16A. When using the periodic inventory system and weighted-average inventory costing method, when is the weighted average cost per unit computed?

17B. What are the two ways that ending merchandise inventory can be estimated?

> Short Exercises

For all short exercises, assume the perpetual inventory system is used unless stated otherwise.

S-1 Determining inventory accounting principles

Davidson Hardware used the FIFO inventory costing method in 2015. Davidson plans to continue using the FIFO method in future years. Which accounting principle is most relevant to Davidson's decision?

Learning Objective 1

Learning Objective 2

S-2 Determining inventory costing methods

Davidson Hardware does not expect costs to change dramatically and wants to use a inventory costing method that averages cost changes.

Requirements

1. Which inventory costing method would best meet Davidson's goal?

2. Assume Davidson wanted to expense out the newer purchases of goods instead. Which inventory costing method would best meet that need?

Use the following information to answer Short Exercises S-3 through S-6.

Mountain Cycles started August with 12 bicycles that cost $42 each. On August 16, Mountain bought 40 bicycles at $68 each. On August 31, Mountain sold 36 bicycles for $84.

Learning Objective 2

S-3 Preparing a perpetual inventory record and journal entries—Specific identification

Requirements

1. Prepare Mountain Cycle's perpetual inventory record assuming the company uses the specific identification inventory costing method. Assume that Mountain sold 8 bicycles that cost $42 each and 28 bicycles that cost $68 each.

2. Journalize the August 16 purchase of merchandise inventory on account and the August 31 sale of merchandise inventory on account.

Learning Objective 2

S-4 Preparing a perpetual inventory record and journal entries—FIFO

Requirements

1. Prepare Mountain Cycle's perpetual inventory record assuming the company uses the FIFO inventory costing method.

2. Journalize the August 16 purchase of merchandise inventory on account and the August 31 sale of merchandise inventory on account.

Learning Objective 2

S-5 Preparing a perpetual inventory record and journal entries—LIFO

Requirements

1. Prepare Mountain Cycle's perpetual inventory record assuming the company uses the LIFO inventory costing method.

2. Journalize the August 16 purchase of merchandise inventory on account and the August 31 sale of merchandise inventory on account.

Learning Objective 2

S-6 Preparing a perpetual inventory record and journal entries—Weighted-Average

Requirements

1. Prepare Mountain Cycle's perpetual inventory record assuming the company uses the weighted-average inventory costing method.

2. Journalize the August 16 purchase of merchandise inventory on account and the August 31 sale of merchandise inventory on account.

S-7 Comparing Cost of Goods Sold under FIFO, LIFO, and Weighted-Average

Learning Objective 3

Refer to Short Exercises S-4 through S-6. After completing those exercises, answer the following questions:

Requirements

1. Which inventory costing method produced the lowest Cost of Goods Sold?

2. Which inventory costing method produced the highest Cost of Goods Sold?

3. If costs had been declining instead of rising, which inventory costing method would have produced the highest Cost of Goods Sold?

S-8 Applying the lower-of-cost-or-market rule

Learning Objective 4

Assume that a Rocket Burger restaurant has the following perpetual inventory record for hamburger patties:

Date	Purchases	Cost of Goods Sold	Merchandise Inventory on Hand
Feb. 9	$ 470		$ 470
22		$ 280	190
28	210		400

At February 28, the accountant for the restaurant determines that the current replacement cost of the ending merchandise inventory is $447. Make any adjusting entry needed to apply the lower-of-cost-or-market rule. Merchandise inventory would be reported on the balance sheet at what value on February 28?

S-9 Determining the effect of an inventory error

Learning Objective 5

California Pool Supplies' merchandise inventory data for the year ended December 31, 2015, follow:

Sales Revenue		$ 60,000
Cost of Goods Sold:		
Beginning Merchandise Inventory	$ 4,200	
Net Cost of Purchases	26,600	
Cost of Goods Available for Sale	30,800	
Less: Ending Merchandise Inventory	6,200	
Cost of Goods Sold		24,600
Gross Profit		$ 35,400

Requirements

1. Assume that the ending merchandise inventory was accidentally overstated by $2,400. What are the correct amounts for cost of goods sold and gross profit?

2. How would the inventory error affect California Pool Supplies' cost of goods sold and gross profit for the year ended December 31, 2016, if the error is not corrected in 2015?

Merchandise Inventory

Learning Objective 6

S-10 Computing the rate of inventory turnover and days' sales in inventory

Santa Fe Communications reported the following figures in its annual financial statements:

Cost of Goods Sold	$ 18,000
Beginning Merchandise Inventory	500
Ending Merchandise Inventory	425

Compute the rate of inventory turnover and days' sales in inventory for Santa Fe Communications. (Round to two decimal places.)

Use the following information to answer Short Exercises SA-11 through SA-13.

The periodic inventory records of Synergy Prosthetics indicate the following for the month of July:

Jul. 1	Beginning merchandise inventory	6 units @ $60 each
8	Purchase	5 units @ $67 each
15	Purchase	10 units @ $70 each
26	Purchase	5 units @ $85 each

At July 31, Synergy counts two units of merchandise inventory on hand.

Learning Objective 7
Appendix A

SA-11 Computing periodic inventory amounts—FIFO

Compute ending merchandise inventory and cost of goods sold for Synergy using the FIFO inventory costing method.

Learning Objectives 7
Appendix A

SA-12 Computing periodic inventory amounts—LIFO

Compute ending merchandise inventory and cost of goods sold for Synergy using the LIFO inventory costing method.

Learning Objective 7
Appendix A

SA-13 Computing periodic inventory amounts—Weighted-Average

Compute ending merchandise inventory and cost of goods sold for Synergy using the weighted-average inventory costing method.

Learning Objective 8
Appendix B

SB-14 Estimating ending inventory by the gross profit method

Glass Company began the year with merchandise inventory of $42,450 and had net cost of purchases of $263,000 during the year. Net sales for the year are $501,000, and Glass's gross profit percentage is 55% of sales. Compute the estimated cost of ending merchandise inventory by the gross profit method.

Learning Objective 8
Appendix B

SB-15 Estimating ending inventory by the retail method

Hartsaw Company had the following cost and retail pricing on its merchandise inventory. In addition, net sales revenue for the time period was $96,000.

	Cost	Retail
Beginning Merchandise Inventory	$ 24,000	$ 47,600
Net Purchases	96,000	190,400
Goods Available for Sale	$ 120,000	$ 238,000

Compute the estimated cost of ending merchandise inventory by the retail method. (Round the cost to retail ratio to the nearest percent.)

> Exercises

For all exercises, assume the perpetual inventory system is used unless stated otherwise.

E-16 Using accounting vocabulary

Learning Objective 1, 2

Match the accounting terms with the corresponding definitions.

1. Specific Identification

2. Materiality Concept

3. Last-In, First-Out (LIFO)

4. Conservatism

5. Consistency Principle

6. Weighted-Average

7. Disclosure Principle

8. First-In, First-Out (FIFO)

a. Treats the oldest inventory purchases as the first units sold.

b. Requires that a company report enough information for outsiders to make knowledgeable decisions.

c. Identifies exactly which inventory item was sold. Usually used for higher cost inventory.

d. Calculates a weighted average cost based on the cost of goods available for sale and the number of units available.

e. Principle whose foundation is to exercise caution in reporting financial statement items.

f. Treats the most recent/newest purchases as the first units sold.

g. Businesses should use the same accounting methods from period to period.

h. Principle that states significant items must conform to GAAP.

E-17 Comparing inventory methods

Learning Objective 2

1. Ending Merch. Inv. $10.60

Express Lane, a regional convenience store chain, maintains milk inventory by the gallon. The first month's milk purchases and sales at its Freeport, Florida, location follow:

Nov. 2	Purchased 8 gallons @ $2.00 each
6	Purchased 2 gallons @ $2.10 each
8	Sold 3 gallons of milk to a customer
13	Purchased 2 gallons @ $2.20 each
14	Sold 4 gallons of milk to a customer

Requirements

1. Determine the amount that would be reported in ending merchandise inventory on November 15 using the FIFO inventory costing method.

2. Determine the amount that would be reported in ending merchandise inventory on November 15 using the LIFO inventory costing method.

3. Determine the amount that would be reported in ending merchandise inventory on November 15 using the weighted-average inventory costing method. Round all amounts to the nearest cent.

Use the following information to answer Exercises E-18 through E-20.

Golf Haven carries an inventory of putters and other golf clubs. The sales price of each putter is $128. Company records indicate the following for a particular line of Golf Haven's putters:

Date	Item	Quantity	Unit Cost
Nov. 1	Balance	17	$68
6	Sale	7	
8	Purchase	20	$74
17	Sale	20	
30	Sale	4	

Learning Objective 2

1. COGS $2,192

E-18 Measuring and journalizing merchandise inventory and cost of goods sold—FIFO

Requirements

1. Prepare a perpetual inventory record for the putters assuming Golf Haven uses the FIFO inventory costing method. Then identify the cost of ending inventory and cost of goods sold for the month.

2. Journalize Golf Haven's inventory transactions using the FIFO inventory costing method. (Assume purchases and sales are made on account.)

Learning Objective 2

1. Ending Merch. Inv. $408

E-19 Measuring ending inventory and cost of goods sold in a perpetual inventory system—LIFO

Requirements

1. Prepare Golf Haven's perpetual inventory record for the putters assuming Golf Haven uses the LIFO inventory costing method. Then identify the cost of ending inventory and cost of goods sold for the month.

2. Journalize Golf Haven's inventory transactions using the LIFO inventory costing method. (Assume purchases and sales are made on account.)

Learning Objective 2

1. COGS $2,204

E-20 Measuring ending inventory and cost of goods sold in a perpetual inventory system—Weighted-Average

Requirements

1. Prepare Golf Haven's perpetual inventory record for the putters assuming Golf Haven uses the weighted-average inventory costing method. Round weighted average cost per unit to the nearest cent and all other amounts to the nearest dollar. Then identify the cost of ending inventory and cost of goods sold for the month.

2. Journalize Golf Haven's inventory transactions using the weighted-average inventory costing method. (Assume purchases and sales are made on account.)

E-21 Comparing amounts for cost of goods sold, ending inventory, and gross profit—FIFO and LIFO

Learning Objectives 2, 3

2. Ending Merch. Inv. $96

Assume that Models and More store bought and sold a line of dolls during December as follows:

Dec. 1	Beginning merchandise inventory	13 units @ $11 each
8	Sale	9 units @ $20 each
14	Purchase	17 units @ $13 each
21	Sale	13 units @ $20 each

Requirements

1. Compute the cost of cost of goods sold, cost of ending merchandise inventory, and gross profit using the FIFO inventory costing method.

2. Compute the cost of cost of goods sold, cost of ending merchandise inventory, and gross profit using the LIFO inventory costing method.

3. Which method results in a higher cost of goods sold?

4. Which method results in a higher cost of ending merchandise inventory?

5. Which method results in a higher gross profit?

E-22 Comparing cost of goods sold and gross profit—FIFO, LIFO, and Weighted-Average methods

Learning Objectives 2, 3

1. COGS $1,900

Assume that JR Tire Store completed the following perpetual inventory transactions for a line of tires:

May 1	Beginning merchandise inventory	16 tires @ $65 each
11	Purchase	10 tires @ $78 each
23	Sale	12 tires @ $90 each
26	Purchase	14 tires @ $80 each
29	Sale	15 tires @ $90 each

Requirements

1. Compute cost of goods sold and gross profit using the FIFO inventory costing method.

2. Compute cost of goods sold and gross profit using the LIFO inventory costing method.

3. Compute cost of goods sold and gross profit using the weighted-average inventory costing method. (Round weighted average cost per unit to the nearest cent and all other amounts to the nearest dollar.)

4. Which method results in the largest gross profit and why?

E-23 Applying the lower-of-cost-or-market rule to merchandise inventories

Eagle Resources, which uses the FIFO inventory costing method, has the following account balances at May 31, 2015, prior to releasing the financial statements for the year:

Merchandise Inventory, ending	$ 13,000
Cost of Goods Sold	69,000
Sales Revenue	118,000

Eagle has determined that the current replacement cost (current market value) of the May 31, 2015, ending merchandise inventory is $12,800.

Requirements

1. Prepare any adjusting journal entry required from the information given.
2. What value would Eagle report on the balance sheet at May 31, 2015, for merchandise inventory?

E-24 Applying the lower-of-cost-or-market rule to inventories

Naturally Good Foods reports merchandise inventory at the lower of cost or market. Prior to releasing its financial statements for the year ended March 31, 2015, Naturally's *preliminary* income statement, before the year-end adjustments, appears as follows:

NATURALLY GOOD FOODS Income Statement (Partial) Year Ended March 31, 2015	
Sales Revenue	$ 117,000
Cost of Goods Sold	45,000
Gross Profit	$ 72,000

Naturally has determined that the current replacement cost of ending merchandise inventory is $17,000. Cost is $18,000.

Requirements

1. Journalize the adjusting entry for merchandise inventory, if any is required.
2. Prepare a revised partial income statement to show how Naturally Good Foods should report sales, cost of goods sold, and gross profit.

E-25 Measuring the effect of an inventory error

Grandma Kate Bakery reported sales revenue of $52,000 and cost of goods sold of $22,000.

Compute Grandma Kate's correct gross profit if the company made either of the following independent accounting errors. Show your work.

a. Ending merchandise inventory is overstated by $6,000.
b. Ending merchandise inventory is understated by $6,000.

E-26 Correcting an inventory error—two years

Learning Objective 5

2. 2015, overstated $4,500

Great Foods Grocery reported the following comparative income statements for the years ended June 30, 2016 and 2015:

GREAT FOODS GROCERY Income Statements Years Ended June 30, 2016 and 2015				
	2016		**2015**	
Sales Revenue		$ 139,000		$ 120,000
Cost of Goods Sold:				
Beginning Merchandise Inventory	$ 13,000		$ 12,000	
Net Cost of Purchases	76,000		70,000	
Cost of Goods Available for Sale	89,000		82,000	
Less: Ending Merchandise Inventory	17,000		13,000	
Cost of Goods Sold		72,000		69,000
Gross Profit		67,000		51,000
Operating Expenses		23,000		18,000
Net Income		$ 44,000		$ 33,000

During 2016, Great Foods discovered that ending 2015 merchandise inventory was overstated by $4,500.

Requirements

1. Prepare corrected income statements for the two years.
2. State whether each year's net income—before your corrections—is understated or overstated and indicate the amount of the understatement or overstatement.

E-27 Computing inventory turnover and days' sales in inventory

Learning Objective 6

2. 77.17 days

New Hope reported the following income statement for the year ended December 31, 2016:

NEW HOPE Income Statement Year Ended December 31, 2016		
Sales Revenue		$ 144,000
Cost of Goods Sold:		
Beginning Merchandise Inventory	$ 10,080	
Net Cost of Purchases	63,840	
Cost of Goods Available for Sale	73,920	
Less: Ending Merchandise Inventory	14,880	
Cost of Goods Sold		59,040
Gross Profit		84,960
Operating Expenses		55,224
Net Income		$ 29,736

Requirements

1. Compute New Hope's inventory turnover rate for the year. (Round to two decimal places.)
2. Compute New Hope's days' sales in inventory for the year. (Round to two decimal places.)

Learning Objective 7
Appendix A

2. COGS $756

EA-28 Comparing ending merchandise inventory, cost of goods sold, and gross profit using the periodic inventory system—FIFO, LIFO, and Weighted-Average methods

Assume that Mesquite Coffee Shop completed the following *periodic* inventory transactions for a line of merchandise inventory:

Jun. 1	Beginning merchandise inventory	20 units @ $20 each
12	Purchase	6 units @ $22 each
20	Sale	14 units @ $35 each
24	Purchase	16 units @ $24 each
29	Sale	20 units @ $35 each

Requirements

1. Compute ending merchandise inventory, cost of goods sold, and gross profit using the FIFO inventory costing method.

2. Compute ending merchandise inventory, cost of goods sold, and gross profit using the LIFO inventory costing method.

3. Compute ending merchandise inventory, cost of goods sold, and gross profit using the weighted-average inventory costing method. (Round weighted average cost per unit to the nearest cent and all other amounts to the nearest dollar.)

Learning Objective 7
Appendix A

EA-29 Computing periodic inventory amounts

Consider the data of the following companies:

Company	Net Sales Revenue	Beginning Merchandise Inventory	Net Cost of Purchases	Ending Merchandise Inventory	Cost of Goods Sold	Gross Profit
Red	$ 101,000	$ 22,000	$ 65,000	$ 17,000	$ (a)	$ 31,000
Yellow	(b)	25,000	95,000	(c)	96,000	40,000
Orange	93,000	(d)	52,000	22,000	62,000	(e)
Green	86,000	12,000	(f)	5,000	(g)	49,000

Requirements

1. Supply the missing amounts in the preceding table.

2. Prepare the income statement for the year ended December 31, 2015, for Red Company, which uses the periodic inventory system. Include a complete heading and show the full computation of cost of goods sold. Red's operating expenses for the year were $11,000.

EB-30 Estimating ending inventory by the gross profit method

Deluxe Auto Parts holds inventory all over the world. Assume that the records for one auto part show the following:

Beginning Merchandise Inventory	$ 220,000
Net Cost of Purchases	800,000
Net Sales Revenue	1,100,000
Gross Profit Percentage	45%

Suppose this inventory, stored in the United States, was lost in a fire. Estimate the amount of the loss to Deluxe Auto Parts. Use the gross profit method.

Learning Objective 8
Appendix B

Estimated COGS, $605,000

EB-31 Estimating ending inventory by the retail method

R K Landscaping and Nursery began November with merchandise inventory that cost $46,800 (retail $65,520). During November, R K made net purchases that cost $33,900 (retail $47,460) and had net sales revenue of $61,800. Use the retail method to estimate the cost of the ending merchandise inventory for November. (Round the cost to retail ratio to the nearest percent. Round all other numbers to the nearest dollar.)

Learning Objective 8
Appendix B

Cost to retail ratio, 71%

> Problems Group A

For all problems, assume the perpetual inventory system is used unless stated otherwise.

P-32A Accounting for inventory using the perpetual inventory system—FIFO, LIFO, and Weighted-Average

Fit World began January with merchandise inventory of 80 crates of vitamins that cost a total of $4,000. During the month, Fit World purchased and sold merchandise on account as follows:

Jan. 5	Purchase	140 crates @ $ 55 each
13	Sale	160 crates @ $100 each
18	Purchase	160 crates @ $ 60 each
26	Sale	170 crates @ $110 each

Learning Objectives 2, 3

2. Ending Merch. Inv., $2,500

Requirements

1. Prepare a perpetual inventory record, using the FIFO inventory costing method, and determine the company's cost of goods sold, ending merchandise inventory, and gross profit.

2. Prepare a perpetual inventory record, using the LIFO inventory costing method, and determine the company's cost of goods sold, ending merchandise inventory, and gross profit.

3. Prepare a perpetual inventory record, using the weighted-average inventory costing method, and determine the company's cost of goods sold, ending merchandise inventory, and gross profit. (Round weighted average cost per unit to the nearest cent and all other amounts to the nearest dollar.)

4. If the business wanted to pay the least amount of income taxes possible, which method would it choose?

Merchandise Inventory

Learning Objectives 2, 3

5. FIFO GP $4,640

P-33A Accounting for inventory using the perpetual inventory system—FIFO, LIFO, and Weighted-Average, and comparing FIFO, LIFO, and Weighted-Average

Decorative Steel began August with 55 units of iron inventory that cost $35 each. During August, the company completed the following inventory transactions:

		Units	Unit Cost	Unit Sale Price
Aug. 3	Sale	45		$83
8	Purchase	75	$52	
21	Sale	70		85
30	Purchase	10	55	

Requirements

1. Prepare a perpetual inventory record for the merchandise inventory using the FIFO inventory costing method.

2. Prepare a perpetual inventory record for the merchandise inventory using the LIFO inventory costing method.

3. Prepare a perpetual inventory record for the merchandise inventory using the weighted-average inventory costing method.

4. Determine the company's cost of goods sold for August using FIFO, LIFO, and weighted-average inventory costing methods.

5. Compute gross profit for August using FIFO, LIFO, and weighted-average inventory costing methods.

6. If the business wanted to maximize gross profit, which method would it select?

Learning Objectives 1, 4

3. COGS $430,000

P-34A Accounting principles for inventory and applying the lower-of-cost-or-market rule

Some of M and T Electronics' merchandise is gathering dust. It is now December 31, 2015, and the current replacement cost of the ending merchandise inventory is $20,000 below the business's cost of the goods, which was $100,000. Before any adjustments at the end of the period, the company's Cost of Goods Sold account has a balance of $410,000.

Requirements

1. Journalize any required entries.

2. At what amount should the company report merchandise inventory on the balance sheet?

3. At what amount should the company report cost of goods sold on the income statement?

4. Which accounting principle or concept is most relevant to this situation?

P-35A Correcting inventory errors over a three-year period and computing inventory turnover and days' sales in inventory

Learning Objectives 5, 6

Evergreen Carpets' books show the following data. In early 2016, auditors found that the ending merchandise inventory for 2013 was understated by $6,000 and that the ending merchandise inventory for 2015 was overstated by $7,000. The ending merchandise inventory at December 31, 2014, was correct.

2. 2015, overstated $7,000

	2015		2014		2013	
Net Sales Revenue		$ 210,000		$ 162,000		$ 169,000
Cost of Goods Sold:						
Beginning Merchandise Inventory	$ 20,000		$ 27,000		$ 41,000	
Net Cost of Purchases	140,000		108,000		98,000	
Cost of Goods Available for Sale	160,000		135,000		139,000	
Less: Ending Merchandise Inventory	29,000		20,000		27,000	
Cost of Goods Sold		131,000		115,000		112,000
Gross Profit		79,000		47,000		57,000
Operating Expenses		53,000		18,000		24,000
Net Income		$ 26,000		$ 29,000		$ 33,000

Requirements

1. Prepare corrected income statements for the three years.

2. State whether each year's net income—before your corrections—is understated or overstated, and indicate the amount of the understatement or overstatement.

3. Compute the inventory turnover and days' sales in inventory using the corrected income statements for the three years. (Round all numbers to two decimals.)

PA-36A Accounting for inventory using the periodic inventory system—FIFO, LIFO, and Weighted-Average, and comparing FIFO, LIFO, and Weighted-Average

**Learning Objectives 3, 7
Appendix A**

Tomorrows Electronic Center began October with 90 units of merchandise inventory that cost $70 each. During October, the store made the following purchases:

1. LIFO Ending Merch. Inv., $7,800

Oct. 3	20 units @ $75 each
12	40 units @ $78 each
18	60 units @ $84 each

Tomorrows uses the periodic inventory system, and the physical count at October 31 indicates that 110 units of merchandise inventory are on hand.

Requirements

1. Determine the ending merchandise inventory and cost of goods sold amounts for the October financial statements using the FIFO, LIFO, and weighted-average inventory costing methods.

2. Sales revenue for October totaled $26,000. Compute Tomorrows' gross profit for October using each method.

3. Which method will result in the lowest income taxes for Tomorrows? Why? Which method will result in the highest net income for Tomorrows? Why?

Merchandise Inventory

Learning Objective 8
Appendix B

2. GP $2,607,600

PB-37A Estimating ending inventory by the gross profit method and preparing the income statement

Halloween Costumes estimates its ending merchandise inventory by the gross profit method. The gross profit has averaged 30% of net sales. The company's merchandise inventory records reveal the following data:

Merchandise Inventory, May 1	$ 270,000
Transactions during May:	
Purchases	7,520,000
Purchase Discounts	146,000
Purchase Returns and Allowances	34,000
Sales	8,719,000
Sales Returns and Allowances	27,000

Requirements

1. Estimate the cost of the May 31 merchandise inventory, using the gross profit method.

2. Prepare the May 2015 partial income statement through gross profit for Halloween Costumes.

Learning Objective 8
Appendix B

1. Cost to retail ratio 83%

PB-38A Estimating ending inventory by the retail method and preparing the income statement

Painting Supplies suffered a terrible tornado, and its entire merchandise inventory was destroyed. Painting Supplies needs to estimate its ending merchandise inventory to collect insurance. The company's merchandise inventory records reveal the following data:

	Cost	Retail
Merchandise Inventory, March 1	$ 108,000	$ 129,600
Transactions during March:		
Purchases	3,000,000	3,600,000
Purchase Discounts	58,000	70,000
Purchase Returns and Allowances	14,000	16,000

Requirements

1. Estimate the cost of the March 31 merchandise inventory, using the retail method. Assume Painting Supplies had net sales revenue of $1,200,000 during March. (Round the cost to retail ratio to the nearest percent.)

2. Prepare the March 2015 partial income statement through gross profit for Painting Supplies.

> Problems **Group B**

For all problems, assume the perpetual inventory system is used unless stated otherwise.

P-39B Accounting for inventory using the perpetual inventory system—FIFO, LIFO, and Weighted-Average

Health World began January with merchandise inventory of 50 crates of vitamins that cost a total of $1,000. During the month, Health World purchased and sold merchandise on account as follows:

Jan. 2	Purchase	100 crates @ $25 each
5	Sale	130 crates @ $40 each
16	Purchase	90 crates @ $30 each
27	Sale	100 crates @ $50 each

Learning Objectives 2, 3

2. Ending Merch. Inv., $200

Requirements

1. Prepare a perpetual inventory record, using the FIFO inventory costing method, and determine the company's cost of goods sold, ending merchandise inventory, and gross profit.

2. Prepare a perpetual inventory record, using the LIFO inventory costing method, and determine the company's cost of goods sold, ending merchandise inventory, and gross profit.

3. Prepare a perpetual inventory record, using the weighted-average inventory costing method, and determine the company's cost of goods sold, ending merchandise inventory, and gross profit. (Round weighted average cost per unit to the nearest cent and all other amounts to the nearest dollar.)

4. If the business wanted to pay the least amount of income taxes possible, which method would it choose?

Learning Objectives 2, 3

5. FIFO GP $3,690

P-40B Accounting for inventory using the perpetual inventory system—FIFO, LIFO, and Weighted-Average, and comparing FIFO, LIFO, and Weighted-Average

Ornamental Iron Works began January with 45 units of iron inventory that cost $24 each. During January, the company completed the following inventory transactions:

		Units	Unit Cost	Unit Sale Price
Jan. 3	Sale	35		$51
8	Purchase	70	$32	
21	Sale	65		73
30	Purchase	25	47	

Requirements

1. Prepare a perpetual inventory record for the merchandise inventory using the FIFO inventory costing method.

2. Prepare a perpetual inventory record for the merchandise inventory using the LIFO inventory costing method.

3. Prepare a perpetual inventory record for the merchandise inventory using the weighted-average inventory costing method.

4. Determine the company's cost of goods sold for January using FIFO, LIFO, and weighted-average inventory costing methods.

5. Compute gross profit for January using FIFO, LIFO, and weighted-average inventory costing methods.

6. If the business wanted to maximize gross profit, which method would it select?

Learning Objectives 1, 4

3. COGS $445,000

P-41B Accounting principles for inventory and applying the lower-of-cost-or-market rule

Some of P and Y Electronics' merchandise is gathering dust. It is now December 31, 2015, and the current replacement cost of the ending merchandise inventory is $30,000 below the business's cost of the goods, which was $95,000. Before any adjustments at the end of the period, the company's Cost of Goods Sold account has a balance of $415,000.

Requirements

1. Journalize any required entries.

2. At what amount should the company report merchandise inventory on the balance sheet?

3. At what amount should the company report cost of goods sold on the income statement?

4. Which accounting principle or concept is most relevant to this situation?

P-42B Correcting inventory errors over a three-year period and computing inventory turnover and days' sales in inventory

Learning Objectives 5, 6

2. 2015, overstated $5,000

Peaceful Carpets' books show the following data. In early 2016, auditors found that the ending merchandise inventory for 2013 was understated by $4,000 and that the ending merchandise inventory for 2015 was overstated by $5,000. The ending merchandise inventory at December 31, 2014, was correct.

	2015	2014	2013
Net Sales Revenue	$ 201,000	$ 161,000	$ 176,000
Cost of Goods Sold:			
Beginning Merchandise Inventory	$ 22,000	$ 25,000	$ 38,000
Net Cost of Purchases	130,000	104,000	92,000
Cost of Goods Available for Sale	152,000	129,000	130,000
Less: Ending Merchandise Inventory	31,000	22,000	25,000
Cost of Goods Sold	121,000	107,000	105,000
Gross Profit	80,000	54,000	71,000
Operating Expenses	56,000	26,000	35,000
Net Income	$ 24,000	$ 28,000	$ 36,000

Requirements

1. Prepare corrected income statements for the three years.

2. State whether each year's net income—before your corrections—is understated or overstated, and indicate the amount of the understatement or overstatement.

3. Compute the inventory turnover and days' sales in inventory using the corrected income statements for the three years. (Round all numbers to two decimals.)

PA-43B Accounting for inventory using the periodic inventory system—FIFO, LIFO, and Weighted-Average, and comparing FIFO, LIFO, and Weighted-Average

Learning Objectives 3, 7 Appendix A

1. LIFO Ending Merch. Inv., $6,960

Easy Use Electronic Center began October with 80 units of merchandise inventory that cost $57 each. During October, the store made the following purchases:

Oct. 3	10 units @ $65 each
12	30 units @ $70 each
18	70 units @ $72 each

Easy Use uses the periodic inventory system, and the physical count at October 31 indicates that 115 units of merchandise inventory are on hand.

Requirements

1. Determine the ending merchandise inventory and cost of goods sold amounts for the October financial statements using the FIFO, LIFO, and weighted-average inventory costing methods.

2. Sales revenue for October totaled $30,000. Compute Easy Uses' gross profit for October using each method.

3. Which method will result in the lowest income taxes for Easy Use? Why? Which method will result in the highest net income for Easy Use? Why?

Learning Objective 8
Appendix B

2. GP $3,413,670

PB-44B Estimating ending inventory by the gross profit method and preparing the income statement

Kids Costumes estimates its ending merchandise inventory by the gross profit method. The gross profit has averaged 39% of net sales. The company's merchandise inventory records reveal the following data:

Merchandise Inventory, July 1	$ 268,000
Transactions during July:	
Purchases	7,661,000
Purchase Discounts	171,000
Purchase Returns and Allowances	32,000
Sales	8,788,000
Sales Returns and Allowances	35,000

Requirements

1. Estimate the cost of the July 31 merchandise inventory, using the gross profit method.

2. Prepare the July 2015 partial income statement through gross profit for Kids Costumes.

Learning Objective 8
Appendix B

1. Cost to retail ratio 71%

PB-45B Estimating ending inventory by the retail method and preparing the income statement

Restaurant Supplies suffered a terrible tornado, and its entire merchandise inventory was destroyed. Restaurant Supplies needs to estimate its ending merchandise inventory to collect insurance. The company's merchandise inventory records reveal the following data:

	Cost	Retail
Merchandise Inventory, June 1	$ 21,600	$ 30,200
Transactions during June:		
Purchases	600,600	840,000
Purchase Discounts	12,000	16,000
Purchase Returns and Allowances	3,000	3,800

Requirements

1. Estimate the cost of the June 30 merchandise inventory, using the retail method. Assume Restaurant Supplies had net sales revenue of $240,000 during June. (Round the cost to retail ratio to the nearest percent.)

2. Prepare the June 2015 partial income statement gross profit for Restaurant Supplies.

> Continuing Problem

P-46 Accounting for inventory using the perpetual inventory system—LIFO

This problem deals with a company named Davis Consulting. Consider the January transactions for Davis Consulting. (Cost data have been removed from the sale transactions.) Davis uses the perpetual inventory system.

Jan. 2	Completed a consulting engagement and received cash of $7,800.
2	Prepaid three months office rent, $1,650.
7	Purchased 80 units software inventory on account, $1,680, plus freight in, $80.
18	Sold 40 software units on account, $3,500.
19	Consulted with a client for a fee of $1,000 on account.
20	Paid employee salary, $2,055, which includes accrued salaries from December.
21	Paid on account, $1,760.
22	Purchased 240 units software inventory on account, $6,240.
24	Paid utilities, $250.
28	Sold 120 units software for cash, $4,680.
31	Recorded the following adjusting entries:
	a. Accrued salaries expense, $686
	b. Depreciation, $100 (Equipment, $30; Furniture, $70)
	c. Expiration of prepaid rent, $550
	d. Physical count of software inventory, 145 units.

Requirements

1. Prepare perpetual inventory records for January for Davis using the LIFO inventory costing method. (Note: You must calculate the cost of goods sold on the 18th, 28th, and 31st.)

2. Open the following T-accounts in the ledger: Cash, $16,400; Accounts Receivable, $1,750; Software Inventory, $0; Office Supplies, $200; Prepaid Rent, $0; Equipment, $1,800; Accumulated Depreciation—Equipment, $30; Furniture, $4,200; Accumulated Depreciation—Furniture, $70; Accounts Payable, $4,700; Salaries Payable, $685; Unearned Revenue, $700; Davis, Capital, $18,165; Davis, Withdrawals, $0; Income Summary, $0; Service Revenue, $0; Sales Revenue, $0; Cost of Goods Sold, $0; Salaries Expense, $0; Rent Expense, $0; Utilities Expense, $0; Depreciation Expense—Equipment, $0; and Depreciation Expense—Furniture, $0.

3. Journalize and post the January transactions using the perpetual inventory record created in Requirement 1. Compute each account balance, and denote the balance as *Bal.*

4. Journalize and post the adjusting entries. Denote each adjusting amount as *Adj.* Compute each account balance, and denote the balance as *Bal.* After posting all adjusting entries, prove the equality of debits and credits in the ledger.

> Practice Set

P-47 Accounting for inventory using the perpetual inventory system—FIFO

Consider the December transactions for Shine King Cleaning. (Cost data have been removed from the sale transactions.) Shine King uses the perpetual inventory system.

Dec. 2	Purchased 600 units of inventory for $3,600 from Sparkle, Co., on terms, 3/10, n/20.
5	Purchased 400 units of inventory from Borax on account with terms 4/5, n/30. The total invoice was for $3,200, which included a $200 freight charge.
7	Returned 100 units of inventory to Sparkle from the December 2 purchase.
9	Paid Borax.
11	Sold 350 units of goods to Happy Maids for $4,900 on account with terms 5/10, n/30.
12	Paid Sparkle.
15	Received 30 units with a retail price of $420 of goods back from customer Happy Maids.
21	Received payment from Happy Maids, settling the amount due in full.
28	Sold 200 units of goods to Bridget, Inc., for cash of $3,000.
29	Paid cash for Utilities of $350.
30	Paid cash for Sales Commission Expense of $225.
31	Recorded the following adjusting entries:
	a. Physical count of inventory on December 31 showed 330 units of goods on hand
	b. Depreciation, $170
	c. Accrued salaries expense of $700
	d. Prepared all other adjustments necessary for December. Assume the cleaning supplies left at December 31 are $50.

Requirements

1. Prepare perpetual inventory records for December for Shine King using the FIFO inventory costing method. (Note: You must calculate the cost of goods sold on the 11th, 28th, and 31st.)

2. Open the following T-accounts in the ledger: Cash, $73,100; Accounts Receivable, $2,000; Merchandise Inventory, $0; Cleaning Supplies, $50; Prepaid Rent, $1,500; Prepaid Insurance, $2,200; Equipment, $2,200; Truck, $8,000; Accumulated Depreciation, $170; Accounts Payable, $945; Unearned Revenue, $3,450; Salaries Payable, $0; Interest Payable, $100; Notes Payable (Long term), $40,000; Hudson, Capital, $44,385; Hudson, Withdrawals, $0; Income Summary, $0; Service Revenue, $0; Sales Revenue, $0; Sales Returns and Allowances, $0; Sales Discounts, $0; Cost of Goods Sold, $0; Sales Commission Expense, $0; Utilities Expense, $0; Depreciation Expense, $0; Salaries Expense, $0; Insurance Expense, $0; Rent Expense, $0; Interest Expense, $0.

3. Journalize and post the December transactions using the perpetual inventory record created in Requirement 1. Compute each account balance, and denote the balance as *Bal.*

4. Journalize and post the adjusting entries. Denote each adjusting amount as *Adj.* Compute each account balance, and denote the balance as *Bal.* After posting all adjusting entries, prove the equality of debits and credits in the ledger.

CRITICAL THINKING

> Decision Cases

Decision Case 1

Assume you are opening a furniture store. To finance the business, you need a $500,000 loan, and your banker requires a set of forecasted financial statements. Assume you are preparing the statements and must make some decisions about how to do the accounting for the business.

Requirements

Answer the following questions:

1. Which type of inventory system will you use: perpetual or periodic? Give your reason.

2. Show how to compute net purchases and net sales revenue. How will you treat the cost of freight in?

3. How often do you plan to do a physical count of inventory on hand? What will the physical count accomplish?

4. Inventory costs are rising. Which inventory costing method would have the effect of

   a. maximizing net income?

   b. minimizing the amount of income tax?

Decision Case 2

Suppose you manage Campbell Appliance. The store's summarized financial statements for 2015, the most recent year, follow:

CAMPBELL APPLIANCE
Income Statement
Year Ended December 31, 2015

Sales	$ 800,000
Cost of Goods Sold	660,000
Gross Profit	$ 140,000
Operating Expenses	100,000
Net Income	$ 40,000

CAMPBELL APPLIANCE
Balance Sheet
December 31, 2015

Assets		Liabilities and Equity	
Cash	$ 30,000	Accounts Payable	$ 35,000
Inventories	75,000	Note Payable	280,000
Land and Buildings, Net	360,000	Total Liabilities	$ 315,000
		Stockholders' Equity	150,000
Total Assets	$ 465,000	Total Liabilities and Equity	$ 465,000

Assume that you need to double net income. To accomplish your goal, it will be very difficult to raise the prices you charge because there is a discount appliance store nearby. Also, you have little control over your cost of goods sold because the appliance manufacturers set the amount you must pay.

Identify several strategies for doubling net income.

> Ethical Issue 1

During 2015, Crop-Paper-Scissors, a craft store, changed to the LIFO inventory costing method of accounting for inventory. Suppose that during 2016, Crop-Paper-Scissors switches back to the FIFO inventory costing method and the following year switches back to LIFO again.

Requirements

1. What would you think of a company's ethics if it changed accounting methods every year?

2. What accounting principle would changing methods every year violate?

3. Who can be harmed when a company changes its accounting methods too often? How?

> Fraud Case 1

Ever since he was a kid, Carl Montague wanted to be a pro football player. When that didn't work out, he found another way to channel his natural competitive spirit: He bought a small auto parts store in Kentucky that was deep in red ink (negative earnings). At the end of the year, he created "ghost" inventory by recording fake inventory purchases. He offset these transactions by "adjustments" to Cost of Goods Sold, thereby boosting profit and strengthening the balance sheet. Fortified with great financials, he got bank loans that allowed him to build up a regional chain of stores, buy a local sports franchise, and take on the lifestyle of a celebrity. When the economy in the region tanked, he could no longer cover his losses with new debt or equity infusions, and the whole empire fell like a house of cards.

Requirements

1. Name several parties that could have been hurt by the actions of Carl Montague.

2. What kind of adjustment to Cost of Goods Sold (debit or credit) would have the effect of boosting earnings?

> Financial Statement Case 1

The notes are an important part of a company's financial statements, giving valuable details that would clutter the tabular data presented in the statements. This case will help you learn to use a company's inventory notes. Visit **www.pearsonhighered.com/ Horngren** to view a link to **Starbucks Corporation** Fiscal 2011 Annual Report. Access the financial statements and related notes, and answer the following questions:

Requirements

1. Which inventory costing method does Starbucks use? How does Starbucks value its inventories? See Note 1.

2. By using the cost of goods sold formula, you can compute net purchases, which are not reported in the Starbucks statements. How much were Starbucks' inventory purchases during the year ended October 2, 2011?

3. Determine Starbucks' inventory turnover and days' sales in inventory for the years ended October 2, 2011. (Round each ratio to one decimal place.) How do Starbucks' inventory turnover and days' sales in inventory compare with **Green Mountain Coffee Roasters, Inc.** for the year ended September 24, 2011? Explain.

> Team Project 1

Obtain the annual reports of as many companies as you have team members—one company per team member. Most companies post their financial statements on their websites.

Requirements

1. Identify the inventory method used by each company.

2. Compute each company's gross profit percentage, inventory turnover, and days' sales in inventory for the most recent two years.

3. For the industries of the companies you are analyzing, obtain the industry averages for gross profit percentage and inventory turnover from Robert Morris Associates, *Annual Statement Studies*; Dun and Bradstreet, *Industry Norms and Key Business Ratios*; or Leo Troy, *Almanac of Business and Industrial Financial Ratios*.

4. How well does each of your companies compare with the average for its industry? What insight about your companies can you glean from these ratios?

> Communication Activity 1

In 75 words or fewer, explain the difference in calculating cost of goods sold using the FIFO, LIFO, and weighted-average inventory costing methods when using a perpetual inventory system.

MyAccountingLab   **For a wealth of online resources, including exercises, problems, media, and immediate tutorial help, please visit** www.myaccountinglab.com.

Try It! Solutions

1. a   3. b

2. d   4. c

5A.

Date	Purchases Quantity	Unit Cost	Total Cost	Cost of Goods Sold Quantity	Unit Cost	Total Cost	Inventory on Hand Quantity	Unit Cost	Total Cost
Aug. 1							10 units	× $15	= $150 } $150
3				3 units	× $15	= $45 } $45	7 units	× $15	= $105 } $105
12	8 units	× $18	= $144				7 units 8 units	× $15 × $18	= $105 = $144 } $249
15				4 units 5 units	× $15 × $18	= $60 = $90 } $150	3 units 3 units	× $15 × $18	= $45 = $54 } $99
20	4 units	× $20	= $80				3 units 3 units 4 units	× $15 × $18 × $20	= $45 = $54 = $80 } $179
28				2 units 3 units	× $18 × $20	= $36 = $60 } $96	3 units 1 unit 1 unit	× $15 × $18 × $20	= $45 = $18 = $20 } $83
Totals	12 units		$224	17 units		$291	5 units		$83

5B.

Date	Purchases Quantity	Unit Cost	Total Cost	Cost of Goods Sold Quantity	Unit Cost	Total Cost	Inventory on Hand Quantity	Unit Cost	Total Cost
Aug. 1							10 units	× $15	= $150 } $150
3				3 units	× $15	= $45 } $45	7 units	× $15	= $105 } $105
12	8 units	× $18	= $144				7 units 8 units	× $15 × $18	= $105 = $144 } $249
15				7 units 2 units	× $15 × $18	= $105 = $36 } $141	6 units	× $18	= $108 } $108
20	4 units	× $20	= $80				6 units 4 units	× $18 × $20	= $108 = $80 } $188
28				5 units	× $18	= $90 } $90	1 unit 4 units	× $18 × $20	= $18 = $80 } $98
Totals	12 units		$224	17 units		$276	5 units		$98

5C.

	Purchases			Cost of Goods Sold			Inventory on Hand		
Date	Quantity	Unit Cost	Total Cost	Quantity	Unit Cost	Total Cost	Quantity	Unit Cost	Total Cost
Aug. 1							10 units	× $ 15	= $ 150 } $ 150
3				3 units	× $ 15	= $ 45 } $ 45	7 units	× $ 15	= $ 105 } $ 105
12	8 units	× $ 18	= $ 144				7 units 8 units	× $ 15 × $ 18	= $ 105 = $ 144 } $ 249
15				8 units 1 unit	× $ 18 × $ 15	= $ 144 = $ 15 } $ 159	6 units	× $ 15	= $ 90 } $ 90
20	4 units	× $ 20	= $ 80				6 units 4 units	× $ 15 × $ 20	= $ 90 = $ 80 } $ 170
28				4 units 1 unit	× $ 20 × $ 15	= $ 80 = $ 15 } $ 95	5 units	× $ 15	= $ 75
Totals	12 units		$ 224	17 units		$ 299	5 units		$ 75

5D.

	Purchases			Cost of Goods Sold			Inventory on Hand		
Date	Quantity	Unit Cost	Total Cost	Quantity	Unit Cost	Total Cost	Quantity	Unit Cost	Total Cost
Aug. 1							10 units	× $ 15	= $ 150 } $ 150 / 10 units = $ 15
3				3 units	× $ 15	= $ 45	7 units	× $ 15	= $ 105
12	8 units	× $ 18	= $ 144				15 units	× $ 16.60	= $ 249 } $ 249 / 15 units = $ 16.60
15				9 units	× $ 16.60	= $ 149	6 units	× $ 16.60	= $ 100
20	4 units	× $ 20	= $ 80				10 units	× $ 18	= $ 180 } $ 180 / 10 units = $ 18
28				5 units	× $ 18	= $ 90	5 units	× $ 18	= $ 90
Totals	12 units		$ 224	17 units		$ 284	5 units		$ 90

6. Antelope Motors should select the LIFO inventory costing method.

7. T. J. Jackson should report merchandise inventory at the lower-of-cost-or-market, which would be $750. The adjusting entry required would be:

Date	Accounts and Explanation	Debit	Credit
Dec. 31	Cost of Goods Sold	550	
	Merchandise Inventory ($1,300 − $750)		550
	To write merchandise inventory down to market value.		

8.

Sales Revenue		$ 48,000
Cost of Goods Sold:		
Beginning Merchandise Inventory	$ 3,360	
Net Cost of Purchases	21,280	
Cost of Goods Available for Sale	24,640	
Less: Ending Merchandise Inventory ($4,960 − $1,920)	3,040	
Cost of Goods Sold		21,600
Gross Profit		$ 26,400

9.

Inventory turnover = Cost of goods sold / Average merchandise inventory
= $484,000 / $100,000
= 4.84 times per year

Average merchandise inventory = (Beginning merchandise inventory + Ending merchandise inventory) / 2
= ($88,800 + $111,200) / 2
= $100,000

Days' sales in inventory = 365 days / Inventory turnover
= 365 days / 4.84
= 75.4 days

10A.

a.

Beginning merchandise inventory (10 units × $15)	$ 150
Net cost of purchases (8 units × $18) + (4 units × $20)	224
Cost of goods available for sale	374
Less: Ending merchandise inventory (1× $18) + (4 × $20)	98
Cost of goods sold	$ 276

b.

Beginning merchandise inventory (10 units × $15)	$ 150
Net cost of purchases (8 units × $18) + (4 units × $20)	224
Cost of goods available for sale	374
Less: Ending merchandise inventory (5 × $15)	75
Cost of goods sold	$ 299

c.

> Cost of goods available for sale / Number of units available = $374 / 22 units
> = $17

Beginning merchandise inventory (10 units × $15)	$ 150
Net purchases (8 units × $18) + (4 units × $20)	224
Cost of goods available for sale	374
Less: Ending merchandise inventory (5 × $17)	85
Cost of goods sold	$ 289

11B.

Beginning merchandise inventory		$ 33,960
Net purchases		210,400
Cost of goods available for sale		244,360
Estimated cost of goods sold		
Sales revenue	$ 400,800	
Less: Estimated gross profit of 40%	160,320	
Estimated cost of goods sold		240,480
Estimated ending merchandise inventory		$ 3,880

> Quick Check Answers

1. c   **2.** a   **3.** b   **4.** b   **5.** d   **6.** a   **7.** b   **8.** b   **9A.** c   **10B.** b

Glossary

Conservatism. A business should report the least favorable figures in the financial statements when two or more possible options are presented.

Consistency Principle. A business should use the same accounting methods and procedures from period to period.

Cost of Goods Available for Sale. The total cost spent on inventory that was available to be sold during a period.

Days' Sales in Inventory. Measures the average number of days that inventory is held by a company. 365 days / Inventory turnover.

Disclosure Principle. A business's financial statements must report enough information for outsiders to make knowledgeable decisions about the company.

First-In, First-Out (FIFO) Method. An inventory costing method in which the first costs into inventory are the first costs out to cost of goods sold. Ending inventory is based on the costs of the most recent purchases. Determines the cost of equivalent units of production by accounting for beginning inventory costs separately from current period costs. It assumes the first units started in the production process are the first units completed and sold. Appendix 20A)

Gross Profit Method. A way to estimate ending merchandise inventory on the basis of the cost of goods sold formula and the gross profit percentage. (Appendix B)

Inventory Costing Method. A method of approximating the flow of inventory costs in a business that is used to determine the amount of cost of goods sold and ending merchandise inventory.

Inventory Turnover. Measures the number of times a company sells its average level of merchandise inventory during a period. Cost of goods sold / Average merchandise inventory.

Last-In, First-Out (LIFO) Method. An inventory costing method in which the last costs into inventory are the first costs out to cost of goods sold. The method leaves the oldest costs—those of beginning inventory and the earliest purchases of the period—in ending inventory.

Lower-of-Cost-or-Market (LCM) Rule. Rule that merchandise inventory should be reported in the financial statements at whichever is lower—its historical cost or its market value.

Materiality Concept. A company must perform strictly proper accounting only for items that are significant to the business's financial situation.

Retail Method. A way to estimate the cost of ending merchandise inventory on the basis of the ratio of the goods available for sale at cost to the goods available for sale at retail. Appendix B)

Specific Identification Method. An inventory costing method based on the specific cost of particular units of inventory.

Weighted-Average Method. An inventory costing method based on the weighted average cost per unit of inventory that is calculated after each purchase. Weighted average cost per unit is determined by dividing the cost of goods available for sale by the number of units available. Determines the average cost of equivalent units of production by combining beginning inventory costs with current period costs.

Photo Credits

Credits are listed in order of appearance.

Photo 1 (top): K. Miri Photography/Shutterstock
Photo 2 (middle): Ari N./Shutterstock
Photo 3 (bottom): Marius Graf/Fotolia and Anankkml/Fotolia
Photo 4: Blend Images/Alamy
Photo 5 (top): Tritooth/Fotolia; (bottom) Steshkin Yevgeniy/Shutterstock
Photo 6: Shutterstock

Accounting Information Systems

Accounting Information Systems

What Should I Do With All This Paperwork?

Sara Faraday stared at the stack of papers on her desk. It was early January, and her accountant had called to remind her that she needed to submit the business's accounting information so that the tax return could be prepared. Sara owns and manages a successful gourmet kitchen store that sells specialty food and kitchen products and also offers cooking classes and workshops. Sara loves interacting with her customers, whether she's helping them find the perfect kitchen product or teaching them a new technique. What she doesn't like about her business is the overwhelming amount of paperwork required to keep the business records. When she first started her business, she kept track of sales to customers and bills paid in a notebook. Now, though, her business has grown so much that it is no longer efficient to keep track of her accounting records in this manner.

Sara is considering asking her accountant to help her set up a more efficient accounting information system. She wants a system that will save her time and make the recordkeeping process easier. In addition, she would like to find a way to record all of her transactions on the computer so that her business's information is easily accessible. Sara also wants a system that will produce reports, such as financial statements, that can help her make business decisions. She knows that there has to be an easier way to record the transactions than what she has been using.

Is There a More Efficient Way?

Before the advent of computers, businesses had to handle all of their accounting transactions manually—that is one journal entry at a time using paper and pencil. As computer technology progressed, more and more accounting information was processed using an automated system. Now, most businesses use some form of computerized accounting software. It might be a very basic system that handles only accounting information, or it might be a very advanced system that stores not only accounting information, but also information about human resources, production, and customer services. For example, Dave's Gourmet, Inc. started with a desire to create the world's hottest hot sauce, but as the business grew into the multinational company that it is today, the owner has had to find a way to keep track of all of the business's accounting information. Dave's Gourmet uses a specialized computerized system that integrates all of its lines of business. In this chapter, we explore how accounting information systems, such as the one that Dave's Gourmet uses, can help a business run more efficiently and effectively.

chapter outline

What is an accounting information system?

How are sales and cash receipts recorded in a manual accounting information system?

How are purchases, cash payments, and other transactions recorded in a manual accounting information system?

How are transactions recorded in a computerized accounting information system?

Learning Objectives

1 Describe an effective accounting information system

2 Journalize and post sales and cash receipts in a manual accounting information system using special journals and subsidiary ledgers

3 Journalize and post purchases, cash payments, and other transactions in a manual accounting information system using special journals and subsidiary ledgers

4 Describe how transactions are recorded in a computerized accounting information system

WHAT IS AN ACCOUNTING INFORMATION SYSTEM?

Learning Objective 1
Describe an effective accounting information system

Accounting Information System (AIS)
A system that collects, records, stores, and processes accounting data to produce information that is useful for decision makers.

An **accounting information system (AIS)** collects, records, stores, and processes accounting data to produce information that is useful for decision makers. Businesses must have a way to collect and store data for a large number of transactions and then use that data to produce reports that investors and management can use to make decisions. Exhibit 1 shows examples of business transactions and activities that are completed when using an accounting information system.

Exhibit 1 | **Business Transactions and AIS Activities**

Business Transactions	AIS Activities
Sell merchandise inventory	Receipt of customer order Approval of credit sale Check availability of merchandise inventory Shipment of inventory to customer Processing of sales invoice Receipt of customer payment
Purchase of goods or services	Request for purchase of goods or services Approval of vendor Receipt of goods or services Processing of vendor invoice Payment for goods or services
Payroll	Approval of new employees Collection of time records Preparation and payment of payroll Preparation and payment of payroll taxes

Effective Accounting Information Systems

An effective accounting information system provides the following:

- Control
- Compatibility
- Flexibility
- Relevance
- Positive cost/benefit relationship

Control

An accounting information system must provide adequate controls of the business's assets and data. Internal controls can safeguard a business's assets and reduce the likelihood of fraud and errors. For example, a business needs procedures for making cash payments. An accounting information system creates the structure to encourage adherence to management procedures.

Compatibility

A compatible system works smoothly with the business's employees and organizational structure. A small business doesn't need a big accounting information system. It could probably do accounting with an entry-level software package such as QuickBooks or Sage 50™ Accounting (formerly called Peachtree). But a large company needs a different system—one that can manage multiple branches and track revenues and expenses in all divisions of the business.

Flexibility

An accounting information system must be flexible to accommodate changes in a business over time. Businesses might start selling some new products, or they might expand to new locations. This will require a more complicated accounting information system.

Relevance

An effective accounting information system provides information that is relevant. In other words, it improves decision making and reduces uncertainty. The information produced must be useful to the business in achieving its overall goals.

Positive Cost/Benefit Relationship

Control, compatibility, flexibility, and relevance can be expensive. A business needs a system that gives the most benefit for the least cost. A relatively inexpensive system, such as QuickBooks, may be the most economical way for a business to do its accounting. Or it may be necessary for a business to invest a large amount of cash in a more complicated system. In addition, the business must consider the cost of training employees to use the system and time spent on entering data into the system. The business must only invest in an accounting information system in which the benefits received outweigh the cost of the system.

An accounting information system can be either manual (completed using paper and pencil) or computerized. All the previously discussed features are needed whether the accounting information system is computerized or manual.

Components of an Accounting Information System

An accounting information system has three basic components:

- Source documents and input devices
- Processing and storage
- Outputs

Source Documents and Input Devices

All data must come from source documents, which provide the evidence for accounting transactions. Examples of source documents include purchase invoices, bank checks, and sales invoices. Many businesses have paper source documents that require employees to transfer data from the paper source document into the accounting information system. This can be done either by data entry procedures using a keyboard and computer or by using computerized scanning equipment.

Source Document
Provides the evidence and data for accounting transactions.

Most businesses now are using computerized accounting information systems to create electronic source documents and capture the data in electronic format. Examples include an electronic invoice and an electronic receiving report.

Source documents also provide control and reliability in an accounting information system. Standardized source documents that require specific data to be inputted ensure that each transaction is recorded accurately and completely. In addition, prenumbered source documents provide necessary control in a system by automatically assigning a sequential number to each new transaction.

Processing and Storage

Once data has been inputted into the system, it must be processed. In a manual accounting information system, processing includes journalizing transactions and posting to the accounts. A computerized system, on the other hand, uses software to process transactions. This software reads and edits transaction data. It allows businesses to process transactions without actually requiring employees to journalize and post to the accounts.

A business's data must also be stored. In a manual system, data are contained in paper documents that are often stored in filing cabinets and off-site document warehouses. Computerized systems now allow businesses to keep data on a main computer, called a **server**, that often allows employees to access information from anywhere in the world. The protection and security of a business's data have become increasingly important. Businesses must be aware of threats to their data such as hacking (unauthorized access) and malware (viruses and spyware). Companies are spending increasingly large amounts of cash to ensure that their data and information are secure.

Server
The main computer where data is stored, which can be accessed from many different computers.

Outputs

Outputs are the reports used for decision making, including the financial statements. In a manual system, reports and financial statements must be created using Word documents, Excel spreadsheets, or PowerPoint. In a computerized system, the software can generate reports instantaneously that can be manipulated easily and used to make business decisions.

> Decisions   How safe are customer data?

Ian Woods had recently been hired as the chief information officer for a start-up Internet-based retail store—ShopUs.com. His main job duties include responsibility for the information technology and computer systems of the business. Ian was reviewing the security of customer data and realized that customer service representatives had access to all customer data including credit card information and billing addresses. What should Ian do?

Solution

The breach of customer data is a key threat to a business. Not only does a business have to be concerned about employees accessing customer data, but there is also a risk that unauthorized individuals outside of the business might hack into the system to obtain customer information. Ian should evaluate whether customer service representatives should have access to all customer data. It might be possible to encrypt some of the data and allow only managers to have access. In addition, Ian should set up guidelines and procedures for how data should be stored and protected. He should also review the federal regulations regarding the security of credit card and personal information to ensure that ShopUs.com is in compliance. Network surveillance, encryption, and software security procedures will all reduce the risk of data breach and abuse.

Exhibit 2 summarizes the three components of an accounting information system.

Exhibit 2 | Accounting Information System Components

| Source Documents And Input Devices | Processing And Storage | Outputs |

> Try It!

Match the benefit of an effective accounting information system with the definition.

Benefit	Definition
1. Control	**a.** Works smoothly with the business's employees and organizational structure.
2. Relevance	**b.** Can accommodate changes in the business over time.
3. Flexibility	**c.** Provides safeguards for a business's assets and reduces the likelihood of fraud and errors.
4. Compatibility	**d.** Benefits received outweigh the cost of the system.
5. Positive cost/ benefit relationship	**e.** Provides information that will improve decision making and reduce uncertainty.

Check your answers at the end of the chapter.

For more practice, see Short Exercises S-1 and S-2. MyAccountingLab

HOW ARE SALES AND CASH RECEIPTS RECORDED IN A MANUAL ACCOUNTING INFORMATION SYSTEM?

We will begin by reviewing how transactions are recorded in a manual accounting information system. You may be wondering why we cover manual accounting information systems when many businesses have computerized systems. There are three main reasons:

1. Learning a manual system equips you to work with both manual and computerized systems. The accounting is the same regardless of the system.
2. Few small businesses have computerized all their accounting. Even companies that use QuickBooks or Sage 50 Accounting, two popular entry-level accounting information systems, keep some manual accounting records.
3. Learning a manual system helps you master accounting.

Learning Objective 2

Journalize and post sales and cash receipts in a manual accounting information system using special journals and subsidiary ledgers

Special Journals

In a manual system, transactions are classified by type. It is inefficient to record all transactions in the general journal, so businesses use special journals. A special journal is an accounting journal designed to record a specific type of transaction. Sales on account, cash receipts, purchases on account, and cash payments are treated as four separate categories and, therefore, create the four special journals. For example:

- Sales on account are recorded in a *sales journal.*
- Cash receipts are recorded in a *cash receipts journal.*
- Purchases of inventory and other assets on account are recorded in a *purchases journal.*
- Cash payments are recorded in a *cash payments journal.*
- Transactions that do not fit in any of the special journals, such as adjusting entries, are recorded in the *general journal,* which serves as the "journal of last resort."

The five types of transactions, the related journal, and the posting abbreviations used in a manual system are summarized in Exhibit 3.

Exhibit 3 | **Manual Accounting Information System**

Transaction	Journal	Posting Abbreviation
Sale on account	Sales journal	S
Cash receipt	Cash receipts journal	CR
Purchase on account	Purchases journal	P
Cash payment	Cash payments journal	CP
All others	General journal	J

Subsidiary Ledgers

In addition to special journals, an accounting information system also uses subsidiary ledgers. A subsidiary ledger holds individual accounts that support a general ledger account. There are two common subsidiary ledgers: accounts receivable subsidiary ledger and accounts payable subsidiary ledger.

Accounts Receivable Subsidiary Ledger

The accounts receivable subsidiary ledger includes a receivable account for each customer. The customer name and account balance is detailed in the subsidiary ledger. In addition, the subsidiary ledger contains detailed information such as the amount each customer purchased, paid, and still owes. The total of the accounts in the accounts receivable subsidiary ledger must equal the Accounts Receivable balance in the general ledger. The is demonstrated in Exhibit 4. The Accounts Receivable balance of $4,319 in the general ledger equals the sum of the accounts in the accounts receivable subsidiary ledger ($935 + $907 + $694 + $1,783).

Exhibit 4 | **Accounts Receivable Subsidiary Ledger**

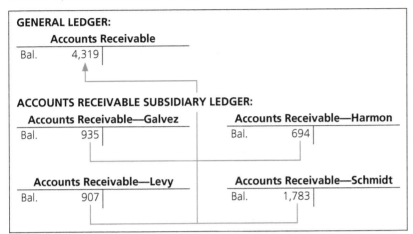

The Accounts Receivable account in the general ledger is called a control account. A control account's balance equals the sum of the balances of accounts in a subsidiary ledger.

Control Account
An account whose balance equals the sum of the balances in a group of related accounts in a subsidiary ledger.

Accounts Payable Subsidiary Ledger

To pay debts on time, a company must know how much it owes each supplier. Accounts Payable in the general ledger shows only a single total for the amount owed on account. It does not indicate the amount owed to each vendor. Companies keep an accounts payable subsidiary ledger that is similar to the accounts receivable subsidiary ledger.

The accounts payable subsidiary ledger lists vendors in alphabetical order, along with amounts paid to the vendors and the remaining amounts owed to them. The total of the individual balances in the subsidiary ledger equals the Accounts Payable (control account) balance in the general ledger.

Accounts Payable Subsidiary Ledger
A subsidiary ledger that includes an accounts payable account for each vendor that contains detailed information such as the amount purchased, paid, and owed.

The Sales Journal

Most merchandisers sell merchandise inventory on account. These credit sales are entered in the sales journal. The sales journal is used when recording the sale of merchandise inventory *on account.* The sale of merchandise inventory for cash is not recorded in the sales journal, but instead, it is recorded in the cash receipts journal. In addition, credit sales of assets other than merchandise inventory—for example, buildings—occur infrequently and are not recorded in the sales journal. They are, instead, recorded in the general journal.

Sales Journal
Special journal used to record credit sales.

Recording Transactions

Exhibit 5 illustrates a sales journal (Panel A) and the related posting to the ledgers (Panel B). When a business completes a sale, the accountant enters the following information in the sales journal:

- Date
- Invoice number
- Customer name
- Transaction amount

Exhibit 5 | Sales Journal With Posting

PANEL A—Sales Journal:

				Sales Journal	Page 3
Date	Invoice No.	Customer Account Debited	Post. Ref.	Accounts Receivable DR Sales Revenue CR	Cost of Goods Sold DR Merchandise Inventory CR
2014					
Nov. 2	422	Maria Galvez	✓	935	505
13	423	Brent Harmon	✓	694	361
18	424	Susan Levy	✓	907	517
27	425	Clay Schmidt	✓	1,783	431
Nov. 30		Total		4,319	1,814
				(115/410)	(511/131)

Individual accounts receivable are posted daily.

Totals are posted at the end of the month.

Totals are posted at the end of the month.

PANEL B—Posting to the Ledgers:

Accounts Receivable Subsidiary Ledger

Maria Galvez

Date	Post. Ref.	Debit	Credit	Balance Debit	Balance Credit
Nov. 2	S.3	935		935	

Brent Harmon

Date	Post. Ref.	Debit	Credit	Balance Debit	Balance Credit
Nov. 13	S.3	694		694	

Susan Levy

Date	Post. Ref.	Debit	Credit	Balance Debit	Balance Credit
Nov. 18	S.3	907		907	

Clay Schmidt

Date	Post. Ref.	Debit	Credit	Balance Debit	Balance Credit
Nov. 27	S.3	1,783		1,783	

General Ledger

Accounts Receivable   No. 115

Date	Post. Ref.	Debit	Credit	Balance Debit	Balance Credit
Nov. 30	S.3	4,319		4,319	·

Merchandise Inventory   No. 131

Date	Post. Ref.	Debit	Credit	Balance Debit	Balance Credit
Nov. 1	Bal.			3,885	
30	S.3		1,814	2,071	

Sales Revenue   No. 410

Date	Post. Ref.	Debit	Credit	Balance Debit	Balance Credit
Nov. 30	S.3		4,319		4,319

Costs of Goods Sold   No. 511

Date	Post. Ref.	Debit	Credit	Balance Debit	Balance Credit
Nov. 30	S.3	1,814		1,814	

Consider the first transaction in Panel A. On November 2, the business sold merchandise inventory on account to Maria Galvez for $935 with a cost of $505. The invoice number is 422. This transaction was recorded as follows when using the general journal:

Date	Accounts and Explanation	Debit	Credit
Nov. 2	Accounts Receivable	935	
	Sales Revenue		935
	Sale on account.		
2	Cost of Goods Sold	505	
	Merchandise Inventory		505
	Recorded the cost of goods sold.		

$$\frac{A\uparrow}{\text{Accounts Receivable}\uparrow}\Big\} = \Big\{ \frac{L}{} + \frac{E\uparrow}{\text{Sales Revenue}\uparrow}$$

$$\frac{A\downarrow}{\text{Merchandise Inventory}\downarrow}\Big\} = \Big\{ \frac{L}{} + \frac{E\downarrow}{\text{Cost of Goods Sold}\uparrow}$$

When using special journals, instead of recording this transaction in the general journal, the business records the transaction in the sales journal. All of the information related to the sale appears on a single line in the sales journal as follows:

Sales Journal					Page 3
Date	Invoice No.	Customer Account Debited	Post. Ref.	Accounts Receivable DR Sales Revenue CR	Cost of Goods Sold DR Merchandise Inventory CR
2014					
Nov. 2	422	Maria Galvez		935	505

The Post. Ref. column is not used until the transaction is posted.

This part of the journal records the sales revenue and associated receivable.

This part of the journal records the expense and the reduction of merchandise inventory.

The entry records the sales revenue and associated accounts receivable by entering the amount of the sale, $935, in the Accounts Receivable DR, Sales Revenue CR column. The entry also records the expense of the sale and the reduction of merchandise inventory by recording the cost of the sale, $505, in the Cost of Goods Sold DR, Merchandise Inventory CR column. By using a sales journal, the recording of sales is streamlined, thus saving a significant amount of time.

It's important to remember that a transaction is recorded in either the general journal or a special journal, but not in both. We are illustrating the general journal entry as a teaching tool to help you understand how the entry is recorded in the special journal. Transactions are not recorded in both journals. To do so would be to record the entry twice.

This business, like most other companies, uses a perpetual inventory system. Throughout this chapter, we illustrate the perpetual system. When recording a sale, the business must record the cost of the goods sold and the decrease in merchandise inventory. If the business, instead, used a periodic inventory system, the sales journal would not need the last column (Cost of Goods Sold DR, Merchandise Inventory CR) because there is no entry recorded to cost of goods sold and merchandise inventory at the time of the sale.

In the sales journal that we are using in this example, there are only two columns used for dollar amounts. One column records the sales revenue and receivable and the other column records the expense of the sale. Businesses that collect sales tax would need to modify the sales journal shown to include an additional column for Sales Taxes Payable. The modified sales journal would have the following headings:

				Sales Journal			Page 3
Date	Invoice No.	Customer Account Debited	Post. Ref.	Accounts Receivable DR	Sales Taxes Payable CR	Sales Revenue CR	Cost of Goods Sold DR Merchandise Inventory CR

Each business will modify its sales journal to fit the types of sales it makes. Remember, though, that only sales on account are recorded in the sales journal.

Posting

Entries in the sales journal are posted to both the accounts receivable subsidiary ledger and the general ledger.

Posting to the Accounts Receivable Subsidiary Ledger Individual accounts receivable are posted daily from the sales journal to the accounts receivable subsidiary ledger. For example, on November 2, the accountant posts the $935 receivable to the individual accounts receivable for Maria Galvez. The sales journal is posted daily to the subsidiary ledger to keep a current record of the amount receivable from each customer.

After posting to the subsidiary ledger, the accountant enters a check mark in the posting reference column of the sales journal (see Exhibit 5). That lets the business know that the transaction was posted to Galvez's account.

Posting to the General Ledger At the end of the month, the accountant totals (commonly called *footing*) the Accounts Receivable DR, Sales Revenue CR and Cost of Goods Sold DR, Merchandise Inventory CR columns. The totals of these columns are posted from the sales journal to the general ledger.

In Exhibit 5 (Panel A), November's credit sales total $4,319. The $4,319 is posted to the Accounts Receivable and Sales Revenue accounts in the general ledger. The account numbers of each account are then printed beneath the total in the sales journal. In Panel B of Exhibit 5, the account number for Accounts Receivable is 115 and the account number for Sales Revenue is 410. Entering these account numbers in the sales journal shows that the $4,319 has been posted to the two accounts.

The debit to Cost of Goods Sold and the credit to Merchandise Inventory for the monthly total of $1,814 are also posted at the end of the month. After posting, these accounts' numbers are entered beneath the total to show that Cost of Goods Sold and Merchandise Inventory have been updated.

As the accountant posts to the ledgers, the journal page number and journal name abbreviation are entered in the ledger account to show the source of the data. All transaction data in Exhibit 5 originated on page 3 of the sales journal, so all posting references are S.3. "S" indicates sales journal. After posting, the Accounts Receivable balance in the general ledger should equal the sum of the individual customer balances in the subsidiary ledger.

Trace all the postings in Exhibit 5. The way to learn an accounting information system is to study the flow of data. The arrows indicate the direction of the information.

The Cash Receipts Journal

Cash Receipts Journal
Special journal used to record cash receipts.

All businesses have lots of cash transactions, and therefore a cash receipts journal comes in handy. The cash receipts journal is a special journal that is used to record cash receipts.

Exhibit 6 illustrates the cash receipts journal. Every transaction recorded in this journal is a cash receipt.

Exhibit 6 | Cash Receipts Journal With Posting

PANEL A—Cash Receipts Journal:

	Cash Receipts Journal							Page 5
Date	Account Credited	Post Ref.	Cash DR	Sales Discounts DR	Accounts Receivable CR	Sales Revenue CR	Other Accounts CR	Cost of Goods Sold DR Merchandise Inventory CR
2014								
Nov. 6			517			517		290
11	Note Payable to First Bank	221	1,000				1,000	
14	Maria Galvez	✓	900	35	935			
19			853			853		426
22	Brent Harmon	✓	300		300			
25	Interest Revenue	460	762				762	
28			1,802			1,802		991
31	Totals		6,134	35	1,235	3,172	1,762	1,707
			(101)	(420)	(115)	(410)	(X)	(511/131)

> Total change to are posted at the end of the month.

> Individual accounts receivable re posted daily.

> Total is not posted.

> Total change to are posted at the end of the month.

> Individual amounts change to are posted at the end of the month.

PANEL B—Posting to the Ledgers:

Accounts Receivable Subsidiary Ledger

Maria Galvez

				Balance	
Date	Post. Ref.	Debit	Credit	Debit	Credit
Nov. 2	S.3	935		935	
14	CR.5		935	0	

Brent Harmon

				Balance	
Date	Post. Ref.	Debit	Credit	Debit	Credit
Nov. 13	S.3	694		694	
22	CR.5		300	394	

Susan Levy

				Balance	
Date	Post. Ref.	Debit	Credit	Debit	Credit
Nov. 18	S.3	907		907	

Clay Schmidt

				Balance	
Date	Post. Ref.	Debit	Credit	Debit	Credit
Nov. 27	S.3	1,783		1,783	

General Ledger

Cash — No. 101

				Balance	
Date	Post. Ref.	Debit	Credit	Debit	Credit
Nov. 30	CR.5	6,134		6,134	

Accounts Receivable — No. 115

				Balance	
Date	Post. Ref.	Debit	Credit	Debit	Credit
Nov. 30	S.3	4,319		4,319	
30	CR.5		1,235	3,084	

Merchandise Inventory — No. 131

				Balance	
Date	Post. Ref.	Debit	Credit	Debit	Credit
Nov. 1	Bal.			3,885	
30	S.3		1,814	2,071	
30	CR.5		1,707	364	

Note Payable to First Bank — No. 221

				Balance	
Date	Post. Ref.	Debit	Credit	Debit	Credit
Nov. 11	CR.5		1,000		1,000

Sales Revenue — No. 410

				Balance	
Date	Post. Ref.	Debit	Credit	Debit	Credit
Nov. 30	S.3		4,319		4,319
30	CR.5		3,172		7,491

Sales Discounts — No. 420

				Balance	
Date	Post. Ref.	Debit	Credit	Debit	Credit
Nov. 30	CR.5	35		35	

Interest Revenue — No. 460

				Balance	
Date	Post. Ref.	Debit	Credit	Debit	Credit
Nov. 25	CR.5		762		762

Cost of Goods Sold — No. 511

				Balance	
Date	Post. Ref.	Debit	Credit	Debit	Credit
Nov. 30	S.3	1,814		1,814	
30	CR.5	1,707		3,521	

The cash receipts journal includes a column for debits to Cash. The next column is for debits to Sales Discounts. The main sources of cash are collections on account and cash sales. Collections on account are recorded in the Accounts Receivable CR column and the Cash DR column. Cash sales are recorded in the Sales Revenue CR column, the Cash DR column, and Cost of Goods Sold DR, Merchandise Inventory CR column. The cash receipts journal also has an Other Accounts CR column that is used to record miscellaneous cash receipt transactions.

Recording Transactions

In Exhibit 6, the first cash receipt occurred on November 6, and was a cash sale for $517 (cost of goods sold, $290). If the transaction had been recorded in the general journal, the following entries would have been recorded:

$$\frac{A\uparrow}{Cash\uparrow} \Big\} = \Big\{ \frac{L}{} + \frac{E\uparrow}{Sales\ Revenue\uparrow}$$

$$\frac{A\downarrow}{Merchandise\ Inventory\downarrow} \Big\} = \Big\{ \frac{L}{} + \frac{E\downarrow}{Cost\ of\ Goods\ Sold\uparrow}$$

Date	Accounts and Explanation	Debit	Credit
Nov. 6	Cash	517	
	Sales Revenue		517
	Cash sale.		
6	Cost of Goods Sold	290	
	Merchandise Inventory		290
	Recorded the cost of goods sold.		

By recording the transaction in the cash receipts journal instead, the entries can be recorded on one line. Observe the debit to Cash and the credit to Sales Revenue ($517) and the debit to Cost of Goods Sold and credit to Merchandise Inventory ($290) for the cost of the merchandise sold.

On November 11, the business borrowed $1,000 from First Bank. If the transaction had been recorded in the general journal, the following entry would have been made:

$$\frac{A\uparrow}{Cash\uparrow} \Big\} = \Big\{ \frac{L\uparrow}{Notes\ Payable\uparrow} + \frac{E}{}$$

Date	Accounts and Explanation	Debit	Credit
Nov. 11	Cash	1,000	
	Note Payable to First Bank		1,000
	Received cash in exchange for note.		

By recording it in the cash receipts journal instead, the accountant would record the $1,000 in the Cash DR column. The Other Accounts CR column is used for the Notes Payable credit because there is no specific credit column for borrowings. For this transaction, the account title, Note Payable to First Bank, is entered in the Account Credited column. The Other Accounts CR column is used when a transaction involves a credit entry that is not listed in the headings (columns) of the cash receipts journal. The entry on November 25 is another example. On November 25, the business received $762 cash of interest revenue. The cash receipts journal does not include a column for credits to interest revenue, therefore the Other Accounts CR column must be used and the credit account must be written in the Account Credited column.

On November 14, the business collected $900 from Maria Galvez. Back on November 2, the business sold $935 of merchandise to Galvez and recorded the sale in the sales journal. This credit sale allowed a $35 discount for prompt payment, and Galvez paid within the discount period. The business records this cash receipt in the cash receipts journal by debiting Cash for $900 and Sales Discounts for $35 and by crediting Accounts Receivable for $935. The customer's name appears in the Account Credited column.

Posting

As with the sales journal, entries in the cash receipts journal are posted daily to the accounts receivable subsidiary ledger and monthly to the general ledger.

Posting to the Accounts Receivable Subsidiary Ledger Amounts from the cash receipts journal are posted to the accounts receivable subsidiary ledger daily. The postings are credits. Trace the $935 credit to Maria Galvez's account. It reduces her balance to zero. The $300 receipt from Brent Harmon reduces his balance to $394. After posting, the accountant enters a check mark in the posting reference column of the cash receipts journal and shows the CR.5 posting reference in the subsidiary ledger. CR.5 signifies that the posting is transferred from the cash receipts journal, page 5.

The posting reference CR.5 should not be confused with the abbreviation for credit, CR. The posting reference for the cash receipts journal always includes a page reference while the abbreviation for credit does not.

Posting to the General Ledger At the end of the month, each column in the cash receipts journal is totaled. The equality of the debits and credits is verified by comparing the sum of all debit columns to the sum of all credit columns.

Debit Columns		Credit Columns	
Cash	$ 6,134	Accounts Receivable	$ 1,235
Sales Discounts	35	Sales Revenue	3,172
Cost of Goods Sold	1,707	Other Accounts	1,762
		Merchandise Inventory	1,707
Total	$ 7,876		$ 7,876

All columns, except for the Other Accounts CR column, are posted in total to the general ledger. For example, the total for Cash ($6,134) is posted as a debit in the Cash account in the general ledger. After posting, the account number is printed below the column total in the cash receipts journal. The account number for Cash (101) appears below the column total, and likewise for the other column totals. The journal reference (CR) and page number (5) are shown in the general ledger as reference of the posting. Follow the arrows in Exhibit 6, which track the posted amounts.

The column total for *Other Accounts* CR is *not* posted. Instead, these credits are posted individually. In Exhibit 6, the November 11 transaction reads "Note Payable to First Bank." This $1,000 credit entry will need to be posted individually to the Note Payable to First Bank account in the general ledger. The account number (221) in the Post. Ref. column shows that the transaction amount was posted individually. The letter X below the column means that the column total was *not* posted.

After posting, the sum of the individual balances in the accounts receivable subsidiary ledger equals the balance of Accounts Receivable in the general ledger, as follows:

GENERAL LEDGER	
Accounts Receivable debit balance	$ 3,084

SUBSIDIARY LEDGER: CUSTOMER ACCOUNTS RECEIVABLE	
Customer	**Balance**
Maria Galvez	$ 0
Brent Harmon	394
Susan Levy	907
Clay Schmidt	1,783
Total Accounts Receivable	$ 3,084

Should be equal.

> **Try It!**

6. Evenson Co. sold merchandise inventory on credit to Brain Crain, $300. The cost of the goods sold was $240. What special journal should the transaction be recorded in, and what is the column used for the $300?

Check your answers at the end of the chapter.

For more practice, see Short Exercises S-3 through S-7.   MyAccountingLab

HOW ARE PURCHASES, CASH PAYMENTS, AND OTHER TRANSACTIONS RECORDED IN A MANUAL ACCOUNTING INFORMATION SYSTEM?

Learning Objective 3

Journalize and post purchases, cash payments, and other transactions in a manual accounting information system using special journals and subsidiary ledgers

Purchases Journal

Special journal used to record all purchases of merchandise inventory, office supplies, and other assets on account.

In the previous section, you learned that when using a manual accounting information system, sales on account are recorded in the sales journal and cash receipts are recorded in the cash receipts journal. We now turn our attention to purchases and cash payments.

The Purchases Journal

A merchandising business purchases merchandise inventory and other items, such as office supplies, equipment, and furniture, on account. The purchases journal handles these transactions plus other purchases incurred *on account*. Cash purchases are not recorded in the purchases journal; instead, they are recorded in the cash payments journal.

Exhibit 7 illustrates a purchases journal (Panel A) and posting to the ledgers (Panel B). The purchases journal has special columns for:

• Credits to Accounts Payable
• Debits to Merchandise Inventory, Office Supplies, and Other Accounts

The Other Accounts DR columns are used for purchases on account of items other than merchandise inventory and office supplies. This business uses a perpetual inventory system. In a periodic inventory system, the Merchandise Inventory DR column would be replaced with a column titled Purchases DR.

Exhibit 7 | Purchases Journal With Posting

PANEL A—Purchases Journal:

							Other Accounts DR		
Date	Vendor Account Credited	Terms	Post. Ref.	Accounts Payable CR	Merchandise Inventory DR	Office Supplies DR	Account Title	Post. Ref.	Amount
2014									
Nov. 2	Hanes Textiles	3/15, n/30	✓	700	700				
5	Pioneer Plastics	n/30	✓	319	319				
9	City Office Supply	2/10, n/30	✓	440			Equipment	191	440
12	Advanced Printing	n/30	✓	236	236				
13	Hanes Textiles	3/15, n/30	✓	451	451				
19	City Office Supply	2/10, n/30	✓	103		103			
23	O'Leary Furniture	n/60	✓	627			Furniture	181	627
Nov. 30	Totals			2,876	1,706	103			1,067
				(210)	(131)	(161)			(X)

Individual accounts payable are posted daily.

Totals are posted at the end of the month.

Total is not posted.

Individual amounts are posted at the end of the month.

PANEL B—Posting to the Ledgers:

Accounts Payable Subsidiary Ledger

Advanced Printing

Date	Post. Ref.	Debit	Credit	Balance Debit	Balance Credit
Nov. 12	P.8		236		236

City Office Supply

Date	Post. Ref.	Debit	Credit	Balance Debit	Balance Credit
Nov. 9	P.8		440		440
19	P.8		103		543

Hanes Textiles

Date	Post. Ref.	Debit	Credit	Balance Debit	Balance Credit
Nov. 2	P.8		700		700
13	P.8		451		1,151

O'Leary Furniture

Date	Post. Ref.	Debit	Credit	Balance Debit	Balance Credit
Nov. 23	P.8		627		627

Pioneer Plastics

Date	Post. Ref.	Debit	Credit	Balance Debit	Balance Credit
Nov. 5	P.8		319		319

General Ledger

Merchandise Inventory — No. 131

Date	Post. Ref.	Debit	Credit	Balance Debit	Balance Credit
Nov. 1	Bal.			3,885	
30	S.3		1,814	2,071	
30	CR.5		1,707	364	
30	P.8	1,706		2,070	

Office Supplies — No. 161

Date	Post. Ref.	Debit	Credit	Balance Debit	Balance Credit
Nov. 30	P.8	103		103	

Furniture — No. 181

Date	Post. Ref.	Debit	Credit	Balance Debit	Balance Credit
Nov. 23	P.8	627		627	

Equipment — No. 191

Date	Post. Ref.	Debit	Credit	Balance Debit	Balance Credit
Nov. 9	P.8	440		440	

Accounts Payable — No. 210

Date	Post. Ref.	Debit	Credit	Balance Debit	Balance Credit
Nov. 30	P.8		2,876		2,876

Recording Transactions

Let's begin by looking at the first transaction. On November 2, the business purchased merchandise inventory costing $700 from Hanes Textiles. If the transaction had been recorded in the general journal, the following entry would have been recorded:

Date	Accounts and Explanation	Debit	Credit
Nov. 2	Merchandise Inventory	700	
	Accounts Payable		700
	Purchased inventory on account.		

By recording the entry in the purchases journal, the transaction can be recorded on one line. The vendor's name (Hanes Textiles) is entered in the Vendor Account Credited column. The purchase terms of 3/15, n/30 are also entered to show the due date and the discount available. Accounts Payable is credited for the transaction amount, and Merchandise Inventory is debited.

Note the November 9 purchase of equipment from City Office Supply. The purchases journal holds no column for equipment, so the business uses the Other Accounts DR columns. Because this was a credit purchase, the accountant enters the vendor name (City Office Supply) in the Vendor Account Credited column and Equipment in the Account Title column.

Posting

Entries from the purchases journal are posted daily to the accounts payable subsidiary ledger and monthly to the general ledger.

Accounts Payable Subsidiary Ledger Individual accounts payable are posted daily from the purchases journal to the accounts payable subsidiary ledger. This allows the business to always have a current record of the accounts payable for each vendor. For example, on November 2, the business would post the $700 accounts payable credit to the Hanes Textiles account in the accounts payable subsidiary ledger. After posting, the accountant enters a check mark in the posting reference column of the purchases journal to indicate that the amount was posted in the subsidiary ledger. In addition, the posting reference (P.8) is printed in the subsidiary ledger.

Posting to the General Ledger Posting from the purchases journal is similar to posting from the other special journals. Exhibit 7, Panel B, illustrates the posting process. At the end of each month, each column in the journal is totaled. All totals, except the Other Accounts DR Amount column, are posted to the general ledger. For example, the $2,876 Accounts Payable CR total is posted to the Accounts Payable account in the general ledger as a credit. After posted, the account number is listed in the purchases journal and the posting reference is listed in the general ledger. The column total for *Other Accounts DR Amount* is *not* posted. Instead, these debits are posted individually to the specific accounts, as done in the cash receipts journal. After all posting is complete, the Accounts Payable balance in the general ledger should equal the sum of the individual vendor balances in the subsidiary ledger.

The Cash Payments Journal

Cash Payments Journal
Special journal used to record cash payments by check and currency.

Businesses make most cash payments by check, and all checks (and payments of cash) are recorded in the cash payments journal. This special journal is also called the *check register* and the *cash disbursements journal.* Exhibit 8 shows the cash payments journal, with the ledgers in Panel B.

Exhibit 8 | **Cash Payments Journal With Posting**

PANEL A–Cash Payments Journal:

Cash Payments Journal							Page 6
Date	Ck. No.	Account Debited	Post. Ref.	Other Accounts DR	Accounts Payable DR	Merchandise Inventory CR	Cash CR
2014							
Nov. 3	101	Rent Expense	541	1,200			1,200
8	102	Office Supplies	161	61			61
15	103	Hanes Textiles	✓		700	21	679
20	104	Pioneer Plastics	✓		119		119
26	105	Merchandise Inventory	131	2,200			2,200
Nov. 30		Totals		3,461	819	21	4,259
				(X)	(210)	(131)	(101)

Total is not posted.

Totals are posted at the end of the month.

Individual accounts payable are posted daily.

PANEL B–Posting to the Ledgers:

Accounts Payable Subsidiary Ledger

Individual accounts are posted at the end of the month.

General Ledger

Advanced Printing

				Balance	
Date	Post. Ref.	Debit	Credit	Debit	Credit
Nov. 12	P.8		236		236

Cash   No. 101

				Balance	
Date	Post. Ref.	Debit	Credit	Debit	Credit
Nov. 30	CR. 5	6,134		6,134	
30	CP. 6		4,259	1,875	

City Office Supply

				Balance	
Date	Post. Ref.	Debit	Credit	Debit	Credit
Nov. 9	P.8		440		440
19	P.8		103		543

Merchandise Inventory   No. 131

				Balance	
Date	Post. Ref.	Debit	Credit	Debit	Credit
Nov. 1	Bal.			3,885	
26	CP.6	2,200		6,085	
30	S.3		1,814	4,271	
30	CR.5		1,707	2,564	
30	P.8	1,706		4,270	
30	CP.6		21	4,249	

Hanes Textiles

				Balance	
Date	Post. Ref.	Debit	Credit	Debit	Credit
Nov. 2	P.8		700		700
13	P.8		451		1,151
15	CP.6	700			451

O'Leary Furniture Co.

				Balance	
Date	Post. Ref.	Debit	Credit	Debit	Credit
Nov. 23	P.8		627		627

Office Supplies   No. 161

				Balance	
Date	Post. Ref.	Debit	Credit	Debit	Credit
Nov. 8	CP.6	61		61	
30	P.8	103		164	

Pioneer Plastics

				Balance	
Date	Post. Ref.	Debit	Credit	Debit	Credit
Nov. 5	P.8		319		319
20	CP.6	119			200

Accounts Payable   No. 210

				Balance	
Date	Post. Ref.	Debit	Credit	Debit	Credit
Nov. 30	P.8		2,876		2,876
30	CP.6	819			2,057

Rent Expense   No. 541

				Balance	
Date	Post. Ref.	Debit	Credit	Debit	Credit
Nov. 3	CP.6	1,200		1,200	

The cash payments journal has two debit columns—one for Other Accounts and one for Accounts Payable. It has two credit columns—one for Merchandise Inventory (for purchase discounts) and one for Cash. This special journal also has columns for the date and check number of each cash payment and the account debited.

Recording Transactions

Let's review the first transaction listed in the cash payments journal. On November 3, the business paid cash of $1,200 for rent. This payment of cash is recorded in the cash payments journal by entering $1,200 in the Cash CR column and the Other Accounts DR column. The Other Accounts DR column is used to record debits to accounts for which no special column exists. The business enters the name of the other account used, Rent Expense, in the Account Debited column. The Other Accounts DR column was also used on November 8 for the purchase of office supplies for cash and on November 26 for the purchase of Merchandise Inventory with cash.

On November 15, the business paid the vendor, Hanes Textiles, on account, with credit terms of 3/15, n/30 (for details, see the first transaction in the purchases journal, Exhibit 7). Paying within the discount period allowed a 3% discount ($21), and the business paid the remaining $679 ($700 less the $21 discount). If the business had recorded the transaction in the general journal, the following would have been recorded:

Date	Accounts and Explanation	Debit	Credit
Nov. 15	Accounts Payable	700	
	Cash		679
	Merchandise Inventory		21
	Paid within discount period.		

Instead, the business will record the transaction in the cash payments journal. The entry will be recorded by entering the $679 in the Cash CR column. The Accounts Payable DR column will be recorded for $700, and the discount of $21 will be entered into the Merchandise Inventory CR column. All transactions involving cash payments are recorded in the cash payments journal.

Posting

Entries in the cash payments journal are posted daily to the accounts payable subsidiary ledger and monthly to the general ledger.

Posting to the Accounts Payable Subsidiary Ledger Posting from the cash payments journal is similar to posting from the cash receipts journal. Individual vendor amounts (accounts payable) are posted daily to the accounts payable subsidiary ledger. The postings are debits and reduce the balance in the individual accounts payable account. Trace the $700 payment to Hanes Textiles. The $700 reduces the balance in the Hanes' subsidiary account to $451. After posting, a check mark is entered in the cash payments journal and the posting reference (CP.6) is printed in the subsidiary ledger.

Posting to the General Ledger At the end of the month, each column is totaled. The totals, except for the Other Accounts DR column, are posted to the specific general ledger accounts. After posting, the account number is printed below the column total in the cash payments journal and the posting reference is printed in the general ledger.

Amounts in the Other Accounts DR column are posted individually (for example, Rent Expense—debit $1,200). When each Other Account DR is posted to the general ledger, the account number is printed in the Post. Ref. column. The letter X below the column signifies that the total is *not* posted.

To review accounts payable, companies list individual vendor balances in the accounts payable subsidiary ledger. The general ledger and subsidiary ledger totals should agree.

GENERAL LEDGER	
Accounts Payable credit balance	$ 2,057

SUBSIDIARY LEDGER: ACCOUNTS PAYABLE	
Vendor	**Balance**
Advanced Printing	$ 236
City Office Supply	543
Hanes Textiles	451
O'Leary Furniture Co.	627
Pioneer Plastics	200
Total Accounts Payable	$ 2,057

Should be equal.

The General Journal

Special journals save time recording repetitive transactions. But some transactions don't fit a special journal. Examples include depreciation, the expiration of prepaid insurance, and the accrual of salaries payable at the end of the period. Companies also use the general journal for sales returns and allowances and purchase returns and allowances. All accounting information systems need a general journal. The adjusting entries and the closing entries are recorded in the general journal, along with other nonroutine transactions.

As we have seen, a manual accounting information system involves five journals: sales journal, cash receipts journal, purchases journal, cash payments journal, and the general journal. It's important to remember that transactions are recorded in either one of the special journals or in the general journal, but not both. Exhibit 9 provides a summary of all five journals that will help you decide which journal to use when recording transactions in a manual system.

Exhibit 9 | Recording Transactions in Special Journals

> **Try It!**

7. Fiscella Co. paid monthly rent of $2,000. What special journal should the transaction be recorded in? What columns will be used?

Check your answers at the end of the chapter.

For more practice, see Short Exercises S-8 through S-12.   MyAccountingLab

HOW ARE TRANSACTIONS RECORDED IN A COMPUTERIZED ACCOUNTING INFORMATION SYSTEM?

A computerized accounting information system has two basic components:

- Hardware
- Software

Hardware is the electronic equipment: computers, monitors, printers, and the network that connects them. Most systems require a network to link computers. In a networked system, the server stores the program and the data.

Software is the set of programs that drives the computer. Accounting software reads, edits, and stores transaction data. It also generates the reports that businesses can use to make decisions. Many software packages are flexible. For example, a small cleaning business may be only partly computerized. This small business may use the computer for employee payrolls, but other parts of the accounting information system may be manual.

Entry-Level Software

With increased availability of affordable computerized accounting information systems, more and more businesses are completing all of their accounting on the computer. Two popular entry-level software packages are QuickBooks and Sage 50 Accounting. Both of these programs allow businesses to enter sales of services and merchandise inventory. In addition, these programs can record expenses and produce reports such as financial statements. These computerized accounting information systems are relatively easy to use, often requiring little knowledge of accounting or GAAP. Computerized accounting software allows businesses to organize finances, track sales and expenses, and complete recordkeeping. QuickBooks and Sage 50 Accounting, though, work best for small businesses. As businesses grow and expand, they need a software system that can handle more advanced processes and transactions.

Enterprise Resource Planning (ERP) Systems

Larger companies will often use an enterprise resource planning (ERP) system to manage their data. ERP systems such as SAP® and Oracle® can integrate all company data into a single database. ERP feeds the data into software for all company activities—from purchasing to production and customer service.

Advantages of ERP systems include:

- Reduce operating costs.
- Help companies adjust to changes.
- Replace separate software systems, such as sales and payroll.

Disadvantages of ERP systems include:

- ERP is expensive. Major installations can cost millions.
- Implementation also requires a large commitment of time and people.

Many ERP systems and entry-level systems can be offered in the "cloud." Cloud computing refers to purchasing software and data storage from a third party. In cloud computing, the software and data are stored on the third-party server instead of by the business. Employees access the software and data via the Internet by using a web browser. Cloud computing can reduce costs by a significant amount for many businesses.

QuickBooks

One way to understand how computerized accounting software works is to view how transactions are handled in this type of system. We are now going to look at a common

Learning Objective 4
Describe how transactions are recorded in a computerized accounting information system

Hardware
Electronic equipment that includes computers, monitors, printers, and the network that connects them.

Network
The system of electronic linkages that allows different computers to share the same information.

Software
Set of programs or instructions that drives the computer to perform the work desired.

Enterprise Resource Planning (ERP)
Software systems that can integrate all of a company's functions, departments, and data into a single system.

Cloud Computing
Software and data are stored on a third-party server instead of by the business and can be accessed by employees via the Internet.

entry-level system, QuickBooks. Although your instructor might not have you complete any assignments using QuickBooks, it will be helpful to view the way QuickBooks handles common accounting entries.

Most computerized accounting information systems are organized by function or task. A user can select a function, such as creating an invoice, from a menu. (A menu is a list of options for choosing computer functions.) QuickBooks uses a Getting Around page to allow users to select from a menu of options. The software also has menu options available at the top of the screen. Exhibit 10 shows the Getting Around page for QuickBooks.

Exhibit 10 | QuickBooks Getting Around Page

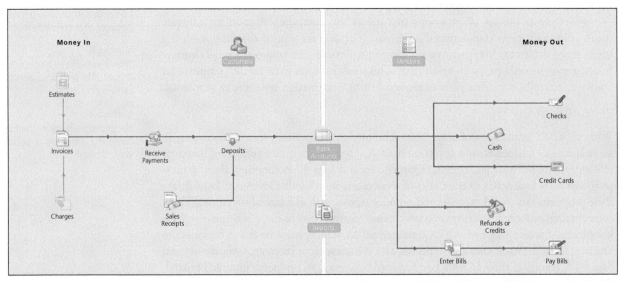

Ethics   Should I change the transaction?

Girmanesh Landin is responsible for recording all of the transactions for Marshall's Home Care. This is Girmanesh's first job as a staff accountant, and she wants to do a good job. Last week, she recorded several cash payments for bills in the computerized accounting information system. She now realizes that she selected the incorrect cash account. She selected the savings account instead of the checking account. Girmanesh knows that she could go back into each transaction and make the correction without anyone knowing that she made the mistake, but she is unsure of what to do. Should Girmanesh make the correction?

Solution

Because Girmanesh is new to the job, she should find out the procedure for making corrections in the accounting information system before she changes each transaction. Attempting to hide her mistakes could cause her integrity to be questioned because it would appear that she was trying to cover up things rather than ask for clarification and help. Most businesses will prefer that Girmanesh make a separate correcting entry instead of going back in and changing the incorrect transaction. This procedure allows for businesses to have a record of the original transaction and then the correcting entry. It is generally never a good idea to change transactions that have already been recorded, and many software systems will not allow such actions as a method to prevent fraud.

QuickBooks separates its Getting Around page into two main sections: Money In and Money Out. The Money In section handles transactions involving customers, including invoices (accounts receivable), receipt of payments, and sales receipts. The Money Out section handles transactions involving vendors, including entering bills (accounts payable), paying bills, and processing refunds. Reports such as the income statement and balance sheet are also accessible from the Getting Around page.

Creating a Sales Invoice

Suppose on June 23, Smart Touch Learning performed $3,000 of services for Richard Michura on account. To record this transaction in QuickBooks, Smart Touch Learning would need to create an invoice for Richard. Exhibit 11 shows the invoice the company created. Notice that there are no debits and credits on the invoice. In a computerized accounting information system, the business does not have to record the transaction in debit and credit format. Instead, by creating the invoice, the software knows automatically to record a debit to Accounts Receivable—Michura and a credit to Sales Revenue. After creating the invoice, the software posts the transaction to the appropriate general ledger accounts. There is no need for the business to manually post the transaction; the software takes care of the posting process.

Exhibit 11 | **Invoice**

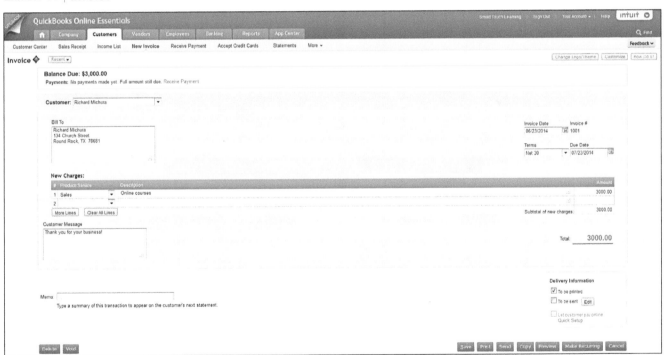

When Smart Touch Learning receives the $3,000 from the customer, the accounting clerk will enter the transaction in the Receive Payment section of QuickBooks. The clerk will select the invoice that is associated with the cash receipt. By doing this, QuickBooks identifies that the invoice has been paid and that Richard Michura has no further outstanding balance.

Entering Bills

When a business needs to record a bill received, it will use the Enter Bills section of QuickBooks. Suppose that on June 25, Smart Touch Learning receives a $580 bill for utilities. Exhibit 12 shows the bill that the company will record in QuickBooks. When Smart Touch Learning saves the bill, the software will automatically record a debit to Utilities Expense and credit to Accounts Payable—Smart Energy.

Exhibit 12 | Bill

On July 5, when Smart Touch Learning makes payment on the bill, it will enter the payment in the Pay Bills section of QuickBooks. The accounting clerk will select the bill to be paid and record the payment to the Cash account. Again, the software takes care of recording the journal entry and posting to the ledger accounts.

Viewing Financial Statements

QuickBooks has the ability to produce numerous reports such as the income statement (called Profit & Loss in QuickBooks), balance sheet, and statement of cash flows. The software can also be used to create accounts receivable and accounts payable aging schedules. Exhibit 13 shows an example of an income statement for Smart Touch Learning.

Exhibit 13 | Income Statement

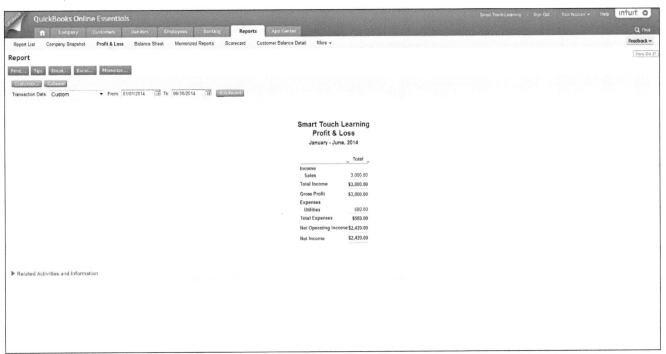

One of the many benefits of using a computerized accounting information system is the ease with which reports are created. For most reports needed, the software includes prebuilt templates that can be used. In addition, the software automatically transfers the amounts from the general ledger to the financial statements. The only thing the accountant needs to do is set the correct time period and review the financial statements for accuracy.

> Try It!

8. Fill in the missing information.

   a. _____ is the set of programs that drives the computer.

   b. Most systems require a(n) _____ to link computers.

   c. _____ is the electronic equipment used in a computerized accounting information system.

   Check your answers at the end of the chapter.

For more practice, see Short Exercise S-13. MyAccountingLab

REVIEW

> Things You Should Know

1. What is an accounting information system?

- An accounting information system (AIS) collects, records, stores, and processes accounting data to produce information that is useful for decision makers.
- An effective accounting information system provides control, compatibility, flexibility, relevance, and a positive cost/benefit relationship.
- An accounting information system has three basic components:
  - Source documents and input devices
  - Processing and storage
  - Outputs

2. How are sales and cash receipts recorded in a manual accounting information system?

- In a manual system, businesses use special journals that are designed to record a specific type of transaction. The four special journals and their uses are:
  - Sales journal—records sales on account
  - Cash receipts journal—records cash receipts
  - Purchases journal—records purchases on account
  - Cash payments journal—records cash payments
- Subsidiary ledgers are used to hold individual accounts that support a general ledger account. Two common subsidiary ledgers are the accounts receivable subsidiary ledger and accounts payable subsidiary ledger.
- Credit sales are recorded in the sales journal, which uses two columns—Accounts Receivable DR, Sales Revenue CR and Cost of Goods Sold DR, Merchandise Inventory CR.
- Cash receipts are recorded in the cash receipts journal, which includes a Cash DR column and various other debit and credit columns.

3. How are purchases, cash payments, and other transactions recorded in a manual accounting information system?

- Purchases on account are recorded in the purchases journal, which includes an Accounts Payable CR column and various other debit columns.
- Cash payments are recorded in the cash payments journal, which includes a Cash CR column and various other debit and credit columns.
- The general journal is used for transactions that aren't recorded in one of the special journals, such as adjusting and closing entries.

4. How are transactions recorded in a computerized accounting information system?

- A computerized accounting information system has two basic components:
  - Hardware—the electronic equipment
  - Software—the set of programs that drives the computer
- Entry-level software, such as QuickBooks and Sage 50 Accounting, is often used by small businesses.
- Larger companies use an enterprise resource planning (ERP) system to manage their data.

> Summary Problem

Houlihan Company completed the following selected transactions during March:

Mar. 4	Received $500 for a cash sale of merchandise inventory to a customer (cost, $319).
6	Received $60 on account from Brady Lee. The full invoice amount was $65, but Lee paid within the discount period to gain the $5 discount.
9	Received $1,080 on a note receivable from Beverly Mann. This amount includes the $1,000 note receivable plus interest revenue.
15	Received $800 for a cash sale of merchandise inventory to a customer (cost, $522).
24	Borrowed $2,200 by signing a note payable to Interstate Bank.
27	Received $1,200 on account from Lance Albert. Collection was received after the discount period, as there was no discount.

Requirements

The general ledger showed the following balances at February 28: Cash, $1,117; Accounts Receivable, $2,790; Note Receivable—Beverly Mann, $1,000; and Merchandise Inventory, $1,819. The accounts receivable subsidiary ledger at February 28 contained debit balances as follows: Lance Albert, $1,840; Melinda Fultz, $885; Brady Lee, $65.

1. Record the transactions in the cash receipts journal, page 7.
2. Compute column totals at March 31.
3. Post from the cash receipts journal to the general ledger and the accounts receivable subsidiary ledger. Use four-column accounts. Use complete posting references, including the following account numbers: Cash, 11; Accounts Receivable, 12; Note Receivable—Beverly Mann, 13; Merchandise Inventory, 14; Note Payable—Interstate Bank, 22; Sales Revenue, 41; Sales Discounts, 42; Interest Revenue, 46; and Cost of Goods Sold, 51. Insert a check mark (√) in the posting reference column for each February 28 account balance.
4. Balance the Accounts Receivable subsidiary ledger with the Accounts Receivable account in the general ledger.

> Solution

Requirements 1 and 2

Cash Receipts Journal								Page 7
Date	Account Credited	Post. Ref.	Cash DR	Sales Discounts DR	Accounts Receivable CR	Sales Revenue CR	Other Accounts CR	Cost of Goods Sold DR Merchandise Inventory CR
2014								
Mar. 4			500			500		319
6	Brady Lee	✓	60	5	65			
9	Note Receivable-Beverly Mann	13	1,080				1,000	
	Interest Revenue	46					80	
15			800			800		522
24	Note Payable-Interstate Bank	22	2,200				2,200	
27	Lance Albert	✓	1,200		1,200			
31			5,840	5	1,265	1,300	3,280	841
			(11)	(42)	(12)	(41)	(x)	(51/14)

Requirement 3

ACCOUNTS RECEIVABLE SUBSIDIARY LEDGER

Lance Albert

Date	Post. Ref.	Debit	Credit	Balance Debit	Balance Credit
Feb. 28	✓			1,840	
Mar. 27	CR.7		1,200	640	

Melinda Fultz

Date	Post. Ref.	Debit	Credit	Balance Debit	Balance Credit
Feb. 28	✓			885	

Brady Lee

Date	Post. Ref.	Debit	Credit	Balance Debit	Balance Credit
Feb. 28	✓			65	
Mar. 6	CR.7		65	0	

GENERAL LEDGER

Cash					No. 11
				Balance	
Date	Post. Ref.	Debit	Credit	Debit	Credit
Feb. 28	✓			1,117	
Mar. 31	CR.7	5,840		6,957	

Accounts Receivable					No. 12
				Balance	
Date	Post. Ref.	Debit	Credit	Debit	Credit
Feb. 28	✓			2,790	
Mar. 31	CR.7		1,265	1,525	

Note Receivable—Beverly Mann					No. 13
				Balance	
Date	Post. Ref.	Debit	Credit	Debit	Credit
Feb. 28	✓			1,000	
Mar. 9	CR.7		1,000	0	

Merchandise Inventory					No. 14
				Balance	
Date	Post. Ref.	Debit	Credit	Debit	Credit
Feb. 28	✓			1,819	
Mar. 31	CR.7		841	978	

Note Payable—Interstate Bank					No. 22
				Balance	
Date	Post. Ref.	Debit	Credit	Debit	Credit
Mar. 24	CR.7		2,200		2,200

Sales Revenue					No. 41
				Balance	
Date	Post. Ref.	Debit	Credit	Debit	Credit
Mar. 31	CR.7		1,300		1,300

Sales Discounts					No. 42
				Balance	
Date	Post. Ref.	Debit	Credit	Debit	Credit
Mar. 31	CR.7	5		5	

Interest Revenue					No. 46
				Balance	
Date	Post. Ref.	Debit	Credit	Debit	Credit
Mar. 9	CR.7		80		80

Cost of Goods Sold					No. 51
				Balance	
Date	Post. Ref.	Debit	Credit	Debit	Credit
Mar. 31	CR.7	841		841	

Requirement 4

GENERAL LEDGER	
Accounts Receivable debit balance	$ 1,525

Accounts Receivable Subsidiary Ledger	
Customer	**Balance**
Lance Albert	$ 640
Melinda Fultz	885
Brady Lee	0
Total accounts receivable	$ 1,525

> Key Terms

Accounting Information System (AIS)

A system that collects, records, stores, and processes accounting data to produce information that is useful for decision makers.

Accounts Payable Subsidiary Ledger

A subsidiary ledger that includes an accounts payable account for each vendor that contains detailed information such as the amount purchased, paid, and owed.

Accounts Receivable Subsidiary Ledger

A subsidiary ledger that includes an accounts receivable account for each customer that contains detailed information such as the amount purchased, paid, and owed.

Cash Payments Journal

Special journal used to record cash payments by check and currency.

Cash Receipts Journal

Special journal used to record cash receipts.

Cloud Computing

Software and data are stored on a third-party server instead of by the business and are accessed by employees via the Internet.

Control Account

An account whose balance equals the sum of the balances in a group of related accounts in a subsidiary ledger.

Enterprise Resource Planning (ERP)

Software systems that can integrate all of a company's functions, departments, and data into a single system.

Hardware

Electronic equipment that includes computers, monitors, printers, and the network that connects them.

Network

The system of electronic linkages that allows different computers to share the same information.

Purchases Journal

Special journal used to record all purchases of merchandise inventory, office supplies, and other assets on account.

Sales Journal

Special journal used to record credit sales.

Server

The main computer where data is stored, which can be accessed from many different computers.

Software

Set of programs or instructions that drives the computer to perform the work desired.

Source Document

Provides the evidence and data for accounting transactions.

Special Journal

An accounting journal designed to record one specific type of transaction.

Subsidiary Ledger

Record of accounts that provides supporting details on individual balances, the total of which appears in a general ledger account.

> Quick Check

Learning Objective 1

1. Which of the following benefits of an effective accounting information system provides safeguards for a business's assets and reduces the likelihood of fraud and errors?

   a. Flexibility   c. Control

   b. Relevance   d. Compatibility

Learning Objective 1

2. The outputs of a computerized accounting information system are called

   a. Reports   c. Processing

   b. Software   d. Purchase invoices

Learning Objective 2

3. Which of the following is not a special journal?

   a. Sales journal   c. Cash receipts journal

   b. General journal   d. Purchases journal

4. Mountain Day Spa sold merchandise inventory on credit to Marvin Smith, $400. Cost of goods sold was $250. When using a manual accounting information system, where should Mountain record this transaction, and what is the appropriate column in which to record the $250?

   Learning Objective 2

   a. Sales journal; Accounts Receivable DR, Sales Revenue CR

   b. Cash receipts journal; Cash DR, Sales Revenue CR

   c. Sales journal; Cost of Goods Sold DR, Merchandise Inventory CR

   d. Cash receipts journal; Cash DR, Accounts Receivable CR

5. Which of the following correctly describes the posting of transactions from the sales journal?

   Learning Objective 2

   a. Individual accounts receivables are posted daily to the general ledger.

   b. At the end of the month, the totals of the columns are posted to the general ledger.

   c. Transactions are posted daily to the general ledger.

   d. The total of the Accounts Receivable DR, Sales Revenue CR column is posted to the accounts receivable subsidiary ledger.

6. Centex Sound Systems purchased merchandise inventory costing $8,000 from Flower Co. on account. Where should Centex record this transaction, and what account is credited?

   Learning Objective 3

   a. Cash payments journal; credit Cash

   b. Sales journal; credit Sales Revenue

   c. Purchases journal; credit Accounts Payable

   d. General journal; credit Inventory

7. Every transaction recorded in the cash payments journal includes a

   Learning Objective 3

   a. Credit to Cash

   b. Debit to Accounts Receivable

   c. Debit to Sales Discounts

   d. Debit to Cash

8. When using a manual accounting information system, which of the following transactions would be recorded in the general journal?

   Learning Objective 3

   a. Depreciation of office furniture

   b. Cash payment of rent

   c. Sale of merchandise inventory on account

   d. Purchase of merchandise inventory on account

9. Disadvantages of an enterprise resource planning (ERP) system include

   Learning Objective 4

   a. Helps companies adjust to changes

   b. Can replace separate software systems

   c. Can reduce costs

   d. Implementation requires a large commitment of time and people

Check your answers at the end of the chapter.

ASSESS YOUR PROGRESS

> Review Questions

1. What is an accounting information system (AIS)?

2. What does an effective accounting information system provide?

3. Explain the three basic components of an accounting information system.

4. What is a special journal?

5. What is the purpose of a subsidiary ledger?

6. What is a control account?

7. List the four special journals often used in a manual accounting information system. What types of transactions are recorded in each of the special journals?

8. Explain the posting process of the sales journal.

9. Provide some examples of transactions that would be recorded in the Other Accounts CR column of the cash receipts journal.

10. What are the columns that are typically used in the purchases journal?

11. Explain the posting process of the cash payments journal.

12. When is the general journal used in a manual accounting information system? Provide some examples of transactions that would be recorded in the general journal.

13. Explain the two components of a computerized accounting information system.

14. What are two common entry-level accounting software systems used by small businesses?

15. What is an enterprise resource planning (ERP) system? What are the advantages and disadvantages of using an ERP?

16. How is QuickBooks organized?

17. How would a business record a sale of services on account in QuickBooks?

18. How would a business record a bill received in QuickBooks?

> Short Exercises

Learning Objective 1

S-1 Evaluating features of an effective accounting information system

In Motion, a T-shirt business, is growing fast, and needs a better accounting information system. Consider the features of an effective system. Which features are most important? Why? Which feature must you consider if your financial resources are limited?

S-2 Defining components of an accounting information system

Match each component of a computerized accounting information system with an example. Components may be used more than once.

Example	Component
1. Server	A. Source documents and input devices
2. Bank checks	B. Processing and storage
3. Reports	C. Outputs
4. Keyboard	
5. Software	
6. Financial statements	
7. Bar code scanner	

S-3 Identifying special journals

Use the following abbreviations to indicate the journal in which you would record transactions a through n.

  J = General journal

  S = Sales journal

CR = Cash receipts journal

  P = Purchases journal

CP = Cash payments journal

Transactions:

_____ **a.** Cash purchase of merchandise inventory

_____ **b.** Collection of dividend revenue earned on an investment

_____ **c.** Prepayment of insurance

_____ **d.** Borrowing money on a long-term note payable

_____ **e.** Purchase of equipment on account

_____ **f.** Cost of goods sold along with a credit sale

_____ **g.** Cash sale of merchandise inventory

_____ **h.** Payment of rent

_____ **i.** Depreciation of computer equipment

_____ **j.** Purchase of merchandise inventory on account

_____ **k.** Collection of accounts receivable

_____ **l.** Expiration of prepaid insurance

_____ **m.** Sale on account

_____ **n.** Payment on account

Learning Objective 2

S-4 Recording transactions in a sales journal

Jun. 1	Sold merchandise inventory on account to Frank Jones, $1,280. Cost of goods, $960. Invoice no. 101.
8	Sold merchandise inventory on account to Iris Fray, $2,000. Cost of goods, $1,560. Invoice no. 102.
13	Sold merchandise inventory on account to Johnny Takac, $320. Cost of goods, $240. Invoice no. 103.
28	Sold merchandise inventory on account to George Westerberg, $800. Cost of goods, $600. Invoice no. 104.

Use the following sales journal to record the preceding transactions.

Sales Journal					Page 1
Date	Invoice No.	Customer Account Debited	Post. Ref.	Accounts Receivable DR Sales Revenue CR	Cost of Goods Sold DR Merchandise Inventory CR
2014					

Note: Short Exercise S-4 should be completed before attempting Short Exercise S-5.

Learning Objective 2

S-5 Posting transactions from a sales journal to subsidiary ledger and general ledger

Review your results from Short Exercise S-4.

Requirements

1. Total each column of the sales journal.

2. Open the following four-column accounts in the accounts receivable subsidiary ledger: Accounts Receivable—Fray; Accounts Receivable—Jones; Accounts Receivable—Takac; Accounts Receivable—Westerberg. Post the transactions to the accounts receivable subsidiary ledger.

3. Open the following selected four-column accounts in the general ledger: Accounts Receivable (112); Merchandise Inventory (118), Bal. $5,000; Sales Revenue (411); Cost of Goods Sold (511). Post the total of each column to the general ledger.

4. Balance the total of the customer balances in the accounts receivable subsidiary ledger against Accounts Receivable in the general ledger.

S-6 Recording transactions in a cash receipts journal

Learning Objective 2

Jul. 5	Sold merchandise inventory for cash, $1,700. Cost of goods, $1,300.
12	Collected interest revenue of $2,000.
18	Received cash from Howie Nathanson, $800, on credit sale. There was no discount.
29	Received $5,000 from Matt Day in full settlement of his account receivable. Day earned a $50 discount by paying early.

Use the following cash receipts journal to record the preceding transactions.

| Cash Receipts Journal | | | | | | | | Page 3 |
Date	Account Credited	Post. Ref.	Cash DR	Sales Discounts DR	Accounts Receivable CR	Sales Revenue CR	Other Accounts CR	Cost of Goods Sold DR Merchandise Inventory CR
2014								

Note: Short Exercise S-6 should be completed before attempting Short Exercise S-7.

S-7 Posting transactions from a cash receipts journal to subsidiary ledger and general ledger

Learning Objective 2

Review your results from Short Exercise S-6.

Requirements

1. Total each column of the cash receipts journal.

2. Open the following four-column accounts in the accounts receivable subsidiary ledger: Accounts Receivable—Day, Bal. $5,050; Accounts Receivable—Nathanson, Bal. $800. Post the transactions to the accounts receivable subsidiary ledger.

3. Open the following selected four-column accounts in the general ledger: Cash (111), Bal. $5,000; Accounts Receivable (112), Bal. $5,850; Merchandise Inventory (118), Bal. $3,000; Sales Revenue (411), Bal. $23,000; Sales Discounts (412); Interest Revenue (419); Cost of Goods Sold (511), Bal. $13,800. Post the total of each column to the general ledger. Also, post the Other Accounts to the general ledger.

4. Balance the total of the customer balances in the accounts receivable subsidiary ledger against Accounts Receivable in the general ledger.

Learning Objective 3 **S-8 Recording transactions in a purchases journal**

Oct. 1	Purchased merchandise inventory on account with credit terms of 2/10, n/30 from Mayer Co., $2,000.
11	Purchased office supplies on account from Battle Co., $300. Terms were n/EOM.
24	Purchased furniture on account with credit terms of 3/10, n/60 from Scott Co., $1,000.

Use the following purchases journal to record the preceding transactions.

							Other Accounts DR		
Date	Vendor Account Credited	Terms	Post. Ref.	Accounts Payable CR	Merchandise Inventory DR	Office Supplies DR	Account Title	Post Ref.	Amount
2014									

Note: Short Exercise S-8 should be completed before attempting Short Exercise S-9.

Learning Objective 3 **S-9 Posting transactions from a purchases journal to subsidiary ledger and general ledger**

Review your results from Short Exercise S-8.

Requirements

1. Total each column of the purchases journal.

2. Open the following four-column accounts in the accounts payable subsidiary ledger: Accounts Payable—Battle Co.; Accounts Payable—Mayer Co.; Accounts Payable—Scott Co. Post the transactions to the accounts payable subsidiary ledger.

3. Open the following selected four-column accounts in the general ledger: Merchandise Inventory (115); Office Supplies (116); Furniture (151); Accounts Payable (211). Post the total of each column to the general ledger. Also, post the Other Accounts to the general ledger.

4. Balance the total of the vendor balances in the accounts payable subsidiary ledger against Accounts Payable in the general ledger.

Learning Objective 3 **S-10 Recording transactions in a cash payments journal**

Jan. 5	Issued check no. 430 to purchase equipment for cash, $1,500.
7	Purchased merchandise inventory for cash, $350, issuing check no. 431.
18	Paid Keane Co. amount owed, $825, less $25 discount. Issued check no. 432.
28	Issued check no. 433 to pay utilities, $280. The bill was just received and there is no liability recorded.

Use the following cash payments journal to record the preceding transactions.

Cash Payments Journal							Page 8
Date	Ck. No.	Account Debited	Post. Ref.	Other Accounts DR	Accounts Payable DR	Merchandise Inventory CR	Cash CR
2014							

Note: Short Exercise S-10 should be completed before attempting Short Exercise S-11.

S-11 Posting transactions from a cash payments journal to subsidiary ledger and general ledger

Learning Objective 3

Review your results from Short Exercise S-10.

Requirements

1. Total each column of the cash payments journal.

2. Open the following four-column accounts in the accounts payable subsidiary ledger: Accounts Payable—Keane Co., Bal. $825. Post the transactions to the accounts payable subsidiary ledger.

3. Open the following selected four-column accounts in the general ledger: Cash (111), Bal. $6,500; Merchandise Inventory (118), $1,800; Equipment (150), $10,000; Accounts Payable (211), $825; Utilities Expense (541). Post the total of each column to the general ledger. Also, post the Other Accounts to the general ledger.

4. Balance the total of the vendor balances in the accounts payable subsidiary ledger against Accounts Payable in the general ledger.

S-12 Recording transactions in a general journal

Learning Objective 3

Mar. 2	Sold merchandise inventory on account to B. Kielman, issuing invoice no. 501 for $300 (cost, $230).
6	Issued credit memo to B. Kielman for $300 for merchandise returned to business by customer. Also accounted for receipt of the merchandise inventory at cost.
21	Purchased merchandise inventory on credit terms of 2/10, n/30 from Poloskey Co., $500.
28	Returned damaged merchandise inventory to Poloskey Co., issuing a debit memo for $500.

Journalize the above transactions that should be recorded in the general journal. If a transaction should not be recorded in the general journal, identify the special journal that should be used. Assume the company uses the perpetual inventory system.

Learning Objective 4

S-13 Understanding components of a computerized accounting information system

Norman Tucker, engineer, is considering using a computerized accounting system for his professional engineering business. Norman has asked that you help him understand the components of a computerized accounting information system by answering the following questions:

Requirements

1. What are the two basic components of a computerized accounting information system?

2. Provide examples of each component.

3. If Norman were interested in an entry-level software system, what software might you recommend?

> Exercises

Learning Objective 2

E-14 Recording transactions—sales journal

Accounts Receivable DR, Sales Revenue
CR column total $1,465

Feb. 1	Sold merchandise inventory on account to Curtis Co., $1,025. Cost of goods, $780. Invoice no. 401.	
	6	Sold merchandise inventory for cash, $860 (cost, $640).
	12	Collected interest revenue of $80.
	15	Received cash from Curtis Co. in full settlement of its account receivable. There was no discount.
	20	Sold merchandise inventory on account to Delgado Co., issuing invoice no. 402 for $440 (cost, $330).
	22	Sold merchandise inventory for cash, $560 (cost $420).
	26	Sold office supplies to an employee for cash of $80.
	28	Received $431 from Delgado Co. in full settlement of its account receivable. Delgado earned a discount by paying early. Terms are 2/10, n/15.

Requirements

1. Prepare headings for a sales journal. Journalize the transactions that should be recorded in the sales journal. (Round the sales discount to a whole dollar.) Assume the company uses the perpetual inventory system.

2. Total each column of the sales journal.

Learning Objective 2

E-15 Recording transactions—cash receipts journal

Accounts Receivable CR column
total $1,465

Refer to information in Exercise E-14.

Requirements

1. Prepare headings for a cash receipts journal. Journalize the transactions that should be recorded in the cash receipts journal.

2. Total each column of the cash receipts journal.

E-16 Using the sales and cash receipts journal

The sales and cash receipts journals of Kincaid Office Products include the following entries:

				Sales Journal	Page 1
Date	Invoice No.	Customer Account Debited	Post. Ref.	Accounts Receivable DR Sales Revenue CR	Cost of Goods Sold DR Merchandise Inventory CR
2014					
May 7	601	L. Ewald	✓	110	76
10	602	T. Ross	✓	60	29
10	603	E. Lovell	✓	60	35
12	604	B. Goebel	✓	120	60
May 31		Total		350	200

					Cash Receipts Journal			Page 5
Date	Account Credited	Post. Ref.	Cash DR	Sales Discounts DR	Accounts Receivable CR	Sales Revenue CR	Other Accounts CR	Cost of Goods Sold DR Merchandise Inventory CR
2014								
May 16	L. Ewald	✓						
19	E. Lovell	✓						
24			300			300		190
30	T. Ross	✓						
May 31	Total							

Identify the missing information in the cash receipts journal for those transactions listed. There are no sales discounts. Also, total the columns in the cash receipts journal and show that total debits equal total credits.

E-17 Analyzing postings from the cash receipts journal

The cash receipts journal of Sironia Plastics follows.

					Cash Receipts Journal			Page 7
Date	Account Credited	Post. Ref.	Cash DR	Sales Discounts DR	Accounts Receivable CR	Sales Revenue CR	Other Accounts CR	Cost of Goods Sold DR Merchandise Inventory CR
2014								
Jan. 2	Annan Corp.	(g)	790	20	810			
9	Kamm, Inc.	(h)	490		490			
19	Note Receivable	(i)	4,480				4,000	
	Interest Revenue	(j)					480	
30	J.T. Franz	(k)	310	10	320			
31			4,230			4,230		3,500
Jan. 31	Total		10,300	30	1,620	4,230	4,480	3,500
			(a)	(b)	(c)	(d)	(e)	(f)

Accounting Information Systems

Sironia's general ledger includes the following selected accounts, along with their account numbers:

Number	Account	Number	Account
110	Cash	510	Sales Revenue
115	Accounts Receivable	512	Sales Discounts
118	Merchandise Inventory	520	Interest Revenue
125	Note Receivable	611	Cost of Goods Sold

Indicate whether each posting reference (a) through (k) should be a

- Check mark (✓) for a posting to a customer account in the accounts receivable subsidiary ledger.
- Account number for a posting to an account in the general ledger. If so, give the account number.
- Letter (X) for an amount not posted.

Learning Objective 2

E-18 Identifying transactions in the accounts receivable ledger

A customer account in the accounts receivable subsidiary ledger of Lyndon Olson Company follows.

JOHN WATERS					
				Balance	
Date	Post. Ref.	Debit	Credit	Debit	Credit
Nov. 1				400	
9	S.5	1,180		1,580	
18	J.8		190	1,390	
30	CR.9		700	690	

Describe the three posted transactions.

Learning Objective 3

E-19 Recording transactions—purchases journal

Accounts Payable CR column
total $4,280

Apr. 2	Purchased merchandise inventory on credit terms of 3/10, n/60 from Valedez Co., $2,800.
5	Issued check no. 820 to purchase equipment for cash, $3,200.
11	Purchased merchandise inventory for cash, $520, issuing check no. 821.
12	Issued check no. 822 to pay Valedez Co. net amount owed from Apr. 2.
19	Purchased office supplies on account from Douglas Supplies, $280. Terms were net end-of-month.
24	Purchased merchandise inventory on credit terms of net 30 from Wade Sales, $1,200.
28	Issued check no. 823 to pay for insurance coverage, debiting Prepaid Insurance for $2,000.
29	Issued check no. 824 to pay rent for the month, $1,450.

Requirements

1. Prepare headings for a purchases journal. Journalize the transactions that should be recorded in the purchases journal. The company uses the perpetual inventory system.

2. Total each column of the purchases journal.

E-20 Recording transactions—cash payments journal

Learning Objective 3

Cash CR column total $9,886

Refer to information in Exercise E-19.

Requirements

1. Prepare headings for a cash payments journal. Journalize the transactions that should be recorded in the cash payments journal.

2. Total each column of the cash payments journal.

E-21 Posting from the purchases journal; balancing the ledgers

Learning Objective 3

The purchases journal of TransEastern Publishing Company follows.

							Other Accounts DR		
Date	Vendor Account Credited	Terms	Post. Ref.	Accounts Payable CR	Merchandise Inventory DR	Office Supplies DR	Account Title	Post. Ref.	Amount
2014									
Sep. 2	Lacer Tech	n/30		800	800				
5	Jupiter Supply	n/30		170		170			
13	Lacer Tech	2/10, n/30		1,400	1,400				
26	Faver Equipment	n/30		900			Equipment		900
Sep. 30	Total								

Purchases Journal — Page 7

Requirements

Merchandise Inventory DR column total $2,200

1. Total each column of the purchases journal.

2. Open four-column ledger accounts for Merchandise Inventory (118), Office Supplies (120), Equipment (150), and Accounts Payable (211). Post to these accounts from the purchases journal. Use dates and posting references in the accounts.

3. Open four-column accounts in the accounts payable subsidiary ledger for Faver Equipment, Jupiter Supply, and Lacer Tech. Post from the purchases journal. Use dates and posting references in the ledger accounts.

4. Balance the Accounts Payable control account in the general ledger with the total of the balances in the accounts payable subsidiary ledger.

E-22 Identifying transactions in the accounts payable ledger

Learning Objective 3

A vendor account in the accounts payable subsidiary ledger of Frazier Company follows.

LARRY CARVER					
				Balance	
Date	Post. Ref.	Debit	Credit	Debit	Credit
Dec. 1					1,800
12	P.4		2,340		4,140
20	J.10	200			3,940
29	CP.6	1,500			2,440

Describe the three posted transactions.

Learning Objectives 2, 3

E-23 Identifying errors in special journals

	Transaction	Recording
a.	Holt Associates paid $490 on account for an earlier purchase of merchandise inventory.	Purchases journal
b.	Recorded depreciation expense for the month.	Cash payments journal
c.	Collected interest revenue.	Cash receipts journal
d.	Sold merchandise inventory on account.	Cash receipts journal
e.	Issued check no. 535 for purchase of merchandise inventory.	Purchases journal
f.	Returned damaged inventory that was purchased on account.	Purchases journal
g.	Sold merchandise inventory for cash.	Sales journal

For each transaction listed, identify the recording error and indicate the journal that should have been used.

Learning Objective 4

E-24 Identifying functions in QuickBooks

	Transaction
a.	$2,000 sale on account to Kim Rhodes.
b.	Received gas and water utility bill, $200.
c.	Received cash from Kim Rhodes.
d.	Received monthly bill for landscaping services, $150.
e.	Paid gas and water utility bill.
f.	Paid landscaping services bill.
g.	Sold merchandise inventory on account to Femi Matthews, $1,500 (cost, $1,250).

For each transaction listed, identify the appropriate function that would be used in QuickBooks. Use the following functions: Invoices, Receive Payments, Enter Bills, Pay Bills.

> Problems **Group A**

All problems can be completed manually or by using either MyAccountingLab General Ledger or QuickBooks.

Learning Objectives 2, 3, 4

Cash Receipts Journal, Accounts Receivable CR column total $12,120

P-25A Using the sales, cash receipts, and general journals

Assume Barton Springs Glass Company uses the perpetual inventory system. The general ledger of Barton Springs Glass Company includes the following selected accounts, along with their account numbers:

Number	Account	Number	Account
11	Cash	19	Land
12	Accounts Receivable	41	Sales Revenue
13	Notes Receivable	42	Sales Discounts
15	Merchandise Inventory	43	Sales Returns and Allowances
16	Office Supplies	51	Cost of Goods Sold
18	Equipment		

All credit sales are on Barton Springs' standard terms of 2/10, n/30. Sales and cash receipts transactions in July were as follows:

Jul. 2	Sold merchandise inventory on credit to Intelysis, Inc., $1,750. Barton Springs' cost of these goods was $600.
3	As an accommodation to a competitor, sold office supplies at cost, $85, receiving cash.
7	Cash sales for the week totaled $1,890 (cost, $1,640).
9	Sold merchandise inventory on account to A. L. Prince, $7,320 (cost, $5,110).
10	Sold land that cost $10,000 for cash of the same amount.
11	Sold merchandise inventory on account to Sloan Electric, $5,100 (cost, $3,520).
12	Received cash from Intelysis in full settlement of its account receivable from July 2.
14	Cash sales for the week were $2,106 (cost, $1,530).
15	Sold merchandise inventory on credit to the partnership of Wilkie & Blinn, $3,650 (cost, $2,260).
18	Received merchandise inventory sold on July 9 to A. L. Prince for $600. The goods shipped were unsatisfactory. These goods cost Barton Springs $440.
20	Sold merchandise inventory on account to Sloan Electric, $620 (cost, $450).
21	Cash sales for the week were $990 (cost, $690).
22	Received $4,000 cash from A. L. Prince in partial settlement of his account receivable. There was no discount.
25	Received cash from Wilkie & Blinn for its account receivable from July 15.
25	Sold merchandise inventory on account to Olsen Co., $1,520 (cost, $1,050).
27	Collected $5,125 on a note receivable. There is no interest.
28	Cash sales for the week totaled $3,774 (cost, $2,460).
29	Sold merchandise inventory on account to R. O. Bankston, $240 (cost, $170).
30	Received merchandise inventory sold on July 25 to Olsen Co. for $40. The cost of these goods was $10.
31	Received $2,720 cash on account from A. L. Prince.

Requirements

1. Use the appropriate journal to record the preceding transactions in a sales journal (omit the Invoice No. column), a cash receipts journal, and a general journal. Barton Springs Glass Company records sales returns and allowances in the general journal.

2. Total each column of the sales journal and the cash receipts journal. Show that total debits equal total credits.

3. Show how postings would be made by writing the account numbers and check marks in the appropriate places in the journals.

Learning Objectives 3, 4

Purchases Journal, Accounts Payable
CR column total $18,950

P-26A Using the purchases, cash payments, and general journals

The general ledger of Crystal Lake Golf Shop includes the following selected accounts, along with their account numbers:

Number	Account	Number	Account
111	Cash	181	Equipment
131	Merchandise Inventory	211	Accounts Payable
161	Prepaid Insurance	564	Rent Expense
171	Office Supplies	583	Utilities Expense

Transactions in December that affected purchases and cash payments follow.

Dec. 2	Purchased merchandise inventory on credit from Timmons, $4,000. Terms were 2/10, n/30.
3	Paid monthly rent, debiting Rent Expense for $2,000.
5	Purchased office supplies on credit terms of 2/10, n/30 from Ross Supply, $450.
8	Received and paid electricity utility bill, $580.
9	Purchased equipment on account from A-1 Equipment, $6,100. Payment terms were net 30.
10	Returned the equipment to A-1 Equipment. It was damaged.
11	Paid Timmons the amount owed on the purchase of December 2.
12	Purchased merchandise inventory on account from Callahan Golf, $4,400. Terms were 3/10, n/30.
13	Purchased merchandise inventory for cash, $650.
14	Paid a semiannual insurance premium, debiting Prepaid Insurance, $1,200.
16	Paid its account payable to Ross Supply, from December 5.
18	Received and paid gas and water utility bills, $190.
21	Purchased merchandise inventory on credit terms of 1/10, n/45 from Dunlop, Inc., $3,900.
21	Paid account payable to Callahan Golf from December 12.
22	Purchased office supplies on account from Office Sales, Inc., $100. Terms were net 30.
26	Returned to Dunlop, Inc. $1,200 of the merchandise inventory purchased on December 21.
31	Paid Dunlop, Inc. the net amount owed from December 21 less the return on December 26.

Requirements

1. Crystal Lake Golf Shop records purchase returns in the general journal. Use the appropriate journal to record the transactions in a purchases journal, a cash payments journal (omit the Check No. column), and a general journal. The company uses the perpetual inventory system.

2. Total each column of the special journals. Show that total debits equal total credits in each special journal.

3. Show how postings would be made from the journals by writing the account numbers and check marks in the appropriate places in the journals.

P-27A Using all journals, posting, and balancing the ledgers

Crestview Computer Security uses the perpetual inventory system and makes all credit sales on terms of 2/10, n/30. Crestview completed the following transactions during May:

Learning Objectives 2, 3, 4

Trial balance, total debits $47,016

May 2	Issued invoice no. 913 for sale on account to K. D. Forbes, $2,000. Crestview's cost of this merchandise inventory was $900.
3	Purchased merchandise inventory on credit terms of 3/10, n/60 from Chicosky Co., $2,467.
5	Sold merchandise inventory for cash, $1,077 (cost, $480).
5	Issued check no. 532 to purchase furniture for cash, $2,185.
8	Collected interest revenue of $1,775.
9	Issued invoice no. 914 for sale on account to Bell Co., $5,550 (cost, $2,310).
10	Purchased merchandise inventory for cash, $1,143, issuing check no. 533.
12	Received cash from K. D. Forbes in full settlement of her account receivable from the sale on May 2.
13	Issued check no. 534 to pay Chicosky Co. the net amount owed from May 3. Round to the nearest dollar.
13	Purchased office supplies on account from Manley, Inc., $441. Terms were n/EOM.
15	Sold merchandise inventory on account to M. O. Brown, issuing invoice no. 915 for $665 (cost, $240).
17	Issued credit memo to M. O. Brown for $665 for merchandise inventory returned by Brown. Also accounted for receipt of the merchandise inventory at cost.
18	Issued invoice no. 916 for credit sale to K. D. Forbes, $357 (cost, $127).
19	Received $5,439 from Bell Co. in full settlement of its account receivable from May 9. Bell earned a discount by paying early.
20	Purchased merchandise inventory on credit terms of net 30 from Sims Distributing, $2,047.
22	Purchased furniture on credit terms of 3/10, n/60 from Chicosky Co., $645.
22	Issued check no. 535 to pay for insurance coverage, debiting Prepaid Insurance for $1,000.
24	Sold office supplies to an employee for cash of $54, which was Crestview's cost.
25	Received bill and issued check no. 536 to pay utilities, $453.
28	Purchased merchandise inventory on credit terms of 2/10, n/30 from Manley, Inc., $675.
29	Returned damaged merchandise inventory to Manley, Inc., issuing a debit memo for $675.
29	Sold merchandise inventory on account to Bell Co., issuing invoice no. 917 for $2,900 (cost, $800).
30	Issued check no. 537 to pay Manley, Inc. in full on account from May 13 purchase.
31	Received cash in full from K. D. Forbes on credit sale of May 18. There was no discount.
31	Issued check no. 538 to pay monthly salaries of $1,950.

Requirements

1. Open four-column general ledger accounts using Crestview's account numbers and balances as of May 1, 2014 that follow. All accounts have normal balances.

Number	Account	Bal.
111	Cash	$ 15,850
112	Accounts Receivable	1,500
114	Merchandise Inventory	6,000
116	Office Supplies	500
117	Prepaid Insurance	0
151	Furniture	2,000
211	Accounts Payable	800
311	Powell, Capital	21,350
411	Sales Revenue	7,000
412	Sales Discounts	0
413	Sales Returns and Allowances	0
419	Interest Revenue	850
511	Cost of Goods Sold	2,250
531	Salaries Expense	1,500
541	Utilities Expense	400

2. Open four-column accounts in the subsidiary ledgers with beginning balance as of May 1, if any: Accounts receivable ledger—Alan Co., $1,500; Bell Co., $0; M. O. Brown, $0; and K. D. Forbes, $0. Accounts payable ledger—Chicosky Co., $0; Manley, Inc., $0; Sims Distributing, $0; Yellow Co., $800.

3. Enter the transactions in a sales journal (page 7), a cash receipts journal (page 5), a purchases journal (page 10), a cash payments journal (page 8), and a general journal (page 6), as appropriate.

4. Post daily to the accounts receivable subsidiary ledger and to the accounts payable subsidiary ledger.

5. Total each column of the special journals. Show that total debits equal total credits in each special journal. On May 31, post to the general ledger.

6. Prepare a trial balance as of May 31, 2014, to verify the equality of the general ledger. Balance the total of the customer balances in the accounts receivable subsidiary ledger against Accounts Receivable in the general ledger. Do the same for the accounts payable subsidiary ledger and Accounts Payable in the general ledger.

P-28A Using all journals, posting, and balancing the ledgers

Learning Objectives 2, 3, 4

Trial balance, total debits $87,127

Soccer Shots uses the perpetual inventory system and makes all credit sales on terms of 2/10, n/30. Soccer Shots completed the following transactions during November:

Nov. 1	Owner contributed $40,000 in exchange for capital.
1	Purchased merchandise inventory on credit terms of 2/15, n/60 from Smith Co., $5,400.
3	Issued invoice no. 1001 for sale on account to Heather Stokes, $4,400. Soccer Shot's cost of this merchandise inventory was $1,980.
3	Collected interest revenue of $3,900.
4	Issued invoice no. 1002 for sale on account to Bookmyer Co., $3,400 (cost, $2,300).
8	Issued check no. 900 to purchase equipment for cash, $4,800.
9	Sold merchandise inventory for cash, $2,300 (cost, $1,500).
10	Received cash from Heather Stokes in full settlement of her account receivable from the sale on Nov. 3. Stokes earned a discount by paying early.
11	Purchased merchandise inventory for cash, $5,500, issuing check no. 901.
11	Purchased office supplies on account from Jordan, Inc., $900. Terms were n/EOM.
13	Issued check no. 902 to pay Smith Co. the net amount owed from Nov. 1. Round to the nearest dollar.
14	Issued invoice no. 1003 for credit sale to Heather Stokes, $357 (cost, $127).
15	Issued credit memo to Bookmyer Co. for $600 for merchandise inventory returned by Bookmyer. Also accounted for receipt of the merchandise inventory at cost, $540.
16	Sold merchandise inventory on account to Robert Mysse, issuing invoice no. 1004 for $665 (cost, $240).
17	Received cash from Bookmyer Co. in full settlement of its account receivable from Nov. 4, less return.
17	Purchased merchandise inventory on credit terms of net 30 from Smith Co., $4,500.
19	Issued check no. 903 to pay for insurance coverage, debiting Prepaid Insurance for $2,000.
20	Purchased equipment on credit terms of 3/10, n/60 from Hildebrand Co., $1,430.
22	Returned damaged merchandise inventory to Smith Co., issuing a debit memo for $500.
22	Purchased merchandise inventory on credit terms of 2/10, n/30 from Smith Co., $675.
25	Issued check no. 904 to pay utilities, $453.
27	Issued check no. 905 to pay Smith Co., in full on account from Nov. 17 purchase, less return.
30	Issued check no. 906 to pay monthly salaries of $4,200.
30	Received cash in full from Heather Stokes on credit sale of Nov. 14. There was no discount.
30	Issued check no. 907 to pay Jordan, Inc. in full on account from Nov. 11 purchase.

Requirements

1. Open the following four-column accounts using the Soccer Shots account numbers and balances as of November 1, 2014 as follows:

Number	Account	Bal.	Number	Account	Bal.
111	Cash	$ 12,450	411	Sales Revenue	$ 6,000
112	Accounts Receivable	2,250	412	Sales Discounts	0
114	Merchandise Inventory	6,500	413	Sales Returns and Allowances	0
116	Office Supplies	450	419	Interest Revenue	1,200
117	Prepaid Insurance	0	511	Cost of Goods Sold	3,600
151	Equipment	1,000	531	Salaries Expense	3,500
211	Accounts Payable	600	541	Utilities Expense	250
311	Golden, Capital	22,200			

2. Open four-column accounts in the subsidiary ledgers with beginning balances as of November 1, if any: Accounts receivable ledger—Adam Co., $2,250; Bookmyer Co., $0; Robert Mysse, $0; and Heather Stokes, $0. Accounts payable ledger—Hildebrand Co., $0; Jordan, Inc., $0; Smith Co., $0; and Zebra Co., $600.

3. Enter the transactions in a sales journal (page 10), a cash receipts journal (page 8), a purchases journal (page 13), a cash payments journal (page 12), and a general journal (page 9), as appropriate.

4. Post daily to the accounts receivable subsidiary ledger and to the accounts payable subsidiary ledger.

5. Total each column of the special journals. Show that total debits equal total credits in each special journal. On November 30, post to the general ledger.

6. Prepare a trial balance at November 30, 2014, to verify the equality of the general ledger. Balance the total of the customer balances in the accounts receivable subsidiary ledger against Accounts Receivable in the general ledger. Do the same for the accounts payable subsidiary ledger and Accounts Payable in the general ledger.

> Problems **Group B**

All problems can be completed manually or by using either MyAccountingLab General Ledger or QuickBooks.

Learning Objectives 2, 3, 4

Cash Receipts Journal, Accounts Receivable CR column total $4,410

P-29B Using the sales, cash receipts, and general journals

Assume the company uses the perpetual inventory system. The general ledger of Suds Soap Company includes the following selected accounts, along with their account numbers:

Number	Account	Number	Account
11	Cash	19	Land
12	Accounts Receivable	41	Sales Revenue
13	Notes Receivable	42	Sales Discounts
15	Merchandise Inventory	43	Sales Returns and Allowances
16	Office Supplies	51	Cost of Goods Sold
18	Equipment		

All credit sales are on Suds' standard terms of 2/10, n/30. Sales and cash receipts transactions in November were as follows:

Nov. 2	Sold merchandise inventory on credit to Bob Thornton, $800. Suds' cost of these goods was $310.
6	As an accommodation to another company, sold new equipment for its cost of $770, receiving cash for this amount.
6	Cash sales for the week totaled $2,100 (cost, $1,360).
8	Sold merchandise inventory to McNair Co. on account, $2,830 (cost, $1,780).
9	Sold land that cost $22,000 for cash of $22,000.
11	Sold merchandise inventory on account to Nickerson Supply, $1,500 (cost, $800).
11	Received cash from Bob Thornton in full settlement of his account receivable from November 2.
13	Cash sales for the week were $1,900 (cost, $1,200).
15	Sold merchandise inventory on credit to Montez and Montez, $900 (cost, $500).
18	Received merchandise inventory from McNair Co. as a sales return, $120. The goods shipped were unsatisfactory. These goods cost Suds $70.
19	Sold merchandise inventory to Nickerson Supply on account, $3,900 (cost, $2,610).
20	Cash sales for the week were $2,330 (cost, $1,570).
21	Received $1,200 cash from McNair Co. in partial settlement of its account receivable. There was no discount.
22	Received cash from Montez and Montez for its account receivable from November 15.
22	Sold merchandise inventory on account to Diamond Co., $2,000 (cost, $1,300).
25	Collected $4,200 on a note receivable. There was no interest.
27	Cash sales for the week totaled $2,900 (cost, $1,900).
27	Sold merchandise inventory on account to Littleton Corporation, $600 (cost, $230).
28	Received merchandise inventory from Diamond Co. as a sales return, $680. The cost of these goods was $390.
30	Received $1,510 cash on account from McNair Co. There was no discount.

Requirements

1. Use the appropriate journal to record the preceding transactions in a sales journal (omit the Invoice No. column), a cash receipts journal, and a general journal. Record sales returns and allowances in the general journal.

2. Total each column of the sales journal and the cash receipts journal. Determine that total debits equal total credits.

3. Show how postings would be made from the journals by writing the account numbers and check marks in the appropriate places in the journals.

Learning Objectives 3, 4

Purchases Journal, Accounts Payable
CR column total $8,960

P-30B Using the purchases, cash payments, and general journals

The general ledger of British Car Specialists includes the following selected accounts, along with their account numbers:

Number	Account	Number	Account
111	Cash	181	Equipment
131	Merchandise Inventory	211	Accounts Payable
161	Prepaid Insurance	564	Rent Expense
171	Office Supplies	583	Utilities Expense

Transactions in January that affected purchases and cash payments were as follows:

Jan. 2	Paid monthly rent, debiting Rent Expense for $900.
5	Purchased merchandise inventory on credit from Sylvania Co., $5,000. Terms were 2/15, n/45.
6	Purchased office supplies on credit terms of 2/10, n/30 from Harmon Sales, $800.
7	Received and paid utility bills, $400.
10	Purchased equipment on account from Lancer Co., $1,050. Payment terms were 2/10, n/30.
11	Returned the equipment to Lancer Co. It was defective.
12	Paid Sylvania Co. the amount owed on the purchase of January 5.
12	Purchased merchandise inventory on account from Lancer Co., $1,100. Terms were 2/10, n/30.
14	Purchased merchandise inventory for cash, $1,585.
15	Paid an insurance premium, debiting Prepaid Insurance, $2,410.
17	Received and paid electricity utility bill, $165.
19	Paid account payable to Harmon Sales, from January 6.
20	Paid account payable to Lancer Co., from January 12.
21	Purchased office supplies on account from Master Supply, $110. Terms were net 30.
22	Purchased merchandise inventory on credit terms of 1/10, n/30 from Linz Brothers, $900.
26	Returned merchandise inventory purchased for $500 on January 22, to Linz Brothers.
31	Paid Linz Brothers the net amount owed from January 22, less the return on January 26.

Requirements

1. Use the appropriate journal to record the preceding transactions in a purchases journal, a cash payments journal (omit the Check No. column), and a general journal. British Car Specialists records purchase returns in the general journal. The company uses the perpetual inventory system.

2. Total each column of the special journals. Show that total debits equal total credits in each special journal.

3. Show how postings would be made from the journals by writing the account numbers and check marks in the appropriate places in the journals.

P-31B Using all journals, posting, and balancing the ledgers

Learning Objectives 2, 3, 4

Trial balance, total debits $49,420

Prudhoe Bay Co. uses the perpetual inventory system and makes all credit sales on terms of 2/10, n/30. During March, Prudhoe Bay Co. completed these transactions:

Mar. 2	Issued invoice no. 191 for sale on account to L. E. Wooten, $2,350. Prudhoe Bay's cost of this merchandise inventory was $1,390.
3	Purchased merchandise inventory on credit terms of 3/10, n/60 from Delwood Plaza, $5,900.
4	Sold merchandise inventory for cash, $3,410 (cost, $1,820).
5	Issued check no. 473 to purchase furniture for cash $1,080.
8	Collected interest revenue of $120.
9	Issued invoice no. 192 for sale on account to Cortez Co., $6,250 (cost, $3,300).
10	Purchased merchandise inventory for cash, $770, issuing check no. 474.
12	Received $2,303 cash from L. E. Wooten in full settlement of her account receivable, net of the discount, from the sale of March 2.
13	Issued check no. 475 to pay Delwood Plaza net amount owed from March 3.
13	Purchased office supplies on account from Havrilla Corp., $680. Terms were n/EOM.
15	Sold merchandise inventory on account to J. R. Wakeland, issuing invoice no. 193 for $740 (cost, $410).
17	Issued credit memo to J. R. Wakeland for $740 for defective merchandise inventory returned by Wakeland. Also accounted for receipt of the merchandise inventory at cost.
18	Issued invoice no. 194 for credit sale to L. E. Wooten, $1,825 (cost, $970).
19	Received $6,125 from Cortez Co. in full settlement of its account receivable from March 9.
20	Purchased merchandise inventory on credit terms of net 30 from Jasper Sales, $2,150.
22	Purchased furniture on credit terms of 3/10, n/60 from Delwood Plaza, $775.
22	Issued check no. 476 to pay for insurance coverage, debiting Prepaid Insurance for $1,345.
24	Sold office supplies to an employee for cash of $80, which was Prudhoe Bay's cost.
25	Received bill and issued check no. 477 to pay utilities, $380.
28	Purchased merchandise inventory on credit terms of 2/10, n/30 from Havrilla Corp., $420.
29	Returned damaged merchandise inventory to Havrilla Corp., issuing a debit memo for $420.
29	Sold merchandise inventory on account to Cortez Co., issuing invoice no. 195 for $1,800 (cost, $1,000).
30	Issued check no. 478 to pay Havrilla Corp. on account from March 13 purchase.
31	Received cash in full from L. E. Wooten on credit sale of March 18. There was no discount.
31	Issued check no. 479 to pay monthly salaries of $1,100.

Requirements

1. Open four-column general ledger accounts using Prudhoe Bay Co.'s account numbers and balances as of March 1, 2014 that follow.

Number	Account	Bal.
111	Cash	$ 10,190
112	Accounts Receivable	2,100
114	Merchandise Inventory	8,400
116	Office Supplies	700
117	Prepaid Insurance	0
151	Furniture	2,800
211	Accounts Payable	1,120
311	Simmons, Capital	17,890
411	Sales Revenue	9,800
412	Sales Discounts	0
413	Sales Returns and Allowances	0
419	Interest Revenue	1,190
511	Cost of Goods Sold	3,150
531	Salaries Expense	2,100
541	Utilities Expense	560

2. Open four-column accounts in the subsidiary ledgers with beginning balances as of March 1, if any. Accounts receivable ledger: Black Co., $2,100; Cortez Co., $0; J. R. Wakeland, $0; and L. E. Wooten, $0. Accounts payable ledger: Delwood Plaza, $0; Havrilla Corp, $0; Jasper Sales, $0; and Patton Co., $1,120.

3. Enter the transactions in a sales journal (page 8), a cash receipts journal (page 3), a purchases journal (page 6), a cash payments journal (page 9), and a general journal (page 4), as appropriate.

4. Post daily to the accounts receivable subsidiary ledger and to the accounts payable subsidiary ledger.

5. Total each column of the special journals. Show that total debits equal total credits in each special journal. On March 31, post to the general ledger.

6. Prepare a trial balance as of March 31, 2014, to verify the equality of the general ledger. Balance the total of the customer account balances in the accounts receivable ledger against Accounts Receivable in the general ledger. Do the same for the accounts payable ledger and Accounts Payable in the general ledger.

P-32B Using all journals, posting, and balancing the ledgers

Soccer Kicks uses the perpetual inventory system and makes all credit sales on terms of 2/10, n/30. Soccer Kicks completed the following transactions during April:

Learning Objectives 2, 3, 4

Trial balance, total debits $103,544

Apr. 1	Owner contributed $48,000 in exchange for capital.
1	Purchased merchandise inventory on credit terms of 2/15, n/60 from Star Co., $6,480.
3	Issued invoice no. 1001 for sale on account to Henrietta Smith, $5,280. Soccer Kicks' cost of this merchandise inventory was $2,376.
3	Collected interest revenue of $4,680.
4	Issued invoice no. 1002 for sale on account to Black Co., $4,080 (cost, $2,760).
8	Issued check no. 900 to purchase equipment for cash, $5,760.
9	Sold merchandise inventory for cash, $2,760 (cost, $1,800).
10	Received cash from Henrietta Smith in full settlement of her account receivable from the sale on Apr. 3. Smith earned a discount by paying early.
11	Purchased merchandise inventory for cash, $6,600, issuing check no. 901.
11	Purchased office supplies on account from Jackson, Inc., $1,080. Terms were n/EOM.
13	Issued check no. 902 to pay Star Co. the net amount owed from Apr. 1. Round to the nearest dollar.
14	Issued invoice no. 1003 for credit sale to Henrietta Smith, $420 (cost, $156).
15	Issued credit memo to Black Co. for $720 for merchandise inventory returned by Black. Also accounted for receipt of the merchandise inventory at cost, $648.
16	Sold merchandise inventory on account to Richard Munoz, issuing invoice no. 1004 for $798 (cost, $288).
17	Received cash from Black Co. in full settlement of its account receivable from Apr. 4, less return.
17	Purchased merchandise inventory on credit terms of net 30 from Star Co., $5,400.
19	Issued check no. 903 to pay for insurance coverage, debiting Prepaid Insurance for $2,400.
20	Purchased equipment on credit terms of 3/10, n/60 from Heavens Co., $1,716.
22	Returned damaged merchandise inventory to Star Co., issuing a debit memo for $600.
22	Purchased merchandise inventory on credit terms of 2/10, n/30 from Star Co., $810.
25	Issued check no. 904 to pay utilities, $540.
27	Issued check no. 905 to pay Star Co., in full on account from Apr. 17, less return.
30	Issued check no. 906 to pay monthly salaries of $5,040.
30	Received cash in full from Henrietta Smith on credit sale of Apr. 14. There was no discount.
30	Issued check no. 907 to pay Jackson, Inc. in full on account from Apr. 11 purchase.

Requirements

1. Open the following four-column accounts using the Soccer Kicks account numbers and balances as of April 1 as follows:

Number	Account	Bal.
111	Cash	$ 10,430
112	Accounts Receivable	3,150
114	Merchandise Inventory	9,100
116	Office Supplies	630
117	Prepaid Insurance	0
151	Equipment	1,400
211	Accounts Payable	840
311	Schuman, Capital	24,080
411	Sales Revenue	8,400
412	Sales Discounts	0
413	Sales Returns and Allowances	0
419	Interest Revenue	1,680
511	Cost of Goods Sold	5,040
531	Salaries Expense	4,900
541	Utilities Expense	350

2. Open four-column accounts in the subsidiary ledgers with beginning balances as of April 1, if any: Accounts receivable ledger—Allen Co., $3,150; Black Co., $0; Richard Munoz, $0; and Henrietta Smith, $0. Accounts payable ledger—Heavens Co., $0; Jackson, Inc., $0; Star Co., $0; and Williams Co., $840.

3. Enter the transactions in a sales journal (page 10), a cash receipts journal (page 8), a purchases journal (page 13), a cash payments journal (page 12), and a general journal (page 9), as appropriate.

4. Post daily to the accounts receivable subsidiary ledger and to the accounts payable subsidiary ledger.

5. Total each column of the special journals. Show that total debits equal total credits in each special journal. On April 30, post to the general ledger.

6. Prepare a trial balance as of April 30, 2014, to verify the equality of the general ledger. Balance the total of the customer balances in the accounts receivable subsidiary ledger against Accounts Receivable in the general ledger. Do the same for the accounts payable subsidiary ledger and Accounts Payable in the general ledger.

> Continuing Problem

P-33 Using all journals

This problem continues the Davis Consulting situation from Problem P-46. Davis
Consulting performs systems consulting. Davis has also begun selling accounting
software and uses the perpetual inventory system to account for software inventory.
During January, Davis completed the following transactions:

Jan. 2	Completed a consulting engagement and received cash of $7,800.
2	Prepaid three months office rent, $1,650.
7	Purchased 80 units software inventory on account from Mraz Co., $1,680, plus freight in, $80.
18	Sold 40 software units on account to Jason Nathanson, $3,500 (cost, $880).
19	Consulted with a client, Louis Fitzgerald, for a fee of $1,000 on account. (Use general journal.)
20	Paid employee salaries, $2,055. Assume there is no accrued salaries payable.
21	Paid Mraz Co. on account, $1,760. There was no discount.
22	Purchased 240 units software inventory on account from White Co., $6,240.
24	Received bill and paid utilities, $250.
28	Sold 120 units software for cash, $4,680 (cost, $2,960).
31	Recorded the following adjusting entries: a. Accrued salaries expense, $686 b. Depreciation, $100 (Equipment, $30; Furniture, $70) c. Expiration of prepaid rent, $550 d. Physical count of software inventory, 145 units, $3,770

Davis Consulting had the following selected accounts with account numbers:

Number	Account	Number	Account
111	Cash	411	Sales Revenue
112	Accounts Receivable	412	Sales Discounts
114	Software Inventory	419	Service Revenue
116	Office Supplies	511	Cost of Goods Sold
117	Prepaid Rent	531	Salaries Expense
171	Accumulated Depreciation—Equipment	541	Utilities Expense
181	Accumulated Depreciation—Furniture	551	Depreciation Expense—Equipment
211	Accounts Payable	561	Depreciation Expense—Furniture
212	Salaries Payable	571	Rent Expense

Requirements

1. Use the appropriate journal to record the preceding transactions in a sales journal (omit the Invoice No. column), a cash receipts journal, a purchases journal, a cash payments journal (omit the Check No. column), and a general journal.

2. Total each column of the special journals. Show that total debits equal total credits in each special journal.

3. Show how postings would be made from the journals by writing the account numbers and check marks in the appropriate places in the journals.

> Practice Set

P-34 Using all journals

Shine King Cleaning has decided that, in addition to providing cleaning services, it will sell cleaning products. Shine King uses the perpetual inventory system. During December 2015, Shine King completed the following transactions:

Dec. 2	Purchased 600 units of inventory for $3,600 on account from Sparkle, Co. on terms 3/10, n/20.
5	Purchased 400 units of inventory from Borax on account with terms 4/5, n/30. The total invoice was for $3,200, which included a $200 freight charge.
7	Returned 100 units of inventory to Sparkle from the December 2 purchase (cost, $600).
9	Paid Borax.
11	Sold 350 units of goods to Happy Maids for $4,900 on account on terms 5/10, n/30. Shine King's cost of the goods was $2,100.
12	Paid Sparkle.
15	Received 30 units with a retail price of $420 of goods back from customer Happy Maids. The goods cost Shine King $180.
21	Received payment from Happy Maids, settling the amount due in full.
28	Sold 200 units of goods to Bridget, Inc. for cash of $3,000 (cost, $1,144).
29	Received bill and paid cash for utilities of $350.
30	Paid cash for Sales Commission Expense of $225.
31	Recorded the following adjusting entries: a. Physical count of inventory on December 31 showed 330 units of goods on hand, $2,541 b. Depreciation, $170 c. Accrued salaries expense of $700 d. Prepared all other adjustments necessary for December Assume cleaning supplies at December 31 are $50.

Shine King Cleaning had the following selected accounts with account numbers:

Number	Account	Number	Account
111	Cash	412	Sales Discounts
112	Accounts Receivable	413	Sales Returns and Allowances
114	Merchandise Inventory	419	Service Revenue
116	Office Supplies	511	Cost of Goods Sold
117	Prepaid Rent	531	Salaries Expense
118	Prepaid Insurance	541	Utilities Expense
171	Accumulated Depreciation	551	Depreciation Expense
211	Accounts Payable	561	Insurance Expense
212	Salaries Payable	571	Rent Expense
213	Unearned Revenue	581	Sales Commission Expense
214	Interest Payable	591	Interest Expense
411	Sales Revenue		

Requirements

1. Use the appropriate journal to record the preceding transactions in a sales journal (omit the Invoice No. column), a cash receipts journal, a purchases journal, a cash payments journal (omit the Check No. column), and a general journal.

2. Total each column of the special journals. Show that total debits equal total credits in each special journal.

3. Show how postings would be made from the journals by writing the account numbers and check marks in the appropriate places in the journals.

CRITICAL THINKING

> Decision Cases

Decision Case 1

A fire destroyed certain accounting records of Golden Books. The owner, Marilyn Golden, asks your help in reconstructing the records. All of the sales are on account, with credit terms of 2/10, n/30. All cash receipts on account reached the store within the 10-day discount period, except as noted. The only accounting record preserved from the fire is the accounts receivable subsidiary ledger, which follows.

Garcia Sales

Date	Post. Ref.	Debit	Credit	Balance Debit	Balance Credit
Apr. 1				450	
3	CR.8		450	0	
25	S.6	3,600		3,600	
29	S.6	1,100		4,700	

Leewright, Inc.

Date	Post. Ref.	Debit	Credit	Balance Debit	Balance Debit
Apr. 1				2,800	
15	S.6	2,600		5,400	
29	CR.8		1,500*	3,900	

*Cash receipt did not occur within the discount period.

Sally Jones

Date	Post. Ref.	Debit	Credit	Balance Debit	Balance Debit
Apr. 1				1,100	
5	CR.8		1,100	0	
11	S.6	400		400	
21	CR.8		400	0	
24	S.6	2,000		2,000	

Jacques LeHavre

Date	Post. Ref.	Debit	Credit	Balance Debit	Balance Debit
Apr. 1				0	
8	S.6	2,400		2,400	
16	S.6	900		3,300	
18	CR.8		2,400	900	
19	J.5		200	700	
27	CR.8		700	0	

Requirements

1. Determine the beginning and ending balances of Accounts Receivable.

2. Determine the sales on account in the month of April.

3. Determine total cash receipts on account from customers during April.

Decision Case 2

MicroData Solutions sells cutting-edge networking software. MicroData's quality control officer estimates that 20% of the company's sales and purchases of merchandise inventory are returned for additional debugging. The company uses the perpetual inventory system. MicroData needs special journals for:

- Sales returns and allowances

- Purchase returns and allowances

Design the two special journals. For each special journal, include a column for the appropriate business document (credit memo or debit memo).

> Ethical Issue 1

On a recent trip to Africa, J. T. Brown, sales manager of Prompt Technology, took his wife along at company expense. Linda White, vice president of sales and Brown's boss, thought his travel and entertainment expenses seemed excessive. But White approved the reimbursement because she owed Brown a favor. White was aware that the company president reviews all expenses recorded in the cash payments journal, so White recorded Brown's wife's expenses in the *general* journal as follows:

Date	Accounts and Explanation	Debit	Credit
	Sales Promotion Expense	9,100	
	Cash		9,100

Requirements

1. Does recording the transaction in the *general* journal rather than in the cash payments journal affect the amounts of cash and total expenses reported in the financial statements?

2. Why did White record these expenses in the *general* journal?

3. What is the ethical issue in this situation? What role does accounting play in this issue?

> Fraud Case 1

Didrikson Rubin, the auditor of Red Barn Farm Equipment, was verifying cash payments to vendors for the past several months. She noticed that several checks had been paid to a specific vendor, but she couldn't find a record of the transaction in the computerized system. Didrikson suspects that an employee is issuing checks to a fictitious "vendor" and then deleting the transactions from the computerized system. How might Didrikson investigate the suspected fraud?

> Team Project 1

Ace Moving is considering investing in an entry-level computerized accounting information system. Ace needs a system that can record customer invoices and receipts. In addition, it would like to track all of its bills and cash payments. As a team, investigate the two common entry-level accounting software products: QuickBooks and Sage 50 Accounting. Prepare a PowerPoint presentation that summarizes the similarities and differences between the two software systems.

> Communication Activity 1

In 150 words or fewer, explain what an accounting information system is and describe an effective system.

Try It! Solutions

1. c

2. e

3. b

4. a

5. d

6. Evenson Co. should use the sales journal. The $300 should be recorded in the Accounts Receivable DR, Sales Revenue CR column.

7. Fiscella Co. should use the cash payments journal. The $2,000 should be recorded in the Cash CR column and the Other Accounts DR column. Rent Expense should be listed in the Account Debited column.

8. **a.** Software

   b. network

   c. Hardware

> Quick Check Answers

1. c **2.** a **3.** b **4.** c **5.** b **6.** c **7.** a **8.** a **9.** d

Glossary

Accounting Information System (AIS). A system that collects, records, stores, and processes accounting data to produce information that is useful for decision makers.

Accounts Payable Subsidiary Ledger. A subsidiary ledger that includes an accounts payable account for each vendor that contains detailed information such as the amount purchased, paid, and owed.

Accounts Receivable Subsidiary Ledger. A subsidiary ledger that includes an accounts receivable account for each customer that contains detailed information such as the amount purchased, paid, and owed.

Cash Payments Journal. Special journal used to record cash payments by check and currency.

Cash Receipts Journal. Special journal used to record cash receipts.

Cloud Computing. Software and data are stored on a third-party server instead of by the business and are accessed by employees via the Internet.

Control Account. An account whose balance equals the sum of the balances in a group of related accounts in a subsidiary ledger.

Enterprise Resource Planning. Software systems that can integrate all of a company's functions, departments, and data into a single system.

Hardware. Electronic equipment that includes computers, monitors, printers, and the network that connects them.

Network. The system of electronic linkages that allows different computers to share the same information.

Purchases Journal. Special journal used to record all purchases of merchandise inventory, office supplies, and other assets on account.

Sales Journal. Special journal used to record credit sales.

Server. The main computer where data is stored, which can be accessed from many different computers.

Software. Set of programs or instructions that drives the computer to perform the work desired.

Source Document. Provides the evidence and data for accounting transactions.

Special Journal. An accounting journal designed to record one specific type of transaction.

Subsidiary Ledger. Record of accounts that provides supporting details on individual balances, the total of which appears in a general ledger account.

Photo Credits

Credits are listed in order of appearance.

Photo 1 (top): Vincent Pen/Fotolia
Photo 2 (middle): Zhukov Oleg/Shutterstock
Photo 3 (bottom): Volff/Fotolia
Photo 4: Nat Ulrich/Shutterstock
Photo 5: Djama/Fotolia

Internal Control and Cash

From Chapter 8 of *Horngren's Accounting*, Tenth edition. Tracie Nobles, Brenda Mattison, Ella Mae Matsumura. Copyright © 2014 by Pearson Education, Inc. All rights reserved.

Internal Control and Cash

Where Did the Cash Go?

Andrew Goard, owner of a sports-themed restaurant located in Brentwood, California, stared at the bank statement on his desk. The business recently experienced record-breaking revenue due to increased customer traffic and expanded menu and drink offerings. Andrew knew that the expenses of the business had also increased, but he had expected the cash in the business's checking account to increase, not decrease, as the bank statement was showing.

Andrew wondered if it was possible that one of his employees was stealing money from the cash register. He really liked all of his employees and didn't think that any of them would steal from the business. But the deposits on the bank statement from customer sales just didn't make sense. Given the increased sales, the cash deposits should have been much higher.

As the owner of the restaurant, Andrew knew that it was his responsibility to ensure that procedures were put into place to be sure the security of cash and other assets of the business. He had thought that completing employee background checks was enough to prevent the theft of the business's assets, but he now suspected that further controls needed to be put into place. Andrew began by reviewing the bank statement and comparing it to the cash records on hand. In doing this, he identified that cash was indeed being stolen from the business by the employee who was responsible for making the daily cash deposits. Andrew realized, though, that it wasn't enough to fire the employee responsible; he needed to put into place security measures that would decrease the likelihood of employee theft happening again.

What Are Internal Controls?

Safeguarding and securing assets should be a concern of all businesses—no matter how small or large the business is. The procedures that businesses put into place to protect assets are called *internal controls* and are a key management responsibility. For example, Buffalo Wild Wings Grill & Bar, a New York–style wing restaurant chain that offers a sports bar atmosphere and a full menu featuring everything from salads to wings, must assure its investors and owners that proper controls have been put into place to protect assets, promote operational efficiency, and ensure accurate and reliable accounting records. In this chapter, we look at the policies and procedures that companies such as Buffalo Wild Wings would use to fulfill this responsibility.

Learning Objectives

1 Define internal control and describe the components of internal control and control procedures

2 Apply internal controls to cash receipts

3 Apply internal controls to cash payments

4 Explain and journalize petty cash transactions

5 Demonstrate the use of a bank account as a control device and prepare a bank reconciliation and related journal entries

6 Use the cash ratio to evaluate business performance

WHAT IS INTERNAL CONTROL AND HOW CAN IT BE USED TO PROTECT A COMPANY'S ASSETS?

Learning Objective 1
Define internal control and describe the components of internal control and control procedures

Internal Control
The organizational plan and all the related measures adopted by an entity to safeguard assets, encourage employees to follow company policies, promote operational efficiency, and ensure accurate and reliable accounting records.

A key responsibility of a business manager is to control operations. Owners set goals, hire managers to lead the way, and hire employees to carry out the business plan. Internal control is the organizational plan and all the related measures designed to accomplish the following:

1. **Safeguard assets.** A company must protect its assets; otherwise it is throwing away resources. If you fail to safeguard cash, the most liquid of assets, it will quickly slip away.

2. **Encourage employees to follow company policies.** Everyone in an organization needs to work toward the same goals. It is important for a business to identify policies to help meet the company's goals. These policies are also important for the company to ensure that all customers are treated similarly and that results can be measured effectively.

3. **Promote operational efficiency.** Businesses cannot afford to waste resources. Business owners and employees work hard to make sales and do not want to waste any of the benefits. Promoting operational efficiency reduces expenses and increases business profits.

4. **Ensure accurate, reliable accounting records.** Accurate, reliable accounting records are essential. Without reliable records, owners and managers cannot tell which part of the business is profitable and which part needs improvement. A business could be losing money on every product sold and not realize it—unless it keeps good records for the cost of its products.

Internal Control and the Sarbanes-Oxley Act

Public Company
A company that sells its stock to the general public.

How critical are internal controls for public companies? They are so important that the U.S. Congress passed a law requiring a public company—one that sells its stock to the general public—to maintain a system of internal controls.

The Enron Corporation and WorldCom accounting scandals rocked the United States in the early years of this millennium. Enron overstated profits and went out of business almost overnight. WorldCom reported expenses as assets and overstated both profits and assets. The same accounting firm, Arthur Andersen LLP, had audited both companies' financial statements. Arthur Andersen voluntarily closed its doors in 2002 after nearly 90 years in public accounting.

As the scandals unfolded, many people asked, "How could this happen? Where were the auditors?" To address public concern, Congress passed the Sarbanes-Oxley Act, abbreviated as SOX. This act requires companies to review internal control and take responsibility for the accuracy and completeness of their financial reports. SOX revamped corporate governance in the United States and affected the accounting profession. Here are some of the SOX provisions:

1. Public companies must issue an internal control report, which is a report by management describing its responsibility for and the adequacy of internal controls over financial reporting. Additionally, an outside auditor must evaluate the client's internal controls and report on the internal controls as part of the audit report.
2. A new body, the Public Company Accounting Oversight Board (PCAOB), oversees the work of auditors of public companies.
3. Accounting firms are not allowed to audit a public company and also provide certain consulting services for the same client.
4. Stiff penalties await violators—25 years in prison for securities fraud and 20 years for an executive making false sworn statements.

The Sarbanes-Oxley Act changed the rules for auditors, limiting what services they can perform in addition to the audit and requiring a report on the internal controls of each public company audited. How does a business achieve good internal control? The next section identifies the components of internal control.

The Components of Internal Control

A business can achieve its internal control objectives by addressing five components listed below:

- **C**ontrol procedures
- **R**isk assessment
- **I**nformation system
- **M**onitoring of controls
- **E**nvironment

You can remember the five components of internal control by using the acronym CRIME.

Control Procedures

Control procedures are designed to ensure that the business's goals are achieved. The next section, "Internal Control Procedures," discusses internal control procedures.

Risk Assessment

A company must identify its risks. For example, food manufacturers face the risk that their food products may harm people; airplane carrier businesses face the possibility that planes may crash; music companies face copyright infringement risks; and all companies face the risk of bankruptcy. Companies facing difficulties might be tempted to falsify their financial statements to make themselves look better than they really are. As part of the internal control system, the company's business risk, as well as the risk concerning individual accounts, must be assessed. The higher the risk, the more controls a company must put in place to safeguard its assets.

Information System

As we have seen, the information system is critical. Controls must be in place within the information system to ensure that only authorized users have access to various parts

Sarbanes-Oxley Act (SOX)
Requires companies to review internal control and take responsibility for the accuracy and completeness of their financial reports.

Internal Control Report
A report by management describing its responsibility for and the adequacy of internal controls over financial reporting.

IFRS

To be IFRS compliant, foreign companies are not required to issue an internal control report or have their internal controls audited by outside auditors. While all companies have internal controls, foreign companies do not have the added expense of an audit of their internal controls. On the other hand, readers of the financial reports of foreign companies have no assurance that the controls are effective.

Internal Auditor
An employee of the business who ensures the company's employees are following company policies, that the company meets all legal requirements, and that operations are running efficiently.

External Auditor
An outside accountant, completely independent of the business, who monitors the controls to ensure that the financial statements are presented fairly in accordance with GAAP.

of the accounting information system. Additionally, controls must be in place to ensure adequate approvals for recorded transactions are required. The decision makers need accurate information to keep track of assets and measure profits and losses.

Monitoring of Controls

Companies hire auditors to monitor their controls. An *internal auditor* is an employee of the business who ensures that the company's employees are following company policies and that operations are running efficiently. Internal auditors also determine whether the company is following legal requirements for internal controls to safeguard assets. An *external auditor* is an outside accountant who is completely independent of the business. External auditors evaluate the controls to ensure that the financial statements are presented fairly, in accordance with the generally accepted accounting principles (GAAP).

>Ethics   Should the liabilities be reported?

Dudley Dorite, CPA, the lead external auditor of Nimron Corporation, thinks that Nimron may be understating the liabilities on its balance sheet. Nimron's transactions are very complex, and outsiders may never figure this out. Dorite asks his CPA firm's audit standards committee how he should handle the situation. The CPA firm's committee replies, "Require Nimron to report all its liabilities." Nimron is Dorite's most important client, and Nimron is pressuring him to certify the liabilities. Dorite can rationalize that Nimron's amounts are okay. What should Dorite do? What would you do?

Solution

Dorite has three options. He can go along with Nimron's liabilities as reported, he can persuade Nimron to report higher amounts of liabilities, or, if Nimron refuses, he can issue a qualified audit report. A qualified audit report is issued when the auditor disagrees with specific items on the financial statements. Dorite should understand that, when he prepares an audit, his responsibility is to the investors and the public. He should follow the recommendation of the audit standards committee. If Dorite went along with misrepresenting the liabilities, he might keep a valuable client, but he could face problems in the future for not disclosing flaws in the presentation of liabilities on the balance sheet.

Environment

The environment is the "tone at the top" or the culture of the business. It starts with the owner or CEO and the top managers. They must behave honorably to set a good example for company employees. Each must demonstrate the importance of internal controls if he or she expects the employees to take the controls seriously.

Internal Control Procedures

Whether the business is a small business that generates less than $10,000 in annual sales or a large business generating $10 billion in annual sales, all companies need the following internal control procedures.

Competent, Reliable, and Ethical Personnel

Employees should be competent, reliable, and ethical. Paying good salaries will attract high-quality employees. Employees should also be trained to do the job, and their work should be adequately supervised.

Assignment of Responsibilities

In a business with good internal controls, no duty is overlooked. Each employee has certain, carefully defined responsibilities. For example, in a large company, the person in charge of signing checks is called the *treasurer*. The chief accounting officer is called the *controller*. Even an entry-level bookkeeper, whose job includes recording accounting transactions accurately, has clear responsibilities. This assignment of responsibilities creates job accountability, thus ensuring all important tasks get done.

Separation of Duties

Smart management policies divide responsibilities between two or more people. Separation of duties limits fraud and promotes the accuracy of the accounting records. Separation of duties can be divided into two parts:

1. **Separating operations from accounting.** Accounting should be completely separate from the operating departments, such as production and sales. What would happen if sales personnel recorded the company's revenue? Sales figures could be inflated, and then top managers would not know how much the company actually sold.
2. **Separating the custody of assets from accounting.** Accountants must not handle cash, and cashiers must not have access to the accounting records. If one employee has both duties, that employee could steal cash and conceal the theft in the accounting records. The treasurer of a company handles cash, and the controller accounts for the cash. Neither person has both responsibilities. This control applies to all assets, not just cash.

Separation of Duties
Dividing responsibility between two or more people to limit fraud and promote accuracy of accounting records.

Audits

To assess the adequacy and accuracy of their accounting records, most companies perform both internal and external audits. Remember, an audit is an examination of a company's financial statements and accounting system by a trained accounting professional called an auditor. Internal audits are performed by employees of the company. External audits are performed by independent auditors who are not employees of the company.

To evaluate the accounting system, auditors must examine the internal controls and test them to ensure the controls are working properly. For example, a control might require authorization by a manager for payments over $50. An auditor would check a sample of payments greater than $50 to determine whether all were properly authorized by a manager.

Documents

Documents provide the details of business transactions and include invoices and orders, which may be paper or electronic. Documents should be pre-numbered to prevent theft and inefficiency. A gap in the numbered sequence draws attention.

For example, for Smart Touch Learning, a key document is the customer invoice. The manager can compare the total cash sales on the invoices with the amount of cash received and deposited into the bank account.

Electronic Devices

Accounting systems are relying less on paper documents and more on electronic documents and digital storage devices. For example, retailers control inventory by attaching an electronic sensor to merchandise. The cashier removes the sensor after a sale is made. If a customer tries to leave the store with the sensor attached, an alarm sounds. Devices such as these can significantly reduce theft.

E-Commerce

E-commerce creates its own unique types of risks. Hackers may gain access to confidential information, such as account numbers and passwords, or introduce computer viruses, Trojans, or phishing expeditions. To address the risks posed by e-commerce, companies have devised a number of security measures. One technique for protecting customer data is encryption. Encryption rearranges plain-text messages by a mathematical process. The encrypted message cannot be read by those who do not know the code. An accounting encryption example uses check-sum digits for account numbers. Each account number has its last digit equal to the sum of the previous digits. For example, consider customer number 2237, where $2 + 2 + 3 = 7$. Any account number failing this test triggers an error message.

Another technique for protecting data is firewalls. Firewalls limit access into a local network. Members can access the network, but nonmembers cannot. Usually several firewalls are built into the system. At the point of entry, additional security measures, such as passwords, PINs (personal identification numbers), and signatures are used. For additional security, more sophisticated firewalls are used deeper in the network to protect more sensitive data.

> **Encryption**
> Rearranging plain-text messages by a mathematical process—the primary method of achieving security in e-commerce.

> **Firewall**
> A device that enables members of a local network to access the network, while keeping nonmembers out of the network.

> Decisions   What e-commerce internal controls should be put into place?

Jason Kane works as an information technology auditor for Netproducts, a retailer that sells merchandise over the Internet. Jason has been assigned the responsibility of reviewing the existing procedures and suggesting internal controls that could best protect the company. Netproducts sells all its merchandise over the Internet and accepts only credit card payments. Netproducts tracks trend information about its sales and maintains all customer, product, and pricing information on the company's intranet. In addition, Netproducts keeps employee information such as annual leave, payroll deposits, and social security numbers on its intranet. What e-commerce controls should Jason suggest?

Solution

Jason should suggest that specific controls be put into place, such as using encryption technology and firewalls, to protect customer and employee information. He should recommend that customers be required to create an online account with a password for the site and that the company only use secured Internet networks. In addition, Netproducts should ensure that the customer and employee data are physically secured and that access to the data can be obtained only by authorized individuals.

Other Controls

The types of other controls are as endless as the types of businesses that employ them. Some examples of other common controls include the following:

- Fireproof vaults to store important documents
- Burglar alarms, fire alarms, and security cameras
- Loss-prevention specialists who train company employees to spot suspicious activity
- Fidelity bonds to reimburse the company for any losses due to employee theft
- Mandatory vacations and job rotation

The Limitations of Internal Control—Costs and Benefits

Unfortunately, most internal controls can be overcome. Collusion—two or more people working together—can beat internal controls. For example, consider the following scenario with Galaxy Theater. Ralph and Lana, employees of Galaxy Theater, can design a scheme in which Ralph, the ticket seller, sells tickets and pockets the cash from 10 customers. Lana, the ticket taker, admits 10 customers to the theater without taking their tickets. Ralph and Lana split the cash. Ralph and Lana have colluded to circumvent controls, resulting in Galaxy Theater losing revenues. To prevent this situation, the manager must take additional steps, such as matching the number of people in the theater against the number of ticket stubs retained, which takes time away from the manager's other duties. It is difficult and costly to plan controls that can prevent collusion.

The stricter the internal control system, the more it costs. A complex system of internal control can strangle the business with red tape. How tight should the controls be? Internal controls must always be judged in light of their costs versus their benefits. Following is an example of a positive cost/benefit relationship: A security guard at a retail store costs about $28,000 a year. On average, each guard prevents about $50,000 of theft each year. The net savings to the retail store is $22,000. An example of a negative cost/benefit relationship would be paying the same security guard $28,000 a year to guard a $1,000 cash drawer. The cost exceeds the benefit by $27,000.

So far we have discussed what internal control is and how it can be used to protect a company's assets. We will now spend the remainder of the chapter concentrating on cash because it is the asset most likely to be stolen. However, it is important to remember that internal controls should be applied to all assets, not just cash.

Collusion

Two or more people working together to circumvent internal controls and defraud a company.

> Try It!

Match the accounting terminology to the definitions.

1. Sarbanes-Oxley Act	a. Organizational plan and all the related measures adopted by an entity to safeguard assets, encourage employees to follow company policies, promote operational efficiency, and ensure accurate and reliable accounting records.
2. Internal control	b. Employees of the business who ensure that the company's employees are following company policies and meeting legal requirements and that operations are running efficiently.
3. Encryption	c. Rearranging plain-text messages by a mathematical process—the primary method of achieving security in e-commerce.
4. Separation of duties	d. Requires companies to review internal control and take responsibility for the accuracy and completeness of their financial reports.
5. Internal auditors	e. Dividing responsibility between two or more people.

Check your answers at the end of the chapter.

For more practice, see Short Exercise S-1. MyAccountingLab

WHAT ARE THE INTERNAL CONTROL PROCEDURES WITH RESPECT TO CASH RECEIPTS?

Learning Objective 2

Apply internal controls to cash receipts

Cash receipts occur primarily when a business sells merchandise or services. All cash receipts should be deposited in the bank for safekeeping shortly after the cash is received. Companies receive cash either over the counter, through the mail, or by electronic funds transfer. Each source of cash has its own security measures. We have already discussed internal control procedures for e-commerce, so this section focuses on over the counter and mail cash receipts.

Cash Receipts Over the Counter

A cash receipt over the counter in a store involves a point-of-sale terminal (cash register) that provides control over the cash receipts. Consider a retail store. For each transaction, the retail store issues a receipt to ensure that each sale is recorded. The cash drawer opens after the clerk enters a transaction, and the machine (cash register) records it. At the end of the day, a manager proves the cash by comparing the cash in the drawer against the machine's record of cash sales. This step helps prevent theft by the clerk.

At the end of the day—or several times a day if business is brisk—the manager deposits the cash in the bank. The machine tape then goes to the accounting department to record the journal entry for cash receipts and sales revenue. These measures, coupled with oversight by a manager, discourage theft.

Cash Receipts by Mail

Many companies receive checks by mail for payments of services or merchandise. Checks sent via mail are considered to be cash receipts. Exhibit 1 shows how companies control cash received by mail.

Exhibit 1 | Cash Receipts by Mail

The process works like this:

Remittance Advice

An optional attachment to a check that tells the business the reason for the payment.

Step 1: All incoming mail is opened by a mailroom employee. The mailroom then sends all customer checks to the treasurer and all remittance advices to the accounting department. A remittance advice is an optional attachment to a check that tells the business the reason for the payment.

Step 2: The treasurer has the cashier deposit the checks in the bank. The cashier receives a deposit receipt.

Step 3: The accounting department (or bookkeeper) uses the remittance advices to record the journal entries to Cash and customer accounts.

Step 4: As a final control, the controller compares the following records for the day:

- Bank deposit amount from the treasurer
- Debit to Cash from the accounting department

The debit to Cash should equal the amount deposited in the bank. If it does, all cash receipts are safe in the bank, and the company's books are up-to-date.

Many companies use a lock-box system as an alternative to accepting cash or checks via the mail or over the counter. In a lock-box system, customers send their checks directly to a post office box that belongs to a bank. A bank employee empties the box daily and records the deposits into the company's bank account. Internal control is tight because company personnel never touch incoming cash. The lock-box system puts a business's cash into the company's bank account quickly.

Lock-Box System

A system in which customers send their checks to a post office box that belongs to a bank. A bank employee empties the box daily and records the deposits into the company's bank account.

> ## Try It!

6. Fill in the missing information concerning how companies control cash received by mail.

a. The _____ opens the mail and sends customer checks to the treasurer.

b. The _____ deposits the customer checks in the bank.

c. The _____ uses the remittance advices to record the journal entries for cash receipts.

d. The _____ compares the bank deposit to the journal entry for cash receipts.

Check your answers at the end of the chapter.

For more practice, see Short Exercises S-2 and S-3. MyAccountingLab

WHAT ARE THE INTERNAL CONTROL PROCEDURES WITH RESPECT TO CASH PAYMENTS?

Companies make many payments by check. They also pay small amounts from a petty cash fund, which is discussed later in the chapter. Let's begin by discussing cash payments by check.

Learning Objective 3

Apply internal controls to cash payments

Controls Over Payment by Check

Companies need a good separation of duties between the operations of the business and writing checks for cash payments. Payment by check is an important internal control for the following reasons:

- The check provides a record of the payment.
- The check must be signed by an authorized official.
- Before signing the check, the official reviews the invoice or other evidence supporting the payment.

Controls Over Purchases and Payments

To illustrate the internal control over cash payments by check, suppose Smart Touch Learning buys its tablets from an electronics manufacturer. The purchasing and payment process follows these steps, as shown in Exhibit 2 (on the next page).

Exhibit 2 | Cash Payments by Check

Step 1: Smart Touch Learning sends a purchase order to the electronics manufacturer that contains the quantity and type of goods needed.

Step 2: The electronics manufacturer ships the inventory and sends an invoice back to Smart Touch Learning.

Step 3: Smart Touch Learning receives the inventory and prepares a receiving report.

Step 4: After approving all documents, Smart Touch Learning sends a check to the electronics manufacturer.

For good internal control, the purchasing agent (the employee who prepares the purchase order) should neither receive the goods nor approve the payment. If these duties are not separated, a purchasing agent could buy goods and have them shipped to his or her home. Or, a purchasing agent could spend too much on purchases, approve the payment, and split the excess with the supplier.

Exhibit 3 shows Smart Touch Learning's payment packet of documents, which may be in either electronic or paper format. Before signing the check for payment of

Exhibit 3 | Payment Packet

goods, the controller or the treasurer should examine the packet to prove that all the documents agree. Only then does the company know the following:

1. It received the goods ordered.
2. It is paying only for the goods received and authorized.
3. It is paying the correct amount.

After payment, the payment packet is marked as paid to prevent the bill from being paid twice. Electronically, paid invoices are automatically marked "paid" by most accounting systems.

The Voucher System

Many companies use the voucher system for internal control over cash payments. A voucher is a sequentially numbered document authorizing a cash payment.

The voucher system uses three items: (1) vouchers, (2) a voucher register, and (3) a check register. All expenditures must be approved before payment. This approval takes the form of a voucher.

Exhibit 4 illustrates a voucher of Smart Touch Learning. To enhance internal control, Smart Touch Learning could add this voucher to the payment packet.

Voucher
A sequentially numbered document authorizing a cash payment.

Exhibit 4 | **Voucher**

VOUCHER			V#1238
Smart Touch Learning			
Payee	Southwest Electronics		
Due Date	June 3		
Terms	3/15, n/30		
Date	Invoice No.	Description	Amount
May 19	620	Tablets	$700
Approved *Andrew Bright*		Approved *John Kolen*	
Controller		Treasurer	

Streamlined Procedures

Technology is streamlining payment procedures. Evaluated Receipts Settlement (ERS) compresses the payment approval process into a single step by comparing the receiving report to the purchase order. If those documents match, then Smart Touch Learning got the tablets it ordered and payment is made to the vendor.

An even more streamlined process bypasses paper documents altogether. In Electronic Data Interchange (EDI), a retailer's computers communicate directly with the computers of suppliers. When the retailer's inventory reaches a low level, the computer creates and sends an electronic purchase order to the supplier. The supplier then ships the inventory and electronically sends an invoice to the retailer. A manager approves the invoice and then an electronic fund transfer (EFT) sends the retailer's payment to the supplier. These streamlined EDI procedures are used for both cash payments and cash receipts in many companies.

Evaluated Receipts Settlement (ERS)
A procedure that compresses the payment approval process into a single step by comparing the receiving report to the purchase order.

Electronic Data Interchange (EDI)
A streamlined process that bypasses paper documents altogether. Computers of customers communicate directly with the computers of suppliers to automate routine business transactions.

> **Try It!**

7. Fill in the missing information.

  a. The vendor ships the inventory and sends a(n) _____ back to the purchaser.

  b. After approving all documents, the purchaser sends a(n) _____ to the vendor.

  c. When ordering merchandise inventory, the purchaser sends a(n) _____ to the vendor.

  d. The purchaser receives the inventory and prepares a(n) _____.

Check your answers at the end of the chapter.

For more practice, see Short Exercise S-4.   MyAccountingLab

HOW CAN A PETTY CASH FUND BE USED FOR INTERNAL CONTROL PURPOSES?

Learning Objective 4

Explain and journalize petty cash transactions

Petty Cash

A fund containing a small amount of cash that is used to pay for minor expenditures.

It is not cost effective for a business to write a check for a taxi fare or the delivery of a package across town. To meet these needs and to streamline record keeping for small cash transactions, companies keep cash on hand to pay small amounts. This fund is called petty cash.

We have already established that cash is the most liquid of assets. Petty cash is more liquid than cash in the bank because none of the bank controls are in place. Therefore, petty cash needs controls such as the following:

- Designate a custodian of the petty cash fund. The custodian is the individual assigned responsibility for the petty cash fund.

- Designate a specific amount of cash to be kept in the petty cash fund.

- Support all petty cash fund payments with a petty cash ticket. These tickets are sequentially numbered. The petty cash ticket serves as an authorization voucher and explanation.

Setting Up the Petty Cash Fund

The petty cash fund is opened when the company writes a check for the designated amount. The company makes the check payable to Petty Cash. Suppose on August 1, Smart Touch Learning creates a petty cash fund of $200. The custodian cashes the $200 check and places the currency in the fund box. The journal entry is as follows:

$$\frac{A\uparrow\downarrow}{\begin{matrix} \text{Petty Cash}\uparrow \\ \text{Cash}\downarrow \end{matrix}} \Big\} = \Big\{ \underline{\quad L \quad} + \underline{\quad E \quad}$$

Date	Accounts and Explanation	Debit	Credit
Aug. 1	Petty Cash	200	
	Cash		200
	To open the petty cash fund.		

For each petty cash payment, the custodian prepares a petty cash ticket like the one in Exhibit 5.

Petty Cash Ticket

PETTY CASH TICKET	#101
Date Aug 25, 2015	
Amount $60	
For Letterhead invoices	
Debit Office Supplies	
Received by *Lewis Wright*	Fund Custodian MAR

Signatures (or initials) identify the recipient of the cash and the fund custodian. The custodian keeps the petty cash tickets in the fund box. The sum of the cash plus the total of the petty cash tickets should equal the fund balance, $200, at all times.

Maintaining the Petty Cash account at its designated balance is the nature of an **imprest system**. The imprest system requires that, at any point in time, the petty cash box contains cash and petty cash tickets that total the amount of the imprest balance. This clearly identifies the amount of cash for which the custodian is responsible, and it is the system's main internal control feature.

Imprest System

A way to account for petty cash by maintaining a constant balance in the petty cash account. At any time, cash plus petty cash tickets must total the amount allocated to the petty cash fund.

Replenishing the Petty Cash Fund

Payments decrease the fund, so periodically the fund must be replenished. Suppose that on August 31 the petty cash fund holds $118 in cash, and $80 in petty cash tickets (ticket #101 for $60 for office supplies and ticket #102 for $20 for a delivery).

You can see $2 is missing:

Fund balance		$ 200
Cash on hand	$ 118	
Petty cash tickets	80	
Total accounted for		198
Amount of cash missing		$ 2

To replenish the petty cash fund, you need to bring the cash on hand up to $200. The company writes a check, payable to Petty Cash, for $82 ($200 imprest balance – $118 cash on hand). The fund custodian cashes this check and puts $82 back in the fund box. Now the fund box holds $200 cash as it should.

The petty cash tickets tell you what to debit and the check amount tells you what to credit, as shown in this entry to replenish the fund:

$$\left.\begin{array}{c} \underline{A\downarrow} \\ \text{Office} \\ \text{Supplies}\uparrow \\ \text{Cash}\downarrow \end{array}\right\} = \left\{\begin{array}{cc} \text{L} + & \underline{E\downarrow} \\ & \text{Delivery} \\ & \text{Expense}\uparrow \\ & \text{Cash Short} \\ & \text{\& Over}\uparrow \end{array}\right.$$

Date	Accounts and Explanation	Debit	Credit
Aug. 31	Office Supplies	60	
	Delivery Expense	20	
	Cash Short & Over	2	
	Cash		82
	To replenish the petty cash fund.		

Missing petty cash funds are debited to a new account, Cash Short & Over. In this case, $2 was missing, so we debit Cash Short & Over for the missing petty cash. Another way to look at this is that we needed another $2 debit to make the journal entry balance.

The Petty Cash account keeps its $200 balance at all times. The Petty Cash account is used only when the fund is started (see the August 1 entry) or when its amount is increased or decreased. If the business increases the fund amount from $200 to $250, this would require a check to be cashed for $50 and the debit would be to Petty Cash. When replenishing the fund, the company debits either the associated expense incurred or the asset purchased with the funds.

At times the sum of cash in the petty cash fund plus the tickets may exceed the fund balance. Consider the previous example. Assume the petty cash ticket #102 for delivery was for $30 instead of $20. Because we know the amount of the petty cash tickets and the amount of cash on hand, we can find out the amount of cash shortage or overage.

> Why wasn't < Petty Cash debited when the fund was replenished?

Fund balance		$ 200
Cash on hand	$ 118	
Petty cash tickets	90	
Total accounted for		208
Amount of cash overage		$ 8

In this case, the cash on hand plus petty cash tickets ($208) is more than the fund balance ($200). A cash overage exists. The journal entry to replenish the fund would be:

$$\left.\begin{array}{c} \underline{A\downarrow} \\ \text{Office} \\ \text{Supplies}\uparrow \\ \text{Cash}\downarrow \end{array}\right\} = \left\{\begin{array}{cc} \text{L} + & \underline{E\downarrow} \\ & \text{Delivery} \\ & \text{Expense}\uparrow \\ & \text{Cash Short} \\ & \text{\& Over}\downarrow \end{array}\right.$$

Date	Accounts and Explanation	Debit	Credit
Aug. 31	Office Supplies	60	
	Delivery Expense	30	
	Cash Short & Over		8
	Cash		82
	To replenish the petty cash fund.		

We know the total debits are $90 ($60 + $30). We know the check to replenish the fund was still $82 (credit to Cash) because the fund balance should total $200 and there was $118 in the petty cash box. For this situation, we need an $8 credit to make the journal entry balance, a gain, which is credited to Cash Short & Over.

Changing the Amount of the Petty Cash Fund

Suppose that on September 1, Smart Touch Learning decides to increase the amount of the petty cash fund from $200 to $300. In order to increase the fund, Smart Touch Learning must write a check for the additional $100, cash the check, and place the additional amount in the petty cash box. Because the amount of the fund has changed, the company must record the following journal entry showing this change:

Date	Accounts and Explanation	Debit	Credit
Sep. 1	Petty Cash	100	
	Cash		100
	To increase the petty cash fund.		

$$\frac{A\uparrow\downarrow}{\begin{array}{c}\text{Petty Cash}\uparrow\\\text{Cash}\downarrow\end{array}}\Bigg\} = \Bigg\{ \underline{\quad L \quad} + \underline{\quad E \quad}$$

Had the Petty Cash fund been decreased, the debit would've been to Cash and the credit to the Petty Cash account. Remember, the only time the Petty Cash account is used in the journal entry is when the account is established, increased, or decreased.

> Try It!

8. The following petty cash transactions of Green Golf Equipment occurred in May:

May 1	Established a petty cash fund with a $200 balance.
31	The petty cash fund has $18 in cash and $180 in petty cash tickets that were issued to pay for Office Supplies ($81), Delivery Expense ($36), Postage Expense ($54), and Miscellaneous Expense ($9). The petty cash custodian replenished the fund and recorded the expenses.

Prepare the journal entries.

Check your answers at the end of the chapter.

For more practice, see Short Exercise S-5. MyAccountingLab

HOW CAN THE BANK ACCOUNT BE USED AS A CONTROL DEVICE?

Learning Objective 5

Demonstrate the use of a bank account as a control device and prepare a bank reconciliation and related journal entries

Cash is the most liquid asset because it is the medium of exchange. Because cash is easy to conceal and relatively easy to steal, most businesses keep their cash in a bank account. The bank has established practices for safeguarding the business's money. This section identifies the most common controls applied to a bank account.

Signature Card

Signature Card
A card that shows each authorized person's signature for a bank account.

Banks require each person authorized to sign on an account to provide a signature card. This helps protect against forgery, because the signature card should be checked frequently by bank personnel to authenticate written checks or deposits made by the business.

Deposit Ticket

Deposit Ticket
A bank form that is completed by the customer and shows the amount of each deposit.

Banks supply standard forms such as a deposit ticket. Completed by the customer, the deposit ticket shows the amount of each deposit. As proof of the transaction, the customer receives a deposit receipt from the bank.

Check

Check
A document that instructs a bank to pay the designated person or business a specified amount of money.

Maker
The party who issues the check.

Payee
The individual or business to whom the check is paid.

To pay cash, the depositor writes a check, which is a pre-numbered document that tells the bank to pay the designated party a specified amount. Exhibit 6 shows a check drawn by Smart Touch Learning. There are three parties to a check: the maker, payee, and bank. The maker is the issuer of the check, in this case, Smart Touch Learning. The payee (California Office Products) is the individual or business to whom the check is paid.

Exhibit 6 | **Check With Remittance Advice**

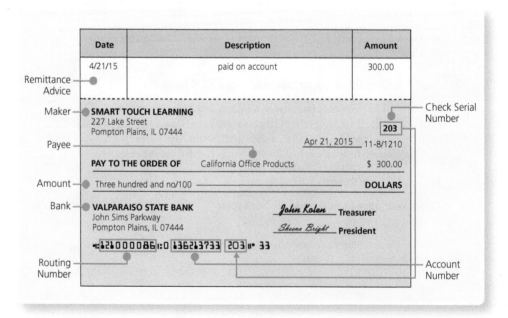

An easy way to remember the difference between the maker and the payee is the maker is the party that is making the promise that the cash is available in the bank to settle the check.

The check has two parts, the check itself and the remittance advice. In addition, the check includes the routing number and account number. The routing number is a 9-digit number that identifies the bank upon which the payment is drawn. The account number identifies the account upon which the payment is drawn.

Bank Statement

Banks send monthly statements to customers. A bank statement reports the activity in the customer's account. The statement shows the account's beginning and ending balances, cash receipts, and payments. Included with the statement are physical or scanned copies of the maker's canceled checks, the checks written by the maker that have been cashed (paid) by the bank. Exhibit 7 is the April 2015 bank statement of Smart Touch Learning.

Routing Number
On a check, the 9-digit number that identifies the bank upon which the payment is drawn.

Account Number
On a check, the number that identifies the account upon which the payment is drawn.

Bank Statement
A document from the bank that reports the activity in the customer's account. It shows the bank account's beginning and ending balances and lists the month's cash transactions conducted through the bank account.

Canceled Checks
Physical or scanned copies of the maker's cashed (paid) checks.

Exhibit 7 | **Bank Statement**

VALPARAISO STATE BANK
JOHN SIMS PARKWAY; POMPTON PLAINS, IL

BANK STATEMENT

Smart Touch Learning
227 Lake Street
Pompton Plains, IL 07444

CHECKING ACCOUNT 136–213733
APRIL 30, 2015

BEGINNING BALANCE	TOTAL DEPOSITS	TOTAL WITHDRAWALS	SERVICE CHARGES	ENDING BALANCE
$12,470	27,080	26,810	20	$12,720

TRANSACTIONS

DEPOSITS	DATE	AMOUNT
Deposit	04/01	19,450
Deposit	04/10	5,500
Deposit	04/22	2,000
EFT—Collection from customer	04/27	100
Interest	04/30	30

CHARGES	DATE	AMOUNT
Service Charge	04/30	20

CHECKS					
Number	Amount	Number	Amount	Number	Amount
202	3,200	203	300		
201	20,000	205	150		
200	1,920				

OTHER DEDUCTIONS	DATE	AMOUNT
EFT—Water Works	04/20	40
NSF	04/25	1,200

Electronic Funds Transfers

Electronic Funds Transfer (EFT)
A system that transfers cash by electronic communication rather than by paper documents.

Electronic funds transfer (EFT) moves cash by electronic communication. Many bills and other payments, such as salaries, rent, utilities, and insurance, are now paid by EFT. It is much cheaper to pay these items by EFT without having to mail a check. Debit card transactions and direct deposits are also considered EFTs.

Bank Reconciliation

Bank Reconciliation
A document explaining the reasons for the difference between a depositor's cash records and the depositor's cash balance in its bank account.

The **bank reconciliation** compares and explains the differences between cash on the company's books and cash according to the bank's records on a specific date. There are two records of a business's cash:

1. The Cash account in the company's general ledger. April's Cash T-account for Smart Touch Learning is shown below.

Cash			
Beg. Bal.	10,550	20,000	Apr. 2
Apr. 1	19,450	3,200	Apr. 15
Apr. 8	5,500	300	Apr. 21
Apr. 22	2,000	2,000	Apr. 30
Apr. 24	9,000	150	Apr. 30
End. Bal.	20,850		

2. The bank statement, which shows the cash receipts and payments transacted through the bank. In Exhibit 7, however, the bank shows an ending balance of $12,720 for Smart Touch Learning.

The books and the bank statement usually show different cash balances. Differences may arise because of a time lag in recording transactions, called **timing differences**. Three examples of timing differences follow:

Timing Difference
Difference that arises between the balance on the bank statement and the balance on the company's books because of a time lag in recording transactions.

- When a business writes a check, it immediately deducts the amount in its checkbook and Cash account. The bank, however, does not subtract the check from the company's account until the bank pays the check a few days later.
- When a company deposits cash in its account, it immediately adds the cash receipt to the checkbook and Cash account. The bank, however, may take a day or two to add deposits to the company's balance.
- EFT payments and EFT cash receipts are often recorded by the bank before a company learns of them.

To obtain accurate cash records, a company must update its Cash account after the company receives its bank statement. A bank reconciliation is used to carry out the updating process. The bank reconciliation explains all differences between the company's cash records and the bank's records of the company's balance. The person who prepares the bank reconciliation should have no other cash duties. This means the reconciler should not be a person who has access to cash or duties that require journalizing cash transactions. Otherwise, he or she could steal cash and manipulate the reconciliation to conceal the theft.

Preparing the Bank Side of the Bank Reconciliation

Here are the items that appear on a bank reconciliation. They all cause differences between the bank balance and the book balance.

The bank side contains items not yet recorded by the bank, but recorded by the company, or errors made by the bank. These items include the following:

Deposit in Transit
A deposit recorded by the company but not yet by its bank.

Deposits in Transit (Outstanding Deposits) A **deposit in transit** has been recorded and has already been added to the company's book balance, but the bank has not yet recorded it. These are shown as "Add: Deposits in transit" on the bank side because when the bank does record these deposits, it will increase the bank balance.

Outstanding Checks An outstanding check is a check that has been recorded and has already been deducted from the company's book balance, but the bank has not yet paid (deducted). Such checks are shown as "Less: Outstanding checks" on the bank side because when the bank does record the checks, it will decrease the bank balance.

Outstanding Check
A check issued by a company and recorded on its books but not yet paid by its bank.

Bank Errors Bank errors are posting errors made by the bank that either incorrectly increase or decrease the bank balance. All bank errors are corrected on the bank side of the reconciliation by reversing the effect of the errors.

> Errors are always recorded on the side of the reconciliation of the party that made the error. If the bank made the error, it is recorded on the bank side. If the business made the error, it is recorded on the book side.

Preparing the Book Side of the Bank Reconciliation

The book side contains items not yet recorded by the company on its books but that have been recorded by the bank, or errors made by the company. Items to show on the book side include the following:

Bank Collections Bank collections are cash receipts the bank has received and recorded for a company's account but that the company has not recorded yet on its books. An example of a bank collection would occur when a business has its customers use a lock-box system. Another example is a bank collecting on a note receivable for a business. A bank collection is often referred to as a credit memorandum. A credit memorandum indicates that the customer's account has been increased. A bank collection (which increases the bank balance) that appears on the bank statement will show as "Add: Bank collections" on the book side of the reconciliation because it represents cash receipts not yet recorded by the company.

Credit Memorandum
An increase in a bank account.

Electronic Funds Transfers The bank may receive or pay cash on a company's behalf. An EFT may be a cash receipt or a cash payment. These will either show up on the book side of the reconciliation as "Add: EFT" for receipts not yet added to the company's books or "Less: EFT" for payments not yet deducted on the company's books.

Service Charge This cash payment is the bank's fee for processing a company's transactions. Service charges can also include the cost of printed checks and other bank fees. A service charge is often referred to as a debit memorandum and represents a decrease in the bank account. This will show as "Less: Service charges" on the book side of the reconciliation because it represents a cash payment not yet subtracted from the company's cash balance.

Debit Memorandum
A decrease in a bank account.

Interest Revenue on a Checking Account A business will sometimes earn interest if it keeps enough cash in its account. The bank statement tells the company of this cash receipt. This will show as "Add: Interest revenue" on the book side of the reconciliation because it represents cash receipts not yet added in the company's cash balance.

Nonsufficient Funds (NSF) Checks Nonsufficient funds (NSF) checks represent checks received from customers for payment of services rendered or merchandise sold that have turned out to be worthless. NSF checks (sometimes called hot checks or bad checks) are treated as subtractions on a company's bank reconciliation. NSF checks are customer checks the company has received and deposited for which the customer doesn't have enough money in his or her bank account to cover. NSF checks will show as "Less: NSF checks" on the book side of the reconciliation.

Nonsufficient Funds (NSF) Check
A check for which the maker's bank account has insufficient money to pay the check.

Book Errors Book errors are errors made on the books of the company that either incorrectly increase or decrease the cash balance in the company's general ledger. All book errors are corrected on the book side of the reconciliation by reversing the effect of the errors.

The bank statement in Exhibit 7 shows that the April 30 bank balance of Smart Touch Learning is $12,720 (upper-right corner). However, the company's Cash account has a balance of $20,850. This situation calls for a bank reconciliation to explain the difference. In completing the bank reconciliation, Smart Touch Learning will review the bank statement and the business's Cash account to determine the timing differences. Exhibit 8, Panel A, lists the reconciling items for your easy reference, and Panel B shows the completed reconciliation.

Exhibit 8 | **Bank Reconciliation**

PANEL A—Reconciling Items

Bank side:

1. Deposit in transit, Apr. 24, $9,000.
2. Outstanding check no. 204, $2,000.

Book side:

3. EFT receipt from customer, $100.
4. Interest revenue earned on bank balance, $30.
5. Bank service charge, $20.
6. EFT payment of water bill, $40.
7. NSF check, $1,200.

PANEL B—Bank Reconciliation

SMART TOUCH LEARNING Bank Reconciliation April 30, 2015					
BANK			**BOOK**		
Balance, April 30, 2015		$ 12,720	Balance, April 30, 2015		$ 20,850
ADD:			ADD:		
1. Deposit in transit		9,000	3. EFT receipt from customer	$ 100	
		21,720	4. Interest revenue earned on bank balance	30	130
					20,980
LESS:			LESS:		
			5. Service charge	20	
2. Outstanding checks			6. EFT payment of water bill	40	
No. 204		2,000	7. NSF check	1,200	1,260
Adjusted bank balance, April 30, 2015		**$ 19,720**	Adjusted book balance, April 30, 2015		**$ 19,720**

These amounts should agree.

SUMMARY OF THE VARIOUS RECONCILING ITEMS:

BANK BALANCE—ALWAYS

- *Add* deposits in transit.
- *Subtract* outstanding checks.
- *Add* or *subtract* corrections of bank errors.

BOOK BALANCE—ALWAYS

- *Add* bank collections, interest revenue, and EFT receipts.
- *Subtract* service charges, NSF checks, and EFT payments.
- *Add* or *subtract* corrections of book errors.

Examining a Bank Reconciliation

Let's go through each side of the bank reconciliation for Smart Touch Learning.

Bank Side of the Reconciliation

Smart Touch Learning begins by recording the bank balance as of April 30, 2015, which is taken from the bank statement, $12,720. The business then identifies any additions or subtractions affecting the bank balance:

1. **Deposit in transit.** Smart Touch Learning reviews the bank statement and the Cash account to determine whether any cash deposits made by the business have not yet been recorded by the bank. Smart Touch Learning identifies that the deposit made on April 24 for $9,000 has not yet been recorded by the bank. This amount is added to the bank balance.

2. **Outstanding check.** The business reviews the canceled checks included with the statement to determine whether any checks written by the business have not yet cleared the bank. Smart Touch Learning identifies check number 204 for $2,000 as outstanding. This amount is subtracted from the bank balance.

After all items affecting the bank side have been identified, the adjusted bank balance is determined.

Book Side of the Reconciliation

The book side of the reconciliation begins by Smart Touch Learning listing the cash account balance as of April 30, 2015. This amount—$20,850—is found in the general ledger. Next, Smart Touch Learning reviews the Cash account and bank statement for items that affect the company's Cash account balance, but are not recorded by the company:

3. **Electronic funds transfer (EFT).** In reviewing the bank statement, Smart Touch Learning identifies an EFT receipt from a customer in the amount of $100. The company has not recorded this receipt in the Cash account; therefore, it will need to be added to the book balance.

4. **Interest Revenue.** Smart Touch Learning identifies a $30 deposit on the bank statement for interest earned that has not yet been recorded in the Cash account. This deposit will be added to the book balance.

5. **Service Charge.** The bank statement shows a $20 service charge. Smart Touch Learning has not recorded this charge in the company's Cash account and will, therefore, need to subtract this amount from the book balance.

6. **Electronic funds transfer (EFT).** Listed in the other deductions section on the bank statement, Smart Touch Learning identifies an EFT payment to Water Works for $40. This payment has not been recorded in the company's Cash account. Smart Touch Learning will subtract this amount from the book balance.

7. **Nonsufficient funds (NSF) check.** Smart Touch Learning identifies an NSF check from a customer on the bank statement. The company had recorded the receipt of this check as an increase to cash originally. The bank has now communicated that the customer's check did not clear and that the customer's payment was never deposited into the business's account. Smart Touch Learning must subtract this amount from the book balance.

After recording all of the items that affect the book balance, Smart Touch Learning determines the adjusted book balance and verifies that it equals the adjusted bank balance. This amount represents the correct cash balance as of April 30, 2015.

Journalizing Transactions From the Bank Reconciliation

The bank reconciliation is an accountant's tool separate from the journals and ledgers. It does *not* account for transactions in the journal. To get the transactions into the accounts, we must make journal entries and post to the ledger. All items on the book side of the bank reconciliation require journal entries. We make no entries on the bank side because we do not have access to the bank's general ledger.

The bank reconciliation in Exhibit 8 requires Smart Touch Learning to make journal entries to bring the Cash account up to date. Numbers in the journal entries correspond to the reconciling items listed in Exhibit 8, Panel A, and to the book side of the reconciliation in Panel B. Note, we chose to list each item in a separate journal entry here, but one compound entry could be made instead of the five separate entries illustrated.

$$\frac{\text{A}\uparrow\downarrow}{\substack{\text{Cash}\uparrow \\ \text{Accounts} \\ \text{Receivable}\downarrow}} \Big\} = \Big\{ \frac{\text{L}}{} + \frac{\text{E}}{}$$

$$\frac{\text{A}\uparrow}{\text{Cash}\uparrow} \Big\} = \Big\{ \frac{\text{L}}{} + \frac{\text{E}\uparrow}{\substack{\text{Interest} \\ \text{Revenue}\uparrow}}$$

$$\frac{\text{A}\downarrow}{\text{Cash}\downarrow} \Big\} = \Big\{ \frac{\text{L}}{} + \frac{\text{E}\downarrow}{\substack{\text{Bank} \\ \text{Expense}\uparrow}}$$

$$\frac{\text{A}\downarrow}{\text{Cash}\downarrow} \Big\} = \Big\{ \frac{\text{L}}{} + \frac{\text{E}\downarrow}{\substack{\text{Utilities} \\ \text{Expense}\uparrow}}$$

$$\frac{\text{A}\uparrow\downarrow}{\substack{\text{Accounts} \\ \text{Receivable}\uparrow \\ \text{Cash}\downarrow}} \Big\} = \Big\{ \frac{\text{L}}{} + \frac{\text{E}}{}$$

Date	Accounts and Explanation	Debit	Credit
3: Apr. 30	Cash	100	
	Accounts Receivable		100
	To record account receivable collected by bank.		
4: 30	Cash	30	
	Interest Revenue		30
	To record interest earned on bank balance.		
5: 30	Bank Expense	20	
	Cash		20
	To record bank service charges incurred.		
6: 30	Utilities Expense	40	
	Cash		40
	To record payment of water bill by EFT.		
7: 30	Accounts Receivable	1,200	
	Cash		1,200
	NSF check returned by bank.		

Cash

Beg. Bal.	10,550	20,000	Apr. 2
Apr. 1	19,450	3,200	Apr. 15
Apr. 8	5,500	300	Apr. 21
Apr. 22	2,000	2,000	Apr. 30
Apr. 24	9,000	150	Apr. 30
Bal.	20,850		
Apr. 30	100	20	Apr. 30
Apr. 30	30	40	Apr. 30
		1,200	Apr. 30
End. Bal.	19,720		

> **Try It!**

For each of the following items, determine whether the item would be:

a. added to the bank balance
b. subtracted from the bank balance
c. added to the book balance
d. subtracted from the book balance

9. Interest revenue earned
10. NSF check
11. Deposit in transit
12. Service charge
13. Outstanding check

Check your answers at the end of the chapter.

For more practice, see Short Exercises S-6 through S-9.   MyAccountingLab

HOW CAN THE CASH RATIO BE USED TO EVALUATE BUSINESS PERFORMANCE?

Cash is an important part of every business. Without an adequate supply of available cash, businesses cannot continue to operate. Businesses, therefore, monitor cash very carefully. One measure that can be used to measure a company's liquidity is the cash ratio. The cash ratio helps to determine a company's ability to meet its short-term obligations. It is calculated as follows:

> Cash ratio = (Cash + Cash equivalents) / Total current liabilities

Notice that the cash ratio includes cash and cash equivalents. Cash equivalents are highly liquid investments that can be converted into cash in three months or less. Examples of cash equivalents are money-market accounts and investments in U.S. government securities.

Let's evaluate Green Mountain Coffee Roasters, Inc.'s liquidity using the cash ratio. Green Mountain's cash and cash equivalents and total current liabilities are presented below (shown in thousands):

	September 24, 2011	September 25, 2010
Cash and cash equivalents	$ 12,989	$ 4,401
Total current liabilities	471,374	238,055

Learning Objective 6
Use the cash ratio to evaluate business performance

Cash Ratio
A measure of a company's ability to pay current liabilities from cash and cash equivalents: (Cash + Cash equivalents) / Total current liabilities.

Cash Equivalent
A highly liquid investment that can be converted into cash in three months or less.

Green Mountain's cash ratio as of September 24, 2011 follows:

$$\text{Cash ratio} = \$12{,}989 / \$471{,}374 = 0.028^*$$

* rounded

In comparison, the cash ratio as of September 25, 2010 was:

$$\text{Cash ratio} = \$4{,}401 / \$238{,}055 = 0.018^*$$

* rounded

The cash ratio has increased slightly from 2010 to 2011 due to an increase in available cash and cash equivalents. This ratio is the most conservative valuation of liquidity because it looks at only cash and cash equivalents, leaving out other current assets such as merchandise inventory and accounts receivable. Notice that for both years, the cash ratio was below 1.0. Having a cash ratio below 1.0 is a good thing. A cash ratio above 1.0 might signify that the company has an unnecessarily large amount of cash supply. This cash could be used to generate higher profits or be taken out for owners' withdrawals. However, a very low ratio doesn't send a strong message to investors and creditors that the company has the ability to repay its short-term debt.

 Try It!

14. The Scott Sun & Shade Company had the following financial data for the year ended December 31, 2015:

Cash and cash equivalents	$ 60,000
Total current liabilities	75,000

What is the cash ratio as of December 31, 2015, for Scott Sun & Shade?

Check your answer at the end of the chapter.

For more practice, see Short Exercise S-10. MyAccountingLab

REVIEW

> Things You Should Know

1. **What is internal control and how can it be used to protect a company's assets?**

   - Internal control is the organizational plan and all the related measures designed to safeguard assets, encourage employees to follow company policies, promote operational efficiency, and ensure accurate and reliable accounting records.

   - The Sarbanes-Oxley Act was passed by Congress to revamp corporate governance in the United States.

   - Internal control includes five components: control procedures, risk assessment, information system, monitoring of controls, and environment.

2. **What are the internal control procedures with respect to cash receipts?**

   - A point-of-sale terminal provides control over cash receipts over the counter.

   - Companies control cash by mail by ensuring appropriate separation of duties when handling cash and recording the transaction.

3. **What are the internal control procedures with respect to cash payments?**

   - Good separation of duties between operations of the business and writing checks for cash payments should exist.

   - A voucher system can be used to control cash payments

4. **How can a petty cash fund be used for internal control purposes?**

   - A petty cash fund allows a business to keep cash on hand to pay for small miscellaneous items such as postage, office supplies, and taxi fare.

   - When the petty cash fund is opened, the company records a debit to Petty Cash and a credit to Cash.

   - The fund is replenished by debiting the associated asset and expense accounts and crediting Cash.

   - Discrepancies in petty cash funds are either debited or credited to the Cash Short & Over account.

5. **How can the bank account be used as a control device?**

   - Bank accounts provide established practices that safeguard a business's money. These controls include use of signature cards, deposit tickets, checks, bank statements, and electronic funds transfers.

   - A bank reconciliation can also be used as a form of internal control. The bank reconciliation compares and explains the difference between cash on the company's books and cash according to the bank's records on a specific date.

   - After the bank reconciliation has been prepared, journal entries must be completed for all items on the book side of the bank reconciliation.

6. **How can the cash ratio be used to evaluate business performance?**

- The cash ratio measures a company's ability to pay its current liabilities from cash and cash equivalents.

- Cash ratio = (Cash + Cash equivalents) / Total current liabilities.

> Summary Problem 1

Misler Company established a $300 petty cash fund on January 12, 2015. Karen Misler (KM) is the fund custodian. At the end of the month, the petty cash fund contains the following:

a. Cash: $163

b. Petty cash tickets, as follows:

No.	Amount	Issued to	Signed by	Account Debited
44	$14	B. Jarvis	B. Jarvis and KM	Office Supplies
45	39	S. Bell	S. Bell	Delivery Expense
47	43	R. Tate	R. Tate and KM	—
48	33	L. Blair	L. Blair and KM	Travel Expense

Requirements

1. Identify three internal control weaknesses revealed in the given data.

2. Journalize the following transactions:

a. Establishment of the petty cash fund on January 12, 2015.

b. Replenishment of the fund on January 31, 2015. Assume petty cash ticket no. 47 was issued for the purchase of office supplies.

3. What is the balance in the Petty Cash account immediately before replenishment? Immediately after replenishment?

> Solution

Requirement 1

The three internal control weaknesses are as follows:

1. Petty cash ticket no. 46 is missing. There is no indication of what happened to this ticket. The company should investigate.

2. The petty cash custodian (KM) did not sign petty cash ticket no. 45. This omission may have been an oversight on her part. However, it raises the question of whether she authorized the payment. Both the fund custodian and the recipient of the cash should sign the petty cash ticket.

3. Petty cash ticket no. 47 does not indicate which account to debit on the actual ticket. If Tate or Karen Misler do not remember where the $43 went, then the accountant will not know what account should be debited.

Requirement 2

Petty cash journal entries:

a. Entry to establish the petty cash fund:

Date	Accounts and Explanation	Debit	Credit
Jan. 12	Petty Cash	300	
	Cash		300
	To open the petty cash fund.		

b. Entry to replenish the fund:

Date	Accounts and Explanation	Debit	Credit
Jan. 31	Office Supplies	57	
	Delivery Expense	39	
	Travel Expense	33	
	Cash Short & Over	8	
	Cash		137
	To replenish the petty cash fund.		

Requirement 3

The balance in the Petty Cash account is *always* its imprest balance, in this case $300.

> Summary Problem 2

The Cash account of Baylor Associates at February 28, 2015, follows.

Cash

Beg. Bal.	3,995	400	Feb. 3
Feb. 6	800	3,100	Feb. 12
Feb. 15	1,800	1,100	Feb. 19
Feb. 23	1,100	500	Feb. 25
Feb. 28	2,400	900	Feb. 27
End. Bal.	4,095		

Internal Control and Cash

Baylor Associates received the following bank statement on February 28, 2015:

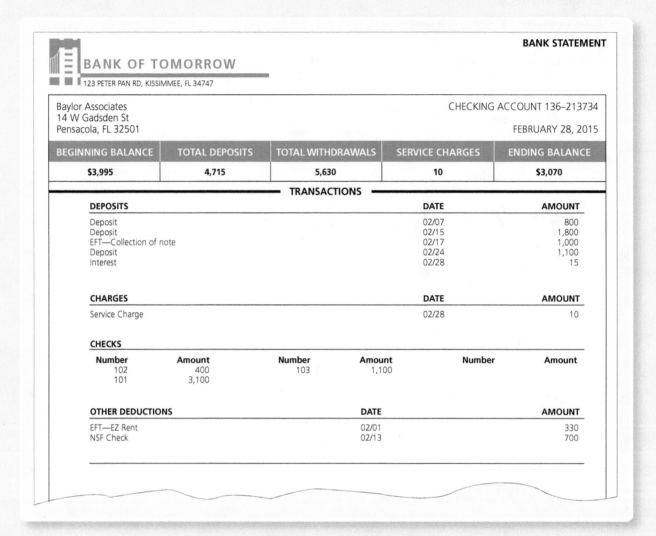

BANK STATEMENT

BANK OF TOMORROW
123 PETER PAN RD, KISSIMMEE, FL 34747

Baylor Associates
14 W Gadsden St
Pensacola, FL 32501

CHECKING ACCOUNT 136–213734

FEBRUARY 28, 2015

BEGINNING BALANCE	TOTAL DEPOSITS	TOTAL WITHDRAWALS	SERVICE CHARGES	ENDING BALANCE
$3,995	4,715	5,630	10	$3,070

TRANSACTIONS

DEPOSITS	DATE	AMOUNT
Deposit	02/07	800
Deposit	02/15	1,800
EFT—Collection of note	02/17	1,000
Deposit	02/24	1,100
Interest	02/28	15

CHARGES	DATE	AMOUNT
Service Charge	02/28	10

CHECKS

Number	Amount	Number	Amount	Number	Amount
102	400	103	1,100		
101	3,100				

OTHER DEDUCTIONS	DATE	AMOUNT
EFT—EZ Rent	02/01	330
NSF Check	02/13	700

Additional data:

Baylor deposits all cash receipts in the bank and makes all payments by check.

Requirements

1. Prepare the bank reconciliation of Baylor Associates at February 28, 2015.
2. Journalize the entries based on the bank reconciliation.

> Solution

Requirement 1

BAYLOR ASSOCIATES Bank Reconciliation February 28, 2015		
Bank:		
Balance, February 28, 2015		$ 3,070
Add: Deposit of February 28 in transit		2,400
		5,470
Less: Outstanding checks issued on February 25 ($500)		
and February 27 ($900)		1,400
Adjusted bank balance, February 28, 2015		**$ 4,070**
Books:		
Balance, February 28, 2015		$ 4,095
Add: Bank collection of note receivable	$1,000	
Interest revenue earned on bank balance	15	1,015
		5,110
Less: Service charge	10	
NSF check	700	
EFT—Rent expense	330	1,040
Adjusted book balance, February 28, 2015		**$ 4,070**

Should be equal.

Requirement 2

Date	Accounts and Explanation	Debit	Credit
Feb. 28	Cash	1,000	
	Notes Receivable		1,000
	Note receivable collected by bank.		
28	Cash	15	
	Interest Revenue		15
	Interest earned on bank balance.		
28	Bank Expense	10	
	Cash		10
	Bank service charge.		
28	Accounts Receivable	700	
	Cash		700
	NSF check returned by bank.		
28	Rent Expense	330	
	Cash		330
	Monthly rent expense.		

> Key Terms

Account Number
On a check, the number that identifies the account upon which the payment is drawn.

Bank Reconciliation
A document explaining the reasons for the difference between a depositor's cash records and the depositor's cash balance in its bank account.

Bank Statement
A document from the bank that reports the activity in the customer's account. It shows the bank account's beginning and ending balances and lists the month's cash transactions conducted through the bank account.

Canceled Checks
Physical or scanned copies of the maker's cashed (paid) checks.

Cash Equivalent
A highly liquid investment that can be converted into cash in three months or less.

Cash Ratio
A measure of a company's ability to pay current liabilities from cash and cash equivalents: (Cash + Cash equivalents) / Total current liabilities.

Check
A document that instructs a bank to pay the designated person or business a specified amount of money.

Collusion
Two or more people working together to circumvent internal controls and defraud a company.

Credit Memorandum
An increase in a bank account.

Debit Memorandum
A decrease in a bank account.

Deposit in Transit
A deposit recorded by the company but not yet by its bank.

Deposit Ticket
A bank form that is completed by the customer and shows the amount of each deposit.

Electronic Data Interchange (EDI)

A streamlined process that bypasses paper documents altogether. Computers of customers communicate directly with the computers of suppliers to automate routine business transactions.

Electronic Funds Transfer (EFT)

A system that transfers cash by electronic communication rather than by paper documents.

Encryption

Rearranging plain-text messages by a mathematical process—the primary method of achieving security in e-commerce.

Evaluated Receipts Settlement (ERS)

A procedure that compresses the payment approval process into a single step by comparing the receiving report to the purchase order.

External Auditor

An outside accountant, completely independent of the business, who monitors the controls to ensure that the financial statements are presented fairly in accordance with GAAP.

Firewall

A device that enables members of a local network to access the network, while keeping nonmembers out of the network.

Imprest System

A way to account for petty cash by maintaining a constant balance in the petty cash account. At any time, cash plus petty cash tickets must total the amount allocated to the petty cash fund.

Internal Auditor

An employee of the business who ensures the company's employees are following company policies, that the company meets all legal requirements, and that operations are running efficiently.

Internal Control

The organizational plan and all the related measures adopted by an entity to safeguard assets, encourage employees to follow company policies, promote operational efficiency, and ensure accurate and reliable accounting records.

Internal Control Report

A report by management describing its responsibility for and the adequacy of internal controls over financial reporting.

Lock-Box System

A system in which customers send their checks to a post office box that belongs to a bank. A bank employee empties the box daily and records the deposits into the company's bank account.

Maker

The party who issues the check.

Nonsufficient Funds (NSF) Check

A check for which the maker's bank account has insufficient money to pay the check.

Outstanding Check

A check issued by a company and recorded on its books but not yet paid by its bank.

Payee

The individual or business to whom the check is paid.

Petty Cash

A fund containing a small amount of cash that is used to pay for minor expenditures.

Public Company

A company that sells its stock to the general public.

Remittance Advice

An optional attachment to a check that tells the business the reason for the payment.

Routing Number

On a check, the 9-digit number that identifies the bank upon which the payment is drawn.

Sarbanes-Oxley Act (SOX)

Requires companies to review internal control and take responsibility for the accuracy and completeness of their financial reports.

Separation of Duties

Dividing responsibility between two or more people to limit fraud and promote accuracy of accounting records

Signature Card

A card that shows each authorized person's signature for a bank account.

Timing Difference

Difference that arises between the balance on the bank statement and the balance on the company's books because of a time lag in recording transactions.

Voucher

A sequentially numbered document authorizing a cash payment.

> Quick Check

Learning Objective 1

1. Which of the following is *not* part of the definition of internal control?

    a. Separation of duties

    b. Safeguard assets

    c. Encourage employees to follow company policy

    d. Promote operational efficiency

Learning Objective 1

2. The Sarbanes-Oxley Act

    a. created the Private Company Accounting Board.

    b. allows accountants to audit and to perform any type of consulting work for a public company.

    c. stipulates that violators of the act may serve 20 years in prison for securities fraud.

    d. requires that an outside auditor must evaluate a public company's internal controls.

Learning Objective 1

3. Encryption

    a. avoids the need for separation of duties.

    b. creates firewalls to protect data.

    c. cannot be broken by hackers.

    d. rearranges messages by a special process.

Learning Objective 1

4. Separation of duties is important for internal control of

    a. cash receipts.

    b. cash payments.

    c. Neither of the above

    d. Both a and b

Learning Objective 2

5. Michelle Darby receives cash from customers. Her other assigned job is to post the collections to customer accounts receivable. Her company has weak

    a. assignment of responsibilities.

    b. ethics.

    c. computer controls.

    d. separation of duties.

Learning Objective 3

6. Payment by check is an important internal control over cash payments because

    a. the check must be signed by an authorized official.

    b. before signing the check, the official reviews the invoice supporting the payment.

    c. Both a and b

    d. None of the above

7. The petty cash fund had an initial imprest balance of $100. It currently has $20 and petty cash tickets totaling $75 for office supplies. The entry to replenish the fund would contain

Learning Objective 4

   a. a credit to Cash Short & Over for $5.

   b. a credit to Petty Cash for $80.

   c. a debit to Cash Short & Over for $5.

   d. a debit to Petty Cash for $80.

8. The document that explains all differences between the company's cash records and the bank's figures is called a(n)

Learning Objective 5

   a. bank collection.

   b. electronic fund transfer.

   c. bank statement.

   d. bank reconciliation.

9. Sahara Company's Cash account shows an ending balance of $650. The bank statement shows a $29 service charge and an NSF check for $150. A $240 deposit is in transit, and outstanding checks total $420. What is Sahara's adjusted cash balance?

Learning Objective 5

   a. $291

   b. $829

   c. $471

   d. $470

10. Espinoza Air Conditioning & Heating had the following select financial data as of June 30, 2015.

Learning Objective 6

Cash	$ 10,000
Cash Equivalents	8,850
Accounts Receivable	3,700
Total current liabilities	29,000

   What is Espinoza's cash ratio?

   a. 0.34

   b. 0.65

   c. 0.78

   d. 1.54

Check your answers at the end of the chapter.

ASSESS YOUR PROGRESS

> Review Questions

1. What is internal control?
2. How does the Sarbanes-Oxley Act relate to internal controls?
3. What are the five components of internal control? Briefly explain each component.
4. What is the difference between an internal auditor and external auditor?
5. What is separation of duties?
6. List internal control procedures related to e-commerce.
7. What are some limitations of internal controls?
8. How do businesses control cash receipts over the counter?
9. How do businesses control cash receipts by mail?
10. What are the steps taken to ensure control over purchases and payments by check?
11. What is a voucher, and how are vouchers used for internal control over cash payments?
12. What are the controls needed to secure the petty cash fund?
13. When are the only times the Petty Cash account is used in a journal entry?
14. What are some common controls used with a bank account?
15. What is a bank reconciliation?
16. List some examples of timing differences, and for each difference, determine if it would affect the book side of the reconciliation or the bank side of the reconciliation.
17. Why is it necessary to record journal entries after the bank reconciliation has been prepared? Which side of the bank reconciliation requires journal entries?
18. What does the cash ratio help determine, and how is it calculated?

> Short Exercises

Learning Objective 1

S-1 Defining internal control

Internal controls are designed to safeguard assets, encourage employees to follow company policies, promote operational efficiency, and ensure accurate accounting records.

Requirements

1. Which objective do you think is most important?
2. Which objective do you think must the internal controls accomplish for the business to survive? Give your reason.

Learning Objective 2

S-2 Applying internal control over cash receipts

Sandra Kristof sells furniture for McKinney Furniture Company. Kristof is having financial problems and takes $650 that she received from a customer. She rang up the sale through the cash register. What will alert Megan McKinney, the controller, that something is wrong?

S-3 Applying internal control over cash receipts by mail

Learning Objective 2

Review the internal controls over cash receipts by mail presented in the chapter. Exactly what is accomplished by the final step in the process, performed by the controller?

S-4 Applying internal control over cash payments by check

Learning Objective 3

A purchasing agent for Franklin Office Supplies receives the goods that he purchases and also approves payment for the goods.

Requirements

1. How could this purchasing agent cheat his company?
2. How could Franklin avoid this internal control weakness?

S-5 Journalizing petty cash

Learning Objective 4

Prepare the journal entries for the following petty cash transactions of Grayson Gaming Supplies:

Mar. 1	Established a petty cash fund with a $150 balance.
31	The petty cash fund has $14 in cash and $148 in petty cash tickets that were issued to pay for Office Supplies ($58) and Entertainment Expense ($90). Replenished the fund and recorded the expenditures.
Apr. 15	Increased the balance of the petty cash fund to $200.

S-6 Understanding bank account controls

Learning Objective 5

Answer the following questions about the controls in bank accounts:

Requirements

1. Which bank control protects against forgery?
2. Which bank control reports the activity in the customer's account each period?
3. Which bank control confirms the amount of money put into the bank account?

S-7 Identifying timing differences related to a bank reconciliation

Learning Objective 5

For each timing difference listed, identify whether the difference would be reported on the book side of the reconciliation or the bank side of the reconciliation. In addition, identify whether the difference would be an addition or subtraction.

a. Deposit in transit

b. Bank collection

c. Debit memorandum

d. EFT cash receipt

e. Outstanding checks

f. $1,000 deposit erroneously recorded by the bank as $100

g. Service charges

h. Interest revenue

i. $2,500 cash payment for rent expense erroneously recorded by the business as $250

j. Credit memorandum

Learning Objective 5

S-8 Preparing a bank reconciliation

The Cash account of First on Alert Security Systems reported a balance of $2,470 at December 31, 2015. There were outstanding checks totaling $700 and a December 31 deposit in transit of $100. The bank statement, which came from Park Cities Bank, listed the December 31 balance of $3,700. Included in the bank balance was a collection of $640 on account from Brendan Ballou, a First on Alert customer who pays the bank directly. The bank statement also shows a $30 service charge and $20 of interest revenue that First on Alert earned on its bank balance. Prepare First on Alert's bank reconciliation at December 31.

Note: Short Exercise S-9 should be used only after completing Short Exercise S-8.

Learning Objective 5

S-9 Recording transactions from a bank reconciliation

Review your results from preparing First on Alert Security Systems' bank reconciliation in Short Exercise S-8. Journalize the company's transactions that arise from the bank reconciliation. Include an explanation with each entry.

Learning Objective 6

S-10 Computing the cash ratio

Budget Banners reported the following figures in its financial statements:

Cash	$ 28,800
Cash Equivalents	2,200
Total Current Liabilities	24,800

Compute the cash ratio for Budget Banners.

> Exercises

Learning Objective 1

E-11 Understanding Sarbanes-Oxley and identifying internal control strengths and weaknesses

The following situations suggest a strength or a weakness in internal control.

a. Top managers delegate all internal control procedures to the accounting department.

b. Accounting department staff (or the bookkeeper) orders merchandise and approves invoices for payment.

c. Cash received over the counter is controlled by the sales clerk, who rings up the sale and places the cash in the register. The sales clerk matches the total recorded by the register to each day's cash sales.

d. The employee who signs checks need not examine the payment packet because he is confident the amounts are correct.

Requirements

1. Define *internal control*.

2. The system of internal control must be tested by external auditors. What law or rule requires this testing?

3. Identify each item in the list above as either a strength or a weakness in internal control and give your reason for each answer.

Internal Control and Cash

E-12 Identifying internal controls

Learning Objective 1

Consider each situation separately. Identify the missing internal control procedure from these characteristics:

- Assignment of responsibilities
- Separation of duties
- Audits
- Electronic devices
- Other controls (specify)

a. While reviewing the records of Quality Pharmacy, you find that the same employee orders merchandise and approves invoices for payment.

b. Business is slow at Amazing Amusement Park on Tuesday, Wednesday, and Thursday nights. To reduce expenses, the owner decides not to use a ticket taker on those nights. The ticket seller (cashier) is told to keep the tickets as a record of the number sold.

c. The same trusted employee has served as cashier for 12 years.

d. When business is brisk, Fast Mart deposits cash in the bank several times during the day. The manager at one store wants to reduce the time employees spend delivering cash to the bank, so he starts a new policy. Cash will build up over weekends, and the total will be deposited on Monday.

e. Grocery stores such as Convenience Market and Natural Foods purchase most merchandise from a few suppliers. At another grocery store, the manager decides to reduce paperwork. He eliminates the requirement that the receiving department prepare a receiving report listing the goods actually received from the supplier.

E-13 Evaluating internal control over cash receipts

Learning Objective 2

Dogtopia sells pet supplies and food and handles all sales with a cash register. The cash register displays the amount of the sale. It also shows the cash received and any change returned to the customer. The register also produces a customer receipt but keeps no internal record of the transactions. At the end of the day, the clerk counts the cash in the register and gives it to the cashier for deposit in the company bank account.

Requirements

1. Identify the internal control weakness over cash receipts.

2. What could you do to correct the weakness?

E-14 Evaluating internal control over cash payments

Learning Objective 3

Gary's Great Cars purchases high-performance auto parts from a Nebraska vendor. Dave Simon, the accountant for Gary's, verifies receipt of merchandise and then prepares, signs, and mails the check to the vendor.

Requirements

1. Identify the internal control weakness over cash payments.

2. What could the business do to correct the weakness?

Learning Objectives 1, 2, 3

E-15 Understanding internal control, components, procedures, and laws

Match the following terms with their definitions.

1. Internal control	**a.** Two or more people working together to overcome internal controls.
2. Control procedures	**b.** Part of internal control that ensures resources are not wasted.
3. Firewalls	
4. Encryption	**c.** Requires companies to review internal control and take responsibility for the accuracy and completeness of their financial reports.
5. Environment	
6. Information system	
7. Separation of duties	**d.** Should be pre-numbered to prevent theft and inefficiency.
8. Collusion	**e.** Limits access to a local network.
9. Documents	**f.** Example: The person who opens the bank statement should not also be the person who is reconciling cash.
10. Audits	
11. Operational efficiency	**g.** Identification of uncertainties that may arise due to a company's products, services, or operations.
12. Risk assessment	
13. Sarbanes-Oxley Act	**h.** Examination of a company's financial statements and accounting system by a trained accounting professional.

i. Without a sufficient one of these, information cannot properly be gathered and summarized.

j. The organizational plan and all the related measures that safeguard assets, encourage employees to follow company policies, promote operational efficiency, and ensure accurate and reliable accounting data.

k. Component of internal control that helps ensure business goals are achieved.

l. Rearranges data by a mathematical process.

m. To establish one, a company's owner/CEO and top managers must behave honorably to set a good example for employees.

Learning Objective 4

2. Cash Short & Over $13

E-16 Accounting for petty cash

Karen's Dance Studio created a $370 imprest petty cash fund. During the month, the fund custodian authorized and signed petty cash tickets as follows:

Petty Cash Ticket No.	Item	Account Debited	Amount
1	Delivery of programs to customers	Delivery Expense	$ 25
2	Mail package	Postage Expense	15
3	Newsletter	Printing Expense	35
4	Key to closet	Miscellaneous Expense	55
5	Copier paper	Office Supplies	80

Requirements

1. Make the general journal entry to create the petty cash fund. Include an explanation.

2. Make the general journal entry to record the petty cash fund replenishment. Cash in the fund totals $147. Include an explanation.

3. Assume that Karen's Dance Studio decides to decrease the petty cash fund to $200. Make the general journal entry to record this decrease.

E-17 Controlling petty cash

Learning Objective 4

2. March 31, Cash CR $91

Hangin' Out Night Club maintains an imprest petty cash fund of $100, which is under the control of Sandra Morgan. At March 31, the fund holds $9 cash and petty cash tickets for office supplies, $77, and delivery expense, $20.

Requirements

1. Explain how an imprest petty cash system works.

2. Journalize the establishment of the petty cash fund on March 1 and the replenishing of the fund on March 31.

3. Prepare a T-account for Petty Cash, and post to the account. What is Petty Cash's balance at all times?

E-18 Classifying bank reconciliation items

Learning Objective 5

The following items could appear on a bank reconciliation:

a. Outstanding checks, $670.

b. Deposits in transit, $1,500.

c. NSF check from customer, #548 for $175.

d. Bank collection of note receivable of $800, and interest of $80.

e. Interest earned on bank balance, $20.

f. Service charge, $10.

g. The business credited Cash for $200. The correct amount was $2,000.

h. The bank incorrectly decreased the business's account by $350 for a check written by another business.

Classify each item as (1) an addition to the book balance, (2) a subtraction from the book balance, (3) an addition to the bank balance, or (4) a subtraction from the bank balance.

E-19 Preparing a bank reconciliation

Learning Objective 5

1. Adjusted Balance $1,230

Harrison Photography's checkbook lists the following:

Date	Check No.	Item	Check	Deposit	Balance
Nov. 1					$ 540
4	622	Quick Mailing	$ 15		525
9		Service Revenue		$ 130	655
13	623	Photo Supplies	55		600
14	624	Utilities	75		525
18	625	Cash	60		465
26	626	Office Supplies	85		380
28	627	Upstate Realty Co.	265		115
30		Service Revenue		1,210	1,325

Internal Control and Cash

Harrison's November bank statement shows the following:

Balance			$ 540
Deposits			130
Debit Checks:	No.	Amount	
	622	$ 15	
	623	55	
	624	115*	
	625	60	(245)
Other charges:			
Printed checks		35	
Service charge		20	(55)
Balance			$ 370

*This is the correct amount for check number 624.

Requirements

1. Prepare Harrison Photography's bank reconciliation at November 30, 2015.

2. How much cash does Harrison actually have on November 30, 2015?

3. Journalize any transactions required from the bank reconciliation.

Learning Objective 5

1. Book Deductions $389

E-20 Preparing a bank reconciliation

Brett Knight Company operates four bowling alleys. The owner just received the October 31 bank statement from City National Bank, and the statement shows an ending balance of $905. Listed on the statement are an EFT rent collection of $410, a service charge of $10, NSF checks totaling $70, and a $30 charge for printed checks. In reviewing his cash records, Knight identified outstanding checks totaling $450 and a deposit in transit of $1,775. During October, he recorded a $310 check by debiting Salaries Expense and crediting Cash for $31. His Cash account shows an October 31 balance of $2,209.

Requirements

1. Prepare the bank reconciliation at October 31.

2. Journalize any transactions required from the bank reconciliation.

> Problems **Group A**

P-21A Identifying internal control weakness in cash receipts

Learning Objective 2

Brother Productions makes all sales on credit. Cash receipts arrive by mail. Justin Broaddus, the mailroom clerk, opens envelopes and separates the checks from the accompanying remittance advices. Broaddus forwards the checks to another employee, who makes the daily bank deposit but has no access to the accounting records. Broaddus sends the remittance advices, which show cash received, to the accounting department for entry in the accounts. Broaddus's only other duty is to grant sales allowances to customers. (A *sales allowance* decreases the amount receivable.) When Broaddus receives a customer check for $375 less a $60 allowance, he records the sales allowance and forwards the document to the accounting department.

Requirements

1. Identify the internal control weakness in this situation.
2. Who should record sales allowances?
3. What is the amount that should be shown in the ledger for cash receipts?

P-22A Correcting internal control weakness

Learning Objectives 1, 2, 3

Each of the following situations has an internal control weakness.

a. Upside-Down Applications develops custom programs to customer's specifications. Recently, development of a new program stopped while the programmers redesigned Upside-Down's accounting system. Upside-Down's accountants could have performed this task.

b. Norma Rottler has been your trusted employee for 24 years. She performs all cash-handling and accounting duties. Ms. Rottler just purchased a new Lexus and a new home in an expensive suburb. As owner of the company, you wonder how she can afford these luxuries because you pay her only $30,000 a year and she has no source of outside income.

c. Izzie Hardwoods, a private company, falsified sales and inventory figures in order to get an important loan. The loan went through, but Izzie later went bankrupt and could not repay the bank.

d. The office supply company where Pet Grooming Goods purchases sales receipts recently notified Pet Grooming Goods that its documents were not pre-numbered. Howard Mustro, the owner, replied that he never uses receipt numbers.

e. Discount stores such as Cusco make most of their sales in cash, with the remainder in credit card sales. To reduce expenses, one store manager ceases purchasing fidelity bonds on the cashier.

f. Cornelius' Corndogs keeps all cash receipts in an empty box for a week because he likes to go to the bank on Tuesdays when Joann is working.

Requirements

1. Identify the missing internal control characteristics in each situation.
2. Identify the possible problem caused by each control weakness.
3. Propose a solution to each internal control problem.

Learning Objective 4

2. June 30, Cash CR $140

P-23A Accounting for petty cash transactions

On June 1, Bash Salad Dressings creates a petty cash fund with an imprest balance of $450. During June, Al Franklin, the fund custodian, signs the following petty cash tickets:

Petty Cash Ticket Number	Item	Amount
101	Office supplies	$ 15
102	Cab fare for executive	10
103	Delivery of package across town	20
104	Business dinner	35
105	Merchandise inventory	65

On June 30, prior to replenishment, the fund contains these tickets plus cash of $310. The accounts affected by petty cash payments are Office Supplies, Travel Expense, Delivery Expense, Entertainment Expense, and Merchandise Inventory.

Requirements

1. Explain the characteristics and the internal control features of an imprest fund.

2. On June 30, how much cash should the petty cash fund hold before it is replenished?

3. Journalize all required entries to create the fund and replenish it. Include explanations.

4. Make the July 1 entry to increase the fund balance to $475. Include an explanation, and briefly describe what the custodian does.

P-24A Accounting for petty cash transactions

Learning Objective 4

2. June 30, Cash CR $175

Suppose that on June 1, Rockin' Gyrations, a disc jockey service, creates a petty cash fund with an imprest balance of $500. During June, Michael Martell, fund custodian, signs the following petty cash tickets:

Petty Cash Ticket Number	Item	Amount
1	Postage for package received	$ 20
2	Office party	25
3	Two boxes of stationery	35
4	Printer cartridges	15
5	Business dinner	75

On June 30, prior to replenishment, the fund contains these tickets plus cash of $325. The accounts affected by petty cash payments are Office Supplies, Entertainment Expense, and Postage Expense.

Requirements

1. On June 30, how much cash should this petty cash fund hold before it is replenished?

2. Journalize all required entries to (a) create the fund and (b) replenish it. Include explanations.

3. Make the entry on July 1 to increase the fund balance to $550. Include an explanation.

P-25A Preparing a bank reconciliation and journal entries

Learning Objective 5

1. Adjusted Balance $16,230

The December cash records of Dunlap Insurance follow:

Cash Receipts		Cash Payments	
Date	Cash Debit	Check No.	Cash Credit
Dec. 4	$ 4,170	1416	$ 860
9	510	1417	130
14	530	1418	650
17	2,180	1419	1,490
31	1,850	1420	1,440
		1421	900
		1422	630

Dunlap's Cash account shows a balance of $16,740 at December 31. On December 31, Dunlap Insurance received the following bank statement:

Bank Statement for December				
Beginning Balance				$ 13,600
Deposits and other Credits:				
Dec.	1	EFT	$ 300	
Dec.	5		4,170	
Dec.	10		510	
Dec.	15		530	
Dec.	18		2,180	
Dec.	22	BC	1,400	9,090
Checks and other Debits:				
Dec.	8	NSF	1,000	
Dec.	11 (check no. 1416)		860	
Dec.	19	EFT	700	
Dec.	22 (check no. 1417)		130	
Dec.	29 (check no. 1418)		650	
Dec.	31 (check no. 1419)		1,940	
Dec.	31	SC	60	(5,340)
Ending Balance				$ 17,350

Explanations: BC–bank collection; EFT–electronic funds transfer; NSF–nonsufficient funds checks; SC–service charge

Additional data for the bank reconciliation follows:

a. The EFT credit was a receipt of rent. The EFT debit was an insurance payment.

b. The NSF check was received from a customer.

c. The $1,400 bank collection was for a note receivable.

d. The correct amount of check 1419, for rent expense, is $1,940. Dunlap's controller mistakenly recorded the check for $1,490.

Requirements

1. Prepare the bank reconciliation of Dunlap Insurance at December 31, 2015.

2. Journalize any required entries from the bank reconciliation.

P-26A Preparing a bank reconciliation and journal entries

The August 31 bank statement of Winchester Healthcare has just arrived from United Bank. To prepare the bank reconciliation, you gather the following data:

a. The August 31 bank balance is $4,870.

b. The bank statement includes two charges for NSF checks from customers. One is for $400 (#1), and the other for $110 (#2).

c. The following Winchester checks are outstanding at August 31:

Check No.	Amount
237	$ 50
288	170
291	520
294	580
295	50
296	140

d. Winchester collects from a few customers by EFT. The August bank statement lists a $1,300 EFT deposit for a collection on account.

e. The bank statement includes two special deposits that Winchester hasn't recorded yet: $970 for dividend revenue, and $80 for the interest revenue Winchester earned on its bank balance during August.

f. The bank statement lists a $30 subtraction for the bank service charge.

g. On August 31, the Winchester treasurer deposited $350, but this deposit does not appear on the bank statement.

h. The bank statement includes a $1,000 deduction for a check drawn by Multi-State Freight Company. Winchester notified the bank of this bank error.

i. Winchester's Cash account shows a balance of $2,900 on August 31.

Requirements

1. Prepare the bank reconciliation for Winchester's Healthcare at August 31, 2015.

2. Journalize any required entries from the bank reconciliation. Include an explanation for each entry.

Learning Objective 5

1. Book Additions $2,350

> Problems Group B

P-27B Identifying internal control weakness in cash receipts

Rocking Chair Productions makes all sales on credit. Cash receipts arrive by mail. Larry Padgitt, the mailroom clerk, opens envelopes and separates the checks from the accompanying remittance advices. Padgitt forwards the checks to another employee, who makes the daily bank deposit but has no access to the accounting records. Padgitt sends the remittance advices, which show cash received, to the accounting department for entry in the accounts. Padgitt's only other duty is to grant sales allowances to customers. (A *sales allowance* decreases the amount receivable.) When Padgitt receives a customer check for $300 less a $40 allowance, he records the sales allowance and forwards the document to the accounting department.

Requirements

1. Identify the internal control weakness in this situation.

2. Who should record sales allowances?

3. What is the amount that should be shown in the ledger for cash receipts?

P-28B Correcting internal control weakness

Each of the following situations has an internal control weakness.

a. Jade Applications' owner has decided that one way to cut costs in the upcoming year is to fire the external auditor. He believes that the internal auditor should be able to efficiently monitor the company's internal controls.

b. In an effort to minimize the amount of paperwork, Ross Homes has decided that it will not keep copies of customer invoices related to sales revenue. Ross believes that this effort will minimize the amount of data storage the company will have to pay for.

c. Elle Bee, a trusted employee for many years, has never taken a vacation. The owner believes that he's lucky that she is so committed to her job.

d. The Medicine Chest Company keeps a small petty cash fund to handle small cash transactions. Because no one wants to volunteer to be the custodian, Lori Robinson, the owner, has decided that all employees should have access to the petty cash. She figures that as long as each employee fills out a petty cash ticket, then there are proper controls in place.

e. Due to the cost of maintaining the security cameras, Mike Bean, owner of Wings and More, has decided that he will remove the cameras that monitor the cash register.

f. Bryan Miller, manager of Hardware Emporium, prides himself on hiring exceptionally skilled employees who need no training to do their jobs.

Requirements

1. Identify the missing internal control characteristics in each situation.

2. Identify the possible problem caused by each control weakness.

3. Propose a solution to each internal control problem.

P-29B Accounting for petty cash transactions

Learning Objective 4

3. Cash Short & Over CR $5

On September 1, Cool Salad Dressings creates a petty cash fund with an imprest balance of $250. During September, Michael Martell, the fund custodian, signs the following petty cash tickets:

Petty Cash Ticket Number	Item	Amount
101	Office supplies	$ 30
102	Cab fare for executive	20
103	Delivery of package across town	35
104	Business dinner	25
105	Merchandise inventory	80

On September 30, prior to replenishment, the fund contains these tickets plus cash of $65. The accounts affected by petty cash payments are Office Supplies, Travel Expense, Delivery Expense, Entertainment Expense, and Merchandise Inventory.

Requirements

1. Explain the characteristics and the internal control features of an imprest fund.
2. On September 30, how much cash should the petty cash fund hold before it is replenished?
3. Journalize all required entries to create the fund and replenish it. Include explanations.
4. Make the October 1 entry to increase the fund balance to $300. Include an explanation, and briefly describe what the custodian does.

P-30B Accounting for petty cash transactions

Learning Objective 4

2. Sep. 30, Cash CR $170

Suppose that on September 1, Bash Gyrations, a disc jockey service, creates a petty cash fund with an imprest balance of $250. During September, Ruth Mangan, fund custodian, signs the following petty cash tickets:

Petty Cash Ticket Number	Item	Amount
1	Postage for package received	$ 30
2	Office party	10
3	Two boxes of stationery	25
4	Printer cartridges	35
5	Business dinner	65

On September 30, prior to replenishment, the fund contains these tickets plus cash of $80. The accounts affected by petty cash payments are Office Supplies, Entertainment Expense, and Postage Expense.

Internal Control and Cash

Requirements

1. On September 30, how much cash should this petty cash fund hold before it is replenished?

2. Journalize all required entries to (a) create the fund and (b) replenish it. Include explanations.

3. Make the entry on October 1 to increase the fund balance to $325. Include an explanation.

Learning Objective 5

1. Adjusted Balance $17,170

P-31B Preparing a bank reconciliation and journal entries

The May cash records of Dickson Insurance follow:

Cash Receipts		Cash Payments	
Date	Cash Debit	Check No.	Cash Credit
May 4	$ 4,150	1416	$ 850
9	540	1417	160
14	560	1418	670
17	2,190	1419	1,690
31	1,870	1420	1,450
		1421	1,200
		1422	640

Dickson's Cash account shows a balance of $16,650 at May 31. On May 31, Dickson Insurance received the following bank statement:

Bank Statement for May			
Beginning Balance			$ 14,000
Deposits and other Credits:			
May	1	EFT	$ 200
May	5		4,150
May	10		540
May	15		560
May	18		2,190
May	22	BC	1,700	9,340
Checks and other Debits:			
May	8	NSF	700
May	11 (check no. 1416)		850
May	19	EFT	400
May	22 (check no. 1417)		160
May	29 (check no. 1418)		670
May	31 (check no. 1419)		1,960
May	31	SC	10	(4,750)
Ending Balance			$ 18,590

Explanations: BC–bank collection; EFT–electronic funds transfer;
NSF–nonsufficient funds checks; SC–service charge

Additional data for the bank reconciliation follows:

a. The EFT credit was a receipt of rent. The EFT debit was an insurance payment.

b. The NSF check was received from a customer.

c. The $1,700 bank collection was for a note receivable.

d. The correct amount of check 1419, for rent expense, is $1,960. Dickson's controller mistakenly recorded the check for $1,690.

Requirements

1. Prepare the bank reconciliation of Dickson Insurance at May 31, 2015.

2. Journalize any required entries from the bank reconciliation.

P-32B Preparing a bank reconciliation and journal entries

The October 31 bank statement of White's Healthcare has just arrived from State Bank. To prepare the bank reconciliation, you gather the following data:

a. The October 31 bank balance is $5,170.

b. The bank statement includes two charges for NSF checks from customers. One is for $420 (#1), and the other is for $120 (#2).

c. The following White's checks are outstanding at October 31:

Check No.	Amount
237	$ 90
288	150
291	580
294	590
295	10
296	150

d. White's collects from a few customers by EFT. The October bank statement lists a $1,400 EFT deposit for a collection on account.

e. The bank statement includes two special deposits that White's hasn't recorded yet: $1,050 for dividend revenue and $50 for the interest revenue White's earned on its bank balance during October.

f. The bank statement lists a $70 subtraction for the bank service charge.

g. On October 31, the White's treasurer deposited $290, but this deposit does not appear on the bank statement.

h. The bank statement includes a $700 deduction for a check drawn by Multi-State Freight Company. White's notified the bank of this bank error.

i. White's Cash account shows a balance of $2,700 on October 31.

Requirements

1. Prepare the bank reconciliation for White's Healthcare at October 31, 2015.

2. Journalize any required entries from the bank reconciliation. Include an explanation for each entry.

Learning Objective 5

1. Book Deductions $610

> Continuing Problem

P-33 Preparing a bank reconciliation and journal entries

This problem deals with a company named Davis Consulting. Davis's March Cash T-account from its general ledger is as follows:

Cash			
Feb. 28 Bal.	23,115	4,300	Mar. 1 (ck. 207)
Mar. 6	2,930	825	Mar. 14 (ck. 208)
Mar. 13	2,800	1,455	Mar. 14 (ck. 209)
Mar. 20	4,800	190	Mar. 28 (ck. 210)
Mar. 27	3,690	550	Mar. 30 (ck. 211)
Mar. 31 Bal.	30,015		

Davis's bank statement dated March 31, 2015, follows:

Bank Statement for March 2015		
Beginning Balance, February 28, 2015		$ 23,510
Deposits and other Credits:		
Mar. 1	$ 700	
Mar. 8	2,930	
Mar. 14	2,800	
Mar. 20 EFT Hip Hop Hats-a customer	400	
Mar. 22	4,800	
Mar. 28 Interest credit	22	11,652
Checks and other Debits:		
Mar. 2 EFT to Paper Products	9	
Mar. 2 ck#206	1,095	
Mar. 18 ck#207	4,300	
Mar. 19 ck#209	1,455	
Mar. 28 EFT to The Cable Co.	85	
Mar. 28 ck#208	825	
Bank Service Charge	18	(7,787)
Ending Balance, March 31, 2015		$ 27,375

Requirements

1. Prepare the March bank reconciliation.

2. Journalize any transactions required from the bank reconciliation. Compute the adjusted account balance for the Cash T-account, and denote the balance as *End. Bal.*

> Practice Set

P-34 Preparing a bank reconciliation and journal entries

Consider the November 2015 transactions for Shine King Cleaning. The bank statement dated November 30, 2015, for Shine King follows.

Bank Statement for November 2015			
Beginning Balance, October 31, 2015		$ 0	
Deposits and other Credits:			
Nov.	2	$ 35,000	
Nov.	10	100	
Nov.	18	4,400	
Nov.	21	40,000	
Nov.	29 EFT Pierre's Wig Stand	600	
Nov.	30 Interest credit	16	80,116
Checks and other Debits:			
Nov.	2 EFT to Check Art	30	
Nov.	5 ck#101	2,000	
Nov.	9 ck#103	1,200	
Nov.	9 ck#102	2,400	
Nov.	26 ck#105	500	
Nov.	28 EFT to Calpine Energy	145	
Nov.	28 ck#106	100	
Bank Service Charge		18	(6,393)
Ending Balance, November 30, 2015			**$ 73,723**

Requirements

1. Prepare the bank reconciliation.

2. Journalize any required entries from the bank reconciliation.

CRITICAL THINKING

> Decision Cases

Decision Case 1

Conduct an Internet search for information on internal control and Sarbanes-Oxley. Write a report of your findings. In your report, discuss some of the advantages and disadvantages of Sarbanes-Oxley. Present it to your class (if required by your instructor).

Decision Case 2

This case is based on an actual situation. Centennial Construction Company, headquartered in Dallas, Texas, built a Rodeway Motel 35 miles north of Dallas. The construction foreman, whose name was Slim Chance, hired the 40 workers needed to complete the project. Slim had the construction workers fill out the necessary tax forms, and he sent their documents to the home office.

Work on the motel began on April 1 and ended September 1. Each week, Slim filled out a timecard of hours worked by each employee during the week. Slim faxed the time sheets to the home office, which prepared the payroll checks on Friday morning. Slim drove to the home office on Friday, picked up the payroll checks, and returned to the construction site. At 5 p.m. on Friday, Slim distributed payroll checks to the workers.

Requirements

1. Describe in detail the main internal control weakness in this situation. Specify what negative result(s) could occur because of the internal control weakness.

2. Describe what you would do to correct the internal control weakness.

Decision Case 3

San Diego Harbor Tours has poor internal control over cash. Ben Johnson, the owner, suspects the cashier of stealing. Here are some details of company cash on September 30:

a. The Cash account in the ledger shows a balance of $6,450.

b. The September 30 bank statement shows a balance of $4,300. The bank statement lists a $200 bank collection, a $10 service charge, and a $40 NSF check.

c. On September 30, the following checks are outstanding:

Amount
$ 100
300
600
200

d. There is a $3,000 deposit in transit on September 30.

e. The cashier handles all incoming cash and makes bank deposits. He also writes checks and reconciles the monthly bank statement.

Requirements

1. Perform your own bank reconciliation using the format illustrated in the chapter. There are no bank or book errors.

2. Assume that the adjusted bank balance is the correct cash amount and that all timing differences have been accounted for. How much has the cashier stolen? How can you tell?

3. Explain how Johnson can improve his internal controls.

> Ethical Issue 1

Mel O'Conner owns rental properties in Michigan. Each property has a manager who collects rent, arranges for repairs, and runs advertisements in the local newspaper. The property managers transfer cash to O'Conner monthly and prepare their own bank reconciliations. The manager in Lansing has been stealing from the company. To cover the theft, he overstates the amount of the outstanding checks on the monthly bank reconciliation. As a result, each monthly bank reconciliation appears to balance. However, the balance sheet reports more cash than O'Conner actually has in the bank. O'Conner is currently putting his entire business up for sale. In negotiating the sale of the business, O'Conner is showing the balance sheet to prospective buyers.

Requirements

1. Identify who, other than O'Conner, could be harmed by this theft. In what ways could they be harmed?

2. Discuss the role accounting plays in this situation.

> Fraud Case 1

Levon Helm was a kind of one-man mortgage broker. He would drive around Tennessee looking for homes that had second mortgages, and if the criteria were favorable, he would offer to buy the second mortgage for "cash on the barrelhead." Helm bought low and sold high, making sizable profits. Being a small operation, he employed one person, Cindy Patterson, who did all his bookkeeping. Patterson was an old family friend, and he trusted her so implicitly that he never checked up on the ledgers or the bank reconciliations. At some point, Patterson started "borrowing" from the business and concealing her transactions by booking phony expenses. She intended to pay it back someday, but she got used to the extra cash and couldn't stop. By the time the scam was discovered, she had drained the company of funds that it owed to many of its creditors. The company went bankrupt, Patterson did some jail time, and Helm lost everything.

Requirements

1. What was the key control weakness in this case?

2. Many small businesses cannot afford to hire enough people for adequate separation of duties. What can they do to compensate for this?

> Financial Statement Case 1

Visit **www.pearsonhighered.com/Horngren** to view a link to **Starbucks Corporation** 2011 Fiscal Year Annual Report. Study the audit opinion (labeled Report of Independent Registered Public Accounting Firm) of Starbucks Corporation and the Starbucks Corporation financial statements. Answer the following questions about the company:

Requirements

1. What is the name of Starbucks' outside auditing firm (independent registered public accounting firm)? What office of this firm signed the audit report? How long after the Starbucks year-end did the auditors issue their opinion?

2. Who bears primary responsibility for the financial statements? How can you tell?

3. Does it appear that Starbucks' internal controls are adequate? How can you tell?

4. What standard of auditing did the outside auditors use in examining the Starbucks financial statements? By what accounting standards were the statements evaluated?

5. By how much did Starbucks' cash balance (including cash equivalents) change during year ended October 2, 2011? What were the beginning and ending cash balances?

6. Review the notes to the consolidated financial statements, specifically Note 1 dealing with Cash and Cash Equivalents. What type of instruments does Starbucks consider to be cash equivalents?

7. Determine Starbucks' cash ratio as of October 2, 2011 and October 3, 2010. How does Starbucks' cash ratio compare with **Green Mountain Coffee Roasters** as illustrated in the chapter? Explain.

> Team Project 1

You are promoting a rock concert in your area. Each member of your team will invest $10,000 of his or her hard-earned money in this venture. It is April 1, and the concert is scheduled for June 30. Your promotional activities begin immediately, and ticket sales start on May 1. You expect to sell all the business's assets, pay all the liabilities, and distribute all remaining cash to the group members by July 31.

Write an internal control manual that will help safeguard the assets of the business. The starting point of the manual is to assign responsibilities among the group members. Authorize individuals, including group members and any outsiders that you need to hire, to perform specific jobs. Separate duties among the group and any employees.

> Communication Activity 1

In 100 words or fewer, explain why there may be a difference between the bank statement ending cash balance and the ending balance in the Cash account. Give at least two examples each of adjustments to the bank balance and to the book balance.

MyAccountingLab **For a wealth of online resources, including exercises, problems, media, and immediate tutorial help, please visit** www.myaccountinglab.com.

Try It! Solutions

1. d
2. a
3. c
4. e
5. b
6. a. mailroom employee; b. cashier; c. accounting department; d. controller
7. a. invoice; b. check; c. purchase order; d. receiving report
8.

Date	Accounts and Explanation	Debit	Credit
May 1	Petty Cash	200	
	Cash		200
	To open the petty cash fund.		
31	Office Supplies	81	
	Delivery Expense	36	
	Postage Expense	54	
	Miscellaneous Expense	9	
	Cash Short & Over	2	
	Cash		182
	To replenish the petty cash fund.		

9. c
10. d
11. a
12. d
13. b
14. Cash ratio = (Cash + Cash equivalents) / Total current liabilities
    = $60,000 / $75,000
    = 0.80

> Quick Check Answers

1. a **2.** d **3.** d **4.** d **5.** d **6.** c **7.** c **8.** d **9.** c **10.** b

Glossary

Account Number. On a check, the number that identifies the account upon which the payment is drawn.

Bank Reconciliation. A document explaining the reasons for the difference between a depositor's cash records and the depositor's cash balance in its bank account.

Bank Statement. A document from the bank that reports the activity in the customer's account. It shows the bank account's beginning and ending balances and lists the month's cash transactions conducted through the bank account.

Canceled Checks. Physical or scanned copies of the maker's cashed (paid) checks.

Cash Equivalent. A highly liquid investment that can be converted into cash in three months or less.

Cash Ratio. A measure of a company's ability to pay current liabilities from cash and cash equivalents: (Cash + Cash equivalents) / Total current liabilities.

Check. A document that instructs a bank to pay the designated person or business a specified amount of money.

Collusion. Two or more people working together to circumvent internal controls and defraud a company.

Credit Memorandum. An increase in a bank account.

Debit Memorandum. A decrease in a bank account.

Deposit in Transit. A deposit recorded by the company but not yet by its bank.

Deposit Ticket. A bank form that is completed by the customer and shows the amount of each deposit.

Electronic Data Interchange (EDI). A streamlined process that bypasses paper documents altogether. Computers of customers communicate directly with the computers of suppliers to automate routine business transactions.

Electronic Funds Transfer (EFT). A system that transfers cash by electronic communication rather than by paper documents.

Encryption. Rearranging plain-text messages by a mathematical process—the primary method of achieving security in e-commerce.

Evaluated Receipts Settlement (ERS). A procedure that compresses the payment approval process into a single step by comparing the receiving report to the purchase order.

External Auditor. An outside accountant, completely independent of the business, who monitors the controls to ensure that the financial statements are presented fairly in accordance with GAAP.

Firewall. A device that enables members of a local network to access the network, while keeping nonmembers out of the network.

Imprest System. A way to account for petty cash by maintaining a constant balance in the petty cash account. At any time, cash plus petty cash tickets must total the amount allocated to the petty cash fund.

Internal Auditor. An employee of the business who ensures the company's employees are following company policies, that the company meets all legal requirements, and that operations are running efficiently.

Internal Control. The organizational plan and all the related measures adopted by an entity to safeguard assets, encourage employees to follow company policies, promote operational efficiency, and ensure accurate and reliable accounting records.

Internal Control Report. A report by management describing its responsibility for and the adequacy of internal controls over financial reporting.

Lock-Box System. A system in which customers send their checks to a post office box that belongs to a bank. A bank employee empties the box daily and records the deposits into the company's bank account.

Maker. The party who issues the check.

Nonsufficient Funds (NSF) Check. A check for which the maker's bank account has insufficient money to pay the check.

Outstanding Check. A check issued by a company and recorded on its books but not yet paid by its bank.

Payee. The individual or business to whom the check is paid.

Petty Cash. A fund containing a small amount of cash that is used to pay for minor expenditures.

Public Company. A company that sells its stock to the general public.

Remittance Advice. An optional attachment to a check that tells the business the reason for the payment.

Routing Number. On a check, the 9-digit number that identifies the bank upon which the payment is drawn.

Sarbanes-Oxley Act (SOX). Requires companies to review internal control and take responsibility for the accuracy and completeness of their financial reports.

Separation of Duties. Dividing responsibility between two or more people to limit fraud and promote accuracy of accounting records.

Signature Card. A card that shows each authorized person's signature for a bank account.

Timing Difference. Difference that arises between the balance on the bank statement and the balance on the company's books because of a time lag in recording transactions.

Voucher. A sequentially numbered document authorizing a cash payment.

Photo Credits

Credits are listed in order of appearance.

Photo 1 (top): Boris Rabtsevich/Shutterstock
Photo 2 (middle): Todd Taulman/Shutterstock
Photo 3 (bottom): Eric Gevaert/Shutterstock
Photo 4: Michaeljung/Shutterstock
Photo 5: Krungchingpixs/Shutterstock
Photo 6: Rido/Shutterstock

Receivables

Receivables

Should Credit Be Extended?

James Hulsey works for a large department store as a credit manager. His main responsibility is handling all credit sales that generate accounts receivable. James must evaluate each customer's request for credit and determine which customers are allowed to purchase goods on credit. He does this by reviewing the customer's credit history and credit score. James has an important decision to make. He understands that granting credit increases the sales of the department store, but it also has its disadvantages.

One of those disadvantages is that the department store has to wait to receive cash. But, for James, the biggest disadvantage—and the most frustrating part of his job—is when customers don't pay. When this happens, the department store suffers a loss because it will never collect the cash associated with the sale. The department store must have a way to take the accounts of customers who will never make payment off the books; this is called a *write-off*. In addition, James must also help the department store estimate the amount of receivables that will be uncollectible. It's important that the department store have a good idea of the amount of cash that will actually be collected on its receivables so it can estimate future cash flows.

How Are Receivables Accounted For?

In this chapter, we determine how companies account for receivables. Receivables represent the right to receive cash in the future from a current transaction. We begin by looking at how companies such as Sears Holdings Corporation (the parent company of Kmart and Sears, Roebuck and Co.) record accounts receivable, including when customers don't make the required payments. Then we review notes receivable, which usually extend over a longer term than accounts receivable and typically involve interest. We finish the chapter by looking at how companies (and investors) can use financial ratios to evaluate the ability to collect cash on accounts receivable.

Learning Objectives

1 Define and explain common types of receivables and journalize sales on credit, credit card sales, and debit card sales

2 Apply the direct write-off method for uncollectibles

3 Apply the allowance method for uncollectibles and estimate bad debts expense based on the percent-of-sales, percent-of-receivables, and aging-of-receivables methods

4 Account for notes receivable including computing interest and recording honored and dishonored notes

5 Use the acid-test ratio, accounts receivable turnover ratio, and days' sales in receivables to evaluate business performance

WHAT ARE COMMON TYPES OF RECEIVABLES AND HOW ARE CREDIT SALES RECORDED?

Learning Objective 1

Define and explain common types of receivables and journalize sales on credit, credit card sales, and debit card sales

Receivable

A monetary claim against a business or an individual.

Debtor

The party to a credit transaction who takes on an obligation/payable.

A **receivable** occurs when a business sells goods or services to another party on account (on credit). It is a monetary claim against a business or an individual. The receivable is the seller's claim for the amount of the transaction. Receivables also occur when a business loans money to another party. A receivable is the right to *receive* cash in the future from a current transaction. It is something the business owns; therefore, it is an asset. *Each* receivable transaction involves two parties:

- The creditor, who receives a receivable (an asset). The creditor will collect cash from the customer or borrower.
- The **debtor**, the party to a credit transaction who takes on an obligation/payable (a liability). The debtor will pay cash later.

Types of Receivables

The three major types of receivables are:

- Accounts receivable
- Notes receivable
- Other receivables

Accounts Receivable

Accounts Receivable

The right to receive cash in the future from customers for goods sold or for services performed.

Accounts receivable, also called *trade receivables*, represent the right to receive cash in the future from customers for goods sold or for services performed. Accounts receivable are usually collected within a short period of time, such as 30 or 60 days, and are therefore reported as a current asset on the balance sheet.

Notes Receivable

Notes Receivable

A written promise that a customer will pay a fixed amount of principal plus interest by a certain date in the future.

Maturity Date

The date when a note is due.

Notes receivable usually have longer terms than accounts receivable. Notes receivable, sometimes called promissory notes, represent a written promise that a customer will pay a fixed amount of principal plus interest by a certain date in the future—called the **maturity date**. The maturity date is the date on which the notes receivable is due. A written document known as a promissory note serves as evidence of the debt and is signed by the debtor. Notes receivable due within one year or less are considered current assets. Notes receivable due beyond one year are long-term assets.

Other Receivables

Other receivables make up a miscellaneous category that includes any other type of receivable where there is a right to receive cash in the future. Common examples include dividends receivable, interest receivable, and taxes receivable. These other receivables may be either current or long-term assets, depending on whether they will be received within one year or less.

Exercising Internal Control Over Receivables

Businesses that sell goods or services on account receive cash (check payments) by mail or online payments (EFT), so internal control over collections is important. A critical element of internal control is the separation of cash-handling and cash-accounting duties.

Most large companies also have a credit department to evaluate customers' credit applications to determine whether they meet the company's credit approval standards. The extension of credit is a balancing act. The company does not want to lose sales to good customers, but it also wants to avoid receivables that will never be collected. For good internal control over cash collections from receivables, separation of duties must be maintained. The credit department should have no access to cash, and those who handle cash should not be in a position to grant credit to customers. If a credit department employee also handles cash, he or she could pocket money received from a customer. The employee could then label the customer's account as uncollectible, and the company would stop billing that customer. In this scenario, the employee may have covered his or her theft.

Recording Sales on Credit

As discussed earlier, selling on account (on credit) creates an account receivable. Businesses must maintain a separate accounts receivable account for each customer in order to account for payments received from the customer and amounts still owed.

For example, Smart Touch Learning sells $5,000 in services to customer Brown on account and $10,000 (sales price) of merchandise inventory to customer Smith on account on August 8. The revenue is recorded (ignore Cost of Goods Sold) as follows:

Date	Accounts and Explanation	Debit	Credit
Aug. 8	Accounts Receivable—Brown	5,000	
	Service Revenue		5,000
	Performed service on account.		
8	Accounts Receivable—Smith	10,000	
	Sales Revenue		10,000
	Sold goods on account.		

$$\underbrace{\text{A}\uparrow}_{\substack{\text{Accounts} \\ \text{Receivable}\uparrow}} \Big\} = \Big\{ \underbrace{\text{L}}_{} + \underbrace{\text{E}\uparrow}_{\substack{\text{Service} \\ \text{Revenue}\uparrow}}$$

$$\underbrace{\text{A}\uparrow}_{\substack{\text{Accounts} \\ \text{Receivable}\uparrow}} \Big\} = \Big\{ \underbrace{\text{L}}_{} + \underbrace{\text{E}\uparrow}_{\substack{\text{Sales} \\ \text{Revenue}\uparrow}}$$

These separate customer accounts receivable (for example, Accounts Receivable–Brown) are called subsidiary accounts. The sum of all balances in subsidiary accounts receivable equals a control account balance. In this case, Accounts Receivable serves as the control. This is illustrated as follows:

Control Account

Accounts Receivable

Bal. 15,000	

Subsidiary Accounts

Accounts Receivable—Brown

Bal. 5,000	

Accounts Receivable—Smith

Bal. 10,000	

Total for subsidiary accounts = $15,000

The control account, Accounts Receivable, shows a balance of $15,000. The individual customer accounts in the subsidiary ledger (Accounts Receivable—Brown $5,000 + Accounts Receivable—Smith $10,000) add up to a total of $15,000.

When the business collects cash from both customers on August 29—$4,000 from Brown and $8,000 from Smith, Smart Touch Learning makes the following entry and posts the entry to the T-accounts:

$$\frac{\textbf{A}\uparrow\downarrow}{\substack{\text{Cash}\uparrow \\ \text{Accounts} \\ \text{Receivable}\downarrow}} = \left\{ \frac{\textbf{L}}{} + \frac{\textbf{E}}{} \right.$$

Date	Accounts and Explanation	Debit	Credit
Aug. 29	Cash	12,000	
	Accounts Receivable—Brown		4,000
	Accounts Receivable—Smith		8,000
	Collected cash on account.		

Control Account

Accounts Receivable

Bal. 15,000	12,000 Aug. 29
Bal. 3,000	

Subsidiary Accounts

Accounts Receivable—Brown

Bal. 5,000	4,000 Aug. 29
Bal. 1,000	

Accounts Receivable—Smith

Bal. 10,000	8,000 Aug. 29
Bal. 2,000	

Total for subsidiary accounts = $3,000

Recording Credit Card and Debit Card Sales

In addition to selling on account, most companies also accept two alternative forms of payment—credit card and debit card. By accepting credit cards and debit cards, such as Visa, MasterCard, and American Express, businesses are able to attract more customers. Credit cards offer the customer the convenience of buying something without having to pay cash immediately. Debit cards, on the other hand, reduce the customer's bank account immediately but allow the customer to pay electronically instead of with currency or by writing a check.

Businesses also benefit from accepting payment by credit and debit cards. They do not have to check each customer's credit rating or worry about keeping accounts receivable records or even collecting from the customer. The card issuer has the responsibility of collecting from the customer. Thus, instead of collecting cash from the customer, the seller will receive cash from the card issuer. There is almost always a fee to the seller to cover the processing costs.

Companies hire a third-party processor to process credit and debit card transactions. Transactions are usually entered into an electronic terminal (card scanner) that the company either purchases or rents from the processor. The fees the card processor charges the company for its processing services vary depending on the type of card and the specific agreement the company has with the card processor. The processor agreement specifies how fees are paid to the processor. The following are two common methods of deposits of proceeds:

- **Net**—The total sale less the processing fee assessed equals the net amount of cash deposited by the processor, usually within a few days of the sale date.
- **Gross**—The total sale is deposited daily within a few days of the actual sale date. The processing fees for all transactions processed for the month are deducted from the company's bank account by the processor, often on the last day of the month.

Proceeds from credit and debit card transactions are usually deposited within a few business days after the sale. Therefore, credit and debit card sales are journalized similar to cash sales. For example, Smart Touch Learning sells merchandise inventory (ignore Cost of Goods Sold) to a customer for $3,000 on August 15. The customer pays with a third party credit card. Smart Touch Learning would record the entry, assuming the card processor assesses a 4% fee and nets the deposit, as follows:

Date	Accounts and Explanation	Debit	Credit
Aug. 15	Cash	2,880	
	Credit Card Expense ($3,000 × 0.04)	120	
	Sales Revenue		3,000
	Recorded credit card sales, net of fee.		

The same entry, assuming the processor uses the gross method, on the sale date would be as follows:

Date	Accounts and Explanation	Debit	Credit
Aug. 15	Cash	3,000	
	Sales Revenue		3,000
	Recorded credit card sales.		

At the end of August, the processor would collect the fees assessed for the month. (*Note:* We assume only the one card sale for this month.)

$$\left.\frac{A\downarrow}{\text{Cash}\downarrow}\right\} = \left\{\frac{L + E\downarrow}{\text{Credit Card Expense}\uparrow}\right.$$

Date	Accounts and Explanation	Debit	Credit
Aug. 31	Credit Card Expense	120	
	Cash		120
	Paid fees assessed by credit card processor.		

Factoring and Pledging Receivables

One of the many drawbacks of accepting sales on account is that the company must wait for the receipt of cash. Sometimes this time period could be delayed as much as 60 to 90 days. In addition, there is always the risk that the company will never collect on the receivable. In the previous section, we looked at credit cards and debit cards as being an option to reduce this risk. Another option for a business is to either factor or pledge its receivables.

When a business factors its receivables, it sells its receivables to a finance company or bank (often called a *factor*). The business receives cash less an applicable fee from the factor for the receivables immediately. The factor, instead of the business, now collects the cash on the receivables. The business no longer has to deal with the collection of the receivable from the customer. The business receives cash associated with the receivable from the factor instead of the customer.

Pledging of receivables is another option for businesses that need cash immediately. In a pledging situation, a business uses its receivables as security for a loan. The business borrows money from a bank and offers its receivables as collateral. The business is still responsible for collecting on the receivables, but it uses this money to pay off the loan along with interest. In pledging, if the loan is not paid, the bank can collect on the receivables.

In both situations, the business has managed to receive cash immediately for the receivables instead of having to wait for collection.

> Decisions   How could we get cash fast?

Peggy Goodman is the owner of a retail furniture store. Her store accepts credit from customers and lately has accumulated a large number of accounts receivable instead of cash. Peggy knows that she will eventually receive the cash, but she is concerned about her cash flow. She needs to pay her employees and doesn't think she has enough cash on hand to do so. She is also concerned that she won't receive all of the cash that is due to the business. What should Peggy do?

Solution

Peggy should consider selling the receivables to a finance company or bank. If the business sells the receivables, it will receive cash immediately, less a fee charged by the finance company or bank. The buyer of the receivables (the finance company or bank) then takes over the receivables and is responsible for collecting the cash when the receivables come due. Peggy's store no longer has the risk of uncollectibles. However, this decision comes at a cost. Peggy must be willing to receive less cash because of the fee the buyer of the receivables charges.

Phoenix Restaurants accepts credit and debit cards as forms of payment. Assume Phoenix had $12,000 of credit and debit card sales on June 30, 2015.

1. Suppose Phoenix's processor charges a 2% fee and deposits sales net of the fee. Journalize the sale transaction for the restaurant.
2. Suppose Phoenix's processor charges a 2% fee and deposits sales using the gross method. Journalize the sale transaction for the restaurant.

Check your answers at the end of the chapter.

For more practice, see Short Exercises S-1 and S-2. MyAccountingLab

HOW ARE UNCOLLECTIBLES ACCOUNTED FOR WHEN USING THE DIRECT WRITE-OFF METHOD?

Selling on account brings both a benefit and a cost:

- The benefit to a business is the potential increased revenues and profits by making sales to a wider range of customers.
- The cost, however, is that some customers do not pay, creating uncollectible receivables.

> **Learning Objective 2**
> Apply the direct write-off method for uncollectibles

Customers' accounts receivable that are uncollectible must be written off or removed from the books because the company does not expect to receive cash in the future. Instead, the company must record an expense associated with the cost of the uncollectible account. This expense is called **bad debts expense**. Bad debts expense is sometimes called *doubtful accounts expense* or *uncollectible accounts expense*.

There are two methods of accounting for uncollectible receivables and recording the related bad debts expense:

- Direct write-off method
- Allowance method

> **Bad Debts Expense**
> The cost to the seller of extending credit. It arises from the failure to collect from some credit customers.

Recording and Writing Off Uncollectible Accounts—Direct Write-Off Method

The **direct write-off method** of accounting for uncollectible receivables is primarily used by small, non-public companies. Under the direct write-off method, accounts receivable are written off and bad debts expense is recorded when the business determines that it will never collect from a specific customer.

For example, let's assume that on August 9 Smart Touch Learning determines that it will not be able to collect $200 from customer Dan King for a sale of merchandise inventory made on May 5. The company would write off the customer's account receivable by debiting Bad Debts Expense and crediting the customer's Accounts Receivable as follows:

> **Direct Write-Off Method**
> A method of accounting for uncollectible receivables in which the company records bad debts expense when a customer's account receivable is uncollectible.

Date	Accounts and Explanation	Debit	Credit
Aug. 9	Bad Debts Expense	200	
	Accounts Receivable—King		200
	Wrote off an uncollectible account.		

$$\left. \begin{array}{c} A\downarrow \\ \text{Accounts} \\ \text{Receivable}\downarrow \end{array} \right\} = \left\{ \begin{array}{ccc} L & + & E\downarrow \\ & & \text{Bad Debts} \\ & & \text{Expense}\uparrow \end{array} \right.$$

Once an account receivable is written off, the company stops pursuing the collection. Some companies might turn delinquent receivables over to an attorney or other collection agency to recover some of the cash for the company, but generally companies do not expect to receive any future payment.

Recovery of Accounts Previously Written Off—Direct Write-Off Method

Occasionally after a company writes off an account, the customer will decide to make payment. To account for this recovery, the company must reverse the earlier write-off. For example, on September 10, Smart Touch Learning unexpectedly receives $200 cash from Dan King. The company will reverse the earlier write-off and then record the cash collection as follows:

$$\left.\frac{\text{A}\uparrow}{\substack{\text{Accounts} \\ \text{Receivable}\uparrow}}\right\} = \left\{\frac{\text{L}}{} + \frac{\text{E}\uparrow}{\substack{\text{Bad Debts} \\ \text{Expense}\downarrow}}\right.$$

$$\left.\frac{\text{A}\uparrow\downarrow}{\substack{\text{Cash}\uparrow \\ \text{Accounts} \\ \text{Receivable}\downarrow}}\right\} = \left\{\frac{\text{L}}{} + \frac{\text{E}}{}\right.$$

Date	Accounts and Explanation	Debit	Credit
Sep. 10	Accounts Receivable—King	200	
	Bad Debts Expense		200
	Reinstated previously written off account.		
10	Cash	200	
	Accounts Receivable—King		200
	Collected cash on account.		

> *In order to keep accurate records about the collection of cash for a previously written off account, the business should re-establish the Accounts Receivable by debiting the receivable account. Then the business can record the receipt of cash for the receivable by debiting Cash and crediting Accounts Receivable. This helps restore the credit history of the customer by showing that the customer did fulfill the promise of payment.*

Limitations of the Direct Write-Off Method

The direct write-off method, as stated earlier, is often used only by small, non-public companies. This is because the direct write-off method violates the matching principle. The matching principle requires that the expense of uncollectible accounts be matched with the related revenue. For example, when using the direct write-off method, a company might record sales revenue in 2014 but not record the bad debt expense until 2015. By recording the bad debts expense in a different year than when the revenue was recorded, the company is overstating net income in 2014 and understating net income in 2015. In addition, on the balance sheet in 2014, Accounts Receivable will be overstated because the company will have some receivables that will be uncollectible but are not yet written off. This method is only acceptable for companies that have very few uncollectible receivables. Most companies must use a method that does a better job of matching expenses to the associated sales revenue. This method is called the *allowance method,* and it is the method required by GAAP.

Williams Company uses the direct write-off method to account for uncollectible receivables. On July 18, Williams wrote off a $6,800 account receivable from customer W. Jennings. On August 24, Williams unexpectedly received full payment from Jennings on the previously written off account.

3. Journalize Williams' write-off on the uncollectible receivable.
4. Journalize Williams' collection of the previously written off receivable.

Check your answers at the end of the chapter.

For more practice, see Short Exercises S-3 and S-4. MyAccountingLab

HOW ARE UNCOLLECTIBLES ACCOUNTED FOR WHEN USING THE ALLOWANCE METHOD?

Most companies use the allowance method to measure bad debts. The allowance method is based on the matching principle; thus, the key concept is to record bad debts expense in the same period as the sales revenue. The offset to the expense is a contra account called Allowance for Bad Debts or the *Allowance for Doubtful Accounts*. The allowance account reduces accounts receivable. The business does not wait to see which customers will not pay. Instead, it records a bad debts expense based on estimates developed from past experience and uses the Allowance for Bad Debts to hold the pool of "unknown" uncollectible accounts.

Recording Bad Debts Expense—Allowance Method

When using the allowance method, companies estimate bad debts expense at the end of the period and then record an adjusting entry. Suppose that as of December 31, 2015, Smart Touch Learning estimates that $80 of its $4,400 accounts receivable are uncollectible. The accounting clerk will record the following adjusting entry:

Learning Objective 3

Apply the allowance method for uncollectibles and estimate bad debts expense based on the percent-of-sales, percent-of-receivables, and aging-of-receivables methods

Allowance Method
A method of accounting for uncollectible receivables in which the company estimates bad debts expense instead of waiting to see which customers the company will not collect from.

Allowance for Bad Debts
A contra account, related to accounts receivable, that holds the estimated amount of uncollectible accounts.

Date	Accounts and Explanation	Debit	Credit
2015			
Dec. 31	Bad Debts Expense	80	
	Allowance for Bad Debts		80
	Recorded bad debts expense for the period.		

$$\underset{\substack{\text{Allowance} \\ \text{for Bad} \\ \text{Debts}\uparrow}}{\underline{\text{A}\downarrow}} \Bigg\} = \Bigg\{ \underset{}{\underline{\text{L}}} + \underset{\substack{\text{Bad Debts} \\ \text{Expense}\uparrow}}{\underline{\text{E}\downarrow}}$$

After posting the adjusting entry, Smart Touch Learning has the following balances in its accounts:

Accounts Receivable		Allowance for Bad Debts		Bad Debts Expense	
Dec. 31 4,400			80 Dec. 31	Dec. 31 80	

Accounts Receivable will be reported on the balance sheet, but it will now be shown at the net realizable value. **Net realizable value** is the net value the company expects to collect from its accounts receivable (Accounts Receivable less Allowance for Bad Debts). Smart Touch Learning would report the following on its balance sheet:

Net Realizable Value
The net value a company expects to collect from its accounts receivable. Accounts Receivable less Allowance for Bad Debts.

Under IFRS, receivables are recognized and reported similarly to what is required by GAAP. Accounts Receivable must be reported at Net Realizable Value and the allowance method is used to accomplish the matching of bad debt expense to the sales of the period and to report receivables at net. Under IFRS, the Allowance for Bad Debts may be called the **Provision** for Bad Debts. IFRS provides more detailed criteria than GAAP for determining when an account is uncollectible.

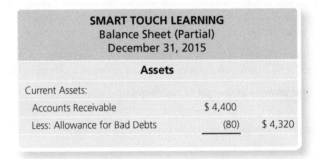

SMART TOUCH LEARNING		
Balance Sheet (Partial)		
December 31, 2015		
Assets		
Current Assets:		
Accounts Receivable	$ 4,400	
Less: Allowance for Bad Debts	(80)	$ 4,320

The balance sheet now reports the amount of accounts receivable that Smart Touch Learning expects to collect, $4,320. The contra account, Allowance for Bad Debts, is subtracted from Accounts Receivable showing that although $4,400 is owed to Smart Touch Learning, the company estimates that $80 of accounts receivable will be uncollectible.

>Ethics   Should the uncollectible accounts be underestimated?

Norah Wang is in the process of recording adjusting entries for her employer, Happy Kennels. She is evaluating the uncollectible accounts and determining the amount of bad debts expense to record for the year. Her employer and owner of Happy Kennels, Gillian Tedesco, has asked that Norah underestimate the amount of uncollectible accounts for the year. Gillian is hoping to get a bank loan for an expansion of the kennel facility, and she is concerned that the net income of the company will be too low for a loan to be approved. What should Norah do?

Solution

It is important that accounts receivable be reported at the appropriate amount on the balance sheet. This involves determining an accurate estimate of uncollectible accounts and recognizing the associated bad debts expense. In understating the amount of uncollectible accounts, Norah would be misleading the bank on the amount of cash that Happy Kennels expects to collect in the future.

Why isn't Bad Debts < Expense debited when writing off an account receivable when using the allowance method?

Writing Off Uncollectible Accounts—Allowance Method

When using the allowance method, companies still write off accounts receivable that are uncollectible. However, instead of recording a debit to Bad Debts Expense (as done when using the direct write-off method), the company will record a debit to Allowance for Bad Debts. Bad Debts Expense is not debited when a company writes off an account receivable when using the allowance method because the company has already recorded the Bad Debt Expense as an adjusting entry. The entry to write off an account under the allowance method has no affect on net income at the time of entry.

For example, on January 10, 2016, Smart Touch Learning determines that it cannot collect a total of $25 from its customer, Shawn Callahan. The accounting clerk would record the following entry to write off the account:

Date	Accounts and Explanation	Debit	Credit
2016			
Jan. 10	Allowance for Bad Debts	25	
	Accounts Receivable—Callahan		25
	Wrote off an uncollectible account.		

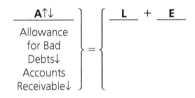

Smart Touch Learning's account balances after the write-off are:

	Accounts Receivable					Allowance for Bad Debts		
Jan. 1, 2016	4,400						80	Jan. 1, 2016
		25	Jan. 10, 2016		Jan. 10, 2016	25		
Bal.	4,375						55	Bal.

The entry to write off a receivable reduces the amount of the Allowance for Bad Debts account and also the Accounts Receivable account, but it does not affect the net realizable value shown on the balance sheet. This is because both Allowance for Bad Debts (contra-asset) and Accounts Receivable (asset) were reduced by the amount of the write-off. In addition, the write-off of a receivable does not affect net income because the entry does not involve revenue or expenses.

	Before Write-Off	After Write-Off
Accounts Receivable	$ 4,400	$ 4,375
Less: Allowance for Bad Debts	(80)	(55)
Net Realizable Value	$ 4,320	$ 4,320

Recovery of Accounts Previously Written Off—Allowance Method

After a company has previously written off an account, the company stops attempting to collect on the receivable. Customers will occasionally make payment on receivables that have already been written off. A business will need to reverse the write-off to the Allowance for Bad Debts account and then record the receipt of cash. In reversing the write-off, the business is re-establishing the receivable account and reversing the write-off from the Allowance for Bad Debts account.

Recall that Smart Touch Learning wrote off the $25 receivable from customer Shawn Callahan on January 10, 2016. It is now March 4, 2016, and Smart Touch

Learning unexpectedly receives $25 cash from Callahan. The entries to reverse the write-off and record the receipt of cash are as follows:

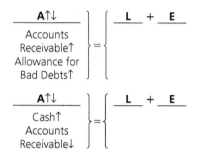

Date	Accounts and Explanation	Debit	Credit
Mar. 4	Accounts Receivable—Callahan	25	
	Allowance for Bad Debts		25
	Reinstated previously written off account.		
4	Cash	25	
	Accounts Receivable—Callahan		25
	Collected cash on account.		

Estimating and Recording Bad Debts Expense—Allowance Method

How do companies determine the amount of bad debts expense when using the allowance method? Companies use their past experience as well as considering the economy, the industry they operate in, and other variables. In short, they make an educated guess, called an *estimate*. There are three basic ways to estimate uncollectibles:

- Percent-of-sales
- Percent-of-receivables
- Aging-of-receivables

Percent-of-Sales Method

Percent-of-Sales Method
A method of estimating uncollectible receivables that calculates bad debts expense based on a percentage of net credit sales.

The percent-of-sales method computes bad debts expense as a percentage of net credit sales. (Some companies will use all sales not just credit sales.) This method is also called the *income-statement approach* because it focuses on the amount of expense that is reported on the income statement.

Let's return to Smart Touch Learning. Based on prior experience, the company's bad debts expense is normally 0.5% of net credit sales, which totaled $60,000 for the year. The accountant calculates bad debt expense using the percent-of-sales method as follows:

> **Percent-of-Sales Method:**
> Bad Debts Expense = Net credit sales × %
> = $60,000 × 0.005
> = $300

When using the allowance method, the only time Bad Debts Expense is recorded is as an adjusting entry.

At December 31, Smart Touch Learning records the following adjusting entry to recognize bad debts expense for the year:

Date	Accounts and Explanation	Debit	Credit
2016			
Dec. 31	Bad Debts Expense	300	
	Allowance for Bad Debts		300
	Recorded bad debts expense for the period.		

After posting the adjusting entry, Smart Touch Learning has the following balances in its balance sheet and income statement accounts. Ignore the previously recorded reversal of the write-off:

Balance sheet accounts:

Accounts Receivable					Allowance for Bad Debts				
Jan. 1, 2016, Bal.	4,400							80	Jan. 1, 2016, Bal.
Net credit sales	60,000	25	Write-offs		Write-offs	25			
		58,000	Collections					55	Unadj. Bal.
Unadj. Bal.	6,375							300	Adj.
Dec. 31, 2016, Bal.	**6,375**							**355**	**Dec. 31, 2016, Bal.**

Income statement account:

Bad Debts Expense		
Jan. 1, 2016, Bal.	0	
Adj.	300	
Dec. 31, 2016, Bal.	**300**	

Percent-of-Receivables Method

The percent-of-receivables and aging-of-receivables methods are based on the balance of accounts receivable. These approaches are also called *balance-sheet approaches* because they focus on the accounts receivable (a balance sheet account) and determine a target allowance balance based on a percentage of the receivable balance.

The first balance sheet approach is the percent-of-receivables method. In the percent-of-receivables method, the business once again determines a percentage of uncollectible accounts based on past experience. This method is different than the percent-of-sales method because it bases the percentage on the *ending* unadjusted balance in the Accounts Receivable account instead of net credit sales.

The calculation for bad debts expense under the percent-of-receivables method is a two-step process. First, the company determines the target balance of Allowance for Bad Debts. Then it uses the target balance to determine the amount of the bad debt expense.

Percent-of-Receivables Method
A method of estimating uncollectible receivables by determining the balance of the Allowance for Bad Debts account based on a percentage of accounts receivable.

Percent-of-Receivables Method:

Step 1: Determine the target balance of Allowance for Bad Debts.

Target balance = Ending balance of accounts receivable × %

Step 2: Determine the amount of bad debts expense by evaluating the allowance account.

Bad debts expense = Target balance − Unadjusted credit balance of Allowance for Bad Debts

OR

Bad debts expense = Target balance + Unadjusted debit balance of Allowance for Bad Debts

---

Let's look at an example for Smart Touch Learning. Assume that at December 31, 2016, the company's unadjusted accounts receivable balance is $6,375. Smart Touch Learning estimates that 4% of its accounts receivable will be uncollectible. In step 1, the company determines the target balance for the Allowance for Bad Debts account: $255 ($6,375 × 0.04). Next, its accountant determines the amount of the bad debts expense adjustment: $255 − $55 = $200.

Allowance for Bad Debts

		80	Jan. 1, 2016, Bal.
Write-offs	25		
		55	Unadj. Bal.
		200	Adj.
		255	**Dec. 31, 2016, Bal.**

Step 2: The bad debts expense adjustment must be calculated based on the target balance.
$255 − $55 = $200

Step 1: Calculate the target balance. It is always reported as a credit balance.
$6,375 × 0.04 = $255

Smart Touch Learning records the following adjusting entry on December 31 to recognize bad debts expense for the year:

$$\left.\begin{array}{c} \text{A}\downarrow \\ \hline \text{Allowance} \\ \text{for Bad} \\ \text{Debts}\uparrow \end{array}\right\} = \left\{\begin{array}{ccc} \text{L} & + & \text{E}\downarrow \\ & & \hline \\ & & \text{Bad Debts} \\ & & \text{Expense}\uparrow \end{array}\right.$$

Date	Accounts and Explanation	Debit	Credit
2016			
Dec. 31	Bad Debts Expense	200	
	Allowance for Bad Debts		200
	Recorded bad debts expense for the period.		

After posting the adjusting entry, Smart Touch Learning has the following balances on its balance sheet and income statement accounts:

Balance sheet accounts:

Accounts Receivable

Jan. 1, 2016, Bal.	4,400			
Net credit sales	60,000	25	Write-offs	
		58,000	Collections	
Unadj. Bal.	6,375			
Dec. 31, 2016, Bal.	**6,375**			

Allowance for Bad Debts

			80	Jan. 1, 2016, Bal.
Write-offs	25			
			55	Unadj. Bal.
			200	Adj.
			255	**Dec. 31, 2016, Bal.**

Income statement account:

Bad Debts Expense

Jan. 1, 2016, Bal.	0	
Adj.	200	
Dec. 31, 2016, Bal.	**200**	

In the preceding example, Smart Touch Learning had an unadjusted *credit* balance in the allowance account. If a company has a debit balance before the adjustment, the calculation for bad debts expense is a little different. Instead of subtracting the unadjusted balance of the Allowance for Bad Debts from the target balance, the unadjusted balance will be added to the target balance.

Let's look at an example. Suppose that Martin's Music has a *debit* balance in its Allowance for Bad Debts account of $150. Assume that it estimates its percentage of uncollectible accounts will be 2% of $40,000 of Accounts Receivable. Martin's Music's bad debt expense adjustment would be calculated as follows:

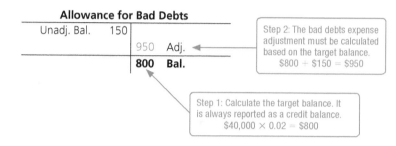

> What if a business had a debit balance in the Allowance for Bad Debts account before the adjustment for bad debts expense?

A company will have a debit balance in the Allowance for Bad Debts account if the company has written off more accounts receivable than it expected to during the year.

Notice that when the allowance account has an unadjusted debit balance, the target balance must be added to the unadjusted balance of the Allowance for Bad Debts to determine the bad debts expense adjustment. Martin's Music would record the following adjusting entry to recognize bad debts expense:

Date	Accounts and Explanation	Debit	Credit
Dec. 31	Bad Debts Expense	950	
	Allowance for Bad Debts		950
	Recorded bad debts expense for the period.		

$$\underbrace{\underline{A\downarrow}}_{\substack{\text{Allowance} \\ \text{for Bad} \\ \text{Debts}\uparrow}} = \Big\{ \underbrace{\underline{L}}_{} + \underbrace{\underline{E\downarrow}}_{\substack{\text{Bad Debts} \\ \text{Expense}\uparrow}}$$

Aging-of-Receivables Method

The aging-of-receivables method is similar to the percent-of-receivables method. However, in the aging method, businesses group individual accounts (Broxson, Andrews, and so on) according to how long the receivable has been outstanding. Then they apply a different percentage uncollectible on each aging category. Exhibit 1 (on the next page) shows the aging schedule for Smart Touch Learning.

Aging-of-Receivables Method
A method of estimating uncollectible receivables by determining the balance of the Allowance for Bad Debts account based on the age of individual accounts receivable.

Exhibit 1 | **Aging of Accounts Receivable**

	Age of Account as of December 31, 2016				
Customer Name	1–30 Days	31–60 Days	61–90 Days	Over 90 Days	Total Balance
Broxson	$ 800				$ 800
Phi Chi Fraternity	2,100				2,100
Andrews		$ 350			350
Jones		480			480
Perez	1,345				1,345
Thompson			$ 1,200		1,200
Clark				$ 100	100
Totals	$ 4,245	$ 830	$ 1,200	$ 100	$ 6,375
Estimated percentage uncollectible	× 1%	× 2%	× 3%	× 90%	
Estimated total uncollectible	$ 42	$ 17	$ 36	$ 90	$ 185

Target balance

At year-end, Smart Touch Learning will need to record the adjusting entry to recognize bad debts expense. The procedure is similar to the percent-of-receivables method.

Aging-of-Receivables Method:

Step 1: Determine the target balance of Allowance for Bad Debts by using the age of each account.

Step 2: Determine the amount of bad debts expense by evaluating the allowance account.

Bad debts expense = Target balance − Unadjusted credit balance of Allowance for Bad Debts

OR

Bad debts expense = Target balance + Unadjusted debit balance of Allowance for Bad Debts

Smart Touch Learning will determine its bad debts expense by subtracting the $55 unadjusted credit balance in the allowance account from the target balance, $185.

Allowance for Bad Debts

		80	Jan. 1, 2016, Bal.
Write-offs	25		
		55	Unadj. Bal.
		130	Adj.
		185	**Dec. 31, 2016, Bal.**

Step 2: The bad debts expense adjustment must be calculated based on the target balance. $185 − $55 = $130

Step 1: Calculate the target balance using the aging schedule. It is always reported as a credit balance.

Smart Touch Learning will record the following adjusting entry on December 31 to recognize bad debts expense for the year:

Date	Accounts and Explanation	Debit	Credit
2016			
Dec. 31	Bad Debts Expense	130	
	Allowance for Bad Debts		130
	Recorded bad debts expense for the period.		

After posting the adjusting entry, Smart Touch Learning has the following balances in its balance sheet and income statement accounts:

Balance sheet accounts:

Accounts Receivable			
Jan. 1, 2016, Bal.	4,400		
Net credit sales	60,000	25	Write-offs
		58,000	Collections
Unadj. Bal.	6,375		
Dec. 31, 2016, Bal.	**6,375**		

Allowance for Bad Debts			
		80	Jan. 1, 2016, Bal.
Write-offs	25		
		55	Unadj. Bal.
		130	Adj.
		185	**Dec. 31, 2016, Bal.**

Income statement account:

Bad Debts Expense	
Jan. 1, 2016, Bal.	0
Adj.	130
Dec. 31, 2016, Bal.	**130**

Comparison of Accounting for Uncollectibles

Exhibit 2 (on the next page) shows the journal entries that are recorded when using both the direct write-off method and the allowance method of accounting for uncollectibles. Take a moment to review the differences in these two methods. Remember that when using the direct write-off method, the business does not use an allowance account and that this method does not conform with GAAP.

Exhibit 2 | **Direct Write-Off Method Versus Allowance Method**

DIRECT WRITE-OFF METHOD	ALLOWANCE METHOD
Write-off of an uncollectible account:	

Bad Debts Expense ... 25
    Accounts Receivable—Customer Name ... 25
 Wrote off an uncollectible account.
	Allowance for Bad Debts ... 25
	    Accounts Receivable—Customer Name ... 25
	 Wrote off an uncollectible account.

Recovery of accounts previously written off:	

Accounts Receivable—Customer Name ... 25
    Bad Debts Expense ... 25
 Reinstated previously written off account.
	Accounts Receivable—Customer Name ... 25
	    Allowance for Bad Debts ... 25
	 Reinstated previously written off account.

Cash ... 25
    Accounts Receivable—Customer Name ... 25
 Collected cash on account.
	Cash ... 25
	    Accounts Receivable—Customer Name ... 25
	 Collected cash on account.

Adjusting entry to recognize bad debts:	
No adjusting entry recorded.	Bad Debts Expense ... 300 Allowance for Bad Debts ... 300 *Recorded bad debts expense for the period.*

Under the allowance method of accounting for uncollectibles, businesses must estimate the amount of the bad debts expense at the end of the accounting period. This is done using one of three methods: percent-of-sales, percent-of-receivables, or aging-of-receivables. Exhibit 3 summarizes the differences in those three methods.

Exhibit 3 | **Comparison of Percent-of-Sales, Percent-of-Receivables, and Aging-of-Receivables Methods**

ALLOWANCE METHOD		
INCOME STATEMENT APPROACH:	**BALANCE SHEET APPROACHES:**	
Percent-of-Sales Method	Percent-of-Receivables Method	Aging-of-Receivables Method
Bad Debts Expense = Net credit sales × %	**Step 1:** Target balance = Ending balance of Accounts Receivable × % **Step 2:** Bad debts expense = Target balance − Unadj. *credit* balance in Allowance for Bad Debts OR Bad debts expense = Target balance + Unadj. *debit* balance in Allowance for Bad Debts	

> **Try It!**

Johnson Company uses the allowance method to account for uncollectible receivables. On September 2, Johnson wrote off a $14,000 account receivable from customer J. Mraz. On December 12, Johnson unexpectedly received full payment from Mraz on the previously written off account. Johnson records an adjusting entry for bad debts expense of $800 on December 31.

5. Journalize Johnson's write-off of the uncollectible receivable.
6. Journalize Johnson's collection of the previously written off receivable.
7. Journalize Johnson's adjustment for bad debts expense.

Check your answers at the end of the chapter.

For more practice, see Short Exercises S-5 through S-8. MyAccountingLab

HOW ARE NOTES RECEIVABLE ACCOUNTED FOR?

Notes receivable are more formal than accounts receivable. The debtor signs a promissory note as evidence of the transaction. Before launching into the accounting, let's define the special terms used for notes receivable:

- **Promissory note**—A written promise to pay a specified amount of money at a particular future date.
- **Maker of the note (debtor)**—The entity that signs the note and promises to pay the required amount; the maker of the note is the debtor.
- **Payee of the note (creditor)**—The entity to whom the maker promises future payment; the payee of the note is the creditor. The creditor is the company that loans the money.
- **Principal**—The amount loaned out by the payee and borrowed by the maker of the note.
- **Interest**—The revenue to the payee for loaning money. Interest is an expense to the debtor and revenue to the creditor.
- **Interest period**—The period of time during which interest is computed. It extends from the original date of the note to the maturity date. Also called the *note term*.
- **Interest rate**—The percentage rate of interest specified by the note. Interest rates are almost always stated for a period of one year.
- **Maturity date**—As stated earlier, this is the date when final payment of the note is due. Also called the *due date*.
- **Maturity value**—The sum of the principal plus interest due at maturity. Maturity value is the total amount that will be paid back.

Exhibit 4 (on the next page) illustrates a promissory note.

Learning Objective 4
Account for notes receivable including computing interest and recording honored and dishonored notes

Principal
The amount loaned out by the payee and borrowed by the maker of the note.

Interest
The revenue to the payee for loaning money—the expense to the debtor.

Interest Period
The period of time during which interest is computed. It extends from the original date of the note to the maturity date.

Interest Rate
The percentage rate of interest specified by the note.

Maturity Value
The sum of the principal plus interest due at maturity.

Exhibit 4 | Promissory Note

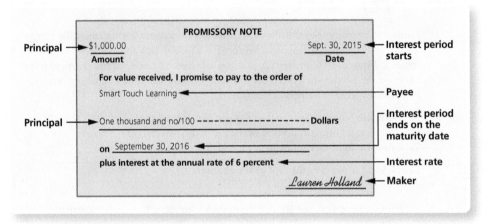

In Exhibit 4, we can see Smart Touch Learning is lending Lauren Holland $1,000 on September 30, 2015, for one year at an annual interest rate of 6%. The accounting clerk would record the following journal entry:

$$\frac{A\uparrow\downarrow}{\substack{\text{Notes}\\\text{Receivable}\uparrow\\\text{Cash}\downarrow}}\Bigg\} = \Bigg\{ \quad \underline{L} \; + \; \underline{E}$$

Date	Accounts and Explanation	Debit	Credit
2015			
Sep. 30	Notes Receivable—Holland	1,000	
	Cash		1,000
	Accepted note in exchange for cash.		

Identifying Maturity Date

Some notes specify the maturity date. For example, September 30, 2016, is the maturity date of the note shown in Exhibit 4. Other notes state the period of the note in days or months. When the period is given in months, the note's maturity date falls on the same day of the month as the date the note was issued. For example, a six-month note dated February 16, 2015, would mature on August 16, 2015.

When the period is given in days, the maturity date is determined by counting the actual days from the date of issue. A 180-day note dated February 16, 2015, matures on August 15, 2015, as shown here:

Month	Number of Days	Cumulative Total
Feb. 2015	28 − 16 = 12	12
Mar. 2015	31	43
Apr. 2015	30	73
May 2015	31	104
Jun. 2015	30	134
Jul. 2015	31	165
Aug. 2015	15	180

In counting the days remaining for a note, remember to

- Count the maturity date.
- Omit the date the note was issued.

Computing Interest on a Note

The formula for computing the interest is as follows:

$$\text{Amount of interest} = \text{Principal} \times \text{Interest rate} \times \text{Time}$$

In the formula, time (period) represents the portion of a year that interest has accrued on the note. It may be expressed as a fraction of a year in months (x/12) or a fraction of a year in days (x/360 or x/365). Using the data in Exhibit 4, Smart Touch Learning computes interest revenue for one year as follows:

$$
\begin{aligned}
\text{Amount of interest} &= \text{Principal} \times \text{Interest rate} \times \text{Time} \\
&= \$1{,}000 \times 0.06 \times 12/12 \\
&= \$60
\end{aligned}
$$

The maturity value of the note is $1,060 ($1,000 principal + $60 interest). The time element is 12/12 or 1 because the note's term is one year.

When the term of a note is stated in months, we compute the interest based on the 12-month year. Interest on a $2,000 note at 10% for nine months is computed as follows:

$$
\begin{aligned}
\text{Amount of interest} &= \text{Principal} \times \text{Interest rate} \times \text{Time} \\
&= \$2{,}000 \times 0.10 \times 9/12 \\
&= \$150
\end{aligned}
$$

When the interest period is stated in days, we sometimes compute interest based on a 360-day year rather than on a 365-day year. (A 360-day year eliminates some rounding and will be used for all calculations in this chapter.) The interest on a $5,000 note at 12% for 60 days can be computed as follows:

$$
\begin{aligned}
\text{Amount of interest} &= \text{Principal} \times \text{Interest rate} \times \text{Time} \\
&= \$5{,}000 \times 0.12 \times 60/360 \\
&= \$100
\end{aligned}
$$

Keep in mind that interest rates are stated as an annual rate. Therefore, the time in the interest formula should also be expressed in terms of a fraction of the year.

Accruing Interest Revenue and Recording Honored Notes Receivable

Some notes receivable may be outstanding at the end of an accounting period. The interest revenue earned on the note up to year-end is part of that year's earnings. Recall that interest revenue is earned over time, not just when cash is received. Because of the revenue recognition principle, we want to record the earnings from the note in the year in which they were earned.

Now, we continue analyzing Smart Touch Learning's note receivable from Exhibit 4. Smart Touch Learning's accounting period ends December 31.

- How much of the total interest revenue does Smart Touch Learning earn in 2015 (from September 30 through December 31)? Smart Touch Learning earns 3 months (October, November, and December) of interest.

$$\$1,000 \times 0.06 \times 3/12 = \$15$$

The accounting clerk makes the following adjusting entry at December 31, 2015:

Date	Accounts and Explanation	Debit	Credit
2015			
Dec. 31	Interest Receivable	15	
	Interest Revenue		15
	Accrued interest revenue.		

- How much interest revenue does Smart Touch Learning earn in 2016 (for January 1 through September 30)? Smart Touch Learning earns 9 months (January through September) of interest.

$$\$1,000 \times 0.06 \times 9/12 = \$45$$

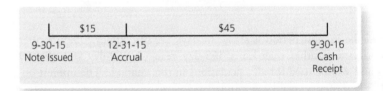

On the maturity date of the note, Smart Touch Learning will receive cash for the principal amount plus interest. The company considers the note honored and makes the following entry:

Date	Accounts and Explanation	Debit	Credit
2016			
Sep. 30	Cash ($1,000 + ($1,000 × 0.06 × 12/12))	1,060	
	Notes Receivable—Holland		1,000
	Interest Receivable		15
	Interest Revenue		45
	Collected note receivable plus interest.		

Some companies sell merchandise in exchange for notes receivable. Assume that on July 1, 2015, Rosa Electric sells household appliances for $2,000 to Dorman Builders. Dorman signs a nine-month promissory note at 10% annual interest. Rosa's entries to record the sale (ignore cost of goods sold), interest accrual, and collection from Dorman are as follows:

Date	Accounts and Explanation	Debit	Credit
2015			
Jul. 1	Notes Receivable—Dorman Builders	2,000	
	Sales Revenue		2,000
Dec. 31	Interest Receivable ($2,000 × 0.10 × 6/12)	100	
	Interest Revenue		100
2016			
Apr. 1	Cash ($2,000 + ($2,000 × 0.10 × 9/12))	2,150	
	Notes Receivable—Dorman Builders		2,000
	Interest Receivable		100
	Interest Revenue ($2,000 × 0.10 × 3/12)		50

$$\underbrace{\frac{A\uparrow}{\text{Notes Receivable}\uparrow}}_{} = \begin{cases} \underline{L} + \underline{E\uparrow} \\ \text{Sales Revenue}\uparrow \end{cases}$$

$$\underbrace{\frac{A\uparrow}{\text{Interest Receivable}\uparrow}}_{} = \begin{cases} \underline{L} + \underline{E\uparrow} \\ \text{Interest Revenue}\uparrow \end{cases}$$

$$\underbrace{\frac{A\uparrow}{\substack{\text{Cash}\uparrow \\ \text{Notes Receivable}\downarrow \\ \text{Interest Receivable}\downarrow}}}_{} = \begin{cases} \underline{L} + \underline{E\uparrow} \\ \text{Interest Revenue}\uparrow \end{cases}$$

A company may accept a note receivable from a credit customer who fails to pay an account receivable. The customer signs a promissory note and gives it to the creditor. Suppose Sports Club cannot pay Blanding Services the amount due on accounts receivable of $5,000. Blanding may accept a 60-day, $5,000 note receivable, with 12% interest, from Sports Club on November 19, 2015. Blanding's entries are as follows:

Date	Accounts and Explanation	Debit	Credit
2015			
Nov. 19	Notes Receivable—Sports Club	5,000	
	Accounts Receivable—Sports Club		5,000
Dec. 31	Interest Receivable ($5,000 × 0.12 × 42/360)	70	
	Interest Revenue		70
2016			
Jan. 18	Cash ($5,000 + ($5,000 × 0.12 × 60/360))	5,100	
	Notes Receivable—Sports Club		5,000
	Interest Receivable		70
	Interest Revenue ($5,000 × 0.12 × 18/360)		30

$$\underbrace{\frac{A\uparrow\downarrow}{\substack{\text{Notes Receivable}\uparrow \\ \text{Accounts Receivable}\downarrow}}}_{} = \begin{cases} \underline{L} + \underline{E} \\ \end{cases}$$

$$\underbrace{\frac{A\uparrow}{\text{Interest Receivable}\uparrow}}_{} = \begin{cases} \underline{L} + \underline{E\uparrow} \\ \text{Interest Revenue}\uparrow \end{cases}$$

$$\underbrace{\frac{A\uparrow}{\substack{\text{Cash}\uparrow \\ \text{Notes Receivable}\downarrow \\ \text{Interest Receivable}\downarrow}}}_{} = \begin{cases} \underline{L} + \underline{E\uparrow} \\ \text{Interest Revenue}\uparrow \end{cases}$$

Exhibit 5 | **Green Mountain Coffee Roasters, Inc.**
Partial Balance Sheet

GREEN MOUNTAIN COFFEE ROASTERS, INC. Balance Sheet (Partial) September 24, 2011 and September 25, 2010 (in thousands)		
Assets	**Sept. 24, 2011**	**Sept. 25, 2010**
Current Assets:		
Cash and Cash Equivalents	$ 12,989	$ 4,401
Restricted Cash and Cash Equivalents	27,523	355
Receivables, less uncollectible accounts and return allowances	310,321	172,200
Inventories	672,248	262,478
Income Taxes Receivable	18,258	5,350
Other Current Assets	28,072	23,488
Deferred Income Taxes, Net	36,231	26,997
Current Assets Held for Sale	25,885	0
Total Current Assets	$ 1,131,527	$ 495,269
Total Current Liabilities	$ 471,374	$ 238,055

Acid-Test (or Quick) Ratio

The current ratio measures a company's ability to pay current liabilities with current assets, and the cash ratio measures a company's ability to meet its short-term obligations with cash and cash equivalents. We now introduce the acid-test ratio (or *quick ratio*), which is also used to measure a company's ability to pay its current liabilities. The acid-test ratio is a more stringent measure than the current ratio but is not as stringent as the cash ratio. The acid-test is a ratio of the sum of cash (and cash equivalents) plus short-term investments plus net current receivables to total current liabilities. The acid-test ratio reveals whether the entity could pay all its current liabilities if they were to become due immediately.

The higher the acid-test ratio, the more able the business is to pay its current liabilities. Green Mountains' acid-test ratio of 0.74 means that the business has $0.74 of quick assets to pay each $1 of current liabilities.

Acid-Test Ratio
The ratio of the sum of cash plus short-term investments plus net current receivables to total current liabilities. The ratio tells whether the entity could pay all its current liabilities if they came due immediately. (Cash + Short-term investments + Net current receivables) / Total current liabilities.

> Acid-test ratio = (Cash including cash equivalents + Short-term investments + Net current receivables) / Total current liabilities
> = ($12,989 + $27,523 + $310,321) / $471,374
> = 0.74 (rounded)

What is an acceptable acid-test ratio? That depends on the industry. In general, an acid-test ratio of 1.00 is considered safe.

Accounts Receivable Turnover Ratio

Accounts Receivable Turnover Ratio
A ratio that measures the number of times the company collects the average accounts receivable balance in a year. Net credit sales / Average net accounts receivable.

The **accounts receivable turnover ratio** measures the number of times the company collects the average accounts receivable balance in a year. The higher the ratio, the faster the cash collections. Green Mountain's accounts receivable turnover ratio, presented below, indicates that the business turns over its receivables almost 11 times a year. Green Mountain's net sales are $2,650,899 for year ended September 24, 2011.

Accounts receivable turnover ratio = Net credit sales / Average net accounts receivable
= $2,650,899 / [($310,321 + $172,200) / 2]
= 10.99 times (rounded)

In calculating the accounts receivable turnover ratio for Green Mountain, we use net sales instead of net credit sales. This is because most companies don't report the level of detail needed to determine net credit sales.

Days' Sales in Receivables

Days' Sales in Receivables
The ratio of average net accounts receivable to one day's sales. The ratio tells how many days it takes to collect the average level of accounts receivable. 365 days / Accounts receivable turnover ratio.

After making a credit sale, the next step is to collect the receivable. **Days' sales in receivables**, also called the *collection period*, indicates how many days it takes to collect the average level of accounts receivable. The number of days' sales in receivables should be close to the number of days customers are allowed to make payment, when credit is extended. The shorter the collection period, the more quickly the organization can use its cash. The longer the collection period, the less cash is available for operations. Green Mountain's days' sales in receivables can be computed as follows:

Days' sales in receivables = 365 days / Accounts receivable turnover ratio
= 365 days / 10.99
= 33 days (rounded)

On average, it takes Green Mountain 33 days to collect its accounts receivable. The length of the collection period depends on the credit terms of the sale. For example, sales on net 30 terms should be collected within approximately 30 days. When there is a discount, such as 2/10, net 30, the collection period may be shorter. Credit terms of net 45 result in a longer collection period.

> Try It!

Lovett Company reported the following selected items at February 28, 2014 (last year's—2013—amounts also given as needed):

Accounts Payable	$ 128,000	Accounts Receivable, net:	
Cash	104,000	February 28, 2014	$ 108,000
Merchandise Inventory:		February 28, 2013	68,000
February 28, 2014	116,000	Cost of Goods Sold	460,000
February 28, 2013	80,000	Short-term Investments	56,000
Net Credit Sales Revenue	1,168,000	Other Current Assets	48,000
Long-term Assets	168,000	Other Current Liabilities	72,000
Long-term Liabilities	52,000		

10. Compute Lovett's (a) acid-test ratio, (b) accounts receivable turnover ratio, and (c) days' sales in receivables for 2014.

Check your answers at the end of the chapter.

For more practice, see Short Exercise S-13.   MyAccountingLab

REVIEW

> Things You Should Know

1. What are common types of receivables and how are credit sales recorded?

- A receivable is a monetary claim against a business or an individual.

- There are three major types of receivables:

  - Accounts receivable—Represent the right to receive cash in the future from customers for goods sold or for services performed.

  - Notes receivable—Represent a written promise that the customer will pay a fixed amount of principal plus interest by a certain date in the future.

  - Other receivables—A miscellaneous category that includes any other type of receivables where there is a right to receive cash in the future.

- A critical component of internal control over receivables is the separation of cash-handling and cash-accounting duties.

- A separate accounts receivable account (called a subsidiary account) must be maintained for each customer in order to account for payments received from the customer and amounts still owed.

- The sum of all balances in the subsidiary accounts receivable will equal a control account balance, Accounts Receivable.

- Sales by credit cards and debit cards are treated as cash sales and typically include a fee (Credit Card Expense) that is paid by the business to the credit card processor.

- As a way to receive cash before receivables are collected, businesses can factor or pledge their receivables.

2. How are uncollectibles accounted for when using the direct write-off method?

- Writing off uncollectible accounts when using the direct write-off method involves a debit to Bad Debts Expense and a credit to Accounts Receivable.

- Recovery of accounts previously written off is recorded by reversing the write-off entry and then recording an entry to receive the cash.

- The direct write-off method violates the matching principle and is not the required method by GAAP.

3. How are uncollectibles accounted for when using the allowance method?

- When using the allowance method, companies estimate bad debts expense at the end of the period and record an adjusting entry that debits Bad Debts Expense and credits Allowance for Bad Debts. There are three ways to estimate bad debts expense:

  - Percent-of-sales method—Computes bad debts expense as a percentage of net credit sales.

  - Percent-of-receivables method—Determines the balance of the Allowance for Bad Debts account based on a percentage of accounts receivable.

  - Aging-of-receivables method—Determines the balance of the Allowance for Bad Debts account based on the age of individual accounts receivable.

- Writing off uncollectible accounts involves a debit to Allowance for Bad Debts and a credit to Accounts Receivable.
- Recovery of accounts previously written off is recorded by reversing the write-off entry and then recording an entry to receive the cash.

4. How are notes receivable accounted for?

- Notes receivable involve interest that is computed as principal times interest rate times time.
- Interest on notes must be accrued at the end of the each period, and an adjusting entry must be recorded by debiting Interest Receivable and crediting Interest Revenue.
- The receipt of cash at a note's maturity includes the principal plus interest.
- When a customer dishonors a note, the business can transfer the note receivable (plus interest earned) to an accounts receivable.

5. How do we use the acid-test ratio, accounts receivable turnover ratio, and days' sales in receivables to evaluate business performance?

- The acid-test ratio reveals whether an entity could pay all its current liabilities if they were due immediately. (Cash + Short-term investments + Net current receivables) / Total current liabilities.
- Accounts receivable turnover ratio measures the number of times the company collects the average accounts receivable balance in a year. Net credit sales / Average net accounts receivable.
- The days' sales in receivables indicates how many days it takes to collect the average level of accounts receivable. 365 days / Accounts receivable turnover ratio.

> Summary Problem 1

Monarch Map Company's balance sheet at December 31, 2014, reported the following:

Accounts Receivable	$ 60,000
Less: Allowance for bad debts	2,000

Requirements

1. How much of the receivables did Monarch expect to collect? Stated differently, what was the net realizable value of these receivables?

2. Journalize, without explanations, 2015 entries for Monarch and post to the Accounts Receivable and Allowance for Bad Debts T-accounts.

   a. Total credit sales for 2015 were $80,000.

   b. Monarch received cash payments on account during 2015 of $74,300.

   c. Accounts receivable identified to be uncollectible totaled $2,700.

3. Record the adjusting entry to recognize bad debts expense using the following independent situations, and then post to the Bad Debts Expense and Allowance for Bad Debts T-accounts.

   a. 3% of credit sales were estimated to be uncollectible.

   b. An aging of receivables indicates that $2,200 of the receivables are estimated to be uncollectible.

> Solution

Requirement 1

Net realizable value of receivables = $60,000 − $2,000 = $58,000

Requirement 2

Date	Accounts and Explanation	Debit	Credit
2015			
(a)	Accounts Receivable	80,000	
	Sales Revenue		80,000
(b)	Cash	74,300	
	Accounts Receivable		74,300
(c)	Allowance for Bad Debts	2,700	
	Accounts Receivable		2,700

Accounts Receivable

Jan. 1, 2015, Bal.	60,000			
(a)	80,000	74,300	(b)	
		2,700	(c)	
Unadj. Bal.	63,000			

Allowance for Bad Debts

		2,000	Jan. 1, 2015, Bal.
(c)	2,700		
Unadj. Bal.		700	

Requirement 3a

Bad debts expense = Net credit sales × % = $80,000 × 0.03 = $2,400

Date	Accounts and Explanation	Debit	Credit
2015			
Dec. 31	Bad Debts Expense	2,400	
	Allowance for Bad Debts		2,400

Allowance for Bad Debts

		2,000	Jan. 1, 2015, Bal.
(c)	2,700		
Unadj. Bal.		700	
		2,400	Adj.
		1,700	**Dec. 31, 2015, Bal.**

Bad Debts Expense

Adj.	2,400	
Dec. 31, 2015, Bal.	**2,400**	

Requirement 3b

Bad debts expense = Target balance + Unadj. debit balance = $2,200 + $700
= $2,900

Date	Accounts and Explanation	Debit	Credit
2015			
Dec. 31	Bad Debts Expense	2,900	
	Allowance for Bad Debts		2,900

Allowance for Bad Debts

		2,000	Jan. 1, 2015, Bal.
(c)	2,700		
Unadj. Bal.	700		
		2,900	Adj.
		2,200	**Dec. 31, 2015, Bal.**

Bad Debts Expense

Adj.	2,900	
Dec. 31, 2015, Bal.	**2,900**	

> Summary Problem 2

Suppose First Fidelity Bank engaged in the following transactions:

2015	
Apr. 1	Loaned $8,000 to Bland, Co. Received a six-month, 10% note.
Oct. 1	Collected the Bland note at maturity.
Dec. 1	Loaned $6,000 to Flores, Inc. on a 180-day, 12% note.
31	Accrued interest revenue on the Flores note.
2016	
May 29	Collected the Flores note at maturity. (Assume 2016 is a leap year.)

Journalize the 2015 and 2016 transactions on First Fidelity's books. Explanations are not needed. Use a 360-day year to compute interest. First Fidelity's accounting period ends on December 31.

> Solution

Date	Accounts and Explanation	Debit	Credit
2015			
Apr. 1	Notes Receivable—Bland, Co.	8,000	
	Cash		8,000
Oct. 1	Cash ($8,000 + $400)	8,400	
	Notes Receivable—Bland, Co.		8,000
	Interest Revenue ($8,000 × 0.10 × 6/12)		400
Dec. 1	Notes Receivable—Flores, Inc.	6,000	
	Cash		6,000
Dec. 31	Interest Receivable	60	
	Interest Revenue ($6,000 × 0.12 × 30/360)		60
2016			
May 29	Cash ($6,000 + ($6,000 × 0.12 × 180/360))	6,360	
	Notes Receivable—Flores, Inc.		6,000
	Interest Receivable		60
	Interest Revenue ($6,000 × 0.12 × 150/360)		300

> Key Terms

Accounts Receivable

The right to receive cash in the future from customers for goods sold or for services performed.

Accounts Receivable Turnover Ratio

A ratio that measures the number of times the company collects the average accounts receivable balance in a year. Net credit sales / Average net accounts receivable.

Acid-Test Ratio

The ratio of the sum of cash plus short-term investments plus net current receivables to total current liabilities. The ratio tells whether the entity could pay all its current liabilities if they came due immediately. (Cash + Short-term investments + Net current receivables) / Total current liabilities.

Aging-of-Receivables Method

A method of estimating uncollectible receivables by determining the balance of the Allowance for Bad Debts account based on the age of individual accounts receivable.

Allowance for Bad Debts

A contra account, related to accounts receivable, that holds the estimated amount of uncollectible accounts.

Allowance Method

A method of accounting for uncollectible receivables in which the company estimates bad debts expense instead of waiting to see which customers the company will not collect from.

Bad Debts Expense

The cost to the seller of extending credit. It arises from the failure to collect from some credit customers.

Days' Sales in Receivables

The ratio of average net accounts receivable to one day's sales. The ratio tells how many days it takes to collect the average level of accounts receivable. 365 days / Accounts receivable turnover ratio.

Debtor

The party to a credit transaction who takes on an obligation/payable.

Direct Write-Off Method

A method of accounting for uncollectible receivables in which the company records bad debts expense when a customer's account receivable is uncollectible.

Dishonor a Note
Failure of a note's maker to pay a note receivable at maturity.

Interest
The revenue to the payee for loaning money—the expense to the debtor.

Interest Period
The period of time during which interest is computed. It extends from the original date of the note to the maturity date.

Interest Rate
The percentage rate of interest specified by the note.

Maturity Date
The date when a note is due.

Maturity Value
The sum of the principal plus interest due at maturity.

Net Realizable Value
The net value a company expects to collect from its accounts receivable. Accounts Receivable less Allowance for Bad Debts.

Notes Receivable
A written promise that a customer will pay a fixed amount of principal plus interest by a certain date in the future.

Percent-of-Receivables Method
A method of estimating uncollectible receivables by determining the balance of the Allowance for Bad Debts account based on a percentage of accounts receivable.

Percent-of-Sales Method
A method of estimating uncollectible receivables that calculates bad debts expense based on a percentage of net credit sales.

Principal
The amount loaned out by the payee and borrowed by the maker of the note.

Receivable
A monetary claim against a business or an individual.

> Quick Check

1. With good internal controls, the person who handles cash can also

   a. account for cash payments.
   b. account for cash receipts from customers.
   c. issue credits to customers for sales returns.
   d. None of the above

   Learning Objective 1

2. When recording credit card or debit card sales using the net method,

   a. cash received equals sales.
   b. cash received equals sales minus the fee assessed by the card processing company.
   c. cash received equals sales plus the fee assessed by the card processing company.
   d. cash isn't received by the seller until the customer pays his or her credit card statement.

   Learning Objective 1

3. Which of the following is a limitation of the direct write-off method of accounting for uncollectibles?

   a. The direct write-off method overstates assets on the balance sheet.
   b. The direct write-off method does not match expenses against revenue very well.
   c. The direct write-off method does not set up an allowance for uncollectibles.
   d. All of the above

   Learning Objective 2

4. The entry to record a write-off of an uncollectible account when using the direct-write off method involves a

   a. debit to Allowance for Bad Debts
   b. credit to Cash
   c. debit to Accounts Receivable
   d. debit to Bad Debts Expense

   Learning Objective 2

Learning Objective 3

5. Brickman Company uses the allowance method to account for uncollectible receivables. At the beginning of the year, Allowance for Bad Debts had a credit balance of $1,000. During the year Brickman wrote off uncollectible receivables of $2,100. Brickman recorded Bad Debts Expense of $2,700. What is Brickman's year-end balance in Allowance for Bad Debts?

    a. $1,600   **c.** $3,700

    b. $4,800   **d.** $600

Learning Objective 3

6. Brickman's ending balance of Accounts Receivable is $19,500. Use the data in the preceding question to compute the net realizable value of Accounts Receivable at year-end.

    a. $16,800   **c.** $17,400

    b. $19,500   **d.** $17,900

Learning Objective 4

7. At December 31 year-end, Crain Company has an $8,400 note receivable from a customer. Interest of 10% has accrued for 10 months on the note. What will Crain's financial statements report for this situation?

    a. The balance sheet will report the note receivable of $8,400.

    b. The balance sheet will report the note receivable of $8,400 and interest receivable of $700.

    c. Nothing because the business has not received the cash yet.

    d. The income statement will report a note receivable of $8,400.

Learning Objective 4

8. Using the data in the preceding question, what will the income statement for the year ended December 31, report for this situation?

    a. Nothing because the business has not received the cash yet

    b. Note receivable of $8,400

    c. Interest revenue of $700

    d. Both b and c

Learning Objective 5

9. At year-end, Schultz Company has cash of $11,600, current accounts receivable of $48,900, merchandise inventory of $37,900, and prepaid expenses totaling $5,100. Liabilities of $55,900 must be paid next year. What is Schultz's acid-test ratio?

    a. 1.08

    b. 0.21

    c. 1.76

    d. Cannot be determined from the data given

Learning Objective 5

10. Using the data in the preceding question, assume accounts receivable had a beginning balance of $67,400 and net credit sales for the current year totaled $807,800. How many days did it take Schultz's to collect its average level of receivables?

    a. 49   **c.** 29

    b. 35   **d.** 26

Check your answers at the end of the chapter.

ASSESS YOUR PROGRESS

> Review Questions

1. What is the difference between accounts receivable and notes receivable?

2. List some common examples of other receivables.

3. What is a critical element of internal control in the handling of receivables by a business? Explain how this element is accomplished.

4. When dealing with receivables, give an example of a subsidiary account.

5. What type of account must the sum of all subsidiary accounts be equal to?

6. What are some benefits to a business in accepting credit cards and debit cards?

7. What are two common methods used when accepting deposits for credit card and debit card transactions?

8. What occurs when a business factors its receivables?

9. What occurs when a business pledges its receivables?

10. What is the expense account associated with the cost of uncollectible receivables called?

11. When is bad debts expense recorded when using the direct write-off method?

12. What are some limitations of using the direct write-off method?

13. When is bad debts expense recorded when using the allowance method?

14. When using the allowance method, how are accounts receivable shown on the balance sheet?

15. When using the allowance method, what account is debited when writing off uncollectible accounts? How does this differ from the direct write-off method?

16. When a receivable is written off under the allowance method, how does it affect the net realizable value shown on the balance sheet?

17. How does the percent-of-sales method compute bad debts expense?

18. How do the percent-of-receivables and aging-of-receivables methods compute bad debts expense?

19. What is the difference between the percent-of-receivables and aging-of-receivables methods?

20. What is the formula to compute interest on a note receivable?

21. Why must companies record accrued interest revenue at the end of the accounting period?

22. How is the acid-test ratio calculated and what does it signify?

23. What does the accounts receivable turnover ratio measure and how is it calculated?

24. What does the days' sales in receivables indicate and how is it calculated?

> Short Exercises

Learning Objective 1

S-1 Ensuring internal control over the collection of receivables

Consider internal control over receivables collections. What job must be withheld from a company's credit department in order to safeguard its cash? If the credit department does perform this job, what can a credit department employee do to hurt the company?

Learning Objective 1

S-2 Recording credit card and debit card sales

Restaurants do a large volume of business by credit and debit cards. Suppose Chocolate Passion restaurant had these transactions on January 28, 2015:

National Express credit card sales	$ 9,300
ValueCard debit card sales	9,000

Requirements

1. Suppose Chocolate Passion's processor charges a 3% fee and deposits sales net of the fee. Journalize these sale transactions for the restaurant.

2. Suppose Chocolate Passion's processor charges a 3% fee and deposits sales using the gross method. Journalize these sale transactions for the restaurant.

Learning Objective 2

S-3 Applying the direct write-off method to account for uncollectibles

Sherman Peterson is an attorney in Los Angeles. Peterson uses the direct write-off method to account for uncollectible receivables.

At January 31, 2014, Peterson's accounts receivable totaled $15,000. During February, he earned revenue of $18,000 on account and collected $19,000 on account. He also wrote off uncollectible receivables of $1,800 on February 28, 2014.

Requirements

1. Use the direct write-off method to journalize Peterson's write-off of the uncollectible receivables.

2. What is Peterson's balance of Accounts Receivable at February 28, 2014?

Learning Objective 2

S-4 Collecting a receivable previously written off—direct write-off method

Gate City Cycles had trouble collecting its account receivable from Sue Ann Noel. On June 19, 2014, Gate City finally wrote off Noel's $700 account receivable. On December 31, Noel sent a $700 check to Gate City.

Journalize the entries required for Gate City Cycles, assuming Gate City uses the direct write-off method.

Learning Objective 3

S-5 Applying the allowance method to account for uncollectibles

The Accounts Receivable balance and Allowance for Bad Debts for Garcia Company at December 31, 2014, was $10,800 and $2,000 (credit balance). During 2015, Garcia completed the following transactions:

a. Sales revenue on account, $268,200 (ignore cost of goods sold).

b. Collections on account, $224,000.

c. Write-offs of uncollectibles, $5,900.

d. Bad debts expense of $5,000 was recorded.

Requirements

1. Journalize Garcia's transactions for 2015 assuming Garcia uses the allowance method.

2. Post the transactions to the Accounts Receivable, Allowance for Bad Debts, and Bad Debts Expense T-accounts and determine the ending balance of each account.

3. Show how accounts receivable would be reported on the balance sheet at December 31, 2015.

S-6 Applying the allowance method (percent-of-sales) to account for uncollectibles

Learning Objective 3

During its first year of operations, Spring Garden Plans earned net credit sales of $322,000. Industry experience suggests that bad debts will amount to 2% of net credit sales. At December 31, 2014, accounts receivable total $36,000. The company uses the allowance method to account for uncollectibles.

Requirements

1. Journalize Spring's Bad Debts Expense using the percent-of-sales method.

2. Show how to report accounts receivable on the balance sheet at December 31, 2014.

S-7 Applying the allowance method (percent-of-receivables) to account for uncollectibles

Learning Objective 3

The Accounts Receivable balance for Clark Company at December 31, 2014, was $18,000. During 2015, Clark earned revenue of $447,000 on account and collected $324,000. Clark wrote off $5,000 receivables as uncollectible. Industry experience suggests that uncollectible accounts will amount to 2% of accounts receivable.

Requirements

1. Assume Clark had a $2,400 credit balance in Allowance for Bad Debts at December 31, 2014. Journalize Clark's December 31, 2015, adjustment to record bad debts expense using the percent-of-receivables method.

2. Assume Clark had a $2,000 debit balance in Allowance for Bad Debts at December 31, 2014. Journalize Clark's December 31, 2015, adjustment to record bad debts expense using the percent-of-receivables method.

Learning Objective 3

S-8 Applying the allowance method (aging-of-receivables) to account for uncollectibles

Summer and Sandcastles Resort had the following balances at December 31, 2014, before the year-end adjustments:

Accounts Receivable	Allowance for Bad Debts
78,000	1,900

The aging of accounts receivable yields the following data:

	Age of Accounts Receivable		
	0–60 Days	Over 60 Days	Total Receivables
Accounts Receivable	$75,000	$3,000	$78,000
Percent uncollectible	× 4%	× 24%	

Requirements

1. Journalize Summer's entry to record bad debts expense for 2014 using the aging-of-receivables method.

2. Prepare a T-account to compute the ending balance of Allowance for Bad Debts.

Learning Objective 4

S-9 Computing interest amounts on notes receivable

A table of notes receivable for 2014 follows:

	Principal	Interest Rate	Interest Period During 2014
Note 1	$ 30,000	8%	4 months
Note 2	10,000	11%	45 days
Note 3	19,000	10%	75 days
Note 4	100,000	7%	10 months

For each of the notes receivable, compute the amount of interest revenue earned during 2014. Round to the nearest dollar.

Learning Objective 4

S-10 Accounting for a note receivable

On June 6, Lakeland Bank & Trust Company lent $110,000 to Samantha Michael on a 90-day, 9% note.

Requirements

1. Journalize for Lakeland the lending of the money on June 6.

2. Journalize the collection of the principal and interest at maturity. Specify the date.

Learning Objective 4

S-11 Accruing interest revenue and recording collection of a note

On December 1, Krauss Company accepted a 120-day, 6%, $4,000 note receivable from J. Oliver in exchange for his account receivable.

Requirements

1. Journalize the transaction on December 1.

2. Journalize the adjusting entry needed on December 31 to accrue interest revenue.

3. Journalize the collection of the principal and interest at maturity. Specify the date.

S-12 Recording a dishonored note receivable

Learning Objective 4

McKenna Company has a three-month, $10,000, 8% note receivable from L. Chambers that was signed on June 1, 2015. Chambers defaults on the loan on September 1.

Journalize the entry for McKenna to record the default of the loan.

S-13 Using the acid-test ratio, accounts receivable turnover ratio and days' sales in receivables to evaluate a company

Learning Objective 5

Southside Clothiers reported the following selected items at September 30, 2014 (last year's—2013—amounts also given as needed):

Accounts Payable	$ 320,000	Accounts Receivable, net:	
Cash	260,000	September 30, 2014	$ 270,000
Merchandise Inventory:		September 30, 2013	170,000
September 30, 2014	290,000	Cost of Goods Sold	1,150,000
September 30, 2013	200,000	Short-term Investments	140,000
Net Credit Sales Revenue	2,920,000	Other Current Assets	120,000
Long-term Assets	420,000	Other Current Liabilities	180,000
Long-term Liabilities	130,000		

Compute Southside's (a) acid-test ratio, (b) accounts receivable turnover ratio, and (c) days' sales in receivables for 2014. Evaluate each ratio value as strong or weak. Southside sells on terms of net 30. (Round days' sales in receivables to a whole number.)

> Exercises

E-14 Defining common receivables terms

Learning Objective 1

Match the terms with their correct definition.

Terms	Definitions
1. Accounts receivable	a. The party to a credit transaction who takes on an obligation/ payable.
2. Other receivables	
3. Debtor	b. The party who receives a receivable and will collect cash in the future.
4. Notes receivable	c. A written promise to pay a specified amount of money at a particular future date.
5. Maturity date	
6. Creditor	d. The date when the note receivable is due.
	e. A miscellaneous category that includes any other type of receivable where there is a right to receive cash in the future.
	f. The right to receive cash in the future from customers for goods sold or for services performed.

Learning Objective 1

E-15 Identifying and correcting internal control weakness

Suppose The Right Rig Dealership is opening a regional office in Omaha. Cary Regal, the office manager, is designing the internal control system. Regal proposes the following procedures for credit checks on new customers, sales on account, cash collections, and write-offs of uncollectible receivables:

- The credit department runs a credit check on all customers who apply for credit. When an account proves uncollectible, the credit department authorizes the write-off of the accounts receivable.

- Cash receipts come into the credit department, which separates the cash received from the customer remittance slips. The credit department lists all cash receipts by customer name and amount of cash received.

- The cash goes to the treasurer for deposit in the bank. The remittance slips go to the accounting department for posting to customer accounts.

- The controller compares the daily deposit slip to the total amount posted to customer accounts. Both amounts must agree.

Recall the components of internal control. Identify the internal control weakness in this situation, and propose a way to correct it.

Learning Objectives 1, 2

E-16 Journalizing transactions using the direct-write off method

On June 1, High Performance Cell Phones sold $23,000 of merchandise to Anthony Trucking Company on account. Anthony fell on hard times and on July 15 paid only $8,000 of the account receivable. After repeated attempts to collect, High Performance finally wrote off its accounts receivable from Anthony on September 5. Six months later, March 5, High Performance received Anthony's check for $15,000 with a note apologizing for the late payment.

Requirements

1. Journalize the transactions for High Performance Cell Phones using the direct write-off method. Ignore Cost of Goods Sold.

2. What are some limitations that High Performance will encounter when using the direct-write off method?

Use the following information to answer Exercises E-17 and E-18.

At January 1, 2015, Windy Mountain Flagpoles had Accounts Receivable of $34,000 and Allowance for Bad Debts had a credit balance of $3,000. During the year, Windy Mountain Flagpoles recorded the following:

a. Sales of $189,000 ($165,000 on account; $24,000 for cash).

b. Collections on account, $133,000.

c. Write-offs of uncollectible receivables, $2,800.

E-17 Accounting for uncollectible accounts using the allowance method (percent-of-sales) and reporting receivables on the balance sheet

Learning Objectives 1, 3

2. AR, Dec. 31 $63,200

Requirements

1. Journalize Windy's transactions that occurred during 2015. The company uses the allowance method.

2. Post Windy's transactions to the Accounts Receivable and Allowance for Bad Debts T-accounts.

3. Journalize Windy's adjustment to record bad debts expense assuming Windy estimates bad debts as 1% of credit sales. Post the adjustment to the appropriate T-accounts.

4. Show how Windy Mountain Flagpoles will report net accounts receivable on its December 31, 2015 balance sheet.

E-18 Accounting for uncollectible accounts using the allowance method (percent-of-receivables) and reporting receivables on the balance sheet

Learning Objectives 1, 3

3. Bad Debts Expense $1,064

Requirements

1. Journalize Windy's transactions that occurred during 2015. The company uses the allowance method.

2. Post Windy's transactions to the Accounts Receivable and Allowance for Bad Debts T-accounts.

3. Journalize Windy's adjustment to record bad debts expense assuming Windy estimates bad debts as 2% of accounts receivable. Post the adjustment to the appropriate T-accounts.

4. Show how Windy Mountain Flagpoles will report net accounts receivable on its December 31, 2015, balance sheet.

E-19 Accounting for uncollectible accounts using the allowance method (aging-of-receivables) and reporting receivables on the balance sheet

Learning Objective 3

2. Allowance CR Bal. $10,720

At December 31, 2014, the Accounts Receivable balance of GPS Technology is $190,000. The Allowance for Bad Debts account has a $1,600 debit balance. GPS Technology prepares the following aging schedule for its accounts receivable:

Accounts Receivable	Age of Accounts			
	1–30 Days	31–60 Days	61–90 Days	Over 90 Days
$190,000	$80,000	$60,000	$40,000	$10,000
Estimated percent uncollectible	0.4%	5.0%	6.0%	50.0%

Requirements

1. Journalize the year-end adjusting entry for bad debts on the basis of the aging schedule. Show the T-account for the Allowance for Bad Debts at December 31, 2014.

2. Show how GPS Technology will report its net accounts receivable on its December 31, 2014, balance sheet.

E-20 Journalizing transactions using the direct write-off method versus the allowance method

During August 2015, Bingham Company recorded the following:

- Sales of $75,600 ($66,000 on account; $9,600 for cash).
- Collections on account, $53,200.
- Write-offs of uncollectible receivables, $1,120.
- Recovery of receivable previously written off, $800.

Requirements

1. Journalize Bingham's transactions during August 2015, assuming Bingham uses the direct-write off method.

2. Journalize Bingham's transactions during August 2015, assuming Bingham uses the allowance method.

E-21 Journalizing credit card sales, note receivable transactions, and accruing interest

Marathon Running Shoes reports the following:

2013	
May 4	Recorded credit card sales of $107,000, net of processor fee of 3%.
Sep. 1	Loaned $17,000 to Jean Porter, an executive with the company, on a one-year, 15% note.
Dec. 31	Accrued interest revenue on the Porter note.
2014	
Sep. 1	Collected the maturity value of the Porter note.

Journalize all entries required for Marathon Running Shoes.

E-22 Journalizing note receivable transactions including a dishonored note

On September 30, 2013, Synergy Bank loaned $88,000 to Kendall Kelsing on a one-year, 12% note. Synergy's fiscal year ends on December 31.

Requirements

1. Journalize all entries for Synergy Bank related to the note for 2013 and 2014.

2. Which party has a

   a. note receivable?
   b. note payable?
   c. interest revenue?
   d. interest expense?

3. Suppose that Kendall Kelsing defaulted on the note. What entry would Synergy record for the dishonored note?

E-23 Journalizing note receivable transactions

Learning Objective 4

Feb. 1, 2014—Cash DR $15,120

The following selected transactions occurred during 2013 and 2014 for Caspian Importers. The company ends its accounting year on April 30.

2013	
Feb. 1	Loaned $14,000 cash to Brett Dowling on a one-year, 8% note.
Apr. 6	Sold goods to Putt Masters, receiving a 90-day, 6% note for $9,000. Ignore Cost of Goods Sold.
Apr. 30	Made a single entry to accrue interest revenue on both notes.
?	Collected the maturity value of the Putt Masters note.
2014	
Feb. 1	Collected the maturity value of the Dowling note.

Journalize all required entries. Make sure to determine the missing maturity date.

E-24 Journalizing note receivable transactions

Learning Objective 4

Oct. 31—Cash DR $18,270

Hot Heat Steam Cleaning performs services on account. When a customer account becomes four months old, Hot Heat converts the account to a note receivable. During 2013, the company completed the following transactions:

Apr. 28	Performed service on account for Sinclair Club, $18,000.
Sep. 1	Received an $18,000, 60-day, 9% note from Sinclair Club in satisfaction of its past-due account receivable.
Oct. 31	Collected the Sinclair Club note at maturity.

Record the transactions in Hot Heat's journal.

Learning Objective 5

E-25 Evaluating ratio data

Algonquin Carpets reported the following amounts in its 2014 financial statements. The 2013 figures are given for comparison.

	2014		2013	
Current Assets:				
Cash		$ 4,000		$ 10,000
Short-term Investments		20,000		9,000
Accounts Receivable	$ 63,000		$ 76,000	
Less: Allowance for Bad Debts	(6,000)	57,000	(5,000)	71,000
Merchandise Inventory		195,000		191,000
Prepaid Insurance		4,000		4,000
Total Current Assets		$ 280,000		$ 285,000
Total Current Liabilities		$ 104,000		$ 106,000
Net Sales (all on account)		$ 732,000		$ 735,000

Requirements

1. Calculate Algonquin's acid-test ratio for 2014. (Round to two decimals.) Determine whether Algonquin's acid-test ratio improved or deteriorated from 2013 to 2014. How does Algonquin's acid-test ratio compare with the industry average of 0.80?

2. Calculate Algonquin's accounts receivable turnover ratio. (Round to two decimals.) How does Algonquin's ratio compare to the industry average accounts receivable turnover of 10?

3. Calculate the days' sales in receivables for 2014. (Round to the nearest day.) How do the results compare with Algonquin's credit terms of net 30?

Learning Objective 5

E-26 Computing the collection period for receivables

Contemporary Media Sign Company sells on account. Recently, Contemporary reported the following figures:

	2013	2012
Net Credit Sales	$ 572,000	$ 600,000
Receivables at end of year	38,700	46,100

Requirements

1. Compute Contemporary's days' sales in receivables for 2013. (Round to the nearest day.)

2. Suppose Contemporary's normal credit terms for a sale on account are "2/10, net 30." How well does Contemporary's collection period compare to the company's credit terms? Is this good or bad for Contemporary?

> Problems **Group A**

P-27A **Accounting for uncollectible accounts using the allowance (percent-of-sales) and direct write-off methods, and reporting receivables on the balance sheet**

Learning Objectives 1, 2, 3

1. Bad Debts Expense $17,700

On August 31, 2014, Daisy Floral Supply had a $155,000 debit balance in Accounts Receivable and a $6,200 credit balance in Allowance for Bad Debts. During September, Daisy made

- Sales on account, $590,000. Ignore Cost of Goods Sold.

- Collections on account, $627,000.

- Write-offs of uncollectible receivables, $7,000.

Requirements

1. Journalize all September entries using the *allowance* method. Bad debts expense was estimated at 3% of credit sales. Show all September activity in Accounts Receivable, Allowance for Bad Debts, and Bad Debts Expense (post to these T-accounts).

2. Using the same facts, assume that Daisy used the direct write-off method to account for uncollectible receivables. Journalize all September entries using the *direct write-off* method. Post to Accounts Receivable and Bad Debts Expense and show their balances at September 30, 2014.

3. What amount of Bad Debts Expense would Daisy report on its September income statement under each of the two methods? Which amount better matches expense with revenue? Give your reason.

4. What amount of *net* accounts receivable would Daisy report on its September 30, 2014, balance sheet under each of the two methods? Which amount is more realistic? Give your reason.

P-28A **Accounting for uncollectible accounts using the allowance method (aging-of-receivables), and reporting receivables on the balance sheet**

Learning Objective 3

2. Allowance CR Bal. $11,551 at Dec. 31, 2014

At September 30, 2014, the accounts of Mountain Terrace Medical Center (MTMC) include the following:

Accounts Receivable	$ 145,000
Allowance for Bad Debts (credit balance)	3,500

During the last quarter of 2014, MTMC completed the following selected transactions:

Dec. 28	Wrote off accounts receivable as uncollectible: Regan, Co., $1,300; Owen Mac, $900; and Rain, Inc., $700
31	Recorded bad debts expense based on the aging of accounts receivable, as follows:

Receivables

Accounts Receivable	Age of Accounts			
	1–30 Days	31–60 Days	61–90 Days	Over 90 Days
$165,000	$97,000	$37,000	$14,000	$17,000
Estimated percent uncollectible	0.3%	3%	30%	35%

Requirements

1. Journalize the transactions.
2. Open the Allowance for Bad Debts T-account, and post entries affecting that account. Keep a running balance.
3. Show how Mountain Terrace Medical Center should report net accounts receivable on its December 31, 2014, balance sheet.

Learning Objectives 1, 3

3. Net AR $119,800

P-29A Accounting for uncollectible accounts using the allowance method (percent-of-sales), and reporting receivables on the balance sheet

Quality Watches completed the following selected transactions during 2013 and 2014:

2013	
Dec. 31	Estimated that bad debts expense for the year was 2% of credit sales of $450,000 and recorded that amount as expense.
31	Made the closing entry for bad debts expense.
2014	
Jan. 17	Sold merchandise inventory to Malcolm Monet, $700, on account. Ignore cost of goods sold.
Jun. 29	Wrote off Malcolm Monet's account as uncollectible after repeated efforts to collect from him.
Aug. 6	Received $700 from Malcolm Monet, along with a letter apologizing for being so late. Reinstated Monet's account in full and recorded the cash receipt.
Dec. 31	Made a compound entry to write off the following accounts as uncollectible: Brian Kemper, $1,600; May Milford, $1,000; and Ronald Richter, $400.
31	Estimated that bad debts expense for the year was 2% on credit sales of $460,000 and recorded the expense.
31	Made the closing entry for bad debts expense.

Requirements

1. Open T-accounts for Allowance for Bad Debts and Bad Debts Expense. Keep running balances, assuming all accounts begin with a zero balance.
2. Record the transactions in the general journal, and post to the two T-accounts.
3. Assume the December 31, 2014, balance of Accounts Receivable is $135,000. Show how net accounts receivable would be reported on the balance sheet at that date.

Receivables

P-30A Accounting for uncollectible accounts (aging-of-receivables method), credit card sales, notes receivable, and accrued interest revenue

Learning Objectives 1, 3, 4

Dec. 31, 2013—Interest Receivable $2,700

Relaxing Recliner Chairs completed the following selected transactions:

2013		
Jul.	1	Sold merchandise inventory to Great Mart, receiving a $45,000, nine-month, 12% note. Ignore cost of goods sold.
Oct.	31	Recorded credit and debit card sales for the period of $21,000. (Use the gross method.)
Nov.	3	Card processor drafted company's checking account for processing fee of $410.
Dec.	31	Made an adjusting entry to accrue interest on the Great Mart note.
	31	Made an adjusting entry to record bad debts expense based on an aging of accounts receivable. The aging schedule shows that $15,200 of accounts receivable will not be collected. Prior to this adjustment, the credit balance in Allowance for Bad Debts is $11,600.
2014		
Apr.	1	Collected the maturity value of the Great Mart note.
Jun.	23	Sold merchandise inventory to Ambiance, Corp., receiving a 60-day, 9% note for $13,000. Ignore cost of goods sold.
Aug.	22	Ambiance, Corp. dishonored its note at maturity; the business converted the maturity value of the note to an account receivable.
Nov.	16	Loaned $21,000 cash to Creed, Inc. receiving a 90-day, 8% note.
Dec.	5	Collected in full on account from Ambiance, Corp.
	31	Accrued the interest on the Creed, Inc. note.

Record the transactions in the journal of Relaxing Recliner Chairs. Explanations are not required. (For notes stated in days, use a 360-day year. Round to the nearest dollar.)

P-31A Accounting for notes receivable and accruing interest

Learning Objective 4

1. Note 3—Jan. 18, 2015

Kelly Realty loaned money and received the following notes during 2014.

Note	Date	Principal Amount	Interest Rate	Term
(1)	Aug.1	$ 24,000	17%	1 year
(2)	Nov. 30	18,000	6%	6 months
(3)	Dec. 19	12,000	12%	30 days

Requirements

1. Determine the maturity date and maturity value of each note.
2. Journalize the entry to record the inception of each of the three notes and also journalize a single adjusting entry at December 31, 2014, the fiscal year-end, to record accrued interest revenue on all three notes. Explanations are not required.
3. Journalize the collection of principal and interest at maturity of all three notes. Explanations are not required.

Learning Objective 4

Dec. 31, 2013—Income
Summary CR $58

P-32A Accounting for notes receivable, dishonored notes, and accrued interest revenue

Consider the following transactions for Jo Jo Music.

2013		
Dec. 6	Received a $7,000, 90-day, 12% note in settlement of an overdue accounts receivable from Dark Star Music.	
31	Made an adjusting entry to accrue interest on the Dark Star Music note.	
31	Made a closing entry for interest revenue.	
2014		
Mar. 6	Collected the maturity value of the Dark Star Music note.	
Jun. 30	Loaned $11,000 cash to Love Joy Music, receiving a six-month, 11% note.	
Oct. 2	Received a $2,400, 60-day, 11% note for a sale to Voice Publishing. Ignore cost of goods sold.	
Dec. 1	Voice Publishing dishonored its note at maturity.	
1	Wrote off the receivable associated with Voice Publishing. (Use the allowance method.)	
30	Collected the maturity value of the Love Joy Music note.	

Journalize all transactions for Jo Jo Music. Round all amounts to the nearest dollar. (For notes stated in days, use a 360-day year.)

Learning Objective 5

1. Acid-test ratio (2014) 0.94

P-33A Using ratio data to evaluate a company's financial position

The comparative financial statements of Lakeland Cosmetic Supply for 2014, 2013, and 2012 include the data shown here:

	2014	2013	2012
Balance sheet—partial			
Current Assets:			
Cash	$ 90,000	$ 70,000	$ 30,000
Short-term investments	145,000	175,000	125,000
Accounts Receivable, Net	290,000	260,000	250,000
Merchandise Inventory	370,000	335,000	325,000
Prepaid Expenses	60,000	15,000	50,000
Total Current Assets	$ 955,000	$ 855,000	$ 780,000
Total Current Liabilities	$ 560,000	$ 600,000	$ 690,000
Income statement—partial			
Net Sales (all on account)	$ 5,860,000	$ 5,140,000	$ 4,200,000

Requirements

1. Compute these ratios for 2014 and 2013:
   a. Acid-test ratio (Round to two decimals.)
   b. Accounts receivable turnover (Round to two decimals.)
   c. Days' sales in receivables (Round to the nearest whole day.)

2. Considering each ratio individually, which ratios improved from 2013 to 2014 and which ratios deteriorated? Is the trend favorable or unfavorable for the company?

> Problems Group B

P-34B Accounting for uncollectible accounts using the allowance (percent-of-sales) and direct write-off methods, and reporting receivables on the balance sheet

Learning Objectives 1, 2, 3

1. Nov. 30 Bal.—AR $133,000

On October 31, 2014, Blossom Floral Supply had a $180,000 debit balance in Accounts Receivable and a $7,200 credit balance in Allowance for Bad Debts. During November, Blossom made the following transactions:

- Sales on account, $560,000. Ignore Cost of Goods Sold.
- Collections on account, $598,000.
- Write-offs of uncollectible receivables, $9,000.

Requirements

1. Journalize all November entries using the *allowance* method. Bad debts expense was estimated at 1% of credit sales. Show all November activity in Accounts Receivable, Allowance for Bad Debts, and Bad Debts Expense (post to these T-accounts).

2. Using the same facts, assume that Blossom used the direct write-off method to account for uncollectible receivables. Journalize all November entries using the *direct write-off* method. Post to Accounts Receivable and Bad Debts Expense and show their balances at November 30, 2014.

3. What amount of Bad Debts Expense would Blossom report on its November income statement under each of the two methods? Which amount better matches expense with revenue? Give your reason.

4. What amount of *net* accounts receivable would Blossom report on its November 30, 2014, balance sheet under each of the two methods? Which amount is more realistic? Give your reason.

Receivables

Learning Objective 3

2. Dec. 31, 2014 Allowance
CR Bal. $5,288

P-35B Accounting for uncollectible accounts using the allowance method (aging-of-receivables), and reporting receivables on the balance sheet

At September 30, 2014, the accounts of Park Terrace Medical Center (PTMC) include the following:

Accounts Receivable	$ 141,000
Allowance for Bad Debts (credit balance)	3,400

During the last quarter of 2014, PTMC completed the following selected transactions:

Dec. 28	Wrote off accounts receivable as uncollectible: Red, Co., $1,600; Jacob Weiss, $1,300; and Star, Inc., $300
31	Recorded bad debts expense based on the aging of accounts receivable, as follows:

	Age of Accounts			
Accounts Receivable	1–30 Days	31–60 Days	61–90 Days	Over 90 Days
$161,000	$99,000	$42,000	$15,000	$5,000
Estimated percent uncollectible	0.2%	2%	20%	25%

Requirements

1. Journalize the transactions.
2. Open the Allowance for Bad Debts T-account, and post entries affecting that account. Keep a running balance.
3. Show how Park Terrace Medical Center should report net accounts receivable on its December 31, 2014, balance sheet.

Learning Objectives 1, 3

1. Dec. 31, 2014, Allowance
CR Bal. $24,600

P-36B Accounting for uncollectible accounts using the allowance method (percent-of-sales), and reporting receivables on the balance sheet

Beta Watches completed the following selected transactions during 2013 and 2014:

2013	
Dec. 31	Estimated that bad debts expense for the year was 3% of credit sales of $440,000 and recorded that amount as expense.
31	Made the closing entry for bad debts expense.
2014	
Jan. 17	Sold merchandise inventory to Manny Vasquez, $800, on account. Ignore cost of goods sold.
Jun. 29	Wrote off Manny Vasquez's account as uncollectible after repeated efforts to collect from him.
Aug. 6	Received $800 from Manny Vasquez, along with a letter apologizing for being so late. Reinstated Vasquez's account in full and recorded the cash receipt.
Dec. 31	Made a compound entry to write off the following accounts as uncollectible: Bill Kappy, $1,400; Mike Venture, $1,100; and Russell Reeves, $200.
31	Estimated that bad debts expense for the year was 3% on credit sales of $470,000 and recorded the expense.
31	Made the closing entry for bad debts expense.

Requirements

1. Open T-accounts for Allowance for Bad Debts and Bad Debts Expense. Keep running balances, assuming all accounts begin with a zero balance.

2. Record the transactions in the general journal, and post to the two T-accounts.

3. Assume the December 31, 2014, balance of Accounts Receivable is $139,000. Show how net accounts receivable would be reported on the balance sheet at that date.

P-37B Accounting for uncollectible accounts (aging-of-receivables method), credit card sales, notes receivable, and accrued interest revenue

Learning Objectives 1, 3, 4

Dec. 31, 2013—Bad Debts Expense $3,900

Sleepy Recliner Chairs completed the following selected transactions:

2013		
Jul.	1	Sold merchandise inventory to Go Mart, receiving a $37,000, nine-month, 8% note. Ignore cost of goods sold.
Oct.	31	Recorded credit and debit card sales for the period of $19,000. (Use the gross method.)
Nov.	3	Card processor drafted company's checking account for processing fee of $420.
Dec.	31	Made an adjusting entry to accrue interest on the Go Mart note.
	31	Made an adjusting entry to record bad debts expense based on an aging of accounts receivable. The aging schedule shows that $14,100 of accounts receivable will not be collected. Prior to this adjustment, the credit balance in Allowance for Bad Debts is $10,200.
2014		
Apr.	1	Collected the maturity value of the Go Mart note.
Jun.	23	Sold merchandise inventory to Appeal, Corp., receiving a 60-day, 12% note for $7,000. Ignore cost of goods sold.
Aug.	22	Appeal, Corp. dishonored its note at maturity; the business converted the maturity value of the note to an account receivable.
Nov.	16	Loaned $23,000 cash to Welch, Inc., receiving a 90-day, 16% note.
Dec.	5	Collected in full on account from Appeal, Corp.
	31	Accrued the interest on the Welch, Inc. note.

Record the transactions in the journal of Sleepy Recliner Chairs. Explanations are not required. (For notes stated in days, use a 360-day year. Round to the nearest dollar.)

Learning Objective 4

1. Note 2—Maturity Value $20,900

P-38B Accounting for notes receivable and accruing interest

Christie Realty loaned money and received the following notes during 2014.

Note	Date	Principal Amount	Interest Rate	Term
(1)	Jun. 1	$ 12,000	10%	1 year
(2)	Sep. 30	20,000	9%	6 months
(3)	Oct. 19	10,000	12%	30 days

Requirements

1. Determine the maturity date and maturity value of each note.

2. Journalize the entry to record the inception of each of the three notes and also journalize a single adjusting entry at October 31, 2014, the fiscal year-end, to record accrued interest revenue on all three notes. Explanations are not required.

3. Journalize the collection of principal and interest at maturity of all three notes. Explanations are not required.

Learning Objective 4

March 6, 2014—Interest Revenue $65

P-39B Accounting for notes receivable, dishonored notes, and accrued interest revenue

Consider the following transactions for Rural Beginnings.

2013		
Dec.	6	Received a $4,000, 90-day, 9% note in settlement of an overdue accounts receivable from AM Publishing.
	31	Made an adjusting entry to accrue interest on the AM Publishing note.
	31	Made a closing entry for interest revenue.
2014		
Mar.	6	Collected the maturity value of the AM Publishing note.
Jun.	30	Loaned $15,000 cash to Jonathon's Publishing, receiving a six-month, 8% note.
Oct.	2	Received a $2,000, 60-day, 8% note for a sale to Ying Yang Music. Ignore cost of goods sold.
Dec.	1	Ying Yang Music dishonored its note at maturity.
	1	Wrote off the receivable associated with Ying Yang Music. (Use the allowance method.)
	30	Collected the maturity value of the Jonathan's Publishing note.

Journalize all transactions for Rural Beginnings. Round all amounts to the nearest dollar. (For notes stated in days, use a 360-day year.)

P-40B Using ratio data to evaluate a company's financial position

Learning Objective 5

1. Days' sales in receivables (2014)
17 days

The comparative financial statements of Perfection Cosmetic Supply for 2014, 2013, and 2012 include the data shown here:

	2014	2013	2012
Balance sheet—partial			
Current Assets:			
Cash	$ 60,000	$ 50,000	$ 60,000
Short-term investments	155,000	155,000	120,000
Accounts Receivable, Net	300,000	240,000	260,000
Merchandise Inventory	355,000	320,000	320,000
Prepaid Expenses	75,000	25,000	55,000
Total Current Assets	$ 945,000	$ 790,000	$ 815,000
Total Current Liabilities	$ 590,000	$ 580,000	$ 680,000
Income statement—partial			
Net Sales (all on account)	$ 5,830,000	$ 5,110,000	$ 4,210,000

Requirements

1. Compute these ratios for 2014 and 2013:

   a. Acid-test ratio (Round to two decimals.)
   b. Accounts receivable turnover (Round to two decimals.)
   c. Days' sales in receivables (Round to the nearest whole dollar.)

2. Considering each ratio individually, which ratios improved from 2013 to 2014 and which ratios deteriorated? Is the trend favorable or unfavorable for the company?

> Continuing Problem

P-41 Accounting for uncollectible accounts using the allowance method

This problem deals with a company named Davis Consulting. Davis reviewed the receivables list from the January transactions. Davis uses the allowance method for receivables, estimating uncollectibles to be 5% of January credit sales, $4,500. Davis identified on February 15 that a customer was not going to pay his receivable of $200.

Requirements

1. Journalize the January 31 entry to record and establish the allowance using the percent-of-sales method for January credit sales.

2. Journalize the entry to record the write-off of the customer's bad debt.

> Practice Set

 P-42 Accounting for uncollectible accounts using the allowance method and reporting net accounts receivable on the balance sheet

Shine King Cleaning uses the allowance method to estimate bad debts. Consider the following January transactions for Shine King Cleaning:

Jan. 1	Performed cleaning service for Debbie's D-list for $8,000 on terms 3/10, n/20.
10	Borrowed money from North Spot Bank, $10,000, 7% for 180 days.
12	After discussions with Pierre's Wig Stand, Shine King has determined that $225 of the receivable owed will not be collected. Wrote off this portion of the receivable.
15	Sold goods to Watertown for $4,000 on terms 4/10, n/30. Cost of goods sold was $600.
28	Sold goods to Bridget, Inc. for cash of $1,200 (cost $280).
28	Collected from Pierre's Wig Stand $225 of receivable previously written off.
29	Paid cash for utilities of $350.
31	Created an aging schedule for Shine King for accounts receivable. Shine King determined that $4,000 of receivables were 2% uncollectible and $9,775 of receivables were 15% uncollectible. Shine King determined the total amount of estimated uncollectible receivables and adjusted the Allowance for Bad Debts assuming a credit balance of $240 in the account. (Round to nearest whole dollar.)

Requirements

1. Prepare all required journal entries for Shine King.
2. Show how net accounts receivable would be reported on the balance sheet as of January 31.

CRITICAL THINKING

> Decision Cases

Decision Case 1

Weddings on Demand sells on account and manages its own receivables. Average experience for the past three years has been as follows:

Sales	$ 350,000
Cost of Goods Sold	210,000
Bad Debts Expense	4,000
Other Expenses	61,000

Unhappy with the amount of bad debts expense she has been experiencing, Aledia Sanchez, owner of Weddings on Demand, is considering a major change in her business. Her plan would be to stop selling on account altogether but accept either cash, credit cards, or debit cards from her customers. Her market research indicates that if she does so, her sales will increase by 10% (i.e., from $350,000 to $385,000), of which $200,000 will be credit or debit card sales and the rest will be cash sales. With a 10% increase in sales, there will also be a 10% increase in Cost of Goods Sold. If she adopts this plan, she will no longer have bad debts expense, but she will have to pay a fee on debit/credit card transactions of 2% of sales. She also believes this plan will allow her to save $5,000 per year in other operating expenses. Should Sanchez start accepting credit cards and debit cards? Show the computations of net income under her present arrangement and under the plan.

Decision Case 2

Pauline's Pottery has always used the direct write-off method to account for uncollectibles. The company's revenues, bad debt write-offs, and year-end receivables for the most recent year follow:

Year	Revenues	Write-Offs	Receivables at Year-End
2013	$150,000	$3,900	$14,000

The business is applying for a bank loan, and the loan officer requires figures based on the allowance method of accounting for bad debts. In the past, bad debts have run about 4% of revenues.

Requirements

Pauline must give the banker the following information:

1. How much more or less would net income be for 2013 if Pauline's Pottery were to use the allowance method for bad debts? Assume Pauline uses the percent-of-sales method.

2. How much of the receivables balance at the end of 2013 does Pauline's Pottery actually expect to collect? (Disregard beginning account balances for the purpose of this question.)

3. Explain why net income is more or less using the allowance method versus the direct write-off method for uncollectibles.

> Ethical Issue 1

E-Z Loan, Co. makes loans to high-risk borrowers. E-Z borrows from its bank and then lends money to people with bad credit. The bank requires E-Z Loan to submit quarterly financial statements in order to keep its line of credit. E-Z's main asset is Accounts Receivable. Therefore, Bad Debts Expense and Allowance for Bad Debts are important accounts.

Slade McMurphy, the owner of E-Z Loan, wants net income to increase in a smooth pattern rather than increase in some periods and decrease in others. To report smoothly increasing net income, McMurphy underestimates Bad Debts Expense in some periods. In other periods, McMurphy overestimates the expense. He reasons that over time the income overstatements roughly offset the income understatements.

Is McMurphy's practice of smoothing income ethical? Why or why not?

> Fraud Case 1

Dylan worked for a propane gas distributor as an accounting clerk in a small Midwestern town. Last winter, his brother Mike lost his job at the machine plant. By January, temperatures were sub-zero, and Mike had run out of money. Dylan saw that Mike's account was overdue, and he knew Mike needed another delivery to heat his home. He decided to credit Mike's account and debit the balance to the parts inventory because he knew the parts manager, the owner's son, was incompetent and would never notice the extra entry. Months went by, and Dylan repeated the process until an auditor ran across the charges by chance. When the owner fired Dylan, he said, "If you had only come to me and told me about Mike's situation, we could have worked something out."

Requirements

1. What can a business like this do to prevent employee fraud of this kind?

2. What effect would Dylan's actions have on the balance sheet? The income statement?

3. How much discretion does a business have with regard to accommodating hardship situations?

> Financial Statement Case 1

Use **Starbucks Corporation**'s Fiscal 2011 Annual Report and the Note 1 data on "Allowance for Doubtful Accounts" to answer the following questions. Visit **www.pearsonhighered.com/Horngren** to view a link to Starbucks Corporation's annual report.

Requirements

1. How much accounts receivables did Starbucks report as of October 2, 2011? As of October 3, 2010?

2. Refer to Note 1, "Allowance for Doubtful Accounts." How does Starbucks calculate allowance for doubtful accounts? What was the amount of the account as of October 2, 2011? As of October 3, 2010?

3. Compute Starbucks' acid-test ratio at the end of 2011. If all the current liabilities came due immediately, could Starbucks pay them?

4. Compute Starbucks' accounts receivable turnover at the end of 2011. Use total net revenues.

5. Compute Starbucks' days' sales in receivables at the end of 2011.

6. How does Starbucks compare to **Green Mountain Coffee Roasters, Inc.** on the basis of the acid-test ratio, accounts receivable turnover, and days' sales in receivables?

> Team Project 1

Companies that process credit cards are often referred to as providing merchant services. Perform an Internet search using the search terms "credit card merchant services" or "credit card processing services." Each member of the team should identify one company or bank that offers credit card services. In a table, compare and contrast the different companies. Some items that you could review would be price/fees, fraud services provided, types of credit cards accepted, whether the service works on the Internet and with POS (point of sale) swipe machines, and how many days it takes to process the credit card transactions. As a team, decide which company would be would be best to use and explain why.

> Communication Activity 1

In 100 words or fewer, explain the difference between the percent-of-sales method and the aging-of-receivables method for calculating the journal entry to adjust the Allowance for Bad Debts.

MyAccountingLab | **For a wealth of online resources, including exercises, problems, media, and immediate tutorial help, please visit** www.myaccountinglab.com.

Try It! Solutions

1.

Date	Accounts and Explanation	Debit	Credit
Jun. 30	Cash	11,760	
	Credit Card Expense ($12,000 × 0.02)	240	
	Sales Revenue		12,000
	Recorded credit card sales, net of fee.		

2.

Date	Accounts and Explanation	Debit	Credit
Jun. 30	Cash	12,000	
	Sales Revenue		12,000
	Recorded credit card sales.		

Receivables

3.

Date	Accounts and Explanation	Debit	Credit
Jul. 18	Bad Debts Expense	6,800	
	Accounts Receivable—Jennings		6,800
	Wrote off an uncollectible account.		

4.

Date	Accounts and Explanation	Debit	Credit
Aug. 24	Accounts Receivable—Jennings	6,800	
	Bad Debts Expense		6,800
	Reinstated previously written off account.		
24	Cash	6,800	
	Accounts Receivable—Jennings		6,800
	Collected cash on account.		

5.

Date	Accounts and Explanation	Debit	Credit
Sep. 2	Allowance for Bad Debts	14,000	
	Accounts Receivable—Mraz		14,000
	Wrote off an uncollectible account.		

6.

Date	Accounts and Explanation	Debit	Credit
Dec. 12	Accounts Receivable—Mraz	14,000	
	Allowance for Bad Debts		14,000
	Reinstated previously written off account.		
12	Cash	14,000	
	Accounts Receivable—Mraz		14,000
	Collected cash on account.		

7.

Date	Accounts and Explanation	Debit	Credit
Dec. 31	Bad Debts Expense	800	
	Allowance for Bad Debts		800
	Recorded bad debts expense for the period.		

8.

Date	Accounts and Explanation	Debit	Credit
Aug. 1	Notes Receivable—King	80,000	
	Cash		80,000
	Accepted note in exchange for cash.		

9.

Date	Accounts and Explanation	Debit	Credit
Oct. 30	Cash	81,000	
	Notes Receivable—King		80,000
	Interest Revenue ($80,000 × 0.05 × 90/360)		1,000
	Collected note receivable plus interest.		

10A.

Acid-test ratio = Cash + Short-term investments + Net accounts receivable / Total current liabilities
= ($104,000 + $56,000 + $108,000) / ($128,000 + $72,000) = 1.34

10B.

Accounts receivable turnover ratio = Net credit sales / Average net accounts receivable
= $1,168,000 / (($68,000 + $108,000) /2) = 13.3 times (rounded)

10C.

Days' sales in receivables = 365 days / Accounts receivable turnover ratio
= 365 days / 13.3 = 27.4 days (rounded)

> Quick Check Answers

1. d **2.** b **3.** d **4.** d **5.** a **6.** d **7.** b **8.** c **9.** a **10.** d

Glossary

Accounts Receivable. The right to receive cash in the future from customers for goods sold or for services performed.

Accounts Receivable Turnover Ratio. A ratio that measures the number of times the company collects the average accounts receivable balance in a year. Net credit sales / Average net accounts receivable.

Acid-Test Ratio. The ratio of the sum of cash plus shortterm investments plus net current receivables to total current liabilities. The ratio tells whether the entity could pay all its current liabilities if they came due immediately. (Cash + Short-term investments + Net current receivables) / Total current liabilities.

Aging-of-Receivables Method. A method of estimating uncollectible receivables by determining the balance of the Allowance for Bad Debts account based on the age of individual accounts receivable.

Allowance for Bad Debts. A contra account, related to accounts receivable, that holds the estimated amount of uncollectible accounts.

Allowance Method. A method of accounting for uncollectible receivables in which the company estimates bad debts expense instead of waiting to see which customers the company will not collect from.

Bad Debts Expense. The cost to the seller of extending credit. It arises from the failure to collect from some credit customers.

Days' Sales in Receivables. The ratio of average net accounts receivable to one day's sales. The ratio tells how many days it takes to collect the average level of accounts receivable. 365 days / Accounts receivable turnover ratio.

Debtor. The party to a credit transaction who takes on an obligation/payable.

Direct Write-Off Method. A method of accounting for uncollectible receivables in which the company records bad debts expense when a customer's account receivable is uncollectible.

Dishonor a Note. Failure of a note's maker to pay a note receivable at maturity.

Interest. The revenue to the payee for loaning money—the expense to the debtor.

Interest Period. The period of time during which interest is computed. It extends from the original date of the note to the maturity date.

Interest Rate. The percentage rate of interest specified by the note.

Maturity Date. The date when a note is due.

Maturity Value. The sum of the principal plus interest due at maturity.

Net Realizable Value. The net value a company expects to collect from its accounts receivable. Accounts Receivable less Allowance for Bad Debts.

Notes Receivable. A written promise that a customer will pay a fixed amount of principal plus interest by a certain date in the future.

Percent-of-Receivables Method. A method of estimating uncollectible receivables by determining the balance of the Allowance for Bad Debts account based on a percentage of accounts receivable.

Percent-of-Sales Method. A method of estimating uncollectible receivables that calculates bad debts expense based on a percentage of net credit sales.

Principal. The amount loaned out by the payee and borrowed by the maker of the note.

Receivable. A monetary claim against a business or an individual.

Photo Credits

Credits are listed in order of appearance.

Photo 1 (top): Nenetus/shutterstock
Photo 2 (middle): Jmiks/Shutterstock
Photo 3 (bottom): Artjazz/Shutterstock
Photo 4: Andresr/Shutterstock
Photo 5: Photobac/Shutterstock
Photo 6: Mike Flippo/Shutterstock
Photo 7: Lithian/Shutterstock

Plant Assets, Natural Resources, and Intangibles

Plant Assets, Natural Resources, and Intangibles

What Do I Do With This Equipment?

Jerry Drake has been working hard at his new landscaping business for several months. Things are great—sales are increasing every month, and he is increasing his customer base. So far, Jerry has been renting lawn equipment or borrowing equipment from his friends. Jerry is now considering buying several new lawn mowers, trimmers, and leaf blowers.

Jerry is trying to figure out how to record the purchase of these items on his books. Should he expense it all or set up asset accounts for each of the items? Jerry is also considering how long each item will last before he needs to purchase new equipment. He knows that his accountant will ask him about depreciation. She has told him there are several methods he should consider. Jerry knows he wants a depreciation method that will match the cost of the equipment with the revenue that the business earns.

In addition, Jerry plans on keeping the equipment as long as he can, which means that he will be making repairs and maintaining the equipment. He is wondering how the cost of the repairs should be recorded. And, what happens when he finally sells the equipment? Jerry realizes there is a lot to consider when a business buys equipment. He knows that his accountant will help answer his many questions so he can properly record the cost of the equipment and any future associated costs.

How Are Plant Assets, Natural Resources and Intangibles Accounted For?

Plant assets, natural resources, and intangibles are some of the most important assets on the balance sheet. These assets help create the revenue of the business. For example, TruGreen, a company that specializes in lawn and landscape services, wouldn't earn a profit without the lawn equipment it uses to service its customers' lawns. ConocoPhillips wouldn't have made a $12.4 billion profit in 2011 without its natural resource of oil reserves. And we are familiar with McDonald's trademark "golden arches." In this chapter, we discuss how to record the purchase, cost allocation, and disposal of these assets.

chapter outline

How does a business measure the cost of a plant asset?

What is depreciation and how is it computed?

How are disposals of plant assets recorded?

How are natural resources accounted for?

How are intangible assets accounted for?

How do we use the asset turnover ratio to evaluate business performance?

How are exchanges of plant assets accounted for? (Appendix A)

Learning Objectives

1 Measure the cost of a plant asset

2 Account for depreciation using the straight-line, units-of-production, and double-declining-balance methods

3 Journalize entries for the disposal of plant assets

4 Account for natural resources

5 Account for intangible assets

6 Use the asset turnover ratio to evaluate business performance

7 Journalize entries for the exchange of plant assets (Appendix A)

HOW DOES A BUSINESS MEASURE THE COST OF A PLANT ASSET?

Learning Objective 1
Measure the cost of a plant asset

Plant Asset
Long-lived, tangible asset, such as land, buildings, and equipment, used in the operation of a business.

Depreciation
The process by which businesses spread the allocation of a plant asset's cost over its useful life.

Cost Principle
A principle that states that acquired assets and services should be recorded at their actual cost.

Plant assets are long-lived, tangible assets used in the operation of a business. Examples include land, buildings, equipment, furniture, and automobiles. Often, plant assets are referred to as *Property, Plant, and Equipment* or *Fixed Assets* in financial statements.

Plant assets are unique from other assets, such as office supplies, because plant assets are long-term (lasting several years). This requires a business to allocate the cost of the asset over the years that the asset is expected to be used. This allocation of a plant asset's cost over its useful life is called **depreciation** and follows the matching principle. The matching principle ensures that all expenses are matched against the revenues of the period. Because plant assets are used over several years, a business will spread the cost of the asset over several years. All plant assets except land are depreciated. We record no depreciation for land because its value typically does not decline with use.

Plant assets are used in the operations of the business. This means that they are not specifically acquired for resale, but instead, they are used to help create the business's revenue. For example, a business that has a vacant building that is not currently being used would classify this asset as a long-term investment instead of as a plant asset. This is because the vacant building is sitting idle and not currently being used in the operations of the business.

Exhibit 1 summarizes the life cycle of a plant asset in a business. The business begins by acquiring the asset and recording the asset on its books. This involves determining the asset cost that is reported on the balance sheet. As the business uses the asset, it must record depreciation expense. In addition, the business also incurs additional expenses (such as repairs and maintenance) related to the asset. And lastly, when the asset has reached the end of its useful life, the business disposes of the asset. Each of these stages in the life of a plant asset must be recorded on the business's books.

Plant assets are recorded at historical cost—the amount paid for the asset. This follows the **cost principle** which states that acquired assets (and services) should be recorded at their actual cost. The *actual cost of a plant asset* is its purchase price plus taxes, purchase commissions, and all other amounts paid to ready the asset for its intended use. Let's begin by reviewing the different categories of plant assets.

Exhibit 1 | Life Cycle of a Plant Asset

| 1. Acquisition of asset | 2. Usage of asset | 3. Disposal of asset |

Land and Land Improvements

The cost of land includes the following amounts paid by the purchaser:

- Purchase price
- Brokerage commission
- Survey and legal fees
- Deliquent property taxes
- Taxes assessed to transfer the ownership (title) on the land
- Cost of clearing the land and removing unwanted buildings

The cost of land does *not* include the following costs:

- Fencing
- Paving
- Sprinkler systems
- Lighting
- Signs

These separate plant assets (fencing, paving, and so on) are called land improvements. Unlike land, land improvements are subject to depreciation.

Suppose Smart Touch Learning needs property and purchases land on August 1, 2015, for $50,000 with a note payable for the same amount. The company also pays cash as follows: $4,000 in property taxes, $2,000 in transfer taxes, $5,000 to remove an old building, and a $1,000 survey fee. What is the company's cost of this land? Exhibit 2 shows all the costs incurred to bring the land to its intended use.

Land Improvement
A depreciable improvement to land, such as fencing, sprinklers, paving, signs, and lighting.

Exhibit 2 | Measuring the Cost of Land

Purchase price of land		$ 50,000
Add related costs:		
Property taxes	$ 4,000	
Transfer taxes	2,000	
Removal of building	5,000	
Survey fee	1,000	12,000
Total cost of land		$ 62,000

The entry to record the purchase of the land on August 1, 2015, follows:

$$\left.\begin{array}{c} \underline{A\uparrow} \\ \text{Land}\uparrow \\ \text{Cash}\downarrow \end{array}\right\} = \left\{\begin{array}{c} \underline{L\uparrow} + \underline{E} \\ \text{Notes} \\ \text{Payable}\uparrow \end{array}\right.$$

Date	Accounts and Explanation	Debit	Credit
Aug. 1	Land	62,000	
	Notes Payable		50,000
	Cash		12,000
	To record purchase of land with cash and note payable.		

Capitalize

Recording the acquisition of land, building, or other assets by debiting (increasing) an asset account.

We would say that Smart Touch Learning *capitalized* the cost of the land at $62,000. Capitalized means that an asset account was debited (increased) because the company acquired an asset. So, for our land example, Smart Touch Learning debited the Land account for $62,000, the capitalized cost of the asset.

Suppose Smart Touch Learning then pays $20,000 for fences, paving, lighting, and signs on August 15, 2015. The following entry records the cost of these land improvements:

$$\left.\begin{array}{c} \underline{A\uparrow\downarrow} \\ \text{Land} \\ \text{Improvements}\uparrow \\ \text{Cash}\downarrow \end{array}\right\} = \left\{\begin{array}{c} \underline{L} + \underline{E} \\ \\ \end{array}\right.$$

Date	Accounts and Explanation	Debit	Credit
Aug. 15	Land Improvements	20,000	
	Cash		20,000
	To record purchase of land improvements for cash.		

Land and land improvements are two entirely separate assets. Recall that land is not depreciated. However, the cost of land improvements *is* depreciated over that asset's useful life.

Buildings

The cost of a building depends on whether the company is constructing the building itself or is buying an existing one. These costs include the following:

Constructing a Building	Purchasing an Existing Building
• Architectural fees	• Purchase price
• Building permits	• Costs to renovate the building to ready the building for use, which may include any of the charges listed under "Constructing a Building"
• Contractor charges	
• Payments for material, labor, and miscellaneous costs	

Machinery and Equipment

The cost of machinery and equipment includes the following:

- Purchase price (less any discounts)
- Transportation charges
- Insurance while in transit

- Sales tax and other taxes
- Purchase commission
- Installation costs
- Testing costs (prior to use of the asset)

After the asset is up and running, the company no longer capitalizes the cost of insurance, taxes, ordinary repairs, and maintenance to the Equipment account. From that point on, insurance, taxes, repairs, and maintenance costs are recorded as expenses.

Furniture and Fixtures

Furniture and fixtures include desks, chairs, file cabinets, display racks, shelving, and so forth. The cost of furniture and fixtures includes the basic cost of each asset (less any discounts), plus all other costs to ready the asset for its intended use. For example, for a desk, this may include the cost to ship the desk to the business and the cost paid to a laborer to assemble the desk.

Lump-Sum Purchase

A company may pay a single price for several assets as a group—a lump-sum purchase (sometimes called a *basket purchase*). For example, Smart Touch Learning may pay a single price for land and a building. For accounting purposes, the company must identify the cost of each asset purchased. The total cost paid (100%) is divided among the assets according to their relative market values. This is called the relative-market-value method.

Relative-Market-Value Method
A method of allocating the total cost (100%) of multiple assets purchased at one time. Total cost is divided among the assets according to their relative market values.

Suppose Smart Touch Learning paid a combined purchase price of $100,000 on August 1, 2015, for the land and building. An appraisal indicates that the land's market value is $30,000 and the building's market value is $90,000. It is clear that the company got a good deal, paying less than fair market value, which is $120,000 for the combined assets. But how will the accountant allocate the $100,000 paid for both assets?

First, calculate the ratio of each asset's market value to the total for both assets combined. The total appraised value is $120,000.

Total market value = Land market value + Building market value
= $30,000 + $90,000
= $120,000

The land makes up 25% of the total market value and the building 75%, as follows:

Percentage of total value = Land market value / Total market value
= $30,000 / $120,000
= 25%

Percentage of total value = Building market value / Total market value
= $90,000 / $120,000
= 75%

For Smart Touch Learning, the land is assigned the cost of $25,000 and the building is assigned the cost of $75,000. The calculation follows:

Asset	Market Value	Percentage of Total Value	× Total Purchase Price	= Assigned Cost of Each Asset
Land	$ 30,000	$30,000 / $120,000 = 25%	× $100,000	= $ 25,000
Building	90,000	$90,000 / $120,000 = 75%	× $100,000	= 75,000
Total	$ 120,000	100%		$ 100,000

Suppose the company purchased the assets by signing a note payable. The entry to record the purchase of the land and building is as follows:

$$\left.\frac{\mathbf{A}\uparrow}{\substack{\text{Land}\uparrow \\ \text{Building}\uparrow}}\right\} = \left\{\frac{\mathbf{L}\uparrow}{\substack{\text{Notes} \\ \text{Payable}\uparrow}} + \frac{\mathbf{E}}{}\right.$$

Date	Accounts and Explanation	Debit	Credit
Aug. 1	Land	25,000	
	Building	75,000	
	Notes Payable		100,000
	To record purchase of land and building in exchange for note payable.		

Capital and Revenue Expenditures

Accountants divide spending on plant assets after the acquisition into two categories:

- Capital expenditures
- Revenue expenditures

Capital Expenditure
An expenditure that increases the capacity or efficiency of a plant asset or extends its useful life. Capital expenditures are debited to an asset account.

A **capital expenditure** is debited to an asset account because it increases the asset's capacity or efficiency or extends the asset's useful life. A capital expenditure is also called a *balance sheet expenditure* because the cost of the expenditure is reported on the balance sheet as an asset.

Examples of capital expenditures include the purchase price plus all the other costs to bring an asset to its intended use, as discussed in the preceding sections. Also, an **extraordinary repair** is a capital expenditure because it extends the asset's capacity or useful life. An example of an extraordinary repair would be spending $3,000 to rebuild the engine on a five-year-old truck. This extraordinary repair would extend the asset's life past the normal expected life. As a result, its cost would be debited to the asset account for the truck as follows:

Extraordinary Repair
Repair work that generates a capital expenditure because it extends the asset's life past the normal expected life.

$$\left.\frac{\mathbf{A}\uparrow\downarrow}{\substack{\text{Truck}\uparrow \\ \text{Cash}\downarrow}}\right\} = \left\{\frac{\mathbf{L}}{} + \frac{\mathbf{E}}{}\right.$$

Date	Accounts and Explanation	Debit	Credit
	Truck	3,000	
	Cash		3,000
	To record cost of rebuilding engine on truck.		

Expenses incurred to maintain the asset in working order, such as repair or maintenance expense, are *not* debited to an asset account. Examples include the costs of maintaining equipment, such as repairing the air conditioner on a truck, changing the oil filter, and replacing its tires. These ordinary repairs are called revenue expenditures and are debited to Repairs and Maintenance Expense. Revenue expenditures, often called *income statement expenditures,* do not increase the capacity or efficiency of an asset or extend its useful life and are reported on the income statement as an expense in the period incurred.

Suppose that Smart Touch Learning paid $500 cash to replace tires on the truck. This expenditure does not extend the useful life of the truck or increase its efficiency. The company's accounting clerk records this transaction as a revenue expenditure as shown:

Revenue Expenditure
An expenditure that does not increase the capacity or efficiency of an asset or extend its useful life. Revenue expenditures are debited to an expense account.

Date	Accounts and Explanation	Debit	Credit
	Repairs and Maintenance Expense	500	
	Cash		500
	To record repairs and maintenance incurred.		

$$\left.\begin{array}{c} A\downarrow \\ Cash\downarrow \end{array}\right\} = \left\{\begin{array}{c} L \quad + \quad E\downarrow \\ \hline \text{Repairs and Maintenance Expense}\uparrow \end{array}\right.$$

Exhibit 3 shows some (a) capital expenditures and (b) revenue expenditures for a delivery truck.

Exhibit 3 | Delivery Truck Expenditures—Capital Expenditure or Revenue Expenditure

CAPITAL EXPENDITURE: Debit an Asset Account	REVENUE EXPENDITURE: Debit Repairs and Maintenance Expense
Extraordinary Repairs:	*Revenue Expenditures:*
Major engine or transmission overhaul	Repair of transmission or engine
Modification for new use	Oil change, lubrication, and so on
Addition to storage capacity	Replacement of tires or windshield
Anything that increases the life of the asset	Paint job

Treating a capital expenditure as an expense, or vice versa, creates an accounting error. Suppose a business replaces the engine in the truck. This would be an extraordinary repair because it increases the truck's life. If the company expenses the cost by debiting Repairs and Maintenance Expense rather than capitalizing it (debiting the asset), the company would be making an accounting error. This error has the following effects:

- Overstates Repairs and Maintenance Expense
- Understates net income
- Understates owner's equity
- Understates the Truck account (asset) on the balance sheet

Incorrectly capitalizing an expense creates the opposite error. Assume a minor repair, such as replacing the water pump on the truck, was incorrectly debited to the asset account. The error would result in expenses being understated and net income being overstated. Additionally, the cost of the truck would be overstated on the balance sheet by the amount of the repair bill.

> Try It!

1. Budget Banners pays $200,000 cash for a group purchase of land, building, and equipment. At the time of acquisition, the land has a market value of $22,000, the building $187,000, and the equipment $11,000. Journalize the lump-sum purchase.

Check your answer at the end of the chapter.

For more practice, see Short Exercises S-1 and S-2. MyAccountingLab

WHAT IS DEPRECIATION AND HOW IS IT COMPUTED?

Learning Objective 2
Account for depreciation using the straight-line, units-of-production, and double-declining-balance methods

As we learned earlier, depreciation is the allocation of a plant asset's cost to expense over its useful life. Depreciation matches the expense against the revenue generated from using the asset to measure net income.

All assets, except land, wear out as they are used. For example, a business's delivery truck can only go so many miles before it is worn out. As the truck is driven, this use is part of what causes depreciation. Additionally, physical factors, like age and weather, can cause depreciation of assets.

Obsolete
An asset is considered obsolete when a newer asset can perform the job more efficiently than the old.

Some assets, such as computers and software, may become *obsolete* before they wear out. An asset is **obsolete** when a newer asset can perform the job more efficiently. As a result, an asset's useful life may be shorter than its physical life. In all cases, the asset's cost is depreciated over its useful life.

Now that we have discussed causes of depreciation, let's discuss what depreciation is *not*.

1. *Depreciation is not a process of valuation.* Businesses do not record depreciation based on changes in the asset's market value.
2. *Depreciation does not mean that the business sets aside cash to replace an asset when it is used up.* Depreciation has nothing to do with cash.

Factors in Computing Depreciation

Depreciation of a plant asset is based on three main factors:

1. Capitalized cost
2. Estimated useful life
3. Estimated residual value

Capitalized cost is a known cost and, as mentioned earlier in this chapter, includes all items spent for the asset to perform its intended function. The other two factors are estimates.

Useful Life
Length of the service period expected from an asset. May be expressed in time, such as months or years, or usage, such as units produced, hours used (for machinery), or miles driven (for a truck).

Estimated **useful life** is how long the company expects it will use the asset. Useful life may be expressed in time, such as months or years, or usage, such as units produced, hours used (for machinery), or miles driven (for a truck). A company's useful life estimate might be shorter than the actual life of the asset. For example, a business might estimate a useful life of five years for a delivery truck because it has a policy that after five years the truck will be traded in for a new vehicle. The business knows that the truck will last longer than five years, but the business uses a useful life of only five years because this is how long the company expects to use the asset.

Useful life is an estimate based on a company's experience and judgment. The goal is to define estimated useful life with the measure (years, units, and so on) that best matches with the asset's decline or use. When determining useful life, a company considers how long it will use the asset and when the asset will become obsolete.

Estimated *residual value*—also called *salvage value*—is the asset's expected value at the end of its useful life. When a company decides to dispose of an asset, the company will sell or scrap it. The residual value is the amount the company expects to receive when the company disposes of the asset. Residual value can sometimes be zero if a company does not plan to receive anything when disposing of the asset. If a company plans on trading the asset in for a new asset, the residual value will be the expected trade-in value. Estimated residual value is *not* depreciated because the company expects to receive this amount at the end. Cost minus estimated residual value is called *depreciable cost*.

Residual Value
The expected value of a depreciable asset at the end of its useful life.

$$\text{Depreciable cost} = \text{Cost} - \text{Estimated residual value}$$

Depreciable Cost
The cost of a plant asset minus its estimated residual value.

Depreciation Methods

There are many depreciation methods for plant assets, but three are used most commonly:

- Straight-line method
- Units-of-production method
- Double-declining-balance method

These methods work differently in *how* they derive the yearly depreciation amount, but they all result in the same total depreciation over the total life of the asset. Exhibit 4 gives the data we will use for a truck that Smart Touch Learning purchases and places in service on January 1, 2014.

Exhibit 4 | **Data for Truck**

Data Item	Amount
Cost of truck	$ 41,000
Less: Estimated residual value	1,000
Depreciable cost	$ 40,000
Estimated useful life—Years	5 years
Estimated useful life—Units	100,000 miles

Straight-Line Method

The straight-line method allocates an equal amount of depreciation to each year and is calculated as follows:

Straight-Line Method
A depreciation method that allocates an equal amount of depreciation each year. (Cost − Residual Value) / Useful Life.

$$\begin{aligned}\text{Straight-line depreciation} &= (\text{Cost} - \text{Residual value}) / \text{Useful life} \\ &= (\$41,000 - \$1,000) / 5 \text{ years} \\ &= \$8,000 \text{ per year}\end{aligned}$$

Because the asset was placed in service on the first day of the year, the adjusting entry to record each year's depreciation is as follows:

Date	Accounts and Explanation	Debit	Credit
Dec. 31	Depreciation Expense—Truck	8,000	
	Accumulated Depreciation—Truck		8,000
	To record depreciation on truck.		

Book Value
A depreciable asset's cost minus accumulated depreciation.

Depreciation Expense is reported on the income statement. Accumulated Depreciation is a contra asset that is reported on the balance sheet following the Truck account. The book value of the plant asset, cost minus accumulated depreciation, is reported on the balance sheet at December 31, 2014 as follows:

Plant Assets:	
Truck	$ 41,000
Less: Accumulated Depreciation—Truck	(8,000)
Truck, Net	$ 33,000

A straight-line depreciation schedule for this truck is shown in Exhibit 5. The final column shows the asset's book value, which is cost less accumulated depreciation. Notice that the depreciation expense amount is the same every year and that the accumulated depreciation is the sum of all depreciation expense recorded to date for the depreciable asset.

Exhibit 5 | **Straight-Line Depreciation Schedule**

Date	Asset Cost	Depreciation for the Year			Accumulated Depreciation	Book Value
		Depreciable Cost	Useful Life	Depreciation Expense		
1-1-2014	$ 41,000					$ 41,000
12-31-2014		($41,000 – $1,000)	/ 5 years	= $ 8,000	$ 8,000	33,000
12-31-2015		($41,000 – $1,000)	/ 5 years	= 8,000	16,000	25,000
12-31-2016		($41,000 – $1,000)	/ 5 years	= 8,000	24,000	17,000
12-31-2017		($41,000 – $1,000)	/ 5 years	= 8,000	32,000	9,000
12-31-2018		($41,000 – $1,000)	/ 5 years	= 8,000	40,000	1,000 ← Residual value

As an asset is used, accumulated depreciation increases and book value decreases. (See the Accumulated Depreciation and Book Value columns in Exhibit 5.) At the end of its estimated useful life, the asset is said to be fully depreciated. An asset's final book value is its residual value ($1,000 in this example).

>Ethics   Capitalize or expense?

Furniture.com uses automated shipping equipment. Early in the year, Furniture.com purchased equipment at a cost of $400,000. Management expects the equipment to remain in service for five years, with zero residual value. Furniture.com plans on using straight-line depreciation. Mason Green is finalizing the depreciation expense calculation for the year when Furniture.com's controller, Flynn Steel, tells Mason to expense the entire cost of the equipment instead of capitalizing the equipment at the time of purchase. Flynn argues that the company won't have to worry about recording depreciation for the next five years—the accounting will "just be easier." What should Mason do? What would you do?

Solution

Mason should explain to Flynn that the cost of an asset that will provide future benefit to the company should be capitalized and then depreciated over the life of the asset. In expensing the entire cost of the equipment in the year of purchase, net income will be understated by $320,000 and the company would not be following GAAP. If the controller still disagrees, Mason should discuss the situation with the company's president.

Units-of-Production Method

The **units-of-production method** allocates a varying amount of depreciation each year based on an asset's usage. Units-of-production depreciates by units rather than by years. As we noted earlier, a unit of output can be miles, units, hours, or output, depending on which unit type best defines the asset's use. When a plant asset's usage varies every year, the units-of-production method does a better of job of matching expenses with revenues.

The truck in our example is estimated to be driven 20,000 miles the first year, 30,000 the second, 25,000 the third, 15,000 the fourth, and 10,000 during the fifth (for a total useful life of 100,000 miles). The units-of-production depreciation for each period varies with the number of units (miles, in the case of the truck) the asset produces. Units-of-production depreciation is calculated as follows:

> **Units-of-Production Method**
> A depreciation method that allocates a varying amount of depreciation each year based on an asset's usage.

Step 1:

> Depreciation per unit = (Cost − Residual value) / Useful life in units
> = ($41,000 − $1,000) / 100,000 miles
> = $0.40 per mile

Step 2:

> Units-of-production depreciation = Depreciation per unit × Current year usage
> = $0.40 per mile × 20,000 miles
> = $8,000 (year 1)

Plant Assets, Natural Resources, and Intangibles

Units-of-production depreciation for the truck is illustrated in Exhibit 6.

Exhibit 6 | **Units-of-Production Depreciation Schedule**

Date	Asset Cost	Depreciation for the Year				Accumulated Depreciation	Book Value
		Depreciation Per Unit	Number of Units		Depreciation Expense		
1-1-2014	$ 41,000						$ 41,000
12-31-2014		$ 0.40	× 20,000	=	$ 8,000	$ 8,000	33,000
12-31-2015		0.40	× 30,000	=	12,000	20,000	21,000
12-31-2016		0.40	× 25,000	=	10,000	30,000	11,000
12-31-2017		0.40	× 15,000	=	6,000	36,000	5,000
12-31-2018		0.40	× 10,000	=	4,000	40,000	1,000 ← Residual value

Double-Declining-Balance Method

Accelerated Depreciation Method
A depreciation method that expenses more of the asset's cost near the start of its useful life and less at the end of its useful life.

Double-Declining-Balance Method
An accelerated depreciation method that computes annual depreciation by multiplying the depreciable asset's decreasing book value by a constant percent that is two times the straight-line depreciation rate.

An **accelerated depreciation method** expenses more of the asset's cost near the start of an asset's life and less at the end of its useful life. The main accelerated method of depreciation is the **double-declining-balance method**. The double-declining-balance method multiplies an asset's decreasing book value by a constant percentage that is twice the straight-line depreciation rate. The straight-line depreciation rate is calculated as *1 / useful life*. Therefore the double-declining-balance method rate will be *2 × (1 / useful life)*. Double-declining-balance amounts can be computed using the following formula:

$$\text{Double-declining-balance depreciation} = (\text{Cost} - \text{Accumulated depreciation}) \times 2 \times (1 / \text{Useful life})$$

For the first year of the truck, the calculation would be as shown:

$$
\begin{aligned}
\text{Double-declining-balance depreciation} &= (\text{Cost} - \text{Accumulated depreciation}) \times 2 \times (1 / \text{Useful life}) \\
&= (\$41,000 - \$0) \times 2 \times (1 / 5 \text{ years}) \\
&= \$16,400 \text{ (year 1)}
\end{aligned}
$$

In year 2, the amount of depreciation would decline because the asset has accumulated some depreciation (the $16,400 for the first year). For the second year of the truck, therefore, the calculation would be as shown:

$$
\begin{aligned}
\text{Double-declining-balance depreciation} &= (\text{Cost} - \text{Accumulated depreciation}) \times 2 \times (1 / \text{Useful life}) \\
&= (\$41,000 - \$16,400) \times 2 \times (1 / 5 \text{ years}) \\
&= \$9,840 \text{ (year 2)}
\end{aligned}
$$

Note that residual value is not included in the formula. Residual value is ignored until the last year. Final-year depreciation is calculated as the amount needed to bring the asset to its residual value. In the case of the truck, residual value was given at $1,000. In the double-declining-balance schedule in Exhibit 7, notice that, after year 4 (12-31-2017), the truck's book value is $5,314. By definition, the truck is to last five years, which ends on 12-31-2018. At the end of the asset's life, its book value should equal the residual value. Therefore, in the final-year, depreciation is book value, $5,314, less the $1,000 residual value, or $4,314 in depreciation expense.

Exhibit 7 | Double-Declining-Balance Depreciation Schedule

Date	Asset Cost	Book Value	DDB Rate		Depreciation Expense	Accumulated Depreciation	Book Value
		Depreciation for the Year					
1-1-2014	$ 41,000						$ 41,000
12-31-2014		$41,000	× $2 \times \frac{1}{5}$	=	$ 16,400	$ 16,400	24,600
12-31-2015		24,600	× $2 \times \frac{1}{5}$	=	9,840	26,240	14,760
12-31-2016		14,760	× $2 \times \frac{1}{5}$	=	5,904	32,144	8,856
12-31-2017		8,856	× $2 \times \frac{1}{5}$	=	3,542	35,686	5,314
12-31-2018					4,314*	40,000	1,000 ← Residual value

*Last-year depreciation is the "plug figure" needed to reduce book value to the residual amount ($5,314 − $1,000 = $4,314).

Comparing Depreciation Methods

Let's compare the depreciation methods. Annual depreciation expense amounts vary, but total accumulated depreciation is $40,000 for all three methods.

	AMOUNT OF DEPRECIATION PER YEAR		
			Accelerated Method
Year	Straight-Line	Units-of-Production	Double-Declining-Balance
1	$ 8,000	$ 8,000	$ 16,400
2	8,000	12,000	9,840
3	8,000	10,000	5,904
4	8,000	6,000	3,542
5	8,000	4,000	4,314
Total Accumulated Depreciation	$ 40,000	$ 40,000	$ 40,000

Deciding which method is best depends on the asset. A business should match an asset's expense against the revenue that the asset produces. The following are some guidelines for which method to use:

Method	Asset Characteristics	Effect on Depreciation	Example Assets
Straight-Line	Generates revenue evenly over time	Equal amount each period	Building
Units-of-Production	Depreciates due to wear and tear rather than obsolescence	More usage causes larger depreciation	Vehicles (miles) Machinery (machine hours)
Double-Declining-Balance	Produces more revenue in early years	Higher depreciation in early years, less later	Computers

Exhibit 8 shows the three methods in one graph for additional comparison. Notice that the straight-line method produces a straight line on the graph because there is an equal amount of depreciation expense each year. The double-declining-balance method produces a line that is decreasing and the units-of-production method's line varies based on usage.

Exhibit 8 | **Annual Depreciation by Method**

> **Decisions**   Which depreciation method should be selected?

Ira Glasier is the owner of Three Junes Weaving. Ira has just purchased an automated weaving machine and is trying to figure out which depreciation method to use: straight-line, units-of-production, or double-declining-balance method. Ira is interested in using a depreciation method that approximates the usage of the weaving machine. He also expects that the weaving machine will have increasing repairs and maintenance as the asset ages. Which method should Ira choose?

Solution

If Ira is interested in using a depreciation method that approximates the usage of the weaving machine, he should use the units-of-production method to depreciate the asset. He could use number of machine hours as the unit of output. This method would best match the usage of the machine to the amount of expense recorded. Ira should be aware, though, that this method could produce varying amounts of depreciation expense each year. For example, if Ira does not use the weaving machine in one year, no depreciation expense would be recorded. This could cause net income to vary significantly from year to year. Because Ira expects the weaving machine to need more repairs as the asset ages, Ira might consider using the double-declining-balance method instead. The double-declining-balance method records a higher amount of depreciation in the early years and less later. This method works well for assets that are expected to have increasing repairs and maintenance in their later years because the total expense (depreciation and repairs and maintenance) can be spread out equally over the life of the asset.

Depreciation for Tax Purposes

The Internal Revenue Service (IRS) requires that companies use a specific depreciation method for tax purposes. This method is the Modified Accelerated Cost Recovery System (MACRS).

Under MACRS, assets are divided into specific classes, such as 3-year, 5-year, 7-year, and 39-year property. Businesses do not get to choose the useful life of the asset. Instead, the IRS specifies the useful life based on the specific classes. For example, office furniture has a 7-year life for tax purposes but might only be depreciated for five years for book purposes.

In addition, the MACRS method ignores residual value. For tax purposes, an asset is fully depreciated to a book value of zero. MACRS is not acceptable for financial reporting under GAAP. This requires that businesses record depreciation for plant assets under two methods—book method (straight-line, units-of-production, or double-declining-balance) and tax method (MACRS).

Modified Accelerated Cost Recovery System (MACRS)
A depreciation method that is used for tax purposes.

> Can the MACRS method be used for financial reporting in accordance with GAAP?

Partial-Year Depreciation

In the previous examples, we calculated depreciation for the entire year. What would happen if the business placed the truck in service on July 1, 2014, instead of January 1, 2014? Would the depreciation for any of the methods change? Yes, but only the methods that are calculated based on a time period, which means only straight-line and double-declining-balance would change. Units-of-production does not consider years in its formula; thus, that calculation remains the same. The revised straight-line calculation under the altered in-service date of July 1, 2014, is as follows:

Straight-line depreciation = [(Cost − Residual Value) / Useful Life] × (Number of Months / 12)
= [($41,000 − $1,000) / 5 years] × (6 / 12)
= $4,000

Because the business used the asset for six months of the year, we only record 6/12 of straight-line depreciation expense, or $4,000, in 2014.

Changing Estimates of a Depreciable Asset

Estimating the useful life and residual value of a plant asset poses a challenge. As the asset is used, the business may change its estimated useful life or estimated residual value. If this happens, the business must recalculate depreciation expense. For example, the business may find that its truck lasts eight years instead of five. This is a change in estimated useful life. Accounting changes like this are common because useful life and residual value are estimates and, as a result, are not based on perfect foresight. When a company makes an accounting change, generally accepted accounting principles require the business to recalculate the depreciation for the asset in the year of change and in future periods. It does not require that businesses restate prior years' financial statements for this change in estimate.

For a change in either estimated asset life or residual value, the asset's remaining depreciable book value is spread over the asset's remaining life. Suppose Smart Touch Learning used the truck purchased on January 1, 2014, for two full years. Under the straight-line method, accumulated depreciation would be $16,000. (Refer to Exhibit 5.)

Straight-line depreciation = (Cost − Residual Value) / Useful Life
= ($41,000 − $1,000) / 5 years
= $8,000 per year × 2 years
= $16,000

Remaining depreciable book value (cost *less* accumulated depreciation) is $25,000 ($41,000 − $16,000). Suppose Smart Touch Learning believes the truck will remain useful for six more years (for a total of eight years). Residual value is unchanged. At the start of 2016, the company would recompute depreciation as follows:

> Revised depreciation = (Book value − Revised residual value) / Revised useful life remaining
> = ($25,000 − $1,000) / 6 years
> = $4,000 per year

Make sure to use the useful life remaining as the denominator in the formula.

In years 2016–2021, the yearly depreciation entry based on the new useful life would be as follows:

$$\left.\frac{A\downarrow}{\substack{\text{Accumulated}\\\text{Depreciation—}\\\text{Truck}\uparrow}}\right\} = \left\{\frac{L \quad + \quad E\downarrow}{\substack{\text{Depreciation}\\\text{Expense—}\\\text{Truck}\uparrow}}\right.$$

Date	Accounts and Explanation	Debit	Credit
Dec. 31	Depreciation Expense—Truck	4,000	
	Accumulated Depreciation—Truck		4,000
	To record depreciation on truck.		

IFRS

IFRS permits the presentation of plant assets at their fair market value because market value may be more relevant and thus more useful to readers of financial statements.

Reporting Plant Assets

Plant assets are reported at book value on the balance sheet. Companies may choose to report plant assets as a single amount, with a note to the financial statements that provides detailed information, or companies may provide detailed information on the face of the statement. The cost of the asset and the related accumulated depreciation should be disclosed. Exhibit 9 shows the two alternative reporting treatments for plant assets.

Exhibit 9 | Reporting Plant Assets

Treatment 1: Plant Assets on the Balance Sheet of Smart Touch Learning (December 31)		
Plant Assets:		
Furniture	$ 18,000	
Less: Accumulated Depreciation—Furniture	(300)	$ 17,700
Building	60,000	
Less: Accumulated Depreciation—Building	(250)	59,750
Land		20,000
Plant Assets, Net		$ 97,450

Treatment 2: Plant Assets on the Balance Sheet of Smart Touch Learning (December 31)	
Plant Assets, Net (See Note 8)	$ 97,450

> Try It!

2. On January 1, Alamo Cranes purchased a crane for $140,000. Alamo expects the crane to remain useful for six years (1,000,000 lifts) and to have a residual value of $2,000. The company expects the crane to be used for 80,000 lifts the first year.

Compute the first-year depreciation expense on the crane using the following methods:

a. Straight-line
b. Units-of-production (Round *depreciation per unit* to two decimals. Round depreciation expense to the nearest whole dollar.)
c. Double-declining-balance (Round depreciation expense to the nearest whole dollar.)

Check your answers at the end of the chapter.

For more practice, see Short Exercises S-3 through S-6. MyAccountingLab

HOW ARE DISPOSALS OF PLANT ASSETS RECORDED?

Eventually, an asset wears out or becomes obsolete. The owner then has several options:

- Discard the plant asset.
- Sell the plant asset.
- Exchange the plant asset for another plant asset.

In this section, we discuss the first two options. Exchanging a plant asset for another asset is covered in the appendix to this chapter (Appendix A).

Plant assets remain on the business's books until they are disposed of. For example, a fully depreciated asset, one that has reached the end of its estimated useful life and is still in service, will still be reported as an asset on the balance sheet. If the asset is still useful, the company may continue using it even though no additional depreciation is recorded. If the asset is no longer useful, it is disposed of. This requires the business to remove the asset and associated accumulated depreciation from the books. In addition, a gain or loss might be recognized by the company.

Regardless of the type of disposal, there are four steps:

1. Bring the depreciation up to date.
2. Remove the old, disposed-of asset and associated accumulated depreciation from the books.
3. Record the value of any cash received (or paid) in the disposal of the asset.
4. Finally, determine the amount of any gain or loss. Gain or loss is determined by comparing the cash received and the market value of any other assets received with the book value of the asset disposed of.

Discarding Plant Assets

Discarding of plant assets involves disposing of the asset for no cash. If an asset is disposed of when it is fully depreciated and has no residual value, then the business simply removes the asset and contra asset, Accumulated Depreciation, from the books

Learning Objective 3
Journalize entries for the disposal of plant assets

(Step 2). There is no need to bring the depreciation up to date (Step 1) because the asset is already fully depreciated. In addition, no cash was received or paid and no gain or loss is recognized.

For example, assume that on July 1, Smart Touch Learning discards equipment with a cost of $10,000 and accumulated depreciation of $10,000. The asset and contra asset accounts are shown below before disposal.

To dispose of the equipment, Smart Touch Learning will need to credit the asset account, Equipment, and debit Accumulated Depreciation—Equipment. The accounting clerk will record the transaction as follows:

Date	Accounts and Explanation	Debit	Credit
Jul. 1	Accumulated Depreciation—Equipment	10,000	
	Equipment		10,000
	Discarded fully depreciated equipment.		

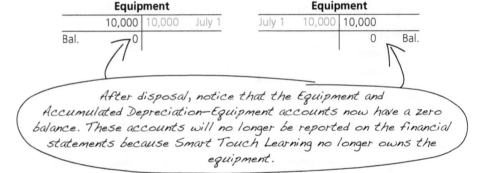

After disposal, notice that the Equipment and Accumulated Depreciation-Equipment accounts now have a zero balance. These accounts will no longer be reported on the financial statements because Smart Touch Learning no longer owns the equipment.

Suppose instead, that on July 1, Smart Touch Learning discarded the equipment, which has a cost of $10,000 but it is not fully depreciated. As of December 31 of the previous year, accumulated depreciation was $8,000. Annual depreciation expense is $1,000 per year. The first step in recording the disposal is to bring the asset up to date on depreciation. Because Smart Touch Learning disposes of the asset on July 1, half a year's depreciation will be recorded ($1,000 × 1/2 = $500) as follows:

Date	Accounts and Explanation	Debit	Credit
Jul. 1	Depreciation Expense—Equipment	500	
	Accumulated Depreciation—Equipment		500
	To record depreciation on equipment.		

Steps 2 through 4 involve recording the disposal of the equipment and accumulated depreciation and calculating any gain or loss. In this situation, there is a $1,500 loss calculated as follows:

Market value of assets received		$ 0
Less: Book value of asset disposed of Cost	$ 10,000	
Less: Accumulated Depreciation ($8,000 + $500)	(8,500)	1,500
Gain or (Loss)		$ (1,500)

When calculating gain or loss, don't forget to update the accumulated depreciation account. In this example, before recording depreciation, the accumulated depreciation account was $8,000; $500 of additional depreciation was recorded at disposal, bringing the total accumulated depreciation to $8,500.

The account, Loss on Disposal, will be used. This account has a normal debit balance and is reported in the Other Expenses and Losses section of the income statement.

Smart Touch Learning records the following entry to dispose of the equipment:

Date	Accounts and Explanation	Debit	Credit
Jul. 1	Accumulated Depreciation—Equipment	8,500	
	Loss on Disposal	1,500	
	Equipment		10,000
	Discarded equipment with a book value of $1,500.		

$$\left. \begin{array}{c} \underline{A\downarrow} \\ \text{Equipment}\downarrow \\ \text{Accumulated} \\ \text{Depreciation—} \\ \text{Equipment}\downarrow \end{array} \right\} = \left\{ \begin{array}{c} \underline{L} + \underline{E\downarrow} \\ \text{Loss on} \\ \text{Disposal}\uparrow \end{array} \right.$$

Equipment

10,000	10,000		July 1
Bal.	0		

Accumulated Depreciation— Equipment

		8,000	
July 1	8,500	500	July 1
		0	Bal.

Loss on Disposal

July 1	1,500

Selling Plant Assets

Companies will often sell a plant asset for cash. We will again use Smart Touch Learning as an example. On July 1, the company sells equipment with a historical cost of $10,000 and accumulated depreciation, as of December 31 of the previous year, of $8,000.

Plant Assets, Natural Resources, and Intangibles

Annual depreciation is $1,000. The first step is to bring the depreciation up to date for the six months through the date of disposal.

Date	Accounts and Explanation	Debit	Credit
Jul. 1	Depreciation Expense—Equipment	500	
	Accumulated Depreciation—Equipment		500
	To record depreciation on equipment.		

This entry brings the accumulated depreciation to $8,500 ($8,000 + $500). The equipment now has a book value of $1,500 ($10,000 − $8,500). Now that we have recorded Step 1, let's look at Steps 2 through 4 for several different scenarios.

Selling a Plant Asset at Book Value

Suppose that Smart Touch Learning sells the equipment for $1,500. Notice that the cash received is equal to the book value of the asset. When a business sells an asset for book value, no gain or loss is recorded. This is because the cash received is equal to the book value of the asset sold.

Market value of assets received		$ 1,500
Less: Book value of asset disposed of Cost	$ 10,000	
Less: Accumulated Depreciation	(8,500)	1,500
Gain or (Loss)		$ 0

In recording the journal entry, Smart Touch Learning will debit cash for $1,500 and then take the equipment and accumulated depreciation off the books as follows:

Date	Accounts and Explanation	Debit	Credit
Jul. 1	Cash	1,500	
	Accumulated Depreciation—Equipment	8,500	
	Equipment		10,000
	Sold equipment for cash.		

Cash

July 1 1,500	

Equipment

10,000	10,000	July 1
Bal. 0		

Accumulated Depreciation—Equipment

		8,000	
July 1	8,500	500	July 1
		0	Bal.

Selling a Plant Asset Above Book Value

If Smart Touch Learning sells the equipment for $4,000, the company will record a gain on sale of the equipment. Notice that the cash received is more than the book value of the asset. When a business sells an asset for more than its book value, a gain is recorded.

Market value of assets received		$ 4,000
Less: Book value of asset disposed of Cost	$ 10,000	
Less: Accumulated Depreciation	(8,500)	1,500
Gain or (Loss)		$ 2,500

The account, Gain on Disposal, will be used. This account has a normal credit balance and is reported in the Other Revenues and Gains section of the income statement.

In recording the journal entry, Smart Touch Learning will remove the old equipment and accumulated depreciation from the books (Step 2), record a debit to Cash for $4,000 (Step 3), and then record a credit to Gain on Disposal (Step 4) as follows:

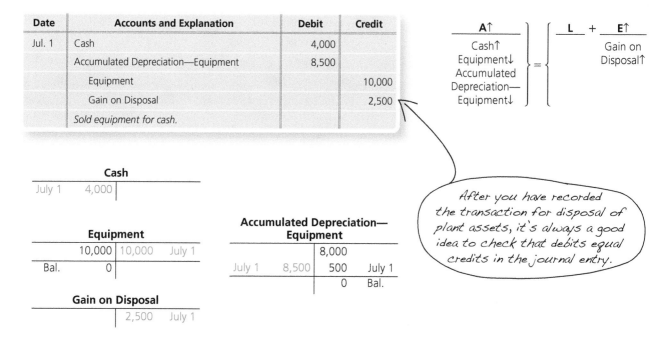

Date	Accounts and Explanation	Debit	Credit
Jul. 1	Cash	4,000	
	Accumulated Depreciation—Equipment	8,500	
	Equipment		10,000
	Gain on Disposal		2,500
	Sold equipment for cash.		

$$\underset{\begin{array}{c}\text{Cash↑}\\\text{Equipment↓}\\\text{Accumulated}\\\text{Depreciation—}\\\text{Equipment↓}\end{array}}{\text{A↑}} \Bigg\} = \Bigg\{ \underset{}{\text{L}} + \underset{\begin{array}{c}\text{Gain on}\\\text{Disposal↑}\end{array}}{\text{E↑}}$$

Cash

July 1	4,000		

Equipment

	10,000	10,000	July 1
Bal.	0		

Gain on Disposal

		2,500	July 1

Accumulated Depreciation—Equipment

		8,000	
July 1	8,500	500	July 1
		0	Bal.

After you have recorded the transaction for disposal of plant assets, it's always a good idea to check that debits equal credits in the journal entry.

Selling a Plant Asset Below Book Value

If Smart Touch Learning sells the equipment for $500, the company will record a loss on sale of the equipment. Notice that the cash received is less than the book value of the asset. When a business sells an asset for less than its book value, a loss is recorded.

Market value of assets received		$ 500
Less: Book value of asset disposed of Cost	$ 10,000	
Less: Accumulated Depreciation	(8,500)	1,500
Gain or (Loss)		($ 1,000)

In recording the journal entry, Smart Touch Learning will remove the old equipment and accumulated depreciation from the books (Step 2), record a debit to Cash for $500 (Step 3), and then record a debit to Loss on Disposal (Step 4) as follows:

$$\frac{A\downarrow}{\begin{matrix}\text{Cash}\uparrow\\\text{Equipment}\downarrow\\\text{Accumulated}\\\text{Depreciation—}\\\text{Equipment}\downarrow\end{matrix}} = \begin{cases} \underline{\quad L \quad} + \underline{\begin{matrix}E\downarrow\\\text{Loss on}\\\text{Disposal}\uparrow\end{matrix}} \end{cases}$$

Date	Accounts and Explanation	Debit	Credit
Jul. 1	Cash	500	
	Accumulated Depreciation—Equipment	8,500	
	Loss on Disposal	1,000	
	Equipment		10,000
	Sold equipment for cash.		

Cash

July 1	500	

Equipment

	10,000	10,000	July 1
Bal.	0		

Accumulated Depreciation— Equipment

		8,000	
July 1	8,500	500	July 1
		0	Bal.

Loss on Disposal

July 1	1,000	

In this section, we have reviewed the journal entries for discarding and selling of plant assets. Exhibit 10 summarizes what you have learned. Before moving on, take a moment to review the exhibit.

Exhibit 10 | Disposals of Plant Assets

Discarding of fully depreciated plant asset

Date	Accounts and Explanation	Debit	Credit
	Accumulated Depreciation	10,000	
	Plant Asset		10,000

Discarding of a plant asset that is not fully depreciated

Date	Accounts and Explanation	Debit	Credit
	Accumulated Depreciation	8,500	
	Loss on Disposal	1,500	
	Plant Asset		10,000

Selling a plant asset at book value

Date	Accounts and Explanation	Debit	Credit
	Cash	1,500	
	Accumulated Depreciation	8,500	
	Plant Asset		10,000

Selling a plant asset above book value

Date	Accounts and Explanation	Debit	Credit
	Cash	4,000	
	Accumulated Depreciation	8,500	
	Plant Asset		10,000
	Gain on Disposal		2,500

Selling a plant asset below book value

Date	Accounts and Explanation	Debit	Credit
	Cash	500	
	Accumulated Depreciation	8,500	
	Loss on Disposal	1,000	
	Plant Asset		10,000

> 3. Counselors of Atlanta purchased equipment on January 1, 2014, for $20,000. Counselors of Atlanta expected the equipment to last for four years and have a residual value of $2,000. Suppose Counselors of Atlanta sold the equipment for $8,000 on December 31, 2016, after using the equipment for three full years. Assume depreciation for 2016 has been recorded. Journalize the sale of the equipment, assuming straight-line depreciation was used.
>
> **Check your answer at the end of the chapter.**

For more practice, see Short Exercises S-7 through S-10. MyAccountingLab

HOW ARE NATURAL RESOURCES ACCOUNTED FOR?

Learning Objective 4
Account for natural resources

Natural resources are assets that come from the earth that are consumed. Examples include iron ore, oil, natural gas, diamonds, coal, and timber. Natural resources are expensed through *depletion*. Depletion is the process by which businesses spread the allocation of a natural resource's cost over its usage. It's called depletion because the company is depleting (using up) a natural resource such that at some point in time, there is nothing left to extract. Depletion expense is computed by the units-of-production method.

Natural Resource
An asset that comes from the earth and is consumed.

For example, an oil well cost $700,000 and is estimated to hold 70,000 barrels of oil. There is no residual value. If 3,000 barrels are extracted and sold during the year, then depletion expense is calculated as follows:

Depletion
The process by which businesses spread the allocation of a natural resource's cost over its usage.

Step 1:

Depletion per unit = (Cost − Residual value) / Estimated total units
= ($700,000 − $0) / 70,000 barrels
= $10 per barrel

Step 2:

Depletion expense = Depletion per unit × Number of units extracted
= $10 per barrel × 3,000 barrels
= $30,000 (year 1)

The depletion entry for the year is as follows:

	A↓			L	+	E↓	
Accumulated Depletion—Oil↑	=					Depletion Expense—Oil↑	

Date	Accounts and Explanation	Debit	Credit
Dec. 31	Depletion Expense—Oil	30,000	
	Accumulated Depletion—Oil		30,000
	To record depletion.		

Accumulated Depletion is a contra asset account similar to Accumulated Depreciation. Natural resources can be reported on the balance sheet as shown for oil in the following example:

Oil	$ 700,000	
Less: Accumulated Depletion—Oil	(30,000)	$ 670,000

> ## Try It!

4. Amplify Petroleum holds huge reserves of oil. Assume that at the end of 2014, Amplify Petroleum's cost of oil reserves totaled $80,000,000, representing 100,000,000 barrels of oil. Suppose Amplify Petroleum removed and sold 20,000,000 barrels of oil during 2015. Journalize depletion expense for 2015.

Check your answer at the end of the chapter.

For more practice, see Short Exercise S-11. MyAccountingLab

HOW ARE INTANGIBLE ASSETS ACCOUNTED FOR?

Intangible assets are assets that have no physical form. Instead, these assets convey special rights from patents, copyrights, trademarks, and other creative works.

In our technology-driven economy, intangibles are very important. The intellectual property of a business is difficult to measure. However, when one company buys another, we get a glimpse of the value of the intellectual property of the acquired company. For example, in 2000, America Online (AOL) acquired Time Warner. AOL said it would give $146 billion for Time Warner's net tangible assets of only $9 billion. Why so much for so little? Because Time Warner's intangible assets were worth billions. Intangibles can account for most of a company's market value, so companies must value their intangibles just as they value merchandise inventory and equipment.

Accounting for Intangibles

Intangible assets that are purchased are recorded at cost. If an intangible is not purchased, only some limited costs can be capitalized. Most purchased intangibles are expensed through amortization, the allocation of the cost of an intangible asset over its useful life. Amortization applies to intangibles exactly as depreciation applies to equipment and depletion to oil and timber.

Intangibles either have a definite life or an indefinite life. Intangibles with an indefinite life have no factors (such as legal and contractual obligations) that limit the usage of the intangible asset. Only intangibles that have a definite life are amortized. Intangible assets with an indefinite life are tested for impairment annually. Impairment occurs when the fair value of an asset is less than the book value. In other words, there has been a permanent decline in the value of the asset. If an impairment occurs, the company records a loss in the period that the decline is identified.

Specific Intangibles

As noted earlier, patents, copyrights, and trademarks are intangible assets. The accounting for the purchase and amortization of each asset is the same.

Patents

A patent is an intangible asset that is a federal government grant conveying an exclusive 20-year right to produce and sell an invention. The invention may be a process, product, or formula—for example, the Dolby noise-reduction process or a prescription drug formula. The acquisition cost of a patent is debited to the Patent account.

Learning Objective 5
Account for intangible assets

Intangible Asset
An asset with no physical form that is valuable because of the special rights it carries.

Amortization
The process by which businesses spread the allocation of an intangible asset's cost over its useful life.

Impairment
A permanent decline in asset value.

Patent
An intangible asset that is a federal government grant conveying an exclusive 20-year right to produce and sell a process, product, or formula.

Like any other asset, a patent may be purchased. Suppose Smart Touch Learning pays $200,000 to acquire a patent on January 1. The accounting clerk records the following entry at acquisition:

$$\left.\begin{array}{c} \mathbf{A\uparrow\downarrow} \\ \text{Patent}\uparrow \\ \text{Cash}\downarrow \end{array}\right\} = \left\{\begin{array}{c} \underline{\mathbf{L} \;+\; \mathbf{E}} \\ \end{array}\right.$$

Date	Accounts and Explanation	Debit	Credit
Jan. 1	Patent	200,000	
	Cash		200,000
	To record purchase of patent.		

Smart Touch Learning believes this patent's useful life is only five years because it is likely that a new, more efficient process will be developed within that time. Amortization expense is calculated using the straight-line method as follows:

$$\begin{aligned} \text{Amortization expense} &= (\text{Cost} - \text{Residual value}) / \text{Useful life} \\ &= (\$200,000 - \$0) / 5 \text{ years} \\ &= \$40,000 \text{ per year} \end{aligned}$$

For most intangibles, the residual value will be zero.

The company's accounting clerk would record the following adjusting entry for amortization:

$$\left.\begin{array}{c} \mathbf{A\downarrow} \\ \text{Patent}\downarrow \end{array}\right\} = \left\{\begin{array}{c} \underline{\mathbf{L} \;+\; \mathbf{E}\downarrow} \\ \text{Amortization} \\ \text{Expense—} \\ \text{Patent}\uparrow \end{array}\right.$$

Date	Accounts and Explanation	Debit	Credit
Dec. 31	Amortization Expense—Patent	40,000	
	Patent		40,000
	To record amortization of patent.		

Why was the account Patent credited instead of Accumulated Amortization—Patent?

Notice that Smart Touch Learning credited the amortization directly to the intangible asset, Patent, instead of using an Accumulated Amortization account. A company may credit an intangible asset directly when recording amortization expense or it may use the account Accumulated Amortization.

At the end of the first year, Smart Touch Learning will report this patent at $160,000 ($200,000 cost minus first-year amortization of $40,000), the next year at $120,000, and so forth. Each year for five years the value of the patent will be reduced until the end of its five-year life, at which point its book value will be $0.

Copyrights and Trademarks

Copyright
Exclusive right to reproduce and sell a book, musical composition, film, other work of art, or intellectual property.

A copyright is the exclusive right to reproduce and sell a book, musical composition, film, other work of art, or intellectual property. Copyrights also protect computer software programs, such as Microsoft® Windows® and the Microsoft® Excel® spreadsheet software. Issued by the federal government, a copyright is granted for the life of the creator plus 70 years.

A company may pay a large sum to purchase an existing copyright. For example, the publisher Simon & Schuster may pay $1 million for the copyright on a popular novel because it thinks it will be able to profit from selling the novel. Even though copyrights have a long legal life (life of creator plus 70 years), most copyrights have short useful lives. Copyrights are amortized over their legal life or useful life, whichever is shorter.

A trademark (also called *trade name*) is an asset that represents distinctive products or services, such as the Nike "swoosh" or the NASCAR number 3 for Dale Earnhardt. Legally protected slogans include Chevrolet's "Like a Rock" and Avis Car Rental's "We try harder." The cost of a trademark or trade name is amortized over its useful life.

Franchises and Licenses

Franchises are privileges granted by a business to sell goods or services under specified conditions. The Dallas Cowboys football organization is a franchise granted by the National Football League. McDonald's and Subway are well-known business franchises. Licenses are privileges granted by a government to use public property in performing services. A radio station might be granted permission by the federal government to use the airwaves to broadcast its music. The acquisition cost of a franchise or license is amortized over its useful life.

Goodwill

In accounting, goodwill is the excess of the cost to purchase another company over the market value of its net assets (assets minus liabilities). Goodwill is the value paid above the net worth of the company's assets and liabilities.

Suppose White Company acquired Mocha Company on January 1, 2014. The sum of the market values of Mocha's assets was $9 million and its liabilities totaled $1 million, so Mocha's net assets totaled $8 million. Suppose White paid $10 million to purchase Mocha. In this case, White paid $2 million above the market value of Mocha's net assets. Therefore, that $2 million is considered goodwill and is computed as follows:

Purchase price to acquire Mocha		$ 10,000,000
Market value of Mocha's assets	$ 9,000,000	
Less: Market value of Mocha's liabilities	(1,000,000)	
Less: Market value of Mocha's net assets		8,000,000
Goodwill		$ 2,000,000

White's entry to record the purchase of Mocha, including the goodwill that White purchased, would be as follows:

Date	Accounts and Explanation	Debit	Credit
Jan. 1	Assets	9,000,000	
	Goodwill	2,000,000	
	Liabilities		1,000,000
	Cash		10,000,000
	To record purchase of Mocha Company.		

$$\left. \begin{array}{c} \underline{A\uparrow} \\ \text{Assets}\uparrow \\ \text{Goodwill}\uparrow \\ \text{Cash}\downarrow \end{array} \right\} = \left\{ \begin{array}{c} \underline{L\uparrow} + \underline{E} \\ \text{Liabilities}\uparrow \end{array} \right.$$

Trademark
An asset that represents distinctive identifications of a product or service.

Franchise
Privilege granted by a business to sell a product or service under specified conditions.

License
Privilege granted by a government to use public property in performing services.

Goodwill
Excess of the cost of an acquired company over the sum of the market values of its net assets (assets minus liabilities).

Goodwill has some special features:

- Goodwill is recorded only by an acquiring company when it purchases another company and pays more for that company than the market value of the net assets acquired (as in our entry above where White purchased Mocha for $2 million more than the value of Mocha's net assets). An outstanding reputation may create goodwill, but that company never records goodwill for its own business.

- According to generally accepted accounting principles (GAAP), goodwill is *not* amortized. Instead, the acquiring company measures the fair value of its goodwill each year. If the goodwill has increased in value, there is nothing to record. But if goodwill's value has decreased, then the company records an impairment loss and writes the goodwill down.

Reporting of Intangible Assets

Intangible assets are reported on the balance sheet similar to plant assets. If a company uses the contra account, Accumulated Amortization, this account is not typically shown on the balance sheet. Instead, intangible assets are shown only at their net book value. Amortization expense is reported on the income statement as part of operations.

Exhibit 11 summarizes our coverage of plant assets, natural resources, and intangibles. Remember that plant assets are those assets that have physical characteristics and are used in operations. Natural resources are assets that come from the physical earth and can be ultimately used up, and intangible assets are assets whose value is not derived from their physical substance.

Exhibit 11 | Assets and Their Related Expenses

Source: © Ford Oval Logo Courtesy of **Ford Motor Company**.

5. On January 1, Orange Manufacturing paid $40,000 for a patent. Although it gives legal protection for 20 years, the patent is expected to provide a competitive advantage for only eight years. Assuming the straight-line method of amortization, record the journal entry for amortization for year 1.

Check your answer at the end of the chapter.

For more practice, see Short Exercises S-12 and S-13. MyAccountingLab

HOW DO WE USE THE ASSET TURNOVER RATIO TO EVALUATE BUSINESS PERFORMANCE?

The asset turnover ratio measures the amount of net sales generated for each average dollar of total assets invested. This ratio measures how well a company is using its assets to generate sales revenue. To compute this ratio, we divide net sales by average total assets. Using net sales and total assets (in thousands) from **Green Mountain Coffee Roasters, Inc.'s** 2011 Annual Report, we can calculate the asset turnover ratio.

Learning Objective 6

Use the asset turnover ratio to evaluate business performance

Asset Turnover Ratio

Measures how efficiently a business uses its average total assets to generate sales. Net sales / Average total assets.

	September 24, 2011	September 25, 2010
Net sales	$ 2,650,899	$ 1,356,775
Total assets	3,197,887	1,370,574

```
Asset turnover ratio = Net sales / Average total assets
                     = $2,650,899 / [($3,197,887 + $1,370,574) / 2]
                     = 1.16 times (rounded)
```

Suppose that the asset turnover ratio for the industry is 1.7 times. Green Mountain's asset turnover ratio of 1.16 times is significantly lower than the industry average. This tells us that Green Mountain is producing $1.16 of sales revenue for each dollar ($1.00) of assets invested. Green Mountain should evaluate ways to increase its asset turnover ratio such as increasing net sales or decreasing average total assets. A high asset turnover ratio is desirable.

6. Maxim Company reported beginning and ending total assets of $140,000 and $160,000 respectively. Its net sales for the year was $240,000. What was Maxim's asset turnover ratio?

Check your answer at the end of the chapter.

For more practice, see Short Exercise S-14. MyAccountingLab

Appendix A: Exchanging Plant Assets

HOW ARE EXCHANGES OF PLANT ASSETS ACCOUNTED FOR?

Earlier in the chapter, we discussed ways that businesses could dispose of plant assets. One way is for a business to exchange a plant asset for another plant asset. In this section, we evaluate how to account for exchanges that have *commercial substance*. An exchange has commercial substance if the future cash flows change as a result of the transaction. In other words, an exchange has commercial substance if in the future, cash flows (receipts of revenue or payment of expenses) of the business will change because of the exchange. For example, exchanging an older asset for a new asset will increase productivity, thereby creating more revenue for the business.

Exchanges that have commercial substance require any gain or loss on the transaction to be recognized. The old asset will be removed from the books and the new asset will be recorded at its market value. Exchanges that lack commercial substance ignore any gain or loss on the transaction, except in limited situations. The new asset is recorded at the old asset's book value plus cash paid and minus cash received instead of at market value.

Exchange of Plant Assets—Gain Situation

Suppose that on December 31, Smart Touch Learning exchanges used equipment for new equipment. The old equipment has a historical cost of $10,000 and accumulated depreciation of $9,000. Its current book value is $1,000 ($10,000 − $9,000). The company acquires the new equipment with a market value of $8,000 and pays cash of $2,000. Assuming this exchange has commercial substance, the gain will be calculated as follows:

Market value of assets received		$ 8,000
Less:		
Book value of asset exchanged	$ 1,000	
Cash paid	2,000	3,000
Gain or (Loss)		$ 5,000

The accounting clerk records the following entry:

Date	Accounts and Explanation	Debit	Credit
Dec. 31	Equipment (new)	8,000	
	Accumulated Depreciation—Equipment	9,000	
	Equipment (old)		10,000
	Cash		2,000
	Gain on Disposal		5,000
	Exchanged old equipment and cash for new equipment.		

Exchange of Plant Assets—Loss Situation

Suppose instead that on December 31, Smart Touch Learning exchanges used equipment for new equipment. The old equipment has a historical cost of $10,000 and accumulated depreciation of $9,000. Its current book value is $1,000 ($10,000 − $9,000). The company acquires the new equipment with a market value of $3,000 and pays cash of $2,500. Assuming this exchange has commercial substance, the loss will be calculated as follows:

Market value of assets received		$ 3,000
Less:		
Book value of asset exchanged	$ 1,000	
Cash paid	2,500	3,500
Gain or (Loss)		$ (500)

The accounting clerk records the following entry:

Date	Accounts and Explanation	Debit	Credit
Dec. 31	Equipment (new)	3,000	
	Accumulated Depreciation—Equipment	9,000	
	Loss on Disposal	500	
	Equipment (old)		10,000
	Cash		2,500
	Exchanged old equipment and cash for new equipment.		

$$A\!\downarrow \quad \begin{Bmatrix} \end{Bmatrix} = \begin{Bmatrix} \end{Bmatrix} \quad L \; + \; E\!\downarrow$$

A↓: Equipment (new)↑ Accumulated Depreciation—Equipment↓ Equipment (old)↓ Cash↓

L + E↓: Loss on Disposal↑

Cash		
	2,500	Dec. 31

Equipment (new)		
Dec. 31	3,000	

Equipment (old)		
	10,000	10,000	Dec. 31
Bal.	0	

Accumulated Depreciation— Equipment		
		9,000	
Dec. 31	9,000	
		0	Bal.

Loss on Disposal		
Dec. 31	500	

> **Try It!**

7A. Arca Salvage Company purchased equipment for $10,000. Arca recorded total depreciation of $8,000 on the equipment. Assume that Arca exchanged the old equipment for new equipment, paying $4,000 cash. The fair market value of the new equipment is $5,000. Journalize Arca's exchange of equipment. Assume this exchange has commercial substance.

Check your answer at the end of the chapter.

For more practice, see Short Exercise SA-15 and SA-16. MyAccountingLab

REVIEW

> Things You Should Know

1. How does a business measure the cost of a plant asset?

- Plant assets are long-lived, tangible assets used in the operations of a business.

- Plant assets are recorded at historical cost—the amount paid for the asset. This includes the purchase price plus taxes, purchase commissions, and all other amounts paid to ready the asset for its intended use.

- A lump-sum purchase involves paying a single price for multiple assets. The cost of each asset purchased must be identified based on the relative-market-value method.

- Two additional types of expenditures are often incurred on plant assets:

  - Capital expenditures—debited to an asset account because it increases the asset's capacity or efficiency or extends the asset's useful life

  - Revenue expenditures—debited to Repairs and Maintenance Expense because they are incurred to maintain the asset in working order

2. What is depreciation and how is it computed?

- Depreciation is the allocation of a plant asset's cost to expense over its useful life.

- Three common depreciation methods are:

  - Straight-line method—allocates an equal amount of depreciation to each year

  - Units-of-production method—allocates a varying amount of depreciation each year based on an asset's usage

  - Double-declining-balance method—an accelerated depreciation method that computes annual depreciation by multiplying the depreciable asset's book value by a constant percent that is two times the straight-line rate

- Modified Accelerated Cost Recovery System (MACRS) is used for tax purposes.

- Occasionally a business may change its estimated residual value or estimated useful life of a depreciable asset. This change requires depreciation to be recalculated in the year of change and moving forward.

- Plant assets are reported on the balance sheet at book value (cost – accumulated depreciation).

3. How are disposals of plant assets recorded?

- There are four steps to recording disposals.

  - Step 1: Bring the depreciation up to date.

  - Step 2: Remove the old, disposed-of asset and associated accumulated depreciation from the books.

  - Step 3: Record the value of any cash received (or paid) for the asset.

  - Step 4: Determine the amount of any gain or loss. (Market value of assets received compared to the book value of the asset disposed of.)

- Review Exhibit 10 for a summary of disposal of plant assets journal entries.

Plant Assets, Natural Resources, and Intangibles

4. How are natural resources accounted for?

- Natural resources are assets that come from the earth and are consumed.
- Depletion is the process by which businesses spread the allocation of a natural resource's cost over its usage.
- Depletion expense is computed by the units-of-production formula.

5. How are intangible assets accounted for?

- Intangible assets are assets that have no physical form and are valuable because of special rights they carry.
- Amortization is the process by which businesses spread the allocation of an intangible asset's cost over its useful life.
- Amortization expense is computed by the straight-line formula.

6. How do we use the asset turnover ratio to evaluate business performance?

- The asset turnover ratio measures the amount of net sales generated for each average dollar of total assets invested.
- Net sales / Average total assets.

7. How are exchanges of plant assets accounted for? (Appendix A)

- Exchanges that have commercial substance require the recording of any gain or loss on the transaction.
- Exchanges that lack commercial substance ignore any gain or loss on the transaction, except in a few limited cases.

> ## Summary Problem

Latté On Demand purchased a coffee drink machine on January 1, 2013, for $44,000. Expected useful life is 10 years or 100,000 drinks. In 2013, 3,000 drinks were sold, and in 2014, 14,000 drinks were sold. Residual value is $4,000.

Requirements

1. Determine the depreciation expense for 2013 and 2014 using the following methods:
   a. Straight-line
   b. Units-of-production
   c. Double-declining-balance

2. Prepare a schedule that shows annual depreciation expense, accumulated depreciation, and book value for 2013 and 2014 using the following methods:
   a. Straight-line
   b. Units-of-production
   c. Double-declining-balance

3. Assume that Latté On Demand sold the equipment for $27,000 cash on July 1, 2015. Assume that management has depreciated the equipment by using the double-declining-balance method. Record Latté On Demand's depreciation for 2015 and the sale of the equipment on July 1, 2015.

> Solution

Requirement 1

a.

> 2013: ($44,000 − $4,000) / 10 years = $4,000
> 2014: ($44,000 − $4,000) / 10 years = $4,000

b.

> Depreciation per unit = ($44,000 − $4,000) / 100,000 drinks = $0.40 per drink
> 2013: $0.40 per drink × 3,000 drinks = $1,200
> 2014: $0.40 per drink × 14,000 drinks = $5,600

c.

> 2013: ($44,000 − $0) × 2 × (1 / 10) = $8,800
> 2014: ($44,000 − $8,800) × 2 × (1 / 10) = $7,040

Requirement 2

a.

Year	Annual Depreciation Expense	Accumulated Depreciation	Book Value
1-1-2013			$ 44,000
12-31-2013	$ 4,000	$ 4,000	40,000
12-31-2014	4,000	8,000	36,000

b.

Year	Annual Depreciation Expense	Accumulated Depreciation	Book Value
1-1-2013			$ 44,000
12-31-2013	$ 1,200	$ 1,200	42,800
12-31-2014	5,600	6,800	37,200

c.

Year	Annual Depreciation Expense	Accumulated Depreciation	Book Value
1-1-2013			$ 44,000
12-31-2013	$ 8,800	$ 8,800	35,200
12-31-2014	7,040	15,840	28,160

Requirement 3

Depreciation expense for 2015:

$$(\$44{,}000 - \$15{,}840) \times (2 / 10) \times (6 / 12) = \$2{,}816$$

Date	Accounts and Explanation	Debit	Credit
2015			
Jul. 1	Depreciation Expense—Equipment	2,816	
	Accumulated Depreciation—Equipment		2,816
	To record depreciation on equipment.		
1	Cash	27,000	
	Accumulated Depreciation—Equipment ($15,840 + $2,816)	18,656	
	Gain on Disposal		1,656
	Equipment		44,000
	Sold equipment for cash.		

> Key Terms

Accelerated Depreciation Method

A depreciation method that expenses more of the asset's cost near the start of its useful life and less at the end of its useful life.

Amortization

The process by which businesses spread the allocation of an intangible asset's cost over its useful life.

Asset Turnover Ratio

Measures how efficiently a business uses its average total assets to generate sales. Net sales / Average total assets.

Book Value

A depreciable asset's cost minus accumulated depreciation.

Capital Expenditure

An expenditure that increases the capacity or efficiency of a plant asset or extends its useful life. Capital expenditures are debited to an asset account.

Capitalize

Recording the acquisition of land, building, or other assets by debiting (increasing) an asset account.

Commercial Substance (Appendix A)

A characteristic of a transaction that causes a change in future cash flows.

Copyright

Exclusive right to reproduce and sell a book, musical composition, film, other work of art, or intellectual property.

Cost Principle

A principle that states that acquired assets and services should be recorded at their actual cost.

Depletion

The process by which businesses spread the allocation of a natural resource's cost over its usage.

Depreciable Cost

The cost of a plant asset minus its estimated residual value.

Depreciation

The process by which businesses spread the allocation of a plant asset's cost over its useful life.

Double-Declining-Balance Method

An accelerated depreciation method that computes annual depreciation by multiplying the depreciable asset's decreasing book value by a constant percent that is two times the straight-line depreciation rate.

Extraordinary Repair

Repair work that generates a capital expenditure because it extends the asset's life past the normal expected life.

Franchise

Privilege granted by a business to sell a product or service under specified conditions.

Goodwill

Excess of the cost of an acquired company over the sum of the market values of its net assets (assets minus liabilities).

Impairment
A permanent decline in asset value.

Intangible Asset
An asset with no physical form that is valuable because of the special rights it carries.

Land Improvement
A depreciable improvement to land, such as fencing, sprinklers, paving, signs, and lighting.

License
Privilege granted by a government to use public property in performing services.

Modified Accelerated Cost Recovery System (MACRS)
A depreciation method that is used for tax purposes.

Natural Resource
An asset that comes from the earth and is consumed.

Obsolete
An asset is considered obsolete when a newer asset can perform the job more efficiently than the old.

Patent
An intangible asset that is a federal government grant conveying an exclusive 20-year right to produce and sell a process, product, or formula.

Plant Asset
Long-lived, tangible asset, such as land, buildings, and equipment, used in the operation of a business.

Relative-Market-Value Method
A method of allocating the total cost (100%) of multiple assets purchased at one time. Total cost is divided among the assets according to their relative market values.

Residual Value
The expected value of a depreciable asset at the end of its useful life.

Revenue Expenditure
An expenditure that does not increase the capacity or efficiency of an asset or extend its useful life. Revenue expenditures are debited to an expense account.

Straight-Line Metho
A depreciation method that allocates an equal amount of depreciation each year. (Cost − Residual Value) / Useful Life.

Trademark
An asset that represents distinctive identifications of a product or service.

Units-of-Production Method
A depreciation method that allocates a varying amount of depreciation each year based on an asset's usage.

Useful Life
Length of the service period expected from an asset. May be expressed in time, such as months or years, or usage, such as units produced, hours used (for machinery), or miles driven (for a truck).

> Quick Check

1. Which cost is *not* recorded as part of the cost of a building?
   a. Real estate commission paid to buy the building
   b. Construction materials and labor
   c. Concrete for the building's foundation
   d. Annual building maintenance

   Learning Objective 1

2. How should you record a capital expenditure?
   a. Debit a liability
   b. Debit capital
   c. Debit an expense
   d. Debit an asset

   Learning Objective 1

3. Which method almost always produces the most depreciation in the first year?
   a. Units-of-production
   b. Straight-line
   c. Double-declining-balance
   d. All produce the same depreciation in the first year.

   Learning Objective 2

Plant Assets, Natural Resources, and Intangibles

Learning Objective 2

4. A Celty Airline jet costs $28,000,000 and is expected to fly 200,000,000 miles during its 10-year life. Residual value is expected to be zero because the plane was used when acquired. If the plane travels 54,000,000 miles the first year, how much depreciation should Celty Airline record under the units-of-production method?

    a. $2,800,000   **c.** $5,600,000

    b. $7,560,000   **d.** Cannot be determined from the data given

Learning Objective 3

5. A copy machine costs $45,000 when new and has accumulated depreciation of $44,000. Suppose Print and Photo Center junks this machine and receives nothing. What is the result of the disposal transaction?

    a. No gain or loss   **c.** Loss of $1,000

    b. Gain of $1,000   **d.** Loss of $45,000

Learning Objective 3

6. Suppose Print and Photo Center in the preceding question sold the machine for $1,000. What is the result of this disposal transaction?

    a. Loss of $44,000   **c.** Loss of $1,000

    b. Gain of $1,000   **d.** No gain or loss

Learning Objective 4

7. Which method is used to compute depletion?

    a. Double-declining-balance method

    b. Straight-line method

    c. Depletion method

    d. Units-of-production method

Learning Objective 5

8. Which intangible asset is recorded only as part of the acquisition of another company?

    a. Patent   **c.** Copyright

    b. Goodwill   **d.** Franchise

Learning Objective 6

9. Liberty Company reported beginning and ending total assets of $25,000 and $22,000, respectively. Its net sales for the year were $18,800. What was Liberty's asset turnover ratio?

    a. 0.75   **c.** 0.80

    b. 0.85   **d.** 1.25

Learning Objective 7
Appendix A

10A. A truck costs $50,000 when new and has accumulated depreciation of $35,000. Suppose Wilson Towing exchanges the truck for a new truck. The new truck has a market value of $60,000 and Wilson pays cash of $40,000. Assume the exchange has commercial substance. What is the result of this exchange?

    a. No gain or loss   **c.** Loss of $5,000

    b. Gain of $5,000   **d.** Gain of $45,000

Check your answers at the end of the chapter.

ASSESS YOUR PROGRESS

> Review Questions

1. What are plant assets? Provide some examples.

2. Plant assets are recorded at historical cost. What does the historical cost of a plant asset include?

3. How do land improvements differ from land?

4. What does the word "capitalize" mean?

5. What is a lump-sum purchase and how is it accounted for?

6. What is the difference between a capital expenditure and a revenue expenditure? Give an example of each.

7. What is depreciation? What are the methods described in the chapter that can be used to compute depreciation?

8. Which depreciation method ignores residual value until the last year of depreciation? Why?

9. How does a business decide which depreciation method is best to use?

10. What is the depreciation method that is used for tax purposes? How is it different than the methods that are used for financial purposes?

11. If a business changes the estimated useful life or estimated residual value for a plant asset, what must the business do in regards to depreciation expense?

12. What financial statement is plant assets reported on and how?

13. How is discarding of a plant asset different from selling a plant asset?

14. How is gain or loss determined when disposing of plant assets? What situation constitutes a gain? What situation constitutes a loss?

15. What is a natural resource? What is the process by which businesses spread the allocation of a natural resource's cost over its usage?

16. What is an intangible asset? Provide some examples.

17. What is the process by which businesses spread the allocation of an intangible asset's cost over its useful life?

18. What is goodwill? Is goodwill amortized? What happens if the value of goodwill has decreased at the end of the year?

19. What does the asset turnover ratio measure and how is it calculated?

20A. What does it mean if an exchange of plant assets has commercial substance? Are gains and losses recorded on the books because of the exchange?

> Short Exercises

S-1 Determining the cost of an asset

Learning Objective 1

Provo Clothing purchased land, paying $80,000 cash plus a $220,000 note payable. In addition, Provo paid delinquent property tax of $1,500, title insurance costing $800, and $4,000 to level the land and remove an unwanted building. Record the journal entry for purchase of the land.

Plant Assets, Natural Resources, and Intangibles

Learning Objective 1

S-2 Making a lump-sum asset purchase

Rural Tech Support paid $130,000 for a group purchase of land, building, and equipment. At the time of the acquisition, the land had a market value of $70,000, the building $56,000, and the equipment $14,000. Journalize the lump-sum purchase of the three assets for a total cost of $130,000, the amount for which the business signed a note payable.

Learning Objective 2

S-3 Computing first-year depreciation and book value

At the beginning of the year, Alaska Freight Airlines purchased a used airplane for $43,000,000. Alaska Freight Airlines expects the plane to remain useful for five years (4,000,000 miles) and to have a residual value of $7,000,000. The company expects the plane to be flown 1,400,000 miles during the first year.

Requirements

1. Compute Alaska Freight Airlines' *first-year* depreciation expense on the plane using the following methods:
   a. Straight-line
   b. Units-of-production
   c. Double-declining-balance
2. Show the airplane's book value at the end of the first year for all three methods.

Learning Objective 2

S-4 Computing second-year depreciation and accumulated depreciation

At the beginning of 2013, Air Canada purchased a used airplane at a cost of $46,000,000. Air Canada expects the plane to remain useful for eight years (5,000,000 miles) and to have a residual value of $6,000,000. Air Canada expects the plane to be flown 1,300,000 miles the first year and 1,000,000 miles the second year.

Requirements

1. Compute *second-year (2014)* depreciation expense on the plane using the following methods:
   a. Straight-line
   b. Units-of-production
   c. Double-declining-balance
2. Calculate the balance in Accumulated Depreciation at the end of the second year for all three methods.

Learning Objective 2

S-5 Calculating partial year depreciation

On July 31, 2013, Logan Services purchased a copy machine for $40,400. Logan Services expects the machine to last for four years and have a residual value of $2,000. Compute depreciation expense on the machine for the year ended December 31, 2013, using the straight-line method.

Learning Objective 2

S-6 Changing the estimated life of an asset

Assume that Alpha Communications paid $75,000 for equipment with a 15-year life and zero expected residual value. After using the equipment for six years, the company determines that the asset will remain useful for only five more years.

Requirements

1. Record depreciation expense on the equipment for year 7 by the straight-line method.
2. What is accumulated depreciation at the end of year 7?

Plant Assets, Natural Resources, and Intangibles

S-7 Discarding of a fully depreciated asset

Learning Objective 3

On June 15, 2013, Ideal Furniture discarded equipment that had a cost of $10,000 and was fully depreciated. Journalize the disposal of the equipment.

S-8 Discarding an asset

Learning Objective 3

On March 31, 2013, Alternative Landscapes discarded equipment that had a cost of $20,000. Accumulated Depreciation as of December 31, 2012, was $18,000. Assume annual depreciation on the equipment is $2,000. Journalize the partial year depreciation expense and disposal of the equipment.

S-9 Selling an asset at gain or loss

Learning Objective 3

Global Positioning Net purchased equipment on January 1, 2013, for $36,000. Suppose Global Positioning Net sold the equipment for $26,000 on December 31, 2014. Accumulated Depreciation as of December 31, 2014, was $16,000. Journalize the sale of the equipment, assuming straight-line depreciation was used.

S-10 Selling an asset at gain or loss

Learning Objective 3

Prine Company purchased equipment on January 1, 2013, for $20,000. Suppose Prine sold the equipment for $7,000 on December 31, 2014. Accumulated Depreciation as of December 31, 2014 was $10,000. Journalize the sale of the equipment, assuming straight-line depreciation was used.

S-11 Accounting for depletion of natural resources

Learning Objective 4

TexAm Petroleum holds huge reserves of oil assets. Assume that at the end of 2013, TexAm Petroleum's cost of oil reserves totaled $72,000,000,000, representing 8,000,000,000 barrels of oil.

Requirements

1. Which method does TexAm Petroleum use to compute depletion?
2. Suppose TexAm Petroleum removed and sold 400,000,000 barrels of oil during 2014. Journalize depletion expense for 2014.

S-12 Accounting for an intangible asset

Learning Objective 5

On October 1, 2013, Soggy Company purchased a patent for $80,000 cash. Although the patent gives legal protection for 20 years, the patent is expected to be used for only five years.

Requirements

1. Journalize the purchase of the patent.
2. Journalize the amortization expense for 2013. Assume straight-line amortization.

S-13 Accounting for goodwill

Learning Objective 5

TMC Advertising paid $170,000 to acquire *Seacoast Report*, a weekly advertising paper. At the time of the acquisition, *Seacoast Report*'s balance sheet reported total assets of $130,000 and liabilities of $70,000. The fair market value of *Seacoast Report*'s assets was $100,000. The fair market value of Seacoast Report's liabilities was $70,000.

Requirements

1. How much goodwill did TMC Advertising purchase as part of the acquisition of *Seacoast Report*?
2. Journalize TMC Advertising's acquisition of *Seacoast Report*.

Plant Assets, Natural Resources, and Intangibles

Learning Objective 6

S-14 Computing the asset turnover ratio

Biagas Company had net sales of $50,200,000 for the year ended May 31, 2014. Its beginning and ending total assets were $51,200,000 and $88,300,000, respectively. Determine Biagas' asset turnover ratio for year ended May 31, 2014.

Learning Objective 7
Appendix A

SA-15 Exchanging plant assets

Brown's Salvage Company purchased a computer for $2,600, debiting Computer Equipment. During 2012 and 2013, Brown's Salvage Company recorded total depreciation of $2,000 on the computer. On January 1, 2014, Brown's Salvage Company traded in the computer for a new one, paying $2,500 cash. The fair market value of the new computer is $4,000. Journalize Brown's Salvage Company's exchange of computers. Assume the exchange had commercial substance.

Learning Objective 7
Appendix A

SA-16 Exchanging plant assets

Purple Company purchased equipment for $15,000. Purple Company recorded total depreciation of $12,000 on the equipment. On January 1, 2014, Purple traded in the equipment for new equipment, paying $18,000 cash. The fair market value of the new equipment is $20,000. Journalize Purple Company's exchange of equipment. Assume the exchange had commercial substance.

> Exercises

Learning Objective 1

1. Land $382,500

E-17 Determining the cost of assets

Ogden Furniture purchased land, paying $70,000 cash plus a $300,000 note payable. In addition, Ogden paid delinquent property tax of $2,500, title insurance costing $2,000, and $8,000 to level the land and remove an unwanted building. The company then constructed an office building at a cost of $700,000. It also paid $55,000 for a fence around the property, $18,000 for a sign near the entrance, and $10,000 for special lighting of the grounds.

Requirements

1. Determine the cost of the land, land improvements, and building.
2. Which of these assets will Ogden depreciate?

Learning Objective 1

Lot 3 $73,500

E-18 Making a lump-sum purchase of assets

Deadwood Properties bought three lots in a subdivision for a lump-sum price. An independent appraiser valued the lots as follows:

Lot	Appraised Value
1	$ 70,500
2	235,000
3	164,500

Deadwood paid $210,000 in cash. Record the purchase in the journal, identifying each lot's cost in a separate Land account. Round decimals to two places, and use the computed percentages throughout.

Plant Assets, Natural Resources, and Intangibles

E-19 Distinguishing capital expenditures from revenue expenditures

Learning Objective 1

Consider the following expenditures:

---

a. Purchase price.

b. Ordinary recurring repairs to keep the machinery in good working order.

c. Lubrication before machinery is placed in service.

d. Periodic lubrication after machinery is placed in service.

e. Major overhaul to extend useful life by three years.

f. Sales tax paid on the purchase price.

g. Transportation and insurance while machinery is in transit from seller to buyer.

h. Installation.

i. Training of personnel for initial operation of the machinery.

Classify each of the expenditures as a capital expenditure or a revenue expenditure related to machinery.

E-20 Computing depreciation—three methods

Learning Objective 2

1. Double-declining-balance, 12/31/14, Exp. $9,750

Papa's Fried Chicken bought equipment on January 2, 2013, for $39,000. The equipment was expected to remain in service for four years and to perform 11,000 fry jobs. At the end of the equipment's useful life, Papa's estimates that its residual value will be $6,000. The equipment performed 1,100 jobs the first year, 3,300 the second year, 4,400 the third, and 2,200 the fourth year.

Requirements

1. Prepare a schedule of *depreciation expense, accumulated depreciation,* and *book value* per year for the equipment under the three depreciation methods. Show your computations. *Note: Three depreciation schedules must be prepared.*

2. Which method tracks the wear and tear on the equipment most closely?

E-21 Changing an asset's useful life and residual value

Learning Objective 2

Yr. 16 $29,350

Everyday Hardware Consultants purchased a building for $540,000 and depreciated it on a straight-line basis over a 40-year period. The estimated residual value is $96,000. After using the building for 15 years, Everyday realized that wear and tear on the building would wear it out before 40 years and that the estimated residual value should be $80,000. Starting with the 16th year, Everyday began depreciating the building over a revised total life of 25 years using the new residual value. Journalize depreciation expense on the building for years 15 and 16.

E-22 Recording partial year depreciation and sale of an asset

Learning Objectives 2, 3

Depr. Exp. $2,200

On January 2, 2013, Repeat Clothing Consignments purchased showroom fixtures for $11,000 cash, expecting the fixtures to remain in service for five years. Repeat has depreciated the fixtures on a double-declining-balance basis, with zero residual value. On October 31, 2014, Repeat sold the fixtures for $6,200 cash. Record both depreciation expense for 2014 and sale of the fixtures on October 31, 2014.

E-23 Recording partial year depreciation and sale of an asset

On January 2, 2012, Pet Oasis purchased equipment for $20,000 cash, expecting the fixtures to remain in service for six years. Pet Oasis has depreciated the fixtures on a straight-line basis, with $2,000 residual value. On April 30, 2014, Pet Oasis sold the fixtures for $8,000 cash. Record both depreciation expense for 2014 and sale of the equipment on April 30, 2014.

E-24 Journalizing natural resource depletion

Sierra Mountain Mining paid $448,500 for the right to extract mineral assets from a 500,000-ton deposit. In addition to the purchase price, Sierra also paid a $500 filing fee, a $1,000 license fee to the state of Nevada, and $60,000 for a geological survey of the property. Because Sierra purchased the rights to the minerals only, it expects the asset to have zero residual value. During the first year, Sierra removed and sold 50,000 tons of the minerals. Make journal entries to record (a) purchase of the minerals (debit Minerals), (b) payment of fees and other costs, and (c) depletion for the first year.

E-25 Handling acquisition of patent, amortization, and change in useful life

Miracle Printers (MP) manufactures printers. Assume that MP recently paid $600,000 for a patent on a new laser printer. Although it gives legal protection for 20 years, the patent is expected to provide a competitive advantage for only eight years.

Requirements

1. Assuming the straight-line method of amortization, make journal entries to record (a) the purchase of the patent and (b) amortization for year 1.

2. After using the patent for four years, MP learns at an industry trade show that another company is designing a more efficient printer. On the basis of this new information, MP decides, starting with year 5, to amortize the remaining cost of the patent over two remaining years, giving the patent a total useful life of six years. Record amortization for year 5.

E-26 Measuring and recording goodwill

Potters has acquired several other companies. Assume that Potters purchased Kittery for $6,000,000 cash. The book value of Kittery's assets is $12,000,000 (market value, $15,000,000), and it has liabilities of $11,000,000 (market value, $11,000,000).

Requirements

1. Compute the cost of the goodwill purchased by Potters.

2. Record the purchase of Kittery by Potters.

Plant Assets, Natural Resources, and Intangibles

E-27 Computing asset turnover ratio

Learning Objective 6

Blackerby Photo reported the following figures on its December 31, 2014, income statement and balance sheet:

Net sales	$ 462,000	
	Dec. 31, 2014	**Dec. 31, 2013**
Cash	$ 15,000	$ 20,000
Accounts Receivable	54,000	73,000
Merchandise Inventory	77,000	69,000
Prepaid Expenses	15,000	9,000
Property, plant, and equipment, net	29,000	14,000

Compute the asset turnover ratio for 2014.

EA-28 Exchanging assets—two situations

Learning Objective 7
Appendix A

2. Loss $(7,000)

Community Bank recently traded in office fixtures. Here are the facts:

Old fixtures:	New fixtures:
Cost, $96,000	Cash paid, $103,000
Accumulated depreciation, $65,000	Market value, $134,000

Requirements

1. Record Community Bank's trade-in of old fixtures for new ones. Assume the exchange had commercial substance.

2. Now let's change one fact. Community Bank feels compelled to do business with Mountain Furniture, a bank customer, even though the bank can get the fixtures elsewhere at a better price. Community Bank is aware that the new fixtures' market value is only $127,000. Record the trade-in. Assume the exchange had commercial substance.

EA-29 Measuring asset cost, units-of-production depreciation, and asset trade

Learning Objectives 1, 2, 7
Appendix A

1. $13,500

Safety Trucking Company uses the units-of-production depreciation method because units-of-production best measures wear and tear on the trucks. Consider these facts about one Mack truck in the company's fleet.

When acquired in 2011, the rig cost $450,000 and was expected to remain in service for 10 years or 1,000,000 miles. Estimated residual value was $150,000. The truck was driven 82,000 miles in 2011, 122,000 miles in 2012, and 162,000 miles in 2013. After 45,000 miles, on March 15, 2014, the company traded in the Mack truck for a less expensive Freightliner. Safety also paid cash of $22,000. Fair market value of the Mack truck was equal to its net book value on the date of the trade.

Requirement

1. Record the journal entry for depreciation expense in 2014.

2. Determine Safety's cost of the new truck.

3. Record the journal entry for the exchange of assets on March 15, 2014. Assume the exchange had commercial substance.

Plant Assets, Natural Resources, and Intangibles

> Problems Group A

Learning Objectives 1, 2

1. Bldg. $482,700

P-30A Determining asset cost and recording partial year depreciation

Drive and Fly, near an airport, incurred the following costs to acquire land, make land improvements, and construct and furnish a small building:

a.	Purchase price of three acres of land	$ 80,000
b.	Delinquent real estate taxes on the land to be paid by Drive and Fly	5,600
c.	Additional dirt and earthmoving	9,000
d.	Title insurance on the land acquisition	3,200
e.	Fence around the boundary of the property	9,100
f.	Building permit for the building	500
g.	Architect's fee for the design of the building	20,700
h.	Signs near the front of the property	9,000
i.	Materials used to construct the building	215,000
j.	Labor to construct the building	173,000
k.	Interest cost on construction loan for the building	9,500
l.	Parking lots on the property	29,000
m.	Lights for the parking lots	11,300
n.	Salary of construction supervisor (80% to building; 20% to parking lot and concrete walks)	80,000
o.	Furniture	11,600
p.	Transportation of furniture from seller to the building	2,200
q.	Additional fencing	6,300

Drive and Fly depreciates land improvements over 20 years, buildings over 40 years, and furniture over 10 years, all on a straight-line basis with zero residual value.

Requirements

1. Set up columns for Land, Land Improvements, Building, and Furniture. Show how to account for each cost by listing the cost under the correct account. Determine the total cost of each asset.

2. All construction was complete and the assets were placed in service on July 1. Record partial-year depreciation expense for the year ended December 31.

Learning Objectives 1, 2

1. Units-of-production, 12/31/14, Exp. $20,250

P-31A Determining asset cost, recording first year depreciation, and identifying depreciation results that meet management objectives

On January 3, 2014, Trusty Delivery Service purchased a truck at a cost of $90,000. Before placing the truck in service, Trusty spent $3,000 painting it, $1,500 replacing tires, and $4,500 overhauling the engine. The truck should remain in service for five years and have a residual value of $9,000. The truck's annual mileage is expected to be 22,500 miles in each of the first four years and 10,000 miles in the fifth year—100,000 miles in total. In deciding which depreciation method to use, Mikail Johnson, the general manager, requests a depreciation schedule for each of the depreciation methods (straight-line, units-of-production, and double-declining-balance).

Requirements

1. Prepare a depreciation schedule for each depreciation method, showing asset cost, depreciation expense, accumulated depreciation, and asset book value.

2. Trusty prepares financial statements using the depreciation method that reports the highest net income in the early years of asset use. Consider the first year that Trusty uses the truck. Identify the depreciation method that meets the company's objectives.

P-32A Recording lump sum asset purchases, depreciation, and disposals

Gretta Chung Associates surveys American eating habits. The company's accounts include Land, Buildings, Office Equipment, and Communication Equipment, with a separate Accumulated Depreciation account for each asset. During 2014, Gretta Chung completed the following transactions:

Jan. 1	Purchased office equipment, $119,000. Paid $80,000 cash and financed the remaining with a note payable.
Apr. 1	Acquired land and communication equipment in a lump-sum purchase. Total cost was $270,000 paid in cash. An independent appraisal valued the land at $212,625 and the communication equipment at $70,875.
Sep. 1	Sold a building that cost $555,000 (accumulated depreciation of $255,000 through December 31 of the preceding year). Chung received $370,000 cash from the sale of the building. Depreciation is computed on a straight-line basis. The building has a 40-year useful life and a residual value of $75,000.
Dec. 31	Recorded depreciation as follows:
	Communication equipment is depreciated by the straight-line method over a five-year life with zero residual value.
	Office equipment is depreciated using the double-declining-balance method over five years with a $2,000 residual value.

Record the transactions in the journal of Gretta Chung Associates.

P-33A Accounting for natural resources

McCabe Oil Company has an account titled Oil and Gas Properties. McCabe paid $6,200,000 for oil reserves holding an estimated 500,000 barrels of oil. Assume the company paid $510,000 for additional geological tests of the property and $490,000 to prepare for drilling. During the first year, McCabe removed and sold 90,000 barrels of oil. Record all of McCabe's transactions, including depletion for the first year.

Learning Objectives 1, 2, 3

Sep. 1 Gain $78,000

Learning Objective 4

Dep. Exp. $1,296,000

Plant Assets, Natural Resources, and Intangibles

Learning Objective 5

1. Goodwill $330,000

P-34A Accounting for intangibles

Midland Telecom provides communication services in Iowa, Nebraska, the Dakotas, and Montana. Midland purchased goodwill as part of the acquisition of Shipley Wireless Company, which had the following figures:

Book value of assets	$ 750,000
Market value of assets	1,000,000
Market value of liabilities	530,000

Requirements

1. Journalize the entry to record Midland's purchase of Shipley Wireless for $320,000 cash plus a $480,000 note payable.

2. What special asset does Midland's acquisition of Shipley Wireless identify? How should Midland Telecom account for this asset after acquiring Shipley Wireless? Explain in detail.

Learning Objectives 2, 3, 7 Appendix A

Jan. 1 Gain $2,000

PA-35A Journalizing partial year depreciation and asset disposals and exchanges

During 2014, Mora Company completed the following transactions:

Jan.	1	Traded in old office equipment with book value of $40,000 (cost of $132,000 and accumulated depreciation of $92,000) for new equipment. Mora also paid $80,000 in cash. Fair value of new equipment is $122,000. Assume the exchange had commercial substance.
Apr.	1	Sold equipment that cost $30,000 (accumulated depreciation of $25,000 through December 31 of the preceding year). Mora received $2,000 cash from the sale of the equipment. Depreciation is computed on a straight-line basis. The equipment has a 5-year useful life and a residual value of $0.
Dec.	31	Recorded depreciation as follows: Office equipment is depreciated using the double-declining-balance method over four years with a $4,000 residual value.

Record the transactions in the journal of Mora Company.

> Problems **Group B**

P-36B Determining asset cost and recording partial year depreciation

Best Parking, near an airport, incurred the following costs to acquire land, make land improvements, and construct and furnish a small building:

Learning Objectives 1, 2

1. Bldg $444,300

a.	Purchase price of three acres of land	$ 89,000
b.	Delinquent real estate taxes on the land to be paid by Best Parking	6,000
c.	Additional dirt and earthmoving	8,000
d.	Title insurance on the land acquisition	3,600
e.	Fence around the boundary of the property	9,100
f.	Building permit for the building	800
g.	Architect's fee for the design of the building	20,200
h.	Signs near the front of the property	9,400
i.	Materials used to construct the building	212,000
j.	Labor to construct the building	172,000
k.	Interest cost on construction loan for the building	9,300
l.	Parking lots on the property	28,900
m.	Lights for the parking lots	10,100
n.	Salary of construction supervisor (75% to building; 25% to parking lot and concrete walks)	40,000
o.	Furniture	11,500
p.	Transportation of furniture from seller to the building	2,000
q.	Additional fencing	6,900

Best Parking depreciates land improvements over 25 years, buildings over 50 years, and furniture over 12 years, all on a straight-line basis with zero residual value.

Requirements

1. Set up columns for Land, Land Improvements, Building, and Furniture. Show how to account for each cost by listing the cost under the correct account. Determine the total cost of each asset.

2. All construction was complete and the assets were placed in service on July 1. Record partial-year depreciation expense for the year ended December 31.

Plant Assets, Natural Resources, and Intangibles

Learning Objectives 1, 2

1. Units-of-production, 12/31/14, Exp. $16,170

P-37B Determining asset cost, recording first year depreciation, and identifying depreciation results that meet management objectives

On January 3, 2014, Speedway Delivery Service purchased a truck at a cost of $65,000. Before placing the truck in service, Speedway spent $4,000 painting it, $2,500 replacing tires, and $8,000 overhauling the engine. The truck should remain in service for five years and have a residual value of $6,000. The truck's annual mileage is expected to be 22,000 miles in each of the first four years and 12,000 miles in the fifth year—100,000 miles in total. In deciding which depreciation method to use, David Greer, the general manager, requests a depreciation schedule for each of the depreciation methods (straight-line, units-of-production, and double-declining-balance).

Requirements

1. Prepare a depreciation schedule for each depreciation method, showing asset cost, depreciation expense, accumulated depreciation, and asset book value.

2. Speedway prepares financial statements using the depreciation method that reports the highest net income in the early years of asset use. Consider the first year that Speedway uses the truck. Identify the depreciation method that meets the company's objectives.

Learning Objectives 1, 2, 3

Sep. 1 Gain $97,440

P-38B Recording lump sum asset purchases, depreciation, and disposals

Hilda Carr Associates surveys American eating habits. The company's accounts include Land, Buildings, Office Equipment, and Communication Equipment, with a separate Accumulated Depreciation account for each asset. During 2014, Hilda Carr completed the following transactions:

Jan.	1	Purchased office equipment, $122,000. Paid $90,000 cash and financed the remaining with a note payable.
Apr.	1	Acquired land and communication equipment in a lump-sum purchase. Total cost was $430,000 paid in cash. An independent appraisal valued the land at $338,625 and the communication equipment at $112,875.
Sep.	1	Sold a building that cost $560,400 (accumulated depreciation of $260,000 through December 31 of the preceding year). Carr received $390,000 cash from the sale of the building. Depreciation is computed on a straight-line basis. The building has a 40-year useful life and a residual value of $90,000.
Dec.	31	Recorded depreciation as follows:
		Communication equipment is depreciated by the straight-line method over a five-year life with zero residual value.
		Office equipment is depreciated using the double-declining-balance method over five years with a $1,000 residual value.

Record the transactions in the journal of Hilda Carr Associates.

Learning Objective 4

Dep. Exp. $1,211,960

P-39B Accounting for natural resources

Garrison Oil Company has an account titled Oil and Gas Properties. Garrison paid $6,400,000 for oil reserves holding an estimated 500,000 barrels of oil. Assume the company paid $530,000 for additional geological tests of the property and $460,000 to prepare for drilling. During the first year, Garrison removed and sold 82,000 barrels of oil. Record all of Garrison's transactions, including depletion for the first year.

Plant Assets, Natural Resources, and Intangibles

P-40B Accounting for intangibles

Heartland Telecom provides communication services in Iowa, Nebraska, the Dakotas, and Montana. Heartland purchased goodwill as part of the acquisition of Shurburn Wireless Company, which had the following figures:

Learning Objective 5

1. Goodwill $540,000

Book value of assets	$ 800,000
Market value of assets	900,000
Market value of liabilities	540,000

Requirements

1. Journalize the entry to record Heartland's purchase of Shurburn Wireless for $360,000 cash plus a $540,000 note payable.

2. What special asset does Heartland's acquisition of Shurburn Wireless identify? How should Heartland Telecom account for this asset after acquiring Shurburn Wireless? Explain in detail.

PA-41B Journalizing partial year depreciation and asset disposals and exchanges

During 2014, Gattis Company completed the following transactions:

Learning Objectives 2, 3, 7
Appendix A

Jan. 1 Gain $5,000

Jan.	1	Traded in old office equipment with book value of $60,000 (cost of $140,000 and accumulated depreciation of $80,000) for new equipment. Gattis also paid $70,000 in cash. Fair value of new equipment is $135,000. Assume the exchange had commercial substance.
Apr.	1	Sold equipment that cost $40,000 (accumulated depreciation of $35,000 through December 31 of the preceding year). Gattis received $3,000 cash from the sale of the equipment. Depreciation is computed on a straight-line basis. The equipment has a five-year useful life and a residual value of $0.
Dec. 31		Recorded depreciation as follows:
		Office equipment is depreciated using the double-declining-balance method over four years with a $4,000 residual value.

Record the transactions in the journal of Gattis Company.

> Continuing Problem

P-42 Calculating and journalizing partial year depreciation

This problem deals with a company named Davis Consulting. Assume Davis Consulting had purchased a computer, $1,800, and office furniture, $4,200, on December 3 and 4, 2014, respectively, and that they were expected to last five years. Assume that both assets have a residual value of $0.

Requirements

1. Calculate the amount of depreciation expense for each asset for the year ended December 31, 2014, assuming the computer is depreciated using the straight-line method and the office furniture is depreciated using the double-declining-balance method.

2. Record the entry for the one month's depreciation.

CRITICAL THINKING

> Decision Case 1

Suppose you are an investment advisor and are looking at two companies to recommend to your clients, Shelly's Seashell Enterprises and Jeremy Feigenbaum Systems. The two companies are virtually identical, and both began operations at the beginning of the current year.

In early January, 2014, both companies purchased equipment costing $143,000, with a 10-year estimated useful life and a $20,000 residual value. Shelly uses the straight-line depreciation method. By contrast, Feigenbaum uses the double-declining-balance method. Both companies' trial balances at December 31, 2014, included the following:

Sales Revenue	$ 270,000
Cost of Goods Sold	70,000
Operating Expenses (other than depreciation)	80,700

Requirements

1. Prepare both companies' income statements. (Disregard income tax expense.)

2. Write a letter to address the following questions for your clients: Which company appears to be more profitable? Which company would you prefer to invest in? Why?

> Ethical Issue 1

Western Bank & Trust purchased land and a building for the lump sum of $3,000,000. To get the maximum tax deduction, Western allocated 90% of the purchase price to the building and only 10% to the land. A more realistic allocation would have been 70% to the building and 30% to the land.

Requirements

1. Explain the tax advantage of allocating too much to the building and too little to the land.

2. Was Western's allocation ethical? If so, state why. If not, why not? Identify who was harmed.

> Fraud Case 1

Jim Reed manages a fleet of utility trucks for a rural county government. He's been in his job for 30 years, and he knows where the angles are. He makes sure that when new trucks are purchased, the salvage value is set as low as possible. Then, when they become fully depreciated, they are sold off by the county at residual value. Jim makes sure his buddies in the construction business are first in line for the bargain sales, and they make sure he gets a little something back. Recently, a new county commissioner was elected with vows to cut expenses for the taxpayers. Unlike other commissioners, this man has a business degree, and he is coming to visit Jim tomorrow.

Requirements

1. When a business sells a fully depreciated asset for its residual value, is a gain or loss recognized?

2. How do businesses determine what residual values to use for their various assets? Are there "hard and fast" rules for residual values?

3. How would an organization prevent the kind of fraud depicted here?

> Financial Statement Case 1

Visit **www.pearsonhighered.com/Horngren** to view a link to Starbucks Corporation's Fiscal 2011 annual report. Refer to the Starbucks Corporation financial statements, including Notes 1 and 6. Answer the following questions.

Requirements

1. Which depreciation method does Starbucks Corporation use for reporting in the financial statements? What type of depreciation method does the company probably use for income tax purposes?

2. What was the amount of depreciation and amortization expense for year ending October 2, 2011?

3. The statement of cash flows reports the purchases of property, plant, and equipment. How much were Starbucks' fixed asset cash purchases during year ending 2011? Did Starbucks' record any proceeds from the sale of fixed assets?

4. What was the amount of accumulated depreciation at October 2, 2011?

5. Compute Starbucks' asset turnover ratio for year ending October 2, 2011. How does Starbucks' ratio compare to **Green Mountain Coffee Roasters, Inc.**?

> Team Project 1

Visit a local business.

Requirements

1. List all its plant assets.

2. If possible, interview the manager. Gain as much information as you can about the business's plant assets. For example, try to determine the assets' costs, the depreciation method the company is using, and the estimated useful life of each asset category. If an interview is impossible, then develop your own estimates of the assets' costs, useful lives, and book values, assuming an appropriate depreciation method.

3. Determine whether the business has any intangible assets. If so, list them and learn as much as possible about their nature, cost, and estimated useful lives.

4. Write a detailed report of your findings, and be prepared to present it to the class.

> Communication Activity 1

In 150 words or fewer, explain the different methods that can be used to calculate depreciation. Your explanation should include how to calculate depreciation expense using each method.

Try It! Solutions

1.

Asset	Market Value	Percentage of Total Value	× Total Purchase Price	= Cost of Each Asset
Land	$ 22,000	$22,000 / $220,000 = 10%	× $200,000	= $ 20,000
Building	187,000	$187,000 / $220,000 = 85%	× $200,000	= 170,000
Equipment	11,000	$11,000 / $220,000 = 5%	× $200,000	= 10,000
Total	$ 220,000	100%		$ 200,000

Date	Accounts and Explanation	Debit	Credit
	Land	20,000	
	Building	170,000	
	Equipment	10,000	
	Cash		200,000
	To record purchase of land, building, and equipment with cash.		

2.

a. Straight-line depreciation = ($140,000 – $2,000) / 6 years = $23,000

b. Depreciation per unit = ($140,000 – $2,000) / 1,000,000 lifts = $0.14 per lift (rounded)

Units-of-production depreciation = $0.14 per lift × 80,000 lifts = $11,200

c. Double-declining-balance depreciation = ($140,000 – $0) × 2 × (1 / 6) = $46,667 (rounded)

3. Accumulated depreciation = [($20,000 – $2,000) / 4 years] × 3 years = $13,500

Date	Accounts and Explanation	Debit	Credit
Dec. 31	Cash	8,000	
	Accumulated Depreciation—Equipment	13,500	
	Gain on Disposal		1,500
	Equipment		20,000
	Sold equipment for cash.		

4. Depletion per unit = ($80,000,000 − $0) / 100,000,000 barrels = $0.80 per barrel

Depletion expense = $0.80 per barrel × 20,000,000 barrels = $16,000,000

Date	Accounts and Explanation	Debit	Credit
Dec. 31	Depletion Expense—Oil	16,000,000	
	Accumulated Depletion—Oil		16,000,000
	To record depletion.		

5. Amortization expense = ($40,000 − $0) / 8 years = $5,000

Date	Accounts and Explanation	Debit	Credit
Dec. 31	Amortization Expense—Patent	5,000	
	Patent		5,000
	To record amortization of patent.		

6. Asset turnover ratio = $240,000 / [($140,000 + $160,000) / 2] = 1.6

7A.

Date	Accounts and Explanation	Debit	Credit
	Equipment (new)	5,000	
	Accumulated Depreciation—Equipment	8,000	
	Loss on Disposal	1,000	
	Equipment (old)		10,000
	Cash		4,000
	Exchanged old equipment and cash for new equipment.		

> Quick Check Answers

1. d **2.** d **3.** c **4.** b **5.** c **6.** d **7.** d **8.** b **9.** c **10A.** b

Glossary

Accelerated Depreciation Method. A depreciation method that expenses more of the asset's cost near the start of its useful life and less at the end of its useful life.

Amortization. The process by which businesses spread the allocation of an intangible asset's cost over its useful life.

Asset Turnover Ratio. Measures how efficiently a business uses its average total assets to generate sales. Net sales / Average total assets.

Book Value A depreciable asset's cost minus accumulated depreciation.

Capital Expenditure. An expenditure that increases the capacity or efficiency of a plant asset or extends its useful life. Capital expenditures are debited to an asset account.

Capitalize. Recording the acquisition of land, building, or other assets by debiting (increasing) an asset account.

Commercial Substance. A characteristic of a transaction that causes a change in future cash flows. (Appendix A)

Copyright. Exclusive right to reproduce and sell a book, musical composition, film, other work of art, or intellectual property.

Cost Principle. A principle that states that acquired assets and services should be recorded at their actual cost.

Depletion. The process by which businesses spread the allocation of a natural resource's cost over its usage.

Depreciable Cost. The cost of a plant asset minus its estimated residual value.

Depreciation. The process by which businesses spread the allocation of a plant asset's cost over its useful life.

Double-Declining-Balance Method. An accelerated depreciation method that computes annual depreciation by multiplying the depreciable asset's decreasing book value by a constant percent that is two times the straight-line depreciation rate.

Extraordinary Repair. Repair work that generates a capital expenditure because it extends the asset's life past the normal expected life.

Franchise. Privilege granted by a business to sell a product or service under specified conditions.

Goodwill. Excess of the cost of an acquired company over the sum of the market values of its net assets (assets minus liabilities).

Impairment. A permanent decline in asset value.

Intangible Asset. An asset with no physical form that is valuable because of the special rights it carries.

Land Improvement. A depreciable improvement to land, such as fencing, sprinklers, paving, signs, and lighting.

License. Privilege granted by a government to use public property in performing services.

Modified Accelerated Cost Recovery System (MACRS). A depreciation method that is used for tax purposes.

Natural Resource. An asset that comes from the earth and is consumed.

Obsolete. An asset is considered obsolete when a newer asset can perform the job more efficiently than the old.

Patent. An intangible asset that is a federal government grant conveying an exclusive 20-year right to produce and sell a process, product, or formula.

Plant Asset. Long-lived, tangible asset, such as land, buildings, and equipment, used in the operation of a business.

Relative-Market-Value Method. A method of allocating the total cost (100%) of multiple assets purchased at one time. Total cost is divided among the assets according to their relative market values.

Residual Value. The expected value of a depreciable asset at the end of its useful life.

Revenue Expenditure. An expenditure that does not increase the capacity or efficiency of an asset or extend its useful life. Revenue expenditures are debited to an expense account.

Straight-Line Method. A depreciation method that allocates an equal amount of depreciation each year. (Cost – Residual Value) / Useful Life.

Trademark. An asset that represents distinctive identifications of a product or service.

Units-of-Production Method. A depreciation method that allocates a varying amount of depreciation each year based on an asset's usage.

Useful Life. Length of the service period expected from an asset. May be expressed in time, such as months or years, or usage, such as units produced, hours used (for machinery), or miles driven (for a truck).

Photo Credits

Current Liabilities and Payroll

From Chapter 11 of *Horngren's Accounting*, Tenth edition. Tracie Nobles, Brenda Mattison, Ella Mae Matsumura. Copyright © 2014 by Pearson Education, Inc. All rights reserved.

Current Liabilities and Payroll

How Much Does One Employee Cost?

Mary Green, MD, recently opened a health care clinic, Family Medicine, that serves low-income families and uninsured individuals. Family Medicine prides itself on keeping its costs low but still providing excellent health care to its patients. When Mary opened the clinic, she hired only one part-time nurse. Now, with the clinic growing, Mary is considering hiring several more nurses and another doctor.

Mary knows that having employees is expensive. Not only does the business have to pay their wages, but there are additional payroll taxes that must also be paid. As Mary is deciding what salary to offer her new employees, she must consider these additional costs. She knows that if she offers the new doctor

a salary of $100,000, the business will end up paying more than $100,000. This is because of additional payroll taxes such as Social Security and unemployment compensation. In addition, Family Medicine will need to offer health care and retirement benefits to each employee. All of these extra expenses cost money—money she could be saving. But Mary knows that in order to provide the quality of service her patients expect, she must pay the cost of hiring new employees.

How Do Businesses Account for Current Liabilities and Payroll?

We now begin our focus on liabilities, or debts, a business owes. Payroll is one of those liabilities. Companies such as UnitedHealth Group Incorporated, a leading health care company that serves more than 75 million people, value hiring smart, committed, and talented people. Part of UnitedHealth's recruiting package is the salary it offers employees. In addition, UnitedHealth Group also offers benefits such as vacation, healthcare, and retirement to reward its employees. Payroll and benefits are reported as current liabilities on the balance sheet until the company makes payment. In this chapter, we look at how businesses, such as UnitedHealth Group, account for and record payroll and other current liabilities.

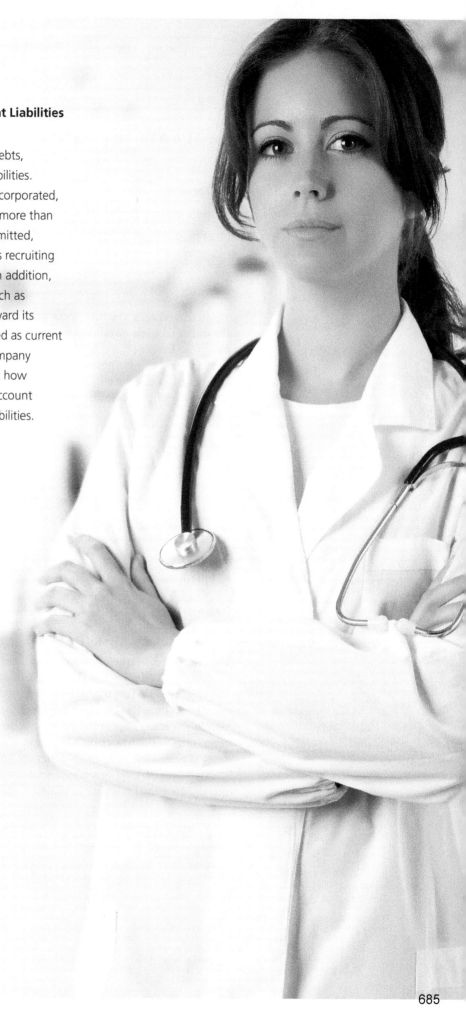

chapter outline

How are current liabilities of known amounts accounted for?

How do companies account for and record payroll?

How are current liabilities that must be estimated accounted for?

How are contingent liabilities accounted for?

How do we use the times-interest-earned ratio to evaluate business performance?

Learning Objectives

1   Account for current liabilities of known amount

2   Calculate and journalize basic payroll transactions

3   Account for current liabilities that must be estimated

4   Account for contingent liabilities

5   Use the times-interest-earned ratio to evaluate business performance

Up to this point, we've been focusing on all the assets a business owns. But what about the bills a business owes? As a business owner or manager, you have to know what you owe (your liabilities) and by what date you have to pay them. Why? To be sure you have cash on hand to pay these bills. In this chapter, we focus on some common current liabilities a business may owe. As with other chapters, we'll continue to focus on Smart Touch Learning and see how it manages its current liabilities.

HOW ARE CURRENT LIABILITIES OF KNOWN AMOUNTS ACCOUNTED FOR?

Learning Objective 1

Account for current liabilities of known amount

Liabilities

Debts that are owed to creditors.

Current Liabilities

Liabilities that must be paid with cash or with goods and services within one year or within the entity's operating cycle if the cycle is longer than a year.

Long-Term Liabilities

Liabilities that do not need to be paid within one year or within the entity's operating cycle, whichever is longer.

IFRS defines current and long-term liabilities in the same manner as GAAP.

Liabilities are debts that are owed to creditors. Liabilities have three main characteristics:

1. They occur because of a past transaction or event.
2. They create a present obligation for future payment of cash or services.
3. They are an unavoidable obligation.

Liabilities can be split into two main categories: current and long-term. In this chapter, we discuss current liabilities. Current liabilities must be paid either with cash or with goods and services within one year or within the entity's operating cycle if the cycle is longer than a year.

Accounts Payable, Notes Payable due within one year, Salaries Payable, Interest Payable, and Unearned Revenue are all current liabilities. Any portion of a long-term liability that is due within the next year is also reported as a current liability. Current liabilities are listed on the balance sheet in the order in which they are due.

Long-term liabilities are liabilities that do not need to be paid within one year or within the entity's operating cycle, whichever is longer. Many Notes Payable are long-term, such as a mortgage on a building.

The amounts of most liabilities are known. For example, a business receives a bill that is due in 30 days or a business takes out a 90-day loan from a bank. We will begin our discussion with current liabilities of a known amount.

Accounts Payable

Amounts owed for products or services purchased on account are *accounts payable*. Because these are typically due in 30 days, they are current liabilities. Businesses can record accounts payable for the purchase of goods or for the receipt of services. Accounts payable occur because the business receives the goods or services before payment has been made.

Sales Tax Payable

Most states assess sales tax on retail sales. Retailers collect the sales tax in addition to the price of the item sold. Sales Tax Payable is a current liability because the retailer must pay the state in less than a year. Sales tax is usually calculated as a percentage of the amount of the sale.

For example, suppose December's taxable sales for Smart Touch Learning totaled $10,000. The company collected an additional 6% sales tax, which would equal $600 ($10,000 × 0.06). The accounting clerk would record that month's cash sales as follows:

Date	Accounts and Explanation	Debit	Credit
Dec. 31	Cash	10,600	
	Sales Revenue		10,000
	Sales Tax Payable ($10,000 × 0.06)		600
	To record cash sales and the related sales tax.		

$$A\uparrow \quad \Big\} = \Big\{ \quad L\uparrow \quad + \quad E\uparrow$$

Cash↑ = Sales Tax Payable↑   Sales Revenue↑

Sales tax is not an expense of the business. It is a current liability. Companies collect the sales tax and then forward it to the state at regular intervals. They normally submit it monthly, but they could file it at other intervals, depending on the state and the amount of the tax. To pay the tax, the company debits Sales Tax Payable and credits Cash.

Date	Accounts and Explanation	Debit	Credit
Jan. 20	Sales Tax Payable	600	
	Cash		600
	To record cash payment for sales tax payable.		

$$A\downarrow \quad \Big\} = \Big\{ \quad L\downarrow \quad + \quad E$$

Cash↓ = Sales Tax Payable↓

Unearned Revenues

Unearned revenue is also called *deferred revenue*. Unearned revenue arises when a business has received cash in advance of providing goods or performing work and, therefore, has an obligation to provide goods or services to the customer in the future. Unearned revenues are current liabilities until they are earned.

Suppose Smart Touch Learning received $900 in advance on May 21 for a month's work beginning on that date. On May 21, because it received cash before earning the revenue, the company has a liability to perform work for the client. The liability is called Unearned Revenue. The entry made by the accounting clerk on May 21 follows:

Date	Accounts and Explanation	Debit	Credit
May 21	Cash	900	
	Unearned Revenue		900
	Collected cash for future services.		

$$A\uparrow \quad \Big\} = \Big\{ \quad L\uparrow \quad + \quad E$$

Cash↑ = Unearned Revenue↑

During May, Smart Touch Learning delivered one-third of the work and earned $300 ($900 × 1/3) of the revenue. On May 31, the accounting clerk would record the following entry to show that some work had been completed and some revenue had now been earned:

$$\left.\begin{array}{c} \underline{\textbf{A}} \end{array}\right\} = \left\{\begin{array}{cc} \underline{\textbf{L}\downarrow} & + & \underline{\textbf{E}\uparrow} \\ \text{Unearned} & & \text{Service} \\ \text{Revenue}\downarrow & & \text{Revenue}\uparrow \end{array}\right.$$

Date	Accounts and Explanation	Debit	Credit
May 31	Unearned Revenue	300	
	Service Revenue		300
	To record service revenue earned that was collected in advance.		

At this point, Smart Touch Learning has earned $300 of the revenue and still owes $600 of work to the customer as shown in the T-accounts:

Unearned Revenue				Service Revenue	
May 31	300	900	May 21		300	May 31
		600	**Bal.**		

Short-Term Notes Payable

Short-term notes payable are a common form of financing. Short-term notes payable represent a written promise by the business to pay a debt, usually involving interest, within one year or less. Assume on May 1, Smart Touch Learning purchased merchandise inventory with a 10%, 90-day note payable, for $8,000. The company uses the perpetual inventory system. The entry to record the note follows:

$$\left.\begin{array}{c} \underline{\textbf{A}\uparrow} \\ \text{Merchandise} \\ \text{Inventory}\uparrow \end{array}\right\} = \left\{\begin{array}{cc} \underline{\textbf{L}\uparrow} & + & \underline{\textbf{E}} \\ \text{Notes} & & \\ \text{Payable}\uparrow & & \end{array}\right.$$

Date	Accounts and Explanation	Debit	Credit
May 1	Merchandise Inventory	8,000	
	Notes Payable		8,000
	Purchased merchandise inventory in exchange for 90-day, 10% note.		

On July 30, when the note is due, Smart Touch Learning will pay the note plus interest and record the following entry:

$$\left.\begin{array}{c} \underline{\textbf{A}\downarrow} \\ \text{Cash}\downarrow \end{array}\right\} = \left\{\begin{array}{cc} \underline{\textbf{L}\downarrow} & + & \underline{\textbf{E}\downarrow} \\ \text{Notes} & & \text{Interest} \\ \text{Payable}\downarrow & & \text{Expense}\uparrow \end{array}\right.$$

Date	Accounts and Explanation	Debit	Credit
Jul. 30	Notes Payable	8,000	
	Interest Expense ($8,000 × 0.10 × 90/360)	200	
	Cash		8,200
	Paid note and interest at maturity.		

Remember that the calculation for interest is principal × interest rate × time.

Current Liabilities and Payroll

Businesses occasionally borrow cash from banks. The bank requires the business to sign a *promissory note* that states that the business will pay the *principal* plus *interest* at a specified *maturity date*. As an example, assume that on November 1, 2014, Smart Touch Learning borrows $10,000 from First Street Bank at 6% for five months. On November 1, the accounting clerk records the following entry:

Date	Accounts and Explanation	Debit	Credit
2014			
Nov. 1	Cash	10,000	
	Notes Payable		10,000
	Received cash in exchange for 5-month, 6% note.		

$$\underline{\begin{array}{c}A\uparrow\\\text{Cash}\uparrow\end{array}} \left.\right\} = \left\{\begin{array}{c}\underline{L\uparrow}\ +\ \underline{E}\\\text{Notes}\\\text{Payable}\uparrow\end{array}\right.$$

At year-end, the matching principle requires the business to accrue interest expense for the two months from November to December as follows:

Date	Accounts and Explanation	Debit	Credit
2014			
Dec. 31	Interest Expense ($10,000 × 0.06 × 2/12)	100	
	Interest Payable		100
	Accrued interest expense at year-end.		

$$\underline{A} \left.\right\} = \left\{\begin{array}{cc}\underline{L\uparrow}\ +&\underline{E\downarrow}\\\text{Interest}&\text{Interest}\\\text{Payable}\uparrow&\text{Expense}\uparrow\end{array}\right.$$

The interest accrual at December 31, 2014, allocated $100 of the interest on this note to 2014. During 2015, the interest on this note for the three remaining months is $150. When Smart Touch Learning records payment for the note, it will record the remaining interest expense and also remove the interest payable and note payable from the books as shown:

Date	Accounts and Explanation	Debit	Credit
2015			
Apr. 1	Notes Payable	10,000	
	Interest Expense ($10,000 × 0.06 × 3/12)	150	
	Interest Payable	100	
	Cash		10,250
	Paid note and interest at maturity.		

$$\underline{\begin{array}{c}A\downarrow\\\text{Cash}\downarrow\end{array}} \left.\right\} = \left\{\begin{array}{cc}\underline{L\downarrow}\ +&\underline{E\downarrow}\\\text{Notes}&\text{Interest}\\\text{Payable}\downarrow&\text{Expense}\uparrow\\\text{Interest}\\\text{Payable}\downarrow\end{array}\right.$$

Current Portion of Long-Term Notes Payable

Long-term notes payable are typically reported in the long-term liability section of the balance sheet. If, however, the long-term debt is paid in installments, the business will report the current portion of notes payable (also called *current maturity*) as a current liability. The current portion of notes payable is the principal amount that will be paid within one year. The remaining portion of the note will be classified as long-term.

Current Portion of Notes Payable
The amount of the principal that is payable within one year.

689

Let's consider a $20,000 note payable that is paid in $5,000 installments over four years. The portion that must be paid within one year, $5,000, is current. The remaining $15,000 will be classified as long-term. No journal entry is needed to reclassify the current portion. It is, instead, only classified as current or long-term for reporting purposes on the balance sheet. Notice that the reclassification does not change the total amount of debt. It only reclassifies $5,000 of the total debt from long-term to current.

On August 10, Swanson Company recorded sales of merchandise inventory on account, $4,000. The sales were subject to sales tax of 4%. The company uses the perpetual inventory system. On September 30, Swanson Company paid $500 of sales tax to the state.

1. Journalize the transaction to record the sale on August 10. Ignore cost of goods sold.
2. Journalize the transaction to record the payment of sales tax to the state.

Check your answers at the end of the chapter.

For more practice, see Short Exercises S-1 through S-5. MyAccountingLab

HOW DO COMPANIES ACCOUNT FOR AND RECORD PAYROLL?

Payroll, also called *employee compensation*, also creates liabilities for a business. For service organizations—such as CPA firms and travel agencies—payroll is *the* major expense. Labor cost is so important that most businesses develop a special payroll system.

There are numerous ways to label an employee's pay:

- *Salary* is pay stated at an annual, monthly, or weekly rate, such as $62,400 per year, $5,200 per month, or $1,200 per week.
- *Wages* are pay amounts stated at an hourly rate, such as $10 per hour.
- *Commission* is pay stated as a percentage of a sale amount, such as a 5% commission on a sale. A realtor who earns 5% commission, for example, earns $5,000 on a $100,000 sale of real estate ($100,000 × 5%).
- *Bonus* is pay over and above base salary (or wage or commission). A bonus is usually paid for exceptional performance—in a single amount after year-end.
- *Benefits* are extra compensation—items that are not paid directly to the employee. Benefits cover health, life, and disability insurance. The employer pays the insurance company, which then provides coverage for the employee. Another type of benefit, retirement, sets aside money for the employee for his or her future retirement.

Businesses pay employees at a base rate for a set period—called *straight time*. For additional hours—*overtime*—the employee may get a higher pay rate, depending on the job classification and wage and hour laws.

Assume Ryan Park was hired to work for Smart Touch Learning. His pay is as follows:

- Ryan earns wages of $15 per hour for straight time (40 hours), so his weekly pay is $600 ($15 per hour × 40 hours).
- The company pays *time-and-a-half* for overtime. That rate is 150% (1.5 times) the straight-time pay rate. Thus, Ryan earns $22.50 per hour of overtime ($15.00 × 1.5).
- For working 42 hours during a week, he earns gross pay of $645, computed as follows:

Straight-time pay for 40 hours	$ 600
Overtime pay for 2 hours: 2 × $22.50	45
Gross Pay	$ 645

Gross Pay and Net (Take-Home) Pay

Two pay amounts are important for accounting purposes. Gross pay is the total amount of salary, wages, commissions, and bonuses earned by the employee during a pay period, before taxes or any other deductions. Gross pay is an expense to the employer. In the preceding example, Ryan Park's gross pay was $645. Net pay is the amount the employee gets to keep. Net pay is also called *take-home pay*. Net pay equals gross pay minus all deductions such as income tax withheld. The employer either writes a paycheck to each employee for his or her take-home pay or directly deposits the employee's take home pay into the employee's bank account.

Employee Payroll Withholding Deductions

The federal government, most states, and many municipalities require employers to deduct taxes from employee paychecks. Insurance companies and investment companies may also get some of the employee's gross pay. Amounts withheld from paychecks are called *withholding deductions*. Payroll withholding deductions are the difference between gross pay and take-home pay. These deductions are withheld from paychecks and sent directly to the government, to insurance companies, or to other entities. Payroll withholding deductions fall into two categories:

- *Required deductions*, such as employee federal and state income tax and Social Security tax. Employees pay their income tax and Social Security tax through payroll deductions.
- *Optional deductions*, including insurance premiums, retirement plan contributions, charitable contributions, and other amounts that are withheld at the employee's request.

After being withheld, payroll deductions become the liability of the employer, who then pays the outside party—taxes to the government and contributions to charitable organizations, for example.

Withholding for Employee Income Tax

United States law and some states, cities, and counties require companies to withhold income tax from employee paychecks. The income tax deducted from gross pay is called income tax withholding. The amount withheld depends on the employee's gross pay and on the number of *withholding allowances* he or she claims. (In this text, we will assume an income tax withholding rate of 20%.)

Gross Pay
The total amount of salary, wages, commissions, or any other employee compensation before taxes and other deductions.

Net Pay
Gross pay minus all deductions. The amount of compensation that the employee actually takes home.

Income Tax Withholding
Income tax deducted from an employee's gross pay.

For federal tax withholdings, an employee files Form W-4 with his or her employer to indicate the number of allowances claimed for income-tax withholding. Each allowance lowers the amount of tax withheld:

- An unmarried taxpayer usually claims one allowance.
- A childless married couple usually claims two allowances.
- A married couple with one child usually claims three allowances, and so on.

Exhibit 1 shows a W-4 for Ryan Park, who claims married with three allowances (lines 3 and 5).

Exhibit 1 | W-4

Withholding for Employee Social Security Tax (FICA)

The Federal Insurance Contributions Act (FICA), also known as the Social Security Act, created the Social Security tax. The Social Security program provides retirement, disability, and medical benefits. The law requires employers to withhold Social Security (FICA) tax from employees' paychecks. The FICA tax has two components:

1. OASDI (old age, survivors, and disability insurance)
2. Medicare (medical benefits)

OASDI provides retirement benefits to individuals based upon age, benefits to survivors of qualified individuals, and disability insurance to individuals who cannot work because of a medical condition. The amount of tax withheld varies from year to year

Federal Insurance Contributions Act (FICA)
The federal act that created the Social Security tax that provides retirement, disability, and medical benefits.

Social Security (FICA) Tax
Federal Insurance Contributions Act (FICA) tax, which is withheld from employees' pay and matched by the employer.

because the wage base is subject to OASDI tax changes each year. For 2012, the OASDI tax applies to the first $110,100 of employee earnings in a year. The taxable amount of earnings is adjusted annually. The OASDI tax rate for employees at the time of this writing is 4.2%. Therefore, the maximum OASDI tax that an employee paid in 2012 was $4,624.20 ($110,100 × 0.042).

The Medicare portion of the FICA tax provides health insurance to individuals based on age or disability. Medicare applies to all employee earnings—that means that there is no maximum tax. At the time of this writing, this tax rate is 1.45%. Therefore, an employee pays a combined FICA tax rate of 5.65% (4.2% + 1.45%) of the first $110,100 of annual earnings ($110,100 is the 2012 cap as it was the most current wage cap at the time of printing), plus 1.45% of earnings above $110,100.

> *The percentage used and the wage base for payroll withholdings and taxes varies from year to year. We are using amounts that are current at the time of printing. You should use these numbers when you complete this chapter's assignments.*

Assume that James Kolen, another employee of Smart Touch Learning, earned $105,800 prior to December. Kolen's salary for December is $10,000. Kolen's FICA tax withheld from his paycheck is calculated as follows:

	FICA	
	OASDI	**Medicare**
Employee earnings subject to tax	$ 110,100	No Max
Employee earnings prior to the current month	− 105,800	
Current pay subject to tax	$ 4,300	$ 10,000
Tax rate	× 0.042	× 0.0145
Tax to be withheld from paycheck	$ 181*	$ 145
Total FICA tax withheld ($181 + $145)	$326	

*Numbers in examples are rounded to nearest dollar for simplicity. Payroll amounts are usually rounded to the nearest cent.

Notice that only $4,300 of Kolen's $10,000 salary is subject to OASDI tax. This is because in December, Kolen reaches the maximum amount of earnings that is subject to OASDI. Once an employee has earned $110,100, no further earnings are taxed for OASDI in that year.

Medicare tax, on the other hand, has no maximum. All earnings are subject to the tax. Kolen pays Medicare tax on the entire $10,000 earned in December.

Optional Withholding Deductions

As a convenience to employees, some companies withhold payroll deductions and then pay designated organizations according to employee instructions. Insurance premiums, retirement savings, union dues, and gifts to charities are examples.

> Why did James Kolen only pay OASDI tax on $4,300 of earnings?

The following table summarizes James Kolen's final pay period on December 31 assuming he authorized a $180 payment for health insurance and a $20 contribution to United Way. Employee income tax is assumed to be 20% of gross pay.

Gross pay		$ 10,000
Withholding deductions:		
Employee income tax (20%)	$ 2,000	
Employee OASDI tax (4.2%)	181	
Employee Medicare tax (1.45%)	145	
Employee health insurance	180	
Employee contribution to United Way	20	
Total withholdings		2,526
Net (take-home) pay		$ 7,474

Payroll Register

Payroll Register
A schedule that summarizes the earnings, withholdings, and net pay for each employee.

Many companies use a **payroll register** to help summarize the earnings, withholdings, and net pay for each employee. Exhibit 2 shows the payroll register for Smart Touch Learning for the month of December.

Exhibit 2 | **Payroll Register**

Employee Name	Earnings			Withholdings						Net Pay	Check No.	Salaries and Wages Expense
	Beginning Cumulative Earnings	Current Period Earnings	Ending Cumulative Earnings	OASDI	Medicare	Income Tax	Health Insurance	Other	Total Withholdings			
James Kolen	$ 105,800	$ 10,000	$ 115,800	$ 181	$ 145	$ 2,000	$ 180	$ 20	$ 2,526	$ 7,474	530	$ 10,000
Benito Munez	62,100	5,500	67,600	231	80	1,100	110	0	1,521	3,979	531	5,500
Ryan Park	37,400	2,580	39,980	108	37	516	110	0	771	1,809	532	2,580
Lisa Smart	0	4,000	4,000	168	58	800	65	0	1,091	2,909	533	4,000
Sharon Zapato	71,500	6,500	78,000	273	94	1,300	180	40	1,887	4,613	534	6,500
Total	$ 276,800	$ 28,580	$ 305,380	$ 961	$ 414	$ 5,716	$ 645	$ 60	$ 7,796	$ 20,784		$ 28,580

A business's payroll register typically includes the following columns:

1. Employee Name
2. Beginning cumulative earnings—the amount the employee has earned through the last pay period.
3. Current period earnings—earnings for the current period (includes regular and overtime earnings, commissions, and bonuses).
4. Ending cumulative earnings—beginning cumulative earnings plus current period earnings.
5. OASDI—4.2% tax on the first $110,100 earnings.
6. Medicare—1.45% tax on all earnings.
7. Income Tax—includes federal, state, and any local government income tax withheld.
8. Health Insurance—withholdings made for employee-paid health care coverage.
9. Other—employees' voluntary withholdings such as charitable contributions and union dues.

10. Total Withholdings—total of all withholdings.
11. Net Pay—current period earnings less total withholdings. This is the amount that is paid to each employee.
12. Check No.—the check number used to make payment for earnings.
13. Salaries and Wages Expense—the amount debited to Salaries and Wages Expense for the current pay period.

Journalizing Employee Payroll

The payroll register is used to record the payroll journal entry. Payroll and payroll withholdings are recorded as liabilities until the amounts are paid. The totals from the payroll register will be used to create the journal entry for Smart Touch Learning.

Date	Accounts and Explanation	Debit	Credit
Dec. 31	Salaries and Wages Expense	28,580	
	FICA—OASDI Taxes Payable		961
	FICA—Medicare Taxes Payable		414
	Employee Income Taxes Payable		5,716
	Employee Health Insurance Payable		645
	United Way Payable		60
	Salaries and Wages Payable		20,784
	To record salaries and wages expense and payroll withholdings.		

$$A \quad \left. \right\} = \left\{ \begin{array}{ccc} \underline{L\uparrow} & + & \underline{E\downarrow} \\ \text{Various} & & \text{Salaries and} \\ \text{Payables}\uparrow & & \text{Wages} \\ \text{Salaries and} & & \text{Expense}\uparrow \\ \text{Wages} & & \\ \text{Payable}\uparrow & & \end{array} \right.$$

In the above journal entry, Salaries and Wages Expense ($28,580) represents the gross pay for all employees. Gross pay includes both the amount owed for salaries and wages ($20,784) and payroll withholdings ($961 + $414 + $5,716 + $645 + $60).

On payday, Smart Touch Learning will make payment of $20,784 to its employees and record the following journal entry:

Date	Accounts and Explanation	Debit	Credit
Jan. 5	Salaries and Wages Payable	20,784	
	Cash		20,784
	To record payment of salaries.		

$$\begin{array}{c} A\downarrow \\ \text{Cash}\downarrow \end{array} \left. \right\} = \left\{ \begin{array}{ccc} \underline{L\downarrow} & + & \underline{E} \\ \text{Salaries} & & \\ \text{and Wages} & & \\ \text{Payable}\downarrow & & \end{array} \right.$$

The other payable accounts, FICA, Income Taxes Payable, Health Insurance, and any charitable contributions, will be removed from the books when payments are made on those specific payables.

Employer Payroll Taxes

In addition to income tax and FICA tax, which are withheld from employee paychecks, *employers* must pay at least three payroll taxes. These taxes are not withheld from employees' gross earnings but instead are paid by the employer:

1. Employer FICA tax (OASDI and Medicare)
2. State unemployment compensation tax (SUTA)
3. Federal unemployment compensation tax (FUTA)

Employer FICA Tax

In addition to the FICA tax withheld from the employee's paycheck, the employer must pay both OASDI and Medicare. The employer portion of OASDI is 6.2% on the first $110,100 of each employee's annual earnings. The employer's tax rate for Medicare is 1.45% on all earnings. The Social Security system is funded by contributions from both the employer and employee.

State and Federal Unemployment Compensation Taxes

Unemployment Compensation Tax Payroll tax paid by employers to the government, which uses the cash to pay unemployment benefits to people who are out of work.

The Federal Unemployment Tax Act (FUTA) and the State Unemployment Tax Act (SUTA) finance workers' compensation for people laid off from work. These unemployment compensation taxes are paid by the employer; they are not deducted from employees' gross pay. (Some states require employees to contribute to SUTA. For our purposes, we will assume that unemployment compensation taxes are paid only by the employer.) In recent years, employers have paid a combined tax of 6.2% on the first $7,000 of each employee's annual earnings for unemployment tax. The proportion paid to the state depends on the individual state, but for many it is 5.6% to the state plus 0.6% to the federal government. For this payroll tax, the employer uses two liability accounts:

- Federal Unemployment Taxes Payable (FUTA Payable)
- State Unemployment Taxes Payable (SUTA Payable)

Exhibit 3 shows the distribution of payroll for an employee who earns $1,000, assuming the employee has not reached the payroll tax limits.

Exhibit 3 | Payroll Costs

Employee's taxes and other withholdings				Employer's taxes			
Net (Take-Home) Pay	OASDI (4.2% on first $110,100)	Medicare (1.45% on all earnings)	Income Tax (20% assumed)	OASDI (6.2% on first $110,100)	Medicare (1.45% on all earnings)	FUTA (0.6% on first $7,000)	SUTA (5.6% on first $7,000)
$743 +	$42 +	$15 +	$200	$62 +	$15 +	$6 +	$56
=$1,000				=$139			
Employer pays a total of $1,139.							

Journalizing Employer Payroll Taxes

Smart Touch Learning's employer payroll taxes for December will be calculated as follows:

Employee Name	Earnings			Employer Payroll Taxes				
	Beginning Cumulative Earnings	Current Period Earnings	Ending Cumulative Earnings	OASDI (6.2%)	Medicare (1.45%)	FUTA (0.6%)	SUTA (5.6%)	Total Taxes
James Kolen	$ 105,800	$ 10,000	$ 115,800	$ 267	$ 145	$ 0	$ 0	$ 412
Benito Munez	62,100	5,500	67,600	341	80	0	0	421
Ryan Park	37,400	2,580	39,980	160	37	0	0	197
Lisa Smart	0	4,000	4,000	248	58	24	224	554
Sharon Zapato	71,500	6,500	78,000	403	94	0	0	497
Total	$ 276,800	$ 28,580	$ 305,380	$ 1,419	$ 414	$ 24	$ 224	$ 2,081

As with employee contributions, the federal FICA—OASDI is determined as 6.2% on the first $110,100 earned by each employee. Smart Touch Learning must pay OASDI tax on all employees; however, the amount paid on James Kolen's earnings is limited to the first $110,100 [($110,100 − $105,800) × 6.2% = $267]. FICA—Medicare applies to all earnings at a rate of 1.45%.

FUTA (0.6%) and SUTA (5.6%) tax is only paid on the first $7,000 of each employee's earnings. Smart Touch Learning will only pay unemployment taxes on Lisa Smart because all other employees have earned more than $7,000 to date.

Smart Touch Learning records the employer's payroll tax expense as a debit to Payroll Tax Expense and a credit to the various payable accounts:

Date	Accounts and Explanation	Debit	Credit
Dec. 31	Payroll Tax Expense	2,081	
	FICA—OASDI Taxes Payable		1,419
	FICA—Medicare Taxes Payable		414
	Federal Unemployment Taxes Payable		24
	State Unemployment Taxes Payable		224
	To record employer's payroll tax expense.		

$$A = \left\{ \begin{array}{ccc} L\uparrow & + & E\downarrow \\ \text{Various} & & \text{Payroll Tax} \\ \text{Payables}\uparrow & & \text{Expense}\uparrow \end{array} \right.$$

Internal Control Over Payroll

There are two main controls for payroll:

- Controls for efficiency
- Controls to safeguard payroll disbursements

Controls for Efficiency

Payroll transactions are ideal for computer processing. The payroll data are stored in a file, and the computer makes the calculations, prints paychecks, and updates all records electronically. In addition, companies may require direct deposits for employees' pay so that paper checks do not have to be written to each employee. Direct deposits also increase efficiency by reducing the amount of reconciling needed on outstanding checks.

Controls to Safeguard Payroll Disbursements

The owner of a small business can monitor his or her payroll by personal contact with employees. Large companies cannot. A particular risk is that a paycheck may be written to a fictitious person and cashed by a dishonest employee. To guard against this, large businesses adopt strict internal controls for payrolls.

Hiring and firing employees should be separated from accounting and from passing out paychecks. Photo IDs ensure that only actual employees are paid. Employees clock in at the start and clock out at the end of the workday to prove their attendance and hours worked.

The foundation of internal control is the separation of duties. This is why all but the smallest companies have separate departments for the following activities:

- The Human Resources Department hires and fires workers.
- The Payroll Department maintains employee earnings records.
- The Accounting Department records all transactions.
- The Treasurer distributes paychecks to employees.

3. Theodore Simpson works for Blair Company all year and earns a monthly salary of $4,000. There is no overtime pay. Blair withholds income taxes at 15% of gross pay. As of July 31, Theodore had $28,000 of cumulative earnings.

Journalize the accrual of salary expense for Blair Company related to the employment of Theodore Simpson for the month of August.

Check your answer at the end of the chapter.

For more practice, see Short Exercises S-6 through S-8. MyAccountingLab

HOW ARE CURRENT LIABILITIES THAT MUST BE ESTIMATED ACCOUNTED FOR?

Learning Objective 3

Account for current liabilities that must be estimated

A business may know that a liability exists, but not know the exact amount. The business cannot simply ignore the liability. It must estimate the amount of the liability and report it on the balance sheet. Common examples of liabilities that are often estimated are bonus plans, vacation pay, health and pension benefits, and warranties.

Under IFRS, current liabilities are sometimes called "provisions" rather than payables, for example, employee provisions or provision for income tax.

Bonus Plans

Many companies give bonuses to their employees in addition to their regular wages. These bonuses are often based on meeting a specific goal, such as the employee meeting an expected sales goal or the business achieving a target profit. Usually a company does not know the amount of the year-end bonus at year-end; the company instead estimates the amount of the bonus based on a set percentage. For example, assume Smart Touch Learning estimates that it will pay a 5% bonus on annual net income. Assume the company reports net income of $315,000 before the calculation of the bonus. The accounting department will calculate the bonus as follows:

Bonus = (Bonus % × Net income before bonus) / (1 + Bonus %)
= (0.05 × $315,000) / (1 + 0.05)
= $15,000

This formula allows you to back into the bonus amount. For example, net income minus the bonus is $300,000 ($315,000 − $15,000). The bonus of $15,000 is really 5% of net income after the bonus has been subtracted ($300,000 × 0.05 = $15,000).

Assuming Smart Touch Learning will not make payment until the next year, it must record a liability for the bonus due to its employees. The accounting clerk will record the following entry:

Date	Accounts and Explanation	Debit	Credit
Dec. 31	Employee Bonus Expense	15,000	
	Employee Bonus Payable		15,000
	To record employee bonus expense.		

$$A \ \Big\}= \Big\{ \ \underline{\text{L}\uparrow} \ + \ \underline{\text{E}\downarrow}$$

Employee Bonus Payable↑   Employee Bonus Expense↑

When Smart Touch Learning makes payment, it will debit Employee Bonus Payable and credit Cash.

Vacation, Health, and Pension Benefits

Businesses typically offer vacation, health, and pension benefits to its employees. A **pension plan** provides benefits to retired employees. Vacation, health, and pension benefits must be estimated and recorded as a liability. Suppose Smart Touch Learning employees earn two weeks of vacation throughout the year. The company estimates that the cost of providing vacation benefits is $1,000 per month. The accounting clerk will record the following journal entry monthly:

Pension Plan
A plan that provides benefits to retired employees.

Date	Accounts and Explanation	Debit	Credit
	Vacation Benefits Expense	1,000	
	Vacation Benefits Payable		1,000
	To record employee vacation benefits expense.		

$$A \ \Big\}= \Big\{ \ \underline{\text{L}\uparrow} \ + \ \underline{\text{E}\downarrow}$$

Vacation Benefits Payable↑   Vacation Benefits Expense↑

When an employee takes paid vacation, Smart Touch Learning will reduce the liability, Vacation Benefits Payable, with a debit and credit Cash. Other benefits, such as health and pension benefits, are recorded in the same manner.

Warranties

Many companies guarantee their products against defects under **warranty** agreements. The time period of warranty agreements vary. The matching principle requires businesses to record Warranty Expense in the same period that the company records the revenue related to that warranty. The expense, therefore, is incurred when the company makes a sale, not when the company pays the warranty claims. At the time of the sale, the company does not know the exact amount of warranty expense but can estimate it.

Assume that Smart Touch Learning made sales on account of $50,000 (cost of merchandise inventory sold, $35,000) subject to product warranties on June 10, and estimates that the cost of warranty repairs will be 3% of sales. The company

Warranty
An agreement that guarantees a company's product against defects.

would record the sales revenue, cost of goods sold, and estimated warranty expense as follows:

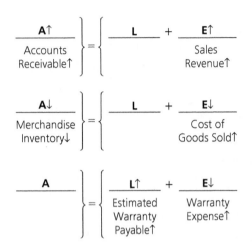

Date	Accounts and Explanation	Debit	Credit
Jun. 10	Accounts Receivable	50,000	
	Sales Revenue		50,000
	Sale on account.		
10	Cost of Goods Sold	35,000	
	Merchandise Inventory		35,000
	Recorded the cost of goods sold.		
10	Warranty Expense	1,500	
	Estimated Warranty Payable		1,500
	To accrue warranty payable.		

Assume that some of Smart Touch Learning's customers make claims that must be honored through the warranty offered by the company. The warranty costs total $800 and are made on June 27. The company replaces the defective goods and makes the following journal entry:

Date	Accounts and Explanation	Debit	Credit
Jun. 27	Estimated Warranty Payable	800	
	Merchandise Inventory		800
	To replace merchandise inventory under warranty.		

Smart Touch Learning's expense on the income statement is $1,500, the estimated amount, not the $800 actually honored. After honoring these warranties, the company's liability account has a credit balance of $700. This $700 balance represents warranty claims Smart Touch Learning expects to pay in the future based on its estimates; therefore, the $700 is a liability to Smart Touch Learning.

Estimated Warranty Payable

Jun. 27	800	1,500	Jun. 10
		700	Bal.

Ethics — How much is the warranty expense?

Henry Stevenson works as the manager of Used Car Superstore. His company prides itself on in-cluding a three-year bumper-to-bumper warranty on all car sales—no matter how old the car is. Henry's job responsibilities include estimating the amount of the warranty on each car sale. Henry knows that the older the car is, the higher the warranty cost will be to the business. Edward Wolf, the owner of the store, has been criticizing Henry for the amount of warranty expense he has been recording. Edward believes that Henry is overestimating the cost of the warranty and has told Henry that he needs to cut the cost in half. What should Henry do? What would you do?

Solution

Accounting for warranties can pose specific ethical challenges because it involves estimates in-stead of actual proven numbers. Businesses like to show high levels of net income in order to look successful. As a result, individuals, such as Edward, may encourage employees to overlook some expenses and liabilities at the end of the accounting period. If Henry does not record the warranty expense or fails to record it at a reasonable amount, total expenses and total liabilities will be un-derstated and net income will be overstated. This might make the company appear to be in better financial condition than it is. Henry should discuss how he determines the estimated cost with his boss. They should decide on a reasonable and accurate number to record as warranty expense.

> **4.** O'Conner guarantees its vacuums for four years. Company experience indicates that warranty costs will be approximately 6% of sales. Assume that O'Conner made sales totaling $200,000 during 2014. Record the warranty expense for the year.
>
> **Check your answer at the end of the chapter.**

For more practice, see Short Exercises S-9 through S-11. MyAccountingLab

HOW ARE CONTINGENT LIABILITIES ACCOUNTED FOR?

A contingent liability is a potential, rather than an actual, liability because it depends on a *future* event. For a contingent liability to be paid, some event (the contingency) must happen in the future. For example, suppose Smart Touch Learning is sued because of alleged patent infringement on one of its online learning videos. The company, there-fore, faces a contingent liability, which may or may not become an actual liability. If the outcome of this lawsuit is unfavorable, it could hurt Smart Touch Learning by increas-ing its liabilities. Therefore, it would be unethical to withhold knowledge of the lawsuit from investors and creditors.

Another contingent liability arises when a company *co-signs a note payable* for another entity. An example of this would occur if a company were to co-sign another company's note payable. The company co-signing has a contingent liability until the note comes due and is paid by the other entity. If the other company pays off the note,

Learning Objective 4
Account for contingent liabilities

Contingent Liability
A potential liability that depends on some future event.

the contingent liability vanishes. If the other company doesn't pay off the note, the co-signing company must pay the debt for the other entity. How businesses record or don't record contingent liabilities is based on one of three likelihoods of the event occurring in the future:

- Remote
- Reasonably possible
- Probable

Remote Contingent Liability

A contingency that is remote has little chance of the event occurring in the future. If a contingency is remote, the company does not need to record a liability and does not need to disclose it in the notes to the financial statements. An example of a remote contingency would be a frivolous lawsuit.

Reasonably Possible Contingent Liability

Contingencies that are reasonably possible have more chance of occurring but are not likely. A reasonably possible contingency should be described in the notes to the financial statements. For example, consider a company that is the defendant in a significant lawsuit. If the company has been advised by legal counsel that it is reasonably possible that they will lose the lawsuit, then they should report the lawsuit in its notes to the financial statements.

Under IFRS, "probable" is defined more broadly as "more likely than not" that the future event will result in a liability. "More likely than not" means more than a 50% chance.

Probable Contingent Liability

If a contingency is probable, it means that the future event is likely to occur. Only contingencies that are probable *and* can be estimated are recorded as a liability and an expense is accrued. An example of an estimable probable contingency is a warranty.

Contingencies that are probable but *cannot* be estimated are disclosed in the notes to the financial statements. A liability is not recorded because the amount of the contingency cannot be estimated. Exhibit 4 summarizes the rules for contingent liabilities.

Exhibit 4 | Contingent Liabilities

Likelihood of Future Event	How to Report the Contingency
Remote	Do not disclose.
Reasonably possible	Describe the situation in a note to the financial statements.
Probable and the amount of the expense *cannot* be estimated	Describe the situation in a note to the financial statements.
Probable and the amount of the expense *can* be estimated	Record an expense and a liability based on estimated amounts.

> Decisions   How should the contingency be reported?

Emily Gallagher is the independent auditor of Tate Manufacturing, a maker of handheld drills and other carpentry tools. Emily is evaluating current lawsuits for the company to determine whether any contingent liabilities should be disclosed. Tate Manufacturing is currently in litigation for a product liability case. The suit claims that a Tate handheld drill heated up quickly and caused a fire. Tate's attorney has told Emily that it is likely that the manufacturer will lose the case, but he does not want to estimate the amount of damages. The attorney is concerned that estimating the amount of damages would establish a dollar amount for settlement and could place their case in jeopardy. What should Emily do?

Solution

GAAP requires that businesses report a contingency if it is probable that the event will occur in the future. The issue here is where the reporting should be made. If the attorney cannot reasonably estimate the amount of the possible damage award, Tate should report the contingent liability in the notes to the financial statements. If an amount can be determined, Tate Manufacturing should record an expense and a liability based on the estimated amount. Emily should determine whether the attorney *can* estimate the damages but just doesn't want to. If the damages can be estimated, Emily should require that the company record a contingent liability.

Alternative Solution

The attorney's concern is understandable. He feels that disclosing the amount of the contingent liability could hurt the determination of the case. If the jury were to find out about the disclosure, it might be more likely to award damages to the plaintiff, or the plaintiff might be able to negotiate a larger settlement with Tate. The attorney has a right to be concerned about the transparency of the financial reporting and potential damage to the outcome of the case. The attorney should only provide an estimate if he is reasonably confident with the amount of damages.

> Try It!

Match the likelihood of future event with the reporting of the contingency. An answer may be selected more than once.

Likelihood of Future Event	How to Report the Contingency
5. Remote	**a.** Do not disclose
6. Reasonably possible	**b.** Record an expense and a liability based on estimated amounts.
7. Probable and the amount of the loss *cannot* be estimated	**c.** Describe the situation in a note to the financial statements.
8. Probable and the amount of the loss *can* be estimated	

Check your answers at the end of the chapter.

For more practice, see Short Exercise S-12.   MyAccountingLab

HOW DO WE USE THE TIMES-INTEREST-EARNED RATIO TO EVALUATE BUSINESS PERFORMANCE?

Investors can use the times-interest-earned ratio to evaluate a business's ability to pay interest expense. This ratio measures the number of times earnings before interest and taxes (EBIT) can cover (pay) interest expense. The times-interest-earned ratio is also called the *interest-coverage ratio*. A high interest-coverage ratio indicates a business's ease in paying interest expense; a low ratio suggests difficulty. The times-interest-earned ratio is calculated as EBIT (Net income + Income tax expense + Interest expense) divided by Interest expense.

Let's evaluate **Green Mountain Coffee Roasters, Inc.'s** ability to pay its interest expense. The following amounts (in thousands) are taken from Green Mountain Coffee Roasters' income statement.

	Year ended September 24, 2011	Year ended September 25, 2010
Net income	$ 199,501	$ 79,506
Income tax expense	101,699	53,703
Interest expense	57,657	5,294

Green Mountain's times-interest-earned ratio for the years ended September 24, 2011, and September 25, 2010, are calculated as follows:

Times-interest-earned ratio = (Net income + Income tax expense + Interest expense) / Interest expense

2011

= ($199,501 + $101,699 + $57,657) / $57,657
= 6.22 (rounded)

2010

= ($79,506 + $53,703 + $5,294) / $5,294
= 26.16 (rounded)

Notice that from 2010 to 2011, Green Mountain experienced a significant increase in interest expense. This is because Green Mountain incurred more debt specifically in its revolving line of credit. This increase in debt decreases Green Mountain's times-interest-earned ratio from 26.16 to 6.22. The 2011 ratio is slightly higher but more in line with the industry average of 5.59. It would appear that although Green Mountain increased its liabilities and incurred more interest expense, it can still easily cover its interest expense.

> **Try It!**

9. Fitzgerald Company reported the following amounts on its 2014 income statement:

	Year Ended December 31, 2014
Net income	$ 19,300
Income tax expense	5,800
Interest expense	900

What is Fitzgerald's times-interest-earned ratio for 2014? (Round your answer to two decimals.)

Check your answer at the end of the chapter.

For more practice, see Short Exercise S-13. MyAccountingLab

REVIEW

> Things You Should Know

1. How are current liabilities of known amounts accounted for?

- Current liabilities are liabilities that must be paid with cash or with goods and services within one year or within the entity's operating cycle if the cycle is longer than a year.

- Some examples of current liabilities are accounts payable, sales tax payable, unearned revenues, and short-term notes payable.

- Current liabilities also include any current portion of long-term notes payable.

2. How do companies account for and record payroll?

- Gross pay is the total amount of salary or wages earned by the employee. Net pay is the amount that each employee gets to keep (take-home pay).

- Payroll withholding deductions are the difference between gross pay and net pay. Examples of payroll deductions that *employees* pay include:

  - Income tax withholding: federal, state, and local income tax
  - Employee FICA tax
    - OASDI: 4.2% on the first $110,100 of annual earnings
    - Medicare: 1.45% on all earnings
  - Optional withholdings: charitable contributions, union dues, and so on.

- A payroll register can be used to help summarize the earnings, withholdings, and net pay for each employee.

- Businesses record a journal entry for payroll and payroll withholdings as a debit to Salaries and Wages Expense and a credit to various liabilities until the amounts are paid.

- *Employers* must pay at least three payroll taxes:

  - Employer FICA tax
    - OASDI: 6.2% on the first $110,100 of each employee's annual earnings
    - Medicare: 1.45% on all earnings
  - State unemployment compensation tax (SUTA): varies by state
  - Federal unemployment compensation tax (FUTA): 0.6% on the first $7,000 of each employee's annual earnings

- Payroll taxes are recorded as a debit to Payroll Tax Expense and a credit to various liabilities until they are paid.

- Internal control over payroll involves efficiency and safeguarding of payroll disbursements.

3. How are current liabilities that must be estimated accounted for?

- Bonuses are based on meeting a specific goal and are considered liabilities (Employee Bonus Payable) until paid.

- Vacation, health, and pension benefits must be estimated and recorded as liabilities.

- Warranty Expense (DR) and Warranty Payable (CR) must be recorded in the same period that the company records the revenue related to the warranty.

- As warranties are honored, the estimated Warranty Payable account is reduced.

4. How are contingent liabilities accounted for?

- A contingent liability is a potential liability that depends on some future event.

- Accounting for contingent liabilities is based on the following likelihoods:

  - Remote: Do not disclose.

  - Reasonably possible: Describe the situation in a note to the financial statements.

  - Probable and the amount of loss *cannot* be estimated: Describe the situation in a note to the financial statements.

  - Probable and the amount of the loss *can* be estimated: Record an expense and a liability based on estimated amounts.

5. How do we use the times-interest-earned ratio to evaluate business performance?

- The times-interest-earned ratio is calculated as (Net income + Income tax expense + Interest expense) / Interest expense.

- It measures the number of times earnings before interest and taxes (EBIT) can cover (pay) interest expense.

> Summary Problem 1

Answer each question independently.

Requirements

1. A restaurant made cash sales of $4,000 subject to a 5% sales tax. Record the sales and the related sales tax. Also record the payment of the tax to the state.

2. On October 1, 2014, Rhodes Company purchased equipment at a cost of $10,000, signing a nine-month, 8% note payable for that amount. Record the October 1 purchase. Also record the adjusting entry needed on December 31, 2014, and payment of the note plus interest at maturity on July 1, 2015.

3. How does a contingent liability differ from a known liability? When would a contingent liability be journalized?

> Solution

Requirement 1

Date	Accounts and Explanation	Debit	Credit
	Cash	4,200	
	Sales Revenue		4,000
	Sales Tax Payable ($4,000 × 0.05)		200
	To record cash sales and the related sales tax.		
	Sales Tax Payable	200	
	Cash		200
	To record cash payment for sales tax payable.		

Requirement 2

Date	Accounts and Explanation	Debit	Credit
2014			
Oct. 1	Equipment	10,000	
	Notes Payable		10,000
	Purchased equipment in exchange for nine-month, 8% note.		
Dec. 31	Interest Expense ($10,000 × 0.08 × 3/12)	200	
	Interest Payable		200
	Accrued interest expense at year-end.		
2015			
Jul. 1	Notes Payable	10,000	
	Interest Expense ($10,000 × 0.08 × 6/12)	400	
	Interest Payable	200	
	Cash		10,600
	Paid note and interest at maturity.		

Requirement 3

A contingent liability is a *potential*, rather than an actual, liability because it depends on a future event. Some event must happen (the contingency) for a contingent liability to have to be paid. Contingent liabilities are journalized when the likelihood of an actual loss is *probable* and the amount of the expense can be reasonably estimated.

> Summary Problem 2

Rags-to-Riches, a clothing resale store, employs one salesperson, Dee Hunter. Hunter's straight-time wage is $10 per hour, with time-and-a-half pay for hours above 40. Rags-to-Riches withholds income tax (20%), FICA—OASDI (4.2%), and FICA—Medicare (1.45%) from Hunter's pay. Rags-to-Riches also pays payroll taxes for FICA—OASDI (6.2%), FICA—Medicare (1.45%), and state and federal unemployment (5.6% and 0.6%, respectively).

During the week ended December 26, Hunter worked 50 hours. Prior to this week, she had earned $2,000.

Requirements

(Round all amounts to the nearest dollar.)

1. Compute Hunter's gross pay and net (take-home) pay for the week.

2. Record the payroll entries that Rags-to-Riches would make for each of the following:

   a. Salaries and wages expense and payment related to Hunter

   b. Employer payroll taxes accrual related to Hunter

   c. Payment of all payroll taxes (employee and employer related)

3. How much was Rags-to-Riches' total payroll expense for the week?

> Solution

Requirement 1

Gross pay:		
Straight-time pay (40 hours × $10 / hour)		$ 400
Overtime pay:		
Rate per hour ($10 × 1.5)	$ 15	
Hours (50 hours − 40 hours)	× 10	
		150
Gross pay		$ 550
Net pay:		
Gross pay		$ 550
Withholding deductions:		
Employee income tax ($550 × 0.20)	$ 110	
Employee OASDI ($550 × 0.042)	23	
Employee Medicare ($550 × 0.0145)	8	
Total withholdings		141
Net (take-home) pay		$ 409

Requirement 2

Date	Accounts and Explanation	Debit	Credit
a.	Salaries and Wages Expense	550	
	FICA—OASDI Taxes Payable		23
	FICA—Medicare Taxes Payable		8
	Employee Income Taxes Payable		110
	Salaries and Wages Payable		409
	To record salaries and wages expense and payroll withholdings.		
	Salaries and Wages Payable	409	
	Cash		409
	To record payment of salaries and wages.		
b.	Payroll Tax Expense	76	
	FICA—OASDI Taxes Payable ($550 × 0.062)		34
	FICA—Medicare Taxes Payable ($550 × 0.0145)		8
	Federal Unemployment Taxes Payable ($550 × 0.006)		3
	State Unemployment Taxes Payable ($550 × 0.056)		31
	To record employer's payroll tax expense.		
c.	FICA—OASDI Taxes Payable ($23 + $34)	57	
	FICA—Medicare Taxes Payable ($8 + $8)	16	
	Employee Income Taxes Payable	110	
	Federal Unemployment Taxes Payable	3	
	State Unemployment Taxes Payable	31	
	Cash		217
	To record payment of payroll tax liabilities.		

Requirement 3

Rags-to-Riches incurred *total payroll expense* of $626 (gross pay of $550 + payroll tax expense of $76).

Contingent Liability
A potential liability that depends on some future event.

Current Liabilities
Liabilities that must be paid with cash or with goods and services within one year or within the entity's operating cycle if the cycle is longer than a year.

Current Portion of Notes Payable
The amount of the principal that is payable within one year.

Federal Insurance Contributions Act (FICA)
The federal act that created the Social Security tax that provides retirement, disability, and medical benefits.

Gross Pay
The total amount of salary, wages, commissions, or any other employee compensation before taxes and other deductions.

Income Tax Withholding
Income tax deducted from an employee's gross pay.

Liabilities
Debts that are owed to creditors.

Long-Term Liabilities
Liabilities that do not need to be paid within one year or within the entity's operating cycle, whichever is longer.

Net Pay
Gross pay minus all deductions. The amount of compensation that the employee actually takes home.

Payroll Register
A schedule that summarizes the earnings, withholdings, and net pay for each employee.

Pension Plan
A plan that provides benefits to retired employees.

Short-Term Note Payable
A written promise made by the business to pay a debt, usually involving interest, within one year or less.

Social Security (FICA) Tax
Federal Insurance Contributions Act (FICA) tax, which is withheld from employees' pay and matched by the employer.

Times-Interest-Earned Ratio
Evaluates a business's ability to pay interest expense. (Net income + Income tax expense + Interest expense) / Interest expense.

Unemployment Compensation Tax
Payroll tax paid by employers to the government, which uses the cash to pay unemployment benefits to people who are out of work.

Warranty
An agreement that guarantees a company's product against defects.

> Quick Check

1. Known liabilities of estimated amounts are

   Learning Objective 1

   a. ignored. (Record them when paid.)
   b. reported on the balance sheet.
   c. reported on the income statement.
   d. reported only in the notes to the financial statements.

2. On January 1, 2014, a business borrowed $18,000 on a five-year, 5% note payable. At December 31, 2014, the business should *record*

   Learning Objective 1

   a. interest payable of $900.
   b. note receivable of $18,000.
   c. cash payment of $18,000.
   d. nothing. (The note is already on the books.)

3. Your company sells $180,000 (selling price) of goods and collects sales tax of 8%. What current liability does the sale create?

   Learning Objective 1

   a. Sales tax payable of $14,400
   b. Sales revenue of $194,400
   c. Unearned revenue of $14,400
   d. None; the company collected cash up front.

4. Jade Larson Antiques owes $20,000 on a truck purchased for use in the business. The company makes principal payments of $5,000 each year plus interest at 8%. Which of the following is true?

   Learning Objective 1

   a. After the first payment is made, the company owes $15,000 plus three years' interest.
   b. After the first payment, $15,000 would be shown as a long-term liability.
   c. After the first payment is made, $5,000 would be shown as the current portion due on the long-term note.
   d. Just before the last payment is made, $5,000 will appear as a long-term liability on the balance sheet.

5. An employee has year-to-date earnings of $107,000. The employee's gross pay for the next pay period is $5,000. If the FICA—OASDI is 4.2% and the wage base is $110,100, how much FICA—OASDI tax will be withheld from the employee's pay? (Answer is rounded to whole dollar.)

    a. $130   **c.** $310

    b. $283   **d.** $203

6. The employer is responsible for which of the following payroll taxes?

    a. 6.2% FICA—OASDI tax

    b. 1.45% FICA—Medicare tax

    c. Federal and state unemployment taxes

    d. All of the above

7. Wells Electric (WE) owed Estimated Warranty Payable of $1,200 at the end of 2013. During 2014, WE made sales of $120,000 and expects product warranties to cost the company 3% of the sales. During 2014, WE paid $2,300 for warranties. What is WE's Estimated Warranty Payable at the end of 2014?

    a. $2,300   **c.** $3,600

    b. $2,500   **d.** $4,800

8. Vega Company expects to pay a 4% bonus on net income of $130,000 after deducting the bonus. The journal entry to record the accrued bonus includes

    a. a debit to Employee Bonus Payable, $5,000.

    b. a debit to Employee Bonus Expense, $5,200.

    c. a credit to Employee Bonus Payable, $5,000.

    d. a credit to Cash, $5,200.

9. Swell Company has a lawsuit pending from a customer claiming damages of $100,000. Swell's attorney advises that the likelihood the customer will win is remote. GAAP requires at a minimum that this contingent liability be

    a. disclosed in the footnotes.

    b. disclosed in the footnotes, with ranges of potential loss.

    c. recorded as a journal entry, as well as disclosed in the footnotes.

    d. No disclosure is required.

10. McDaniel Company reported the following amounts on its 2014 income statement:

	Year ended December 31, 2014
Net income	$ 60,500
Income tax expense	12,100
Interest expense	5,000

What was McDaniel's times-interest-earned ratio for 2014?

    a. 12.10   **c.** 13.10

    b. 15.52   **d.** 14.52

Check your answers at the end of the chapter.

ASSESS YOUR PROGRESS

> Review Questions

1. What are the three main characteristics of liabilities?

2. What is a current liability? Provide some examples of current liabilities.

3. How is sales tax recorded? Is it considered an expense of a business? Why or why not?

4. How do unearned revenues arise?

5. What do short-term notes payable represent?

6. Coltrane Company had a $5,000 note payable that is paid in $1,000 installments over five years. How would the portion that must be paid within the next year be reported on the balance sheet?

7. What is the difference between gross pay and net pay?

8. List the required employee payroll withholding deductions and provide the tax rate for each.

9. How might a business use a payroll register?

10. What payroll taxes is the employer responsible for paying?

11. What are the two main controls for payroll? Provide an example of each.

12. When do businesses record warranty expense and why?

13. What is a contingent liability? Provide some examples of contingencies.

14. Curtis Company is facing a potential lawsuit. Curtis's lawyers think that it is reasonably possible that it will lose the lawsuit. How should Curtis report this lawsuit?

15. How is the times-interest-earned ratio calculated and what does it evaluate?

> Short Exercises

For all payroll calculations, use the following tax rates and round amounts to the nearest cent.

Employee: OASDI: 4.2% on first $110,100 earned; Medicare: 1.45%.

Employer: OASDI: 6.2% on first $110,100 earned; Medicare: 1.45%; FUTA: 0.6% on first $7,000 earned; SUTA: 5.6% on first $7,000 earned.

S-1 Determining current versus long-term liabilities

Learning Objective 1

Rios Raft Company had the following liabilities.

a. Accounts Payable

b. Note Payable due in 3 years

c. Salaries Payable

d. Note Payable due in 6 months

e. Sales Tax Payable

f. Unearned Revenue

Determine whether each liability would be considered a current liability (CL) or a long-term liability (LTL).

S-2 Recording sales tax

On July 5, Keller Company recorded sales of merchandise inventory on account, $20,000. The sales were subject to sales tax of 6%. On August 15, Keller Company paid $850 of sales tax to the state.

Requirements

1. Journalize the transaction to record the sale on July 5. Ignore cost of goods sold.

2. Journalize the transaction to record the payment of sales tax to the state.

S-3 Recording unearned revenue

On July 1, *Fly Fishing Magazine* collected cash of $80,000 on future annual subscriptions starting on August 1.

Requirements

1. Journalize the transaction to record the collection of cash on July 1.

2. Journalize the transaction required at December 31, the magazine's year-end, assuming no revenue earned has been recorded. (Round adjustment to the nearest whole dollar.)

S-4 Accounting for a note payable

On December 31, 2013, Edgmont purchased $10,000 of merchandise inventory on a one-year, 10% note payable. Edgmont uses a perpetual inventory system.

Requirements

1. Journalize the company's purchase of merchandise inventory on December 31, 2013.

2. Journalize the company's accrual of interest expense on June 30, 2014, its fiscal year-end.

3. Journalize the company's payment of the note plus interest on December 31, 2014.

S-5 Determining current portion of long-term note payable

On January 1, Beck Company purchased equipment of $100,000 with a long-term note payable. The debt is payable in annual installments of $20,000 due on December 31 of each year. At the date of purchase, how will Beck Company report the note payable?

S-6 Computing and journalizing an employee's total pay

Gloria Traxell works at College of San Bernardino and is paid $20 per hour for a 40-hour workweek and time-and-a-half for hours above 40.

Requirements

1. Compute Traxell's gross pay for working 48 hours during the first week of February.

2. Traxell is single, and her income tax withholding is 10% of total pay. Traxell's only payroll deductions are payroll taxes. Compute Traxell's net (take-home) pay for the week.

3. Journalize the accrual of salaries and wages expense and the payments related to the employment of Gloria Traxell.

S-7 Computing payroll amounts considering FICA tax ceilings

Learning Objective 2

Xinia Poehler works for MRK all year and earns a monthly salary of $12,000. There is no overtime pay. MRK withholds income taxes at 15% of gross pay. In addition to payroll taxes, Xinia elects to contribute 5% monthly to United Way. MRK also deducts $150 monthly for co-payment of the health insurance premium. As of September 30, Xinia had $108,000 of cumulative earnings.

Requirements

1. Compute Xinia's net pay for October.
2. Journalize the accrual of salaries expense and the payments related to the employment of Xinia Poehler.

S-8 Computing and journalizing the payroll expense of an employer

Learning Objective 2

Barnett Company has monthly salaries of $20,000. Assume Barnett pays all the standard payroll taxes and no employees have reached the payroll tax limits. Journalize the accrual and payment of employer payroll taxes for Barnett Company.

S-9 Computing bonus payable

Learning Objective 3

On December 31, Vazquez Company estimates that it will pay its employees a 3% bonus on $40,000 of net income after deducting the bonus. The bonus will be paid on January 15 of the next year.

Requirements

1. Journalize the December 31 transaction for Vazquez.
2. Journalize the payment of the bonus on January 15.

S-10 Journalizing vacation benefits

Learning Objective 3

Neal Company has five employees. Each employee earns one vacation day a month. Neal pays its employees a weekly salary of $1,000 for a five-day workweek.

Requirements

1. Determine the amount of vacation expense for one month.
2. Journalize the entry to accrue the vacation expense for the month.

S-11 Accounting for warranty expense and warranty payable

Learning Objective 3

Trekster Corrector guarantees its snowmobiles for three years. Company experience indicates that warranty costs will be approximately 4% of sales.

Assume that the Trekster dealer in Colorado Springs made sales totaling $533,000 during 2014. The company received cash for 30% of the sales and notes receivable for the remainder. Warranty payments totaled $17,000 during 2014.

Requirements

1. Record the sales, warranty expense, and warranty payments for the company. Ignore cost of goods sold.
2. Post to the Estimated Warranty Payable T-account. At the end of 2014, how much in Estimated Warranty Payable does the company owe? Assume the Estimated Warranty Payable is $0 on January 1, 2014.

Current Liabilities and Payroll

Learning Objective 4

S-12 Accounting treatment for contingencies

Farley Motors, a motorcycle manufacturer, had the following contingencies.

a. Farley estimates that it is reasonably possible but not likely that it will lose a current lawsuit. Farley's attorneys estimate the potential loss will be $1,200,000.

b. Farley received notice that it was being sued. Farley considers this lawsuit to be frivolous.

c. Farley is currently the defendant in a lawsuit. Farley believes it is likely that it will lose the lawsuit and estimates the damages to be paid will be $80,000.

Determine the appropriate accounting treatment for each of the situations Farley is facing.

Learning Objective 5

S-13 Computing times-interest-earned ratio

Hale Electronics reported the following amounts on its 2013 income statement:

Year Ended December 31, 2013	
Net income	$ 48,400
Income tax expense	7,260
Interest expense	4,000

What is Hale's times-interest-earned ratio for 2013? (Round the answer to two decimals.)

> Exercises

Learning Objective 1

Sales Tax Payable $14,400

E-14 Recording sales tax

Consider the following transactions of Pearl Software:

Mar. 31	Recorded cash sales of $180,000, plus sales tax of 8% collected for the state of New Jersey.
Apr. 6	Sent March sales tax to the state.

Journalize the transactions for the company. Ignore cost of goods sold.

Learning Objective 1

May 1, 2015 Interest Expense $340

E-15 Recording note payable transactions

Consider the following note payable transactions of Creative Video Productions.

2014	
May 1	Purchased equipment costing $17,000 by issuing a one-year, 6% note payable.
Dec. 31	Accrued interest on the note payable.
2015	
May 1	Paid the note payable plus interest at maturity.

Journalize the transactions for the company.

E-16 Recording and reporting current liabilities

Learning Objective 1

Dec. 31 Subscription Revenue $165

TransWorld Publishing completed the following transactions during 2014:

Oct. 1	Sold a six-month subscription (starting on November 1), collecting cash of $330, plus sales tax of 9%.
Nov. 15	Remitted (paid) the sales tax to the state of Tennessee.
Dec. 31	Made the necessary adjustment at year-end to record the amount of subscription revenue earned during the year.

Journalize the transactions (explanations are not required).

E-17 Journalizing current liabilities

Learning Objectives 1, 2

Salaries Expense $3,400

Edmund O'Mally Associates reported short-term notes payable and salaries payable as follows:

	2014	2013
Current Liabilities—partial:		
Short-Term Notes Payable	$ 16,400	$15,600
Salaries Payable	3,400	3,100

During 2014, O'Mally paid off both current liabilities that were left over from 2013, borrowed money on short-term notes payable, and accrued salaries expense. Journalize all four of these transactions for O'Mally during 2014. Assume no interest on short-term notes payable of $15,600.

E-18 Computing and recording gross and net pay

Learning Objective 2

1. Net Pay $495.83

Henry Striker manages a Frosty Boy drive-in. His straight-time pay is $10 per hour, with time-and-a-half for hours in excess of 40 per week. Striker's payroll deductions include withheld income tax of 8%, FICA tax, and a weekly deduction of $5 for a charitable contribution to United Way. Striker worked 52 hours during the week.

Requirements

1. Compute Striker's gross pay and net pay for the week. Assume earnings to date are $10,000.

2. Journalize Frosty Boy's wages expense accrual for Striker's work. An explanation is not required.

3. Journalize the subsequent payment of wages to Striker.

E-19 Recording employer payroll taxes

Learning Objective 2

Payroll Tax Expense $6,026.50

Ricardo's Mexican Restaurant incurred salaries expense of $65,000 for 2014. The payroll expense includes employer FICA tax, in addition to state unemployment tax and federal unemployment tax. Of the total salaries, $17,000 is subject to unemployment tax. Also, the company provides the following benefits for employees: health insurance (cost to the company, $2,060), life insurance (cost to the company, $350), and retirement benefits (cost to the company, 7% of salaries expense). Journalize Ricardo's expenses for employee benefits and for payroll taxes. Explanations are not required.

Learning Objective 2

2. Salaries & Wages Payable $13,980

E-20 Recording employee and employer payroll taxes

Park Company had the following partially completed payroll register:

Earnings			Withholdings									Salaries and
Beginning Cumulative Earnings	Current Period Earnings	Ending Cumulative Earnings	OASDI	Medicare	Income Tax	Health Insurance	United Way	Total Withholdings	Net Pay	Check No.	Wages Expense	
$ 83,000	$ 4,200				$ 840	$ 80	$ 5			801	
105,000	7,000				1,400	130	10			802	
45,000	2,500				500	45	0			803	
62,500	3,500				700	60	5			804	
0	2,000				400	40	0			805	
$ 295,500	$ 19,200				$ 3,840	$ 355	$ 20				

Requirements

1. Complete the payroll register.
2. Journalize Park's wages expense accrual for the current pay period.
3. Journalize Park's expenses for employer payroll taxes for the current pay period.

Learning Objective 3

1. Warranty Expense $10,880

E-21 Accounting for warranty expense and warranty payable

The accounting records of Clay Ceramics included the following at January 1, 2014:

Estimated Warranty Payable	
	4,000 Beg. Bal.

In the past, Clay's warranty expense has been 8% of sales. During 2014, Clay made sales of $136,000 and paid $7,000 to satisfy warranty claims.

Requirements

1. Journalize Clay's warranty expense and warranty payments during 2014. Explanations are not required.
2. What balance of Estimated Warranty Payable will Clay report on its balance sheet at December 31, 2014?

Learning Objective 3

Dec. 31 Employee Bonus Expense $392

E-22 Accounting for warranties, vacation, and bonuses

McCarthy Company completed the following transactions during 2014:

Nov. 1	Made sales of $8,000. McCarthy estimates that warranty expense is 4% of sales. (Record only the warranty expense.)	
20	Paid $100 to satisfy warranty claims.	
Dec. 31	Estimated vacation benefits expense to be $1,200.	
31	McCarthy expected to pay its employees a 2% bonus on net income after deducting the bonus. Net income for the year is $20,000.	

Journalize the transactions (explanations are not required).

E-23 Accounting treatment for contingencies

Learning Objective 4

Analyze the following independent situations.

a. McKinney Company is being sued by a former employee. McKinney believes that there is a remote chance that the employee will win. The employee is suing McKinney for damages of $1,000.

b. Reeves Oil Refinery had a gas explosion on one of its oil rigs. Reeves believes it is likely that it will have to pay environmental clean-up costs and damages in the future due to the gas explosion. Reeves cannot estimate the amount of the damages.

c. Love Company estimates that it will have to pay $20,000 in warranty repairs next year.

Determine how each contingency should be treated.

E-24 Computing times-interest-earned ratio

Learning Objective 5

Griffith Ratio 142.20 times

The following financial information was obtained from the year ending 2014 income statements for Griffith Automotive and Bowen Automotive:

	Griffith	Bowen
Net income	$ 27,200	$ 60,800
Income tax expense	8,100	23,000
Interest expense	250	2,400

Requirements

1. Compute the times-interest-earned ratio for each company.
2. Which company was better able to cover its interest expense?

> Problems Group A

P-25A Journalizing and posting liabilities

The general ledger of Speedy Ship at June 30, 2014, the end of the company's fiscal year, includes the following account balances before adjusting entries.

Accounts Payable	$ 114,000
Interest Payable	0
Salaries Payable	0
Employee Payroll Taxes Payable	0
Employer Payroll Taxes Payable	0
Unearned Rent Revenue	6,900
Long-Term Notes Payable	210,000

The additional data needed to develop the adjusting entries at June 30 are as follows:

a. The long-term debt is payable in annual installments of $42,000, with the next installment due on July 31. On that date, Speedy Ship will also pay one year's interest at 8%. Interest was paid on July 31 of the preceding year. Make the adjusting entry to accrue interest expense at year-end.

b. Gross unpaid salaries for the last payroll of the fiscal year were $4,300. Assume Employee Payroll Taxes Payable are $970.

c. Employer payroll taxes owed are $850.

d. On February 1, the company collected one year's rent of $6,900 in advance.

Requirements

1. Using T-accounts, open the listed accounts and insert the unadjusted June 30 balances.

2. Journalize and post the June 30 adjusting entries to the accounts that you opened. Identify each adjusting entry by letter.

3. Prepare the current liabilities section of the balance sheet at June 30, 2014.

P-26A Computing and journalizing payroll amounts

Louis Welch is general manager of United Salons. During 2014, Welch worked for the company all year at a $10,200 monthly salary. He also earned a year-end bonus equal to 10% of his annual salary.

Welch's federal income tax withheld during 2014 was $850 per month, plus $924 on his bonus check. State income tax withheld came to $70 per month, plus $40 on the bonus. FICA tax was withheld on the annual earnings. Welch authorized the following payroll deductions: Charity Fund contribution of 1% of total earnings and life insurance of $5 per month.

United incurred payroll tax expense on Welch for FICA tax. The company also paid state unemployment tax and federal unemployment tax. In addition, United provides Welch with health insurance at a cost of $150 per month. During 2014, United paid $4,000 into Welch's retirement plan.

Requirements

1. Compute Welch's gross pay, payroll deductions, and net pay for the full year 2014. Round all amounts to the nearest dollar.

2. Compute United's total 2014 payroll expense for Welch.

3. Make the journal entry to record United's expense for Welch's total earnings for the year, his payroll deductions, and net pay. Debit Salaries Expense and Bonus Expense as appropriate. Credit liability accounts for the payroll deductions and Cash for net pay. An explanation is not required.

P-27A Journalizing liability transactions

The following transactions of Denver Pharmacies occurred during 2013 and 2014:

Learning Objectives 1, 3

Jan. 29 Cash $16,960
Dec. 31 Interest Expense $360

2013		
Jan.	9	Purchased computer equipment at a cost of $9,000, signing a six-month, 6% note payable for that amount.
	29	Recorded the week's sales of $64,000, three-fourths on credit and one-fourth for cash. Sales amounts are subject to a 6% state sales tax. Ignore cost of goods sold.
Feb.	5	Sent the last week's sales tax to the state.
Jul.	9	Paid the six-month, 6% note, plus interest, at maturity.
Aug.	31	Purchased merchandise inventory for $12,000, signing a six-month, 9% note payable. The company uses the perpetual inventory system.
Dec.	31	Accrued warranty expense, which is estimated at 2% of sales of $603,000.
	31	Accrued interest on all outstanding notes payable.
2014		
Feb.	28	Paid off the 9% note plus interest at maturity.

Journalize the transactions in Denver's general journal. Explanations are not required.

P-28A Journalizing liability transactions

The following transactions of Brooks Garrett occurred during 2014:

Learning Objectives 3, 4

1. June 30 Warranty Expense $8,000

Apr.	30	Garrett is party to a patent infringement lawsuit of $200,000. Garrett's attorney is certain it is remote that Garrett will lose this lawsuit.
Jun.	30	Estimated warranty expense at 2% of sales of $400,000.
Jul.	28	Warranty claims paid in the amount of $6,000.
Sep.	30	Garrett is party to a lawsuit for copyright violation of $100,000. Garrett's attorney advises that it is probable Garrett will lose this lawsuit. The attorney estimates the loss at $100,000.
Dec.	31	Garrett estimates warranty expense on sales for the second half of the year of $500,000 at 2%.

Requirements

1. Journalize required transactions, if any, in Garrett's general journal. Explanations are not required.

2. What is the balance in Estimated Warranty Payable?

P-29A Computing times-interest-earned ratio

The income statement for Colorado Communications follows. Assume Colorado Communications signed a 120-day, 6%, $4,000 note on June 1, 2015, and that this was the only note payable for the company.

COLORADO COMMUNICATIONS Income Statement Year Ended July 31, 2015		
Sales Revenue	$ 28,000	
Less: Sales Returns and Allowances	5,040	
Sales Discounts	3,360	
Net Sales Revenue		$ 19,600
Cost of Goods Sold		12,600
Gross Profit		7,000
Operating Expenses:		
Selling Expenses	700	
Administrative Expenses	1,750	
Total Expenses		2,450
Operating Income		4,550
Other Revenues and (Expenses):		
Interest Expense	?	
Total Other Revenues and (Expenses)		?
Net Income before Income Tax Expense		?
Income Tax Expense		900
Net Income		$?

Requirements

1. Fill in the missing information for Colorado's year ended July 31, 2015, income statement.
2. Compute the times-interest-earned ratio for the company.

> Problems Group B

P-30B Journalizing and posting liabilities

The general ledger of Pack-N-Ship at June 30, 2014, the end of the company's fiscal year, includes the following account balances before adjusting entries.

Accounts Payable	$ 111,000
Interest Payable	0
Salaries Payable	0
Employee Payroll Taxes Payable	0
Employer Payroll Taxes Payable	0
Unearned Rent Revenue	6,300
Long-Term Notes Payable	220,000

The additional data needed to develop the adjusting entries at June 30 are as follows:

a. The long-term debt is payable in annual installments of $44,000, with the next installment due on July 31. On that date, Pack-N-Ship will also pay one year's interest at 10%. Interest was paid on July 31 of the preceding year. Make the adjusting entry to accrue interest expense at year-end.

b. Gross unpaid salaries for the last payroll of the fiscal year were $4,900. Assume Employee Payroll Taxes Payable are $960.

c. Employer payroll taxes owed are $810.

d. On February 1, the company collected one year's rent of $6,300 in advance.

Requirements

1. Using T-accounts, open the listed accounts and insert the unadjusted June 30 balances.

2. Journalize and post the June 30 adjusting entries to the accounts that you opened. Identify each adjusting entry by letter.

3. Prepare the current liabilities section of the balance sheet at June 30, 2014.

P-31B Computing and journalizing payroll amounts

Learning Objective 2

1. Net Pay $96,608

Lenny Worthington is general manager of Crossroad Salons. During 2014, Worthington worked for the company all year at a $9,200 monthly salary. He also earned a year-end bonus equal to 5% of his annual salary.

Worthington's federal income tax withheld during 2014 was $810 per month, plus $928 on his bonus check. State income tax withheld came to $80 per month, plus $60 on the bonus. FICA tax was withheld on the annual earnings. Worthington authorized the following payroll deductions: Charity Fund contribution of 1% of total earnings and life insurance of $15 per month.

Crossroad incurred payroll tax expense on Worthington for FICA tax. The company also paid state unemployment tax and federal unemployment tax. In addition, Crossroad provides Worthington with health insurance at a cost of $110 per month. During 2014, Crossroad paid $7,000 into Worthington's retirement plan.

Requirements

1. Compute Worthington's gross pay, payroll deductions, and net pay for the full year 2014. Round all amounts to the nearest dollar.

2. Compute Crossroad's total 2014 payroll expense for Worthington.

3. Make the journal entry to record Crossroad's expense for Worthington's total earnings for the year, his payroll deductions, and net pay. Debit Salaries Expense and Bonus Expense as appropriate. Credit liability accounts for the payroll deductions and Cash for net pay. An explanation is not required.

Current Liabilities and Payroll

Learning Objectives 1, 3

Jan. 29 Cash $17,755
Dec. 31 Interest Expense $220

P-32B Journalizing liability transactions

The following transactions of Plymouth Pharmacies occurred during 2013 and 2014:

2013

Jan.	9	Purchased computer equipment at a cost of $7,000, signing a six-month, 9% note payable for that amount.
	29	Recorded the week's sales of $67,000, three-fourths on credit and one-fourth for cash. Sales amounts are subject to a 6% state sales tax. Ignore cost of goods sold.
Feb.	5	Sent the last week's sales tax to the state.
Jul.	9	Paid the six-month, 9% note, plus interest, at maturity.
Aug.	31	Purchased merchandise inventory for $6,000, signing a six-month, 11% note payable. The company uses a perpetual inventory system.
Dec.	31	Accrued warranty expense, which is estimated at 4% of sales of $608,000.
	31	Accrued interest on all outstanding notes payable.

2014

Feb.	28	Paid off the 11% note plus interest at maturity.

Journalize the transactions in Plymouth's general journal. Explanations are not required.

Learning Objectives 3, 4

1. June 30 Warranty Expense $12,900

P-33B Journalizing liability transactions

The following transactions of Dunn Miles occurred during 2014:

Apr.	30	Miles is party to a patent infringement lawsuit of $230,000. Miles's attorney is certain it is remote that Miles will lose this lawsuit.
Jun.	30	Estimated warranty expense at 3% of sales of $430,000.
Jul.	28	Warranty claims paid in the amount of $6,400.
Sep.	30	Miles is party to a lawsuit for copyright violation of $130,000. Miles's attorney advises that it is probable Miles will lose this lawsuit. The attorney estimates the loss at $130,000.
Dec.	31	Miles estimates warranty expense on sales for the second half of the year of $510,000 at 3%.

Requirements

1. Journalize required transactions, if any, in Miles's general journal. Explanations are not required.

2. What is the balance in Estimated Warranty Payable?

P-34B Computing times-interest-earned ratio

The income statement for Wyoming Communications follows. Assume Wyoming Communications signed a 120-day, 4%, $6,000 note on June 1, 2015, and that this was the only note payable for the company.

Learning Objectives 5

1. Net Income $6,210

WYOMING COMMUNICATIONS
Income Statement
Year Ended July 31, 2015

Sales Revenue	$ 48,000	
Less: Sales Returns and Allowances	8,640	
Sales Discounts	5,760	
Net Sales Revenue		$ 33,600
Cost of Goods Sold		21,600
Gross Profit		12,000
Operating Expenses:		
Selling Expenses	1,200	
Administrative Expenses	3,000	
Total Expenses		4,200
Operating Income		7,800
Other Revenues and (Expenses):		
Interest Expense	?	
Total Other Revenues and (Expenses)		?
Net Income before Income Tax Expense		?
Income Tax Expense		1,550
Net Income		$?

Requirements

1. Fill in the missing information for Wyoming's year ended July 31, 2015, income statement.

2. Compute the times-interest-earned ratio for the company.

> Continuing Problem

P-35 Accounting for liabilities of a known amount

This problem deals with a company named Davis Consulting. Davis Consulting believes the company will need to borrow $300,000 in order to expand operations. Davis consults the bank and secures a 10%, five-year note on March 1, 2014. Davis must pay the bank principal in five equal installments plus interest annually on March 1.

Requirements

1. Record the $300,000 note payable on March 1, 2014.

2. Record the entry to accrue interest due on the note at December 31, 2014.

3. Record the entry Davis would make to record the payment to the bank on March 1, 2015.

CRITICAL THINKING

> Decision Cases

Decision Case 1

Golden Bear Construction operates throughout California. The owner, Gaylan Beavers, employs 15 work crews. Construction supervisors report directly to Beavers, and the supervisors are trusted employees. The home office staff consists of an accountant and an office manager.

Because employee turnover is high in the construction industry, supervisors hire and fire their own crews. Supervisors notify the office of all personnel changes. Also, supervisors forward the employee W-4 forms to the home office. Each Thursday, the supervisors submit weekly time sheets for their crews, and the accountant prepares the payroll. At noon on Friday, the supervisors come to the office to get paychecks for distribution to the workers at 5 pm.

The company accountant prepares the payroll, including the paychecks. Beavers signs all paychecks. To verify that each construction worker is a bona fide employee, the accountant matches the employee's endorsement signature on the back of the canceled paycheck with the signature on that employee's W-4 form.

Requirements

1. Identify one way that a supervisor can defraud Golden Bear Construction under the present system.

2. Discuss a control feature that the company can use to *safeguard* against the fraud you identified in Requirement 1.

Decision Case 2

Sell-Soft is the defendant in numerous lawsuits claiming unfair trade practices. Sell-Soft has strong incentives not to disclose these contingent liabilities. However, GAAP requires that companies report their contingent liabilities.

Requirements

1. Why would a company prefer *not* to disclose its contingent liabilities?

2. Describe how a bank could be harmed if a company seeking a loan did not disclose its contingent liabilities.

3. What ethical tightrope must companies walk when they report contingent liabilities?

> Ethical Issue 1

Many small businesses have to squeeze down costs any way they can just to survive. One way many businesses do this is by hiring workers as "independent contractors" rather than as regular employees. Unlike rules for regular employees, a business does not have to pay Social Security (FICA) taxes and unemployment insurance payments for independent contractors. Similarly, it does not have to withhold federal income taxes or the employee's share of FICA taxes.

The IRS has a "20 factor test" that determines whether a worker should be considered an employee or a contractor, but many businesses ignore those rules or interpret them loosely in their favor. When workers are treated as independent contractors, they do not get a W-2 form at tax time (they get a 1099 instead), they do not have any income taxes withheld, and they find themselves subject to "self-employment" taxes, by which they bear the brunt of both the employee and the employer's share of FICA taxes.

Requirements

1. When a business abuses this issue, how is the independent contractor hurt?
2. If a business takes an aggressive position—that is, interprets the law in a very slanted way—is there an ethical issue involved? Who is hurt?

> Fraud Case 1

Sara Chung knew the construction contractors in her area well. She was the purchasing manager at the power plant, a business that was the major employer in the region. Whenever a repair or maintenance job came up, Sara's friends would inflate the invoice by 10%. The invoice would then be passed through the accounts payable department, where the clerk was supposed to review and verify the charges before processing the payment. The accounts payable clerk, Valerie Judson, was happy to have a job and didn't want anything to jeopardize it. She knew the deal but kept her mouth shut. Sara's contractor friends would always "kick back" the 10% extra to Sara under the table. One day, Valerie had a heart attack and went into the hospital. The company hired a new accounts payable clerk, Spencer Finn. He had worked construction in his college days and suspected something was fishy, but he couldn't prove it. He did, however, wish to protect himself in case the fraud came to light.

Requirements

1. How could an auditor detect fraud of this sort?
2. What can a business do to prevent this kind of fraudulent activity?
3. What should the new accounts payable clerk do to protect himself?

> Financial Statement Case 1

Details about a company's liabilities appear in a number of places in the annual report. Visit **www.pearsonhighered.com/Horngren** to view a link to Starbucks Corporation's Annual Report. Use **Starbucks Corporation**'s fiscal 2011 financial statements to answer the following questions.

Requirements

1. Give the breakdown of Starbucks' current liabilities at October 2, 2011.
2. Calculate Starbucks' times-interest-earned ratio for the years ending October 2, 2011, and October 3, 2010. How did Starbucks do compared to **Green Mountain Coffee Roasters** in its ability to pay its interest expense?

Current Liabilities and Payroll

> Team Project 1

In recent years, the airline industry has dominated headlines. Consumers are shopping Priceline.com and other Internet sites for the lowest rates. The airlines have also lured customers with frequent-flyer programs, which award free flights to passengers who accumulate specified miles of travel. Unredeemed frequent-flyer mileage represents a liability that airlines must report on their balance sheets, usually as Air Traffic Liability.

Southwest Airlines, a profitable, no-frills carrier based in Dallas, has been rated near the top of the industry. Southwest controls costs by flying to smaller, less expensive airports; using only one model of aircraft; serving no meals; increasing staff efficiency; and having a shorter turnaround time on the ground between flights. The fact that most of the cities served by Southwest have predictable weather maximizes its on-time arrival record.

With a partner or group, lead your class in a discussion of the following questions, or write a report as directed by your instructor answering the following questions:

Frequent-flyer programs have grown into significant obligations for airlines. Why should a liability be recorded for those programs? Discuss how you might calculate the amount of this liability. Can you think of other industries that offer incentives that create a similar liability?

> Communication Activity 1

In 150 words or fewer, explain how contingent liabilities are accounted for.

MyAccountingLab — **For a wealth of online resources, including exercises, problems, media, and immediate tutorial help, please visit** www.myaccountinglab.com.

Try It! Solutions

1.

Date	Accounts and Explanation	Debit	Credit
Aug. 10	Accounts Receivable	4,160	
	Sales Revenue		4,000
	Sales Tax Payable ($4,000 × 0.04)		160
	To record sales of merchandise inventory and the related sales tax.		

2.

Date	Accounts and Explanation	Debit	Credit
Sep. 30	Sales Tax Payable	500	
	Cash		500
	To record cash payment for sales tax payable.		

3. OASDI: $4,000 × 0.042 = $168

Medicare: $4,000 × 0.0145 = $58

Income Taxes: $4,000 × 0.15 = $600

Date	Accounts and Explanation	Debit	Credit
Aug. 31	Salaries Expense	4,000	
	FICA—OASDI Taxes Payable		168
	FICA—Medicare Taxes Payable		58
	Employee Income Taxes Payable		600
	Salaries Payable		3,174
	To record salaries expense and payroll withholdings.		

4.

Date	Accounts and Explanation	Debit	Credit
	Warranty Expense ($200,000 × 0.06)	12,000	
	Estimated Warranty Payable		12,000
	To accrue warranty payable.		

5. a

6. c

7. c

8. b

9. Times-interest-earned ratio = (Net income + Income tax expense + Interest expense) / Interest expense
= ($19,300 + $5,800 + $900) / $900
= 28.89

> Quick Check Answers

1. b **2.** a **3.** a **4.** c **5.** a **6.** d **7.** b **8.** c **9.** d **10.** b

Glossary

Contingent Liability. A potential liability that depends on some future event.

Current Liabilities. Liabilities that must be paid with cash or with goods and services within one year or within the entity's operating cycle if the cycle is longer than a year.

Current Portion of Notes Payable. The amount of the principal that is payable within one year.

Federal Insurance Contributions Act (FICA). The federal act that created the Social Security tax that provides retirement, disability, and medical benefits.

Gross Pay. The total amount of salary, wages, commissions, or any other employee compensation before taxes and other deductions.

Income Tax Withholding. Income tax deducted from an employee's gross pay.

Liabilities. Debts that are owed to creditors.

Long-Term Liabilities. Liabilities that do not need to be paid within one year or within the entity's operating cycle, whichever is longer.

Net Pay. Gross pay minus all deductions. The amount of compensation that the employee actually takes home.

Payroll Register. A schedule that summarizes the earnings, withholdings, and net pay for each employee.

Pension Plan. A plan that provides benefits to retired employees.

Short-Term Note Payable. A written promise made by the business to pay a debt, usually involving interest, within one year or less.

Social Security (FICA) Tax. Federal Insurance Contributions Act (FICA) tax, which is withheld from employees' pay and matched by the employer.

Times-Interest-Earned Ratio. Evaluates a business's ability to pay interest expense. (Net income + Income tax expense + Interest expense) / Interest expense.

Unemployment Compensation Tax. Payroll tax paid by employers to the government, which uses the cash to pay unemployment benefits to people who are out of work.

Warranty. An agreement that guarantees a company's product against defects.

Photo Credits

Credits are listed in order of appearance.

Photo 1 (top): Valentyn Volkov/Shutterstock
Photo 2 (middle): Y.H. Lim/Alamy
Photo 3 (bottom): Wavebreakmedia/Shutterstock
Photo 4: Carlo Dapino/Shutterstock
Photo 5: Pan Xunbin/Shutterstock
Photo 6 Shutterstock

Index

statement of, 23, 58-59, 216